Foundations of
Social Work Practice

A GRADUATE TEXT

4TH EDITION

MT

Cheryl Y. Bradley, Publisher
Marcia D. Roman, Managing Editor, Journals and Books
Kathie P. Baker, Editor
Caroline Polk, Copy Editor
Juanita J. Ruffin, Proofreader
Bernice Eisen, Indexer

Cover design by Britt Engen, Metadog Design Group
Interior design by Cynthia Stock, Electronic Quill Publishing Services
Printed and bound by Port City Press, Baltimore, Maryland

Library of Congress Cataloging-in-Publication Data

Foundations of social work practice : a graduate text / Mark A.
   Mattaini, Christine T. Lowery, editors. —4th ed.
      p. cm.
   Includes bibliographical references and index.
   ISBN-13: 978-0-87101-374-3
   1. Social service. I. Mattaini, Mark A. II. Lowery, Christine T.
HV40.F683 2007
361.3—dc22

                                        2006030101

1/2/09

For all the emerging women
leaders in postcolonial societies
and
for Paul Farmer, and all others who struggle
for justice and liberation in solidarity
with the poor and the oppressed

Contents

PART 2. FOUNDATIONS OF SOCIAL WORK PRACTICE

APPENDIXES

□□□
A Note to Instructors

Mark A. Mattaini and Christine T. Lowery

*B*eginning social work students are naturally concerned about learning skills that are immediately applicable in fieldwork practice, but only by integrating a skills focus with immersion in the underlying knowledge base can students move beyond the role of technicians to that of autonomous professionals. This text is an integration of knowledge and practice skills. The chapters can be used in any order; one approach that we have found useful is to interweave practice skills chapters with knowledge chapters. Most master's students are in concurrent fieldwork and are therefore eager to focus on "what to do." Material on social justice, values and ethics, and other knowledge areas clearly needs to be covered at the same time and can often best be integrated by interspersing those chapters with those that are more applied. No single book can provide everything students need, so instructors are encouraged to use this text in conjunction with the most current journal articles and other readings, given the educational assessment of their own students and context.

Although fieldwork can provide a great deal of opportunity to learn skills (and knowledge), it is a rare field placement that can offer adequate exposure to systems of all sizes, the wide range of practice challenges, and grounding in the best current knowledge. In addition, in some schools students are not in the field until later in their programs. Ideally, therefore, a skills lab is integrated with classroom content. We have included a beginning set of skill-building exercises as Appendix C; those exercises are conceptually linked to the chapters in this text. Instructors and students are encouraged, however, to use those exercises simply as starting points in co-creating their own teaching and learning approaches.

Part I

□ □ □

Foundation Knowledge

1

□□□

Foundations of
Social Work Practice

Mark A. Mattaini and *Christine T. Lowery*

Social work is an exciting and tremendously challenging profession, perhaps more so now than ever before. What could be more exhilarating than working with individuals, families, groups, and communities to help them reach their goals, overcome serious life obstacles, and contribute to social justice and human rights?

One can visualize social work practice as a continuous rope of events stretching through time. This rope is made of many intertwining strands, all of which are required for the rope to do its work. The strands include knowledge, skills, values and ethics, and true commitment—each of which inform every practice event and decision. Each strand, in turn, consists of multiple threads (for example, the many forms of knowledge, from the scientific to the experiential, needed for practice, and differential skills for intervention with different client groups). A rope can be stretched out linearly, but it can also curve and loop back upon itself, and social work practice over time has done this as well. Social work practice, in other words, is enormously complex. Graduate-level social workers need certain core knowledge from each strand but will pursue specific threads differentially as guided by the needs of their practice.

All the threads and strands of the profession are of necessity intertwined and interdependent; none can be forgotten without weakening the whole. Every social worker therefore requires "foundation knowledge" about the work of the profession as a whole. Many practical examples of the need for this broad preparation are found throughout this text; challenges faced by homeless families, for example, might involve personal struggles (perhaps mental health or addiction issues), depleted community resource networks, and even national policy dimensions, any or all of which may require attention in practice with the family.

Social work graduate students are adult learners. This text is therefore rooted in "web teaching" (Patterson & Jaffe, 1994), an approach to adult learning in which the basic map or outline of a subject is initially sketched. At later stages, knowledge of different areas and connections on the map is refined and deepened, and the final result is a richly elaborated and interconnected understanding. This introductory chapter sketches the contours of factors that come to a nexus in each practice event and places those events within a wider contextual field. The basic map for this work is shown in Figure 1-1; note that this image can be thought of as a cross-section of the conceptual rope discussed above.

FIGURE 1-1

Dimensions of Social Work Practice in Context

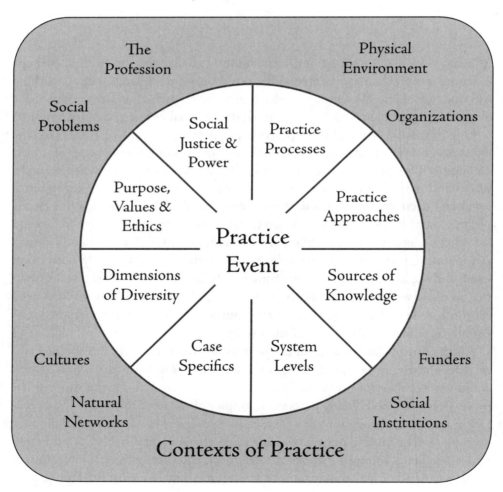

Subsequent chapters elaborate on sections of this web in increasing detail. In fact, one's professional education, both in graduate school and continuing throughout one's career, will continue to deepen knowledge and skills within this conceptual map. (Evidence suggests that many social workers fail to continue this lifelong learning process [Mullen & Bacon, 2003]. Such failure does an injustice to clients and the human community.) Deciding what to emphasize within this interconnected whole is a major conceptual skill in social work.

THE PURPOSE AND MISSION OF SOCIAL WORK

The purpose of social work is to enhance adaptations among clients and the ecological field within which they are embedded, consistent with social justice. *Clients* include individuals, families, communities, or other collective entities. (In some cases, terminology such as "consumers," "members," or "participants" may be preferable, although one must take care to avoid defining deeply human services as mere commodities.) Professionals in other disciplines are often interested in some of the same issues, but their core professional missions are different (Meyer, 1993). Medicine—including psychiatry—is concerned with curing illness and enhancing the health of individuals, although public health expands this function somewhat. Psychology is primarily a science (sometimes applied) of individuals, with special but not exclusive emphasis on mental phenomena and individual behavior. In contrast, social work—at its very core—is holistically concerned with the person-in-situation and with viewing and intervening in that social reality to further client goals within a social justice framework (Marsh, 2005). This focus is fundamentally different from the foci of allied professions, although certain skills and knowledge are shared.

Given the professional mission of the social work field, social workers need to understand individuals, collectives, and environments and how they interrelate; this is perhaps the most complex assignment of any profession. Issues with which contemporary social workers and their clients grapple every day (for example, the HIV/AIDS crisis in the United States and around the world; family breakdown and violence associated with deep, intergenerational poverty; or the failure of education for an enormous number of children in urban centers) illustrate this complexity, but it has been present since the beginning of social work. One has only to read the work of Charles Loring Brace (1872/1973) or Mary Richmond (1917) to see that problems and solutions to the most serious human challenges have never been easy to understand or to address.

In the early development of the profession, caseworkers looked at both the person and his or her environment, maintaining a dual focus in which each could be alternately foreground or background. It was difficult to find ways of conceptualizing the interactions and largely impossible to see the interconnections between person and environment as foreground. Rather, early social workers often were forced to operationalize person-in-situation by using lists of personal and environmental factors to be examined in the course of the social study. The contemporary perspectives discussed in chapter 2 can be of enormous help in moving beyond this relatively static approach.

Although many social work practice functions can be performed effectively by paraprofessional and bachelor's-level staff, the primary function of the graduate-level social worker is not so much to simply act as to think—to understand the perplexing intricacies of each client's unique dilemma and to develop intervention strategies that are based on that understanding. Professional practice cannot be based on simple formulas or uniform step-by-step prescriptions, although practice guidelines may be of significant use (see chapter 2). As the social worker and client face the full complexities of practice situations, comprehensive understanding becomes elusive, and one can never know enough. While recognizing this reality, the professional social worker, with the client, must still decide what is to be done, even when the limits of what is possible are distressingly evident. Much more can often be done than is immediately evident.

THE COMPLEXITY OF SOCIAL WORK

The social worker needs to see—and, to the extent possible, know—everything at once. For example, it is not possible to look at and deal separately with a client's emotional state, then the possible effects of family dynamics, and then the effects of racial and cultural factors. Adequate assessment in social work often requires "thinking big"—seeing the full transactional situation all at once (Meyer, 1993)—while "doing small"—providing a highly focused intervention. The practice setting; realities of the issues being addressed; and the effects of oppression, domination, disadvantage, and other sociocultural factors are all part of the social work case.

The scope of social work reaches from attention to the individual, family, group, and community to the arena of social policy, increasingly at an international level. Social workers work with adults and children of all economic classes, racial and ethnic groups, cultures, gender identifications, and sexual orientations in hospitals, clinics, social agencies, homes, schools, institutions, community centers, and on the street. Their interventions span prevention and protection, rehabilitation, and capacity building. *Given all of this variation, however, social work as a profession is bound by mission to "preferential treatment for the poor"* [italics added] (Farmer, 2003, p. 227), focusing particularly on those most in need, those who find themselves in "entrapping niches" (Sullivan & Rapp, 2006, p. 267), and those whose human rights are commonly ignored. Poverty and structural violence, racism, sexism, heteronormativity, and other injustices form a matrix of challenges that requires the work of the best-prepared minds and hearts, working in solidarity with those most affected.

The postindustrial, globalized society has engendered a new level of social isolation; value systems that, more than ever, privilege the individual over the collective; and heightened tensions and misunderstandings among cultures and generations that sometimes reach a fever pitch. People (and groups) have responded differently with depression, violence, or withdrawal. At the same time, changing realities bring new opportunities for society and for social work practice that range from increased access to information and tools important for empowerment to new possibilities for forging social connections, even globally, via dramatic advances in communications.

Social work is a social institution, and as such, it carries certain mandates in the arenas of health, welfare, and education. Except in the area of family and child welfare, in which social work has traditionally been the primary discipline, most social workers practice in "host agencies" such as schools; the Red Cross; institutions for the elderly, children, and people with disabilities; or correctional settings. These fields and social institutions represent the concerns of the public and are supported by statutes that provide legal sanction and funding from multiple levels of government, by contributions from individuals and private organizations, or both. The social welfare, health, and educational institutions of this country represent an enormous social and economic investment, and social work is deeply embedded in those institutions. In a very real sense, therefore, social work carries collective public responsibility for its work; it is not simply an individual professional endeavor.

Historically, the social work profession has been organizationally based, in part because of the early social assignment and commitment of social workers to working with the poor and dispossessed and in part because the breadth and complexity of necessary social services require organizational support. Because the resources controlled by the poor are often severely limited, publicly supported and organizationally based services are often the only possible route to the assistance needed; at the same time, such services may seriously limit choice and options. Over time, much has been learned by social workers and others about humanizing bureaucracies, both for employees and for service consumers. Organizations can only "work for people" (Meyer, 1979), however, if they are deeply grounded in a dynamic of shared power, which remains uncommon in social and human services (Lowery & Mattaini, 2001). In an interlocking organizational culture of shared power, all participants have strong voices, all make contributions from their strengths and gifts, and all share responsibility for outcomes (Lowery & Mattaini, 1999; see also chapter 2). Bureaucracies grounded in competitive, coercive, and exploitive adversarial power cannot facilitate true collaboration with clients or communities, nor can they be adequately responsive to the needs of the increasingly diverse contemporary practice world (Gutierrez, GlenMaye, & DeLois, 1995). Unfortunately, most contemporary social institutions rely to a substantial extent on adversarial power (Sidman, 2001); social workers often need to challenge that reliance and construct alternatives.

Historically, practitioners in most professions have recognized that the work they do is somehow sacred in that it carries obligations to other individuals and the human collective that go beyond self-interest. Social work is not about self, image, or ego. Social work is not a "job"; it is not a "career." Social work, to a substantial degree, carries the responsibilities of society for social and economic justice. It is mission-driven, liberating work with the deep and complex fabric of humanity. Practice that recognizes this reality is not an ideal; it is an ethical responsibility.

THE CONCEPTUAL MAP

Professional social work skills are differentially applied on the basis of the collaborative understanding of the case developed by practitioner and client. The actions taken are responsive to the complexities of the case and to the social context within which the case is embedded. All the dimensions shown in Figure 1-1 must be addressed simultaneously.

Imagine that you are working with a neglected girl. It probably makes sense to you that your purpose relates to doing something about the fit between the child and her ecological environment; that factors related to culture and social class, as well as to her mother's mental illness, may be relevant; and that is it important to know about the girl's emotional stability as well as about what her mother does and does not do as a parent. It is also crucial to apply what is known from research related to promoting resilience in children in high-risk situations and to supporting parents as they strive to provide what their children need. Agency and policy structures may guide and limit what can be done, as will your knowledge of applicable practice models or approaches. While you are thinking about all of these factors and gathering specific information about the case, you also need to build genuine, empathic, respectful relationships with the child, the parent and, perhaps, a "kinship" foster parent (a relative serving as a foster parent) within a matrix of shared power.

The challenge in this, a rather typical social work case, is clear. You certainly cannot deal with each related factor sequentially, because the factors are inextricably interwoven. The factors and their interconnections must be considered "all at once," as a transactional conceptual network. Graphic tools can be helpful in this process (Hartman, 1995/1978; Mattaini, 1993) because they enable the social worker and client(s) to see both the "big picture" and the critical details of

FIGURE I-2

◻◻◻◻◻

Sequential Ecomaps

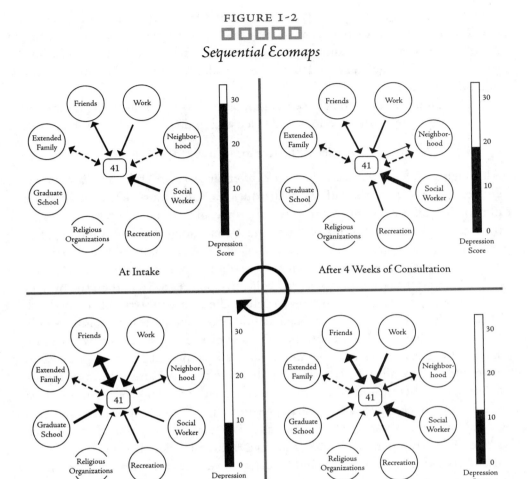

Note: These ecomaps portray the changing life situation and level of depression (shown on the thermometer graphs) of a client. Depression measured using the Beck Depression Inventory II (Beck, Steer, & Brown, 1996) over 12 sessions of interpersonal therapy.

Source: Reprinted with permission from Mattaini, M. A. (1993). *More than a thousand words: Graphics for clinical practice* (p. 159). Washington, DC: NASW Press. © National Association of Social Workers.

the case simultaneously. Figure 1-2, for example, is a sequential ecomap portraying transactional changes over time in the case of a depressed, single 41-year-old man. At the beginning of the case (the upper left panel), one can see not only particular positive and negative interactions that the client has experienced but also the dynamic, holistic configuration of the case: The client is isolated, with few meaningful connections anywhere, and his level of depression is significant. Moving clockwise, one can observe concurrent shifts in specific ecological transactions, the balance of positive and negative transactions over time, and how those transactions appear to relate to levels of depression and the construction of a fulfilling life.

Major dimensions of the conceptual map portrayed in Figure 1-1 are briefly sketched in the following sections and discussed in depth in later chapters.

Social Justice and Power

Although social workers perform many different tasks and take on many different roles in a wide variety of social institutions, fulfilling social work's historic purpose requires a commitment to social justice and human rights that emerges from an authentic recognition of the connections among all people (and peoples) and their world. Social workers carry a solemn responsibility not to do charity work or treat people's disorders but to contribute from their personal gifts and training and to use their personal and collective power to strengthen the human and natural web within which they and their clients are inextricably embedded. Historically, "justice" has often been defined to systematically exclude whole groups (see chapter 3). A contemporary view of social justice, however, can be defined by transactions that genuinely value all people, all peoples, and all life; foster inclusion while deeply respecting diversity of values and cultures; support the human rights of individuals and the collective rights of groups; and reduce reliance on adversarial power operating through coercion, oppression, and violence. Justice is not a static state; it is realized (made real) in action. Social justice is one of the core perspectives on social work practice sketched in chapter 2, is discussed in depth in chapter 3, and is deeply woven into the fabric of the remaining chapters of this book.

As implied in the preceding paragraph, justice cannot be understood without understanding adversarial and shared power. As the profession has evolved, so has our recognition of the crucial importance of practicing within a framework of shared power, in which clients, social workers, and others involved (for example, family members or foster parents) all have crucial roles to play, roles that that carry obligations and responsibilities (Lowery & Mattaini, 2001). Shared power practice leaves no room for paternalism or ego because the social worker lets go of the role of "expert" in exchange for something more genuine. Sharing power minimizes the need to rely on adversarial processes and ensures recognition of the voice and value of everyone involved. The resulting practice is a constructive process of co-creation rather than the treatment of pathology. For this reason, conceptualizing social work practice as merely "therapy" is far too limited.

The developing strengths approach to practice (Saleebey, 2006) is an important advance for the profession because it offers tools for operationalizing shared power and moves the field away from a primary focus on pathological processes and toward practice that capitalizes on what the client and social worker bring to the table. The strengths approach has been important in helping social workers view clients as competent human beings who bring their own strengths to the social work consultation. Clients are not seen as bundles of pathology or as problems to be solved but as partners in a collaborative process. The shift is much more profound than may be apparent at first because much of social work in recent decades has relied heavily on diagnosing "what is wrong," in part because of an overreliance on psychiatric models of understanding human beings. The strengths perspective also brings hope and excitement to practice—a major contribution in itself. Most contemporary statements of social work practice models, at least to some extent, incorporate the strengths perspective, and it truly has much to offer practice, despite significant limitations. The strengths perspective is discussed further in chapter 2.

Professional Purpose, Values, and Ethics

Carol Meyer, a seminal figure in the development of social work practice theory, in reference to a classic definition of clinical social work (Ewalt, 1979), wrote that "social work claims as its central purpose the enhancement of adaptations among individuals, families, groups, communities—and their particular environments" (Meyer, 1993, p. 18). She noted that this central focus on the person-in-environment construct is unique in social work, despite interdisciplinary overlaps in skills and selected knowledge. Adding explicit attention to social justice further refines a current understanding of social work, although this emphasis has always been present to some extent. Social work has always involved both "cause" (the organized effort to advocate for oppressed populations) and "function" (a set of direct practice activities carried out with the sanction of the larger society) (Lee, 1929). The distinction and balance between the two has ebbed and flowed and has been an ongoing tension within the profession since its beginnings.

In addition to purpose, common values and professional ethics are characteristic of all professions, including social work. Neither values nor ethics are easy to enact in practice, although they may seem straightforward in the abstract. For example, residual homophobia and heteronormativity (the attitude that regards heterosexual relationships and orientation as the norm against which all others are measured) are often challenges for people entering the social work field despite abstract commitments to the value of respect for all, the ethical mandate not to condone discrimination of any kind, and the central place of social justice as the organizing value of the profession (Marsh, 2005).

Realities also complicate the application of social work values. Although the importance of the professional value of "client self-determination" may seem evident, the social worker also recognizes that not all human behavior is under the unconstrained, conscious control of the client, and therefore the reality of limitations in the potential for self-determination emerges. In addition, individuality is viewed by many cultures as less important than the collective good. Only ethnocentrism would suggest that the individualistic alternative is better; indeed, strong arguments can be made to the contrary. Social workers must find ways to be responsive to such value complexities as they play themselves out in day-to-day social work practice. Practice consistent with professional values and ethics, therefore, requires constant questioning, self-awareness, and growth. Chapter 4 explores those issues in detail.

Client Diversity

Social workers' clients, as would be expected in the contemporary world, are extremely diverse along many interwoven dimensions. In fact, most social workers will spend a large proportion of their time working with people who are quite different from themselves. Broad and deep understanding of this diversity is therefore a crucial area of professional knowledge that has critical implications for practice. Clients differ in age, gender identification, health and physical ability, race, education, occupation, sexual orientation, physical attractiveness (as culturally defined), intellectual and verbal abilities, behavior, and in many other ways. In addition, individuals play out their lives as members (central or peripheral) of multiple cultural entities and identities, from families to social classes to ethnic and religious groups. Social workers commonly need to learn to be effective across deep, historically rooted rifts of credibility and trust. In a multicultural society, differences need to be understood and valued as sources of potentially useful variations that could enrich the lives of members of all cultures. Unfortunately, as a result of many groups' long histories of oppression and disrespect in the United States, divisions are often bitter, and bridging those gaps is a critical professional—and cultural—challenge.

Oppression is a serious issue in much of social work. In contemporary U.S. culture, and in many of the European cultures from which it emerged, major institutions and those receiving primary benefit from them have consistently relied on the exercise of coercive and adversarial power: exploitation, violence, threat, punishment, and individualistic competition (Sidman, 2001). This power has been and often continues to be exercised within a context of privilege—white privilege, male privilege, and class privilege, for example. Coercive oppression is commonly characteristic of the judicial system, education, major economic institutions, government agencies, international relations—and, in many cases, even families (for example, battering, child abuse, or sexual coercion). These coercive and adversarial arrangements are maintained by the results they produce for those in power, but they ultimately have profoundly negative results for the collective (Sidman, 2001). And that collective is the province of social work.

A good deal is known about sensitivity to differences and, to some extent, about specific approaches that tend to be valuable in practice with members of particular groups (e.g., Castillo, 1997; McGoldrick, Giordano, & Garcia-Preto, 2005; U.S. Surgeon General, 2001). Every client is an individual, however, not just an accumulation of descriptive categories; levels of biculturalism and acculturation differ widely, and personal life experiences are unique. Hence, almost paradoxically, although deep awareness of difference sensitizes the worker, the essence of culturally sensitive practice is to be able to individualize a case without being blinded by categorical labels.

Culturally sensitive or culturally competent practice is not enough. The very design of social work services and entire service systems needs to emerge from the diverse voices of those served, resulting in genuinely *ethnoconscious* services (Gutierrez, 1997). The social worker must recognize that clients, program participants, and community collaborators often see the world in ways genuinely different from those of the social worker because of their cultural experiences. People who are deeply grounded in traditional African values, for example, are likely to see issues and evaluate solutions in ways that are dramatically different from many European Americans; they are more likely to emphasize connectedness and spirituality, for example (Schiele, 1996).

Ethnoconscious social services that emerge from deep cultural roots may offer possibilities that would never occur to practitioners otherwise. For example, agencies guided by the *Ma'at* (Seven Cardinal Virtues: order, balance, harmony, compassion, reciprocity, justice, and truth) and the *Nguzo Saba* (Seven Pillars of Strength: unity, self-determination, collective work and responsibility, cooperative economics, purpose, creativity, and faith) are likely to deal with funders, communities, and clients in quite different ways than do agencies who see their operations as part of consumer society (O'Donnell & Karanja, 2000).

Human beings and human society are rooted in the physical world and the natural environment, which includes the web of human connections. Modern Western society has done tremendous damage to that environment—damage that has produced serious health and social justice issues that have the most immediate impact on the poor but ultimately affect everyone (Besthorn & McMillen, 2002). Indigenous cultures carry particular knowledge about how to live collectively as part of the natural world, including knowledge essential to the survival of human and other species (LaDuke, 1999; Martin, 1999), and knowledge of how to heal the terrible damage that modern society sometimes creates in both the human web and the natural environment (Ross, 2006). Social work has much to learn from indigenous cultures; those lessons can have an immediate impact on how social work is practiced and how social agencies are organized (Lowery & Mattaini, 2001). The emphasis on shared power found throughout this book is a key example.

One important aspect of human life is the spiritual dimension, and true social work practice is spiritual work. Religious and spiritual practices and experiences are core to many people's lives, and to most cultures, and cannot be ignored in work with the human web. Many Latino people, for example, rely on both traditional healers and organized religion; traditional and Western practices are often amalgamated and integrated in contemporary Latino celebrations, rituals, and other practices. It is important to wonder about and honor this dimension of people's lives. Clients appreciate respect for their worldviews, values, and practices, including the religious and spiritual dimensions; only by respecting those elements can the social worker see the whole person. Social workers need to examine how their own religious and spiritual beliefs and practices may influence their work for better (for example, by enriching recognition for human connection) or for worse (for example, by tempting one to impose one's own beliefs on others).

Case Specifics

Every case is unique, and the client (whether an individual, family, or other system) and the environmental context within which the client is embedded provide a good deal of particularized information that can guide collaborative assessment and intervention. Data-based "practice guidelines" for particular issues or practice goals can be useful (Rosen & Proctor, 2003), but they need to be flexibly adapted to fit case realities. Because client experiences and knowledge must be part of the shared worker–client knowledge base for intervention to be effective, a social worker usually asks a number of questions and gives clients real opportunities to share their stories during the initial engagement and throughout the intervention process.

The client may not know or understand everything that is relevant, but it is a mistake to dismiss information—even partial and relatively subjective information—that the client provides; the social worker's own view is likely to include just as much distortion (Saleebey, 2006), and, except when a clear reason exists not to, it is far better to begin by believing the client. It is therefore always important to understand the client's perceptions as important case data. Providing opportunities for clients to tell their stories in their own way, in their own voices, is more likely to produce meaningful information than interrogating them with a barrage of questions.

Observation of clients and client systems can also provide valuable knowledge. For example, combining observations of repetitive patterns of exchange—positive and negative—in a couple or a family with research about the importance of such patterns (see, for example, Burman, John, & Margolin, 1992) can provide a great deal of direction to the family clinician. Viewing such observations within the matrix of the family's environmental transactions (Mattaini, Grellong, & Abramovitz, 1992)—information about which often comes from the family and segments of their social networks—enhances the potential for broadly based, family-centered practice that transcends the limitations of family therapy alone.

Systems Thinking

Social workers are professionally concerned with individuals, groups, couples, families, neighborhoods, formal and informal organizations, communities, and societies. Each system is made up of subsystems and itself constitutes a subsystem of higher order systems. System levels are organized hierarchically, so a particular system (for example, an individual) may at one moment be viewed as the focal system and at the next moment as a subsystem of another system (a family). General systems theory and recent advances in systems thinking (see chapter 2) have proven helpful in identifying common systemic characteristics (for example, exchange of resources and energy with environments across boundaries) that can guide practice thinking.

Each systemic level (individuals as systems, family systems, community systems, and so forth) has its own integrity. What emerges in families, for example, is more than the aggregate of what individuals do: Families establish and maintain regular patterns, their own "cultural practices." Those practices tend to continue over time, even when they may be emotionally, physically, or otherwise costly to the individuals involved. For example, as discovered by Patterson (1976; Reid, Patterson, & Snyder, 2002), parent–child dyads often become trapped in a chronic pattern of escalating coercive exchange, which can be understood only if one looks at the pattern through a transactional lens. The best predictor of satisfaction and stability within a couple is the pattern of positive and aversive exchange present in their relationship, and the most effective approaches to working with entire families focus on the dynamics of interpersonal transactions (Mattaini, 1999). Groups, organizations, and communities similarly have their own systemic integrity, and intervention therefore needs to emerge from an understanding of transactional dynamics. Given its importance, chapter 2 emphasizes systems thinking, and the concept is interwoven throughout the subsequent chapters.

Knowledge

An organized knowledge base is crucial to any profession. Anyone can simply act; the professional is expected to act deliberately, taking the steps that are most likely to be helpful, parsimonious, and consistent with a client's welfare. Deciding on those steps requires an extensive knowledge base. Practice that is based entirely on intuition or "common sense" not only is, by definition, not professional but also—far more importantly—is likely to be ineffective. Effectiveness, when it can be achieved, is an ethical mandate.

Practice Wisdom. Practice wisdom—one form of knowledge for practice—is a slippery concept, yet there can be little doubt that much of what happens in practice is rooted in it. In this discussion, *practice wisdom* refers to two separate but related phenomena: (1) explicit rules, handed down to others by experienced practitioners, that appear to "work"—heuristic rules viewed as "good enough" to guide much of practice—and (2) patterns of professional behavior, articulated or not, that have been shaped and refined through years of practice and often serve as models for other workers. These two forms of knowledge are passed on from generation to generation of social workers, sometimes as a form of oral tradition. Experienced social workers have often learned a tremendous amount that can be of value to others, and the importance of this type of knowledge should not be minimized. Reliance on such rules has associated risks, however. The rules may be inaccurate but passed on persuasively by practitioners who strongly believe them to be true; their application may then result in less-than-adequate services to clients. For example, social workers in the field of substance abuse often rely on codependency theory, which "assert[s] that a woman married to an alcoholic contribute[s] to her husband's addiction because of her own disturbed personality needs" (Collins, 1993, p. 471)—an assertion for which it turns out there is no persuasive evidence (Collins; Peele, 1995). "Codependency" is perhaps a useful narrative for some situations, but it carries clear risks; in some of its common forms, codependency theory defines most families as dysfunctional, characterizes shared responsibility for collective outcomes as bad, and suggests that attention should be directed primarily to dysfunction rather than strengths and power (Collins). It has also resulted in unjustifiably blaming women and labeling them as pathological. The term "codependence" is not found in most evidence-based work related to the families of those addicted to substances, who often prove to be among the most powerful resources for treatment of the addicted (Collins; Miller & Carroll, 2006).

The second type of practice wisdom—patterns of professional behavior shaped by practice experience—is also essential, although it is more difficult to capture. Sometimes social workers know what they are doing and why, and they can accurately explain it verbally. At other times, effective practitioners cannot explain exactly what they do or why, but by observing their timing or the inflection of their voices during clinical sessions, for example, others can learn to do much the same thing. For this reason, among others, videotaped and audiotaped sample sessions and real or simulated clinical presentations are valuable. The observers can notice the principles that are the particular focus of a session or demonstration, and they may be able to learn, consciously or not, from the many subtle behavioral events that occur simultaneously.

In response to the limitations of practice wisdom, contemporary social workers have increasingly come to value *evidence-based practice*—practice that relies on neither intuition nor authority but on critical examination of the best available evidence, particularly evidence that has been tested in rigorous, scientific ways (Gambrill, 1999, 2003). Certainly, practice involves much more than this, but the importance of testing what one does and of seeking the best-validated information on which to base decisions can hardly be overemphasized. Evidence-based practice is discussed in depth in chapter 2 and subsequently.

Biological, Behavioral, and Sociocultural Sciences. Moving beyond practice wisdom, much of the foundational knowledge for social work practice has scientific roots. Social workers work with people (who are biological, emotional, behavioral, and social beings); with families, groups, communities, and organizations (which are sociocultural entities); and with the relationships among and between people, social entities, and the physical world. Because these are the "raw materials" of practice, it is important to understand as much as possible about them. Thus, social workers must know not only about practice and social issues but also about the basic sciences that undergird them, including biology and genetics; ecological science; and behavioral science and the disciplines that examine large systems, including sociology, anthropology, and cultural analysis.

Some conditions that social workers deal with have clear physiological dimensions; for instance, although the effects of the environment appear to be important determinants of the course and severity of schizophrenia, many of the underlying processes involved are usually biological in nature. The extent and nature of the biological basis of the disorder is not yet entirely clear, however, and serious issues exist regarding the diagnosis (Bola & Pitts, 2005; Wong, 2006). In another example, serious depression is associated with changes in the levels and actions of neurotransmitters in the brain (Sadock & Sadock, 2003). That "psychological" interventions are nonetheless effective for many cases of depression (Nathan & Gorman, 1998) demonstrates the essential unity of the human organism. Many psychophysiological connections exist in substance abuse (Miller & Carroll, 2006; National Institute on Alcohol Abuse and Alcoholism, 2000; Sadock & Sadock, 2003). For example, children of people with severe addictions to alcohol are at substantially increased risk for alcohol problems themselves. Therefore, knowledge of biological and medical information in whatever area the social worker is practicing is essential.

E. O. Wilson (1992) noted that

humanity is part of nature, a species that evolved among other species. The more closely we identify ourselves with the rest of life, the more quickly we will be able to discover the sources of human sensibility and acquire the knowledge on which an enduring ethic, a sense of preferred direction, can be built. (p. 348)

Since the 1960s, social workers have recognized that ecological science has much to offer them for understanding practice in a complex, interconnected world. First, human beings are literally part of the natural world and, like other animals, need to be able to obtain certain resources, including food, shelter, and social interaction, from their environments to survive. (Those basic needs are missing or at continuous risk for many homeless and poor people.) The connectedness among people and other parts of the natural world is an essential underpinning of shared power in social work practice, which requires recognizing that service is not about doing something *for* someone else but rather about contributing to the interconnected web within which each of us is simply a nexus. Ecofeminists emphasize that ecological connectedness is not just a metaphor but the reality of the human species (Besthorn & McMillen, 2002). An ecological perspective profoundly changes the definition of practice and clarifies the importance of exploring the interlocking environmental events, human actions, and cultural practices within which client struggles occur. Ecological science is one of the theoretical roots of the ecosystems perspective (see chapter 2), which has proven important for conceptualizing practice.

Social workers draw on a tremendous wealth of information from the behavioral and social sciences; most graduate programs include substantial coursework focused on human behavior in the social environment. Knowledge from psychology, behavior analysis, social psychology, sociology, anthropology, economics, demography, epidemiology, and political science, as well as from professions such as medicine, psychiatry, and family therapy, is critical for effective practice. For example, recent work in the analysis of cultural practices can be useful for determining what needs to change in an ecological field to reduce the incidence of social problems such as youth and collective violence (Mattaini, 2001, 2002) and to increase the rates of prosocial acts like effective parenting at a community level (Irvine, Biglan, Smolkowski, Metzler, & Ary, 1999).

Practice Approaches

It is essential to be forthright in representing social work to graduate students. The profession is currently fragmented on several dimensions; one of the most potentially divisive has to do with practice approaches, or practice models, which reflect different and often conflicting worldviews. Although individual cases, and, therefore, specific interventions, are unique, the social worker seldom must, or should, develop intervention strategies *de novo*. Practice approaches are organized systems of intervention designed to be applied in relatively consistent ways across multiple cases (including groups and communities). Not only do practice approaches permit social workers to apply what has been learned from other cases to the current one, they are valuable in making explicit how the worker understands the case situation and what is to be done about it. In other words, when using a practice approach, the worker does not depend exclusively on amorphous, unarticulated intuition—which is no doubt always present—but engages in critical analysis consistent with a coherent conceptual framework.

Social work practice, like other helping professions, is grounded in the practitioner's understanding of the phenomena involved, including individual experiences and action, social phenomena, and the environmental context within which they occur. In the roughly 100 years during which the profession has evolved, many different practice approaches have emerged. A few key clusters, however, encompass most practice approaches. Each approach has contributed something to professional practice, and the graduate social worker should certainly have some exposure to each, if for no other reason than to be able to communicate with colleagues. At the same time, it is critical to avoid an eclectic stew that randomly mixes concepts from multiple approaches. Different approaches see the multiple causes of human action in different and, to some extent, incompatible ways. A "moral" model for understanding addictions, for example, would indicate the need for an act of will on the part of an alcoholic person while denying much of what has been learned about substance abuse in recent decades; a disease model would suggest the need to acknowledge powerlessness as an early step toward treatment. A social worker's core understanding of human action is unlikely to change from moment to moment and person to person, although much can be said for taking a fresh perspective at times. Because different theoretical frameworks often understand human behavior and other social forces in incompatible ways, practice approaches grounded in the most adequate and well-established underlying conceptual understandings should be privileged.

Psychosocial Practice. The oldest professional practice framework in social work is the psychosocial approach, which has continually evolved since Richmond's (1917) *Social Diagnosis.* This approach has, for at least six decades, relied primarily on psychodynamic theory (including modern developments in ego psychology, self psychology, and object relations). The key to understanding human behavior and emotion in this approach is the developmental process over the life course, much of which is seen as outside of the client's conscious awareness. Because development occurs primarily through experience, this approach has a place for the social and physical environment, but that place may primarily be historical. Current environmental forces are certainly recognized by psychosocial social workers but are somewhat difficult to work into a single conceptual framework. Among the best contemporary statements of this approach, both of which have attempted to address historical limitations of the model, are those of Goldstein (1995, 2001) and Woods and Hollis (1999).

Ecological Practice. Partly in response to the bias toward identifying individual dysfunction rather than transactional issues that is often found in psychosocial work, the ecological approach (particularly the *life model* [Germain & Gitterman, 1996]) emphasizes mutual adaptation between person and environment. The life model applies ecological constructs such as habitat, niche, parasitism, and stress and coping directly to the social world. (Note the overlap with the ecosystems perspective. It is possible, however, to practice ecosystemically from any practice approach; see chapter 2.) This approach also is grounded in process, including human development over the life course and the processes of helping over time. The model focuses particularly on certain classes of problems, including life transitions, traumas, dysfunctional relationship patterns, and coping with environmental stressors. Related approaches include *person–environment practice* (Kemp, Whittaker, & Tracy, 1997), which heavily emphasizes assessing and enriching social support networks, based on both well-explicated theory and emerging research.

Ecobehavioral Practice. The third major cluster of practice approaches is the ecobehavioral approach, which encompasses traditional behavioral, cognitive, and cognitive–behavioral approaches, but in most contemporary variants pays extensive attention to the social, cultural, and physical contexts of practice rather than focusing tightly on client behavior (whether overt or cognitive). Like other early approaches, behavioral models were initially largely limited to work with overt client behavior; similarly, early cognitive models, and most cognitive–behavioral approaches, tended to focus too narrowly on client self-talk without adequately addressing environmental transactions. Both emphasized the importance of well-supported theory and research, however, which led to their expansion. Modern ecobehavioral practice encompasses both overt action and private experiences (cognitive and emotional), and it recognizes both environmental origins (as does the psychosocial model) and current environmental influences (as does the ecological model) that shape human experience. In its contemporary manifestations, ecobehavioral practice places a heavy focus on shared power in the practice relationship and on the co-construction of an improved personal reality (in contrast to "treating problems") (Mattaini, 1997, 1999). Berlin's (2002) cognitive–integrative approach, one ecobehavioral variation, attends not only to cognitive factors but also to environmental events and conditions and overt behavioral work. These approaches are deeply grounded in behavioral, cognitive, and cultural analytic science.

Alternative Models. In addition to the broad, theory-grounded practice approaches, a number of other contemporary and emerging approaches deserve special note. Particularly important are culturally specific models of practice. For example, Afrocentric models structure practice according to traditional African values and cultural practices (O'Donnell & Karanja, 2000; Schiele, 1996); other models are specific to a single indigenous nation (e.g., a Lakota-specific approach, as described by Voss, Douville, Little Soldier, & Twiss, 1999). Many such approaches, not surprisingly, incorporate a heavy focus on family and community context and de-emphasize individual, pathology-focused diagnosis. Such models can be implemented independently, or components of the models can be integrated with other approaches to practice. This is also true of feminist practice, which can be implemented as a primary model but has also contributed a great deal to nearly every contemporary practice model.

All practice approaches that survive evolve and change over time. For example, the task-centered approach as originally formulated (Reid & Epstein, 1972) was explicitly atheoretical and was designed for practice by a broad range of social workers , but particularly those with psychodynamic backgrounds (the norm at the time). Recent statements of the model (Reid, 2000; Tolson, Reid, & Garvin, 2003) can probably best be described as fitting within the ecobehavioral cluster (Gambrill, 1994) and are heavily evidence based. Most contemporary models evolved from earlier approaches; for an extensive consideration of this history and useful diagrams tracing it, see Germain (1983). Germain predicted that the major practice approaches in the field would converge in important ways, and that indeed has happened during the past two decades. Psychosocial theorists like Goldstein (1995, 2001), for example, now include a significant amount of ecological content in their work, and the ecobehavioral approach integrates ecological, behavioral, and cognitive content. Proponents of differing approaches appear to have considerable mutual respect for each other—a recent and healthy development for the field.

Selecting Practice Approaches. So, how is a practitioner to decide what practice approach to use? Up to a point, a disciplined eclecticism in which techniques and strategies drawn from multiple approaches are selected on the basis of their empirical support can be useful. Random eclecticism, however, in which practice is not shaped by any coherent understanding but simply emerges from momentary preference, intuition, or whim, is neither professional nor likely to be effective—and therefore poses serious ethical problems. When a social worker decides to use "rebirthing" techniques simply because those techniques somehow appeal to her, and a healthy child dies of asphyxiation as a result (as happened recently in Colorado) (Nicholson, 2001), it becomes clear that selection of approaches involves more than personal preference.

Choosing a practice approach, of course, is where evidence-based practice becomes important (Gambrill, 1999). The evidence-based practice process (see chapter 2) guides the social work practitioner toward locating and relying on intervention strategies that have withstood rigorous, critical evaluation, to the extent that such strategies are known. If "what works" is at least partially known, the social worker has an ethical imperative to use that knowledge. Some authors (e.g., Thyer, 2001) involved in the movement toward evidence-based practice believe that it could eventually replace concern with models and approaches and that social workers will then simply do what has been shown to be most effective. In some areas, progress toward that point is occurring. Still, unique problems and situations will always require comprehensive theoretical frameworks to decode and understand.

In general, each social worker needs to achieve a coherent understanding of human behavior in its social and environmental context and decide what practice approaches to use and what actions to take based on that understanding. The social worker develops that understanding on the basis of careful reading of the available evidence and understanding of the adequacy of the theory underlying specific practice approaches. In some cases, psychosocial and behavioral theory may suggest similar approaches, but in others they will suggest dramatically different courses of action; deciding what approach to take may be of profound importance to clients. For example, for a moderately depressed client, traditional psychodynamic treatment may increase risk of deterioration and suicide, whereas strong evidence suggests that certain other approaches (for example, behavioral activation, interpersonal therapy, pharmacological treatments, or cognitive therapy) are likely to help (Nathan & Gorman, 1998). As a general rule, skilled social workers practice from a relatively consistent, coherent theoretical understanding of human behavior while remaining open to integrating possibilities drawn from alternative frameworks.

An additional, crucial determinant of practice approach must be the extent to which it can be applied with clients whose worldviews and experiences may be very different from the social worker's own. Many of the bodies of theory from which practice approaches evolved have European and Anglo American roots, and some can be extended to other cultural groups more comfortably than others. An approach that emphasizes individual autonomy as "healthy," for example, may be damaging to clients whose cultural reality is fundamentally collective. Alternative approaches, therefore, may be more effective with such groups (see, for example, Ross, 2006). Most contemporary practice approaches are paying increasing attention to cultural factors, but some have advanced much further than others in these directions.

Finally, because social work cases are complex, social workers must achieve a high level of theoretical sophistication in their chosen areas. If, for example, one adopts ecological theory as the core of his or her practice and, perhaps, the life model (Germain & Gitterman, 1996) as the primary practice approach, it is not enough simply to know that from this perspective, client issues are seen as problems related to traumatic events, stressful life transitions, environmental problems, or dysfunctional patterns of interpersonal relationships and communication. Responsible professionals must also strive to stay current with emerging findings in ecological science (Hudson, 2000; Wilson, 1992), in the evolutionary biology and natural history in which ecology is itself based, and in the social sciences that are closely tied to these fields (see Harris, 2000). Because the life model also relies on scientific findings related to the life course, stress and coping, and risk and resilience (for example, Fraser, 2004), social workers practicing from this model should be immersed in those additional areas. They should be familiar with popular treatments of these fields and should achieve the sophistication needed to understand the primary sources.

The chapters that follow provide substantial guidance that is based on the current state of the art related to selecting practice approaches at different system levels. It is the responsibility of each social work professional to stay current with emerging knowledge and evidence to provide the quality of services that clients deserve.

Practice Processes

Practice is nonlinear, but it is not random or chaotic. Certain processes must occur if social workers are to be helpful. Those processes tend to occur in a particular but not invariant order. They also are recursive, and social workers will often find themselves cycling back to move ahead.

First, the social worker must be able to engage the client in a genuine human relationship of shared power—not as a separate process, but organically throughout the work. A good deal of research supports what every skilled social worker knows: The facilitating conditions of empathic communication, warmth and respect, and authenticity are crucial. Those principles were first elaborated by Carl Rogers and were subsequently explicitly adopted and adapted by social workers (for example, Hepworth, Rooney, Rooney, Strom-Gottfried, & Larsen, 2005), who had for many years recognized the centrality of the helping relationship (Perlman, 1979). The worker who cannot achieve those necessary (but not sufficient) conditions will fail with most clients. A complication is that we are often not the best judges of our own interpersonal skills, so supervised practice, including feedback, is essential to ensuring competence. The strengths perspective, as discussed in the next chapter, has contributed additional skills for achieving genuinely respectful human relationships with clients. In addition, the emphasis on hope, resilience, and capacity to change that the strengths perspective brings to practice can help both social worker and clients move into their work together with a level of energy and excitement that often is not characteristic of pathology-focused approaches.

Next, assuming that a social worker has these basic skills, he or she must know how to intervene to help. Intervention is always rooted in data about a particular case that are uncovered during exploration and organized in a coherent way in an individualized assessment. Because not everything tried works, an integrated process of monitoring and evaluation is also core to practice. These processes, which are central to effective practice, are emphasized in subsequent chapters, particularly chapter 8.

Contexts of Practice

All practice occurs in a *context*, which shapes the practice. "Context" as used here refers to the systems and conditions that constitute the environment of the case, sometimes at a substantial distance. The results of welfare reform and the changing economy, for example, have had major effects on the way social workers work with clients and communities. In health and, increasingly, in other fields of practice, managed care networks have become the norm, and there is much less emphasis on a private, entrepreneurial model of care. Therefore, the importance of focused, short-term work—which has been growing for some time—continues to grow.

Clients, workers, agencies, and service systems are always embedded in contexts. In work with an individual, for example, family or informal natural networks are often resources for the work, but they can also be sources of the problem and obstacles to intervention (Tolson et al., 2003). Contextual factors that influence practice include policy and funding mechanisms, the physical environment, natural networks, institutions, cultures, and the profession itself. In every case, potential positive and negative effects of contextual factors must inform the social worker's thought. Factors that are particularly salient in a case are likely to occupy the foreground, but it is important not to ignore other factors that may have less obvious but nevertheless meaningful effects on the case. It can also be valuable to think through contextual factors that affect cases within organizational and community networks, to take a fresh look at them now and then, and to think about implications of those forces for achieving the organizational mission. For example, family service agencies have recently moved toward a substantially strengthened recognition of the potential of community-centered practice, as opposed to more traditional approaches, which tend—conceptually and, sometimes, actually—to amputate families from neighborhoods and community networks.

Social work's mission relates primarily to the severe social problems with which people, families, and communities grapple, to ameliorating (or preventing) difficulties, and to intervening in crises. Issues such as violence (domestic and nondomestic), the maltreatment of children, addictions, homelessness, poverty, racism, natural and manmade disasters, effects of war and terrorism (and their complex roots), isolation, and mental and physical illnesses constitute both the content and the context of social work practice. Social workers know a good deal about many of these problems, about their epidemiology and etiology, and about what may be helpful when a client system faces them. For example, a substantial knowledge base exists about what practice strategies are effective and under what circumstances for work with clients struggling with substance abuse and addictions (Higgins & Katz, 1998; Miller & Carroll, 2006). For instance, the *community reinforcement approach* (CRA), has been demonstrated in multiple studies to be substantially superior to traditional treatment for inpatients and outpatients with serious alcohol and drug problems (Meyers & Miller, 2001). Although social workers need not apply this approach with every client with a substance abuse problem, if they will be working with such clients they probably have an ethical mandate to know about it. They and their clients can then reach an informed, collaborative decision about whether to use some variation of CRA or whether they should take a different route.

Most social work practice—even private practice—occurs as part of service systems within fields of practice, organizations, and social institutions. Contemporary fields include families and children, health care, aging, mental health, school-based services, and industrial social work. Conceptual difficulties in finding the bright lines that separate fields are many; note, for example, that the partial list just provided includes fields discriminated by setting, developmental stage, and type of problem. Despite this conceptual inelegance, each field has a certain ad hoc coherence because institutional structures, funding streams, and social policies tend to be organized along those lines and because each field provides access to clients at an important crossroad of life. Fields are continually evolving; some are fading, and others are emerging at any given point in time. Table 1-1 identifies important dimensions that must be taken into account in truly understanding one's field of practice.

Students often find it useful to explore the major elements of the framework depicted in Table 1-1 as a course assignment because doing so clarifies important variables that usually have a powerful impact on practice. It is also a good idea to spend time with agency staff exploring those factors whenever moving into a new field of practice.

A FINAL WORD

This book recognizes that social work is a complex professional field and deals with that complexity; it thus is not an "easy read." The authors, however, have made every effort to write as teachers and practitioners engaged in a collaborative, progressive learning endeavor with the reader. The central purpose of this book is to support courses focused on the foundations of practice by (1) introducing

TABLE I-I

□ □ □ □ □

A Framework for Assessing a Field of Practice

I.   The target population (such as children, youths, older people, or women), the problem addressed in the field (for example, substance abuse, homelessness, AIDS, or immigrant and refugee status), or the specialized settings (including schools, the workplace, hospitals and clinics, or prisons)
II. Earlier historical responses to the problem, population, or settings
III. Framework for provision
     A. Laws and regulations
     B. Explicit and implicit policies (manifest and latent goals, objectives, and purposes)
     C. Funding
     D. Policy-making agency and distribution of responsibility among the levels of government: federal, state, and local
     E. Criteria for eligibility
     F. Coverage (the proportion of the population with the problem or need that is eligible for the service) and take-up (the proportion of eligible people who receive the service)
     G. Comparative perspectives (optional, as relevant)
IV. Program models and delivery systems
     A. Program function: access, entry, or liaison service; case or treatment service; social utility or developmental service; or a combination (specify which)
     B. Community service (neighborhood- or home-based), residential facility, or both
     C. Formal or informal service (self-help or mutual aid)
     D. Administrative auspices (public or private nonprofit or private for-profit, sectarian or nonsectarian, autonomous freestanding or part of a system other than the personal social services)
     E. Funding
     F. Mission
     G. Access (how clients or consumers find out about and obtain the service)
     H. Channeling (How do clients or consumers get processed through the organization or agency?)
     I. Characteristics of the clientele: criteria for eligibility and the number and types of clients served
     J. Links with other services in the same field or in different fields
V.   Practice modes and staffing patterns
     A. Types of services provided and interventions used
     B. Innovative practice modes
     C. Staffing patterns
        1. Professional and paraprofessional roles
        2. Specialist, generalist, case manager roles
        3. Individual or team roles
        4. Unidisciplinary or multidisciplinary staff
VI. Research, evaluation, outcomes
     A. Theoretical knowledge base used or not
     B. Knowledge of effects, effectiveness, impact, and costs
     C. Program innovations
     D. Critiques
VII. An overview of issues, trends, and debates, including positions taken by interest groups and professional associations, new legislative proposals, and quantitative and qualitative adequacy of service provisions

Note: This framework builds on an earlier formulation developed during the 1970s by a committee at the Columbia University School of Social Work.

graduate students to the core knowledge and values of professional practice and (2) encouraging the development of practical skills consistent with that knowledge and those values while (3) viewing the work of social work as supporting social justice within the web of human and wider environmental connectedness. Specialized knowledge and experience accumulated beyond this course will then strike a familiar note because the broad contours of practice have been sketched here.

REFERENCES

Beck, A. T., Steer, R. A., & Brown, G. K. (1996). *Manual for the Beck Depression Inventory* (2nd ed.). San Antonio, TX: Psychological Corporation.

Berlin, S. B. (2002). *Clinical social work practice: A cognitive-integrative perspective.* New York: Oxford University Press.

Besthorn, F. H., & McMillen, D. P. (2002). The oppression of women and nature: Ecofeminism as a framework for an expanded ecological social work. *Families in Society, 83,* 221–232.

Bola, J. R., & Pitts, D. B. (2005). Assessing the scientific status of "schizophrenia." In S. A. Kirk (Ed.), *Mental disorders in the social environment* (pp. 120–136). New York: Columbia University Press.

Brace, C. L. (1973). *The dangerous classes of New York, and twenty years' work among them.* Silver Spring, MD: National Association of Social Workers. (Original work published 1872)

Burman, B., John, R. S., & Margolin, G. (1992). Observed patterns of conflict in violent, nonviolent, and nondistressed couples. *Behavioral Assessment, 14,* 15–37.

Castillo, R. J. (1997). *Culture and mental illness: A client-centered approach.* Pacific Grove, CA: Brooks/Cole.

Collins, B. G. (1993). Reconstruing codependency using self-in-relation theory: A feminist perspective. *Social Work, 38,* 470–476.

Ewalt, P. (Ed.). (1979). *Toward a definition of clinical social work.* Washington, DC: National Association of Social Workers.

Farmer, P. (2003). *Pathologies of power: Health, human rights and the new war on the poor.* Berkeley: University of California Press.

Fraser, M. W. (2004) *Risk and resilience in childhood: An ecological perspective* (2nd ed.). Washington, DC: NASW Press.

Gambrill, E. (1994). What's in a name? Task-centered, empirical, and behavioral practice. *Social Service Review, 68,* 578–599.

Gambrill, E. (1999). Evidence-based practice: An alternative to authority-based practice. *Families in Society, 80,* 341–350.

Gambrill, E. (2003). Evidence-based practice: Implications for knowledge development and use in social work. In A. Rosen & E. K. Proctor (Eds.), *Developing practice guidelines for social work intervention* (pp. 37–58). New York: Columbia University Press.

Germain, C. B. (1983). Technological advances. In A. Rosenblatt & D. Waldfogel (Eds.), *Handbook of clinical social work* (pp. 26–57). San Francisco: Jossey-Bass.

Germain, C. B., & Gitterman, A. (1996). *The life model of social work practice* (2nd ed.). New York: Columbia University Press.

Goldstein, E. G. (1995). *Ego psychology and social work practice* (2nd ed.). New York: Free Press.

Goldstein, E. G. (2001). *Object relations theory and self psychology in social work practice.* New York: Free Press.

Gutierrez, L. (1997). Multicultural community organizing. In M. Reisch & E. Gambrill (Eds.), *Social work in the 21st century* (pp. 249–259). Thousand Oaks, CA: Pine Forge.

Gutierrez, L., GlenMaye, L., & DeLois, K. (1995). The organizational context of empowerment practice: Implications for social work administration. *Social Work, 40,* 249–258.

Harris, M. (2000). *The rise of anthropological theory* (updated edition). Walnut Creek, CA: AltaMira Press.

Hartman, A. (1995). Diagrammatic assessment of family relationships. *Families in Society, 76,* 111–122. (Original work published 1978)

Hepworth, D. H., Rooney, R., Rooney, G. D., Strom-Gottfried, K., & Larsen, J. A. (2005). *Direct social work practice* (7th ed.). Belmont, CA: Wadsworth.

Higgins, S. T., & Katz, J. L. (Eds.). (1998). *Cocaine abuse: Behavior, pharmacology, and clinical applications.* San Diego, CA: Academic Press.

Hudson, C. G. (2000). From social Darwinism to self-organization: Implications for social change theory. *Social Service Review, 74,* 533–559.

Irvine, A. B., Biglan, A., Smolkowski, K., Metzler, C. W., & Ary, D. V. (1999). The effectiveness of a parenting skills program for parents of middle school students in small communities. *Journal of Consulting and Clinical Psychology, 67,* 811–825.

Kemp, S. P., Whittaker, J. K., & Tracy, E. M. (1997). *Person-environment practice.* New York: Aldine de Gruyter.

LaDuke, W. (1999). *All our relations.* Cambridge, MA: South End Press.

Lee, P. R. (1929). Social work: Cause and function. In *Proceedings of the National Conference of Social Work* (pp. 3–20). New York: Columbia University Press.

Lowery, C. T., & Mattaini, M. A. (1999). The science of sharing power: Native American thought and behavior analysis. *Behavior and Social Issues, 9,* 3–23.

Lowery, C. T., & Mattaini, M. A. (2001). Shared power in social work: A Native American perspective of change. In H. Briggs & K. Corcoran (Eds.), *Social work practice: Treating common client problems* (pp. 109–124). Chicago: Lyceum Books.

Marsh, J. C. (2005). Social justice: Social work's organizing value. *Social Work, 50,* 293–294.

Martin, C. L. (1999). *The way of the human being.* New Haven, CT: Yale University Press.

Mattaini, M. A. (1993). *More than a thousand words: Graphics for clinical practice.* Washington, DC: NASW Press.

Mattaini, M. A. (1997). *Clinical practice with individuals.* Washington, DC: NASW Press.

Mattaini, M. A. (1999). *Clinical intervention with families.* Washington, DC: NASW Press.

Mattaini, M. A. (with the PEACE POWER Working Group). (2001). *Peace power for adolescents: Strategies for a culture of nonviolence.* Washington, DC: NASW Press.

Mattaini, M. A. (2002). Understanding and reducing collective violence. *Behavior and Social Issues, 12,* 90–108.

Mattaini, M. A., Grellong, B. A., & Abramovitz, R. (1992). The clientele of a child and family mental health agency: Empirically derived household clusters and implications for practice. *Research on Social Work Practice, 2,* 380–404.

McGoldrick, M., Giordano, J., & Garcia-Preto, N. (Eds.). (2005). *Ethnicity and family therapy* (3rd ed.). New York: Guilford Press.

Meyer, C. H. (1979). Introduction: Making organizations work for people. In C. H. Meyer (Ed.), *Making organizations work for people* (pp. 1–12). Washington, DC: National Association of Social Workers.

Meyer, C. H. (1993). *Assessment in social work practice.* New York: Columbia University Press.

Meyers, R. J., & Miller, W. R. (2001). *A community reinforcement approach to addiction treatment.* New York: Cambridge University Press.

Miller, W. R., & Carroll, K. M. (2006). *Rethinking substance abuse: What the science shows, and what we should do about it.* New York: Guilford Press.

Mullen, E. J., & Bacon, W. F. (2003). Practitioner adoption and implementation of practice guidelines and issues of quality control. In A. Rosen & E. K. Proctor (Eds.), *Developing practice guidelines for social work intervention* (pp. 223–235). New York: Columbia University Press.

Nathan, P. E., & Gorman, J. M. (Eds.). (1998). *A guide to treatments that work.* New York: Oxford University Press.

National Institute on Alcohol Abuse and Alcoholism. (2000). *10th special report to the U.S. Congress on alcohol and health.* Rockville, MD: Author.

Nicholson, K. (2001, June 19). "Rebirth" therapists get 16 years. *Denver Post,* p. A-01.

O'Donnell, S. M., & Karanja, S. T. (2000). Transformative community practice: Building a model for developing extremely low income African-American communities. *Journal of Community Practice, 7*(3), 67–84.

Patterson, D. A., & Jaffe, J. (1994). Hypermedia computer-based education in social work education. *Journal of Social Work Education, 30,* 267–277.

Patterson, G. R. (1976). The aggressive child: Victim and architect of a coercive system. In E. J. Mash, L. A. Hamerlynck, & L. C. Handy (Eds.), *Behavior modification and families* (pp. 267–316). New York: Brunner/Mazel.

Peele, S. (1995). *Diseasing of America: How we allowed recovery zealots and the treatment industry to convince us we are out of control.* San Francisco: Jossey-Bass.

Perlman, H. H. (1979). *Relationship, the heart of helping people.* Chicago: University of Chicago Press.

Reid, J. B., Patterson, G. R., & Snyder, J. J. (Eds.). (2002). *Antisocial behavior in children and adolescents: A developmental analysis and the Oregon model for intervention.* Washington, DC: American Psychological Association.

Reid, W. J. (2000). *The task planner.* New York: Columbia University Press.

Reid, W. J., & Epstein, L. (1972). *Task-centered casework.* New York: Columbia University Press.

Richmond, M. E. (1917). *Social diagnosis.* New York: Russell Sage Foundation.

Rosen, A., & Proctor, E. K. (2003). *Developing practice guidelines of social work intervention.* New York: Columbia University Press.

Ross, R. (2006). *Returning to the teachings: Exploring aboriginal justice* (2nd ed.). Toronto: Penguin Canada.

Sadock, B. J., & Sadock, V. A. (2003). *Kaplan and Sadock's concise textbook of clinical psychiatry.* Philadelphia: Lippincott Williams & Wilkins.

Saleebey, D. (Ed.). (2006). *The strengths perspective in social work practice* (4th ed.). Boston: Allyn & Bacon.

Schiele, J. H. (1996). Afrocentricity: An emerging paradigm in social work practice. *Social Work, 41*, 284–294.

Sidman, M. (2001). *Coercion and its fallout* (Rev. ed.). Boston: Authors Cooperative.

Sullivan, W. P., & Rapp, C. A. (2006). *Honoring philosophical traditions: The strengths model and the social environment.* In D. Saleebey (Ed.), The strengths perspective in social work practice (4th ed., pp. 261–278). Boston: Allyn & Bacon.

Thyer, B. A. (2001). Introductory principles of social work research. In B. A. Thyer (Ed.), *The handbook of social work research methods* (pp. 1–24). Thousand Oaks, CA: Sage Publications.

Tolson, E. R., Reid, W. J., & Garvin, C. D. (2003). *Generalist practice: A task-centered approach.* New York: Columbia University Press.

U.S. Surgeon General. (2001). *Youth violence: A report of the Surgeon General.* Washington, DC: Department of Health and Human Services. (Also available through www.surgeongeneral. gov/library/youthviolence)

Voss, R. W., Douville, V., Little Soldier, A., & Twiss, G. (1999). Tribal and shamanic-based social work practice: A Lakota perspective. *Social Work, 44*, 228–241.

Wilson, E. O. (1992). *The diversity of life.* Cambridge, MA: Belknap/Harvard University Press.

Wong, S. E. (2006). Behavior analysis of psychotic disorders: Scientific dead end or casualty of the mental health political economy? *Behavior and Social Issues, 15*, 152–177.

Woods, M. E., & Hollis, F. (1999). *Casework: A psychosocial therapy* (5th ed.). New York: McGraw-Hill.

2

□□□

Perspectives for Practice

Mark A. Mattaini and Christine T. Lowery

Given the complexities involved in practice, social workers need to develop ways of looking at client realities that help them sort out what is happening and where to begin to work. Perspectives are not practice models, and they are not meant to tell the social worker what to do. Rather, they clarify how to look at and think about cases in a comprehensive way. For example, the purpose of the ecosystems perspective is to ensure that the practitioner pays attention to the multiple interacting elements that are always present in a case, particularly in assessment. Several other perspectives—ways of looking at complicated case realities—however, have also proven to be critically important. This chapter presents four perspectives on practice, each of which yields different but essential information about the case, as portrayed in Figure 2-1.

In addition to the ecosystems perspective, the other perspectives considered in depth here are those of *shared power*, *social justice*, and *evidence-based practice*. The emerging *strengths* perspective is also important in contemporary social work; for reasons explained below, it is subsumed here under the perspective of shared power. To understand the case, the social worker metaphorically moves around the wheel shown in the figure, examining the case from multiple standpoints. With experience, it often becomes possible to attend to more than one perspective at once, but it is essential that none of these important dimensions be ignored. As will become clear in the discussion that follows, these ways of looking at a case are not truly separate but are, in fact, deeply intertwined.

FIGURE 2-1
□ □ □ □ □
Four Perspectives on Social Work Practice

THE ECOSYSTEMS PERSPECTIVE

Although the *person-in-environment* concept has governed practice since the work of Mary Richmond (1917) nearly a century ago and has been defined and redefined (Hamilton, 1951; Hollis, 1972) over the years, its hyphenated structure (the separation between "person" and "environment") has contributed to a continuing imbalance—that is, greater emphasis on either the person or the environment. One consequence has been the tendency of practitioners to avoid environmental interventions in favor of changing people in isolation from their life situations because the environment is often seen as intractable and difficult to affect (Kemp, Whittaker, & Tracy, 1997). Research by Rosen and Livne (1992) demonstrated that social workers tend to focus on intrapersonal issues at the expense of transactional problems that have significant environmental roots. Lindsey (1998) found that social workers often do not recognize limited financial resources, shortages of services (for example, housing assistance, substance abuse treatment), lack of social support, or battering as significant obstacles to restabilizing homeless families (although they are known to be). Clinical social workers' choice to focus on the person to the exclusion of the environment may also have had something to do with the view that their professional status was dependent on their engaging in practice similar to that of psychiatrists and psychotherapists.

The *ecosystems perspective* (Auerswald, 1968; Meyer, 1976) emerged from two sets of ideas: the science of ecology (DuBos, 1972) and general systems theory (von Bertalanffy, 1968). The perspective was adopted in social work beginning in the 1960s as a way of seeing the person and the environment in their interconnected and transactional reality—to order and comprehend complexity while avoiding oversimplification and reductionism. It provides a way of placing conceptual boundaries around cases to provide limits and define the parameters of practice with individuals, families, groups, and communities.

Ecology

Ecology is the science concerned with the adaptive fit of organisms and their environments and the means by which they achieve a dynamic balance. Ecological science captures the organic interdependence among all living things as people and their environments adapt to each other through time. Ecological thinking has been applied as a metaphor in the life model of practice; it has also been applied in a somewhat abstract but nonmetaphoric way by, for example, the ecofeminists. In the *life model* (Germain & Gitterman, 1996), ecological constructs such as *habitat* (the physical and social settings within a cultural context in which people live out their lives) and *niche* (the status of a person or group within a social structure) are used to understand human relatedness. The life model also identifies human analogues to pollution and parasitism as ways of ecologically conceptualizing oppression. This approach is grounded in process, including human development over the life course and the processes of helping over time. The foci of work emphasized in this approach include life transitions, traumatic experiences, dysfunctional relationship patterns, and coping with environmental stressors, all of which are understood in terms of establishing stable but dynamic ecological adaptations.

Ecofeminists, by contrast, understand human beings and human communities as inextricably embedded in the natural world, parts of a single natural ecology (Besthorn & McMillen, 2002). Nature is viewed as one with and beneficial for humanity, and "radical interconnectedness" is seen as the reality. The goal of practice becomes revitalization of each person's direct, lived, sensual experience within the complex web of which we are a part. Ecofeminism is concerned with the dynamics of all forms of domination and patriarchy, and it views all oppressions (for example, of women and nature) as inextricably linked. This view challenges traditional hierarchical views, whether grounded in gender, race, culture, species, or other characteristics, and it suggests that issues of environmental degradation and understandings of the human place in nature cannot be separated from systemic forces that maintain multiple oppressions. The consistency of ecofeminist thought with indigenous worldviews around the world is notable.

Ecological concepts are powerful ideas that move far beyond a primary focus on individual dynamics while viewing the person as a key actor in a much larger systemic field. This perspective suggests, for example, that a gay man being battered by his partner can be understood only in the context of cultures grounded in heteronormativity and the associated oppression; transactional patterns within the couple, family, and friendship networks; and the physical realities of his life. (*Heteronormativity* is a pattern of thinking or acting demonstrating an expectation that everyone is heterosexual; for example, seeing a wedding ring and asking about a woman's "husband" rather than her spouse or partner.) Adequate intervention may then need to address several or all of these dimensions. Ecological dynamics are clearly complex; general systems theory has proven useful for understanding how transactional processes actually play out.

General Systems Theory

General systems theory (GST) is often seen as a genuinely different way of thinking about the world that involves a shift from linear thinking (cause → effect) to a view in which events are seen as multiply and reciprocally caused. For example, a teenage client is not viewed as using drugs simply because he was sexually abused by a stepfather; rather, what has transpired between the two of them is one small part of an ongoing, transactional field of events. As a result, many routes may be available for assisting the client in shaping a more fulfilling life (reflecting a systems concept called "equifinality"). Systems thinking is increasingly seen as a way of viewing self-regulating systems in transaction with their environments (for example, cells, organisms, even entire ecosystemic communities) that is consistent with emerging science (Mattaini, in press). Beginning in the late 1960s, social work thinkers—Carel Germain (for example, Germain, 1973) and Carol Meyer (for example, Meyer, 1976, 1983, 1988) in particular—recognized the utility of systems concepts for understanding the complicated transactional realities with which the profession works.

Among useful GST concepts are the following:

+ *Boundaries.* Living systems (persons, families, organizations) construct boundaries that determine what is inside and what is outside the system, and they exchange energy across that boundary. Overly rigid boundaries result in relatively closed systems that cannot import adequate energy and gradually run down. Overly permeable boundaries, by contrast, result in loss of systemic integrity; systems with such diffuse boundaries dissipate into the environment. Boundaries that are either too rigid or too open are common among troubled families, for example.

+ *Structure.* Living systems are in constant flux, but they maintain a dynamic stability of structure through the change. The structure of such a system is not like the static stability of a mobile, which collapses if something changes (like a thread being cut), but rather like a whirlpool, in which the water flows constantly but the pattern of events remains relatively stable. Families again offer a good example; flexibility and adaptability are known to be key to effective family functioning (see chapter 9), but conservation of family culture and routine is also critical.

+ *Hierarchy.* Systems are organizations of lower-level subsystems and may be organized into higher-level supersystems. For instance, a human body requires the interaction of multiple subsystems, such as the circulatory and neurological systems, to survive. Family therapists have found Minuchin's (1974) concepts of the parental, couple, and child subsystems of the family system to be particularly useful for determining where intervention should focus, and communities (supersystems) are constituted of families (which are subsystems of those communities) This implies that the same system, say the family, may at sometimes be viewed as the focal system, sometimes as a subsystem, and sometimes as a supersystem. This nested organization is the core of GST.

+ *Equifinality.* A satisfactory case outcome may often be reached by multiple routes; if one approach is not available, another may be. For example, finding a "passion" may help resolve demoralization for a teen who refuses psychotherapy (and may, in fact, be a better approach).

+ *Multifinality.* Many outcomes may be possible, given a single beginning state. An impoverished African American woman who is being beaten by her partner may become mired in depression and despair; may become an advocate for legal action to end the human rights violations involved in battering; or may become a womanist activist working with other people experiencing multiple oppressions associated with the intersections of race, gender, and class, depending on her experiences with her world. Multifinality is hopeful and contradicts strong determinism; where a person is today does not determine where he or she will be tomorrow.

Other systems concepts, including feedback; energy flow; input, output, and throughput; differentiation and specialization; and positive and negative entropy can also be useful in social work and are often considered in detail in courses on human behavior and the social environment (see Anderson, Carter, & Lowe, 1999, for additional detail).

Recent Advances in Systems Thinking

As in other sciences, knowledge in ecological systems thinking continues to advance. Several principles with direct application to social work have emerged from recent systemic research and theory. (For additional detail, see Capra, 1996, who provides a readable summary. Hudson [2000] provided a good review of material on emergence and self-organization, which are key constructs in modern systems thinking. Emergent ideas related to complexity theory are summarized in Warren, Franklin, & Streeter, 1998.) Important emerging concepts in systems thinking include

- a shift to viewing webs of transactional relationships, rather than objects, as the basic elements of reality
- the central importance of self-organization in those networks
- the crucial place of diversity in those self-organizing systems.

Brief summaries of work in each of these areas may be useful for deepening understanding of the value of systems thinking.

Primacy of Relationships. Contemporary biology and physics have come to recognize that reality consists not of a collection of objects but of an "inseparable web of relationships" (Capra, 1996, p. 37). The primary components of this web are *patterns of transactional events*; objects (including organisms) are secondary and have reality only in networks of relationships. Figures 2-2 and 2-3 illustrate this change of perspective. Cells, organisms, families, ecosystems—all systems, large or small, are organized in this network pattern. Figures 2-2 and 2-3, therefore, can be viewed as depicting the dynamics of any nested systems; the primacy of transactions over objects applies in all cases. For example, a community may be seen as a network of transactions among families, businesses, and institutions, each of which is itself a network of transactions among people, which in turn are organic networks of biological organs in transaction, and so forth. "Members of an ecological community are interconnected in a vast and intricate network of relationships, the web of life. They derive their essential properties and, in fact, their very existence from their relationships to other things" (Capra, p. 298). This understanding has profound implications for social work practice; all of practice is ultimately work not with a client but with a network of transactions within which that person's existence is embedded.

FIGURE 2-2

FIGURE 2-2

□ □ □ □ □

Traditional View of Systemic Reality

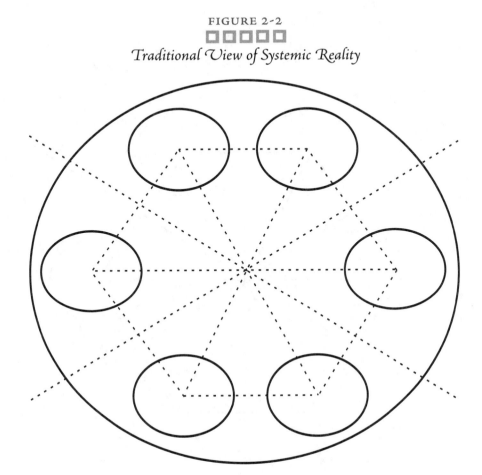

Note: In the traditional view of systemic reality, *objects* (for example, people, families, and communities) are viewed as the core of reality, and relationships among them are considered incidental.

Self-Organizing Networks. Recent systems work has also expanded our understanding of the structure and boundaries of such transactional networks (Hudson, 2000). These networks, technically termed "autopoietic" (Maturana & Varela, 1980), are self-organizing and "self-making." The dynamic patterns of transactions that constitute the network are organized by the network itself and establish their own self-constructed boundaries. The boundaries—for example, that of a family or a network of fictive kin constructed among a group of gay persons—provide a natural structure for practice.

Such networks "couple" with their contextual environments through transactions across the boundary. How a network responds to an influence from outside

FIGURE 2-3

□□□□□

Emerging Contemporary Systems View

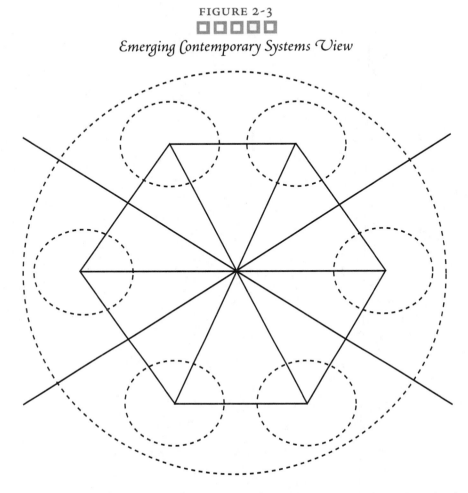

Note: In this view, the essential reality consists of *transactions*; objects are the emergent results of patterns of transactions. A family, for example, only exists in the transactions among its members, and a person lives only so long as transactional biological events continue.

is determined by the state and structure of the network. For example, two families may be coupled to a dangerous neighborhood. One may respond by collapsing, its boundaries diffuse and its members lost to the street. Another may respond with great resilience, by taking collective steps to couple with healthier networks (churches and youth organizations, for example). The response of each family cannot be predicted from knowledge of the impinging environment because the enduring patterns of transactions within each family are key determinants. At the same time, increasing environmental stresses will gradually overwhelm the resilience of increasing numbers of families. Responses to major disasters like Hurricane Katrina in New Orleans in 2005 offer examples. Many families who had managed quite adequately under normal circumstances were unable to maintain their balance in the aftermath of the disaster. Others, however, proved enormously resilient and found ways to emerge intact, even when largely left on their own to cope.

Role of Diversity. Diversity is regarded as key to ecological stability and balance in ecology. "A diverse ecosystem will also be resilient. . . . The more complex the network is, the more complex its pattern of interconnections, the more resilient it will be" (Capra, 1996, p. 303). In human society, many people regard respect and appreciation for diversity as primarily a matter of "political correctness," but systems thinking tells us that diversity may be key to cultural and spiritual survival. One culture may offer possible solutions to problems that are intractable for other groups. Consider the criminal justice system in the United States: Incarceration produces profound emotional, social, and spiritual damage for those enmeshed in the system—not just prisoners, but also those who work in the system. Ultimately, we are all damaged, for we are all connected. The damage is serious and continuous, but no way out of this cycle is apparent within the practices of dominant culture. Indigenous groups, however, have developed entirely different responses to socially damaging actions from their very different worldviews, responses that can be much less expensive, more effective, and more humane (Ross, 2006). Tragically, cultural diversity is disappearing as rapidly as is biodiversity (Davidson, 1994), creating profound implications for human society.

Advantages and Limitations of the Ecosystems Perspective for Practice

Although the ecosystems perspective has been almost universally accepted in social work over the past three decades, some critiques (for example, Wakefield, 1996a, 1996b) have drawn the profession's attention to the perspective's inevitable limitations and have been helpful in sharpening ecosystemic thought. Perspectives (and practice theories) are valuable to the extent that they contribute to positive outcomes. No single perspective, theory, or worldview is universally best; note again the importance of diversity for survival of any living system, including that of the social work profession. Nonetheless, the ecosystems perspective has demonstrated its usefulness in a number of ways, outlined below.

The importance of expanding social workers' view of cases is more than rhetorical, given research indicating that practitioners tend to focus on some areas at the expense of others. Social workers, like everyone else, pay attention to the questions they ask themselves or are asked. As discussed above, considerable research indicates that social work practitioners and students tend not to look at multiple transactional levels of their cases unless they rely on a structure for ensuring that they do so. The function of the ecosystems perspective is to ensure that questions about the broad contextual fields that structure cases are asked.

Assessment. Wakefield (1996a), in his critique of the ecosystems perspective, suggested that the perspective is not useful for assessment. Several arguments can be made for its utility for that purpose, however. First, the perspective has stimulated considerable development of assessment tools, including the ecomap (Jordan & Franklin, 2003), all of which direct the practitioner's attention to potentially critical areas that are otherwise often missed.

Second, the perspective draws attention to factors that have a major effect on cases, even if they cannot be addressed directly. For example, the experiences of a person of color with personal and institutional oppression need to be acknowledged—and often directly addressed—in practice. Despite claims to the contrary, many social workers who do not ask the core ecosystems question "What are the principal positive and aversive transactions the client experiences or could experience, and how can they be addressed?" simply miss such factors (Mattaini, in press). As one of the author's clients replied in response to his question about a problem with a potential landlord, "Race is always part of the issue!" So are gender, social class, sexual orientation, the physical and social environments, and the other variables toward which the ecosystems perspective points.

Third, practitioners operating without an ecosystems framework may agree with Wakefield's (1996a) assertion that "assessment is, to a large extent, a matter of defining the client's problem. . . . A framework that does not help with problem definition cannot be said in any significant sense to help in assessment" (p. 14). Social work assessment, however, is *not* primarily about diagnosing a client's problem but rather about determining what new reality should be constructed within a framework of social justice, how that reality differs from the present reality, and what resources will be required to move from the latter to the former. A medical model suggests that finding a simple diagnosis of client pathology and treating it is the essence of the work, but social work practice is far broader than that. Assessment is a shared process between social worker and client, in which they co-construct a vision of an improved life configuration and develop a realistic plan to get there (see chapter 8; also Cowger, Anderson, & Snively, 2006). Problem definition is only one, often minor, dimension of such assessment.

Connectedness. The ecosystems perspective emphasizes the connectedness among case elements and is consistent with contemporary physical, behavioral, and ecological science as well as many important philosophic traditions. This emphasis has been criticized, however. For example, Wakefield (1996a) suggested that more linear, "domain-specific clinical theories" are required to decide which of the possible or actual connections are relevant to a case and doubted the "general existence of the proposed circular transactions in social work cases" (p. 11). The first observation is, in one sense, true: One needs both a coherent theoretical model and a broad ecosystemic view of cases to practice social work.

The examples given to support Wakefield's doubts about reciprocal transactions, however, are problematic. For example, Wakefield (1996a) indicated that the notion of connectedness and transactional causation might suggest false circular causes (for example, that "institutionalized mental patients' symptoms are due to feedback from the asylum's social structure"; p. 12). Wakefield believed that symptoms are almost entirely biologically determined. Wakefield also indicated that "almost all instances of abuse of children seem to be best explained by linear causal processes originating entirely in the environment" (p. 13). (Wakefield's meaning is less clear here; he may be referring to environmental stresses. Whatever "the environment" means here, however, from the context he apparently does mean that some single set of causal processes leads directly to abuse.) These illustrations are actually excellent examples of complexity and reciprocal transaction. Although the underlying causes of schizophrenia appear to be primarily biological, for example, the form and severity of symptoms are extensively shaped by the institutional or family environment within which the patient is embedded (Wong, 2006), and the course of the illness is profoundly affected by cultural factors (Castillo, 1997). The child maltreatment research indicates that children with more difficult temperaments (generally viewed as present from birth) are at higher risk for abuse (Rutter, 1987); that many transactional factors within and outside the family appear to be involved in the etiology of abuse; and that intervention with child, parent, and environment may be needed (see chapter 13).

Note that this analysis says nothing about blame or responsibility, only that psychosocial phenomena are, at root, deeply interconnected. A child born with a difficult temperament is not responsible for being abused, for example. However, helping children who are "difficult" learn to get what they need in less challenging ways does reduce the chances that they will be abused and increase the chances that they will receive affection and attention from parents, teachers, and peers; we do them no favor by ignoring that fact. In addition, although the primary intervention in cases of child maltreatment involves work with the parent, the outcome of that work is profoundly affected by other social transactions experienced by the parent (Dumas & Wahler, 1983). Similarly, the batterer is responsible for domestic violence. Nevertheless, the most effective approach to protecting women from domestic violence consists of limiting the batterer's access to his or her victim (who certainly bears no responsibility for the abuse), helping the victim make a safety plan, and offering opportunities for social support and building critical consciousness regarding the oppression involved. In many cases, the most effective preventive and interventive programming for human problems focuses on recognizing and manipulating indirect variables rather than on simple unicausal or linear approaches. Connectedness is real.

SHARED POWER PERSPECTIVE

The second major perspective on practice shown in Figure 2-1, that of shared power, is rooted in "web thinking" (Lowery & Mattaini, 1999, 2001) and requires the connectedness principle of ecosystems. From this view (which is grounded in Native American thought), all actions on the part of the social worker, client, and other actors in the case either contribute to or damage the interconnected reality within which the actors are embedded. The focus of practice is on working toward a point at which all actors with a stake in the case (for example, biological parents, foster parents, foster child, social worker, and other professionals) have strong voices in planning, make contributions from their respective strengths, and share responsibility for the outcome. (Note the link to the strengths perspective here.) All actors do not bear "equal" responsibility; each actor carries different responsibilities. All collectively share responsibility for the child's welfare. This approach is possible only if the essential interconnections among case elements are recognized.

Power and Empowerment

Social workers are often quite comfortable talking about "empowerment"; the term seems nonthreatening and affirming. A number of issues must be faced, however. First, "empower" is a transitive verb; someone or something empowers someone else. If the social worker empowers the client, the real power lies not with the client but with the worker. If the client empowers him- or herself, the role of the worker is not entirely clear; this lack of clarity presents a question that some empowerment theorists have found difficult to resolve. Empowerment is a good thing, but the issues are deeper than may be immediately evident. One critical consideration is that the root of the word empowerment is *power*; not all social workers are comfortable thinking of their work or their clients' situations in terms of power dynamics. But reality involves power.

A clear understanding of power is essential to discussions of empowerment and shared power. Within a traditional social work view of power, one seeks to achieve a "power balance between workers and clients" (Hasenfeld, 1987, p. 476). "A has power *over* B when A has the potential to obtain favorable outcomes *at B's expense.* Moreover, the power of A *over* B indicates the dependence of B on A" [italics added] (Hasenfeld, p. 473). Power, within this view, is adversarial, limited, coercive, and potentially exploitive. If that is what power really is, the social worker needs to give it up, of course; it is not clear that this is the kind of power that clients need to develop, either. Some empowerment and feminist social workers offer "shared power" as an alternative, but they continue to view power as limited and adversarial, suggesting that the social worker must "give up power" so the client can get it. Power, in each of these understandings, is limited, adversarial, and essentially hydraulic—if someone's power increases, someone else's must decrease. No wonder social workers have not universally embraced this view!

Adversarial power is real, however. Contemporary U.S. society relies heavily on coercive, egocentric, and competitive practices in most major social institutions. A scaffolding of adversarial power is used by dominant (note the word) society to maintain social order within the justice system, institutions of social welfare, many schools and workplaces, many religious institutions, and even many families (Sidman, 2001). As discussed in a later section, many social justice and human rights issues are involved in this matrix of adversarial power, within which many clients find themselves inextricably entrapped. Those who lack the repertoires or resources required to meet educational or work expectations, for example, are often punished and may ultimately be excluded from opportunities to access essential economic and other resources. A homeless person for whom no adequate living situation exists is often blamed for his or her condition not only by the larger society but often by overworked professionals within the social welfare system, who are frustrated when they have no resources to offer and the client continues to stand in front of them in need. A well-intentioned social worker can be absorbed into such adversarial systems without recognizing that it is happening. A social worker operating from some views of empowerment might encourage the client in this situation to "empower himself" to find housing—even though it is actually difficult or impossible for the client to do so. The worker here is shifting responsibility, but not offering a real alternative— "giving up" power that she never had. When the client fails, it can then be seen as the client's failure. Genuine sharing of power, however, offers an authentic and truly powerful alternative.

Shared Power

We suggest here that the social worker adopt a dramatically distinct view of power that emerges from certain indigenous worldviews (Lowery & Mattaini, 1999) and leads to a different path toward empowerment. This approach emerges from a worldview that recognizes that every person lives his or her life as part of a web of visible and invisible connections that we as human beings share with each other and with all other life forms. Every action either contributes to or damages that web. Opening prayers at Native American gatherings often include a phrase such as "We pray that we will do things in a good way, with a good spirit, so that everyone may benefit." Interconnections among persons (and the rest of the living world) are viewed not only as environmental but as essential to who one is and as spiritual in nature.

Within this perspective, power is not limited, nor need it be adversarial. Power is viewed as a gift, and one begins with the assumption that everyone carries many kinds of power and can learn other kinds. Resources may be limited, but power is not a material resource. Power is not a possession, not something that one "has" but rather an expression of who one is and what one can do. Rather than having power, one "does" power—power emerges only in action, it is process. And it is a gift, not something one "takes credit" for in an egocentric way. Recognizing one's own power as a gift is humbling and prepares one for appreciation of the power of others and for a process of mutual contribution from the gifts of each. If someone increases his or her power (a process the social worker can nurture using her own power), no one loses power; rather, the total power available to do what needs to be done increases. This approach is neither abstract nor idealistic; it simply recognizes that using all available personal resources well is more likely to produce good results.

Acting from an understanding of shared power requires honoring the gifts and power of everyone involved, which in turn requires actively reaching for the voices of all, so that each has a strong voice in establishing direction and taking action together. One goes into a dynamic of shared power speaking, thinking, and feeling that the people involved are doing this together, that they share responsibility for what happens, that they each have something critically important to offer. No one is giving up power; instead, everyone is actively pooling power to work toward a goal that is good for all. Empowerment, then, is mutual, transactional, and active. Within a shared power perspective, the social worker and client are in it together and work toward an outcome that is good for all. It is not good for the human web, for example, if a child is abused—and because I am part of that web, it is not good for me. The contrast with a view of practice in which "I as expert treat your pathology" is stark.

The strengths perspective, discussed next, has several important contributions to make to the sharing of power. Social work practice does, of course, occur within a sociocultural matrix that relies extensively on adversarial power; following the discussion of strengths, this chapter turns to that critical issue. Liberation from oppression, discussed later, is ultimately a collective endeavor.

Strengths

Dennis Saleebey and his colleagues have spent the past two decades developing a genuinely different perspective on practice, the *strengths perspective* (Saleebey, 2006). Strengths theorists early on noted a "fascination with problems and pathology" among social workers and other professionals and suggested that the way this fascination structured practice led to "a relentless march toward hemming in each aspect of the human condition, even human nature itself, as reflective of some behavioral, emotional, and/or cognitive ills" (Saleebey, 2006, p. 3). As a result, mental health, rather than a desirable condition, has "turned into a thriving and handsomely rewarding business" (Saleebey, p. 3). The strengths approach, although not denying problems or oppression, begins with and works with the client's strengths, which have often been largely or entirely ignored in traditional practice. (Strengths can be viewed as reflections of personal power.) The practice process, from this perspective, really is different; attention to strengths is not just one component of practice, but rather is seen as the core of the work that needs to be done.

Table 2-1 lists a number of core values and principles underlying strengths-based practice; those values and principles overlap extensively with shared-power practice. Beginning with the notion that every person, group, family, and community has strengths suggests that each entity brings potential power to the table. The notion that "we serve clients best by collaborating with them" clearly reflects at least some of the dynamics of shared power (although these dynamics are not, as discussed below, fully developed in the strengths approach). Assessment in this perspective involves identifying with the client the social and political strengths and obstacles in the environment, as well as identifying the psychological and physical strengths and obstacles within the client. These lists then provide tools for working toward achieving an improved outcome for the client.

The principles listed in Table 2-1 and the specific guidance that strengths-based practitioners offer regarding the range of potential strengths are enormously important for practice and should not be minimized, even given the obstacles to strengths-based practice within current practice structures. Although practitioners have much to learn from this approach, it has clear limitations. First, strengths are usually described as something a client "has" and, as such, are somewhat static; power, by contrast, is something that is only realized in action. Strengths are also not usually described in transactional terms; power, however, is transactional and ecosystemic by its very nature. If poorly conducted, a strengths assessment can come across as patronizing—as simply a list of affirmations in the face of real struggle. Although the developers of the strengths perspective are working hard to address this issue, it can sometimes be operationalized in too naïve a way, thus minimizing real obstacles. For example, it is true that people are often resilient in the face of serious trouble, but it is also clear that as risks accumulate, such resilience can ultimately be overwhelmed. Finally, it is not entirely clear what "pooling strengths" (as is sometimes discussed in strengths literature) means in action; sharing power, however, is collaborative at its core. In our view, therefore, strengths-based practice has much to contribute to social work, but it is only one dimension of sharing power.

TABLE 2-1
□□□□□
Values and Principles of the Strengths Perspective

- Every person, human collective, and environment is rich with strengths: Every person, groups and environment has a wealth of assets, resources, wisdom, and knowledge; they may be evident only if the social worker actively seeks them out, but they are the seeds of transformation and growth.

- Heroism and hope: Clients are viewed through a lens of liberation and hope. The assumption is that whatever pain and oppression life may have dealt, a craving to survive and affirm life remains and can be released in the work.

- Plasticity: People carry the potential for change, whatever their life experiences. Behavior, feelings, and thinking all can change, given the opportunity. The upper limits of the capacity to grow and change are not known, so clients' aspirations should be taken seriously.

- Membership: Everyone is born with a natural need for belonging and is entitled to a valued place in the human community.

- Resilience: People have the strength to rebound from and overcome trials and adversity, to bear up and ultimately thrive despite damage that has been done. Trauma and struggle can do serious harm, but they may be sources of strength and opportunity.

- Healing and wholeness: Human beings are born with a natural capacity for healing and health. Rather than "curing" the client, the social worker takes action to catalyze the client's own capacity for healing.

- Dialogue: "Humans can only come into being through a creative and emergent relationship with others" (Saleebey, 2006, p. 14). Humanity is confirmed and supported through dialogue that recognizes the unique perspective of each person and group.

- Collaboration: The role of expert is not the best stance for practice, because it closes the door to client expertise and the emergence of the client's wisdom and personal narratives. A collaborative stance may also reduce the risk of paternalism, victim blaming, and victim creating.

- Suspension of disbelief: Social workers often have been trained to expect that client perceptions will be distorted and biased and that clients are likely to be dishonest. Affirming clients' views, perspectives, and values and avoiding the creation of a dynamic in which clients must be dishonest to receive services are key to genuine engagement.

Sharing Power in Practice

The social worker using a shared power perspective enters the case with a commitment to finding and working with the power carried by those involved along with a humble and honest recognition of the gifts and power he or she brings to the case. This commitment plays itself out at every stage. Imagine that the case involves a low-income, single mother who is struggling with her 14-year-old daughter around involvement with a 17-year-old boy, curfew issues, and concern about possible beginning substance use. During early engagement, the worker actively reaches for the experiences, feelings, and emotions of both family members (and perhaps other members of their social network, where appropriate) with full faith that each person brings important strengths and potential to their work together. The worker is hopeful, seeing both mother and daughter in their power. Perhaps the girl brings real enthusiasm and energy for building a fulfilling life for herself and genuine love for her mother, and the mother brings active concern for her daughter and a capacity for listening. The social worker brings her knowledge of evidence-based practice (see below), her ecosystemic eye that attends to factors outside the relationship that are affecting it, and skills honed over time for practice with families. Knowing her own skill in assisting the healing of damaged relationships and her ability to engage across age differences, the worker early in the process discusses with the family her confidence that the three of them together have the power to construct a future that works for both the mother and the daughter—and that they each carry real responsibility for making that happen. What the mother and daughter each brings to the table is discussed to clarify that each person does have much to contribute—and that each truly needs the other.

Shared power continues to play itself out at every stage of the practice process. Mother and daughter are helped to envision how they each would like the family to look upon conclusion of their work together. The social worker's responsibility here is to emphasize commonalities while ensuring that both the mother's and the daughter's voices are truly heard. Assessment pays considerable attention to how each client, and both together, have previously faced challenges and what gifts they bring that they can leverage toward improving communication and healing the relationship. Each participant—social worker and family member—will be consistently involved in determining exactly what steps to take, in evaluating progress, and in designing a plan to maintain progress that has been made.

A graduate-level social worker is ultimately an autonomous professional and has responsibility for ensuring that practice occurs within a dynamic of shared power. Without doubt, doing so in a comprehensive way is easier within an agency structure that supports practice of this kind. Lorraine Gutierrez, who has made important contributions to empowerment theory and practice, and her colleagues have conducted research into ways in which social service agencies can support or impede empowerment practice (Gutierrez, GlenMaye, & DeLois, 1995). Among their important findings are that the primary barriers to such practice include funding arrangements, the larger social context of the organization, and interpersonal and intrapersonal factors. They also found, however, that these factors could be counterbalanced to a substantial degree through empow-erment-oriented staff development, a culture of shared power within the organi-zation, and strong administrative leadership for empowerment practice.

Within agency cultures, certain practices appear to be common and impor-tant for establishing a climate of shared power:

- high levels of mutual recognition for positive actions
- low levels of aversive (coercive, adversarial, exploitive) exchanges among organizational actors
- active reaching for alternative perspectives and voices
- high levels of honesty and authenticity
- exploration of multiple and long-term consequences of decisions being considered
- particular attention to possible negative consequences—to anyone—of decisions taken
- attention to satisfaction of all important stakeholder groups (Lowery & Mattaini, 1999).

Finally, the individual social worker is not powerless in helping to move agency practices closer to those consistent with shared power. Action supporting organi-zational change has a long history in social work (see chapter 7), and social work-ers who recognize their own power and the potential power of those around them can often marshal support for important shifts in agency practices. See chapter 12 for an extensive discussion of strategic action for organizational change.

EVIDENCE-BASED PRACTICE

As discussed in chapter 1, an important component of what the social worker brings to a relationship of shared power is knowledge. Critical dimensions of that knowledge are what approaches to healing have the best available empirical support and how to work with clients within a dynamic of shared power to fit what is known to the realities of the case. Metaphorically moving to the next quadrant of the wheel (see Figure 2-1), the worker looks at the case through the lens of an evidence-based practice perspective. The term "evidence-based" has been used in several ways in recent years in the professions and in some cases has produced controversy. One issue is that some forms of evidence are clearly better than others; in the evidence-based literature, the preference is for interventions that have strong research-based support. Of course, in many areas such support is limited; the social worker can only work with what evidence is available, which in some cases may be incomplete and of limited rigor. (Some authors have sug-gested that a research base is not central to evidence-based practice, but this is a distortion of standard usage.)

Within this framework are two relatively distinct ways in which the term "evidence-based" is used; neither is wrong, but it is important to distinguish the two. The first refers to evidence-based intervention strategies, the second to the *process* of evidence-based practice. Some intervention strategies and procedures have strong empirical support from multiple studies. One example is behavioral activation (BA) treatment for depression. BA is one component of the well-established cognitive therapy approach to depression (Beck, Reinecke, & Clark, 2003). Recent studies have indicated that the BA procedure by itself produces results as strong as, and possibly stronger than, those for the full (and much more complicated) cognitive therapy model (Dimidjian et al., 2006; Lejuez, Hopko, LePage, Hopko, & McNeil, 2001). Given this evidence, along with the fact that BA is simpler and, therefore, easier to learn and implement, the social worker working with a client with significant depression has an ethical obligation to be familiar with this procedure.

In the prevention area, attention has begun turning to the use of *evidence-based kernels* and *behavior vaccines* (Embry, 2004), in part because of discouraging outcomes for common approaches. An evidence-based kernel is "an irreducible unit of behavior-change technology that produces an observable, reliable result" (Embry, p. 578), a simple intervention procedure (for example, writing recognition notes to improve classroom behavior) that anyone can implement without expensive add-on programs that are difficult to maintain over the long term (Erickson, Mattaini, & McGuire, 2004). A behavior vaccine is an assemblage of evidence-based kernels that can be widely and inexpensively implemented and that preventively inoculates against a serious problem such as violence or substance abuse. A multitude of evidence-based interventions, kernels, and behavior vaccines are available; the challenge is to find them and to select those that are most likely to fit a particular case. The evidence-based process can help with that challenge.

Authority-Based and Evidence-Based Practice

Historically, most social work practice has been authority based, meaning that the practitioner relies on some authority—a dynamic instructor, supervisor, untested practice wisdom—to decide what to do. In some areas, little well-tested knowledge is available, but that has become less and less true in recent years (Gibbs & Gambrill, 2002). In addition, some authority-based approaches can be demonstrably harmful (Gambrill, 2005), including seemingly attractive innovations, such as some forms of "holding therapy," and common traditional approaches, such as nondirective psychodynamic therapy for serious depression. At the community level, the Fighting Back prevention project to reduce substance abuse, which was well funded by the Robert Wood Johnson Foundation, integrated what were generally regarded in the prevention field as best practices, including involvement of multiple community stakeholders and a strong emphasis on community empowerment. The results were more than disappointing: No effects on child and youth outcomes and an *increase* in substance abuse among adults were found, and community strategies showed no impact (Hallfors, Hyunsan, Livert, & Kadushin, 2002). The continuing primary reliance on authority-based practice, given the increasing existence of well-validated strategies and procedures, raises critical ethical issues. Can a social worker continue to use demonstrably damaging approaches or approaches with unknown results when approaches that are known to be useful may be available? This is the central question that has led social work to emphasize evidence-based practice.

Accepting the argument that evidence-based practice is to be preferred to authority-based practice, when possible, still leaves significant challenges. One challenge is that empirical knowledge accumulates and, in some cases, is refined in dramatic ways over time. Traditional approaches to continuing education appear to be quite ineffective in keeping professionals informed of emerging knowledge (Gambrill, 1999). Worse, social workers refer to practice journals far less often than do psychiatrists and psychologists and, when asked, prefer guidelines for practice developed by professional consensus (an authority-based strategy in which respondents are simply asked what they think works best) to guidelines grounded in the best available research (Mullen & Bacon, 2003). Given this backdrop, Gambrill (1999, 2005) brought the evidence-based process, which is well-developed in medicine, into social work.

Evidence-Based Practice Process

Gambrill (2006) characterized the evidence-based practice process as involving the following five steps, slightly adapted here:

1. Developing answerable questions, the answers to which can specifically guide practice. (For example, do Head Start programs prevent later dropout? For what types of depression is medication indicated?)
2. Searching for the answers to those questions in effective and efficient ways, often through the use of extensive online databases and professional literature.
3. Critically appraising the information obtained. (For example, how valid and reliable is it? How powerful are the effects found? How applicable is it to this case?)
4. Determining how well those strategies and procedures fit the case, especially given the values and preferences of the client. Within the evidence-based framework, under almost all circumstances, clients are informed of the results of the search for information, whether the search produces several options from which the client can then make an informed choice or

produces no useful guidance, leaving client and social worker to turn to well-established theory or other sources to decide what to do. (Note the consistency with shared power here; see Gambrill, 2006, for more information about the involvement of clients in the evidence-based practice process.)

5. Evaluating the effectiveness and efficiency of steps taken, modifying the approach on the basis of that data, and clarifying outcomes for future reference.

To use this process, of course, the social worker needs to be prepared to frame the right questions, find answers to those questions, assess the quality and utility of the answers found, and work collaboratively with the client to use the information effectively. Developing skills in those areas, then, is an ethical obligation, and those repertoires are part of what the social worker brings to the shared power process.

Practice Guidelines

One tool for evidence-based practice is *practice guidelines* (Rosen & Proctor, 2003). In a number of professions, including social work, recognition that many cases have much in common is increasing. Research-based guidelines suggesting steps likely to be effective for those cases can be developed, refined, and shared with practitioners who may be too busy to do all of this work themselves. Potential and real challenges are involved in the development of such guidelines. Work on guidelines across disciplines has focused nearly exclusively on disorders, problems, or pathologies; such guidelines can move the focus quite dramatically away from transactional realities, strengths, and power and can obscure the continuing impact of oppression. Social work is also often much more complex than medicine, the field in which practice guidelines have primarily been developed: In many cases, a disease is the result of a single organism, whereas a social work client's struggles may involve substantial and interlocking conditions and events at the sociocultural, neighborhood, family, peer, intrapersonal, and other levels. Those complexities make the development of guidelines challenging and may create significant risk of oversimplifying a case in critical ways.

Rosen and Proctor (2003) have suggested the development of *target-based* practice guidelines, which focus on constructing a desirable situation—using specific target goals—rather than on problems and disorders. This approach is a genuine advance, although it is challenging, given the extent to which the literature is currently organized around problems, particularly around psychiatric diagnoses grounded in the *Diagnostic and Statistical Manual of Mental Disorders* (fourth ed., text revision) (American Psychiatric Association [APA], 2000).

Social Justice

"Our commitments, our loyalties, must be primarily to the poor and vulnerable" (Farmer, 2003, p. 229). In this simple statement, Paul Farmer, a physician and human rights activist, expressed a value stance that must characterize social work practice at all system levels. Jeanne Marsh, the former editor of the core professional journal *Social Work*, stated that social justice is the "organizing value" of social work—the value underlying all professional social work practice (Marsh, 2005). As we will see in chapter 7, that has not always been true, and it is not always true in practice, either. Only if the social worker looks at every case through a social justice lens is he or she likely to notice issues of oppression and human rights that need to be addressed in some way in practice.

Oppression. Most social work clients experience oppression in some form, whether we notice it or not. About 20 percent of all children live in poverty, but that is true for nearly 40 percent of African American children, including most African American children born to single mothers. Roughly a quarter of African American boys will be seriously involved in the criminal justice system as young adults. Millions of people in the United States and hundreds of millions in the world lack adequate health care. Tens of millions of women in the United States and hundreds of millions in the world fear for their safety due to threats of battering and sexual assault. Homeless children in Brazil are routinely killed, but the lives of homeless and other poor children in the United States are also precarious. Millions of children are bullied mercilessly, even in "good" schools, with effects that persist through life. The self-worth of millions of young girls is subtly but profoundly eroded through their social experiences. People struggling with substance abuse are viewed as moral failures rather than as being trapped in a biological and behavioral disorder that cannot simply be escaped by choice. Collective violence worldwide killed at least 200 million people in the 20th century (Krug, Dahlberg, Mercy, Zwi, & Lozano, 2002), and the new century does not appear to promise better.

It is common in the helping professions to focus on "what is wrong" with the client; that way of framing the work, however, risks overlooking social forces and structural violence that create the kinds of experiences described in the previous paragraph. Oppression takes many forms. Young (1990) noted that some oppression is the result of tyrannical coercion (slavery, for example), but other oppression is the result of unquestioned habits and actions that are deeply rooted in contemporary culture and require no evil intentions to maintain. Young described "five faces of oppression" (p. 39):

1. Exploitation. (This term can be defined as the inequitable transfer of the results of the labor of one group to another, as in unfair labor practices.)

2. Marginalization. (Some people simply have no place economically or socially within society; the homeless are a good example.)

3. Powerlessness. (Some people lack a real voice in their own lives and in shaping their world; powerlessness is characteristic, for example, among the poor living in hypersegregated neighborhoods in many major cities, who can do little to address inequities of education, housing, medical care, and other resources.)

4. Cultural imperialism. (Members of nondominant cultures are made invisible and forced to adopt practices that are inconsistent with who they are as individuals and as cultural groups.)

5. Violence. (This term can be defined as the threat and reality of danger to self, family, and property, often for no reason other than to demonstrate dominance and to humiliate.)

Most social work clients, particularly those who are poor and vulnerable, experience some of these forms of oppression, which are deeply interwoven with the surface issues that may bring them to the attention of the social worker. Power dynamics are clearly deeply interwoven with social justice, as discussed in the section above on adversarial and shared power. Social justice and injustice, and the way in which power is distributed and exercised in the client's world, are at the core of practice.

Social Justice and Human Rights. Social justice can be understood in many ways. Social policy courses often emphasize *distributive justice*, which is concerned with how limited resources are distributed among a population, who deserves how much of the total resources available, and why. This is certainly an important dimension of justice, and one with which social workers need to be deeply concerned. This is not the only way of thinking about social justice, however, and it may not be the most useful for practice. One critical dimension of justice, for many, has to do with who has a voice in making critical social decisions. This is sometimes referred to as *participatory* or *procedural* justice (Longres & Scanlon, 2001). One of the criticisms of an exclusive focus on distributive justice is that if only the powerful are involved in making distributive decisions, the vulnerable are likely to be poorly served (see chapter 3 for clear evidence that this criticism is justified). An exclusively distributive framework thinks of resources as necessarily limited. Free speech, civil rights, and many other nonmaterial "goods," however, are not adequately conceptualized in this manner. Mental health is not a finite resource, for example, such that if you have more, I have less. A commonsense understanding of justice seems to suggest that all would and should benefit from "more mental health."

The distributive paradigm has often been used to maintain status quo social arrangements by distributing just enough to prevent social disorder. Such minimal distribution may, in fact, be inherent in the paradigm (Alejandro, 1998). After major urban riots, for example, distributive pronouncements about addressing social inequities typically flow, but the accompanying resources generally do not. Distributive theories also typically focus on the rights of individuals and fail to consider the need for *communal* rights. Distinct groups within a diverse society often wish to maintain what is important to them within their own cultural value system; what is important to them, however, may be undervalued or invisible to dominant-society representatives who make distributive decisions (Young, 1990). Deep down, we are NOT all the same (see chapter 5).

An alternative framework for understanding social justice, and the one emphasized in this book, is that of human rights. As discussed in the next chapter, the Universal Declaration of Human Rights (United Nations, 1948; reprinted in Appendix B) identifies key rights that everyone should have. Some rights are protective. For example, no one should be subjected to torture or to cruel, inhumane, or degrading treatment, and everyone has a right to protection from discrimination. Other rights are affirmative: Everyone has a right to participate in government, and everyone has a right to adequate medical care; to food, clothing, and shelter; and to security in old age. Note that none of the examples cited are universally available to social work clients, so issues of human rights are constantly present in social work practice settings. A great deal of social work practice is with clients whose human rights are being violated and who are systematically disempowered from acting to achieve redress. Many social workers recognize these realities, yet it is not always clear what this recognition means for their practice.

Social Justice and Human Rights in Practice. It may seem evident that if one's clients are being systematically deprived of their basic human rights, both individually and collectively, advocacy should be a core component of practice. Advocacy for the rights of individual clients (case advocacy) is one dimension of nearly every social worker's practice. Less common is an emphasis on the rights of groups of clients (class advocacy). Social workers in many fields of practice best serve their clients by becoming involved in political action and working with those in positions of power who can address distributive and participatory issues (Hoeffer, 2006).

In addition to advocacy practice, human rights can be supported in practice in least two other ways. Even in clinical practice, many moments arise that involve issues with human rights dimensions. For example, one of the authors was once working in a small city with a young man with a severe mental illness. At one point, every possible housing option had been foreclosed, either because of the client's lack of financial resources or because of his inability to maintain himself in a communal setting because of his illness. He had, essentially, burned out every service provider in the city, and no one was willing to take him back. At that point, the social worker, who had worked with this client for several years, naturally experienced considerable frustration; days and days of work over all that time had come to naught. Yet, the problem was the result of the client's mental illness, not of voluntary obstinacy, and housing is a basic human right that the United States has committed to guaranteeing as a signatory to the Universal Declaration of Human Rights. Sadly, in some cases all that can be done immediately is to acknowledge the injustice present and commit to continued advocacy. In this case, for example, rather than blaming the client, the social worker needed to acknowledge the injustice present, work with the client to survive until he was again eligible to be considered for housing, and work for more housing options for those with severe mental illness.

Many times, the social worker's frustration or biases may interfere with just practice. In another example, it was previously quite common—and is still by no means unknown—for professionals working with women who had been battered or raped to use words (or nonverbals) that communicate that the responsibility for what happened lay at least in part with the women. Such small, private encounters are themselves a violation of the client's human rights and support structural oppression and violence. The alternative is (1) to explicitly address the oppression, to surface it and validate the woman's experience; (2) to help her to find ways to heal from what has happened; and (3) within a dynamic of shared power, to find the power to build a life in which her rights will be honored (often collectively with others). These steps involve what Paulo Freire called "conscientization" (the development of critical consciousness) and movement toward collective action for mutual liberation (Freire, 1970/2000).

In addition, some organizations and social work practitioners have structured practice in ways that explicitly address human rights, often collectively among multiple clients. Several such examples are sketched here, and students are encouraged to seek out the full articles and consider how the underlying concepts might inform their own agency practice now and in the future.

Attention to social justice should begin with engagement; the social worker with a justice orientation sees the client not as a collection of pathologies but as a person who has struggled to find a path through challenging obstacles, some of which may well be grounded in oppression. Cowger and associates (2006) reminded us that assessment is, in part, a political process and exposure and response to oppression should be one factor examined in assessment. They indicate that "social ills such as patriarchy, racism, economic brutality, and homophobia all routinely violate individual, group, and community integrity, and in the face of overwhelming personal and institutional forces, people are repeatedly rendered powerless" (p. 100). The ways in which clients have resisted oppression, although perhaps costly, should be viewed as indications of strength. An inner-city adolescent who has struggled with multiple manifestations of structural violence (poverty, racism, community violence, failing schools, and lack of opportunity) may be difficult for a social worker to engage, for example. His resistance, however, should be viewed as a survival strategy and should be acknowledged and honored as his way of coping with oppression, rather than taken personally.

Parker (2003) discussed the structure of services at the Institute for Family Services in Somerset, New Jersey. The program, which uses a feminist and human rights framework, is explicitly designed to address justice and oppression in clinical practice. As described in Parker's study,

> The structure of the program runs counter to most therapeutic programs that limit the experience of change to the interior boundary of individual and family life. In contrast, the cultural context model breaks through perceived barriers around the nuclear family by creating a community that directly links families to one another. Within this multifamily, or community milieu, clients are helped to examine gender, class, and other systemic patterns that contribute to their dilemmas. The walls of the therapy room are further extended by inviting other significant persons into the therapeutic process, including community and religious leaders. The model focuses on dismantling traditional rules of privacy and access to power and social opportunity via open dialogues that focus on the principles of empowerment and maintaining accountability over time. (p. 276)

The primary modality used is that of "culture circles": same-sex groups that are designed to enhance critical consciousness and deal explicitly with power issues within the family and the larger society.

Finn and Jacobson (2003) formulated what they described as a *just practice paradigm*. Their approach is in an early state of development, but emphasizes five factors that are useful to consider for any social worker attempting to contribute to social justice in practice: (1) meaning (how people understand themselves and their world); (2) context (emotional, cultural and physical surroundings); (3) power (including power over, power within, power with, and power to do); (4) history (as it has shaped reality and is continually being shaped); and (5) possibility (a hopeful sense of what may be). Finn and Jacobson's work noted the impact of global forces, oppression, and a human rights perspective on everyday practice; these factors play out through the five dimensions noted.

Vodde and Gallant (2002) developed an approach organized around understanding power and oppression that is designed to bridge micro and macro practice. Their approach, grounded in narrative–deconstructive theory, involves a three-step process, beginning with what they termed "first order externalization." In this process, the problem itself, not the person struggling with it, is identified as "the problem," which is grounded in oppression. In "second order externalization," the emphasis is on identifying the social forces that structure that oppression. That process leads to the final step, the development of self as one member of a class of oppressed persons, and ultimately through connections with others in that class to the construction of a "community of resistance." Vodde and Gallant also present specific suggestions and examples of moving through this process, which could otherwise seem rather abstract. As will be evident in the next chapter, the steps outlined in their work mirror those used in a good deal of human rights work around the world.

Action for social justice and supporting human rights, then, can and should be central to social work practice. The connections are explored in depth in the next chapter and will emerge repeatedly throughout the rest of this book.

MAPPING PRACTICE

A simple example may help clarify how the social worker "walks around" a case, looking at it from multiple perspectives. For example, assume the client system is a neighborhood. In the community under consideration (drawn from a real case), a neighborhood social services center serves young people and their families. The center has become deeply embedded in the neighborhood, which is significantly economically distressed but not devastated. The immediate neighborhood is bordered by a commercial area that includes three small stores, a restaurant, and a movie theater. A nearby park, a primary school, a police station, a health care center, and two churches constitute the community within the boundary of the case. Figure 2-4 is a simplified ecomap of the community.

The social services center thought about its work broadly, not just as counseling but as community building. The problem brought to the attention of the center was that a group of about a dozen 11-year-old boys had been harassing the storekeepers by menacing customers and drawing graffiti. The police could not catch them, their parents felt helpless to stop them, they resisted the pleas of their pastor and priest, they would not attend group sessions at the neighborhood center, and no after-school programs were available.

Thinking ecosystemically, the social worker at the neighborhood center assessed the situation of the aggressive boys and the lack of neighborhood resources. Many actors are concerned about what is happening (store owners, parents, pastors, police); the social worker and the young boys are also involved. A shared-power perspective would suggest bringing the talents and resources of many of those people to the table and structuring opportunities for each actor to contribute to addressing the collective challenge.

FIGURE 2-4

Community Ecomap Showing Families in Their Ecological Context

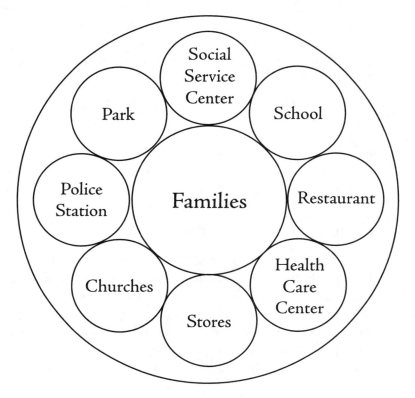

From the perspective of evidence-based practice, one of the roles of the social worker is to ask the questions "What kind of services are helpful in supporting positive youth development?" and "What may set these boys on a healthy path, rather than one leading to further and more serious antisocial behavior?" A good deal is known about this subject (Fraser, 2004; Reid, Patterson, & Snyder, 2002). A thorough examination of the support for various strategies would result in a few promising options, which could then be taken back to the table for consideration and adaptation. Among the things the literature would emphasize is the value of adult mentors, monitoring, and opportunities for community participation and involvement.

Finally, note that the boys should not be viewed primarily as damaged or as problems to be solved in some way. They lived in challenging circumstances; they were children of color whose schools were of poor quality, who lacked adequate supervision and opportunities for healthy development, who were at high risk for future legal involvement and incarceration, and about whom social institutions did not seem to much care. Their relative disadvantage in a wealthy society involves serious issues of justice, even though observers may be tempted simply to see them as delinquents.

The social worker relied at least in part on each perspective in assessing and planning in the case. The central challenge was to shift the relationships among the store owners and the boys. To assist with this process, she approached the store owners and, after a heated exchange, worked with them to consider alternative ways of dealing with the boys. In the process, she helped them see that they could have power to address the situation, but not through the adversarial methods they had tried. Chasing and scolding the boys was not working. The store owners (facilitated by the social worker) called the boys together for lunch at the neighborhood restaurant and, working with the youth, created a neighborhood baseball team. The store owners bought the boys uniforms (with the names of the stores on them) and equipment and took turns managing the team during games. All the people in the neighborhood who had felt the effects of the boys' destructive behavior (which was eliminated) were relieved.

Other possible options for intervention included clinical treatment with the boys and their families (if the boys could be corralled!). The social worker, however, chose what proved to be both a parsimonious and a powerful intervention. One can only speculate about the later well-being of the neighborhood: the increase in the boys' sense of competence and the relief of the parents, the police, the pastor and priest, and the store owners and their customers. Developmentally, it was crucial that something be done immediately, before the emerging group of youths began to move more deeply into gang culture. Systemic principles illustrated in this case example include identification of meaningful boundaries, connectedness and reciprocity, equifinality, and the shifting of dynamic balances. Shared power was present, although perhaps bringing others to the (restaurant) table (family, religious leaders) might have increased the options by expanding the collective power brought to bear. The intervention grew from the empirical literature related to positive youth development, and some support was offered to youth who were at high risk for marginalization (one form of oppression).

The neighborhood social services center offered many traditional services (including individual and family counseling, and treatment and socialization group work), and over time it developed strong recreation, mentoring, tutoring, and after-school programs. Program development and specific services offered clearly benefited from looking at the community from multiple perspectives and making a primary commitment to the poor and vulnerable, consistent with Farmer's (2003) call. The next chapter further promotes an understanding of social justice and human rights.

REFERENCES

Alejandro, R. (1998). *The limits of Rawlsian justice.* Baltimore: Johns Hopkins University Press.

American Psychiatric Association. (2000). *Diagnostic and statistical manual of mental disorders* (4th ed., text revision). Washington, DC: Author.

Anderson, R. E., Carter, I., & Lowe, G. R. (1999). *Human behavior in the social environment: A social systems approach* (5th ed.). Hawthorne, NY: Aldine de Gruyter.

Auerswald, E. H. (1968). Interdisciplinary versus ecological approach. *Family Process, 7,* 202–215.

Beck, A. T., Reinecke, M. A., & Clark, D. A. (2003). *Cognitive therapy across the lifespan: Evidence and practice.* New York: Cambridge University Press.

Besthorn, F. H., & McMillen, D. P. (2002). The oppression of women and nature: Ecofeminism as a framework for an expanded ecological social work. *Families in Society, 83,* 221–232.

Capra, F. (1996). *The web of life.* New York: Anchor Books.

Castillo, R. J. (1997). *Culture and mental illness: A client-centered approach.* Pacific Grove, CA: Brooks/Cole.

Cowger, C. D., Anderson, K. M., & Snively, C. A. (2006). Assessing strengths: The political context of individual, family, and community empowerment. In D. Saleebey (Ed.), *The strengths perspective in social work practice* (4th ed., pp. 93–196). Boston: Allyn & Bacon.

Davidson, A. (1994). *Endangered peoples.* San Francisco: Sierra Club Books.

Dimidjian, S., Hollon, S. D., Dobson, K. S., Schmaling, K. B., Kohlenberg, R. J., Addis, M. E., Gallop, R., McGlinchey, J. B., Markley, D. K., Gollan, J. K., Atkins, D. C., Dunner, D. L., & Jacobson, N. S. (2006). Randomized trial of behavioral activation, cognitive therapy, and antidepressant medication in the acute treatment of adults with major depression. *Journal of Consulting and Clinical Psychology, 74,* 658–670.

DuBos, R. (1972). *The god within.* New York: Charles Scribner's Sons.

Dumas, J. E., & Wahler, R. G. (1983). Predictors of treatment outcome in parent training: Mother insularity and socioeconomic disadvantage. *Behavioral Assessment, 5,* 301–313.

Embry, D. D. (2004). Community-based prevention using simple, low-cost, evidence-based kernels and behavior vaccines. *Journal of Community Psychology, 32,* 575–591.

Erickson, C., Mattaini, M. A., & McGuire, M. S. (2004). Constructing nonviolent cultures in schools: The state of the science. *Children and Schools, 26,* 102–116.

Farmer, P. (2003). *Pathologies of power: Health, human rights, and the new war on the poor.* Berkeley: University of California Press.

Finn, J. L., & Jacobson, M. (2003). Just practice: Steps toward a new social work paradigm. *Journal of Social Work Education, 39,* 57–78.

Fraser, M. W. (2004). *Risk and resilience in childhood: An ecological perspective* (2nd ed.). Washington, DC: NASW Press.

Freire, P. (2000). *The pedagogy of the oppressed.* New York: Continuum. (Original work published 1970)

Gambrill, E. (1999). Evidence-based practice: An alternative to authority-based practice. *Families in Society, 80,* 341–350.

Gambrill, E. (2005). Critical thinking, evidence-based practice, and mental health. In S. A. Kirk (Ed.), *Mental disorders in the social environment: Critical perspectives* (pp. 247–269). New York: Columbia University Press.

Gambrill, E. (2006). Evidence-based practice and policy: Choices ahead. *Research on Social Work Practice, 16,* 338–357.

Germain, C. B. (1973). An ecological perspective in casework practice. *Social Casework, 54,* 323–330.

Germain, C. B., & Gitterman, A. (1996). *The life model of social work practice* (2nd ed.). New York: Columbia University Press.

Gibbs, L. F., & Gambrill, E. (2002). Evidence-based practice: Counterarguments to objections. *Research on Social Work Practice, 12*(3), 452–476.

Gutierrez, L., GlenMaye, L., & DeLois, K. (1995). The organizational context of empowerment practice: Implications for social work administration. *Social Work, 40,* 249–258.

Hallfors, D., Hyunsan, C., Livert, D., & Kadushin, C. (2000). Fighting back against substance abuse: Are community coalitions winning? *American Journal of Preventive Medicine, 23,* 237–324.

Hamilton, G. (1951). *Theory and practice of social casework.* New York: Columbia University Press.

Hasenfeld, Y. (1987). Power in social work practice. *Social Service Review, 61,* 469–483.

Hoeffer, R. (2006). *Advocacy practice for social justice.* Chicago: Lyceum Books.

Hollis, F. H. (1972). *Casework: A psychosocial therapy* (2nd ed.). New York: Random House.

Hudson, C. G. (2000). From social Darwinism to self-organization: Implications for social change theory. *Social Service Review, 74,* 533–559.

Jordan, C., & Franklin, C. (2003). *Clinical assessment for social workers: Quantitative and qualitative methods* (2nd ed.). Chicago: Lyceum Books.

Kemp, S. P., Whittaker, J. K., & Tracy, E. M. (1997). *Person-environment practice.* New York: Aldine de Gruyter.

Krug, E. G., Dahlberg, L. L., Mercy, J. A., Zwi, A. B., & Lozano, R. (2002). *World report on violence and health.* Geneva: World Health Organization.

Lejuez, C. W., Hopko, D. R., LePage, J. P., Hopko, S. D., & McNeil, D. W. (2001). A brief behavioral activation treatment for depression. *Cognitive and Behavioral Practice, 8,* 164–175.

Lindsey, E. W. (1998). Service providers' perception of factors that help or hinder homeless families. *Families in Society, 79,* 160–172.

Longres, J. F., & Scanlon, E. (2001). Social justice and the research curriculum. *Journal of Social Work Education, 37,* 447–463.

Lowery, C. T., & Mattaini, M. A. (1999). The science of sharing power: Native American thought and behavior analysis. *Behavior and Social Issues, 9,* 3–23.

Lowery, C. T., & Mattaini, M. A. (2001). Shared power in social work: A Native American perspective of change. In H. Briggs & K. Corcoran (Eds.), *Social work practice: Treating common client problems* (pp. 109–124). Chicago: Lyceum Books.

Marsh, J. C. (2005). Social justice: Social work's organizing value. *Social Work, 50,* 293–294.

Mattaini, M. A. (in press). The ecosystems perspective: A scientific view. In K. M. Sowers & C. N. Dulmus (Eds.), *The comprehensive handbook of social work and social welfare.* Hoboken, NJ: John Wiley & Sons.

Maturana, H., & Varela, F. (1980). *Autopoiesis and cognition.* Dordrecht, the Netherlands: D. Reidel.

Meyer, C. H. (1976). *Social work practice: The changing landscape* (2nd ed.). New York: Free Press.

Meyer, C. H. (Ed.). (1983). *Clinical social work practice in an ecosystems perspective*. New York: Columbia University Press.

Meyer, C. H. (1988). The eco-systems perspective. In R. A. Dorfman (Ed.), *Paradigms of clinical social work* (pp. 275–294). New York: Brunner/Mazel.

Minuchin, S. (1974). *Families and family therapy*. Cambridge, MA: Harvard University Press.

Mullen, E. J., & Bacon, W. F. (2003). Practitioner adoption and implementation of practice guidelines and issues of quality control. In A. Rosen & E. K. Proctor (Eds.), *Developing practice guidelines for social work intervention* (pp. 223–235). New York: Columbia University Press.

Parker, L. (2003). A social justice model for clinical social work practice. *Affilia, 18*, 272–288.

Reid, J. B., Patterson, G. R., & Snyder, J. (2002). *Antisocial behavior in children and adolescents: A developmental analysis and model for intervention*. Washington, DC: American Psychological Association.

Richmond, M. E. (1917). *Social diagnosis*. New York: Russell Sage Foundation.

Rosen, A., & Livne, S. (1992). Personal versus environmental emphases in formulation of client problems. *Social Work Research & Abstracts, 29*(4), 12–17.

Rosen, A., & Proctor, E. K. (2003). *Developing practice guidelines for social work intervention*. New York: Columbia University Press.

Ross, R. (2006). *Returning to the teachings: Exploring aboriginal justice* (2nd ed.). Toronto: Penguin Canada.

Rutter, M. (1987). Psychosocial resilience and protective mechanisms. *American Journal of Orthopsychiatry, 57*, 316–331.

Saleebey, D. (Ed.). (2006). *The strengths perspective in social work practice* (4th ed.). Boston: Allyn & Bacon.

Sidman, M. (2001). *Coercion and its fallout* (Rev. ed.). Boston: Authors Cooperative.

United Nations. (1948). *Universal Declaration of Human Rights*. New York: Author.

Vodde, R., & Gallant, J. P. (2002). Bridging the gap between micro and macro practice: Large scale change and a unified model of narrative-deconstructive practice. *Journal of Social Work Education, 38*, 439–460.

von Bertalanffy, L. (1968). *General system theory*. New York: George Braziller.

Wakefield, J. C. (1996a). Does social work need the eco-systems perspective? Part 1: Is the perspective clinically useful? *Social Service Review, 70*, 1–32.

Wakefield, J. C. (1996b). Does social work need the eco-systems perspective? Part 2: Does the perspective save social work from incoherence? *Social Service Review, 70*, 183–213.

Warren, K., Franklin, C., & Streeter, C. L. (1998). New directions in systems theory: Chaos and complexity. *Social Work, 43*, 357–372.

Wong, S. E. (2006). Behavior analysis of psychotic disorders: Scientific dead end or casualty of the mental health political economy? *Behavior and Social Issues, 15*, 152–177.

Young, I. M. (1990). *Justice and the politics of difference*. Princeton, NJ: Princeton University Press.

3

□□□

Social Justice and International Human Rights

Christine T. Lowery

Women must be included in any satisfactory theory of justice.

(Okin, 1989, p. 14)

During the "16 Days of Activism against Gender Violence" in 1991, a petition was faxed around the world that advocated "women's rights as human rights" across the globe. The petition, called for the 1993 UN World Conference in Vienna, Austria, to "comprehensively address women's human rights at every level of its proceedings" and to recognize gender-based violence "as a violation of human rights requiring immediate action" (Friedman, 1995, p. 28). Originally distributed in Spanish, French, and English and ultimately translated into 23 languages, the petition cited the *Universal Declaration of Human Rights*. The International Women's Tribune Center (IWTC) and the Center for Women's Global Leadership shared original sponsorship (Bunch & Reilly, 1994).

> Copies were returned to IWTC in languages staff could not recognize and signed with fingerprints. . . . Batches [of faxes] were received from U.S.-based organizations that had received the petition from overseas. The petition drive lasted until the World Conference with batches of 75,000 periodically sent to the UN to urge conference organizers to include women's issues on their agenda. (Friedman, p. 28)

When the World Conference convened in Vienna in 1993, more than 1,000 groups had signed up to cosponsor the petition, and almost 500,000 signatures had been gathered from 124 countries (Bunch & Reilly, 1994). People around the world could relate to the simple and broad meaning the petition carried; the petition informed and involved them; people "translated it into whatever issue was most pressing for the group of people they were working with" (Carillo, cited in Friedman, 1995, p. 28). Timing for the petition tapped into organizing efforts on behalf of women all over the world that had gained international momentum in the past 20 years. Two years later, the 1991 petition led to a global tribunal that presented violence against women as human rights violations.

Why are women's issues so important? Half the world's population is female, and before equality can be discussed, people must understand how gender is enacted through labor and economics, social upheavals and war, immigration, race, class, religion, and ethnicity and how gender is marginalized and violated in societies around the world. The time for human rights and the contribution of women worldwide to world policy is now. Why should social workers understand a human rights perspective? Research findings have revealed that "verbal support for civil liberties and human rights is weak and limited" (Devall, 1976, p. 346). The rights of whole groups of people are lost "overnight" with no outcry from the general population. "Opinion leadership sometimes emerges to counter human rights violations" (Devall, p. 346), but political strength and timing are limiting factors.

The power behind human rights and a human rights ethic is information and an educated public opinion. International tribunals; "courts, ombudsmen, study commissions, private groups, educational institutions" (Devall, 1976, p. 347); and responsible media serve to educate. Social workers are part of a professional body that educates through practice, education, research, and advocacy. A basic tenet of the social work profession is the dignity and worth of human beings, and social workers have advocated for the rights of others in health, mental health, education, and social services even while relatively less engaged in the political and social policy arena (Midgley, 1997). Knowledge of human rights encourages the support and enforcement of those rights through supporting institutions. The goal of human rights and enforcement is not punishment; it is prevention (Devall, 1976).

How people treat each other as human beings reflects their morality. How social workers treat others shapes their ethics in a professional relationship. If social workers hope to shape their future as human beings in a global village, they must place human rights at the nexus of social justice. The goal of this chapter is to help the student think about social justice principles centered on human rights with an emphasis on global women's rights. Principles of justice and human rights must be reflected in social policy, acted out in everyday morality, and implemented through relationships in social work practice and advocacy.

An international perspective exposes the realities of living in a world where a global economy, consumption patterns of rich countries, exploitation of human and environmental resources in poor countries, and the desperate poverty of a billion people worldwide alter gender roles, ethnic groups, cultures, philosophies, worldviews, and how peoples live (Rasmussen, 1994). From these perspectives, issues of diversity—gender, ethnicity, race, age, sexual orientation, and physical and mental challenges—are woven into international justice issues, and oppression and domination are subsumed in the continuum of violence that is poverty, injustice, and corruption.

This chapter has two intersecting components: (1) foundational knowledge, including history and policy, and (2) social justice concepts and examples. First, the reader is exposed to a short review of moral philosophy followed by a discussion of rights and relationships, including legal, moral, and human rights. Building on this base, the five instruments of the UN-sponsored *International Bill of Human Rights* are described as an example of social policy. The UN *Declaration on the Rights of Indigenous Peoples* is briefly discussed as an example of those voices that have not been heard, despite the universalistic nature of the *International Bill of Human Rights*. Second, the chapter explores issues of justice and violence, using violence against women (including war crimes, trafficking in prostitution, and human rights abuses within the family) to illustrate the violation of human rights. The chapter includes a discussion of international advocacy strategies on behalf of women.

A PHILOSOPHICAL BASE:
RIGHTS AND RELATIONSHIPS

Social justice theories—or moral rules and principles—emerged from moral philosophy. It is important to understand whose moral philosophy and purposes those rules and principles served. The Western concepts of liberty, justice, and contract have seeds in the writings of St. Thomas Aquinas (1224–1274), descended through feudal systems of the Middle Ages, and were later shaped by Locke (1632–1704), Hume (1711–1776), Rousseau (1712–1778), and others (Barker, 1962). These politically liberal ideas were built on doctrines concerning the relationship of society and government as described in the Bible (God ordained powers and made covenants), Roman law (authority), and Aristotelian principles (king–tyrant; accountability to the masses) (Barker). Benhabib (1992) argued that the modern universalist moral theorists from Hobbes (1588–1679) to Rawls (1921–) are substitutionalist and depend on the experiences of one group—white, male, propertied professionals—to substitute for those of all. This is, essentially, the cultural imperialism of colonialism.

Ancient and medieval moral systems considered man-as-he-ought-to be, man-as-he-is, and rules for "just relations in his human community" and included man's place in relation to natural forces. Indigenous peoples worldwide still claim moralities based on a Mother Earth relationship or one's relationship to natural forces. As Benhabib (1992) wrote, "The attack of medieval nominalism and modern science, the emergence of capitalist exchange relations and the subsequent division of the social structure into the economy, the polity, civil associations and the domestic-intimate sphere, radically alter[ed] moral theory" (p. 154) from the ancient systems. Modern theorists claimed a disconnection from the limitations of nature, and morality was no longer bound by this relationship.

Autonomy and the Public–Private Sphere

The early contract theorists of the 18th century defended privacy and the autonomy of the self, distinguished justice from "the good life," and consolidated the split between public and private domains (Benhabib, 1992). The public–private divide separates the sphere of home and family from paid work and facilitates the power of men over women in the public domain. This experience is characteristic of Western industrialized nations over the past two centuries (Boyd, 1997). Autonomy of the self was privatized in this process, and women and the domestic–familial sphere were swallowed up in this privacy. This privacy has hampered the exposure of violence in the home and has made gender equality and child care needs difficult to achieve in the workplace. In essence, an entire domain of human activity, namely, nurture, reproduction, love, and care, which became women's lot in the course of the development of modern bourgeois society, has been excluded from moral and political considerations and relegated to the realm of "nature" (Benhabib, p. 155).

The transition from subsistence economies in developing countries to money economies ripples through cultures and affects gender roles worldwide. Women's status in traditional cultures is enhanced by their contributions to food gathering, childbearing, and care for families. What has happened to women in the West is now happening to women in developing countries, which are moving from agricultural to industrial to technological phases, sometimes all at once. As a woman's work of household production and maintenance is devalued, she is excluded from social and economic power and resources (Pietilä & Vickers, 1996). As at the end of the 20th century, the role of gender in the shaping of economic and political realities is crucial. Jean-Bertrand Aristide, former president of Haiti, recognized the role of women in world affairs:

Studies around the world have shown that when household budgets are in the hands of women, they are more likely to be spent for primary needs (food, education, and health care). I predict that when the budgets of nations are in the hands of women we will see the same result. (Aristide, 2000, p. 41)

Rights and Relationships

The concept of "rights" stands at the intersection of morality, justice, and relationships as a triangulated base of social justice. Smith (1994) described rights as "the obligations embedded in some social or institutional context where expectation has moral force" (p. 25). From a feminist perspective, Young (1990) considered rights in terms of relationships:

> Rights are not fruitfully conceived as possessions. Rights are relationships, not things; they are institutionally defined rules specifying what people can do in relation to one another. Rights refer to doing more than having, to social relationships that enable or constrain action. (p. 25)

Rights differ from wants or needs in that they are specific entitlements. "Rights emphasize morality in the *relational and reciprocal nature* of the concept, in the obligation or duty required, and in the contribution to well-being, an inherent quality of morality" [italics added] (Smith, 1994, p. 23).

Legal and Moral Rights. Rights may protect people from the power of the state (for example, the right to a fair trial) or delineate entitlements from the state (Smith, 1994). Legal rights can be defended in the courts, whereas moral rights appeal to general principles—democracy and the right to have a voice, for example. Legal and moral rights can be further divided into *liberty-oriented* rights and *security-oriented* or *claim* rights that protect people's physical and material status. Freedom of action expressed in civil or political rights is a liberty-oriented right. Property rights, unemployment compensation, and social security are examples of security-oriented rights.

Relationship is emphasized when the interests of one group must be negotiated in some way with the interests of another group in light of a "more important moral or political ideal. . . . Struggles are frequently engaged to make moral rights legal, the vote for black South Africans being an obvious case" (Smith, 1994, p. 38). Human beings are treated differently from place to place, and the justification for such treatment also varies. Hence, rights are relative in their importance, interpretation, and practice from society to society. Smith gave a broad example of how the nature of different societies is reflected in struggles for rights:

Capitalist societies tend to prioritize individual liberty and property rights, while socialist societies place more emphasis on collective entitlements from the state. Basic civil liberties are more of an issue in South Africa than in Britain, where social security is a major concern. (p. 38)

Human Rights. Human rights are moral rights supported by the belief in the moral worth and dignity of human beings. Ideally, people have entitlement to these rights as human beings, regardless of age, race, class, gender, religion, national origin, or language. For the social work student, human rights serves as a foundation for a personal perspective on social justice and social policy woven into the ethics of the profession and translated concretely into social work practice day to day.

Economic, social, and cultural rights were linked with civil and political rights as a body of rights at the UN-sponsored First International Conference on Human Rights in Teheran, Iran, in 1968. Twenty-five years later, the UN World Conference on Human Rights in Vienna (in 1993), recognized the universal nature of human rights to address racism, discrimination, xenophobia (fear of foreigners), and intolerance and emphasized the rights of women; children; members of ethnic, religious, and linguistic minority groups; and indigenous peoples.

How are human rights related to social justice? Peffer (cited in Smith, 1994) provided the following criteria: Both concepts are concerned with fundamental human needs; both create obligations that the state or other individuals can legitimately force people to meet; and both provide a basis for justifying actions and seeking protection of others and provide grounds for justifying or criticizing social institutions, programs, or policies. The work of the United Nations on human rights and the struggle of indigenous peoples to save their lands, cultures, and resources are examples of this critical relationship.

The International Bill of Human Rights as Social Policy

Social policy requires at least three elements: moral authority (rights), legal force (implementation and review), and commitment of partnerships (ratification). Five major UN legal instruments define and guarantee the protection of human rights: (1) The *Universal Declaration of Human Rights* (United Nations, 1948); (2) the *International Covenant on Economic, Social and Cultural Rights* (United Nations, 1966b); and (3) the *International Covenant on Civil and Political Rights* (United Nations, 1966a). The fourth and fifth instruments are the operational protocols to the two covenants. The *Declaration* is a manifesto with primarily moral authority, whereas the covenants are treaties binding on the states that ratify them. Together, the five documents constitute the UN *International Bill of Human Rights* (United Nations, 1993b), which provides one example of social policy in process.

The *Universal Declaration of Human Rights* (United Nations, 1948; reprinted in Appendix B of this volume) was adopted in 1948 and serves as a standard against which member states can measure their progress, but the declaration requires enforcement procedures, which are provided by the covenants and protocols cited above. Among the rights in the 30 articles of the *Declaration* is a right to a free elementary education. "Men and women of full age" have the right to marry and have a family with equal rights in the marriage and at its dissolution (United Nations, 1993b, p. 6). (Same-sex marriage or marriage equality is the purview of religious dictates in some views.) People have a right to a nationality, to freedom of movement, to seek asylum, to social and international order, and to participate in the cultural life of the community. Most important, social justice ideals are actualized through legal means (procedural justice) through incorporation of human rights standards into policies of member states. If the system is working, policies are sanctioned; ensuing practices are examined; information is fed back into the process; and policies are refined, changed, updated, or eliminated.

The Covenant on Civil and Political Rights (United Nations, 1966a) recognizes the rights to life, liberty, and safety; the right to privacy; and the right to a fair trial. The Covenant on Economic, Social, and Cultural Rights (United Nations, 1966b) recognizes equal rights of men and women; the rights to work, to fair wages, and to form and join unions; and the right to adequate standards of living, among others. The two covenants (economic, social, and cultural; civil and political) create the legal force required for implementation and include protocols for review of implementation and commitment to specified relationships among the partners who have ratified the document.

A Declaration of Human Rights for Indigenous Peoples

Despite the noble and far-reaching language of the UN declaration, some peoples (preinvasion, precolonial societies) have not been heard in this process, and any analysis of social justice must ask, Who is being excluded from this list of human rights? Who has not been heard? Who is not here? Julian Burger, of the UN Center for Human Rights, calculated that "in half of the 161 states in the UN, the rights of indigenous peoples to self-determination are being denied or restricted" (Burger, cited in Davidson, 1994, p. 67). Davidson contended that the UN declaration becomes "empty sentiment" as member governments try to eradicate small, scattered groups of indigenous peoples for their land and resources. For example, Brazil is one of several countries in which Amazonian rain forests are burned to create open grazing land to feed cattle for the world beef market and to build roads for mining operations. This practice challenges rights and changes the cultures of indigenous peoples.

Since 1982, leaders of the 200 million to 250 million indigenous peoples have worked on UN drafts of what has become the UN *Declaration on the Rights of*

Indigenous Peoples (United Nations, 2006). In 1995, the draft was approved by a UN subcommission but until recently faced a stalemate at the level of the Human Rights Council (formerly the Commission on Human Rights). Refusal to acknowledge indigenous peoples as partners has been as central to the struggle as the language of the document, particularly as it applies to self-determination and to lands, territories, and resources.

There is hope, however. "Indigenous rights are on the radar screen, and the language is showing up in documents which contain references to indigenous rights and the special status of indigenous peoples," reported Elizabeth Homer, former director of the Office of American Indian Trust (personal communication, October 5, 2000). The Organization of American States has drafted an *American Declaration for Rights of Indigenous Peoples* (Inter-American Commission on Human Rights, 1997), although without funds to actively support working groups (Homer). Midway through the International Decade of the World's Indigenous People (1995–2004), the United Nations approved the establishment of the Permanent Forum for Indigenous Peoples.

In May 2005, members of the Permanent Forum set two goals regarding indigenous children, youth, and women: to eradicate poverty and extreme hunger and to achieve universal primary education. Indigenous representatives pleaded for inclusion in poverty-reduction decisions and warned against embedded injustices in such policies, including deprivation of land. Poverty indicators, they said, should be based on the indigenous experience with attention to the protection of collective rights (International Work Group for Indigenous Affairs [IWGIA], 2005). In January 2006, the United Nations sponsored a seminar, Indigenous Peoples' Permanent Sovereignty over Natural Resources and on Their Relationship to Land, which featured examples from the Amazigh People in Morocco, the Innu Nation and the government of Canada, and the Uro People in Puno, Peru (IWGIA, 2005).

Why is relationship to the land—both political and spiritual—and environmental knowledge significant? In a comparative analysis of how societies collapse, Diamond (2005) developed a five-point framework of interrelated factors to help understand societal vulnerability: environmental damage, climate change, hostile neighbors, and friendly trade partners. The fifth point is the response to environmental problems, which is always critical in whether a society succeeds or fails. Indigenous peoples worldwide carry an ancient understanding of their ecological environments, now being scientifically "discovered." This knowledge base has not been consulted as dams are erected, migration sites are eradicated in favor of land development, and rivers are polluted through destruction of the rain forests. This knowledge, however, may prove useful in attempts to understand and reconcile the worldwide destruction to physical and social environments.

In February 2006, the 11th session of the working group submitted another draft of the *Declaration on the Rights of Indigenous Peoples* to the Human Rights Council, and in June 2006 that draft was approved by the Council and forwarded to the UN General Assembly with a recommendation for approval. The Declaration as approved by the Human Rights Council includes a statement that because of colonization and dispossessed lands, territories, and resources, indigenous peoples are prevented from exercising the right to development that is based on their own needs and interests. Indigenous peoples ask for

redress, by means that can include restitution or, when this is not possible, of a just, fair and equitable compensation, for the lands, territories and resources which they have traditionally owned or otherwise occupied or used, and which have been confiscated, occupied, used or damaged without their free, prior and informed consent. (United Nations, 2006, Article 28, ¶1)

Approval of the Declaration by the General Assembly is by no means assured, and continuing advocacy will be critical.

JUSTICE AND VIOLENCE:
SOCIAL EMPOWERMENT AND
SOCIAL DISEMPOWERMENT

Social justice and human rights are empowering for societies if commitments to relationships through just policies are honored. On the other end of the continuum, social disempowerment is experienced when there is violence in the form of poverty, corruption, and injustice. Violence affects quality of life and opportunity through fear and poverty, including educational, social, economic, cultural, and political deprivation. Violence takes the lives of women and children through physical and sexual abuse; erodes social justice through graft, crime, and political corruption; exploits and destroys the physical environment; and savagely plows through nations, their peoples, and cultures in acts of war, territorial disputes, and terrorism. Injustice is evident through domination and what Young (1990) called the five faces of oppression: cultural imperialism, marginalization, exploitation, powerlessness, and violence.

To understand the disempowering role of violence and injustice as a continuum engulfing private and public spheres in society, the definition of violence must be expanded. The Panel on Understanding and Control of Violent Behavior of the National Academy of Sciences defined violence as "behaviors by individuals that intentionally threaten, attempt, or inflict physical harm on others" (Reiss & Roth, 1993, p. 2). Admittedly, this definition masks the diversity of violence that causes death or is hidden in "statistical classifications of nonfatal crimes" (Reiss & Roth, 1993, p. 2). The UN *Declaration on the Elimination of Violence against Women* (United Nations, 1993a) expands gender-based violence to include "physical, sexual or psychological harm or suffering to women including threats of such acts, coercion or arbitrary deprivation of liberty, whether occurring in public or private life" (Pietilä & Vickers, 1996, p. 143). Famine of the mind (educational deprivation), body (starvation), and spirit (poverty) must also be included in the continuum of violence. From indigenous worldviews, violence is not only physical but also contains emotional, environmental, spiritual, spatial, and geographical components as well as generational time—past, present, and future.

Who perpetrates violence on whom? What type of violence (poverty, injustice, and corruption) is being perpetrated? For what purpose? Whose rights are acknowledged, protected, or violated? If one looks closely enough, control of resources, social control, and coercion are at the heart of violence. (For the interested reader, Noam Chomsky [1999] documented U.S. policies that contradict human rights, including sanctions, in *The Umbrella of U.S. Power*.) The political nature of both culture and religion must also be questioned, and practitioners must "listen with skepticism and care" (Rao, 1995, p. 174). Rao used women within culture as an example when she cautioned,

> without questioning the political uses of culture, without questioning whose culture this is and who its primary beneficiaries are, without placing the very notion of culture in historical context and investigating the status of the interpreter, we cannot understand the ease with which women become instrumentalized in larger battles of political, economic, military, and discursive competition in the international arena. (p. 174)

The continuum from social justice and human rights to violence (or social empowerment to social disempowerment) forces social work students to redefine how they conceptualize social problems and to acknowledge how social power is used, on whose behalf, and for what purposes.

Social Power: Force, Wealth, and Knowledge

Toffler (1990) included violence as part of the triad of social power: force, wealth, and knowledge. Force is seen as a low-quality power because one can use it only to punish. Wealth has greater flexibility and is considered a medium-quality power. Knowledge, "the most democratic form of power" (Toffler, p. 20), has the greatest flexibility and efficiency: "to punish, reward, persuade . . . transform" (p. 16). Wealth is the least "maldistributed" source of power. Toffler argued that "an even greater chasm separates the armed from the unarmed and the ignorant from the educated" (p. 20). The power behind human rights and environmental justice is an educated public opinion. Global communication helps people enter the international dialogue to organize education and resistance across the world while working locally. And although the "digital divide" separates people, global comparisons and patterns help us recognize who is absent and who controls the global dialogue.

In the analysis of social justice (morality, justice, and relationship) or violence (poverty, injustice, and corruption), social work students must examine the quality and relationship among the elements of social power in social policies and their implementation and interventions in an era of global change. For example, countries with technological power rely less on agricultural or industrial countries and use technologies (knowledge) to make wealth with each other by creating multinational organizations and magnifying the chasm between rich and poor countries (Toffler & Toffler, 1995). Economic apartheid can be described as a pyramid, at the apex of which are the transnational corporations; below that is a middle class. At the ever-widening base is "an underclass of people who are unimportant both as producers and as consumers, for which the system has absolutely no plans" (George, cited in Pietilä & Vickers, 1996, p. 154). The limited gains in global health and global economics of recent decades (in South Korea and Indonesia, for example) are being swallowed in the gap between rich and poor. The gains are swept away as the movement from rural to urban areas and immigration from the south to the north overload social structures (Barten, 1994) and environmental resources (Diamond, 2005).

In contrast, knowledge is becoming available to more people in countries worldwide, and shifts in power can occur. For example, alliances among small and medium states from both the northern and the southern hemispheres have forged bans on antipersonnel land mines (International Campaign to Ban Land Mines, 2006). Multinational corporations, which have power to influence governments around the world, can be held accountable for their human rights practices through the collective power of nongovernmental organizations (NGOs) using moral force (Human Rights Watch, 2006a). Globally, countries of the south with fresh experiences in fighting repression bring new and bold leadership to these coalitions by upholding the principle of universality and defending human rights in the face of the waning commitment of the major powers (China, the United States, and Russia) (Human Rights Watch, 2006b).

Intentional Human Commitment. Social empowerment on a global basis is highly complex and politically entangled and requires long-term, intentional human commitment (Robertson, 2000). For example, in 1998 collective work and alliances among small and medium states—through the auspices of the United Nations—established the International Criminal Court (ICC) (Robertson). The idea of a world criminal court was proposed in 1937 by the League of Nations and resurfaced in the face of terrorism and drug trafficking in the 1980s.

War crimes, genocide, and crimes against humanity; systematic or widespread murder; torture; and rape and other forms of sexual violence would come to the attention of the international court, and the court would try international criminals and terrorists. The United States, China, Israel, and India were among the seven nations abstaining from the vote to ratify, yet the United States and China manipulate to control politics in the ICC through the UN Security Council (Robertson). What should have been the "the triumph of international law over superpower expediency" instead demonstrated the gap in human rights rhetoric and the reality (Robertson, p. 324). The human rights challenge to international law is essential, and intentional human commitment must reference what is right and good instead of "what states have done in the past in their selfish national interests" (Robertson, p. 89).

In another example, addressing world poverty at the macro level, no dearth of expertise and knowledge exists regarding interconnecting global issues. Yet, harmonized action at the global level is confounded by power and politics (Sachs, 2006). The best of international evidence and science can be offered to address poverty and sustainable development through effective UN Country Teams, which include UN agencies operating in developing countries, the International Monetary Fund (IMF) and the World Bank (Sachs). That is not usually the case, however. The IMF and the World Bank are generalist institutions: The World Bank focuses on development, and the IMF addresses macroeconomic issues (for example, budgets, financial practices, exchange rates). Currently the IMF and the World Bank have a privileged position influenced by the power of wealthy countries: "one dollar, one vote" (Sachs, p. 287).

The UN General Assembly also operates on a "one country, one vote" basis. The UN agencies are specialized institutions, offer expertise in development, and are less influenced by rich countries. They offer knowledge in child health and education (UNICEF), family planning (UN Population Fund), agriculture (Food and Agriculture Organization), public health and disease control (World Health Organization [WHO]), and capacity building and governance (UN Development Program) (Sachs, 2006). Yet, they "rarely have the macroeconomic overview at work in the IMF–World Bank perspective. . . . Without a much closer partnership of the specialized UN agencies with the IMF and the World Bank, none of these institutions can do their work properly" (Sachs, p. 287).

The next section examines an example of social empowerment and intentional human commitment in the face of gender-based violence. Thirty years of incremental, painstaking organization; coalition building; and the work of many women in many organizations around the world have laid the groundwork for interrelated issues: violence against women, women's rights, and the role of women in economic development and the environment. Advocacy in social work requires the same in-depth attention and work to change policies on behalf of vulnerable populations. Lessons learned from human rights work can advance student knowledge in this domain.

Human Rights Abuses against Women and Advocacy for the World's Women

"How have women been affected by limited forms of democracy? What has been the impact on women of narrow definitions of human rights? Why have so many degrading life experiences of women not been understood as human rights issues?" (Bunch, 1995, p. 11). How did women's rights become a worldwide issue in the 1990s, and how will attention to women's rights be maintained in the new century? Integrating women's issues into the human rights agenda is process building on an international scale. Such process building needs to be deeply integrated into social work practice at all levels, from social policy advocacy at the national and international level to direct practice with survivors of such abuse. Three strategies are briefly discussed in this section: (1) making relationships through worldwide women's conferences and networks, (2) mainstreaming women's rights agendas into human rights agendas with moral force, and (3) dealing with women's everyday lives. Creative, committed social workers have been and are involved in all of these strategies as means for standing in solidarity with populations experiencing some of the most serious oppressions in human history.

Making Relationships through Worldwide Conferences and Agendas. Although women had organized worldwide against injustices in their own political contexts, Friedman (1995) acknowledged the UN Decade for Women (1975–1985) as "the watershed both for placing women on the international intergovernmental agenda and for facilitating women's cooperation" (p. 23). The role of NGOs at the World Conferences for Women in Mexico (1975), Copenhagen (1980), Nairobi (1985), and Beijing (1995) was critical. NGO forums provided venues for women from all over the world to talk, form relationships, and construct strategies for making their governments accountable (Friedman).

In 2000, the United Nations hosted Beijing +5 in New York City. Summarizing the conference, Human Rights Watch reported that although greater attention had been given to the abuses of women's human rights and use of human rights rhetoric, the legal and moral force required to change policies and practices in many countries are still culturally bound, politically entangled, contradictory, and difficult to address:

> The South African government, for example, could proudly declare its commitment to women's rights at Beijing +5, yet thousands of South African women farm workers had no ability to establish work contracts independently of their husbands. Similarly, the government of Peru condemned

violence against women, while obliging domestic violence victims to undergo mandatory conciliation sessions with their abusers; the Uzbekistan government maintained constitutional guarantees of women's equality but women wishing to divorce their husbands faced major, gender-specific obstacles; the Taliban administration in Afghanistan shrouded its denial of women's rights in the rhetoric of protection but its forces raped ethnic Hazara and Tajik women with impunity; and Japan's government treated trafficked women not as victims of abuse but as criminals. (Human Rights Watch, 2000, ¶11)

Growing out of the Decade for Women, the *Convention on the Elimination of All Forms of Discrimination Against Women* (CEDAW) (United Nations, 1979), which came into force in 1981 was a powerful tool for women's equality—"from family to workplace to government" (Friedman, 1995, p. 23). A network of international organizations to ensure education and compliance with CEDAW followed: the International Women's Rights Action Watch; Latin American Committee for the Defense of Women's Rights; the Asia-Pacific Forum on Women, Law, and Development; and Women in Law and Development in Africa (Friedman, p. 23). National and international women's organizations facilitate information sharing in England, Canada, the Philippines, France, and the United States. In December 2000, CEDAW began considering petitions for hearings from individual women and groups of women who have exhausted all national remedies.

Mainstreaming Women's Rights Agendas into Human Rights Agendas. The rights of marginalized social groups are typically treated as special issues without full integration into the political agenda. Not until the 1970s did the UN agenda specifically address women's issues and recognize women as resources (Pietilä & Vickers, 1996). Still, women's rights were viewed as a subissue of human rights, the public sphere of state-sanctioned oppression, without considering the private sphere in which most violations of women's rights occur (Peters & Wolper, 1995). Historically, the United Nations did not see women's oppression as a political issue; thus, sex discrimination and violence were also excluded from the human rights agenda (Stamatopoulou, 1995). The creation of specialized bodies to address women's rights allowed major UN human rights bodies to "absolve themselves of this responsibility" (Stamatopoulou, p. 45) and relegated women's rights to add-ons (a common political tactic with minority concerns) rather than politically integrated issues.

Focusing attention on violence against women, however, was a powerful tool for reshaping human rights through women's experience. An international human rights framework already existed and had political power and protocols supported by governments. Slavery, torture, and terrorism represented everything the human rights community was combating, but did not include women's experiences. Women's human rights advocates used the continuum of violence in the public and private spheres to educate and hold governments accountable (Friedman, 1995). "The process of including women transforms agendas" and challenges "the hierarchy of rights, with civil and political rights at the pinnacle" (Friedman, p. 20) with the notion that all human rights—political, civil, social, economic, cultural—are indivisible. What frameworks exist for mainstreaming social work issues? How are women's experiences used to "transform agendas"? The Global Tribunal on Violations of Women's Human Rights (in Vienna, Austria, 1993) (discussed below) is an example of mainstreaming agendas.

In another example, violence and discrimination against women were acknowledged as lifelong patterns of abuse. By 1995, following the Beijing conference, the strategic objectives of the *Platform for Action and the Beijing Declaration* were formally extended to the "girl-child," nurturing her education, her safety, and her health care and encouraging the development of her social, economic, and political power. These objectives were built on the pre-existing Convention on the Rights of the Child. Note that thinking about practice with girls and young women, especially those from the most at-risk groups, as human rights work changes the terms of social work in important ways.

Dealing with Women's Everyday Lives. How can women influence the international agenda on a local level? Work at the international level must be based on life experiences of women, and grassroots organizations can supply this critical information. The Vienna conference connected women from government and from specialized agencies with human rights advocates at the grassroots. Despite work at the international level, many women have felt little impact locally. Yet, gains for such women in their own communities have often been the result of their own courageous work.

Suarez Toro (1995) focused on the everyday lives of women in Central America and described a process of grassroots exploration and analysis in a region where "equality before the law is not equality in life for women" (p. 190) and political violence—torture, rape, execution, disappearance—continues. In this process, using their own life experiences as starting points, women themselves popularize women's issues and educate one another. In groups, the women identify the first time their human rights were violated because they are women and determine the first time they reclaimed their rights. They analyze international human rights instruments to see what protects them and what does not, and they determine what needs to be changed. Next, the women concretely name strategies that can help change their daily lives and construct strategies for influencing policy at the local, national, and international levels. The women discuss their own resistance, fears, and excitement and support each other as they act. This methodology places in context the "facts of their lives, as part of larger social, political, and cultural constructs as well—as part of a global problem" (Suarez Toro, p. 193).

What is the place of social work here? Recognizing the connectedness of women's experiences of oppression worldwide, social workers have clear opportunities and obligations both to advocacy supporting the mainstreaming of women's issues as human rights issues and to assisting women with whom they work to see their struggles within a global context. For example, some social agencies are now structuring services not in terms of treating the pathology of individual women, but rather by helping women (and men) working in groups ("culture circles") examine systemic patterns of oppression that contribute to the dilemmas faced by clients (Parker, 2003).

Global Tribunal on Violations of Women's Human Rights

New women's coalitions have made old divisions—those along north–south lines and those among women working in nongovernmental, governmental, and UN agencies—obsolete in the active lobbying to get women and human rights on the agenda for the World Conference in Vienna (Bunch & Reilly, 1994). Starting in November 1992, grassroots hearings on violations of women's human rights took place from India to Costa Rica, from the United States to Argentina. This evidence was sent to the UN Centre for Human Rights (Bunch & Reilly). The hearings culminated at the Global Tribunal on Violations of Women's Human Rights (in Vienna, 1993), which coincided with the World Conference in June of that year. In one day, 33 women testified to the "failure of existing human rights mechanisms to protect and promote women's human rights" (Friedman, 1995, p. 30). Four judges documented joint recommendations at the end of the hearings:

> We affirm the principle of universality that protects all of humanity, including women. Universal human rights standards are rooted in all cultures, religions, and traditions, but those cultural, religious and traditional practices that undermine universality and prove harmful to women cannot be tolerated. (Bunch & Reilly, p. 32)

In this section, the testimonies from the Tribunal are followed by current references to organizations working on behalf of women across the world. The struggles documented by the tribunal may once have seemed to be happening far away, but this is clearly no longer the case. Similar violations of the rights of women cross international boundaries, and the policies of governments including that of the United States have a profound impact on the extent to which human rights are honored or violated. In addition, contemporary social workers commonly see in their practice immigrant and refugee women who have experienced extreme violence, torture, and mutilation. Social workers therefore need to have a clear-eyed appreciation of the realities in which their clients have been embedded.

War Crimes. The Universal Declaration of Human Rights (United Nations, 1948) states, "No one shall be subject to torture or to cruel, inhuman or degrading treatment or punishment." The Fourth Geneva Convention states "in case of conflict or occupation" and in noninternational conflicts, women are protected against "attack on their honour . . . rape, enforced prostitution and any form of indecent assault" (Bunch & Reilly, 1994, p. 33).

In the 1930s, the Japanese established army brothels, sexually enslaving and serially raping some 200,000 women, mostly girls under age 20. Eighty to 90 percent of the women were from Korea; the remainder were from China, Taiwan, the Philippines, Indonesia, and some European countries (Bunch & Reilly, 1994). In 1992, the University of Zagreb School of Medicine reported 10,000 rapes in Bosnian Serbian army camps; estimates from other reports are as high as 60,000 (cited in Bunch & Reilly). Rape and forced pregnancy used to promote ethnic cleansing by Serbians are but one side of the corruption of war; another side is the complicity of governments that use statistics on rape to incense hatred of the enemy (Bunch & Reilly). And male violence against women, aggressively supported by governments, is anesthetized in terms such as "Japanese comfort women" and "ethnic cleansing" as women's lives are smothered.

Palestine and Darfur. Uncovering violence is crucial on the international agenda. To bring global attention to these areas, the Special Rapporteur (representative) on Women and Violence to the UN Commission on Human Rights visited the occupied Palestinian territory and the Darfur region of the Sudan and reported on both situations in 2005 (UN High Commission on Human Rights, 2005). The current results of war and occupation on women can be clearly seen.

According to the Special Rapporteur's report, the Israeli "security situation," or occupation of Palestine, represents "an integrated system of violence at the intersection of occupation and patriarchy subjugates women through a continuum of violence linking all spheres of life" (UN High Commission on Human Rights, 2005, ¶8). The report called on the government of Israel to observe international law to ensure the rights and protection of Palestinian civilians, particularly the right to health and medical care for expectant mothers and the ill. Speaking on behalf of Palestine, Nadine Hassassian summarized details for the record:

> Killings, arrests and detentions, dispersion, restrictions on movements, house demolitions [resulting in homelessness] and expropriation of property were among the list of Israeli practices which made the lives of Palestinian women unbearable and insecure. The deteriorating economic and

social conditions brought about by the Israeli closure regime and the wall [Apartheid Wall begun in 2002] led to abject poverty and an alarmingly high unemployment rate, thus rendering many women increasingly dependent on emergency assistance including food aid. (UN High Commission on Human Rights, 2005)

Israeli aggression and oppression have an impact on the health and development of the children of the women of Palestine because the occupation has severely taxed women's physical and psychological abilities to cope. Hassassian concluded that condemning Israeli violations of rights is no relief at this point; the international community must put pressure on Israel to end its occupation of Palestine. Itzhak Levanon of Israel, acknowledged the destruction and adverse effects of the conflict. Because of the multiple factors that contribute to violence, Israel could not support the conclusion that violence against women had increased as a direct result of the occupation (UN High Commission on Human Rights, 2005).

In the Darfur region of Sudan, women report that violence—murder, rape, attacks on their villages, burning of their homes, and loss of their livestock—takes place at the hands of the government-backed militia (the Janjaweed) and

---

Sidebar 3-1: *Hypocrisy Forces a Change in Name*

On March 15, 2006, the United Nations voted to replace the Commission on Human Rights, founded in 1946, with a new UN Human Rights Council (Farley, 2006). It was finally recognized that the politicization (poor reputation, hypocrisy, and double standards) of the Commission undermined its purpose and duty to human rights protections (UN General Assembly, 2006). Too many countries had sought membership on the old Commission to prevent criticism of their own records or to target others. The new structure provides a series of new procedural safeguards, including periodic universal review of the record of all member countries, and raised the Commission's status to that of a Council, which would report directly to the General Assembly rather than to the UN bureaucracy. The United States, however, contended that the filter to bar member countries with serious human rights abuses from membership on the Council was not adequate and that the Council would therefore not be powerful enough to address violations by countries such as Sudan, Cuba, Iran, Zimbabwe, Belarus, and Burma (Farley). The United States proposed unsuccessfully to require a two-thirds vote by the General Assembly for Council membership and to bar countries under UN sanction for rights abuses. A review of the council's status will take place in 2011 (Farley).

❐❐❐❐❐

Sidebar 3-2: *Who Monitors Compliance?*

Seven committees (listed below), as well as the new Human Rights Council, monitor the compliance of states, parties to specific treaties, and laws listed above. Committees may call on governments to respond to allegations and may make recommendations for appropriate remedies where violations are found. Should governments not comply, a series of other steps may be taken, including specific requests for action from government officials and publication of findings. *Rapporteurs* (representatives) or experts gather facts, visit prisons, interview victims, and make recommendations on how to increase respect for human rights in specific areas: torture, religious intolerance, racism, sale of children, and violence against women. Reports of the rapporteurs help mobilize international attention.

Committee against Torture
http://www.unhchr.ch/html/menu2/6/cat/index.html

Committee on Education, Social and Cultural Rights
http://www.ohchr.org/english/bodies/cescr/

Committee on Migrant Workers
http://www.ohchr.org/english/bodies/cmw/index.htm

Committee on the Elimination of Discrimination against Women
http://www.un.org/womenwatch/daw/cedaw/committee.htm

Committee on the Elimination of Racial Discrimination
http://www.unhchr.ch/html/menu2/6/cerd.htm

Committee on the Rights of the Child
http://www.ohchr.org/english/bodies/crc/

Human Rights Committee
http://www.unhchr.ch/html/menu2/6/hrc.htm

security forces. Women who are raped face multiple obstacles in obtaining justice and health intervention. Ilham Ahmed of Sudan asserted that Sudan's penal code imposed the maximum sentence for rape, that men who staffed the police stations are trained, and that the militias who committed crimes were apprehended and were being prosecuted. In spite of these efforts, observers in the region noted that rebels had been committing crimes against women and that "a number of women" had been killed in this conflict (UN High Commission on Human Rights, 2005).

Trafficking in Prostitution. From the 1985 Nairobi Forward-Looking Strategies for the Advancement of Women (United Nations, 1986) come the following:

> Forced prostitution is a form of slavery imposed on women by procurers. It is . . . the result of economic degradation that alienates women's labour through processes of rapid urbanization and migration resulting from underemployment and unemployment. It also stems from women's dependence on men. . . . Sex tourism [and] forced prostitution . . . reduce women to mere sex objects and marketable commodities. (United Nations, ¶ 290)

In the Netherlands in 1993, the Foundation against Trafficking in Women reported assisting women from Asia and Central and Eastern European countries—Poland, Bulgaria, the Ukraine, Russia—where economic changes had not stabilized. Women paid low wages in other countries are lured to the Netherlands with promises of legitimate work and better pay; once there, they are trafficked into prostitution (Bunch & Reilly, 1994).

The *Medium Term Philippine Development Plan,* or *Philippines 2000* (Largoza-Maza, 1995), follows the transition of an economy based on U.S. military bases to U.S. "rest and relaxation preserves" and multinationals, propped up by Filipino women as cheap labor and sexual commodities. Where farmlands are being displaced by industrial estates fueled by foreign investment and increasing sex tourism, women are easily exploited in an economic environment where a daily wage averages $4.20 and daily cost of living for an average family of six is $10.20 (Largoza-Maza). GABRIELA (General Assembly Binding Women for Reforms, Integrity, Equality, Leadership, and Action) is a coalition of Filipino women's organizations that emerged from the anti-Marcos struggle (1983–1986). GABRIELA addresses issues ranging from

> U.S. military bases to nuclear power plants to rape, domestic violence and prostitution; from U.S. imperialism to the stranglehold of multinational companies to militarization to Filipino "comfort women" through organizing, research, and education; legislative action, campaigns, mobilization; welfare and crisis intervention; and local and international networking. (Largoza-Maza, p. 65)

It is important to note that trafficking in prostitution is not limited to other parts of the world; at least 50,000 women, mostly from Latin America, countries of the former Soviet Union, and Southeast Asia are trafficked into the United States each year, and the problem appears to be increasing (Raymond, Hughes, & Gomez, 2001)

In 2000, the Coalition Against Trafficking in Women (which has offices around the world), with the International Human Rights Network (with offices in Ireland and Uganda), gained ground in a strong and inclusive definition of trafficking, a definition central to the new UN *Protocol to Prevent, Suppress and Punish Trafficking in Persons, Especially Women and Children* (United Nations, 2000c). This protocol supplements the UN *Convention against Transnational Organized Crime* (United Nations, 2000a). In 2005, the United States ratified the convention and three protocols: the aforementioned protocol against trafficking in persons, as well as the *Protocol Against the Smuggling of Migrants by Land, Sea, and Air* (United Nations, 2000b) and the *Protocol Against the Illicit Manufacturing of and Trafficking in Firearms, Their Parts and Components and Ammunition* (United Nations, 2001). (See http://www.unodc.org/unodc/en/trafficking_convention. html#top for discussion of the definition of trafficking.)

Violations of the Body. Female genital mutilation (FGM) is the excision of genitalia in the name of cultural and social constructions of femininity and wifely obedience. FGM "affects 100 million women who live in 26 African countries, a few minorities in some Asian countries, and immigrants in Europe, Canada, Australia, and the United States" (Bunch & Reilly, 1994, p. 53). Nahid Toubia, a medical doctor from the Sudan, asserted that "as women, we too have the right to decide what parts of our culture we want to preserve and what we want to abandon . . . . These women [who have been mutilated] are holding back a silent scream so strong it could shake the earth" (Bunch & Reilly, p. 53). Asma Abedel Haleem, a human rights lawyer and Islamic scholar from the Sudan, reported, "It is not sufficient for religion to shun the practice. Religion should be used as a tool for condemning and preventing its occurrence. The participation of women in the reinterpretation of religion will be crucial" (Bunch & Reilly, p. 54).

Sexuality. Rebeca Sevilla, co-chair of the International Lesbian and Gay Association, reported that in Brazil 2,000 murders of gay people were documented in the media from 1983 to 1993. About 90 percent of the cases had been analyzed, and most cases are unresolved or the aggressor is free. Social cleansing has claimed lesbians, gay men, prostitutes, and street kids (Bunch & Reilly, 1994). The International Lesbian and Gay Association (ILGA) Web site (http://www. ilga.org) documented the second international retreat for lesbian and gay Muslims and their friends, which took place in 2000. The focus of the retreat was on reconciling homosexuality and Islam and discussing ideological differences among the participants, who represented more than a dozen nationalities and ethnic groups. In 2006, ILGA held its world conference in Geneva and organized four panels on lesbian, gay, bisexual, and transgender (LGBT) issues at the UN Human Rights Council. In December of the same year, the UN Economic and Social Council granted consultative status to three LGBT organizations (ILGA-Europe and two member groups of that association). Continuing advocacy for international recognition and protection of the rights of LGBT persons is ongoing.

   Disability, Reproduction, and Population Control. At the Tribunal, Nicaraguan Petrona Sandoval recounted her experience of becoming paralyzed from epidural anesthesia during childbirth, one of 600 to 2,000 estimated cases in 10 years, according to a study by a Swedish group (Bunch & Reilly, 1994). No thorough investigation has occurred, and the cause is uncertain, but it was "most likely" expired medications (Bunch & Reilly). Lack of informed consent, "coerced abortions and sterilization, unsafe contraceptive devices, unnecessary hysterectomies, and the incompetent use of epidural anesthesia and episiotomies" are some of the reproduction and population control violations of women's rights in health (Bunch & Reilly, p. 57).
   In August 2005, the first UN treaty on the rights of persons with disabilities underwent article-by-article review and comment. Independent living, inclusion in the community, women with disabilities, children with disabilities, education, participation in political and public life, personal mobility, and international cooperation were key topics. Expertise came from several organizations, including Inclusion International, Disabled People International, the International Disability Coalition, and the World Federation of the Deaf. The lead agency in the United Nations is Enable (UN General Assembly, 2005).

   Human Rights Abuses within the Family. The *New York Times* reported that the Women Rights Awareness Program, an advocacy group in Kenya, found that 70 percent of the men and women they interviewed knew their neighbors beat their wives; almost 60 percent blamed the women. Agnes Siyiankoi, age 30, was beaten by her husband with a cattle club and carried to the hospital. Hospitalization requires an official complaint, which often deters victims from speaking out. With support from her brother, who is a lawyer, she filed assault charges after 13 years of abuse. She formally challenged the traditional power structure among the Masai tribal peoples in Kenya and suffered the anger of other women, for "it is unheard of in Masailand to put your husband in jail" ("Kenyan Tradition Confronted," 1997, p. A5).
   Gayla Thompson, an African American woman living in New York, testified as follows before the Global Tribunal on Violations of Women's Human Rights:

> [My husband] beat me bad enough to cause an abortion. . . . I was able to get away at one point and call the police and when they arrived—because my husband was in his police uniform and had me on the floor kicking me and beating me and punching me—the other officers thought I was fair game and so they joined in. (Bunch & Reilly, 1994, p. 26)

Political persecution is narrowly defined, and when intersecting with citizenship and discrimination, these complex realities are not addressed by institutions and systems. Maria Olea, an immigrant to the United States, escaped domestic violence in a Chilean "dictatorial political system" (Bunch & Reilly, 1994, p. 78) that supports men who can legally abuse women and sought refugee status with her two children. Domestic violence is not considered grounds for obtaining refugee status in the United States, and she faces death if she is returned to Chile. Maria Olea's invisibility as an undocumented woman subjects her to another set of laws that further diminish her chances and the lives of her undocumented children in the United States (Bunch & Reilly).

According to a *New York Times* article (Simons, 1998), migration to cities in Morocco and other countries around the Mediterranean has encouraged more couples to live alone rather than within a Muslim family network. Urban living has contributed to improved education for women, but it has also removed them from protection by their fathers and brothers and exposed them to more abuse, repudiation of the marriage, and divorce, according to Fatima Zahra Tamouth, a professor of African history at the University of Rabat (Simons). In 1993, women's groups collected one million signatures to move divorce and child custody rules from the Mudawana, the Muslim family law, into the Moroccan civil code (Simons). Subsequent reforms, which were made without the input of women, have had little impact, and women now want a part in abolishing repudiation and making rules for child custody and divorce, which now affect 50 percent of couples. Activists cited the UN International Women's Conference in Beijing (1995) as a catalyst for women "among the more emancipated of the Arab world" in Morocco, Tunisia, and Algeria (Simons, p. A6).

Intersecting Issues. HIV/AIDS intersects with violence against women, trafficking in persons, and gender inequality and vulnerability worldwide. Reports from special rapporteurs and national delegations during hearings at the UN Commission on Human Rights in April 2005 indicated that the number of women living with HIV had increased in every region of the world (UN High Commission on Human Rights, 2005). Violence from domicile to the transnational arena increases the risks of HIV transmission. For example, human trafficking directly exposes girls and women trafficked for sex tourism to the virus, yet trafficking is seen as a law-and-order issue, not a human rights issue. Victims are criminalized and prosecuted as illegal aliens, undocumented workers, or irregular migrants.

The World Health Organization Media Centre (2005) conducted a study on women's health and domestic violence across countries to help inform policies and strategies, particularly those designed to integrate violence prevention into initiatives for children in schools, youth, HIV/AIDS, and sexual and reproductive health, including prenatal care, family planning, and postabortion care. The report stated,

> In this study, women who were in physically or sexually abusive relationships were more likely to report that their partner had multiple sexual partners and had refused to use a condom than women in non-violent relationships. Women who reported physical or sexual violence by a partner were also more likely to report having had at least one induced abortion or miscarriage than those who did not report violence. (World Health Organization Media Centre, ¶6)

SOCIAL JUSTICE AND ECONOMIC DEVELOPMENT

People who are marginalized are easily exploited; the labor of one social group (class, gender) is used to benefit another social group in pursuit of profit and power (Young, 1990). The global search for cheap labor, exploitation of Hispanic garment workers in California, trafficking in prostitution, and child labor in Pakistan are examples. The resulting powerlessness is a function of position in a hierarchical structure and inhibits the realization of one's capacity and decision making in working life and increases exposure to disrespectful and dehumanizing treatment because of status (Young).

In 1992, equity, social justice, and eliminating poverty were linked to sustainable development at the Earth Summit in Rio de Janeiro, Brazil (Rasmussen, 1994). Questions, interventions, and policies framed in terms of social justice and social empowerment must reflect the diversities of philosophies, cultures, realities, and environmental limits, along with a promise of a quality future for the coming generations. Women are collectively asking, "What kind of economic development is best suited to the promotion of human development?" rather than "What kind of human development would promote competition and growth?" (Pietilä & Vickers, 1996). In 1984, Devaki Jain, an essayist from India, assessed development:

> Economic development, that magic formula, devised sincerely to move poor nations out of poverty, has become women's worst enemy. Roads bring machine-made ersatz goods, take away young girls and food and traditional art and culture; technologies replace women, leaving families even further impoverished. Manufacturing cuts into natural resources (especially trees), pushing fuel and fodder sources further away, bring home-destroying floods or life-destroying drought, and adding all the time to women's work burdens. (cited in Pietilä & Vickers, p. 35)

And where does the road go? Kunstler (1993) wrote about the modern American landscape and reflected similar pessimism about economic development:

The [American] road is now like television, violent and tawdry. The landscape it runs through is littered with cartoon buildings and commercial messages. We whiz by them at fifty-five miles an hour and forget them, because one convenience store looks like the next. They do not celebrate anything beyond their mechanistic ability to sell merchandise. We don't want to remember them. We did not savor the approach and we were not rewarded upon reaching the destination, and it will be the same next time, and every time. There is little sense of having arrived anywhere, because everyplace looks like no place in particular. (p. 131)

SUMMARY

This discussion has centered on social justice and violence, viewing each as a continuum bridging the public and private spheres. Morality, justice, and relationships support social justice. Social power is contained in force, wealth, and knowledge. Social policy can structure social justice but requires moral authority, legal force, and commitment to relationship. Violence is embedded in poverty, corruption, and injustice—including cultural imperialism, exploitation, marginalization, and powerlessness.

International human rights, including women's rights as human rights, are examined as the central focus of social justice. In this chapter, the *International Bill of Rights*, the UN *Declaration on the Rights of Indigenous Peoples*, and violence against women as violations of human rights—from war crimes in the public sphere to domestic violence in the private sphere—have served as the primary examples of social justice activism. Advocacy strategies take place at all levels, from international to local. The act of writing this chapter is another strategy, because its placement in a textbook for social work students serves to educate, to inform, and to move to action.

Indigenous peoples understand that, spiritually and in reality, justice is shaped every day through attitudes and reinforced through interactions with others and with the environment. These attitudes and actions can nurture or contaminate future generations. To help shape social justice, social work students must understand that social work must be more than a paycheck, more than a career. Social justice requires the understanding that diversity fuels life and that the Earth and its populations are vulnerable to violence, the misuse of power, and oppression. Social workers who respond to social justice understand that this requires continual study and vigilance, self-reflection, the courage to change as new information comes to light, and the responsibility to act, both individually and collectively, as new understandings are formed. Above all, social justice requires the recognition of that which is dead and temporary, that which is living, that which must be respected, and that which must be preserved.

REFERENCES

Aristide, J. B. (2000). *Eyes of the heart: Seeking a path for the poor in the age of globalization.* Monroe, ME: Common Courage.

Barker, F. (1962). *Social contract.* New York: Oxford University Press.

Barten, F. (1994). Health in a city environment. *World Health, 47*(3), 24–25.

Benhabib, S. (1992). *Situating the self: Gender, community and postmodernism in contemporary ethics.* New York: Routledge.

Boyd, S. (1997). Challenging the public/private divide: An overview. In S. Boyd (Ed.), *Challenging the public/private divide: Feminism, law, and public policy* (pp. 3–33). Toronto: University of Toronto Press.

Bunch, C. (1995). Transforming human rights from a feminist perspective. In J. Peters & A. Wolper (Eds.), *Women's rights, human rights: International feminist perspectives* (pp. 11–17). New York: Routledge.

Bunch, C., & Reilly, N. (1994). *Demanding accountability: The global campaign and Vienna Tribunal for Women's Human Rights.* New Brunswick, NJ: Rutgers University, Center for Women's Global Leadership.

Chomsky, N. (1999). *The umbrella of U.S. power: The Universal Declaration of Human Rights and the contradictions of U.S. policy.* New York: Seven Stories Press.

Davidson, A. (1994). *Endangered peoples.* San Francisco: Sierra Club Books.

Devall, W. B. (1976). Social science research on support of human rights. In R. P. Claude (Ed.), *Comparative human rights* (pp. 326–352). Baltimore: Johns Hopkins University Press.

Diamond, J. (2005). *Collapse: How societies choose to fail or succeed.* New York: Viking Penguin.

Farley, M. (2006, March 16). U.S. explains objection to new rights panel. *Chicago Tribune*, p. 15.

Friedman, E. (1995). Women's human rights: The emergence of a movement. In J. Peters & A. Wolper (Eds.), *Women's rights, human rights: International feminist perspectives* (pp. 18–35). New York: Routledge.

Human Rights Watch. (2000). *Women's human rights.* Retrieved December 30, 2006, from http://www.hrw.org/wr2k1/women/index.html

Human Rights Watch. (2006a). *Business and human rights.* Retrieved December 30, 2006, from http://www.hrw.org/doc/?t=corporations

Human Rights Watch. (2006b). Introduction. In *World Report 2006.* New York: Author. Retrieved December 30, 2006, from http://hrw.org/wr2k6/introduction/1.htm#_Toc121910420

Inter-American Commission on Human Rights. (1997). *Proposed American declaration on the rights of indigenous peoples.* Retrieved December 30, 2006, from http://www.cidh.oas.org/Indigenous.htm

International Campaign to Ban Land Mines. (2006). *Campaign history.* Retrieved December 30, 2006, from http://www.icbl.org/campaign/history

International Work Group for Indigenous Affairs. (2005). *The UN permanent forum on indigenous issues.* Retrieved June 5, 2006, from http://www.iwgia.org/sw218.asp

Kenyan tradition confronted: A beaten wife goes to court. (1997, October 31). *New York Times*, p. A5.

Kunstler, J. H. (1993). *The geography of nowhere.* New York: Simon & Schuster.

Largoza-Maza, L. (1995). The Medium Term Philippine Development Plan toward the year 2000: Filipino women's issues and perspectives. In J. Peters & A. Wolper (Eds.), *Women's rights, human rights: International feminist perspectives* (pp. 62–65). New York: Routledge.

Midgley, J. (1997). *Social welfare in a global context.* Thousand Oaks, CA: Sage Publications.

Okin, S. M. (1989). *Justice, gender, and the family.* New York: Basic Books.

Parker, L. (2003). A social justice model for clinical social work practice. *Affilia, 18,* 272–288.

Peters, J., & Wolper, A. (1995). *Women's rights, human rights: International feminist perspectives.* New York: Routledge.

Pietilä, H., & Vickers, J. (1996). *Making women matter: The role of the United Nations* (3rd ed.). Atlantic Highlands, NJ: Zed Books.

Rao, A. (1995). The politics of gender and culture in international human rights discourse. In J. Peters & A. Wolper (Eds.), *Women's rights, human rights: International feminist perspectives* (pp. 167–175). New York: Routledge.

Rasmussen, L. L. (1994). And earth ethic for survival. *Ethics & agenda 21: Moral implications of a global consensus* (pp. 54–57). New York: United Nations.

Raymond, J. G., Hughes, D. M., & Gomez, C. J. (2001). *Sex trafficking of women in the United States: International and domestic trends.* North Amherst, MA: Coalition Against Trafficking in Women. Retrieved from http://action.web.ca/home/catw/readingroom.shtml?x=16939

Reiss, A., & Roth, J. A. (Eds.). (1993). *Understanding and preventing violence* (Vol. 1). Washington, DC: National Academy Press.

Robertson, G. (2000). *Crimes against humanity: The struggle for global justice.* New York: New Press.

Sachs, J. D. (2006). *The end of poverty: Economic possibilities for our time.* New York: Penguin Books.

Simons, M. (1998, March 9). Cry of Muslim women for equal rights is rising. *New York Times,* pp. A1, A6.

Smith, D. M. (1994). *Geography and social justice.* Oxford, England: Blackwell.

Stamatopoulou, E. (1995). Women's rights and the United Nations. In J. Peters & A. Wolper (Eds.), *Women's rights, human rights: International feminist perspectives* (pp. 36–48). New York: Routledge.

Suarez Toro, M. (1995). Popularizing women's human rights at the local level: A grassroots methodology for setting an international agenda. In J. Peters & A. Wolper (Eds.), *Women's rights, human rights: International feminist perspectives* (pp. 189–194). New York: Routledge.

Toffler, A. (1990). *Powershift: Knowledge, wealth, and violence at the edge of the 21st century.* New York: Bantam Books.

Toffler, A., & Toffler, H. (1995). *Creating a new civilization: The politics of the third wave.* Atlanta: Turner.

United Nations. (1948). *Universal declaration of human rights.* New York: Author. Retrieved December 2, 2006, from http://www.un.org/Overview/rights.html

United Nations. (1966a). *International covenant on civil and political rights.* Retrieved December 30, 2006, from http://www.unhchr.ch/html/menu3/b/a_ccpr.htm

United Nations. (1966b). *International covenant on economic, social and cultural rights.* Retrieved December 30, 2006, from http://www.unhchr.ch/html/menu3/b/a_cescr.htm

United Nations. (1979). *Convention on the elimination of all forms of discrimination against women (CEDAW).* Retrieved December 30, 2006, from http://www.un.org/womenwatch/daw/cedaw/text/econvention.htm

United Nations. (1986). *Nairobi forward-looking strategies for the advancement of women.* Retrieved December 30, 2006, from http://www.un.org/womenwatch/confer/nfls/Nairobi1985report.txt

United Nations. (1993a). *Declaration on the elimination of violence against women.* Retrieved December 30, 2006, from http://www.un.org/documents/ga/res/48/a48r104.htm

United Nations. (1993b). *International bill of human rights.* New York: Author.

United Nations. (2000a). *Convention against transnational organized crime.* Retrieved December 30, 2006, from http://www.unodc.org/unodc/crime_cicp_convention.html

United Nations. (2000b). *Protocol against the smuggling of migrants by land, sea, and air.* Retrieved December 30, 2006, from http://www.ohchr.org/english/law/organizedcrime.htm

United Nations. (2000c). *Protocol to prevent, suppress and punish trafficking in persons, especially women and children.* Retrieved December 30, 2006, from http://www.unodc.org/unodc/en/trafficking_protocol.html

United Nations. (2001). *Protocol against the illicit manufacturing of and trafficking in firearms, their parts and components and ammunition.* Retrieved December 30, 2006, from www.unodc.org/pdf/crime/a_res_55/255e.pdf

United Nations. (2006). *Declaration on the rights of indigenous peoples.* Retrieved December 30, 2006, from http://www.ohchr.org/english/issues/indigenous/declaration.htm

United Nations General Assembly, Department of Public Information. (2005, August 8). *Disability convention committee forges ahead on articles affecting daily life of people with disabilities* [Press release] (SOC 4678). Retrieved June 3, 2006, from www.un.org/News/Press/docs/2005/soc4678.doc.htm

United Nations General Assembly, Department of Public Information. (2006, March 15). *General Assembly establishes new Human Rights Council by vote of 170 in favour to 4 against* [Press release] (GA/10449). Retrieved June 3, 2006, from www.un.org/News/Press/docs/2006/ga10449.doc.htm

United Nations High Commission on Human Rights. (2005, April 6). *Commission hears from special rapporteurs on violence against women, trafficking in persons, UN adviser on gender issues.* Retrieved December 30, 2006, from http://domino.un.org/unispal.NSF/99818751a6a4c9c6852560690077ef61/f5f047910e94596785256fdc005071db!OpenDocument

World Health Organization Media Centre. (2005, November 24). *WHO report finds domestic violence is widespread and has serious impact on health.* Retrieved June 5, 2006, from http://www.who.int/mediacentre/news/releases/2005/pr62/en/index.html

Young, I. M. (1990). *Justice and politics of difference.* Princeton, NJ: Princeton University Press.

HUMAN RIGHTS RESOURCES

The UN Human Rights Umbrella

Central portal to United Nations human rights information (including International Bill of Human Rights, UN High Commissioner for Human Rights, and UN Human Rights Council)

http://www.un.org/rights

UN Human Rights Council (human rights complaints; human rights database)
http://www.ohchr.org/english/bodies/hrcouncil/

Womenwatch (central gateway to information and resources on the promotion of gender equality and the empowerment of women throughout the United Nations system)
http://www.un.org/womenwatch

International Labor Organization (UN specialized agency that seeks the promotion of social justice and internationally recognized human and labor rights)
http://www.ilo.org

Office of the UN High Commissioner for Refugees (legal and humanitarian protection for refugees)
http://www.unhcr.org

UN Children's Fund (UNICEF; works for children's rights; their survival, development, and protection)
http://www.unicef.org

UN Commission on the Status of Women (global policy-making body for women's rights)
http://www.un.org/womenwatch/daw/csw/

UN Development Program (the United Nations' global development network, focused on economic and social development respectful of human rights)
http://www.undp.org

UN Educational, Scientific, and Cultural Organization (encourages international peace and universal respect by promoting collaboration among nations)
http://www.unesco.org

Other Resources

Human Rights Watch
http://www.hrw.org

World Health Organization (right to health)
http://www.who.int/en/

Major Human Rights Laws

Convention on the Prevention and Punishment of the Crime of Genocide (1948)
http://www.unhchr.ch/html/menu3/b/p_genoci.htm

Convention Relating to the Status of Refugees (1961) http://www.unhchr.ch/html/menu3/
b/o_c_ref.htm

International Convention on the Elimination of All Forms of Racial Discrimination (1965)
http://www.unhchr.ch/html/menu3/b/d_icerd.htm

Convention on the Elimination of All Forms of Discrimination against Women (1979)
http://www.unhchr.ch/html/menu3/b/e1cedaw.htm

Convention against Torture and Other Cruel, Inhuman or Degrading Treatment or
Punishment (1984)
http://www.unhchr.ch/html/menu3/b/h_cat39.htm

Convention on the Rights of the Child (1989)
http://www.unhchr.ch/html/menu3/b/k2crc.htm

International Convention on the Protection of the Rights of All Migrant Workers and
Members of their Families (1990; ratified by nine countries, requires 20)
http://www.unhchr.ch/html/menu3/b/m_mwctoc.htm

4
□□□
Professional Values and Ethics

Marian Mattison

Social work education has always reserved a central role for subject matter on values and ethics in the training and development of its professionals. "The compelling importance of social work's value base and ethical principles" (Reamer, 1995, p. 5) has historically defined the mission of the profession and helped distinguish it from other allied helping professions. The structure and purpose of ethics training in social work education have been continuously influenced by forces from within the profession and by external sociopolitical forces and evolving societal norms.

In the earliest stage of the profession, social workers were cast as "rescuers of the poor," and little attention was paid to the moral and ethical behavior of the workers themselves. The charge of these early workers was narrowly focused on helping the poor reform themselves by overcoming their alleged "character defects," including thriftlessness, laziness, intemperance, and immorality. It was assumed that the altruistic nature of the early social workers' efforts would ensure that they had their clients' best interests at heart. That assumption contrasts starkly with today's contemporary social work ethics education. In the current educational climate, the expectation is that social work graduates will be well instructed in the responsibilities associated with the moral conduct of professional practice. The curriculum at the undergraduate and graduate levels routinely includes specific instruction in meeting the ethical standards, duties, and responsibilities of the profession; an exposure to procedures for systematic ethical decision making; information about strategies for avoiding ethics complaints; and content on ethical risk management strategies.

SHIFTS IN THE FOCUS OF PROFESSIONAL ETHICS

The significance placed on ethics and values in social work parallels the profession's historical vacillation between its mission to serve the vulnerable through social action and its efforts to generate therapeutic change at the individual level. The charitable acts of the late 19th century's "friendly visitors" were concentrated on the moral obligation of visitors "to discern the moral lapse responsible for the problem and then to supply the appropriate guidance" (Trattner, 1979, p. 85). The moral and ethical motives and resulting behaviors of early volunteers were assumed to be pure, and questions of unethical conduct did not surface as a subject for professional discussion or attention.

Around the turn of the century, moral emphasis shifted as the settlement house movement raised questions about the roles played by social and economic institutions in denying the poor access to the resources necessary for full participation as citizens. The structural flaws of social and economic institutions were judged to be the cause of the social ills that kept the poor underserved and resulted in poverty and oppression. This viewpoint not only characterized the settlement house era but also created the foundation for the social justice movement of the 1960s.

It was not until the 1920s that social work began to consider the morality of professional behavior and engaged in a professionwide conversation about how to define professional ethics. This shift in focus from the moral development of clients to the values of the profession was driven, in part, by the recognition that a professional code of conduct in the form of a written ethical code was essential "to formalize the transformation of the occupation into a profession" (Loewenberg, Dolgoff, & Harrington, 2000, p. 39). The effort to describe expectations for the ethical practice of professional social work introduced a fundamental redirection of attention to the accountability of practitioners to the public. Although novel at the time, the initial effort to draft ethical principles sparked a continual process of defining the conduct, duties, and responsibilities of social workers in relationships with clients and organizations that continues today. At the same time, a rudimentary effort to codify value preferences was begun in an effort to provide guidance regarding the use of values in practice.

As society transitioned into the "scientific" period of the 1930s to the 1950s, the era's prioritization of intellectual, clinical, and research-based knowledge affected how social work developed. The changing priorities led the social work profession to temporarily abandon the centrality of "softer" traditional values in favor of recasting its image in the eyes of the public. During this period, social work, like other professions, focused on issues that could be addressed empirically rather than on concerns involving ethics and values. In an effort to establish itself as an objective field and to be recognized as a credible profession, social work cultivated its casework techniques and clinical methodologies. "Carrying out the altruistic motivation of the profession" (Brill, 2001, p. 227) took a back seat to efforts aimed at improving social work's professional status.

Following the turbulence of the 1960s and a reexamination of the appropriateness of professional involvement with social activism, an increasing majority of social workers established themselves in clinical and casework activities. In the decades to follow, practitioners were increasingly confronted with complex issues and ethical tensions never before imagined. Shrinking financial and programmatic resources, restricted eligibility criteria for services, competition for funding sources, the advent of managed care, and technological advances presented questions about how social workers were to operationalize the core values of the profession into a new era of practice. This period witnessed consumers' challenges to the assumed authority of professionals and widespread publicity in the media about egregious violations of client rights. Lawsuits and litigation alleging ethics violations followed. The public became more aware of their rights against breaches of privacy, sexual misconduct by professionals, fraudulent practices, and incompetent service delivery. Not only did the public need protection against misconduct by professionals, but practitioners were also in need of information and training to avoid lawsuits and litigation. It was apparent that existing educational practices and training on values and ethics were failing to prepare social workers for the problems they faced in their work with clients and client systems.

Spawned by the emergence of the field of biomedical ethics and a burgeoning interest in applied ethics across the professions, there was a "renaissance" of moral education throughout higher education in the 1970s and 1980s. "Social work education also experienced a renewal of interest in ethical issues and ethics teaching" (Morelock, 1997, p. 72) and paid increased attention to dilemmas involving ethics and values along with ways to reduce subjectivity in decision making. A decisive shift occurred in the direction of values education, in which the topics of applied ethics and ethical decision making took a central role. As the literature devoted to the subject of social work ethics expanded, many graduate and undergraduate programs introduced content on ethics and ethical decision making into their curricula. Attention shifted toward the ethical behavior of practitioners, and social work instruction focused on the ethical standards for practice and the analytic skills needed to resolve difficult ethical choices.

Professional preparation for social work practice has since progressed from the gradual and voluntary inclusion of content on applied ethical decision making to a mandate to teach values and ethics in the social work curriculum. This directive is defined by the Council on Social Work Education (CSWE) in its Educational Policy and Accreditation Standards (EPAS), which require that

social work education programs integrate content about values and principles of ethical decision making as presented in the National Association of
Social Workers [NASW] Code of Ethics. The educational experience provides students with the opportunity to be aware of personal values; develop,
demonstrate, and promote the values of the profession; and analyze ethical
dilemmas and the ways in which these affect practice, services, and clients.
(CSWE, 2001, p. 8)

Although the EPAS require that "graduates demonstrate the ability to . . .
understand the value base of the profession and its ethical standards and principles, and practice accordingly" (CSWE, 2001, p.7), it is left to the discretion of
individual programs to design and position this content in their curricula. Some
programs require or offer discrete courses in social work ethics, although most
programs infuse ethics instruction across courses.

During the late 1980s, research and literature on the subject of social work
ethics flourished, and the subject matter found a permanent place in the consciousness of professional activity. The profession initiated efforts to refocus
its attention on a more contemporary, applied, and practical approach to teaching the subjects of values and ethics. An ardent interest in strategies and
approaches to training students in applying skillful reasoning when confronted
with moral or ethical dilemmas began. The field recognized that the complexities of ethical dilemmas require a systematic and deliberate approach that
should not be left to the intuitive resolve of individual practitioners. Proponents of guides or structured approaches agreed that an approach grounded in
thoughtful reasoning and open to the consideration of competing arguments
for and against particular courses of action would improve the quality of ethical decisions.

As a result, alternative teaching methods were woven into curricula, and a
notable shift occurred from theoretical and abstract discussions of values and
moral theory to an approach that emphasized applied ethical decision making
grounded in the use of case material. The goal of this type of education was never
to teach moral behavior or present solutions to ethical dilemmas but rather "to
encourage students to be alert in discovering and perceiving ethical issues, in
considering competing arguments, in examining both the strengths and limitations of their own positions, and in reaching thoughtfully reasoned conclusions"
(Loewenberg et al., 2000, p. xvi). The changes reflect the transition over the past
century of the role of values and ethics in both social work education and practice. It is no longer sufficient for social workers to be well intentioned. Changes
from within the profession and from the public demand that social workers make
ethical decisions in a systematic, reasoned way that can endure objective
scrutiny.

DISTINGUISHING VALUES FROM ETHICS

Although the terms "values" and "ethics" are often used interchangeably, they refer to different concepts. "Values are concerned with what is *good* and *desirable*, whereas ethics deal with what is *right* and *correct*" (Loewenberg et al., 2000, p. 22). Values are "essentially preferences" (Levy, 1993, p. 2) that inspire and underscore social work's professional relationships, duties, and obligations, whereas "ethics are the application of values to human relationships and transactions" (Levy, 1993, p. 1). For example, a core social work value is social justice, which obligates practitioners to meet the ethical standards and practices described in Standard 6, Social Workers' Ethical Responsibilities to the Broader Society, of the NASW *Code of Ethics* (NASW, 1996). It includes responsibilities to "advocate for living conditions conducive to the fulfillment of basic human needs" (Standard 6.01), "to promote policies and practices that demonstrate respect for difference" (Standard 6.04[c]), and to act "to prevent and eliminate domination of, exploitation of, and discrimination against any person, group, or class on the basis of race, ethnicity, national origin, color, sex, sexual orientation, age, marital status, political belief, religion, or mental or physical disability" (Standard 6.04[d]). Although professional values offer social workers directives and "conceptions of the desirable" (Kluckhohn, 1951, p. 403), they are frequently stated in general, abstract terms and, thus, cannot provide social workers with sufficient behavioral directives to make practice decisions (Perlman, 1976).

THE CENTRALITY OF SOCIAL WORK VALUES

As a profession, social work is values driven. Professional attitudes, approaches, and behaviors are unified by adherence to the values context that permeates all aspects of social work interventions. This infusion extends beyond engagement with clients to include interactions with colleagues and social systems. The internalization of core professional social work values, such as service, social justice, client worth, and integrity, define and shape a collective belief system that places the interest of clients before personal interests. The overarching values of the profession provide a structure to social workers' interactions with and reactions to clients and client systems. The values base of social work not only determines which interventions are used but also provides an operational framework for how those interventions are translated into relationships with clients and client systems.

Socialization into the profession includes the internalization of a belief system that commits practitioners to acting purposefully, to promoting the best interests of clients, and to resisting the impulse to act in a self-serving manner. Social workers are characterized by internalized dispositions toward actions, desires, and feelings that promote social justice and equality. Elements of those commitments to social justice are evidenced in the kinds and qualities of interactions among social workers, clients, and social institutions. Social workers are committed to moral virtues, "those that are explicit forms of regard for the interests of others, such as honesty, caring about justice, sincerity, truthfulness, benevolence, trustworthiness, and nonrecklessness" (Pincoffs, as cited in Van Wyk, 1990, p. 162).

Although repeated debates about how to best implement social work values into practice have occurred throughout the profession's history, no disagreement exists about the need to socialize students into the adoption of and commitment to the profession's values base. Social work education ensures that students "fit" within professional norms and attitudes and that they demonstrate an *ethic of care*, or a moral orientation to care for those in need. Caring about others involves a stable, reliable, and fixed disposition to act consistently out of a regard for the dignity, worth, and value of others as members of the human community. These are the basic values of the social work profession.

The Preamble to the NASW *Code of Ethics* identifies the core values of the social work profession as "the foundation of social work's unique purpose and perspective"; they reflect "what is unique to the social work profession" (NASW, 1996). The core values are the basis upon which the profession's mission statement is derived and underscore the *Code's* broad ethical principles, which delineate the "ideals to which all social workers should aspire" (NASW, Ethical Principles). The values, as listed in the preamble to the *Code*, are *not* ordered to give priority or precedent to one value over others (NASW). The six core values are as follows:

+ service
+ social justice
+ dignity and worth of the person
+ importance of human relationships
+ integrity
+ competence.

These values address why and how social workers carry out their professional duties. Discussions of social work values frequently evoke ideals such as facilitating client self-determination; demonstrating respect for cultural, racial, and spiritual diversity; providing access to opportunities and resources needed for maximizing client potential; and fostering client empowerment. They also address promoting social justice and combating social injustices, safeguarding client confidentiality, showing respect for colleagues, and the assumption of responsibility for one's professional conduct. The values are clear and straightforward. What is less clear is how to operationalize the values into ethical practice behavior (Perlman, 1976).

OPERATIONALIZING VALUES

Social workers agree to accountability for standardized values, but the manner in which those values are best implemented in practice often remains unclear and vague. For example, the expectation that social workers will respect the dignity of clients is operationalized by a commitment to full participation of clients in treatment practices and maximizing "responsible self-determination" (NASW, 1996, Ethical Principles). What should be the boundaries and limits to client self-determination? At what point should self-determination be sacrificed if the client engages in behavior that the social worker views as self-destructive? When the social worker's judgment about what constitutes risky or self-destructive behaviors differs from that of the client, whose definition should prevail? If client self-determination begins to conflict with another social work value, such as protecting the client from harm, which one should take precedence?

Consider the case of a 14-year-old girl who discloses in confidence to the social worker that she is pregnant and is committed to having her child. The client cannot be persuaded to inform her parents that she is pregnant. She is determined to get past the legal time limit for abortion so that her stepfather cannot pressure her to terminate the pregnancy. The social worker knows that the young woman is less likely to get the medical and social support she needs to stay healthy and have a healthy baby if the pregnancy is kept secret. In addition, at age 14 the client is not old enough to consent to sex or legally make health decisions for herself. On the basis of this knowledge, is it responsible for the social worker to sanction the client's right to determine her own best interests? What is the social worker's responsibility to disclose the pregnancy to the minor's guardians? Should client confidentiality be sacrificed when it may result in perceived health risks to the adolescent and her unborn child? To whom does the social worker owe primary loyalty in a case such as this, in which the interests of the adolescent, the unborn child, and the guardians are in conflict? How should the social worker's own views on abortion and adolescent parenting be taken into account?

ETHICAL DILEMMAS IN SOCIAL WORK PRACTICE

Cases such as the one described above represent the types of ethical dilemmas that are common in social work. Ethical dilemmas arise when social workers are confronted by a situation in which two or more of the values the social worker is committed to upholding conflict with one another. The social worker is unable to meet all the obligations at once and must ultimately make judgments about which obligation(s) to meet. Hospital social workers, for example, are often conflicted as they arrange discharge plans for elderly clients when questions remain about clients' abilities to care for themselves at home. The social worker respects the client's rights to decide where to live and whether to accept home health care (client self-determination). At the same time, the social worker is aware of the potential danger to the client's well-being if discharged to the home alone (duty to protect). Similarly, a social worker who has a strong working relationship with a mother in substance abuse recovery may learn of an instance of relapse, which resulted in a degree of neglectful behavior toward the child. Extenuating circumstances, such as an unanticipated layoff or an isolated contact with an abusive former partner, may give the social worker cause to contemplate whether the greater good is served by reporting the relapse (adhering to agency and legal mandates) or by assuming a wait-and-see approach (client empowerment). Social workers commonly encounter situations like these and are forced to make decisions between two valid ethical points of view.

When ethical tensions are embedded in decision making, the social worker must confront the fact that two or more courses of action cannot be realized simultaneously and that each choice is potentially compromising or unsatisfying. As in the examples above, a social worker may need to choose between promoting client self-determination and protecting the client's well-being. In other cases, the social worker will have to decide whether the duty to uphold agency and legal mandates should take priority over the duty to act in the best interests of the client. The challenge inherent in resolving ethical dilemmas like these is determining which value should supersede others; it often requires determining which party is owed the social worker's primary loyalty. The social worker will also need to decide whether the main obligation is to the identified client, the family system, the agency, or the provider or payer of the services.

NASW CODE OF ETHICS

Ethics are the rules of conduct that direct people to act in a manner consistent with the values they profess (Lewis, 1982). The importance of having standards or guidelines for ethical practice in social work cannot be overstated. Ethical standards are necessary points of reference to assist social workers in determining preferred professional practices and for making judgments about acceptable and unacceptable courses of action in cases of values conflicts. Such standards, which are typical of and specific to each profession, are organized into codes of ethics that set expectations for professional conduct. The NASW *Code of Ethics* represents this set of rules for social workers (see Appendix A). The *Code* is designed to guide the everyday conduct of professional social workers by articulating the profession's basic values, ethical principles, and ethical standards. Based on the fundamental values of the profession, the *Code* specifies standards of behavior for professional social workers' ethical responsibilities to clients, colleagues, the social work profession, and society. The *Code* is also recognized as a source of "ethical standards to which the general public can hold the social work profession accountable" (NASW, 1996, Purpose) and against which such behavior will be measured in cases of alleged ethical misconduct.

Current Edition of the NASW Code of Ethics

In 1996, the social work profession adopted its current code of ethics, an entirely new version that represents a contemporary understanding of and appreciation for the complexities of the ethical tensions routinely faced by practitioners. The need for a comprehensive rewrite, not merely a revision of the 1979 code, which had already been modified twice, was created by the realities of the new and unique ethical issues facing social work practitioners today. With the advance of the field of applied ethics,

> social workers had developed a firmer grasp of the wide range of ethical issues facing practitioners, many of which were not addressed in the 1979 code. The broader field of applied and professional ethics, which had begun in the early 1970s, had matured considerably resulting in the identification and greater understanding of novel ethical issues not cited in the 1979 code. (Reamer, 1998, p. 4)

The new and expanded NASW *Code of Ethics* (NASW, 1996), totaling 27 pages, is more specific, practical, and detailed than the previous version. It identifies a total of 155 ethical standards to guide the professional activities of social workers. Although they are not prescriptive in nature, the standards establish practice expectations, some of which are "enforceable guidelines for professional conduct" (NASW, 1996, Ethical Standards). Other standards are aspirational and therefore open to the interpretation and "discretionary latitude" (Goldmeir, 1984) of the decision maker.

> Social workers cannot expect their code of ethics to provide simple, quick, and formulaic solutions to all ethical problems and issues. Rather, they can expect it to acquaint them with compelling ethical issues and dilemmas and offer reasonable guidance in light of current knowledge. In the final analysis, social workers must rely on their own good judgment to discern the relevance of the code to their particular circumstances." (Reamer, 1998, p. 261)

The *Code* does not provide answers to ethical dilemmas and decisions, but it provides a guide for the issues that should be considered when resolving them.

Newer Sections and Standards

The revised code (NASW, 1996), which is broader in scope than the preceding version, introduces detailed directives and widens the variety of subjects addressed. In addition to the modification and revision of previous standards, new standards address the provision of services in the contemporary era. For example, the expansion of the standards on privacy and confidentiality (Standard 1.07) addresses confidentiality in the modern age of technology. Social workers are advised "to take precautions to ensure and maintain the confidentiality of information transmitted to other parties through the use of computers, electronic mail, facsimile machines, telephones and telephone answering machines, and other electronic or computer technology" (Standard 1.07[m]). Managed care standards have necessitated that clients now be informed of the "limits to services because of the requirements of a third-party payer" (Standard 1.03[a]) and apprised of the protocols regulating the insurer's access to client information. "Social workers should not disclose confidential information to third-party payers unless clients have authorized such disclosure" (Standard 1.07[h]). These provisions address technology and constructs that did not exist in previous versions of the *Code* and alert social workers to modern social work practices.

In addition to expanded provisions regarding privacy and confidentiality, the current *Code* includes a caution against physical contact with clients (Standard 1.10) and extends previous prohibitions against sexual relationships with clients to include prohibiting sexual relationships with former clients and their relatives. Social workers "should not engage in sexual activities or sexual contact with clients' relatives or other individuals with whom clients maintain a close personal relationship when there is risk of exploitation or potential harm to the client" (Standard 1.09[b]). The *Code* addresses several other issues that have emerged over the past two decades:

+ the requirement of cultural competency on the part of practitioners (Standard 1.05[a])
+ the need to avoid dual or multiple relationships with clients or former clients (Standard 1.06[c])
+ the obligation to be alert to and address colleagues' impairment (Standards 2.09[a], 2.09[b])
+ the ethical obligations of agency administrators to advocate for adequate resources and the just distribution of resources (Standards 3.07[a]–[c])
+ +the responsibilities of social work educators and field instructors (Standards 3.02[a]–[d])
+ the responsibilities of social workers when terminating services to clients (Standards 1.16[a]–[f])
+ the misrepresentation of competence on the part of social workers (Standards 1.04[a]–[c]).

It is critical that all professional social workers and social work students be knowledgeable about the standards in the *Code* and to behave accordingly. Most state regulatory agencies and courts will use the *Code* as the standard for best practices and rely on its provisions to determine whether social workers charged with violations or ethical misconduct have acted in accordance with accepted professionals standards. Although the *Code* instructs social workers to "take into consideration all the values, principles, and standards in this Code that are relevant to any situation in which ethical judgment is warranted" (NASW, 1996, Purpose), research confirms that, all too often, social workers are insufficiently acquainted with the specific standards of the *Code* (Mattison, 1994) and that "even advanced social work practitioners are not that aware of new code provisions" (Congress, 2000, p. 3). Despite the impact the *Code* has on daily practice and its legal ramifications in cases of alleged misconduct, many social workers are not knowledgeable about its content.

LEGAL RESPONSIBILITIES

In the early days of social work, few, if any, laws governed professional practice. Since the 1970s, however, regulatory mechanisms designed to govern the behavior of social workers and other human services professionals have expanded. Social work values and ethics reflect the field's collective voluntary preferences and decisions about practice behaviors. Many of those values and ethical standards are also embodied in state laws and regulations and in court decisions that govern professional social work practice. Because "conduct valued by law and conduct valued by social work ethics may not always coincide . . . the demands of law may thus conflict with principles of social work ethics to which social workers are committed and to which they are expected to conform" (Levy, 1993, p. 40). In many cases, what is legally mandated diverges from what the social worker judges to be ethically sound. "Social workers frequently encounter circumstances involving [both] ethical and legal issues. In many instances, relevant ethical and legal standards complement each other; however, in some circumstances, ethical and legal standards conflict" (Reamer, 2005, p. 163).

For example, when a high school student discloses, in confidence, to the school social worker that he is HIV-positive, is currently having unprotected sex, and refuses to disclose his health status to his sexual partners, the social worker may feel compelled to alert known partners (students in the school) to the imminent danger. The laws protecting the confidential disclosure of HIV/AIDS status are clear but may conflict with the social worker's inclination to ensure that other students are informed of the need to protect themselves. Is there an obligation on the part of the social worker to disclose the confidential information to protect third parties?

"The professional obligation to warn a third party of a potential danger has been widely discussed starting with the now famous case of *Tarasoff v. The Regents of the University of California* (1976)" (Parsons, 2001, p. 124). This decision was fundamental in establishing the duty of mental health providers to warn intended victims of "foreseeable risks," and the law protects providers from criminal charges alleging a violation of confidentiality. "The general expectation that social workers will keep information confidential does not apply when disclosure is necessary to prevent serious, foreseeable, and imminent harm to a client or other identifiable person" (Standard 1.07[c]). In the case of HIV transmission, is the social worker obligated to protect third parties? Is the possible transmission of HIV a "foreseeable risk" of harm under the law?

In addition to being proficient in the standards of practice and skilled in making ethical judgments, social work practitioners must have an active knowledge of the laws and regulations they are obliged to obey. Knowledge of applicable laws is necessary for good practice as well as self-preservation. Awareness of legal obligations and prevailing legal standards is no longer a subject that social workers can afford to ignore. Across all fields of practice, federal, state, and local laws have a bearing on social work practice decisions. "Issues defining the rights of clients, the rights of the practitioner, the way in which services are selected and provided, and the nature of the relationship between the practitioner and client are all being shaped by the professional codes of conduct and now by extension of those codes into law" (Parsons, 2001, p. 65). Social workers who neglect to learn about the laws that apply to their practice may unwittingly act illegally and be subject to the consequences.

CONFLICTS BETWEEN THE LAW AND ETHICAL DUTIES

Social workers are continually challenged by the tensions between legal imperatives and ethical practices. Under what circumstances can a social worker disclose confidential information against client wishes? Is a school social worker free to reveal a minor's reported drug use to parents or guardians? What are the circumstances under which social workers are mandated to divulge confidential information "to prevent serious, foreseeable, and imminent harm to a client or other identifiable person" (Standard 1.07[c])? Must the legal mandate to report suspected abuse or neglect be met unequivocally when doing so presents a potential harm to clients' well-being? Is the social worker ever justified in disobeying the law to serve a greater good? These types of questions are common to contemporary social work practice and must be resolved.

Consider the following case example:

A social worker practicing in child welfare has been working with the Sullivan family over a period of nine months. Julie, age 23, is the mother of two children: Thomas, age four, and Alisa, who is now 10 months old. Julie is a capable and motivated parent who has worked cooperatively with the social worker at building parenting skills, particularly in the area of discipline. The case first came to the attention of authorities through Tommy's involvement in Head Start. Julie was abusing drugs and alcohol at the time, and teachers were concerned about her neglectful behavior. The threat of having her children removed from the home provided sufficient motivation for Julie to enter and complete a drug rehabilitation program. She has been drug free for nine months.

A recent encounter with a former live-in partner caused a setback in Julie's sobriety. She admitted, in confidence, that she had an overnight binge. Julie slept through a scheduled home visit with the social worker. When contact was made with Julie late in the day, the social worker arrived at the home to find the children hungry and unbathed. Julie expressed sincere regret and begged the social worker not to include her lapse in the report being prepared for an upcoming court appearance.

As a mandated reporter, the social worker is aware of her legal responsibility to report cases of suspected abuse and neglect. In this case, though, she is reluctant to file a report, because her judgment is that the legal imperative conflicts with what is in the best interests of the client and her children. The social worker believes that Julie's progress will be compromised or even undermined by a report at this time. In the estimation of the social worker, this was truly an isolated incident and the client's repentance is genuine. The social worker judges that maintaining the therapeutic relationship she and Julie have developed will sustain the progress Julie has made and will be instrumental in continued progress. Should the therapeutic relationship be destabilized, both Julie and her children may be worse off. The worker's familiarity with local resources indicates that placement of the children outside of the home would be destructive and destabilizing at many levels.

In this case, the practitioner judges that ethical obligations conflict with the legal duty and agency protocol to report the incident to protective services. The social worker must weigh causing harm to the family against the legal obligation to report. Is the worker justified in disobeying the law for a perceived greater good? Adhering to the law may resolve the ethical dilemma if the social worker does what is legally obligated. But what if the worker judges that the possible harms from reporting would cause greater damage to the family than the isolated incident of neglect? What if, in light of past experience, the social worker believes that the child protective services system is ill equipped to provide services to this family? Is that justification to not report? Is it ever justifiable for a social worker to disregard a legal obligation when the worker thinks it is in the client's best interests? Is compliance with the law to report suspected abuse an obligation that assumes priority above all other considerations? At what point should the social worker risk legal exposure by not reporting in order to prevent possible harms that may result from reporting? Is there more than one ethically justifiable course of action in this case?

Cases like this create more questions than answers. The questions, however, are an important part of the ethical decision-making process.

RESOLVING ETHICAL DILEMMAS
IN SOCIAL WORK PRACTICE

Although the profession does not sanction a particular paradigm for resolving ethical dilemmas, the consensus is that a systematic analysis is essential. This analysis should include a step-by-step consideration of the entirety of facts and interests relevant to the dilemma and its resolution. Many authors have proposed frameworks to structure the decision-making process, and those frameworks share many commonalities (Linzer, 1999; Loewenberg et al., 2000; Mattison, 2000; Reamer, 1995). The guidelines have given form and shape to the ethical decision-making process by calling the practitioner's attention to the range of factors deemed necessary for a comprehensive evaluation of competing interests, options, and loyalties.

Analyzing ethical dilemmas and reaching resolution involves due consideration of the ethical aspects of the case in light of the standards for best practice. The process of resolving ethical dilemmas emphasizes both the precepts (rules and principles) that apply to the situation and the contemplative moral reasoning that produces an outcome. It is widely accepted that reasoned solutions result from first recognizing the ethical aspects of case circumstances and then engaging in a systematic and rational analysis of competing arguments and possible courses of action.

In ethical dilemmas, the facts, details, and circumstances of the case are inevitably open to interpretation by the individual practitioner and, thus, different outcomes result. By their nature, dilemmas have no single accepted standard interpretation of the details, nor do they have a simple or easily rendered resolution. "Decisions about ethical questions are rarely idiosyncratic and usually follow an individual's consistent patterns. Since such decisions involve questions of right and wrong, they are deeply rooted in that value system which is most important to the decision maker" (Loewenberg et al., 2000, p. 45). As long as the decision maker engages in a systematic process of reasoning that considers the range of options and their possible outcomes, however, an ethically sound decision is likely to result.

MODEL FOR ANALYZING ETHICAL DILEMMAS

Resolving ethical dilemmas requires thoughtful contemplation and reasoning on the part of the decision maker and the use of self in the application of a framework to guide the decision-making process. A guide to the steps in the decision-making process follows. The steps are illustrated by examples from the "Julie" case above.

Step 1: Gather and Assess Case Background Information and Case Details

The process of ethical decision making begins with a comprehensive understanding of the facts and circumstances of the case and the identification of the stakeholders affected by the outcome of the decision. Information gathering and assessment is by no means a value-free process. The inclusion and omission of certain information about the case, the decision as to the primary client to whom the social worker is obligated, and the interpretation of the facts all are keenly influenced by the decision maker. Social workers must be aware of personal values, biases, pressures, and experiences that may influence their ability to objectively interpret the case circumstances. The worker may be aware of such influences, or they may lie at the unconscious level but nonetheless influence the process. Does the social worker "hold a grudge" against the protective services unit? Has the social worker "risked" not reporting in a previous case that had a tragic end? Was the social worker previously involved in the transfer of a child to foster care where the child was tragically and subsequently injured? Would factors related to clients' sexual orientation or race affect decision making?

In the case of Julie, the social worker not only assembles case details but also interprets their meaning. The stakeholders in this case (those who stand to gain or lose or will be affected in some way) include Julie and her children, the social worker, the agency, and society at large.

Step 2: Separate the Practice Considerations from the Ethical Components

Social workers' success in responding to ethical dilemmas depends, in part, on their ability to distinguish the ethical factors of a case from the practice issues involved. The worker must be able to delineate the ethical components of the case to fully engage in the decision-making process. Without differentiating the practice considerations from the ethical issues, the worker may unwittingly select a course of action that is based on practice standards without acknowledging the aspects of the decision-making process that are grounded in moral reasoning.

When a legal obligation to report suspected neglect conflicts with a worker's ethical duties to the client, which obligation takes priority? In Julie's case, the following questions help separate practice issues from ethical concerns:

+ Is the legal obligation to report the suspected neglect absolute?
+ Given the possible consequences of reporting, is it possible that a greater good might be served by not reporting?
+ If removal of the children from the home is judged to be detrimental to the client's best interests, is a decision to not report justifiable?
+ If agency rules require written documentation of client activity, can an act of omission (not recording the social worker's observations) be justified?
+ Should the social worker risk an ethics complaint for violating the mandate to report the suspected neglect in order to serve the client's interest foremost?

In the face of competing obligations and loyalties, social workers often find that professional obligations, as described in the code, contradict one another and cannot be met simultaneously.

> The NASW Code of Ethics does not specify which values, principles, and standards are most important and ought to outweigh others in instances when they conflict. Reasonable differences of opinion can and do exist among social workers with respect to the ways in which values, ethical principles, and standards should be rank ordered when they conflict." (NASW, 1996, Purpose).

Social workers are expected to reconcile conflicts between ethical obligations and relevant laws "in a manner that is consistent with the values, principles, and standards expressed" in the Code and to "seek consultation" from a supervisor "before making a decision" (NASW, 1996, Purpose).

Step 3: Identify Possible Courses of Action

Social workers select possible courses of action after considering the potential risks and benefits of each course in light of perceived obligations to relevant rules, policies, and laws. The decision maker must first identify the possible courses of action available and the extent to which the needs of different stakeholders might be served or disserved by each option. By its nature, the resolution of an ethical dilemma will result in harms and benefits to different parties simultaneously.

In Julie's case, the social worker can choose to comply with mandated reporting laws or adopt a "wait-and-see" approach. Compliance with reporting laws may offer the following benefits and harms:

Potential benefits:
+ reduction of the social worker's legal vulnerability
+ support for the social order that the law was established to maintain
+ prevention of more serious acts of neglectful behavior toward the children.

Potential harms:

+ threat to the therapeutic relationship
+ risk of further harm to the children if removed from the home
+ client feelings of anger and betrayal
+ client feelings of mistrust for helping professionals in general
+ erosion of client progress.

Continued monitoring of the case without filing a report may offer the following benefits and harms:

Potential benefits:

+ maintenance of the therapeutic relationship and continued client progress
+ preservation of trust in helping professionals
+ protection of family unity.

Potential harms:

+ legal ramifications for failure to comply with reporting laws
+ collusion with client creates client's expectations for future exceptions to rules
+ serious injury or death to children
+ worsening of client's substance abuse problems
+ legal sanctions against the agency
+ social order undermined by selective compliance with laws.

Step 4: Identify Legal Obligations and Relevant Principles and Standards in the NASW Code of Ethics

If they are not already aware of them, social workers should determine the laws and legal obligations that apply to the case. Social workers must also consult the NASW *Code of Ethics* (1996) and judge which ethical standards and principles describe relevant ethical duties. The process of identifying which standards apply to a particular case is conditioned by the perspective and values of the decision maker, and differences of opinion can and will exist.

As a mandated reporter, the social worker is obligated by state law to report Julie's suspected neglect. As an agency employee, the practitioner is obligated to agency practices and policies that require her to record the incident in her progress notes and report it to authorities. Simultaneously, the value of service, as described in the *Code*, states that "social workers elevate service to others above self interest" (NASW, 1996, Ethical Principles). Avoidance of risk to the practitioner should not serve as the primary motivation for acting.

The *Code's* ethical standards describing the social worker's duties and obligations that relate to Julie's case include the following:

Standard 1.01 Commitment to Clients
Social workers' primary responsibility is to promote the well-being of clients.

Standard 1.07 Privacy and Confidentiality
(c) Social workers should protect the confidentiality of all information obtained in the course of professional service, except for compelling professional reasons.

(d) Social workers should inform clients, to the extent possible, about the disclosure of confidential information and the potential consequences, when feasible before the disclosure is made. This applies whether social workers disclose confidential information on the basis of a legal requirement or client consent.

Standard 2.05 Consultation
(a) Social workers should seek the advice and counsel of colleagues whenever such consultation is in the best interests of the clients.

Standard 3.04 Client Records
(a) Social workers should take reasonable steps to ensure that documentation in records is accurate and reflects the services provided.

Standard 3.09 Commitments to Employers
(a) Social workers generally should adhere to commitments made to employers and employing agencies.

Standard 4.01 Competence
(c) Social workers should base practice on recognized knowledge, including empirically based knowledge, relevant to social work and social work ethics.

Step 5: Determine Which Obligation or Duty to Prioritize, and Justify One's Course of Action

This step involves weighing and measuring the information gathered in previous steps to determine which priority, obligation, or value will take priority over others. This step gives explicit consideration to the reasons a particular choice of action is selected or preferred. The process of determining a course of action requires the decision maker to articulate how he or she decided which factors were relevant (or irrelevant) and how he or she deliberated to reach a conclusion. The ethical justifications of an action and judgments about what is right or good are expressions of the moral values associated with ethical theories (Box 4-1). Because ethical theories presuppose differing conceptions of rightness and goodness, and each conception involves a set of beliefs about what we should and

Sidebar 4-1: Moral Theories as the Basis for Action

Utilitarian versus Deontological Assumptions

Although social workers may be unfamiliar with formal theories of contemporary philosophy, justification for choices of action are commonly based on the moral theories and traditions associated with either *utilitarian* or *deontological* thinking and practice. It therefore may be helpful for social workers to develop an understanding of these theories.

In utilitarian thinking, the ultimate criterion for what is morally right or wrong is the amount of good produced as a result of the action. Actions in themselves are not defined as inherently good or bad, but they are judged as good or bad by virtue of their anticipated consequences. Traditionally, social workers incorporate utilitarian principles into their work, making choices that they judge will produce the greatest good. In considering possible choices of action (Step 3) the goodness or correctness of an act is evaluated on the basis of future consequences. In accordance with utilitarian principles, the social worker could justify the decision to not comply with the reporting law in Julie's case because the greater good will result from carefully monitoring the situation and postponing a report.

In contrast, the deontological theory argues that some types of action are inherently right or wrong. It emphasizes the importance of fixed moral rules, such as the duty to obey laws or the obligation to respect a client's right to self-determination. Under this theory, duties are binding and ethical rules should be applied universally to all circumstances, regardless of the consequences they produce. In this "psycholitigious world" (Bergantino, 1996, p. 31), the threat of litigation may motivate social workers to place additional moral value on following laws and agency policies. Depending on which duty the social worker in Julie's case considers most absolute, the worker may feel compelled to uphold the law and report to authorities, or she may judge that not reporting serves the "best interests" of the client.

Virtue Ethics

Justifying actions on the basis of utilitarian or deontological assumptions have, at their center, an emphasis on the rightness of the act, action, or outcome that results. Less attention is paid to the *agent* or to the character of the person making the decision. The idea that the decision maker does engage in the decision-making process from a value-laden perspective is not readily accounted for in these theories. Within the virtue ethics framework, however, issues of character and moral personality of the practitioner, his or her private preferences, and reference points for right and wrong are considered. "A principal reason why people are disposed to act in certain ways is that they have certain values and character traits" (Williams, 1985, p. 175). Under the principles of virtue ethics, decisions about right or wrong

(continues)

⊡⊡⊡⊡⊡

Sidebar 4-1: Moral Theories as the Basis for Action (continued)

are judged "by appealing to what a virtuous [person] would do. . . . It thus offers us an explanation of right and wrong action in terms of facts about a virtuous [person]: an act is right *because* it is what a virtuous person does or would do" (Timmons, 2002, p. 222).

Because ethical theories differ, what is perceived to be "a harm by one theory may not even look like a harm by another or may look like a different sort of harm, of a different kind and different weight" (Robison & Reeser, 1999, p. 47). Although social workers' capacity for rational decision making and use of a systematic process are clearly important, the character and nature of the decision maker provide a foundation for the embodiment of their beliefs in choosing courses of action. Virtue ethics is distinguished from other moral theories by being *agent* centered rather than *act* centered; being concerned with "being rather than doing"; and attempting to answer the question "What sort of person should I be?" rather than "What should I do?" (Timmons, 2002, p. 220). Instead of questioning the right action to take in given circumstances, the language of virtue ethics calls attention to the acquisition of character-based qualities, virtues, and predilections and the propensity to act in accordance with one's moral character. Actions are not chosen in light of their potential consequences, to maximize the greatest good, or in consideration of moral rules or prescriptions. Instead, actions flow from a person's inner dispositions or character and dispose them to act in accordance with the core values or virtues they embody. If Julie's social worker solved the ethical dilemma using virtue ethics, the rightness or wrongness of the course of action would stem from the workers' goodwill and explicit regard for the Julie and her children. It would not be determined by "legislatively top heavy" (McBeath & Webb, 2002, p. 1016) mandates or the worker's interest in self-preservation.

should not do, many authors "recommend group deliberations to solve ethical dilemmas" (Freud & Krug, 2002, p. 481). Social workers should consult with supervisors and peers to weigh the benefits and harms of potential actions and come to a conclusion. "The process works best if people with different moral intuitions are involved" (Freud & Krug, p. 481).

Step 6: Resolution and Reflection

After the course of action has been selected, justified, and implemented, it is important to monitor the decision and its consequences. The practitioner should observe whether assumptions made about harms and benefits were accurate and examine the effects of the decision on the stakeholders involved. It is also beneficial for the practitioner to reflect on the values, ethical principles, ethical standards, and theories that shaped the decision-making process. Giving thought to one's individualized style of decision making may highlight a pattern of response of which the social worker was unaware. Consciousness of these patterns may inform future resolution of ethical dilemmas.

In addition to facilitating decision making, the use of a step-by-step process or decision-making model can supply documented evidence of an informed process of decision making. This type of documentation is critical in the event that a decision is challenged legally or charges of professional misconduct are brought forward. When a practitioner is called upon to justify assessment and assignment of relative value to ambiguous facts associated with the case, careful documentation of the decision-making process offers reason and insight into the logic of the decision.

RISK MANAGEMENT

Because lawsuits alleging professional malpractice and liability have grown significantly over the past few decades, education for social workers needs to address protecting oneself from lawsuits. The potential legal ramifications associated with professional misconduct can be minimized and legal vulnerability can be reduced when social workers are informed about strategies for "risk management." Heightened emphasis on risk management adds a new dimension to ethics education and necessitates that students be instructed in both the traditional normative values of the profession and their practice application, as well as the prevention of malpractice and liability claims. In professional social work ethics education, greater emphasis is now placed on teaching students about the risks to self and agency when acts of commission or omission leave legal imperatives unmet or compromised. These situations occur when abiding by the law was judged to be the secondary priority to other, preferred choices of action. "Without knowledge of the legal issues, processes and language, clinical social workers place themselves in an extremely alienated and vulnerable position (Bullis, 1995, p. xiii).

Risk management involves avoiding misconduct by becoming well versed in responsibilities at the practice, ethical, and legal levels and practicing in accord with those responsibilities. Social workers are encouraged to be alert to local, state, and federal laws and court rulings that have implications for practice. This awareness does not guarantee that charges of incompetence, malpractice, and negligence will not be brought against social workers. Social workers who are familiar with liability claims, however, can be alert to conditions, mistakes, and misjudgments that trigger claims and can strive to avoid active violations of client rights and misapplication of practice standards. "Knowledge, information, and good practice are the best defenses against liability" (Loewenberg et al., 2000, p. 33).

SERVING CLIENT INTERESTS VERSUS MINIMIZING WORKER RISKS

Increased vulnerability to legal action has raised concerns about social workers opting "to play it safe at the expense of providing the best service for their clients" (Parsons, 2001, p. 65). The demands of a litigious society may have resulted in "defensive forms of social work" (McBeath & Webb, 2002, p. 1016), which emphasize compliance with legal mandates and protection of the practitioner. In this type of environment, social workers may be attracted to the choice of action that can be justified as compliance with agency policy and legal mandates rather than putting client interests first. The influential disincentives to considering various options in ethical decision making make it even more important for social workers to use a systematic process to solve ethical dilemmas.

In addition to legal pressures, social workers are subject to other influences from society that affect the way they work. Brill (2001) argued that the ability of professional social workers to put the client first and to work for social justice has been compromised by the social, economic, and political contexts of contemporary social work. Social workers today are less willing "to be advocates and to tackle social justice issues as part of their practice" (Brill, 2001, p. 227). Despite these deterrents, the current NASW *Code of Ethics* reaffirms the responsibility of social workers to actively engage in practices directed toward social justice and the promotion of basic rights (NASW, 1996, Standard 6.01). Contemporary social workers are challenged to meet the standards of their field despite the increasingly complex social and political forces that come to bear on their practice.

CONCLUSION

Ethical decision making is an integral component of social work practice, both past and present. With the development of the NASW *Code of Ethics*, social workers now have well-defined ethical standards that can guide the resolution of ethical dilemmas. Because the *Code* is only a guide, social workers must still engage in decision making on a case-by-case basis and exercise "discretionary latitude" (Goldmeir, 1984). The most sound ethical decisions are made through a systematic process that considers all the practice and ethical issues involved, weighs the harms and benefits of various courses of action, and documents a well-reasoned decision-making process upon which the social worker later reflects. In addition to ethical philosophies and societal pressures, social workers' decision-making processes are affected by the workers' alignment with personally held and professionally adopted values. All of these influences come together to shape decisions that social workers make when faced with ethical dilemmas. Although ethical choices are situation specific and require nuanced responses, social work decisions need to be unified by the characteristic of care that gives shape to their judgments and leads them to promote justice while serving humanity.

REFERENCES

Bergantino, L. (1996). For the defense: Psychotherapy and the law. *Voices, 32,* 29–33.

Brill, C. K. (2001). Looking at the social work profession through the eye of the NASW Code of Ethics. *Research on Social Work Practice, 11,* 223–234.

Bullis, R. K. (1995). *Clinical social work misconduct: Laws, ethics and interpersonal dynamics.* Chicago: Nelson-Hall.

Congress, E. P. (2000). What social workers should know about ethics: Understanding and resolving practice dilemmas. *Advances in Social Work, 1,* 1–25.

Council on Social Work Education. (2001). *Educational policy and accreditation standards.* Alexandria, VA: Author.

Freud, S., & Krug, S. (2002). Beyond the code of ethics, part 1: Complexities of ethical decision making. *Families in Society: Journal of Contemporary Social Services, 83,* 474–482.

Goldmeir, J. (1984). Ethical styles and ethical decisions in health care settings. *Social Work in Health Care, 10*(1), 46–60.

Kluckhohn, C. (1951). Values and value-orientations in the theory of action: An explanation in definition and clarification. In T. Parsons & F. E. Shils (Eds.), *Toward a general theory of action* (pp. 388–433). Cambridge, MA: Harvard University Press.

Levy, C. S. (1993). *Social work ethics on the line.* New York: Haworth Press.

Lewis, H. (1982). *The intellectual base of social work practice.* New York: Haworth Press.

Linzer, N. (1999). *Resolving ethical dilemmas in social work practice.* Boston: Allyn & Bacon.

Loewenberg, F. M., Dolgoff, R., & Harrington, D. (2000). *Ethical decisions for social work practice* (6th ed.). Itasca, IL: F. E. Peacock.

Mattison, M. (1994). *Ethical decision making in social work practice* (Doctoral dissertation, Columbia University, New York, 1994). *Dissertation Abstracts International, 55*(06), 1695A.

Mattison, M. (2000). Ethical decision making: The person in the process. *Social Work, 45,* 201–212.

McBeath, G., & Webb, S. A. (2002). Virtue ethics and social work: Being lucky, realistic, and not doing one's duty. *British Journal of Social Work, 32,* 1015–1036.

Morelock, K. T. (1997). The search for virtue: Ethics teaching in MSW programs. *Journal of Teaching in Social Work, 14*(1/2), 69–87.

National Association of Social Workers. (1996). *Code of Ethics of the National Association of Social Workers.* Washington, DC: Author.

Parsons, R. D. (2001). *The ethics of professional practice.* Boston: Allyn & Bacon.

Perlman, H. H. (1976). Believing and doing: Values in social work education. *Social Casework, 57,* 381–390.

Reamer, F. G. (1995). *Social work values and ethics.* New York: Columbia University Press.

Reamer, F. G. (1998). *Ethical standards in social work: A critical review of the NASW Code of Ethics.* Washington, DC: NASW Press.

Reamer, F. G. (2005). Ethical and legal standards in social work: Consistency and conflict. *Families in Society: Journal of Contemporary Social Services, 86*(2), 163–169.

Robison, W., & Reeser, L. C. (1999). *Ethical decision making in social work.* Boston: Allyn & Bacon.

Timmons, M. (2002). *Moral theory: An introduction.* Lanham, MD: Rowman & Littlefield.

Trattner, W. I. (1979). *From poor law to welfare state* (2nd ed.) New York: Free Press.

Van Wyk, R. N. (1990). *Introduction to ethics.* New York: St. Martin's Press.

Williams, B. (1985). *Ethics and the limits of philosophy.* Cambridge, MA: Harvard University Press.

5

Diversity, Ethnic Competence, and Social Justice

Christine T. Lowery

The problem is we're not seeing or hearing the same things. Even church bells mean something different to us. She hears them and sets her watch. I hear them and remember the endless funerals in the villages outside the capital. But what right do I have to be angry with her? It is not her fault that her culture has made her who she is.

—Demetria Martìnez (1994, p. 128)

Illana Harlow, a folklorist, highlights the exchange of cultural symbols in her photographic exhibitions. The subject of one exhibition was Cypress Hills, a nonsectarian cemetery in the "graveyard belt" along the Brooklyn–Queens border, where Jackie Robinson, "the Brooklyn Dodger who integrated baseball" is buried (Dugger, 1997, p. B1). In the photos, one can see a crucifix juxtaposed with the Jewish custom of placing small rocks on a gravestone; a food offering of shrimp dumplings, soy chicken, and sticky rice is accompanied by White Castle miniburgers. A Puerto Rican woman leaves a yellow napkin topped by a stone, "a visual echo" of the prayers for the dead left on the Chinese tombstones nearby. Older Greek and Lithuanian tombstones coexist with newer forms. Now popular with black and Hispanic people, "black granite markers, etched with photographic likenesses of the dead, are common and were brought by Jewish refugees who began pouring into New York following the collapse of the Soviet Union" (Dugger, p. B3). Among the living, Italian bands, remnants of the Little Italy-to-Chinatown immigrant transition, still play Christian hymns for Buddhist services at Chinese funeral parlors on New York City's Mulberry Street.

How do Buddhists view the transition from life to death? How have those views been integrated into a multicultural setting? How do Christian influences manifest among these groups? How have the expression of grief and remembrance changed from immigrant generations through first, second, third, and fourth American-born generations? How have language, education, new occupations, geographical mobility, interracial marriage, and multiracial children influenced the social life and the cultural practices and rituals of families in their multiple communities? Social work focuses on people in their cultural environments, whether these families were new immigrants in the tenements of the 1930s or constructed families in the gay community, including people of color, facing AIDS in the 1980s and 1990s. The movement of social services from monocultural and ethnocentric perspectives to ethnically sensitive perspectives and culturally competent approaches holds limited promise because inequalities in societal power are not addressed (Gutierrez & Nagda, 1996). An ethnoconscious or empowerment approach not only includes but incorporates the power of communities of color in advocacy, partnership, and social transformation (Gutierrez & Nagda). In this global age, a multicultural perspective, coupled with a sense of social justice, becomes imperative, not just for social workers but for anyone who must negotiate power differentials, multiple cultures, and multiple environments—all in unsynchronized transformation—from birth to the grave.

This chapter examines the complexities of diversity in social work, including political, historical, and sociological factors. How those elements are woven into issues of social justice are illustrated by promises made to the Hmong, who fought on behalf of the United States in Vietnam, to assurances that Native Americans would run their own welfare programs. Students are encouraged to think of issues in social work at the intersections of diversity (including time, both present and historical) and contexts, rather than in lists (race, gender, and ethnicity). Anthropologist James W. Green (1995) has contributed thoughtful work on multiethnic approaches, and this chapter relies on his work for general concepts, including ethnicity and culture.

MULTICULTURALISM, PLURALISM, AND ETHNIC COMPETENCE

Multiculturalism and pluralism, celebrated and debated as they are (D'Souza, 1992), evoke responses from tolerance to appreciation for differences; those responses, however, are often without enthusiastic intercultural learning or transcultural understanding (Gould, 1996). In a *New York Times* essay drawing on his book *One Nation, After All* (Wolfe, 1998b; note the claim in the title), Wolfe (1998a) reported the outcomes of in-depth interviews with 200 people living in the suburbs of Tulsa, Oklahoma; Atlanta; San Diego; and Boston. Wolfe

◻◻◻◻◻

Sidebar 5-1: Hmong Veterans, Their Families, and Welfare

Social workers must be aware of the sociopolitical–cultural position of refugees and their collective histories with the United States—of their existence amid changing sentiments, forgotten promises, and newly constructed policies. One such example is the Hmong, tribal people from the mountains of Laos who aided the Central Intelligence Agency (CIA) during the Vietnam War (1961–1974) for 13 years. Acting on promises made by the United States, the Hmong made their way to refugee camps in Thailand in the late 1970s, where they stayed, sometimes for years, while refugee status was reviewed and granted. In the United States, they settled primarily in California, Wisconsin, and Minnesota.

Weiner (1997) reported that the earliest groups of Hmong refugees faced the loss of food stamps and welfare benefits as a group (170,000) among 1.8 million legal immigrants in the United States (pp. A1, A5). The Hmong who fought with the CIA were then in their mid-40s to mid-50s, suffered age and racial discrimination, lack of education, and the physical and mental wounds of war. Their families were large, usually eight to 10 members, and minimum wage jobs could not support families of this size. A formal statement in the budget act acknowledged the wartime contributions of the Hmong, categorized them as Vietnam veterans, and asserted that their families deserved assistance, but the statement lacked the force of law (Weiner, p. A5). The cuts to the Hmong people's benefits, which constitute "1/30th of one percent of the annual Federal food stamp budget" (about $9 million), had an impact on about 16,000 veterans and thousands more of their family members (Weiner, p. A5). At that time, the feelings of despair were demonstrated in the suicides, despite cultural taboos, of three women (one an elder), two in California and one in Wisconsin (Weiner, p. A5).

By the mid-1990s, the Hmong were running their own social service programs in California and later in Wisconsin and Minnesota, and young people were attending state universities and entering professional life.

asserted that American middle-class morality promotes what he called *nonjudgmentalism*—from racial integration to working mothers to multiculturalism—while holding firm to a strict moral code for one's own behavior. Wolfe predicted no culture wars with this brand of pluralism, but he did predict battles for gay rights because homosexuality lies "outside the circle of middle-class nonjudgmentalism." This difference cannot be reconciled when homosexuality is viewed as a moral issue (or as a choice, as those most hostile to gay rights frame homosexuality).

For gay activists, the shift from marginality to the "heartland" was symbolized by a short-lived victory involving discrimination in public accommodations in

New Jersey (Bruni, 1998). James Dale, the son of a military man, was dismissed as assistant scoutmaster in 1990 and thrown out of the Boy Scouts when it was discovered that he was gay (Wadler, 1998, p. B2). In *Boy Scouts of America v. James Dale*, the New Jersey Supreme Court ruled "against excluding openly gay young men from the Boy Scouts of America" and shifted from "fundamental legal protections in employment and housing to the inclusion of homosexuals in some of the most traditional, conservative institutions in American society" (Bruni, p. 36). In California, however, the state supreme court "ruled that the Boy Scouts could exclude homosexuals, agnostics and atheists from its ranks because it is a private membership group not covered by the state's civil rights laws" (Purdum, 1998, p. A1).

Because of the conflict in state rulings, the U.S. Supreme Court agreed to review *Boy Scouts of America v. James Dale*. In a 5–4 decision in June 2000, the Court upheld the Boy Scouts' policy of excluding gay men and lesbians on the basis that the law cannot compel an organization to accept members in opposition to its purpose. In response, school systems in New York, Chicago, Minneapolis, and San Francisco severed ties with the Boy Scouts because they did not tolerate discrimination on the basis of sexual orientation.

Six years later, by June 2006, 20 states had voted to ban same-sex marriage, and six more states were scheduled to vote on the issue that November (Goldberg, 2006). The Human Rights Campaign, a gay and lesbian civil rights group, was focusing on a piecemeal, long-term strategy of education and acceptance "from gay adoption to anti-discrimination rules to domestic partnership policies" (Goldberg, p. 5). The day-to-day work of "moving American people toward marriage equality is about moving people toward a greater understanding and respect of same-sex relationships" (Goldberg, p. 5).

Many issues stand outside the circle of middle-class nonjudgmentalism, a position reinforced by suburban isolation and monoculturalism. Cultural homogeneity—the belief that underneath we are all the same—is far less threatening than cultural dissimilarity, particularly when that dissimilarity is associated with redistribution of resources, status, power, or special privileges (Green, 1995), such as affirmative action, bilingual programs, recognition of Native American fishing and land claims, and acknowledgment of the rights of immigrants or people who are transgendered. Dissimilarity engenders reactions ranging from discomfort and aversion to distrust and fear of loss, to hostility and hatred.

Green (1995) credited James Leigh, a social worker and former instructor at the University of Washington, with coining the term *ethnic competence*, defined as the idea that someone who is ethnically competent "can provide professional services in a way that is congruent with behavior and expectations that are normative for a given community" (Green, p. 89). The ethnically competent social worker may be uncomfortable until he or she becomes familiar with the cultural terrain. However, he or she understands three realities: (1) Social workers must be lifelong learners; (2) culture is augmentative, complex, and changing; and (3) attention to social justice is a necessary component in unraveling ignorance, biases, prejudices, and racism.

Most schools of social work combine an ecological (micro) and systemic (macro) orientation with social justice and cultural diversity. Nevertheless, social work directors surveyed in 89 homeless shelters in North Carolina and Georgia who worked with homeless families "were no less likely to attribute successful restabilization to client's attitude and motivation" (Lindsey, 1998, p. 170) than were non–social workers. How does worker perception of the causes of homelessness influence services to parents trying to stabilize their family's lives when macro-level factors such as affordable housing or employment opportunities are lacking? Johnson, Renaud, Schmidt, and Stanek (1998), who surveyed 302 social workers, suggested that clinical social workers may overlook the environmental contexts (for example, neighborhood violence, economic distress, drugs, and stress of caring for a child with mental and emotional disabilities) of parental behaviors. Focusing primarily on the micro elements, two-thirds of the clinical social workers in the Lindsey study agreed with blaming statements such as "Family dynamics are usually the major cause of children's emotional disorders" (Lindsey, p. 181).

Lifelong Learning

Social workers must understand that to develop cultural understanding, they must become lifelong learners, listeners, and participant observers. They become practitioner–scientists in that their learning is systematic and, at times, experimental. Significantly, meaningful learning requires feedback loops of self-reflection and community feedback, both formal and informal, to enrich social workers' self-knowledge and practice.

Social workers must be authentic about their own discomfort in cross-cultural situations and examine their value base, biases, prejudices, and racism as part of a self-assessment. They must be critical thinkers and recognize that there are multiple perspectives and interpretations of events and experiences. They must recognize that resources are not always formal, but often informal as well.

> It is not our role to speak to people about our own view of the world, nor to attempt to impose that view on them, but rather to dialogue with the people about their view and ours. We must realize that their view of the world, manifested variously in their action, reflects their situation in the world. (Freire, 1994, p. 77)

Dialogue is co-created and transforming and requires humility (Freire, 1994). Critical thinking contributes to dialogue, and only dialogue contributes to critical thinking (Freire):

> Critical thinking contrasts with naive thinking, which sees "historical time as a weight, a stratification of the acquisitions and experiences of the past," from which the present should emerge normalized and "well-behaved." For the naive thinker, the important thing is accommodation to this normalized "today." For the critic, the important thing is the continuing transformation of reality, in behalf of the continuing humanization of men. (p. 73)

Social workers must be open to lessons that present themselves through clients who teach us how they survive under difficult circumstances and through people who share histories and past experiences of their communities. Practitioners must recognize that although they bring a certain expertise to their work, the people with whom they work bring their own expertise. It is the ethnically competent social worker who can help facilitate work that makes room for others to contribute to advocacy and the work of solving social problems. "The oppressors are the ones who act upon the people to indoctrinate them and adjust them to a reality which must remain untouched" (Freire, 1994, p. 75). It is the ethnically competent social worker who recognizes that he or she is not the only one with power, but one of many with power and that social work is an opportunity where powerful work can take place.

Culture Is Augmentative, Complex, and Changing

Cultural contacts made under conditions of choice (as opposed to colonization or domination) can be expansive, but not without engendering complexities and stresses that must be processed. Buriel (1984) analyzed generational patterns in Mexican American families. Integration in Mexican American culture "represents a highly adaptive strategy" for adjusting to Anglo American society and a freedom and fluidity in choice of "skills, roles and standards of behavior that are necessary to translate their native ability into conventional forms of success" (Buriel, 1984, p. 126). In his award-winning sociological study *Streetwise*, Anderson (1990) explained that the young black man is caught in a "cultural catch-22, negotiating symbols and action in the borderlands between black neighborhoods and white gentrification. The young black man dresses the part to "act right" by tough "ghetto standards" (Anderson, p. 181) to avert victimization by strangers in his peer group or ridicule by his peers. Whether he is law abiding or crime prone, law-abiding white and black people may interpret his pose as threatening or "predatory."

As a culture comes into contact with other cultures, new traits do not simply replace old ones. Rather, old traits are modified and new ones appear. . . . To recognize new forms of social complexity as they emerge in the behavior of individuals or families, and to value the creativity of people's responses to social change, is to acknowledge the integrity and capability inherent in their traditions and values. This view of culture, as a source of creative complexity rather than substitutive replacement, is the philosophical essence of ethnic competence. (Green, 1995, p. 96)

Sidebar 5-2: Black Nationalism and Islam

The pairing of black nationalism and Al-Islam offers a strong example of how the intersection of political, religious, and ethnic cultures create new structures through time; shapes leaders; creates followers, practitioners, and dissidents; and shapes communities (McAdams-Mahmoud, 2005). Cultural changes generated by Noble Drew Ali, who founded the Moorish American Science Temples in 1913, and of Marcus Garvey and the United Negro Improvement Association, influenced the Honorable Elijah Muhammad, who combined principles from Garvey and Ali in creating his organization, the Nation of Islam. Malcolm X, the son of a Garveyite, was born Malcolm Little and changed his name when he joined the Nation of Islam; the X represented his lost African tribal name. He later changed his name to Al-Hajj Malik al-Shabazz. Malcolm X eventually pulled away from Elijah Muhammad and was later assassinated. In the late 1970s, Muhammad's son "led a massive number of his father's followers into the orthodox practice of Islam" (McAdams-Mahmoud, p. 139). Minister Louis Farrakhan and his followers now maintain the pairing of black nationalism and Islam in the tradition of Muhammad.

International contacts among Muslims of different sects from the United States, Africa, and Saudi Arabia and other Middle Eastern countries will continue to shape the cultures of African American Muslims. Social workers who work with these populations must be aware of the cultural changes through time and the challenges of being Muslim in a non-Islamic society. An ethnically competent social worker preparing to work with this population would relish the challenge of long-term study about Islam and Muslim culture (including participation in the community, observation, reading, and processing experiences and self-reflection) and gradually incorporating lessons learned as he or she matured personally and professionally.

Social Justice

The ethnically competent social worker understands that although ethnicity is significant in one's identity, it extends to access to social and economic privileges and broadens into social justice issues. Devore and Schlesinger (1996) approached this reality with the term *ethclass*, defined as the intersection of social class and ethnicity.

Separate and unequal—issues of injustice are glaring enough for all to see. "Different and unequal" are tightly braided into the social and economic fabric of North America. "Different and feared"—xenophobia—remain a volatile combination. For example, it was assumed that Middle Eastern terrorists were involved in the 1995 bombing of the Murrah Federal Building in Oklahoma City before two white American men were described. When the first television pictures of the destruction caused in the bombing were transmitted, many Arab American, Iranian American, and Iraqi American people and international students from the Middle East endured the suspicion and rejection of their neighbors and colleagues.

Separate and Unequal: "Calculated Unfairness"

Many children outside the circle of nonjudgmentalism experience a lack of opportunity to engage in a democratic society at all. In *Savage Inequalities*, Kozol (1991) wrote about the school systems of Camden, New Jersey; Chicago; Detroit; East St. Louis, Missouri; New York City; and San Antonio, Texas. Recent research by Fine, Burns, Payne, and Torre (2004) suggested that little has changed since Kozol's classic work. School systems are still primarily funded by property taxes supplemented by state and federal funds. States should provide enough funds to equalize poor and rich districts at a "foundation" level, but they do not. The reality "guarantees that every child has an equal minimum" but not the same education (Fine et al., 2004, p. 209). A 14-year-old girl described these injustices succinctly:

> Every year in February we are told to read the same old speech of Martin Luther King. . . . "I have a dream." . . . We have a school in East St. Louis named for Dr. King. . . . The school is full of sewer water and the doors are locked with chains. Every student in that school is black. It's like a terrible joke on history. (Kozol, 1991, p. 35)

Similarly, a survivor of such schools who made it to college said, "Every day, every hour, talented students are being sacrificed. . . . [The schools are] destroying lives" (Fine et al., 2004, p. 53).

"Children reach the heart of these hypocrisies much quicker than the grown-ups and the experts do" (Kozol, 1991, p. 35). "About injustice, most poor children in America cannot be fooled" (Kozol, p. 57). Similarly, Fine and colleagues (2004) found that high school student Alondra Jones had this to say:

> It makes me, you know what, in all honesty, I'm going to break something down to you. It make you feel less about yourself, you know, like you sitting here in a class where you have to stand up because there's not enough chairs and you see rats in the buildings, the bathrooms is nasty, you got to pay. And then you, like I said, I visited Mann Academy, and these students, if they want to sit on the floor, that's because they choose to. And that just makes me feel real less about myself because it's like the state don't care about public schools. If I have to sit there and stand in the class, they can't care about me. It's impossible. So in all honesty, it really makes me feel bad about myself. (p. 63)

Kozol (1991) quoted a teacher in Camden, New Jersey, who commented that what impressed her is that kids get up and come to school at all: "They're old enough to know what they are coming to." Few textbooks, no laboratory equipment, few computers per student—where computers are found—toxic waste

---

Sidebar 5-3: The Copenhagen Consensus

Where should the world (rich nations and 1 percent of their gross domestic product) invest $50 billion through 2008, to do the most good? What should we do first? To inform democratic decision-making processes, the Copenhagen Consensus (a group consisting primarily of international economists) researched the world's challenges and paired them with cost-efficient solutions (Lomburg, 2004). The list of priorities included communicable diseases, conflicts and arms proliferation, financial stability, governance and corruption, malnutrition and hunger, migration, sanitation and access to clean water, and subsidies and trade barriers. The Copenhagen Consensus listed climate change as the first priority and access to education as fourth.

The lack of global education is, in part, the result of children not attending available schools, children dropping out of school early, and low levels of learning achievement while in school (Pritchett, 2004); the same is true of education in the United States. As in developing countries, schools in the United States lack infrastructure, instructional materials, and teacher training and supervision. Lomburg (2004) asserted that the Copenhagen Consensus process could be used to make a list of American educational challenges, to identify economists to evaluate the evidence, and to produce a prioritized list to show where we might get the most for our educational investments.

dumps nearby, buildings that are falling apart, poorly paid teachers, rote learning for standardized tests that compare them unfavorably with white students who have access to so much more in school districts just minutes away. Roughly half of the freshmen that start junior high never make it to high school in some of the poorest school districts in these cities, systems that "bear the appearance of calculated unfairness" (p. 57). "There exists no more powerful force for rigidity of social class and the frustration of natural potential . . . than a differential magnitude between the education of two children, the sole justification for which is an imaginary school district line" (Coons et al., cited in Kozol, 1991, pp. 206–207).

Culture and Ethnicity

Culture and ethnicity are not essential or innate properties of persons; they are the meanings that two people act on in a specific relationship. This emphasis on relational rather than essentialist aspects of culture may, in fact, be the only useful way to think about cultural differences in a complex, heterogeneous society such as our own.

—Hannerz, cited in Green (1995, p. 15)

Behavior and meanings in relationship with individuals (family) and in subgroups (work), within even larger systems of other people (geographic region), form a culture. This concept of culture is broad and adaptable, moving from the association primarily with ethnicity and race to systems and communities. Consider social work as a professional culture; academic cultures; organizational cultures in hospitals, nursing homes, and child welfare entities; addiction treatment cultures (for example, Alcoholics Anonymous); cultures in mental health clinics, schools for people who are deaf, and homeless shelters; family cultures; neighborhood cultures; regional cultures; and national cultures.

Consider the Farm Belt and the generational transformation to a culture of aging. Nebraska, Iowa, the Dakotas, and Kansas lead the nation with the highest proportion of people age 85 and older, "the oldest old" (Rimer, 1998, p. A1). Red Cloud, Nebraska, where almost half the residents are age 65 or older, is being reshaped by the generational erosion of young families looking for jobs and leaving behind their grandparents and great-grandparents (Rimer). Raymond T. Coward, dean of the School of Health and Human Services at the University of New Hampshire, compared retirement communities of the Sunbelt and the Plains states. Demographically, they are similar; environmentally, they are "distinct cultural and social environments in which to grow old" (Rimer, p. A1). In the Sunbelt, retirees migrate to the area, seasonally or permanently, and community roles are not restricted to older people. In rural communities, "when everyone else leaves, somebody has to be mayor, head of the cemetery committee, and the school board. Older people step up, and do those jobs very well" (Rimer, p. A14). Some rural communities offer meaningful roles that help maintain a vigorous older community. The older members help sustain the economy and psychologically support one another. Ultimately, however, a balance of old and young will ensure Red Cloud's future as a community. As the elderly residents gradually die, communities like Red Cloud struggle with the question of who will fill those community roles.

In Iowa, some communities have encouraged the arrival of Hispanic immigrant families to help repopulate their communities, but transitions for the immigrants are still bounded by differences, "American" expectations, and discrimination. Three million Latinos are in the Midwest, mostly in Chicago and in concentrations in rural Kansas, Nebraska, and Minnesota (Maharidge, 2006). In Iowa, small rural towns like Dennison and Storm Lake, as well as cities like Davenport and Des Moines, have a Latino population consisting mostly of indigenous peoples from Mexico, Central America, and South America. In 2002, Latinos were the largest minority in Iowa and made up 3.1 percent of the state population (Maharidge).

Cultures become more complex as ethnicity is added to the context of behaviors in relationship. Ethnicity encompasses a sense of peoplehood. The essential elements of peoplehood are kinship (the biological nature of unity over generations); commensuality (eating together); social intimacy despite distance (geographic, genealogic); and core beliefs that explain the world in the collective present with a collective history (Nash, 1989). Normally, surface features of ethnicity are observed: family rituals and physical characteristics (kinship); food preferences and sharing patterns; and behaviors, values, norms, ethnohistory, and celebrations (beliefs) (Nash). Two different examples that express how ethnicity is interpreted follow.

Interpreting Barbie. Within-ethnicity perceptions are diverse and complex, and in this example, they intersect with popular culture, marketing and sales, ethnicity, and geography. In 1997, when Mattel introduced the Puerto Rican Barbie doll, Puerto Rican people on the island were delighted. Americans of Puerto Rican descent, however, saw the doll as Anglo-looking (Puerto Ricans are racially mixed) and thought the inscription on the box, "The U.S. lets us govern ourselves," was "condescending" (Navarro, 1997). (Puerto Rico was ceded to the United States by Spain at the end of the Spanish-American War a century ago [Navarro]. As a commonwealth of the United States, Puerto Rico has options for statehood, independence, or the status quo. Currently, residents are U.S. citizens who can be drafted and to whom federal laws apply. They do not pay federal income taxes, vote for president, or elect members of Congress ["Choice for Puerto Rico," 1998].)

Navarro (1997) compared the sociopolitical position of the 2.8 million Puerto Ricans in the United States, who struggle with stereotypes in a multiethnic society, with that of the four million Puerto Rican people, who constitute a majority in Puerto Rico and to whom the doll represented recognition of the island's culture. The two perspectives on boundaries and boundedness reflect the relationship of each group in its respective societal context in relation to other cultures.

Who Is a Jew? In another example of the cultural perspective and practice, the reshaping of ideologies in the context of religion and politics—engendered by cross-continental perspectives, experiences, history, and tradition—intersect in the question "Who is a Jew?" The question centers on who can carry out conversions to Judaism. In the United States, religious leaders of conservative, reform, and orthodox Judaism movements may carry out conversions; in Israel, only conversions by orthodox rabbis are legally valid and "confer eligibility for citizenship" (Schmemann, 1998, p. A7). Underlying the issue of conversion and citizenship is the challenge to orthodox rabbis in Israel from the reform and conservative branches of Judaism, which is stronger in the United States than in Israel. The reform movement gives women equality, sanctions mixed marriages, and "is anathema to the stern, black-garbed keepers of the faith in Israel" (Schmemann, p. A7), who resist any acknowledgment of these branches.

Categorical and Transactional Ethnicity, Politics, and Race

Green (1995) interpreted the work of Bennett (1975) in *The New Ethnicity: Perspectives from Ethnology,* and he focused on Barth (1969) in *Ethnic Groups and Boundaries.* Green distinguished between *categorical* and *transactional* concepts of ethnicity. Categorical concepts are rigid, but transactional concepts are evolving; one is simple, the other complex. Those who hold categorical concepts of ethnicity expect assimilation as an intervention, but those who see ethnicity as transactional look to indigenous models to guide intervention and "anticipate resistance to politics and cultural dominance" (p. 28).

Categorical ethnicity has permeated North American thinking and beliefs; specific cultural traits, usually stereotypical, are assumed. Seductively, strengths that ethnicity contributes are recognized, but acculturation into a homogeneous whole is tacitly expected. The concept of *cultural pluralism,* the "separate-but-equal harmony" or "tossed salad" model of ethnic celebration, is based on categorical ethnicity (Green, 1995). Green contended that white people define ethnicity for themselves in "surface features"—food, clothing, rituals and celebrations, geography, and national labels. Politically, this perspective "locates ethnicity exclusively in others and excuses [white people] from having to consider their own participation in the management and enforcement of *separateness*" (Green, p. 21), exercising their white privilege.

The dark side of pluralism is political, and the following examples illustrate this; the dominant group defines the categories and controls resources, and differences become a threat (Green, 1995). Pluralistic social services are satisfied with semi-inclusive agency policies and abound with empowerment terminology, but focus more on territorial funding issues with no intention of confronting social injustice and inequalities. Payne (1997) cautioned against embracing political empowerment ideology, whose goal is to limit state services while placing responsibility on individuals for providing their own needs. Indeed, national policy in the 1970s reflected such an ideology in the guise of pluralism and called for "nonintervention in human issues as though that were a benevolent respect for cultural differences" (Green, p. 26).

For example, the work rules of the Personal Responsibility and Work Opportunity Reconciliation Act of 1996 not only strike hard in geographically isolated regions but also create barriers to implementation. When the law was passed, Native American tribal governments saw an opportunity to exercise their tribal sovereignty and to develop realistic welfare-to-work requirements for tribal members within their own economic and cultural contexts (Belluck, 1997). This started a process of negotiation from the cultural and tribal levels to the state and federal levels. Under the federal law, tribal governments negotiated to have the right, as states do, "to set rules on who can receive welfare and for how long" (Belluck, p. A1). Although states pay up to one third of the costs of welfare-to-work programs, the law does not require them to contribute a share for welfare services delivered by tribes within a state. Tribes receive the federal share, but tribes without money are essentially denied participation. Oregon and Arizona were among the first states that agreed to transfer funds that would have been spent had tribal members remained on state welfare rolls. States are mandated to coordinate Medicaid and food stamp programs with tribal welfare programs (Belluck).

As of January 1999, the U.S. Department of Health and Human Services had approved 18 tribes and one urban/tribal consortium (out of 22 applications from 557 federally recognized programs) to run their own programs (Pandey, Brown, Scheuler-Whitaker, & Gundersen, 2004). Evaluation in 2004 showed that problematic communication and collaboration within tribes, between tribes and states, and between tribes and the federal government had improved (Pandey et al.). A lack of state matching funds, support costs, start-up money, and federal rewards for programs that are successful, however, hampered first transfers.

Among the first tribal plans came from South Dakota. Tribes in South Dakota make up 7.4 percent of the population but 53 percent of the welfare recipients (Belluck, 1997). The Sisseton–Wahpeton Sioux is the only tribe in South Dakota that can supplement the federal share, and it provides $200,000 per year from tribal funds. Among other innovations, the tribe combines welfare and training at the tribal college, supporting those on welfare for two years and allowing time for completion of an associate's degree; in contrast, the state plan provides one year of support for students on welfare. As of October 1, 1997, the Sisseton–Wahpeton Sioux had 80 families (from a population of 5,500) on the welfare rolls (Belluck, 1997). Recently, the economy and employment situation on the reservation has benefited from a plastic bag factory and three casinos that cater to gamblers from North Dakota and Canada.

The Rosebud Sioux reservation in the south of the state borders Nebraska and presents a common scenario. Rosebud has a population of 20,000, and 11 percent of eligible adults work (Belluck, 1997). Rosebud, too, has a casino, the only major employer. Profits pay water and electricity bills for destitute families and provide $75 clothing vouchers for schoolchildren. If Rosebud could afford its own welfare program, even more flexibility would be built in for its people. For example, suggested work activities would include hunting, fishing, and making quilts, all of which are part of tribal life and normal work activity.

Although transactional ethnicity can be seen in these examples, tribes must balance the political work to strengthen tribal sovereignty while holding the federal government responsible for treaty accords and contracts, as well as to tribes for historical agreements, including land concessions, right of ways across tribal lands, and water and mineral rights.

Transactional Ethnicity and Race. The transactional model of ethnicity presents a pattern of evolving values within "boundaries . . . using cultural traits as markers for inclusion and exclusion as situations require" (Green, 1995, p. 27). The model suggests that maintaining "boundedness" with those like us and maintaining boundaries to distinguish ourselves from others in multiethnic milieus are what motivates ethnic distinctions to be "continuously defined, redefined, and reinforced" (Green, p. 27). Changing ethnic group names (black, African American, Chicano, Hispanic, Latino, Native American, American Indian, and First Nations) reflect changing perceptions of ethnic boundaries *in relationship to others*, including dominant society. Within this framework, is it possible that a dialogue about race can take place?

Kotlowitz (1998) documented the racial stasis in southwestern Michigan, symbolized by the St. Joseph River between Benton Harbor and St. Joseph. As Kotlowitz moved between black and white communities when he was doing research for his book in the 1990s, he found he could more easily talk with black people about race. In spite of Clinton's presidential call for a national conversation on race, for white people in the United States, race "poses no urgency . . . does not impose on their daily routines. . . . Among whites, there's a reluctance— or lack of opportunity—to engage" (Kotlowitz, p. 23).

Sidebar 5-4: Reconstructing the World

Essayist Nancy Mairs writes of her life and the effects of multiple sclerosis on her body in *Waist-High in the World* (1996), indicating the view from her wheelchair:

> As one of my idiosyncrasies, I prefer to call myself a cripple. . . . For one thing, because it is a word many people with disabilities find deeply offensive, I apply it only to myself, and so it reminds me that I am not speaking for others. For another, it lets you know what my condition is: I can't use my limbs as I once could. Blindness, deafness, intellectual impairment all qualify as "disabilities" (or "differing abilities" to people with mealy mouths), but the circumstances they impose are nothing like mine. "Mobility impaired," the euphemizers would call me, as though a surfeit of syllables could soften my reality. No such luck, I still can't sit up in bed, can't take an unaided step, can't dress myself, can't open doors (and I get damned sick of waiting in the loo until some other woman needs to pee and opens the door for me.)
>
> My choice may reflect a desire for accuracy more than anything else. In truth, although I am severely crippled, I am hardly disabled at all, since, thanks to technology and my relatively advantaged circumstances, I'm not prevented from engaging in the meaningful activities and relationships the human spirit craves. . . . *But I think it is very, very important to distinguish "disability" . . . from some of the circumstances associated with it, often by people who have little direct knowledge of physical and mental limitations and their consequences.* Like all negative terms, "disability" is part of a binary, existing in relation to a privileged opposite: that is, one is "disabled" only from the point of view of another defined by common social values as "able". . . . "I" am disabled, then, only from "your" point of view. . . . When I have occasion to refer to a class with a broader spectrum of impairments, I use the more conventional "people with disabilities," or the "disabled" for short; and people who lack them I call "the nondisabled," since in relation to me, they are the deficient ones. Already, in this way, I begin to reconstruct the world. (pp. 12–14)

Source: *Waist-high in the world* (pp. 12–14), by Nancy Mairs. Copyright © 1996 by Nancy Mairs. Reprinted by permission of Beacon Press, Boston.

Boundedness, Race, and Power in a Changing South Africa. In an international example of boundedness, race, and power, white people in South Africa have a fervent dedication to race. Religion, the Afrikaans language, color (white, colored, black), and political power have served to ensure the ethnic boundedness of the Afrikaners—the descendants of Dutch, German, and French settlers who make up approximately 7 percent of the population (Goodwin & Schiff, 1995).

The Afrikaner supremacy ended in 1999, when the coalition government between the African National Congress and the National Party ended.

The postapartheid transitions for Afrikaners provide a stark example of the struggle of "identity work" on many levels: individual, national, ethnic, political, and ideological. Afrikaner culture "blended Europe and Africa in ways seen nowhere else" (Daley, 1998, p. 11). At the same time, rigid boundaries were established under apartheid and—justified as the "will of God"—denied black people a decent education, the right to vote, the right to own land where they wanted, the right to live where they wanted, and the right to move about in freedom.

What does an 11th-generation Afrikaner teach his children about their heritage in the transition from apartheid to black majority leadership? (Daley, 1998). Generational, geographical, and emotional responses to the new era in South Africa varied. Some people still control segregation when and where they can, some were angered by the loss of Afrikaans television, and others avoided the "moral debate about their culpability" or participated in "the new martyrdom" (Daley, p. 11)—the backlash against being blamed. New-order Afrikaners questioned the culpability of their institutions, created new opportunities for investment that use a black empowerment model, and created opportunities for university students to work in poor areas (Daley). Goodwin and Schiff (1995) contended that no moral transformation occurred; for most Afrikaners, the shift was political, and their motivation was to hold on to as much power as possible. Separatist messianism—"bringing Christianity to Africa while remaining separate" (Goodwin & Schiff, p. 13)—is still the "volk's true calling" for some Afrikaners.

Goodwin and Schiff (1995) interviewed Elna Trautmann, an Afrikaner, in their book. From a different perspective, one couched in anxiety, uncertainty, and hope, Trautmann, who has spent time in intercultural learning, suggested that "the only way the Afrikaners can guarantee their continued existence" is to acknowledge "the great reservoirs of compassion among South Africa's blacks":

> One thing about the black man is that in essence he's not aggressive. I don't believe at all that Africa hasn't got compassion. Here they call it *ubuntu* (a belief that a person exists through other people). I don't believe that any black wants to do to the Afrikaner what the Afrikaner has done to him. I have never in a discussion with anyone found any black who said he wanted to do that. (Goodwin & Schiff, p. 375)

But can the *volk* change? Trautmann despaired as she considered people who are not educating their children for the political change or for changing their inherited racism. Change will come only when those who do not know how to renegotiate status and power die out.

In December 2000, an apology for apartheid was published by a group of 450 prominent white intellectual and civic leaders in South Africa. The *Declaration of Commitment* unexpectedly reopened wounds and sparked bitter debate among whites about their place in South Africa (Salopek, 2001a). President Thabo Mbeki of the African National Congress led a stable South African economy, but the huge disparities in black and white incomes, the racialized politics, and privileged lifestyles of whites also prevailed. Antijie Krog, a poet and writer who led the effort to create the declaration, saw the white angst and public debate as useful. In spite of their history, this public debate among whites had not honestly occurred and "may open political space for whites to criticize the present" (Salopek, p. 12).

External pressures to negotiate relationships between blacks and whites exist as well. The isolation of apartheid insulated both whites and blacks from the rest of the continent. When 46 years of apartheid was lifted in South Africa, the "rest of Africa literally came pouring in" (Salopek, 2001b, p. 1). As in the United States, immigration and border control are volatile issues; unlike the United States, South Africa's immigration is relatively new. Estimates are that 500,000 to 4 million illegal immigrants have come from Angola, Botswana, Congo, Mozambique, Senegal, and Zimbabwe (Salopek). The competition for jobs and housing has produced a black backlash against strangers, and hate crimes against *makwerekwere* (outsiders) are rising (Salopek). Human Rights Watch has criticized South Africa's lack of due process in expelling thousands of legal and illegal immigrants, and human rights investigations of anti-immigrant abuses continue (Salopek).

Under apartheid, South Africa was economically isolated. Now, the country has become an "economic powerhouse in sub-Saharan Africa" (Goering, 2006, p. 10). South African investments dominate, "providing cell phones in the Congo, building hotels in Nigeria, providing bank loans in Angola, smelting aluminum in Mozambique, running power plants in Mali and selling decent pizza or hamburgers just about everywhere" (Goering, p. 10). South Africa's resources are contributing to infrastructure for energy sources from "building and running power plants from Libya to Zambia, building a gas pipeline with Mozambique, producing oil in Gabon, and converting natural gas to diesel in Nigeria" (Goering, p. 10). This explosive economic expansion has an impact on race, immigration, culture, and the politics of South Africa.

In June 2006, the 30-year anniversary of the 1976 Soweto student protest against the apartheid regime was commemorated in Johannesburg (Zavis, 2006). Black students languished in inferior schools and were forced to learn in Afrikaans, the language of the oppressors. In 1976, unarmed students protested in Soweto township and were met with brutal police force; 13-year-old Hector Pieterson was shot and killed. "There was tear gas, people were screaming, running, and police chasing everybody" said Mandla Malinga, 51, who was among the student protesters (Zavis, p. 9). In the nationwide rioting that followed, an esti-mated 500 youths were killed, and "thousands were maimed, disappeared into detention or fled the country to join the guerrilla fight" (Zavis, p. 9). This upris-ing turned the tide in the struggle against apartheid. Today, the challenges for black South Africa continue: poverty, unemployment, alcohol and drug abuse, AIDS, illiteracy, women and child abuse, and uneven education.

Boundedness is created and negotiated amid the changing economic, politi-cal, and social complexities in a certain time for groups of people. The blacks and whites of South Africa have experienced complex changes in racial power in the past 20 years. Students in social work must understand these complexities at the individual, group, family, and community levels. International social work requires an even more studied analysis of the histories of the many peoples who come together in a nation or state.

Intersection: Race, Imperialism, and Democracy

A democracy flourishes when its citizens know and understand multiple per-spectives, the complexity of issues, and "painful truths" (West, 2004, p. 39). Part of this "critical cultivation of an active citizenry" is looking at our history as well as our present through the lens of race and U.S. imperialism at home and abroad (West, p. 39). Cornel West, described by *Newsweek* as an "eloquent prophet with attitude," is a professor of religion at Princeton. He asserts that we have yet to struggle with our imperialist nihilism because we have yet to honestly look at our deep racism. Whole groups of peoples (indigenous peoples, Mexican peasants, Asian laborers, and African slaves) have struggled in this country, and our his-tory is knotted with anti-Semitism, anti-Catholicism, and anti-unionism. It is our legacy of white supremacy, West concludes, that has "inflicted deeper wounds on the American landscape" and "yielded painful truths about the limits of democracy in America" (West, p. 40).

Ralph Waldo Emerson called for a "cultural declaration of independence that required a creative appropriation of the humanist tradition for democratic aims" (Emerson, cited in West, 2004, p. 76) and the "worth of each individual and the potential of all people to re-create and remake themselves" (West, p. 78). West's *Democracy Matters* is an attempt to forge an integration with Emersonian ideals. West writes, "The special focus of this other tradition is the excoriating critique of America's imperialist and racist impediments to democratic individuals, com-munity, and society. It explicitly makes race and empire the two major limits of the American democratic experiment" (West, p. 86) and truly limits embracing and supporting democracies across the world (West, p. 143).

What are we denying? America is not pure, and our history is not clean. Our ideals are not upheld without selection and exclusion, and our hypocrisies are exposed. West (2004) acknowledged that "democratic projects in human history—from Athens to America—have xenophobic and imperial roots" (West, p. 42). If ever there is great revolution in America, the continued inequality of conditions, the notions of inferior and superior, and the crushing weight of imperialism will foment the unrest (West, p. 46).

The critique of America's racism may well be forced by Hispanics and blacks. Together, blacks and Hispanics compose almost 25 percent of the U.S. population, and their economic and political power cannot be ignored.

Democracy and Mexican Immigration: Imperative Realities and Outdated Policies.

Democracy is always a movement of energized public to make elites responsible—it is at its core and most basic foundation the taking back of one's powers in the face of misuse of elite power. . . . Democracy is not just a system of governance, as we tend to think of it, but a cultural way of being.

—West (2004, p. 68)

The "browning of America" found a political face in massive numbers in spring 2006. Unprecedented democratic (of the people) participation in marches began in Chicago and spread throughout the United States from California to Washington, DC. Millions of immigrants and undocumented workers, primarily from Mexico, peacefully called for justice in the development of policies regarding the freedom to come to the United States, to work, and to support their families. For many people facing poverty, survival is the primary goal; for many more, crossing the border is the only option.

The 2006 immigrant rights movement was the startling response to a bill passed by the U.S. House of Representatives in December 2005. The catalyst was the bill's intention to "raise illegal immigration to felony status and extend a fence along the U.S.–Mexico border, a barrier that many immigrants abhor" (Martinez, 2006, p. 20). In Chicago, collective action was harnessed—in less than a month before the first demonstration in March—through an existing network in which experienced activists had already registered expatriate voters for the Mexican presidential elections slated for July 2006 (Martinez). Substantially more vigorous were the "275 immigrant associations—with memberships from a few dozen to 2,000—in the Chicago area that represent Mexicans from a certain hometown or state" (Martinez, p. 20). "Through these associations, the factory workers, roofers and waitresses who represent the Mexican grass roots have helped plan events, even modest ones such as banquets or picnics" (Martinez, p. 20). Spanish-language radio connected everyone, the Internet played its role, and "the tree bore fruit like an explosion" (Martinez, p. 20).

Jose Gonzalez, a human rights activist from San Diego, understands the major impetus for legal and illegal immigration. Gonzalez, a U.S. citizen, came from Mexico illegally 25 years ago. He understands that the indigenous peoples of Mexico have little future in a country where government and elites work for their own purposes (Navarette, 2006). Mexico does not have enough jobs, so $20 billion is sent home by Mexicans abroad to support family. "The elite want to help get more rights for Mexicans in the United States; the immigrants themselves just want better-paying jobs at home so they won't have to go to United States in the first place" (Navarette, p. 23). If he were president of Mexico, Gonzalez's prescription would be systemic:

+ Work to eliminate police corruption. Police corruption dissolves trust, erodes incentive, and leaves people unprotected.
+ Impose realistic licensing fees, which would no longer penalize employers and small businesses but would encourage more businesses, more jobs, and better wages.
+ Address the problem of environmental pollution. Companies that devour natural resources and pollute waterways need to be punished (Navarette).

Policies of Exclusion. Although immigration was favored in the British colonies, charters excluded Catholics and steered away from paupers and convicts. Inferiority, anti-Semitism, and racism have always been undercurrents in U.S. immigration policy, which blatantly excluded the Chinese from 1882 to 1943 (Reimers, 1998). Policies of immigration have a history of "compromises, exceptions, and idiosyncratic features," including literacy tests imposed in 1917, which were unsuccessful in reducing the numbers of southern Europeans, and the Immigration Act of 1952, which was intended to stem the "communist threat" (Mackie, 1995, p. 288). After World War II, the "refugee" category was mostly a product of Cold War foreign policy (Mackie). In an attempt to limit immigration, overpopulation and depletion of environmental resources momentarily entered the debate in the 1960s and remerged in the 1990s regarding quality-of-life issues in opposition to illegal immigration (Reimers).

Ethnic balance and protecting self-interest have always been concerns of nativists, although racial criteria and nationality quotas were eliminated in the Immigration Act of 1965, when kin-based immigration was introduced. By 1978, the unintended consequences of this act had concentrated immigration among people from countries in Central America and Asia (Mackie, 1995). According to Mackie, illegal immigration stemmed from a wartime foreign agricultural worker program formally ending in 1965. Market forces and labor shortages influenced practices of agricultural employers, even under formal prohibition of illegal immigration in 1986. The 1990 immigration reforms opened immigration to other regions, and illegally immigrating Europeans (Irish and Poles) found legal entry here (Mackie).

After September 11, 2001, national security became a priority. According to the National Immigration Forum (2006) online, "Immigration laws were selectively enforced for people from predominantly Muslim, Arab, and South Asian countries." Hundreds of people were arrested for violations and held without charges or notification of family, friends, or lawyers. (National Immigration Forum, 2006). In the wake of September 11, approval of visa applications for refugees and those seeking asylum, who are "among those most rigorously screened," were reduced to a fraction of their annual allotted numbers (National Immigration Forum online).

Since 1980, analysis of the impact of immigration on the economy and labor market has become more scholarly and includes new research by sociologists and economists (Reimers, 1998). Issues of immigrants' impact on social welfare programs (food stamps, public health and medical care, and public schools) and the taxpayer burden of immigration are other areas of study. Reimers cautioned that the use of scholarly material, whether to support critics of immigration or "defenders of liberal policies," furthers a political agenda (p. 88).

Political machinations and old ways of thinking about immigration fail the new reality. Poverty in Mexico—a poverty not understood by most Americans—is driving an "exodus" of biblical proportions (Cooper, 2006, p. 126). A million people are caught each year by the Border Patrol; after multiple attempts, half of those caught eventually make it across (Cooper). Since stricter controls were implemented in 1994, between 400 and 500 people have died each year, mostly in the high desert of southern Arizona. According to Cooper, 15 million to 20 million people have crossed the border, and another 20 million will cross in the next two decades. Charles Bowden's (2003) *Down by the River* and Luis Urrea's (1996, 2004) *By the Lake of Sleeping Children* and *The Devil's Highway* are imperative reading for the social work student to understand the extent of this issue.

As populations continue to escape poverty and economic and social injustice worldwide, immigration will continue to rise. Will massive democratic action like the 2006 immigration marches make a difference for the United States, or will political compromise, exceptions, and historical events continue to be the dominating influences for immigration policies?

Disasters, Displacement, Cultural Shifts, Political Shake-Ups, and Economic Quakes

It's like there's a rumbling and a quake is coming. One group got their ear to the ground, waiting to see how it all shakes out. The other group is waiting to be shaken, and we don't know where they're going to wind up. But that ain't just in the Delta, right now that's everywhere.

—Sara Claree White, cited in Trice (2006, p. 1)

Hurricane Katrina slammed into the Gulf Coast, tearing away the levees and exposing the complacent underbelly of the federal government and "unprepared-for-disaster" agencies. Businesses and commerce stopped, infrastructure crumbled, and municipalities lost their tax base. Hundreds of thousands of people were displaced, left homeless, and abandoned. Instantly, media images of our racism in practice were sent across the world. The outrage has since passed. Other than reporting on cases of fraud, the national media has largely forgotten about the aftermath of Katrina: the hypocrisy, the racism, the poverty, the shame. When there is inaction and injustice by government, the organized voices of the many peoples—some with their own media outlets—can be activated and, most important, linked. The stories of the Vietnamese in the shrimping industry, the Mexican immigrants, and blacks in the south follow. Social workers can find a niche in community work following disaster and in policy building with those affected by disaster.

The Vietnamese and Katrina. Originally, the stories of Hurricane Katrina survivors focused mostly on the hardest hit, the black poor, 67 percent of the population in New Orleans proper. "To deflect sole blame from the powerful," wrote Tang (2006, p. 1), spinmeisters switched to stories of people who got out without government help. Stories of Vietnamese shrimpers were shaped, extolling the virtues of the Vietnamese: "ethnic solidarity, war-tested survival skills, and their trusted shrimping boats" (Tang, p. 1). The reality is meaner and more stark and no longer a feature story.

More than 35,000 Vietnamese residents of Gulf Port and Biloxi, Mississippi, will probably never return to those communities (Tang, 2006). The shrimping industry has all but disappeared, taking with it the livelihood of about 15 percent of the adult Vietnamese working population. Another 45 percent of the Vietnamese population worked in the New Orleans tourism industry, including hotels and casinos. Two thousand Vietnamese in Mississippi, the poorest state in the Union, were displaced from Biloxi. Many of the Vietnamese displaced from the region (about 15,000), including those from three waves of refugees since the Vietnam War ended, are now in Houston, already home to the largest ethnic enclave of Vietnamese in the nation.

An awakening is in progress, and a shift in allegiance is occurring, according to Tang (2006). "Vietnamese-American politics has been characterized by an abiding loyalty to the U.S. government, a no-nonsense anti-communism and deep distrust for those who seek to shift the community toward socially progressive trends" (Tang, p. 3). In the first three weeks after Katrina, Vietnamese service agencies handled immediate relief and relocation without government help. They were among the first to make assessments about long-term plans for displaced Vietnamese people. A month post-Katrina, a Congressional briefing on the hurricane's impact on the Vietnamese Americans in the gulf was convened by Vietnamese organizations—Boat People SOS, National Association of Vietnamese American Service Agencies, and the National Congress of Vietnamese Americans. Here, Vietnamese community leaders publicly called for government accountability. Personal accountability over government accountability would no longer loyally be supported. In a change of political and social will, Vietnamese leaders promoted a three-phase plan that placed responsibility squarely on the government for assistance with housing, income, food, employment, and, in the future, rebuilding homes or permanently relocating families (Tang, 2006).

The Congressional Black Caucus (CBC) echoed this plan in H.R. 4197, which addressed the eradication of poverty and hurricane recovery (Bacon, 2006). The CBC called for authorizing funds for housing, health care, federal unemployment insurance, and Temporary Assistance to Needy Families payments. Money for rebuilding homes and schools for returning residents and apprenticeships for employment stability are part of the bill.

Immigrants and Katrina. Four months after Katrina, the Census Bureau estimated that 450,000 people left the Gulf Coast region in the wake of Hurricanes Katrina and Rita. (Hurricane refugees in hotels and shelters were not counted) (Associated Press, 2006). Federal estimates for the influx of refugees to Houston and Harris County, Texas, totaled 93,000 people, but city and county estimates placed the influx at about 150,000. The black population in the New Orleans metropolitan area dropped from 37 percent to 22 percent; the white population increased to 73 percent from 60 percent. The largest influx into the Gulf Coast region consisted of Hispanics, totaling almost 100,000 in the four months after Katrina (Associated Press).

As flood waters receded, federal no-bid contracts went to politically connected contractors (Bacon, 2006). According to immigrant rights groups, the FEMA contract pays about $35 for removal of each cubic yard of debris, but multiple subcontractors siphon their share, and the people who actually remove the debris get $10 for each cubic yard. Affirmative action was suspended, which excluded local firms and local workers and lowest wages from competition (Bacon). Employers wanted workers without families because schools and community services would not be available (Bacon). Although some contractors brought their own workers, word of mouth traveled, and immigrant workers became part of the clean-up work force (Bacon).

Conditions for immigrant workers are predictably exploitive. Workers sleep in tents, abandoned trailers, or school buses. Health standards are not enforced, safety rules are often suspended, and tetanus immunizations are not readily available (Bacon, 2006). "Migrants work from sunup to sundown without any benefits, and sometimes even without paychecks," reported representatives from

Sidebar 5-5: *Blacks, Latinos, and Cultural Change in the Mississippi Delta*

The influx of Hispanics into the South has been in the making for more than 10 years. The Hispanic population is growing faster in the South than in any other part of the country, and Mississippi's Hispanic population—people from Mexico, Honduras, Guatemala, El Salvador, Colombia, and Argentina—grew 150 percent between 1990 and 2000. It now totals nearly 40,000 and makes up 1.8 percent of the Mississippi population, most of whom live in the Mississippi Delta (Trice, 2006). In the Delta, "one of the poorest parts of the poorest state" (Trice, p. 22), 64.7 percent of the population is black, 32.5 percent is white, and 1.0 percent is categorized as "other," but 36.2 percent of the total state population is black and 60.7 percent is white (1.7 percent is categorized as "other") (Trice, p. 22).

In the Mississippi Delta, cotton fields gave way to catfish ponds in the 1980s, and African American low-skilled workers, many of them women, still labor in the $275 million-a-year catfish-processing industry (Trice, 2006). In the 1980s, "slave wages" kept the labor pool in poverty, women suffered carpal tunnel syndrome from skinning 25 to 28 catfish per minute, sexual harassment was alive, and bathroom breaks were timed (Trice, p. 22). The Delta Pride catfish-processing plant was fined for violation of safety laws; the company appealed, but it eventually complied. In 1985, black women organized and formed a union in 1986. However, conditions did not improve until a 1,200-worker walkout and boycott. After three months, the workers won a $1.50 per hour increase, bringing pay to $5.50 per hour (Trice).

In the mid-1990s, the U.S. Department of Labor sponsored a program to allow employers in the hospitality, poultry, forestry, construction, and catfish industries to hire short-term foreign workers to fill jobs for which Americans were not competing (Trice, 2006). That program created many changes in workforce composition. Now, in 2006, about 30 percent of the 5,000-person catfish-processing workforce is Hispanic, and cultural changes signal a new community. A Spanish-language church and the Supermercado El Mexicano on U.S. Highway 82 opened in 2004. In Indianola, Wal-Mart is stocking Mexican-brand staples to accommodate its Hispanic market. Social service agencies, hospitals, and schools have added Spanish to posted signs (Trice).

In May 2006, one plant owner gave notice to immigrant workers to provide documentation or lose their jobs (Trice, 2006). Other plant owners may follow. If huge numbers of undocumented workers lose their jobs and plant owners cannot replace the workers they need to remain competitive, will black union workers then have more leverage for improved pay and pensions? Will immigrant workers use the unions to change their futures? These consequences are not clearly predictable, but for the social worker in the Delta, a systemic view that includes history, economics, politics in the South, and cultural change is required to understand the process of change.

the Mississippi Immigrant Rights Alliance who gathered complaints with other labor and immigrant rights groups (Bacon, p. 17).

> This is the dark side of the neoliberal American dream. The net result is the casualization of the workforce throughout the hurricane-affected areas. Temporary jobs instead of permanent ones. Jobs for mobile, single men, rather than for families. No protection for wages. Hiring through contractors and temporary agencies, instead of a long-term commitment from an employer. (Bacon, p. 17)

Essentially, this is the model that is proposed for the immigrant guest worker programs supported by some politicians. Companies could recruit outside the country and bring in 300,000 to 400,000 workers under temporary visas. Bacon (2006) warned that a downward spiral in wages, exacerbated by layers of competing contractors, recruiters, and labor agencies that ultimately exploit and dehumanize workers, is ignored. "In the wake of Katrina, the contractors now in the Gulf would have a more systematic way to recruit the same kind of contingent workforce, with the active assistance of the federal government" (Bacon, p. 17).

Rodolfo de la Garza, a scholar with the Tomas Rivera Policy Institute and a professor of political science at Columbia University, provided an analysis connecting Latinos and blacks (Richardson, 2006). The civil rights agenda was about "equality under the law and integration"; it was a broad, inclusive agenda that brought benefits to white women, Latinos, and Asians through the 1960s and 1970s. Antidiscrimination laws are used for legal protection for gays and lesbians. When the Voting Rights Act was passed in 1965, revisions to immigration policy that year benefited from the momentum of the civil rights legislation and aided Latino immigration.

Today, however, fewer similarities may be found between African Americans and Latinos in their struggle for rights, de la Garza concludes (Richardson, 2006). Systemic racism oppresses blacks in a way Latinos do not experience. In the labor market, immigrants compare their wages here with wages in their own countries, and they see benefits; African Americans compare their wages to white workers, and they see significant gaps. Latinos face the disparagement of the use of Spanish and immigrant rights. This has "transformed and focused the Latino community's national political priorities" (Richardson, p. 4). If voting rights and civil rights form the core of African American issues, "a Latino civil rights agenda would include working-class concerns": education, jobs, and immigration (Richardson, p. 4).

Indeed, leaders of the immigrant rights movement are identifying broad concerns. In their effort to "grow the movement" and include non-Latinos, movement leaders want to encompass more than rights and include broad reforms:

education, housing, a living wage, accountability in policing, and English-language training (Martinez, 2006, p. 20). Even more broadly, the movement may find common ground with the global labor and human rights movements, particularly as they work against exploitation and modern-day slavery (Richardson, p. 4).

The Gulf Coast, a ground zero for racial and cultural change brought about by internal displacement and immigration, will surely suffer more hurricanes. It is a new era, and the global and human rights perspective—political, cultural, economic, environmental—expands our ability to see and to understand the quaking beneath our feet.

CONCLUSION

We can legitimately say that in the process of oppression someone oppresses someone else; we cannot say that in the process of revolution someone liberates someone else, nor yet that someone liberates himself, but rather that human beings in communion liberate each other.

—Paulo Freire (1994, p. 114)

What does this all mean for the social work profession? How must we now prepare ourselves to meet the challenges of an era that mimics the turn of the 20th century but in which changes occur at hyperspeed and with high-powered technology and in which both violence and progress—in all forms—can touch us personally? As learners sitting next to each other in class, with all our differences, we must recognize that there is someplace that we can go together. As social workers, we must be aware that in the absence of dialogue and understanding lies the absence of self-reflection and the opportunity for self-knowledge, followed by the absence of shared reason and the danger for a misuse of power.

REFERENCES

Anderson, E. (1990). *Streetwise: Race, class, and change in an urban community.* Chicago: University of Chicago Press.

Associated Press. (2006, June 7). Hispanics move into hurricane regions. *Chicago Tribune,* p. 3.

Bacon, D. (2006). Looking for common ground. *Colorlines: Race, Culture, Action, 9,* 15–18.

Barth, F. (1969). *Ethnic groups and boundaries.* Boston: Little, Brown.

Belluck, P. (1997, September 9). Tribe's new power over welfare may come at too high a price. *New York Times,* pp. A1, A20.

Bennett, J. W. (1975). *The new ethnicity: Perspectives from ethnology.* St. Paul, MN: West Publishing.

Bowden, C. (2003). *Down by the river: Drugs, money, murder and family.* New York: Simon & Schuster.

Bruni, F. (1998, March 8). A battlefield shifts: Gay scout's court victory shows how far movement has progressed. *New York Times*, p. 36.

Buriel, R. (1984). Integration with traditional Mexican-American culture and sociocultural adjustment. In J. L. Martinez, Jr., & R. H. Mendoza (Eds.), *Chicano psychology* (pp. 95–130). Orlando, FL: Academic Press.

Choice for Puerto Rico. (1998, March 9). *New York Times*, p. A18.

Cooper, M. (2006, May). Exodus: The ominous push and pull of the U.S.–Mexican border. *The Atlantic Monthly*, 297(4), 123-127.

Daley, S. (1998, February 22). Africa's "White Tribe" fears dark past is prologue. *New York Times*, pp. A1, A11.

Devore, W., & Schlesinger, E. G. (1996). *Ethnic-sensitive social work practice* (4th ed.). Boston: Allyn & Bacon.

D'Souza, D. (1992). *Illiberal education: The politics of race and sex on campus*. New York: Vintage Books.

Dugger, C. W. (1997, October 28). Outward bound from the mosaic: Where dead are mourned, many traditions mingle. *New York Times*, pp. B1, B3.

Fine, M., Burns, A., Payne, Y., & Torre, M. E. (2004). Civics lessons: The color and class of betrayal. In L. Weis & M. Fine, *Working method: Research and social justice* (pp. 53–74). New York: Routledge.

Freire, P. (1994). *Pedagogy of the oppressed* (Rev. ed.). New York: Continuum.

Goering, L. (2006, December 4). In gold mines of S. Africa, a duel with pirates. *Chicago Tribune*, pp. 1, 10.

Goldberg, M. (2006, June 10). Different tack on gay rights. *Chicago Tribune*, p. 5.

Goodwin, J., & Schiff, B. (1995). *Heart of whiteness: Afrikaners face black rule in the new South Africa*. New York: Scribner.

Gould, K. H. (1996). The misconstruing of multiculturalism: The Stanford debate and social work. In P. L. Ewalt, E. M. Freeman, S. A. Kirk, & D. L. Poole (Eds.), *Multicultural issues in social work* (pp. 29–42). Washington, DC: NASW Press.

Green, J. W. (1995). *Cultural awareness in the human services: A multi-ethnic approach* (2nd ed.). Boston: Allyn & Bacon.

Gutierrez, L., & Nagda, B. A. (1996). The multicultural imperative in human services organizations: Issues for the twenty-first century. In P. R. Raffoul & C. A. McNeece (Eds.), *Future issues for social work practice* (pp. 203–213). Needham Heights, MA: Allyn & Bacon.

Johnson, H. C., Renaud, E. F., Schmidt, D. T., & Stanek, E. J. (1998). Social workers' views of parents of children with mental and emotional disabilities. *Families in Society*, 79, 173–187.

Kotlowitz, A. (1998, January 11). Colorblind: How can you have a dialogue on race when blacks and whites can see no gray? *New York Times Magazine*, pp. 22–23.

Kozol, J. (1991). *Savage inequalities: Children in America's schools*. New York: HarperPerennial.

Lindsey, E. W. (1998). Service providers' perceptions of factors that help or hinder homeless families. *Families in Society*, 79, 160–172.

Lomborg, B. (2004). Introduction. In B. Lomborg (Ed.), *Global crises, global solutions* (pp. 1–12). Cambridge, England: Cambridge University Press.

Mackie, G. (1995). U.S. immigration policy and local justice. In J. Elster (Ed.), *Local justice in America* (pp. 227–290). New York: Russell Sage Foundation.

Maharidge, D. (2006). The white buffalo. *Colorlines: Race, Culture, Action, 9,* 34–36.

Mairs, N. (1996). *Waist-high in the world.* Boston: Beacon Press.

Martinez, D. (1994). *Mother tongue.* New York: Ballantine Books.

Martinez, M. J. (2006, May 1). March: Organizers reach out to non-Latinos. *Chicago Tribune,* pp. 1, 20.

McAdams-Mahmoud, V. (2005). African American Muslim families. In M. McGoldrick, J. Giordano, & N. Garcia-Prieto (Eds.), *Ethnicity and family therapy* (3rd ed., pp. 138–150). New York: Guilford Press.

Nash, M. (1989). *The cauldron of ethnicity in the modern world.* Chicago: University of Chicago Press.

National Immigration Forum. (2006). *Due process—post 9/11.* Retrieved June 11, 2006, from http://www.immigrationforum.org/DesktopDefault.aspx?tabid=541

Navarette, R., Jr. (2006, June, 2). Immigrant's take on Mexico's Fox: "What a shame." *Chicago Tribune,* p. 23.

Navarro, M. (1997, December 27). A new Barbie in Puerto Rico divides island and mainland. *New York Times,* pp. A1, A9.

Pandey, S., Brown, E. F., Scheuler-Whitaker, L. & Gundersen, B. (2004). *Promise of welfare reform: Development through devolution on Indian reservations.* Retrieved June 16, 2006, from http://gwbweb.wustl.edu/buder/papers/article22a.pdf

Payne, M. (1997). Empowerment and advocacy. In *Modern social work theory* (2nd ed., pp. 266–285). Chicago: Lyceum Books.

Personal Responsibility and Work Opportunity Reconciliation Act of 1996, Pub. L. 104-193, 110 Stat. 2105.

Pritchett, L. (2004). Access to education. In B. Lomborg (Ed.) *Global crises, global solutions.* Cambridge, England: Cambridge University Press.

Purdum, T. S. (1998, March 23). California justices allow Scouts to bar gay and atheist members. *New York Times,* pp. A1, A19.

Reimers, D. M. (1998). *Unwelcomed strangers: American identity and the turn against immigration.* New York: Columbia University Press.

Richardson, S. S. (2006). Perspective: Dream takes a new direction. *Chicago Tribune,* Section 2, pp. 1, 4.

Rimer, S. (1998, February 2). Rural elderly create vital communities as young leave void. *New York Times,* pp. A1, A14.

Salopek, P. (2001a, January 8). Apology exposes anger, angst of S. Africa whites. *Chicago Tribune,* pp. 1-1, 1-12.

Salopek, P. (2001b, January 16). Intolerance in "rainbow nation." *Chicago Tribune,* pp. 1-1, 1-12.

Schmemann, S. (1998, January 27). "Who's a Jew" puzzle gets more tangled. *New York Times,* p. A7.

Tang, E. (2006, June). Boat people. *Color Lines, 9*(1). Retrieved December 30, 2006, from http://colorlines.com/article.php?ID=28

Trice, D. T. (2006, June 11). Immigration issues real in Delta: "Struggle to hold on to what we have." *Chicago Tribune,* pp. 1, 22.

Urrea, L. A. (1996). *By the lake of sleeping children.* New York: Anchor.

Urrea, L. A. (2004). *The devil's highway.* New York: Little, Brown & Company.

Wadler, J. (1998, March 10). A matter of scout's honor, gay victor says. *New York Times*, p. B2.

Weiner, T. (1997, December 27). Many Laotians in U.S. find their hopes betrayed. *New York Times*, pp. A1, A5.

West, C. (2004). *Democracy matters*. Newark, NJ: Penguin Books.

Wolfe, A. (1998a, February 8). The homosexual exception: A new study shows that suburban Americans are surprisingly tolerant—of everyone but gay men and lesbians. *New York Times Magazine*, pp. 46–47.

Wolfe, A. (1998b). *One nation, after all: What Americans really think about God, country, family, racism, welfare, immigration, homosexuality, work, the right, the left and each other*. New York: Viking.

Zavis, A. (2006, June 17). Lessons of Soweto recalled. *Chicago Tribune*, p. 9.

6

Monitoring Social Work Practice

Mark A. Mattaini

In chapters 8 through 13, which outline practice with individuals, families, groups, communities, and organizations, the authors repeatedly note the need for ongoing monitoring and evaluation of practice. Two central questions about monitoring cut across practice at all system levels and have critical ethical and professional implications: (1) How is the client doing? and (2) Is my practice working (that is, helping)? This chapter sketches a framework for addressing those questions at all system levels; the framework is further elaborated in subsequent chapters.

The framework is not meant to provide a complete description of how to go about monitoring practice. This rich and complex area requires book-length treatment to achieve adequate coverage (for example, Bloom, Fischer, & Orme, 2006; Nugent, Sieppert, & Hudson, 2001). Rather, this chapter is meant as an introduction to essential concepts for practice monitoring and evaluation with which students should be familiar as they move into their fieldwork settings.

All social workers want to believe that their practice is making a difference, and they need to communicate that message if they want financial support and community sanction. Still, believing that one is effective is not the same as knowing that one is effective or being able to demonstrate it to oneself and to others. A serious debate about practice effectiveness emerged in the profession in the 1970s and continued through the 1990s (for example, Fischer, 1973, 1976; Gordon, 1983; Mullen & Dumpson, 1972; Raw, 1998; Reid & Hanrahan, 1982; Thomlison, 1984; Thyer & Myers, 1999; Wood, 1978). Some analysts (for example, Raw) have argued that social work is an art whose effectiveness cannot be measured, whereas others (for example, Thyer & Myers) have vigorously asserted that clients have a right to effective treatment and that effectiveness must be measured.

It is now clear that some practice "works" well and that some does not. Although there is much yet to be learned about effective practice and many questions about monitoring complex goals and issues remain, the profession has, by and large, embraced the need to use evidence-based intervention strategies and the need to track how clients are doing over time, recognizing that such monitoring will inevitably be less than perfect.

Social workers are responsible to themselves, the community, and especially their clients for trying to determine how their cases are progressing in as objective a way as possible. At a minimum, they simply must know whether the clients are or are not moving toward their goals (Question 1, above). (For clients for whom avoiding deterioration or relapse is the objective, the question shifts to whether or not they are maintaining a particular level of functioning.) It clearly matters, for example, whether a parent is using alternatives to abusive physical punishment; whether an overstressed family achieves a more satisfying balance with its environment; whether several depressed members of a treatment group are becoming less depressed; or whether a neighborhood is achieving an increased level of empowerment leading to economic development, family stability, and increases in social capital. Collaboratively determining how to track changes in cases is also critical to a shared power approach to practice, because involvement in self-monitoring can be empowering for clients (Kopp, 1993). Clarity about intervention goals also demystifies the social work consultation process because both client and worker can see whether change is occurring in the areas important to the client. With the continued expansion of managed care, monitoring of practice may be essential to ensure funding for agencies, because managed care companies often require clinicians to demonstrate that progress is being made and that their intervention strategies are effective.

Social workers naturally also want to know whether their practice is contributing to changes they observe in their clients. Question 2, above, can be restated as "Is the joint work being done by the client and social worker responsible for whatever change is being achieved?" Determining the extent to which the intervention is responsible for the change requires a level of experimental control that is generally not easily available in practice settings, and answering this question rigorously may not be possible, as discussed below. It is always possible, however—although not always simple—to find some way to address Question 1, to determine at least whether progress toward client goals is being achieved. In some cases, monitoring the *process* of practice—what clients and workers are doing—is also important, although ultimately, outcome matters most.

The basic principles of monitoring are the same regardless of the size or complexity of the client system involved. If focal issues (client goals or target problems) have been clearly specified and agreed on at any system level, the creative, thoughtful practitioner can find a way to track whether they are being achieved in a manner that is organic to, rather than imposed on, the practice. The limited evidence available suggests that clients prefer that some clear method of monitoring outcome be used as opposed to relying on practitioners' global opinions (Campbell, 1988).

Given the complexity of the transactional realities that social work deals with, however, monitoring is often not straightforward. The behavior of individual clients is easier to measure, for example, than are environmental events or the actions of representatives of large, bureaucratic systems: A wider range of individual-level measures exists, and it is easier to gain access to individual clients. In some cases, what is monitored may be at some remove from where intervention is needed. If the issue is depression, for example, it may make sense to monitor the case using a standardized rapid assessment instrument, such as the Beck Depression Inventory–II (Beck, Steer, & Brown, 1996). However, if the depression is deeply rooted in situational factors over which the client has limited control (for example, severe and persistent battering), lack of progress should not be attributed to the client's resistance, a personality disorder, or other factors that fail to take the full case situation into account. In this case, the client's depression is the focal issue and is appropriate to track, but intervention should be directed toward the causal factors in the social and physical environment (an assessment issue).

Social workers must be familiar with at least two major bodies of knowledge before they can effectively monitor their practice. First, they need to know about *measurement*, defined here as approaches for measuring progress on focal issues. Second, they need to know how to *design* their ongoing measurement approach— how to apply those measures and structure treatment so as to track what is going on. Although measurement and design are research terms, no unfamiliar, complex approach is being suggested here. Research is really nothing more than a rigorous way of seeking the answers to questions; in this case, the interest is in finding relatively rigorous ways to answer the practice questions "Is the client doing better?" and "Is my work helping the client?" Monitoring is an indivisible aspect of practice, not something extraneous that is artificially appended to it.

MEASUREMENT

The progress of people or systems toward achieving their goals can be measured in many ways, some of which are more reliable and valid than others. Some methods are narrow and some are broad, and some require more specific training than others. Professional social workers who use any monitoring strategy must be familiar with certain technical aspects of measurement, such as reliability and validity (just as physicians must understand how to read laboratory tests). Although it is not possible to review all the available approaches to measurement, and practitioners commonly must develop new ones to fit case situations, the discussion of a few approaches may help the reader think about possibilities that may fit a particular form of practice or a particular case.

Validation of Measures

In using any form of measurement, it is important to know the following information:

+ Is the measure *valid?* Does it measure what it is supposed to measure, not something else?
+ Is the measure *reliable?* Does it produce stable scores with little measurement error?
+ Is the measure is *sensitive* enough to pick up changes that occur?
+ If the instrument is generally valid, is it valid for the population of which the client is a member?

Details about each of these elements are emphasized in research courses and in books on practice evaluation and measurement; this section provides a brief review.

A valid measure of depression should measure depression, not anger or anxiety, for example, although it is common for those issues to be intertwined. A valid measure of community empowerment should measure just that, and not ethnicity, although ethnicity may in many cases be correlated with empowerment due to patterns of oppression and racism. These examples suggest the complexities of testing validity.

Considerable research has refined measures of validity. For example, testing the validity of a measure of depression is sometimes done by comparing scores of a group of people with clear clinical diagnoses of depression with scores of another group with no depression (the *known groups* method). In other cases, the measure may be validated by testing the extent to which the measure correlates with other constructs. For example, depression should have a substantial correlation with hopelessness and low self-esteem, a moderate correlation with anxiety, and very little correlation with certain demographic variables. This process is called *construct validation.*

If a client completes a scale for hopelessness on two different days when she feels equally hopeless, but the measurement instrument used yields very different scores for the two days, a problem clearly exists. Similarly, if two people count the number of times an autistic child complies with a parental request over the course of a one-hour videotape, their counts should be nearly the same. In each of those situations, a strong measure should yield about the same score—it should be *reliable*. All items on an instrument should also measure the same thing (*internal consistency* reliability). Reliability is actually one dimension of validity. A measure that is not reliable cannot be valid—if the instrument is not measuring anything in a stable way, it cannot be measuring the construct or issue of interest accurately.

Clearly, given the technical complexities involved in validating measures, real advantages exist in using instruments for which reliability and validity have already been established whenever possible, rather than trying to test the validity of measures one develops oneself. Nevertheless, one must often settle for measures with only moderate levels of demonstrated validity; such measures should be interpreted cautiously.

Some instruments may be reasonably reliable and valid, but they may not be *sensitive* enough to pick up the often subtle shifts that can happen in work with clients. A scale constructed with only two possible scores (for example, 0 for no depression and 1 for depression) would be nearly useless for monitoring clinical progress. Some scales are sensitive enough to pick up differences between populations (levels of anxiety among the poor and the rich, for example) but are not sensitive enough to use for clinical purposes.

Many scales and other forms of measurement have been validated with limited populations, often college undergraduates. The validity of such scales for other populations is often unknown and cannot be assumed. Considerable effort is now going into testing existing measures and developing new measures for particular populations, and those efforts often uncover considerable cultural differences and biases. Selection of a measure therefore involves looking not just at reported measures of validity, reliability, and sensitivity but also at the populations that have been sampled in the validation process. It may seem that some issues, such as depression, would be similar across cultures. But it turns out, for example, that depression among some Asian groups is more likely to manifest in somatic complaints than in statements of emotion. Many measures that are grounded primarily in affect and cognition (common areas in which depression is evident among white Americans) may therefore miss the problem when used with Asian immigrants and refugees.

Measurement Methods

The most accurate way to measure is usually through direct observation (especially, of course, if done by multiple observers so reliability can be measured). In many practice settings, such observation may be impractical, but this strategy is often dismissed too quickly. In working with parents to teach parenting skills, for example, social workers can observe parents' and children's behavior directly, and such observations may provide extraordinarily useful data for ongoing intervention planning. The wide availability of videotaping equipment can simplify this process (see, for example, Mattaini, McGowan, & Williams, 1996). Such simple methods as a chart tracking an autistic child's successful efforts at toileting (see Figure 6-1) or the number of times partners in an intimate relationship perform simple actions that the other appreciates (as in the "caring days" procedure) (Mattaini, 1999; Stuart, 1980) are helpful for planning intervention and motivating clients as well. Note, as in Figure 6-1, that observational monitoring forms can and should be developed in ways that are immediately accessible and comprehensible for clients.

Various types of rating scales can be useful when direct observation is not realistic. One is Task Attainment Scaling (Reid, 1992), in which the level of achievement of agreed-on tasks is rated on a scale of 1 (minimally or not achieved), 2 (partially achieved), 3 (substantially achieved), to 4 (completely achieved)—or "no" (no opportunity to attempt) (see also Nugent et al., 2001, for a computerized approach to monitoring task completion). This technique can be applied in every session, in any form of practice in which client, worker, or joint tasks are relevant (as they are in most practice). This is a form of process monitoring, and it is based on the empirically supported assumption that completion of tasks contributes to outcome (Reid).

Self-anchored scales, on which a client is asked to rate, for example, how sad he or she feels on a scale of 1 to 10, are relatively straightforward and have been used to monitor situations ranging from pathological jealousy to depression (Nugent et al., 2001). Such scales are usually easy for clients to relate to and can have excellent psychometric properties (that is, validity and reliability; Nugent et al.). Several such scales can be used together, as in the Mood Thermometers (Tuckman, 1988) (Figure 6-2). Clinician rating scales, such as the Clinical Rating Scale (Epstein, Baldwin, & Bishop, 1983) for family assessment (on which the clinician rates family functioning on six dimensions and overall), are easy to use and can have excellent measurement properties (Miller, Epstein, Bishop, & Keitner, 1985). A particularly useful resource for locating available instruments for clinical practice is Corcoran and Fischer's (2000) two-volume *Measures for Clinical Practice*. Measures for larger systems are also available, and they can be located by searching online abstract services such as Social Work Abstracts and PsycINFO.

Reliability and validity can be enhanced by adding behavioral descriptions to the points on a rating or self-anchored scale, to clarify what is meant by, for example, a 3 on a 5-point scale of conflict containment in a family. Figure 6-3 provides an example of two such behaviorally anchored rating scales (Daniels, 2000), which were developed to monitor a clinical case (Seidenfeld & Mattaini, in press). Ratings on such scales can be graphed over time and can be combined and quantified on standardized Goal Attainment Follow-Up Guides (Bloom et al., 2006; Kiresuk, 1973) for program evaluation purposes.

FIGURE 6-1
□ □ □ □ □
Chart of Toileting Successes, Kept by Parent and Child

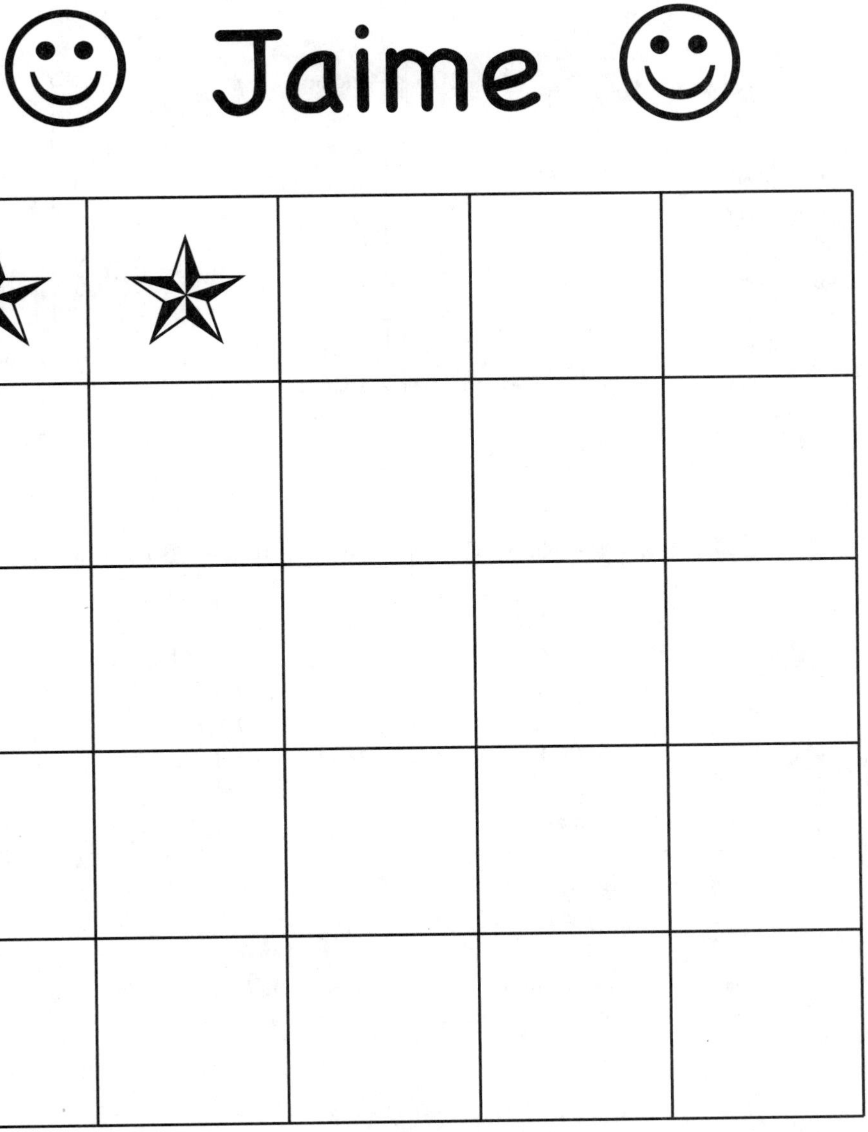

☺ **Jaime** ☺

Note: Stickers, smiling faces, or stars can be drawn or attached—preferably by the child—each time he or she uses the toilet properly. When a row is completed (five correct toiletings on the chart shown here), the child can be rewarded with something he or she enjoys, like having a story read. (Latham, 1994, also suggested pasting a picture of the child seated on the potty chair or toilet at the top of the chart as a reminder of the desired behavior.)

FIGURE 6-2

Mood Thermometers

How I Feel Right Now

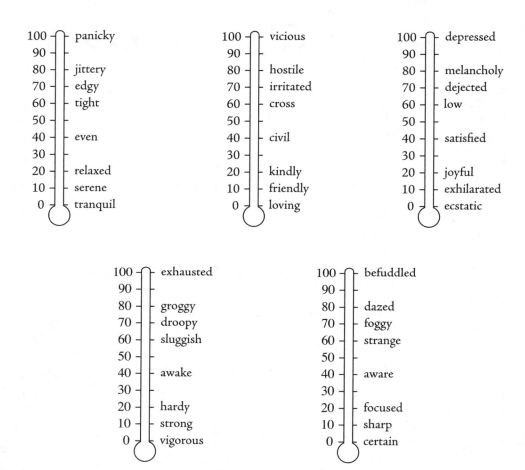

Source: Tuckman, B. W., *Educational and Psychological Measurement* (Vol. 48, No. 2), pp. 419–427, copyright 1988 Sage Publications, reprinted by permission of Sage Publications, Inc.

Graphing

Both the client and the social worker may find it reinforcing to see progress on the graph—or motivating not to see such progress. Graphing is usually an integral part of self-monitoring and is an empowering strategy for client systems of all sizes (Biglan, Ary, & Wagenaar, 2000; Kopp, 1988, 1993; O'Reilly et al.,

FIGURE 6-3

□ □ □ □ □

Behaviorally Anchored Rating Scales for Two Clinical Issues

Level of Goal Attainment	Decision Making	Social Contacts
5	Client regularly seeks opportunities to make choices, tracks consequences effectively, and readily takes reasonable risks to obtain valued reinforcement.	Client engages in a rich and varied social life in which he can identify the sources and nature of social reinforcers that he experiences; readily engages with new people who may be potential friends.
4	Client independently identifies available choices and possible outcomes for each, and acts on those data with only limited need for support under most circumstances.	Client can identify several people other than his regular contacts (girlfriend, consultant, coworkers) who provide a variety of valued social reinforcers on a regular basis.
3	Client makes some decisions after consultant assists him to identify possible choices and clarify possible consequences for each; acts on those choices only with substantial encouragement.	Client can identify at least two friends (other than girlfriend) who provide valued social reinforcement.
2	Client avoids acting on decisions until he experiences significant aversives for failing to act.	Client's primary social contacts are with consultant, girlfriend, and coworkers.
1	Client fails to make or act on decisions, even when lack of action results in significant aversives.	Client's social contacts are limited to those required for survival.

Source: Reprinted with permission from Seidenfeld, M., & Mattaini, M. A. (in press). Personal and family consultation services: An alternative to therapy. *Behavior and Social Issues.* © M. Seidenfeld and M. A. Mattaini.

2002). By graphing multiple self-anchored or rating scales concurrently, clients and social workers can examine connections among various aspects of client and environmental functioning over time, which may help identify relationships and, not incidentally, also protect them from oversimplifying complex cases. For example, Figure 6-4 depicts three dimensions of the Marital Happiness Scale (Azrin, Naster, & Jones, 1973), which was completed before each

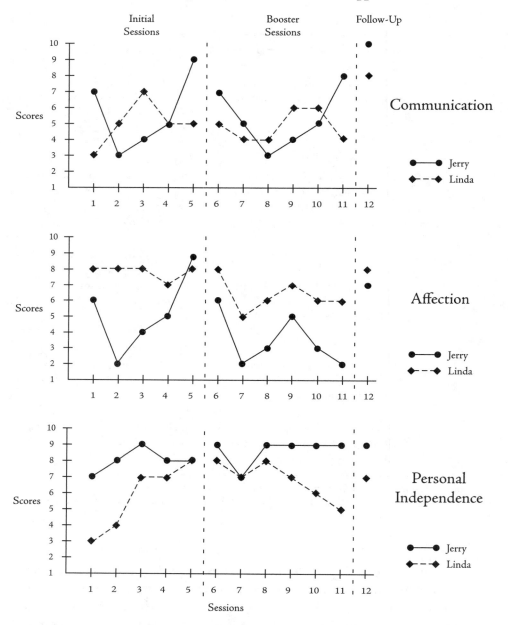

FIGURE 6-4

🔲🔲🔲🔲🔲

A Couple's Scores on Communication, Affection, and Personal Independence on the Marital Happiness Scale

Notes: These scores were for a five-session block of joint work and for six booster sessions scheduled when the couple requested them. Also included are scores for a single follow-up point several months after the last booster session. Refer to Exercise 6-1 in Appendix C for further analysis of these data.

session by both partners in a couples case seen by the author. Each dimension on this 10-dimension scale is rated on a scale ranging from 1 (completely dissatisfied) to 10 (completely satisfied), so higher scores reflect higher satisfaction. For each dimension, each partner is asked, "If my partner continues to act in the future as he/she is acting *today* with respect to this relationship area, how happy will I be *with this area of our relationship?*" The scale can be used for all types of intimate partnerships, including gay and straight, marital and cohabiting.

The first five sessions occurred during five consecutive weeks. Subsequently, booster sessions were available on an "as-needed" basis (when difficulties arose—note the lower scores when the instrument was completed just before each booster). A single follow-up data point (suggesting a high level of satisfaction several weeks after the final session) is also shown. Note that the male partner believed at intake that communication was not a significant problem, whereas the female partner saw it differently. During the first few sessions, progress in communication was uneven, as is typical in early stages of couples work. In other areas, however, initial progress was evident; for example, although Jerry was always fairly satisfied with his own level of independence, Linda's satisfaction with her own independence improved considerably (as was also true of overall happiness with the relationship, not shown). Some other areas, such as affection, showed a much more uneven pattern, requiring work throughout the phases.

Data such as these, in which multiple factors can be tracked together, can be enormously informative for tracing ongoing client satisfaction with their lives and with the intervention. Similar multivariable procedures can be used to examine concurrent changes among levels of support and aversives (conditions with which one tends to minimize contact) from environmental systems and a client's mood or family functioning. Associations among these factors can be traced over time using quantified sequential ecomaps (see Figure 1-2).

Also available are a wide variety of rapid assessment instruments (RAIs), which are brief, paper-and-pencil instruments that are designed to be completed quickly and often by a client. Such instruments can be used to measure moods, self-talk, assertiveness, family functioning, peer relations and social interactions, magical thinking, and many other dimensions of human and social functioning (see Corcoran & Fischer, 2000, for examples of such measures). Hudson and his colleagues have done extensive work over the course of more than two decades to develop an integrated package of instruments that are specifically targeted for use with social work clients (Nugent et al., 2001). It is important to learn how to select and use such instruments, usually through specific course content, because it is essential to understand their psychometric properties, how cultural differences may affect responses and interpretation, and how to correctly integrate data from RAIs with other information to complete a comprehensive clinical assessment. RAIs offer tremendous flexibility, however, and they often have excellent reliability and validity.

Many such instruments can be used with clients who are seen in groups. Another strategy, useful at all systemic levels but demonstrated here for use with a group, is the qualitative matrix (Miles & Huberman, 1994), which is used to track, for example, group members' progress in learning social skills in a structured skills training group (see Figure 6-5).

Other qualitative strategies may be useful in tracing the intervention process with individuals, families, groups, and communities. Reid's (1988) Case Process Chart, for example, relies primarily on rich narrative data, rather than numbers, but it allows the relationships among events to emerge using a matrix structure.

Although monitoring change at a community level may be more complicated, the same basic principles used with smaller systems apply (Biglan et al., 2000). Changes can be tracked by interviews or questionnaires, which may include many of the types of measures just described; by direct observation (for example, of the number of people hanging out on a street or the number of vacant buildings on a block); and especially by examining incidence data related to focal issues (for example, juvenile arrests or dropouts).

The list of tools discussed here is by no means exhaustive, and professional social workers will find that they often must adapt or even create tools that will adequately capture the critical data elements in a particular case or group of cases at whatever systemic level. Bloom and associates (2006) provided much detail about such measurement (as well as about design; see below). The challenge is to find an approach that can capture the most important complexities of a case in ways that are practical and realistic. How often these measures are taken, and how, are design questions, which are discussed next.

DESIGN

Technically, "design" refers to ways of structuring data collection to help determine the extent to which an intervention is causally related to outcomes. Many of the designs that are practical for everyday practice monitoring can address this question only in limited ways and provide only limited control over what are called "alternative explanations" of change. For example, it is sometimes difficult to rule out seasonal changes that co-occur with intervention. Nonetheless, a certain amount of rigor—provided by design—is often possible in practice.

Two general classes of design can be valuable for monitoring and evaluating practice: *single-system* designs and *group* designs. Practice ultimately takes place with single systems (a person, a family, a community, or an organization). Even in group work, the primary goal is often to improve or maintain the level of functioning or quality of life of each member, and results for each may vary. (In some

FIGURE 6-5

Tracking Matrix for a Social Skills Group Showing Skills for Which Group Members Have Met the Established Criterion Level

SESSION 1

Member	Skill # 1	2	3	4	5	6	7	8	9	10
Jill										
George		✓	✓		✓					
Mary Kay		✓	✓		✓					
Ernie				✓						✓
Sarah										
Kate		✓								
Sharee										
Maxine										

SESSION 2

Member	Skill # 1	2	3	4	5	6	7	8	9	10
Jill	✓	✓								
George	✓	✓	✓		✓					
Mary Kay	✓		✓		✓					
Ernie		✓	✓	✓						✓
Sarah										
Kate		✓	✓							
Sharee	✓									
Maxine										

SESSION 3

Member	Skill # 1	2	3	4	5	6	7	8	9	10
Jill	✓	✓	✓	✓	✓				✓	✓
George	✓	✓	✓	✓	✓	✓		✓	✓	
Mary Kay	✓	✓	✓	✓	✓					
Ernie		✓		✓						
Sarah										
Kate	✓	✓	✓							
Sharee	✓	✓	✓							
Maxine										

SESSION 4

Member	Skill # 1	2	3	4	5	6	7	8	9	10
Jill	✓	✓			✓					
George	✓	✓	✓		✓				✓	
Mary Kay	✓		✓		✓					✓
Ernie		✓		✓	✓					
Sarah	✓			✓	✓					
Kate	✓	✓	✓	✓	✓					
Sharee	✓									
Maxine										

SESSION 5

Member	Skill # 1	2	3	4	5	6	7	8	9	10
Jill	✓	✓	✓	✓	✓	✓	✓			
George	✓	✓	✓	✓	✓	✓	✓		✓	
Mary Kay	✓		✓	✓	✓	✓	✓			✓
Ernie		✓	✓	✓	✓	✓	✓			
Sarah	✓		✓	✓	✓	✓	✓			
Kate	✓	✓	✓	✓	✓	✓	✓			
Sharee	✓		✓	✓						
Maxine										

SESSION 6

Member	Skill # 1	2	3	4	5	6	7	8	9	10
Jill	✓	✓	✓	✓	✓	✓	✓	✓	✓	✓
George	✓	✓	✓	✓	✓	✓	✓	✓	✓	✓
Mary Kay	✓	✓	✓	✓	✓	✓	✓	✓	✓	
Ernie		✓	✓	✓	✓	✓	✓	✓		
Sarah	✓	✓	✓	✓	✓	✓	✓			
Kate	✓	✓	✓	✓	✓	✓	✓			
Sharee	✓	✓	✓	✓	✓					
Maxine										

Source: Reprinted with permission from M. A. Mattaini (1993). *More than a thousand words: Graphics for clinical practice* (p. 163). Washington, DC: NASW Press. ©National Association of Social Workers.

cases, however, the goal is change at the level of group culture, in which case the entire group should be regarded as the single focal system.) For those reasons, the main emphasis in this chapter is on single-system, or single-case, designs. A brief consideration of group designs, which can be useful for some program evaluation purposes, especially when combined with single-system designs, is presented later in the chapter.

Many research courses focus on group designs. Although some of the concepts learned in such courses (such as internal validity or generalizability) apply regardless of the type of design, group designs are generally inappropriate for the routine monitoring of practice. Group designs require a relatively large number of similar clients and the use of untreated control groups or comparison groups receiving different treatments, preferably with random assignment. Group studies also "wash out" differences among cases, which may not matter for research purposes but does matter a great deal for clinical purposes. For example, on average a group of cases may improve, but this aggregate may include some clients who do much better, some who do a bit better, and some who deteriorate badly. In practice, intervention should be varied for each case to achieve the best possible outcome, but such variation would fatally compromise rigorous group designs. For these and other conceptual and practical reasons (Johnston, 1988), practitioners ordinarily use some form of single-case design instead of group designs. To the extent possible, the social worker wants to rule out alternative explanations for apparent change—such as seasonal variations, a sudden family crisis, or the effects of testing—so as to demonstrate that the intervention itself is responsible for the change. In single-case designs, whatever controls for alternative explanations are present are provided by the case itself, rather than a separate control group (as is common in group designs).

Single-Case Designs

Many types of single-case designs are in use, but only a few with considerable applicability to practice monitoring are highlighted here. The reader should refer to the specialized literature for further detail (for example, Bloom et al., 2006; Nugent et al., 2001). In some circumstances, particularly in emergencies, the social worker simply starts to intervene and at the same time tracks the level of problems experienced. For example, with a client with severe depression, one would ordinarily begin treatment immediately and monitor the level of depression over time, using perhaps an RAI or a self-anchored scale. This approach is called a *B design*, because the accepted convention is to label the baseline phase (that is, measurements of the problem taken before intervention begins) "A" and to label intervention phases "B" (and "C," "D," and so forth if multiple types of interventions are used). In the example with the depressed client described above, baseline data are not collected; therefore, it is a B design. Note that a B design is adequate for showing that depression is declining during the course of treatment, but it does not provide a stable picture of how depressed the client was at the beginning (that would require collecting baseline data at several time points before initiating intervention—which would clearly be inappropriate here). B designs also cannot demonstrate that the intervention was responsible for the change, because something else may be the cause of the improvement, including artifacts (for example, clients tend to enter treatment when things are at their worst, so data often improve to some extent simply as a result of what is called "regression toward the mean"—extreme scores typically tend to move closer to the average over time). Even if alternative explanations cannot be ruled out, however, monitoring the level of depression is clearly essential.

In other cases, social workers can collect some baseline data (sometimes retrospectively) and then continue to collect data during intervention and, ideally, during follow-up. Figure 6-6 is an example of an A–B design with a single follow-up point. (In single-case designs, data are usually graphed to simplify analysis, and visual analysis is characteristic of such designs.) The figure illustrates an interesting case, in which the client was disturbed by jealous thoughts about her husband's first wife, who had died before the client and her husband met (Slomin-Nevo & Vosler, 1991).

The extent of client change is clear in Figure 6-6, and it is reasonable to suppose that the intervention may have contributed to the change, although it cannot be proved. If the primary goal were scientific knowledge building, such uncertainty would be an issue, but for clinical purposes, the data are probably persuasive enough. In other cases, the first intervention does not have the desired effect, and the worker may use a clinical analytic design with multiple sequential intervention phases, some of which may include combinations of several interventions, until a satisfactory outcome is achieved (see Figure 6-7 for an example).

Generally, the goal in social work practice is to achieve a clear and obvious change that is immediately evident on the graph (a "slam-bang" effect). Clinically significant effects that are truly meaningful ordinarily should emerge clearly and persuasively on the graph, because client goals usually involve quite substantial change that will be visually evident. It is also possible, however—and in some cases desirable—to supplement visual analysis of single-case data with simple or complex statistical tests that have been developed for time-series data (Bloom et al., 2006; Nugent et al., 2001).

Other, more involved designs enable social workers to better untangle causality (for example, multiple baseline, changing criterion, or withdrawal designs) as well as to select the best of several possible intervention strategies to pursue with a particular case (for example, alternating treatment designs). Refer to the specialized literature (for example, Bloom et al., 2006; Nugent et al., 2001) for more

FIGURE 6-6
□□□□□
*Single-Case Evaluation of Brief Problem-Solving Therapy
for Obsessive Jealousy*

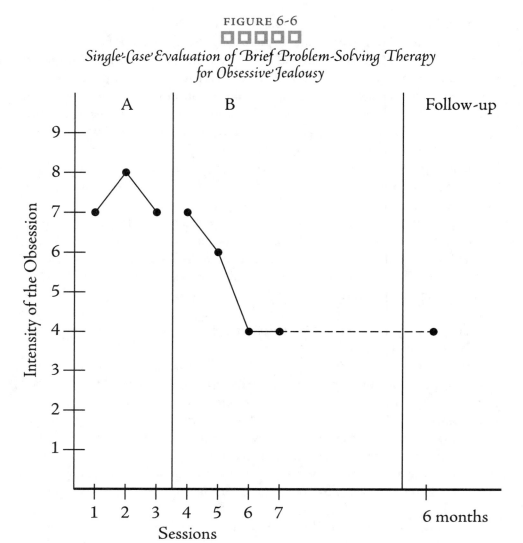

Source: Slomin-Nevo, V., & Vosler, N. R. (1991). The use of single-system design with systemic brief problem-solving therapy. *Families in Society, 72,* 42. Reprinted with permission from *Families in Society* (www.familiesinsociety.org), published by the Alliance for Children and Families.

detail about such designs, which can be of particular use for social workers wishing to contribute to the practice research literature. In most cases, however, social workers in practice will rely on the simpler designs discussed here.

Single-system designs are applicable even when the system involved includes many people or groups. For example, if a neighborhood organization wished to reduce the rate of violent crimes on the street, it might test two different approaches, such as increased patrolling by the police (negotiated with the local

FIGURE 6-7

Example of a Clinical Analytic Design

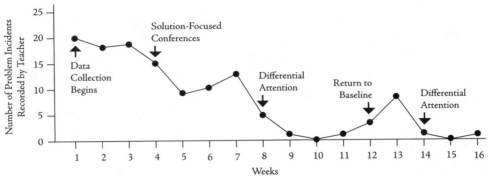

Notes: In this hypothetical case of a child displaying behavior problems in a classroom, the social worker begins by gathering baseline data. After three weeks, she might begin twice-weekly, solution-focused conferences with the student and teacher to shift perceptions by emphasizing positive exceptions and work toward the student's own goals (for example, Watkins & Kurtz, 2001). Note that although the problems appear to abate somewhat with this intervention, they continue at a distressing level and are trending toward the baseline level. As a result, the social worker might introduce an additional procedure, such as designing a program to ensure high levels of peer attention to appropriate behavior and extinction of inappropriate behavior (Ervin, Miller, & Friman, 1996). If this program resolved the problem, as seems to be the case here, the social worker and the teacher might try to withdraw this somewhat demanding procedure to see whether it is still required. On the graph, withdrawal led to a resurgence of the classroom problems, which again remitted after the differential reinforcement procedure was reinstated. (Naturally, when inappropriate behavior has resulted in attention for years, it may take some time to eliminate that behavior.) The graph suggests both that the problems have been brought under control and that the intervention was responsible for the improvement.

precinct) and establishment of a youth antiviolence board, and determine the relative effectiveness of each approach. This strategy might involve establishing a baseline from data on violent crimes over the past year (A), followed by two months of increased patrolling (B), then two months of youth work (C), or two months of both (B–C). Note that although the crime data involve multiple people, the neighborhood organization would trace the aggregate data for the neighborhood—a single-system strategy. Other possibly confounding effects (seasonal patterns, for instance) should also be considered in such evaluations. Refer to Biglan et al. (2000) for more information about the use of single-system time-series designs with larger systems like communities.

Group Designs

Although single-system designs have particular power for practice monitoring, group designs may be useful at times, particularly at programmatic or community levels. For example, if an agency decided to implement a new short-term treatment project, it might want to compare the effectiveness of that approach with the standard open-ended approach currently being used. No clients would go untreated—this would be a *contrast group design*, rather than one relying on an untreated control group. As long as the same measures (for example, a package of RAIs) were used with both groups, and reasonable decisions could be made about when to use them (perhaps every 90 days for a year, or six months after intake), such a design could be practical. Note, however, that single-case designs could be incorporated within this group design—and probably ought to be (Nugent et al., 2001). It is not enough to know that the average outcome is as good or better for the new program as it was for the old, although that information is important. It is still critical for clinical purposes to monitor how each client is doing. One intervention stream would last longer than the other in this example, but what happens during those periods for each client should be driven by the specifics of the case.

Comparison-group studies would be useful if a social worker and a community group were working to prevent school dropouts, for example. They might establish a new tutoring and support program in one school and compare the dropout data for students in that school with data for students in similar schools in which such a program was not in place during a specified period of time. Although it would be a weak design (other factors—alternative explanations—may be responsible for differences found), it would provide at least some basis for comparison. It is important to examine such data because some "prevention" programs may have a range of benefits but may not actually have any effect on the problem to be prevented and some may even be damaging (Embry, 2004). In a world of limited resources, it is essential to know whether one's program is associated with positive change.

Monitoring at the programmatic level blends into program evaluation (see chapter 13). Although evaluation is a specialized field and evaluation research can become extremely complex (Rossi, Freeman, & Lipsey, 2003), completing a simple evaluation that may include tracking clients' satisfaction and simple measures of goal attainment or task achievement need not require major effort, particularly given the current widespread availability of personal computers. Data that are routinely collected can often be used for simple evaluations that require few agency resources (see, for example, Patterson & Basham, 2006, on using standard office spreadsheets for statistical analysis).

CONCLUSION

Monitoring of practice need not be arcane and does not require advanced mathematical and research skills. Poorly done monitoring carries risks, however, because a requirement for monitoring may lead poorly prepared social workers to focus on what is easiest to see (often, the behavior of clients) rather than what is most important—which may include larger systemic factors. Social workers have no choice, however. A professional cannot practice ethically without paying attention to whether clients are achieving their goals. Therefore, social workers must learn the skills of monitoring and learn them well. This is a special challenge because awareness of the importance of, and the development of tools for, monitoring practice are relatively recent advances in the profession. Some of the methods and instruments available are rough and need a good deal more elaboration. Many social workers, administrators, and supervisors in the field have limited knowledge in this area, so recent graduates are increasingly looked to as the "experts." In many settings, demands by funders to document effectiveness and measure outcomes have become intense and are another reason to develop expertise in monitoring. The primary reason to find ways to track progress and outcomes, however, is that it is the only way in which one can know whether a client is reaching his or her goals and whether one is helping the client to do so.

REFERENCES

Azrin, N. H., Naster, B. J., & Jones, R. (1973). Reciprocity counseling: A rapid learning-based procedure for marital counseling. *Behaviour Research & Therapy, 11*, 365–382.

Beck, A. T., Steer, R. A., & Brown, G. K. (1996). *Manual for the Beck Depression Inventory* (2nd ed.). San Antonio, TX: Psychological Corporation.

Biglan, A., Ary, D., & Wagenaar, A. C. (2000). The value of interrupted time-series experiments for community intervention research. *Prevention Science, 1*, 31–49.

Bloom, M., Fischer, J., & Orme, J. (2006). *Evaluating practice: Guidelines for the accountable professional* (5th ed.). Boston: Allyn & Bacon.

Campbell, J. A. (1988). Client acceptance of single-system evaluation procedures. *Social Work Research & Abstracts, 24*(2), 21–22.

Corcoran, K., & Fischer, J. (2000). *Measures for clinical practice: A sourcebook* (3rd ed., Vols. 1 & 2). New York: Free Press.

Daniels, A. C. (2000). *Bringing out the best in people* (2nd ed.). New York: McGraw-Hill.

Embry, D. D. (2004). Community-based prevention using simple, low-cost, evidence-based kernels and behavior vaccines. *Journal of Community Psychology, 32*, 575–591.

Epstein, N. B., Baldwin, L. M., & Bishop, D. S. (1983). The McMaster Family Assessment Device. *Journal of Marital and Family Therapy, 9*, 171–180.

Ervin, R. A., Miller, P. M., & Friman, P. C. (1996). Feed the hungry bee: Using positive peer reports to improve the social interactions and acceptance of a socially rejected girl in residential care. *Journal of Applied Behavior Analysis, 29*, 251–253.

Fischer, J. (1973). Is casework effective? A review. *Social Work, 18*, 5–20.

Fischer, J. (1976). *The effectiveness of social casework*. Springfield, IL: Charles C Thomas.

Gordon, W. E. (1983). Social work revolution or evolution? *Social Work, 28*, 181–185.

Johnston, J. M. (1988). Strategic and tactical limits of comparison studies. *Behavior Analyst, 11*, 1–9.

Kiresuk, T. J. (1973). Goal attainment scaling at a county mental health service. *Evaluation Monograph, 1*, 12–18.

Kopp, J. (1988). Self-monitoring: A literature review of research and practice. *Social Work Research & Abstracts, 24*(4), 8–20.

Kopp, J. (1993). Self-observation: An empowerment strategy in assessment. In J. B. Rauch (Ed.), *Assessment: A sourcebook for social work practice* (pp. 255–268). Milwaukee, WI: Families International.

Latham, G. I. (1994). *The power of positive parenting*. North Logan, UT: P&T Ink.

Mattaini, M. A. (1993). *More than a thousand words: Graphics for clinical practice*. Washington, DC: NASW Press.

Mattaini, M. A. (1999). *Clinical intervention with families*. Washington, DC: NASW Press.

Mattaini, M. A., McGowan, B. G., & Williams, G. (1996). Child maltreatment. In M. A. Mattaini & B. A. Thyer (Eds.), *Finding solutions to social problems: Behavioral strategies for change* (pp. 223–266). Washington, DC: American Psychological Association.

Miles, M. B., & Huberman, A. M. (1994). *Qualitative data analysis: An expanded sourcebook*. Thousand Oaks, CA: Sage Publications.

Miller, I. W., Epstein, N. B., Bishop, D. S., & Keitner, G. I. (1985). The McMaster Family Assessment Device: Reliability and validity. *Journal of Marital and Family Therapy, 11*, 345–356.

Mullen, E. J., & Dumpson, J. R. (1972). *Evaluation of social intervention*. San Francisco: Jossey-Bass.

Nugent, W. R., Sieppert, J. D., & Hudson, W. W. (2001). *Practice evaluation for the 21st century*. Belmont, CA: Brooks/Cole.

O'Reilly, M., Tiernan, R., Lancioni, G., Lacey, C., Hillery, J., & Gardiner, M. (2002). Use of self-motivating and delayed feedback to increase on-task behavior in a post-institutionalized child within regular classroom settings. *Education & Treatment of Children, 25*, 91–102.

Patterson, D. A., & Basham, R. E. (2006). *Data analysis with spreadsheets*. Boston: Allyn & Bacon.

Raw, S. D. (1998). Who is to define effective treatment for social work clients? *Social Work, 43*, 81–86.

Reid, W. J. (1988). The metamodel, research, and empirical practice. In E. R. Tolson (Ed.), *The metamodel and clinical social work* (pp. 167–192). New York: Columbia University Press.

Reid, W. J. (1992). *Task strategies*. New York: Columbia University Press.

Reid, W. J., & Hanrahan, P. (1982). Recent evaluations of social work: Grounds for optimism. *Social Work, 27*, 328–340.

Rossi, P. H., Freeman, H. E., & Lipsey, M. W. (2003). *Evaluation: A systematic approach* (7th ed.). Thousand Oaks, CA: Sage Publications.

Seidenfeld, M., & Mattaini, M. A. (in press). Personal and family consultation services: An alternative to therapy. *Behavior and Social Issues*.

Slomin-Nevo, V., & Vosler, N. R. (1991). The use of single-system design with systemic brief problem-solving therapy. *Families in Society, 72*, 38–44.

Stuart, R. B. (1980). *Helping couples change*. New York: Guilford Press.

Thomlison, R. J. (1984). Something works: Evidence from practice effectiveness studies. *Social Work, 29,* 51–56.

Thyer, B. A., & Myers, L. L. (1999). On science, antiscience, and the client's rights to effective treatment. *Social Work, 44,* 501–504.

Tuckman, B. W. (1988). The scaling of mood. *Educational and Psychological Measurement, 48,* 419–427.

Watkins, A. M., & Kurtz, P. D. (2001). Using solution-focused intervention to address African American male overrepresentation in special education: A case study. *Children & Schools, 23,* 223–234.

Wood, K. M. (1978). Casework effectiveness: A new look at the research evidence. *Social Work, 23,* 437–459.

7

Compassion, Control, and Justice in Social Work History

Jerry R. Cates

Compassion, social control, and social justice are deep themes in social work history. Research is threaded with controversy about the extent to which these powerful motifs have been actualized in our profession as well as what they mean for its identity and future. The theme of compassion—the identification with people who suffer coupled with the desire to alleviate their suffering through increasingly professionalized actions—is unequivocally intrinsic to our history. Paradoxically, however, this record of compassionate response is intertwined with one of social control that, at times, has been extraordinarily oppressive. This social control has sometimes derived from factors internal to the profession and, at other times, has been imposed by forces external to the profession. Despite this troubling and paradoxical combination, it nevertheless remains the case that individual and collective pursuit of social justice by social workers is a strong current in the profession's history, one that possesses the power to inspire contemporary professionals. As a prime example, consider the case of Jane Addams, whose social justice achievements made her an international icon far beyond the boundaries of social work.

Rather than begin with a famous figure such as Jane Addams, however, this chapter opens with a brief introduction to three little-known social workers who grappled with social justice issues emerging from the daily rounds of their work and who did so in ways that contributed to historic turning points of reform. The work of Elizabeth Chief, Bennie Parish, and Peter Buxton shows that one does not have to be famous or occupy a powerful position to make social justice contributions that have historic impact.

ELIZABETH CHIEF

An American Indian social worker in the federal Bureau of Indian Affairs (BIA) in the late 1940s, Elizabeth Chief had firsthand knowledge of the desperate conditions faced by Native Americans of the Southwest. Indian disease rates were among the highest and life spans among the shortest of any group in the United States. Chief had often "traveled on horseback over rough trails to assist mothers with malnourished small children and to investigate the condition of Indians who were drinking polluted water from irrigation ditches" (Philp, 1999, p. 58). She was well acquainted with the link between this suffering and the long-standing illegal actions of New Mexico and Arizona in totally excluding Indians residing on reservations from the public assistance benefits of the Social Security Act. This discrimination had been in place since the passage of the act in 1935, and it had been well known to, tolerated by, and even condoned by the federal agencies responsible for policy oversight: the BIA and the Social Security Board (Cates, 1988). The exclusion of the needy aged, the blind, and dependent children was undergirded by southwestern denial of the Indian right to vote. Using photographs, needs data, and details of her own observations, she conveyed the dimensions of the desperate situation, coupled with strong statements about the culpability of the New Mexico State Department of Public Welfare, to the National Conference of Indian Affairs. This information, in turn, became the basis of a remarkable "Starvation without Representation" article by Will Rogers, Jr., in the national publication *Look Magazine* (Rogers, 1948). The BIA, stung by Chief's actions, retaliated by ordering her to relocate from her New Mexico home to a new assignment on the Pine Ridge Reservation in South Dakota (Philp, p. 59). But it was too late to prevent her impact: Chief had made a significant contribution to a complex series of political events in 1948 and 1949 that eventually led to Indian voting rights and Indian access to public welfare in the Southwest.

BENNIE PARISH

In 1962, Bennie Parish was a public welfare caseworker in Oakland, California, when he refused to go on a midnight raid against his welfare clients. For this refusal, he was fired as insubordinate (Piven & Cloward, 1971, p. 166).

California, as did many states, routinely subjected welfare recipients to stark degradation rituals to force them off welfare rolls. These rituals were directed with particular force against African American clients. Among the most notorious degradation rituals was the midnight raid (Bell, 1965; Piven & Cloward, 1971). Caseworkers were ordered to visit clients' homes, unannounced and usually late at night, to look for signs of a male presence. If such signs were found (e.g., a shoe, a child's response to the worker's questioning about mother's boy-friends) or if the client refused to open the door to the unannounced visit, the woman and her children would be cut from the welfare roll without a hearing or right of appeal. Midnight raids combined with the "man-in-the-house" rule to produce the following "logical" sequence:

+ If a woman receiving Aid to Families with Dependent Children (AFDC) benefits was suspected of "seeing a man," she must be engaging in sexual intercourse outside of marriage, which meant she was immoral, which, in turn, meant she was an "unfit" parent to whom welfare payments should not be made and whose children might be removed for this reason alone.
+ The man she was seeing could be assumed to be the father of her children and should be held responsible for their financial support.

Thus, it was justifiable to terminate a woman in this situation immediately from the rolls (Bell, 1965).

These practices had gone on for decades, with federal oversight agencies—the Department of Health, Education, and Welfare (HEW) and HEW's subordinate, the Bureau of Public Assistance—doing virtually nothing to challenge the states, even though the federal agencies carried statutory authority and responsibility for seeing that the federal–state welfare system was administered with equity. When Parish was fired, he protested and filed a lawsuit. As part of his case, the unconstitutionality of midnight raids was highlighted. Eventually, he won his court case and was reinstated. In part as a reaction to national publicity about the case, HEW eventually did what it could have done all along: It issued new federal rules prohibiting midnight raids in the AFDC program. The rules, in turn, became part of a substantial series of legal cases and other developments, which, by the late 1960s, had vindicated welfare clients' rights to fair hearings and other aspects of due process.

PETER BUXTON

After his experience as a military psychiatric social worker, Peter Buxton became a San Francisco public health caseworker. In the late 1960s, he came across published accounts of the ongoing (now infamous) Tuskegee syphilis experiment. He was outraged to learn that impoverished African American men in rural Alabama were being subjected to a decades-long, federally funded human experiment to study the crippling and lethal effects of syphilis. The men had both treatment and knowledge of their diagnosis withheld from them by federal and local health officials so that medical researchers could study the disease's progression. Upon learning about the experiment, Buxton immediately protested to top levels of the U.S. Public Health Service. Despite initial rebuffs and attempts to intimidate him, he persisted and, as the book *Bad Blood* (Jones, 1981) put it, "In the end it was Peter Buxton (and the press) that stopped Tuskegee" (p. 203). Congressional hearings were conducted, national and international outrage ensued, and the human experimentation was brought to an end. In the wake of these events, federal legislation was enacted that permanently altered the national research landscape by establishing federal requirements for informed consent and other procedures to protect humans involved in federally supported research.

The examples of Chief, Parish, and Buxton illustrate several points. They demonstrate the historically conditioned and "given" nature that injustice often takes. In each situation, knowledge of the oppression's long-standing existence may not have been widely dispersed among the general public, but it was no secret in professional and policy circles. In the course of their normal work, each social worker was presented with "normal" oppressions that had a dismaying degree of acceptance by those in authority at the time.

The examples also carry the theme of people of color being excluded from full citizenship. The exclusion of Indians from welfare and electoral politics was a key factor in maintaining a structure of Anglo dominance in the Southwest. The AFDC midnight raids, although not applied exclusively to African Americans, were applied to them with selective force and frequency and served as tool in a structure of racial domination. The Tuskegee experiment was drenched in racist assumptions in all its aspects.

The examples illustrate social workers operating in the terrain of the modern social welfare state. The 20th-century emergence of the massive bureaucratic social welfare state as the ground on which much of the profession operates dramatically affected virtually every aspect of the profession. The welfare state has accomplished much good, but the examples given here show that when turned to the wrong ends, it can inflict numbing degrees of oppression. When professionals follow commitments to social justice and resources are mobilized, however, reform can follow.

The profession to which Chief, Parish, and Buxton belonged and into which many readers of this text are preparing to enter has a history that extends back to the Progressive Era. Its origins are rooted in the dislocations and anxieties the country was experiencing at the time.

A PROFESSION TAKES FORM: 1880 TO 1930

In the late 19th and early 20th centuries, a profession recognizable as modern social work emerged. It came about in a period of great change. As the 19th century closed, the rapidly expanding industrial economy experienced severe economic fluctuations, bringing hardship for the working classes clustered in urban centers and jammed into crowded, unhealthy tenements. Labor unrest was met with violent repression. This was a time of enormous immigration: The labor of these new workers was essential to the economy, but native-born Americans were often unsettled by the influx of newcomers.

The new profession descended from the work of a group of reformers collectively known as the Charity Organization Societies (COS) movement, which sought to reshape the ways in which American poor had been receiving help. In the 50-year period from 1880 to 1930, COS currents mingled with those of a very different development, the settlement movement. Adding to the mixture were the efforts of various other urban reformers, some of whom overlapped with the settlement movement; these included the child-saving movement as well as researchers and writers with journalistic and academic connections. All this made for a rich and complex situation, full of options for shaping a new profession. The choices made in this period fundamentally shaped the course of the profession for many years, and they still, in large part, frame contemporary debates about the proper mission of social work. Those choices revolved around the themes of individual casework, the place of community, and the role of social reform in the profession.

COS Lineage: 1880s to 1920s

"Scientific charity" was the approach taken by the COS movement; it was an attempt to be organized, planful, and, above all, controlling with regard to the perceived menace of poverty, or "pauperism," as it was usually labeled. Led by upper-class representatives, mostly Protestant women, the movement sought to curb, if not totally eliminate, all publicly financed aid to the poor and to make relief strictly a private exercise of charity. This was to be done in a businesslike fashion, through careful investigation and coordination of casework to determine need, to distinguish those "worthy" of help from the "unworthy." It marked a break from the past in that religious proselytizing was to be banned from the work of helping the poor and replaced with a bureaucratic approach. Cities were divided into districts; records were maintained to ensure that no cases received overlapping help. Salaried staff known as "paid agents" performed necessary administrative and investigative functions.

The heart of the whole system, however, was the "friendly visitor," the volunteer who went to the homes of the poor to provide help to her social inferiors. "Scientific charity," according to its leading theorist, Josephine Lowell, "must be toward a person in an inferior circumstance to his benefactor. We cannot be charitable to our equals—in the sense of the word with which we are dealing" (Katz, 1996, p. 74). The help to be given was the advice and sterling moral example of a middle- or upper-class visitor who could somehow show them a better way—precisely how this was to be done was not very clear. The advice given was to be "friendly," yet dispensed without sentiment and—very important—to be given without money. Tangible expressions of aid, such as cash, were an absolute threat to the poor and could be given only in the most extreme situations because they would undermine the work ethic. "Not alms but a friend" was a gentle framing of the approach; "repressing pauperism" was a tougher frame.

Poverty was automatically assumed to be the result of personal moral failure; most often, the culprits were seen as sheer idleness and drink. If it proved absolutely impossible to avoid provision of publicly financed cash support, then the COS movement insisted that such aid be given only behind the walls of a residential institution for the poor—the poorhouse—and never in the form of "outdoor relief," or cash support given to people in their own homes. Under strict supervision in the poorhouse, proper discipline would impart moral renewal and ensure that appropriate deference was shown by the paupers to their benefactors.

These attitudes were codified into a "theory of scientific charity," as expressed in the writings of leaders such as Josephine Lowell (1884). Some leaders of the COS movement clung to their theory into the early 1900s, despite the fact that it was never possible to reach their goal of abolishing outdoor relief. The number of needy people fluctuated dramatically as the volatile late 19th-century economy underwent recessions and depressions that threw large numbers of even the most devoted adherents of the American work ethic into deep poverty (Katz, 1996, pp. 60–87; Lubove, 1969, pp. 1–20).

The COS movement was the response of uneasy upper classes to the social and economic dislocations of the time. The social control functions of the efforts were not disguised: Helping explicitly went hand in hand with self-conscious attempts to keep in their place immigrants, laboring classes, and the impoverished, who were seen as posing serious threats to American stability and well-being. Fear that the working class might come to demand help as a right was never far from the minds of COS leaders. Katz (1996) wrote that one such figure, Humphreys Gurteen, explicitly compared the threat of a rising class of poor demanding their "rights" to a Frankenstein monster accidentally created through too-liberal alms giving (Katz, p. 77). Friendly visiting was to be a method of calming class relations, a supplement to other forms of control, such as the use of armed troops to control strikes—something that first happened in the 1870s (Katz, p. 69). Ultimately, the COS movement drastically failed to achieve its goals; some of its most prominent leaders began to see that scientific charity was impotent in the face of structural causes of mass unemployment. In time, the intense moralizing and resistance to tangible help on the part of COS workers came to be seen as useless and even cruel by some of the movement's leading theorists. For example, by 1896 Josephine Lowell had left the COS behind and was advocating for higher wages for the working classes, union organizing, and economic reform. Another major COS leader, Edward Devine, would observe by the 1920s that he and others in the COS movement had actually "caused . . . pauperism by our failure to provide for the necessities of life" (Katz, p. 86).

For all its failures and negative features, it remains the case that modern social work can see in the COS work crude prototypes of some of its cherished features. The movement disengaged helping from religious proselytizing, established a focus on the individual situation, and enunciated the importance of individual investigation of situations. The movement promoted the value of careful administrative coordination of activities and the necessity of an objective, scientific approach to helping (even if the actual implementation of this imperative was anything but scientific or objective). However imperfectly these elements were implemented in COS activities, their importance as ideals was passed on to later caseworkers, who sought to improve upon them (Leiby, 1984).

Individual Casework Focus and Emergent Professional Identity: 1900s to 1920s

One COS caseworker who sought to better the COS movement's sorry track record was Mary Richmond. She provided national leadership in moving casework beyond the limits of friendly volunteer visiting by replacing the visitor with a professionally trained and salaried social caseworker. In her book *Social Diagnosis* (Richmond, 1917), the first major theoretical treatise of professional casework, Richmond presented her schema for analyzing individual need in the context of the dynamic interplay among six sets of "forces": family, personal, neighborhood, civic, private charity, and public relief. As Specht and Courtney (1994) put it, she was groping toward something later generations would term a *social systems approach*, but she was doing so before such theoretical formulations were available to her (p. 76). Her book was of enormous importance to caseworkers as they sought to define themselves as members of a new profession. The book, although short on what to do in terms of actual intervention once the careful social diagnosis was made, still stands out as a landmark on the road to professionalization because of its systematic approach, its focus on understanding the client in context of the environment, its theme of learning from the client through careful listening, and the goal of actually helping clients chart their own courses rather than imposing morally superior advice on them. Even before the appearance of her book, the COS movement had been inspired by Richmond's pleas for professionalization and professional education, leading to the establishment of the first formal training for professional social casework in 1897 at the New York School of Philanthropy (which eventually evolved into the Columbia University School of Social Work). By 1919, there were 17 such schools. Richmond joined the Russell Sage Foundation and used her position to encourage the development of social work education, publishing another important book, *What Is Social Case Work?* (Richmond, 1922).

Community Focus and Emergent Professional Identity: 1900s to 1920s

Katz, a leading historian of American social welfare, referred to the settings in which social work emerged as "the city wilderness" (1996, p. 163), a reference to how overwhelming the urban centers were for the flood of migrants and immigrants, many of whom spoke little, if any, English. The turn-of-the-century urban world was a daunting one for those at the lower ends of the social order: It featured crowded, unsanitary housing; an absence of government protections for workers; exploitation of child labor; political corruption; and intense poverty—all of which underscored the need for help.

As 20th-century casework evolved out of the failures of COS, the attention to environment flagged by Richmond led to a considerable focus on community, producing what historian Katz (1996) viewed as the use of a "mediation" approach. The mediators stood between individuals and families, on the one hand, and the complex, intense world of the industrial urban centers, on the other. When operating at their best, some of the COS workers drew on common sense and knowledge of the city's workings to help bewildered clients. Not promoted as part of the formal theory of scientific charity and done almost as an afterthought, Katz portrays this work as one of the most genuinely useful things COS workers did for clients. They "interceded with churches, relief agencies, and relatives. They accompanied clients to doctors, hospitals, and courts. They helped them find housing and jobs. In short, they became experts on urban survival" (Katz, p. 170).

Lubove (1969) provided a revealing, detailed examination of this mediation and linking function. The new, Richmond-style caseworkers became links between large institutional systems (medical hospitals, schools, mental institutions, and justice systems) and the neighborhoods and families from which clients came. Lubove identified a pattern that was repeated in a variety of institutional settings: Institutional administrators, realizing that their own professional goals could be enhanced if they had better knowledge of clients' lives outside the professional setting, turned to caseworkers and their home visits for this information. The emergence of medical social work illustrates the pattern of social workers as the eyes and ears of other professionals. In 1905, physician John Cabot instituted social services at the Massachusetts General Hospital in Boston. Influenced by earlier COS work in Baltimore and New York, Cabot's medical social service initiative marked an important development in the emergence of social casework. It established the precedent of social work in a host setting and use of the home visit as a key tool.

The new medical social workers were seen as enhancing three distinct medical purposes: (1) improving medical diagnoses, (2) enhancing patient compliance with prescribed medical interventions, and (3) helping alter the environment itself through public health initiatives. Physicians' diagnoses were aided by case-worker-provided information; for example, one Boston General doctor asked a caseworker to check out the validity of a patient's remarks: "This patient tells us stories of abuse at home by his sons. He is depressed and moody—Can you tell us what the conditions are there?" (Lubove, 1969, p. 28). Caseworkers could improve patient compliance with treatment plans by helping them understand and accept what must be done. As Lubove observed, "Immigrants and workers crowding the hospital clinics might comprehend a dispensary physician's diagnosis of tuberculosis but not necessarily the relevance of his prescription—plenty of sunlight, fresh air, ventilation, and high standards of personal hygiene to protect others" (p. 27). Social workers, too, had to struggle to see the relevance of the prescriptions, given the misery of the overcrowded tenement houses and the scarcity of sunlight, fresh air, and hygienic conditions there. Such observations eventually led some social workers to move into the realm of community and policy reform in an attempt to make such prescriptions meaningful. For example, social worker John Kingsbury became New York's Commissioner of Public Charities by moving up through COS ranks as a caseworker. His casework notebooks (Kingsbury, 1912) contain poignant descriptions of his attempts to implement the "sunshine, ventilation, good food, and sanitation" prescriptions of physicians for his poor tubercular clients in New York's tenements. For instance, the notes describe one young woman who regularly wrapped herself as warmly as she could, climbed the stairs of her tenement to the roof, and sat next to the chimney in her wooden chair, hoping the fresh air and sunshine would allow her to survive the disease and carry out her marriage plans. Kingsbury was not alone in being propelled in the direction of social reform and policy advocacy by such experiences.

The third, community, aspect of the new casework helped reduce the incidence of disease. Through such efforts as the crusade against tuberculosis, in which early social workers played leadership roles, it was shown that the community itself could organize in the interest of improved health. The net effect was to begin to "socialize" the hospital in the sense of extending health promotion efforts beyond the walls of the hospital into the community and bringing environmental information and resources inside the institutions (Lubove, 1969, p. 28).

The multiple, community-focused functions of the new casework, in hindsight, are impressive and seem eminently logical. Acceptance of them at the time, though, was anything but smooth. Despite Cabot's support, other physicians were often suspicious of the new caseworkers. Some doctors were intolerant of newcomers who might want to infringe on medical prerogatives. These attitudes were aggravated when the new caseworkers quickly decided to reject nurses as professional role models (in the sense that nurses were aides to doctors) and sought to emulate the professional standing of doctors themselves. The new social workers wanted to move beyond being the "eyes and ears" of physicians and relate to the doctors as one professional to another. Other physicians simply did not believe in the new environmental perspective and insisted that medicine was about the business of curing diseases, not making social calls. Acceptance of the new caseworkers proceeded by fits and starts, but the role did take hold, and a professional niche was created (although not necessarily on the "one professional-relating-to-another" terms the early social workers wanted).

The pattern of "socializing an institution" that Lubove (1969) described for medical social work is found in other professional areas. School social workers emerged when large, urban school systems needed someone to reach out beyond the walls of the school building. Similar developments occurred in mental institutions as new caseworkers helped psychiatrists strengthen their approach by cultivating community and family connections (Lubove, pp. 22–84).

Settlements, Social Reform, and Emergent Professional Identity: 1880s to 1930s

The Progressive Era, which extended approximately from 1880 to the outbreak of World War I, contained a remarkable outpouring of urban reform efforts, and the settlement movement is of particular interest to the history of social work. Settlements emerged side by side with Richmond-style, environmentally anchored casework. At times overlapping, at times in tension, and in some ways converging, the two developments were central to the emergence of social work. Other reform impulses of the time were important as well, such as the child-saving movement and the work of journalists and university-affiliated researchers.

"Spearheads for reform" is the apt term used by Davis (1967) to describe the settlement movement:

> The settlement house became one of the principal instruments in this first war on poverty. Located in the middle of the worst neighborhoods . . . it provided a center of sympathy, help, and hope to nearby slum dwellers. The settlement house, at its best became a social center, school, homemaking class, kindergarten, play and recreation center, and an informal housing and employment bureau. (pp. ii–vii)

Neighborhood improvement efforts drew settlement workers quickly into the larger arena of urban reform and politics:

> Settlement leaders quickly learned that it would be impossible to transform the neighborhood without also "reforming" urban society. Nearly all the questions they dealt with—education, labor standards, housing improvements, the condition of women and children parks and playgrounds, sanitation and so on—involved public policy . . . settlement workers, often

against their own predilections, were pulled into the vortex of politics. (Davis, 1967, p. viii)

The "house" of the settlement movement was the residence in which settlement workers lived in the midst of their impoverished neighbors. Some residents were volunteers, others had stipends, and others, including famous people of the day, came for visits. Beginning simply as "good neighbors" to the poor, they sought to learn from their neighbors, to teach them, and, bit by bit, to find their paths to ever-increasing usefulness to the neighborhood, city, and nation. Like their casework colleagues, settlement workers were intent on being systematic and scientific in their work (although they were less concerned about achieving professional status than were the caseworkers). They pioneered neighborhood surveys that documented residential patterns and community needs. This activity naturally led to university research connections. Settlement workers also formed partnerships with journalists such as Paul Kellogg, who gained social work fame with his comprehensive survey of community needs in Pittsburgh and his long tenure as editor of *Survey*, the leading social work journal of its time.

The American settlement movement was inspired by an English prototype, Toynbee Hall, although a distinctively American model quickly emerged. Katz (1996) summarized the American model's characteristics: It was more democratic, less sectarian, more likely to deal with immigrant populations, and had more pronounced social reform, social research, and social activism commitments than its British counterparts (Katz, p. 164). To this list, Skocpol (1992) added distinctively American gender dynamics: Women were much more important than in Britain; women outnumbered men, and, "perhaps most telling, the United States had many successful mixed-gender settlements in which women were leaders" (p. 346). A new generation of college-educated American women had found an opportunity to exercise their talents, and they went to it with vigor and success.

The first American settlement house was the Neighborhood Guild on the Lower East Side of New York (it eventually became the College Settlement). Settlement houses spread to many urban centers, numbering 400 by 1910 (Katz, 1996, p. 164). Lillian Wald's Henry Street Settlement gained a national reputation for social reform successes. By far the most famous settlement house was Hull House, established on Chicago's Halsted Street by Jane Addams and Ellen Gates Starr.

In addition to their pioneering work in policy and community advocacy, social research, and civic improvement, settlement house residents originated what has become one of the mainstays of social work practice: group work. As described by Schopler and Galinsky (1995), settlement workers discovered the value of group formats to pursue a wide-ranging agenda including advocacy "to fight for

improved housing, better working conditions, and increased recreational opportunities," educational groups for citizenship lessons, and early, experimental
efforts "to promote therapeutic groups . . . classes for treating tuberculosis in the
homes of the poor in 1907, meetings for youthful drug addicts at Hull House in
1909, and experimental groups for the emotionally disturbed at Chicago State
Hospital in 1918" (p. 1131). These early efforts emphasized the congruence of
group work with democratic principles and often stressed contact across cultural
and ethnic groups. By the 1940s, a more narrowly defined group treatment
approach, heavily influenced by psychoanalytic thought, prevailed. Over the
coming decades, a wide range of group models emerged, but the original group
work ideals of the settlement movement were not lost.

Another strand of reform mingling with all of the above approaches but having its own, distinctive roots is known as the *child-saving movement*, a term that
encompasses a large number of reform movements focused on rescuing and protecting children. Among the best-known early names associated with this movement is Charles Loring Brace, who, through the New York Children's Aid society,
pioneered the practice of relocating large numbers of needy and presumably
homeless children from the East to new homes in the North Atlantic and Midwest, often with farmers who needed labor. Between 1853 and 1929, it is estimated that more than 31,000 children were placed in homes through the work
of this society. In many ways, the practice was a revival of the colonial practice of
indentured servitude; as Costin (1985) put it, "There were charges that Brace's
program was based on prejudices against immigrants [and] that many of the
children were unnecessarily removed from their parents" (p. 39). By the beginning of the 20th century, greater attention was being placed to how foster placements were being handled and the process of professionalization had begun in
child welfare.

Women in the Settlement Movement. The women of the American settlement
movement have long fascinated scholars, and they occupy a central place in
women's history. Gordon (1991) furthered understanding of the intermingling
of race and gender among settlement women and other reformers in this period
by comparing the experiences of African American and white women reformers.
In an important study of women welfare activists extending from the Progressive
Era to World War II, Gordon found three main areas of differences. First, black
women were more likely to emphasize universal social programs with benefits
open to all citizens, whereas white women emphasized services delivered under
the supervision of caseworkers and dependent on detailed investigations of eligibility. In part, Gordon suggested, this difference indicates a higher level of con-
descension and suspicion of clients on the part of white reform leaders. Second,
black women were much more accepting of women working outside the home.

Finally, black women were much more likely than white women to openly advocate for the need to protect women from sexual victimization.

The ideal of the unmarried, professionally dedicated settlement worker who had no room in her life for marriage and the traditional family was prominent among white settlement workers of the Progressive Era, but it faded in importance after World War I. Walkowitz (1990) provided an accounting of the second generation of women social workers, who framed their gender identity in very different ways. In contrast to pre-World War I white settlement ideals, women social workers of the 1920s wanted to be both homemakers and professionals. They also sought full membership in the booming consumer economy of the 1920s, mistakenly anticipating that social work positions would pay well enough to guarantee them white-collar middle-class status. Seeking to blend "domesticity, career, and consumption," women social workers found no ready-made role models at hand and struggled to fashion new identities (p. 1052). As Walkowitz saw it, their struggles to attain a high level of consumerism (when in actuality the average social worker salary did not support it), high levels of professional autonomy (when the reality of much agency life emphasized routinization and high levels of supervision), and high levels of traditional domesticity framed many of the gender identity issues for women social workers over the coming decade.

Drawn from a close examination of eastern, urban, white, and Jewish women social workers, Walkowitz's (1990) account is intriguing, but it is limited in its application. To what extent was there a "second-generation" change in gender identity issues for black women social workers or women in rural areas of the country? Further research is needed to explore these ideas.

The Special Case of Jane Addams. By the early 20th century, settlement leader Jane Addams had become one of the best-known and admired Americans, eventually compiling a list of achievements (including the Nobel Peace Prize) so deep and rich that it continues to inspire to the present day. As Katz (1996) put it, "for people across the country, she embodied the transcendence of stale political division, the reconciliation of social divisions, the active service in the public interest central to the ideals of grass-roots progressivism" (p. 167). A recent upsurge in scholarly interpretations of her life, career, and political thought is testimony to her continuing and evolving impact on American culture as well as her status as an internationally acknowledged icon of social justice (Diliberto, 1999; Elshtain, 2002).

In terms of social work history, two things stand out. First, Addams's accomplishments have had enormous impact on the profession; they fundamentally helped shape it and made her a key figure in its development. Second, it is doubtful that she spent much time thinking about the professionalization of social work and that she thought of herself as a professional social worker in any meaningful way. Her concerns were with social justice, democratic ideals, and the protection of society's vulnerable—not professional identity, and not the development of professional standards and guidelines. As eminent historian Elshtain (2002) wrote, Addams "thought of those who came and went at Hull-House as citizens, or citizens-in-the-making, not as clients or receivers of service" (p. xxi).

It is true that she was elected as president of the National Conference on Charities and Corrections in 1910 (a forerunner of the National Conference of Social Work) and unsuccessfully sought the presidency of the National Conference of Social Work in 1922 (withdrawing when it became clear that she would lose, in part because of the public opinion backlash against her pacifist opposition to World War I). She did work closely with those who self-consciously identified themselves as social workers, and many contemporaries referred to her as one. However, it remains the case that she simply did not give high priority to profession-building efforts in the way, for example, that Hull House colleagues Sophonisba Breckenridge and Edith Abbott did when they devoted themselves to the establishment of social work education at University of Chicago and fought for high standards in the new profession (Shoemaker, 1998). Her impact on the profession came through her power to inspire rather through self-conscious attempts to build a profession. Although it is understandable and justifiable for social work to see her as one of its founding figures because of her inspirational example, it is a mistake to attempt to limit her to the role of social worker or see her as self-consciously devoting herself to the forging of a new profession in any sustained way.

Addams's personal qualities were memorable and were marked by a patient, humane respect for all who came her way. "She was a larger-than-life figure, of whom contemporaries, years after her death, still spoke with awe and reverence" (Elshtain, 2002, p. xxii). The narrative of her life and career is a compelling one: "As she made her way from a small town in rural Illinois to become the most famous female public figure of her time—an extraordinary pilgrimage, likened by some of Addams's admirers to that of Abraham Lincoln" (Elshtain, p. xxii). Her achievements in creating social services and leading various reforms were numerous and long lasting. Addams's leadership in pacificist opposition to American participation in World War I raised her international profile but brought about a decline in her public support—from "saint" to "villain" is how Davis (1973) referred to the transition. By 1931, four years before her death, she was awarded the Nobel Prize, and her standing as one of the country's most admired persons had recovered. Addams's role as original political thinker is a profound one, and one that only recently has come into its own. As Elshtain pointed out, full appreciation of her political thought, as distinct from her social service achievements, has been slow in coming, but signs suggest a contemporary resurgence of interest in it as seen, for example, in the widespread attention given to Knight's (2005) analysis of Addams's role as a political philosopher as well as social activist.

THE PROFESSION COALESCES: PIVOTAL DECISION IN THE 1930S AND CONTINUING DEBATE

A rich mixture of elements was available to shape the new profession: Richmond's version of casework, with its strong environmental focus; the settlement movement's emphasis on community development, social reform, and political involvement; and a commitment to systematic, careful procedures that were as scientific as possible to undergird helping efforts. By 1930, a fascinating development had occurred that stands as a landmark in the profession's history: Leadership of the profession had passed firmly into the hands of casework, but not the environmentally focused casework pioneered by Richmond. Instead, an inner-directed psychiatric version emerged. What accounts for this turn of events? Most scholars agree that it was shaped in large part by the new profession's intense drive to be accepted as a "real" profession with a unique mission, a scientific base for practice and strict control, by way of education, over who could enter it. That most prestigious of all professions, medicine, was adopted as a role model.

Lubove (1969) provided the classic account of developments. The early psychiatry—social work link proved to be important to the emerging field of casework, and at first it followed the familiar pattern of reaching out beyond the walls of clinics and institutions into patients' homes and communities. Psychiatric social workers, however, quickly began to de-emphasize environment as they emulated their psychiatrist mentors. Increasingly, inner-directed psychology came to dominate this branch of casework: The emphasis was "personality" over "environment." Around 1920, as Lubove observed, it was clear that "a critical decision facing social workers . . . was whether to continue along the lines of the psycho-social casework expounded by Mary Richmond . . . or to embrace the psychotherapy which some psychiatric social workers were beginning to view with favor" (p. 83). As it turned out, the psychiatric framework eclipsed the Richmond model. The psychiatric caseworker emerged as the "queen of the caseworkers" in terms of status, pay, and professional visibility (p. 86). This triumph went hand in hand with another development: growing social work acceptance of Freudian thought. It was the Freudian—psychiatric—caseworker model that prevailed. Although illustrations of psychoanalytic fervor are plentiful in the historical literature, Lubove let social worker Ethel Ginsberg's comment represent them all as she looked back, from the vantage point of 1940, on the great inroads Freudian thought had made in American social work by then: "How sterile our work was before Freud and how fertile it has become through his genius" (p. 88).

By 1930, Freudian-influenced, psychiatric casework was presented in much of the professional literature as the leading model of social work practice in virtually all areas of casework, including school social work, medical social work, and family guidance.

Freudian thought provided a new, "scientific" body of theory for the profession that would, one hoped, give social work a unique niche in the world of professions. (A nagging problem remained, though: How, exactly did psychiatric casework differ from psychiatry?) Another way to look at these developments is to consider the famous Abraham Flexner speech of 1915. Flexner, a physician and leading medical educator who was fresh on the heels of revolutionizing medical education in the United States, was asked by the National Conference of Charities and Corrections, the largest organization of social workers, to address its members on the question of whether social work was a profession. "Definitely not" was his response, and, moreover, social work would never be a profession until it met criteria that seemed reasonable to him. His criteria, unsurprisingly, reflected an idealized accounting of medicine's professional contours. A profession, he pronounced, must have a unique role in society, a scientific basis, a method for translating the knowledge produced by science into practical ends, a specific technique that could be passed on through professional education, and its own professional literature (Austin, 1983).

Chief among Flexner's criteria was the need to develop a unique professional "technique" that could be passed on through formal education. Much of the professional development in the 1920s can be seen as a drive to live up to Flexner's charge by narrowing the profession's focus to one particular framework: psychiatry. In considering these efforts, however, it is important to keep in mind Lubove's (1969) observation that when one says that psychiatric casework dominated the profession by 1930 and kept its leadership position well into the 1950s, one is speaking primarily in terms of nationally visible spokespersons, leading publications, and dominant influences in schools of social work. These were certainly hugely important matters, but they were not the totality of social work. This leading influence was primarily an urban (Eastern and Midwestern), white, and largely women's phenomenon. Despite this high-profile, public face of the profession, the actual extent to which psychiatric, particularly Freudian, frameworks were implemented in day-to-day social work practice is still open to question (Field, 1980). Even with this caveat in mind, though, it remains true that the psychiatric turning point was a profoundly important professional development because it determined the leading public face of the profession.

The decision to embrace a narrow, psychiatric version of casework as the profession's core identity by 1930 remains a flashpoint for debate about the historical legacy and true mission of social work in light of the growth of private practice and popularity of clinical social work in recent decades. Lubove (1969) described the consequences of the 1930 turning point as momentous: It "deflected social work's attention from the social and cultural environment and from relevant insights provided by the social sciences" (p. 117). Ironically, he pointed out, when the profession turned from Richmond's environmentally anchored casework to the inner-focused, psychotherapeutic model, it actually undermined, rather than strengthened, the new profession's search for security and a unique identity:"

> If psychiatric knowledge and technique were fundamental to social work, then what distinguished the social worker from the psychiatrist, and social casework from psychotherapy, except the social worker's inferior training? It was one thing to reject Mary Richmond's formulation, or minimize social work's liaison and resource mobilization function, but quite another to fail in substituting some specific alternative function which really differentiated the social worker from the psychiatrist. (p. 117)

Another influential historian, Katz (1996) visited the same point in a trenchant, if not caustic, summary: Social work

> chose the wrong alternative. As social workers rejected urban mediation and abandoned social reform, they became second-class therapists, inferior in standing, if not in competence, to psychologists and psychiatrists. . . . With some irony social workers did not in fact become either therapists or professionals. Instead, they became badly paid servants of bureaucracies and the state. (p. 172)

To be sure, the intense search for a unique identity, status, prestige, and improved salaries was fundamental to the psychiatric turning point. That quest, however, is not the whole story. The dramatic impact of World War I (1914–1918) on society must be taken into account. As Davis (1967) demonstrated, the war, in the name of patriotism, snuffed out much of the Progressive Era's lively debate about societal reform. Following the war, a conservative backlash produced a national Red Scare (a wave of paranoia about the threat of communist subversion from within accompanied by large-scale political repression—a forerunner of a similar phenomenon in the early 1950s). In this period of social and political backlash, social criticism became a risky enterprise, and Jane Addams saw society undergoing a general "political and social sag" (Davis, p. 229). Jane Addams also saw her own popularity plunge as she was branded a socialist and communist for her peace efforts during World War I and her social reform positions (for example, the Daughters of the American Revolution ejected her from their membership). Although her standing as one of the country's most admired figures had recovered by the time of her death in 1935, the drastic fluctuation in her popularity signified the rapid pace of change in society as a whole.

Other limitations to the Lubove (1969) and Katz (1996) analyses must be kept in mind. Lubove's history ends in the early 1930s; thus, it misses the meaningful resurgence of activism and reform in social work circles produced in the 1930s New Deal era (Leighninger, 1987, p. 75). A similar process occurred in the 1960s, spurred by the civil rights movement and the War on Poverty (Jansson, 1997, pp. 232–234).

Katz's (1996) assertion that social work has never become a profession is a highly sensitive one that is not infrequently heard (Hopps & Collins, 1995) and is extremely controversial. The charge, though, is not sustainable—however much the profession's history is marked by a nearly obsessive worry over this very point. Austin (1983) offered a breath of fresh air and a wider perspective on the issue. He visited, yet again, the psychiatric turning point, this time by means of a systematic analysis of the Flexner speech, which he saw as a leading impetus of the drive toward medical–psychiatric professionalism. Flexner's pronouncement that social work was not a profession and could only become one by emulating medicine, Austin concluded, was "probably . . . the most significant event in the development of the intellectual rationalization for social work as an organized profession" (p. 357). Social work, he argued, too naively took Flexner to heart. In a compelling analysis, he dissected logical flaws in the Flexner argument and concluded that social work should stop trying to live up to the physician's long-ago pronouncement: "It is time to exorcise his ghost and turn our attention to the significant issues that emerge from the distinctive social responsibilities of professional social work" (Austin, p. 375). To exorcise that ghost, it is time for social work to, in effect, relax and accept that it already is an established, major profession, regardless of what some sociologists or historians might say: "When, or if, social workers themselves believe that social work is an established profession, and act on that belief, other groups in society are likely to agree" (p. 375).

Austin (1983) argued that an occupation is recognized as a profession when it asserts "the right to be accorded such recognition by other professional groups and can make it hold" (p. 374). In seeking too hard to prove to others that social work is, indeed, a scientifically based profession, wrote Austin, there occurred a nonproductive preoccupation with (a) defining a unitary model of social work practice that would smoothly integrate the strikingly wide range of tasks and functions addressed by social work and (b) a de-emphasis of such things as case management, social care, and mediating tasks as being "not professional." Both preoccupations should be set aside. The profession should make peace with the facts that it is a diverse, multifaceted enterprise and that a single, intellectually elegant "unitary model" of practice is not likely to be reached any time soon. Acceptance of those facts, coupled with increased self-assurance about social work's existing, achieved professional status, will allow social workers to accept that increased attention to case management, linking–mediating tasks, and social reform will enhance, not diminish, professional status, because those activities speak to unique functions not addressed by other professions and are faithful to original elements in social work's historic mission.

Debate about the "true" nature of social work and the competing claims for leadership that come from the multiple sectors of the profession will undoubtedly continue (for example, see Specht & Courtney, 1994). As it does, interpretations of the profession's historical record will play an important role. An important element of the historical record is the place of the modern welfare state in the development of the profession.

MODERN WELFARE STATE DEVELOPMENT: GENDER, RACE, AND INEQUALITY

The emergence of the modern welfare state is intimately involved with social work's development. Blurred boundaries between public and private service sectors (caused by developments such as contracting, licensing, accreditation, and other regulatory functions) mean that even social workers not working for a government agency are deeply affected by the decisions made by local and federal governments. The welfare state is not simply a backdrop for the profession's historical development: Social workers have played key roles in shaping the welfare state, and the state, in turn, has profoundly shaped the profession.

Maternalist, Paternalist, and "Manly" Welfare State Construction: Post–Civil War to 1920s

The remarkable outpouring of reform energy shown in the Progressive Era was, in large part, women's energy. This characteristic led one prominent scholar (Skocpol, 1992) to assess these early steps toward an American welfare state as an exercise in "maternalist" welfare state construction. The maternalist framing fits because of the leadership role of women; because women themselves framed their social reform goals in maternal conceptualizations such as national "social housekeeping" efforts and roles as "mothers of the nation"; and, finally, because the substance of the policy reforms targeted women and children (Skocpol). In a famous phrase of the time, American culture relegated women to a "separate sphere" of activity, apart from men—a sphere dominated by emotions and the nurturing of family and economic dependence on men. Historians, most notably Skocpol, have shown how Progressive-era women worked within the separate-sphere social identities assigned them, expanded those identities, and succeeded in redefining themselves as politically powerful caretakers for the community and nation.

Maternalist successes are more fully appreciated when put in the context of American paternalist policy failures. In the late 19th century, when western

European countries were developing early versions of the modern welfare state centered on benefits for working men and their dependents, the United States was conspicuously devoid of such developments—with one exception. The one arena in which the United States showed dramatic welfare growth was the rise of a national system of Civil War pensions for Union veterans. This system, however, was extinguished by the 1920s. Its ending was something of a temporary dead end in welfare state development.

The Civil War pension system story is important and not widely known (Skocpol, 1992). Although it has been common to argue that the federal government did not involve itself in a major way in welfare programs until the New Deal era, Skocpol pointed out the inaccuracy of this view. The federal government actually developed its first large-scale welfare program in the aftermath of the Civil War, when Congress passed retirement and disability benefits for Union veterans. Over time, benefits were liberalized and benefits for dependents added. Largely because of Republican and Democratic competition to liberalize benefits to win elections, the Civil War pension system evolved into a large, fairly generous for its time, welfare system that was administered without the stigma often associated with welfare. Skocpol summed up the reach of this early welfare system: "In 1910, approximately 35% of northern men aged 65 and over were on the pension rolls, whereas less than 10 percent of men residing in the South were federal pensioners (some of these were ex-slave veterans and many others were white Union veterans who had migrated from the North)" (pp. 135–136).

The Civil War generation died away by the 1920s, and the generous system of social provision died with it and was not replaced with a European-style, "paternalist" welfare state. That style of welfare state can be thought of as paternalist because the typical pattern in Europe was for male-operated state bureaucracies to administer social provisions (various industrial social insurances) to male workers and their dependents. One might have expected that the large-scale federal involvement in welfare represented by the Civil War pension system would have paved the way for a permanent federal welfare role by the early 20th century. The first two decades of the 20th century, however, saw a series of unsuccessful attempts to establish paternalist national policies in the areas of health insurance, unemployment insurance, and old-age insurance, and courts and various levels of American government were highly resistant to the proposals. (Yet, in some policy areas modest achievements occurred at individual state levels, as in the case of experimentation with state-level unemployment insurance and workmen's compensation). In part, resistance to institutionalizing a paternalistic national welfare state structure in the 1920s grew out of reformers' fear of the manner in which electoral politics had propelled the growth of the Union pension system. In a manner that showed a direct line of descent from the COS fear of welfare and "outdoor relief," reformers by the 1920s were fearful that institutionalizing social welfare on the generous, dignified terms found in the pension system would be a corrupting step—in effect, buying votes with welfare.

In contrast to the stalled paternalist welfare structure of the 1920s, the same period saw a string of remarkable American successes in establishing social provisions for women and children, in effect creating significant steps in the direction of a maternalist welfare state. Creation of the federal Children's Bureau, widespread adoption of state-level mother's pensions (an early form of welfare for women and dependent children), and an array of protections for women in the workplace all constituted remarkable achievements in an era when most comparable initiatives for male workers were rejected. The contrast is all the more striking when one considers that before 1920 most American women were not allowed to vote. Women achieved these successes through a massive, highly coordinated national system of women's clubs and social reform movements. A crucial element in their successes was the formulation of an ideology of civic improvement framed in terms of women as caretakers of modern civilization. In the words of Skocpol (1992), there was a "remarkable kind of maternalist political consciousness at a time when U.S. industrial workers were not very politically class-conscious . . . American women used their clubs and federations to engage in 'municipal housekeeping' and to propose new public social policies to help mothers, children, and families" (p. 529). Important leadership elements in this drive for maternalist social welfare policy came from women in the newly developing social work profession—although social work was only one among many sectors involved.

The incipient national maternalist welfare state did not come to be, however. The important steps taken in the 1920s were not followed by a maternalist wave of development in the next phase of social welfare state development: the creation of the 1930s New Deal array of policies and programs, created in response to the economic devastation and political turmoil created by the 1929 crash in the economy and the resulting Great Depression. In the New Deal era, the country took a different direction than that envisioned by the women social welfare leaders of the 1920s; nevertheless, their achievements stand out as a remarkable chapter in the history of social welfare and social work. By putting their stamp on the proto-welfare state developments of the 1920s, women leaders, including social workers, had put in place policies, organizations, and arguments that would have a prominent place in the next phase of welfare state development: the New Deal.

As influential as Skocpol's (1992) interpretation of maternalist and paternalist welfare state efforts has been, it is not without its critics. For example, Gordon (1994) emphasized the long-term oppressive consequences of the separate sphere concept and underscored the low level of payments under the mother's pensions and the worthiness-based behavioral controls that accompanied such payments, thus questioning the reality of the reform represented by the Progressive Era mother's pension. Instead, Gordon saw the creation of a "two-track" system of social welfare: The lower track (public assistance) targeted and discriminated against women, and a higher track (social insurance) provided better treatment for men, which institutionalized gender inequality in the welfare state.

Critics also point out that not all women's achievements in this period can be seen as working within the constraints of the separate sphere. For example, Wilkerson-Freeman (2002) described a "subversive feminist dominion" of interracialist social workers in Georgia that emerged in the 1920s and 1930s. Using strategies different from the maternalist ones described by Skocpol (1992), female social workers in Georgia succeeded in federalizing previously federal–state New Deal relief activities and, in so doing, created a temporary "domain" in which long-standing, racist state social welfare policies were explicitly challenged.

Willrich (2000) drew attention to another aspect of gender relations in the Progressive Era. He argued that insufficient attention has been paid to the regulation of male breadwinners by women of the time and suggested refining Gordon's (1994) two-track (male and female) thesis of Progressive Era welfare to include the creation of a "third policy track: the criminalization, regulation, and punishment of able-bodied male breadwinners who failed to support their families" (Willrich, p. 461). Willrich analyzed the growth of family courts, such as the one created in Chicago that worked hand in hand with women from Hull House and other social reform circles to punish men who were not performing their family support role (judges came to rely heavily on presentencing recommendations from women caseworkers). Without minimizing the overriding issue of hegemonic patriarchy in the society of the time, Willrich enriched our understanding by pointing to the creation of a woman's domain in which men were subjected to corrective interventions for not fulfilling societally defined gender roles.

Yet another fascinating and important view of gender issues in the Progressive Era is found in Murphy's (2001) research on Progressive Era ideals of "manliness" in New York City reform politics. In his analysis, the struggle between Progressive Era reformers and the New York City political machine was not simply a contest between political machines and reformers. Instead, male reformers, in effect, sought to create their own, noncorrupt political and social machine; that is, they "attempted to replace what they believed was a corrupt system with new sets of institutions and associations that organized men across class, ethnic, and generational lines" (Murphy, p. 3). In the first wave of Progressive Era reform, machine opponents fought back with language that sought to characterize male reformers as sentimental, impractical, effeminate, mollycoddles—in sum, less than masculine. These categories, says Murphy, "emerged, in part, from a discourse in which nonpartisan male reformers were alleged to be members of a 'third sex' or 'intermediate sex'" (p. 4).

In an interesting turn of events, in the second stage of reform, divisions occurred within the reform camp itself, often over U.S. imperialist foreign policy. Militarist reform leaders, such as Theodore Roosevelt, seized on charges of deficient masculinity to stigmatize their opponents within their own reform circles ("unmanly" was one of Roosevelt's most common epithets in describing men who differed with his policy positions). Thus, reform circles themselves adopted "the sexual invective of party politicians to cast aspersions on reform opponents, many of whom held anti-imperialist and socialist views" (Murphy, 2001, p. 4). Murphy traced the emergence of "militarist" and "pacifist" wings of New York reform circles, with men of the latter group subjected to repeated sexual identity aspersions.

In summary, gender issues in the Progressive Era are fascinatingly complex. In the midst of a patriarchal society, a new generation of college-educated women, still without the vote, took the lead in carving out an area of substantial social welfare accomplishment for women and children by working with and pushing the boundaries of the separate sphere of women's activities. Concurrently, a woman's domain of control over men who were failing to support their families was created by way of family courts. Finally, among men (at least in New York City and probably in other locales), reform became intertwined with battles, often invective filled, over ideals of masculinity, struggles that reached within and split male Progressive Era reform circles.

Bifurcated Welfare State: 1930s New Deal to 1960s War on Poverty and Beyond

Central, distinguishing characteristics of the modern American welfare state that emerged from Franklin Roosevelt's New Deal administration are its "bifurcated" and "reluctant" nature (Jansson, 1997; Skocpol, 1988). It is reluctant because the American version of welfare was late in emerging, has less generous benefits, and is incomplete compared with Western European systems (for example, the United States has no comprehensive national health insurance or national family allowance system). It is bifurcated because it has a two-part, or split-level, structure that consists of a fundamental institutional and political division between the "respectable," politically strong Social Security level and a stigmatized, politically vulnerable "welfare" level (Skocpol, 1988, p. 295). The top tier has a long history of powerful connotations of being "earned" benefits for the "worthy." The lower, welfare, level exists in what Katz (1996) called "the shadow of the poorhouse" and has ungenerous benefits and a history of stigmatizing "unworthy" beneficiaries.

The differences between the two are not accidental. New Deal architects were careful to distinguish between social insurance and welfare, and they invested considerable resources and ingenuity in elevating the image of social insurance in the public mind and derogating the image—and reality—of welfare (Cates, 1983). Separation of the two parts of the social welfare system was reinforced by New Deal failure to embrace national full employment policies—which, if achieved, would have placed more people under the protection of the work-related upper tier (Skocpol, 1988).

Former settlement house participants and social workers from the preceding decades played key roles in the creation of the New Deal welfare state and its evolution over the following decades. Such social work figures included Frances Perkins (first Secretary of Labor), Julia Lathrop (first director of the federal Children's Bureau), Grace Abbot (another director of the Children's Bureau), Florence Kelly (leader of the Consumer League), Harry Hopkins (Roosevelt's first director of national relief efforts), and John Collier (New Deal director of the Bureau of Indian Affairs) (Trattner, 1986).

Much of social work's efforts have been focused on poorer clients occupying the lower tier of the bifurcated welfare state. This emphasis has had important, complex ramifications. At times the profession has had a good track record of advocating for the needy in policy circles, particularly during the New Deal and War on Poverty eras (Spano, 1982; Specht & Courtney, 1994). Conversely, the profession has a history of ambivalence about its association with poverty, welfare, and the stigmatized. One manifestation of this ambivalence has been the sometimes wide gap between professional social work circles and the realm of public welfare officials. The gap is an ironic and unfortunate phenomenon for many reasons, not the least being the central role played by social workers in the creation of the federal–state system of public assistance programs. From 1935 until the early 1950s, social worker Jane Hoey directed the federal Bureau of Public Assistance, which had administrative oversight for federal–state public assistance. The energy and commitment Hoey showed over nearly two decades of leadership were formidable. Leighninger (1987) told of one governor who telephoned Washington, DC, to complain about the "red-haired devil" in his office (Hoey) ordering him around on welfare matters (p. 91). She fought for a just implementation of welfare that would provide benefits with respect and dignity. Too often, however, she was overruled and even censured for her efforts by administrative superiors in the Social Security Board/Social Security Administration who either feared the development of a too-liberal welfare program or simply did not see the programs as worth the effort (Cates, 1983, 1988).

Given the historically close alignment between economic and racial divisions in this country, the bifurcated, or split-level, construction of the welfare state has meant the lines have been "racially charged" (Skocpol, 1988, p. 302). African

Americans were overwhelmingly excluded from the top (social insurance) portion of the welfare state at the time of its creation. The original 1935 Social Security Act excluded agricultural and small-firm labor from both unemployment and old-age social insurance. Consequently, most African Americans were excluded from initial coverage, a situation that had deep, long-lasting consequences. Too much New Deal labor and social welfare legislation was "a sieve with holes sized so that the majority of our workers would drop through," observed the National Association for the Advancement of Colored People's (NAACP's) Charles Houston (1935, p. 4). In the lower tier, public assistance features were built into the New Deal public assistance provisions of the Social Security Act that gave the South a free hand to treat African Americans in a severely discriminatory way.

Between World War I and the mid-1950s, African Americans transformed themselves from a predominantly rural to a predominantly urban population, and they emerged as powerfully concentrated clusters of swing votes in national elections. Then, as a result of victories achieved in the modern civil rights victories of the 1960s, African Americans became powerfully incorporated into national electoral processes. They were then positioned to press for improved access to all aspects of the modern welfare state and, in effect, to undo the racial overlay of the welfare state division.

Unfortunately, this change did not occur. The 1960s War on Poverty achieved many successes (Levitan & Taggert, 1976; Plotnick & Skidmore, 1975), but it failed utterly to eliminate the deep pockets of northern, inner-city, African American poverty that originated in Progressive Era migration and segregation. In fact, many scholars believe the War on Poverty inadvertently escalated racial polarization in the welfare state as a result of its failure to abolish poverty and to overcome the New Deal's exclusion of African Americans from full participation in the upper tier of the welfare state. In addition, the proximity of the War on Poverty to both the civil rights movement and the devastating urban riots of the 1960s precipitated a serious white backlash in which perceptions of race, violence, and welfare were blurred in a confused, stereotyped, and powerful fashion (Lieberman, 1998; Quadagno, 1994). Racial divisions in the welfare state have a long history and remain a central concern that is discussed in the next section.

Racial Duality in the Welfare State and the Profession: Post–Civil War to the 1960s

As Orfield (1988), a leading scholar of segregation and desegregation, observed, "Race is the most fundamental cleavage in American history" (p. 314). This view resonates both with legendary African American scholar W.E.B. DuBois's (1996) famous declaration that "the problem of the twentieth century is the problem of the colour-line" (p. 625) and with contemporary social policy analyst William

Julius Wilson's (1999) plea, on the eve of the 21st century, to overcome the nation's racial divide.

Ringer's (1983) conceptual framework of racial duality is a useful way to view the historical intertwining of racism, social welfare, and social work. In this formulation, the United States' history is situated in the total history of "five centuries of white European expansion throughout the world" by forceful conquest and domination of nonwhite populations (Ringer & Lawless, 1989, p. xiii). In the emerging American nation–state, white colonists (colonialists) built a two-part sociopolitical structure that was a template for the nation's future struggles over racial equality. One realm, which Ringer termed the domain of "we the people," was "rooted in the rights and sovereignty of the people and regulated by the normative code of the American creed" (p. 8). The American creed enshrined the democratic rights of full citizenship. Entry into this "people's domain" was initially restricted to whites. The other domain, outside the circle of we the people, has been governed by a racial creed legitimating the use of force, exploitation, and fraud to subordinate nonwhite groups. In this analysis, the concept of race has been a sociopolitical construction, not a biological one. The term has often been used as shorthand for both race and ethnicity—a point vividly demonstrated by the fact that definitions of white and nonwhite vary considerably throughout history. The coexistence of these two domains (we the people and others) is a fundamental structural duality in American history. Much of that history is one of struggles by the excluded to achieve entry into the full democratic rights of the people's domain. Each racial or ethnic group's history has been a series of unique encounters with this structure of duality, and those encounters permeate the history of social welfare and social work in ways not yet fully understood.

African American Struggles with Duality. The size of the African American population, the extent to which black exclusion and segregation were written into the legal and political foundations of the country, and the intensity of the struggles to overcome those obstacles have in many ways made the African American the "central nonwhite figure in a [national] racial drama" (Ringer, 1983, p. 153). African American duality was enforced through three distinct systems of separation and control, discussed by Orfield (1988): slavery, Jim Crow segregation, and the modern urban ghetto. Slavery was overturned only after a long struggle that culminated in the United States' bloodiest war. Jim Crow segregation emerged after the Civil War and produced a rigid system of racial separation and discrimination backed by the use of lethal force, including lynchings. Although the precise origins of the phrase "Jim Crow" are obscure and uncertain, the label refers to a system of local and state laws that, peaking in southern and border states, codified a system of racial segregation that touched virtually all aspects of life (Vann, 1966). By 1880, the system of Jim Crow segregation had achieved acceptance at the national level by leading white intellectuals, political leaders, and most of the general white population. It was not overturned until the African American civil rights successes of the 1960s.

The third system of separation and control has been the modern urban ghetto: racially segregated pockets of inner-city poverty. This system has its origins in the fierce residential segregation that faced African Americans as they migrated north in the first half of the 20th century. This system has changed little since the last major national antipoverty effort in the 1960s, and it constitutes the central dilemma of the modern welfare state.

The profession of social work emerged in the midst of national white acceptance of Jim Crow segregation. The emergent profession was overwhelmingly white. Systematic denial of African American access to education of all types, coupled with growing insistence on graduate education as the key to professional entry, meant that racial duality was deeply imprinted into the structure of the new profession. Every facet was affected: who joined the profession, who was served by it, the nature of its interventions, its knowledge base, the profession's policy and reform priorities, and the content of social work education. For the most part, social workers of the Progressive Era functioned within limits set by prevailing white racist norms. This theme is encapsulated in an incident that is often pointed to as one of the high points of social work's political influence during the Progressive Era.

In 1912, Theodore Roosevelt bolted the Republican Party and ran for president as the candidate of the Progressive party, a campaign many progressive social workers saw as "the climax of their long struggle for social justice" (Davis, 1967, p. 194). Social workers had written the industrial and social planks of the party platform, and the best-known social worker in the country, Jane Addams, was chosen to speak in favor of the Roosevelt's nomination. Addams was presented with a dilemma, however: White southern progressives objected to the seating of African American delegates from their states. Coming on the heels of an earlier, losing fight to have a "Negro equality" plank written into the Progressive Party platform, Addams found their objections hard to take. Roosevelt, however, decided against challenging the white supremacists, fearing he would lose the national election without southern support. Jane Addams, too, reluctantly acquiesced, and the southern African American delegates were rejected. Addams subsequently tried to explain to the African American community both her own and the Progressive Party's positions on race in an article published in the NAACP's journal, *Crisis*, arguing that if the Progressives achieved national office, a general era of reform would ensue that would, over the long run, improve race relations (Addams, 1912).

This incident illustrates that racial justice was seen as too much to add to the progressive reform agenda: It was feared that standing up to racism would undermine the ability to achieve anything else of substance. In addition to this calculation of what appeared politically feasible, the thinking of white settlement leaders and caseworkers was not free of the racist stereotyping of the day. Even Jane Addams, as Iglehart and Becerra (2000) pointed out, was capable of telling 1908 African Americans that their progress was, in part, blocked by their own cultural disadvantages in that they lacked "some of the restraints of the traditions which . . . [Italians, Greeks, and Russians] bring with them." (p. 122)

For the most part, white social workers were indeed, in the words of Allen (1974), "reluctant reformers" when it came to racial justice. Katz's (1996) summary of Chicago settlement leaders' attitudes toward racial justice also captured the tone of most of the national white settlement and caseworker movement:

> Jane Addams, Edith Abbott, Sophonisba Breckenridge, and Florence Kelley led the left wing of the settlement movement. They understood how blacks had been exploited. . . . Nonetheless, when it came to practical policies, no differences separated them from their more openly racist colleagues. . . . The more liberal settlement leaders advocated economic and political equality, but not social equality; worked hard to improve black living conditions within the ghetto; and accepted segregation either as inescapable or desirable. All of them refused to integrate their settlement houses. Even when the racial compositions of their neighborhoods changed, most settlements remained white islands, and [only a] . . . handful of settlements opened to serve blacks. (p. 183)

Katz (1996) and Kusmar (1976) traced the origins of the modern inner-city pockets of African American poverty to the Progressive Era racial segregation that was imposed on the newly arriving African American migrants. Katz argued that Progressive Era leadership's acceptance of residential segregation implicates them in the creation of the modern black urban ghetto (p. 181). The experiences of black urban communities have been fundamentally different from the experiences of immigrants:

> The history of Chicago's blacks and of blacks in every other city, did not recapitulate the experiences of European immigrants. No immigrant group ever lived in neighborhoods as segregated as the black ghetto. With each decade, as they left the center of cities for new homes in the suburbs, European immigrants and their children lived in less segregated surroundings. By contrast, black segregation, higher from the start, continued to increase. European immigrants were allowed, even encouraged to move out of ethnic enclaves; blacks were prevented from leaving the ghetto. (Katz, p. 182)

White tactics to enforce segregation included a wide range of devices, including the use of force against blacks who tried to move into white neighborhoods; the burning of crosses on lawns; the creation of restrictive covenants (home purchase contracts that prohibited reselling to African Americans); the formation of white neighborhood organizations (ostensibly to promote neighborhood well-being but actually intended to monitor the racial composition of the neighborhood); agreements among real estate agents to "steer" African American customers away from white neighborhoods; and "redlining," the practice of racial discrimination in the mortgage and insurance industries (Dreier, 1996; Farley, 1996). Another key factor was the de facto underwriting of residential segregation by the federal government itself in its post-1930s Federal Housing Administration home mortgage programs, which were operated for decades in a manner that was "whites only" (Calmore, 1996).

Although the white face put to professional social work in the Progressive Era dominated until the civil rights movement of the 1950s and 1960s, important African American currents of social work practice and education had existed from the turn of the century onward. African Americans created their own settlement houses and other social welfare systems, developed their own schools of social work, and created their own approaches to social work practice while they fought against exclusion and oppression. In so doing, they not only served their own communities but made vital contributions to the social work profession as a whole (Carlton-LaNey, 2001; Gordon, 1991; Iglehart & Becerra, 2000; Ross, 1978).

One of the first professionally trained African American social workers was George Edmund Haynes, who in 1910 graduated from the New York School of Philanthropy. Attending school on a New York COS fellowship, he specialized in the study of social problems of blacks who had migrated to the urban north (Carlton, 1982). His growing expertise in this area eventually led to his leadership role in the founding of the National League on Urban Conditions Among Negroes, later to become the National Urban League (NUL). This organization grew to national scope and became the first major social welfare agency designed to serve the needs of urban African Americans. As executive director of the NUL, Haynes established the country's first formal training program in social services (although not a full-fledged school of social work) for African Americans at Fisk University in Nashville. He was clear about the need for black social workers and black-focused professional social work education: "To know people very well one must live with them . . . [and] share with them the life of the Negro world. . . . Only Negroes live within that world" (Carlton, p. 90).

Except for token representation in some white schools, African Americans, until the midpoint of the 20th century, turned primarily to Atlanta University and Howard University for graduate social work education—and before 1920, even those options were not available. Another early African American social worker, Jesse O. Thomas (1967), observed, "In 1919–1920 there was not a colored person who had received training at an accredited school of social work south of Washington or east of St. Louis" (p. 117). Thomas, head of the southern branch of the NUL at the time, had been asked to address the 1920 National Conference of Social Workers in New Orleans. In a setting that graphically embodied the intersection of social work and Jim Crow segregation, African American social workers were made to sit in the gallery while white social workers sat on the main floor of the conference hall. Thomas refused to give his speech under these segregated conditions, upon which the whites moved to the gallery and listened to his appeal for the creation of a black school of social work at Atlanta University, something that was accomplished within the year. When Howard University, in Washington, DC, began to offer social work training in 1935 (a fully accredited school of social work was developed by 1943), the two universities became the nation's leading sources of professionally educated African American social workers.

Forrester B. Washington, long-time dean of the Atlanta school, was an early leader in the development of black social work curriculum content because he believed white social work schools simply were not capable of preparing social workers—of any race—to work in black communities. African Americans, he said in 1929, had "a different social background which has nothing to do with heredity and a great deal to do with environment" (Yabura, 1970). He pointed to the long tradition of distinctive helping institutions in black communities— resources that had been developed in response to white exclusion. Social workers who had learned to work successfully with the problems faced by African Americans had eventually "developed an elaborate technique to meet these difficulties—but it was not learned in school. They had to acquire it by trial and error method and of course during the 'learning period' the clients are the sufferers" (Yabura). Washington was intent on institutionalizing such knowledge. From 1927 through the early 1940s, the school offered what must have been the largest collection of social work courses in the country on topics such as "The Techniques of Community Work Among Negro People; Industrial Problems of Negro People; The Conduct of Social Surveys in Negro Communities" (Yabura). Such black content declined by the mid-1940s, the victim of the growing clout of white social work accreditation circles, which were not receptive to such courses (Yabura).

During the 1920s and for decades after, the Atlanta school worked with a remarkable African American community activist, Lugenia Burns Hope. In 1908, Hope, building on her COS experiences in Chicago, had established the Neighborhood Union, which adapted the settlement house movement to the black communities around Atlanta University. Her work epitomizes the contributions of large numbers of African American community builders, North and South, who labored to develop services for their communities. For 30 years, she led the organization and developed a striking array of services—kindergartens, health facilities, day care centers, playgrounds, neighborhood centers, tuberculosis drives, and citizenship schools—as well as providing leadership in the development of low-cost housing for the poor. Her work inspired similar efforts by African American community leaders around the South. As a faculty member at the Atlanta school of social work, she was able integrate her community-based practice with teaching (Gary, 1986; Rouse, 1989).

Forrester B. Washington's focus on a distinctively African American identity for the Atlanta school of social work was different from the approach taken by Inabel Burns Lindsay, African American social worker and first dean of the Howard University School of Social Work. Deeply committed to fostering social work responsiveness to the African American community, she nevertheless resisted attempts to frame the school as a "Negro school," instead wanting one with a reputation as being open to students of all races. She was alert to racism in social work education and practice and was the first to speak out again a long-standing practice in schools of social work around the country of "assigning Black students to field placements in public welfare agencies, but seldom . . . to the much sought after placements in hospitals and mental health agencies" (Hawkins & Daniels, 1985, p. 3). Upon her urging, the accreditation body of the time mandated a stop to the practice. Similarly, in the days before the modern civil rights movement, she helped organized a boycott with Johns Hopkins Hospital social workers to protest that institution's refusal to allow African Americans, including her social work field students, to eat in the whites-only cafeteria. She monitored field agencies closely and removed students from social work agencies that refused to change their practices of segregating restroom facilities or calling African American clients by first names while addressing whites with titles (Hawkins & Daniels). By the 1960s, both Atlanta University and Howard University transformed their curricula to make black content increasingly visible as an educational theme. In the case of Howard, this produced a school of social work mission known as the "Black Perspective in Social Work," a distinctive approach to the profession that has structured the social work education of students of all races enrolled there.

The work of African American social workers in the era of Jim Crow segregation constitutes a profound professional heritage. It documents community strength and responsiveness in the face of oppression. The achievements constitute a legacy for all social work. In an era when narrow, psychiatric-oriented casework dominated the profession, African American communities and schools helped keep alive what is now termed "community-based practice." The early efforts of leaders such as Washington and Haynes to forge African American curriculum content were forerunners of contemporary Africentric and Afrocentric social work practice models (Everett, Chipungu, & Leashore, 1991; Schiele, 2000), and they prefigured the profession's much later commitment to multiculturalism and cultural competence in practice (Fellin, 2000).

As the welfare state developed in the New Deal era of the 1930s, and in accordance with prevailing Jim Crow segregation, the cluster of white New Deal reformers who helped shaped policies was accompanied by an informal and segregated "black cabinet" of so-called "race advisors." Confined to an advisory role, these African Americans were given the challenging task, to say the least, of "advising" the Roosevelt administration about how to demonstrate some degree of responsiveness to the severe Depression-era needs of African Americans. This was a daunting task: Roosevelt, bowing to southern demands, would not even support legislative proposals to make lynching a federal crime (Kirby, 1980). Included in this group, for a brief period, was Forrester B. Washington, who left Atlanta University to become a New Deal race advisor, only to resign after six months and return to his social work deanship, frustrated by the tokenism of the race-advising effort (Kirby). "Those who think that because these Negro advisors are in Washington they can lay back and be assured of good care" were in for disillusionment, he told the *Afro-American* newspaper and pointed to the extent to which the new Social Security legislation ignored the plight of blacks (Washington, 1935).

Other black social workers in the coming decades played nationally important roles in challenging racial duality in the welfare state. Lester Granger, as head of the NUL, promoted a social casework, employment-preparation approach toward improving the lot of African Americans and also served as an important advisor to the military about integration of the armed forces in the late 1940s (Brown, 1991; Parris & Brooks, 1971; Weiss, 1974). Whitney M. Young, after spending time himself as dean of the Atlanta University School of Social Work, succeeded Granger at NUL and led that organization into the era of the modern civil rights movement. Presidents Johnson and Nixon turned to him for advice on poverty and race issues. He became an important bridge between black America and U.S. corporate leadership.

Young also served as president of the National Association of Social Workers and the National Conference on Social Welfare in the 1960s. In those roles, he helped move both organizations in the direction of social activism (Weiss, 1989). "Social work was born in an atmosphere of righteous indignation, of divine discontent," he told the National Conference on Social Welfare in his 1967 inaugural address, but the drive for professional status had diminished the commitment to social action, and social work had "made a fetish of methodology." As paraphrased by Weiss, Young believed "too many social workers looked down their noses at the poor; too many were uncomfortable with issues of race and religion.

They had come to be seen not as crusaders but as 'experts in adjustment and accommodation'" (Weiss, p. 207).

Other Racial and Ethnic Groups and the Struggle with Duality. Each racial and ethnic group in American history has had a unique encounter with the nation's structure of racial duality, and for encounters occurring after the birth of the profession, social work has been a part of the experience. The Native American encounter is strikingly different from the African American one in that treaty rights and tribal sovereignty have been important structural features that, especially in recent decades, have helped shape the social welfare and social work roles. One whole sector of the New Deal era is known as the Indian New Deal (Parman, 1976; Philp, 1999; Taylor, 1980) and points to a fundamental shift in national policy from assimilation and destruction of Indian and tribal identity to a new policy of preserving Indian cultural heritage and land. John Collier, former community social worker, led this reformist drive as BIA Commissioner from 1933 to 1945 (Kelly, 1983). The intersection of this reform effort with the developing welfare state had decidedly mixed outcomes. On the one hand, Collier backed Indian involvement in New Deal work relief programs such as the Indian Civilian Conservation Corps. On the other hand, he was a key player in an illegal New Deal era agreement to exclude Southwest reservation residents from participation in the new federal–state public assistance programs (Cates, 1983).

The rise of Indian tribal and pan-tribal political activism following World War II (Cornell, 1988) led to increasing levels of Indian self-determination in all aspects of Indian life, including social welfare and social work arenas. This shift is demonstrated, for example, by the passage of the 1978 Indian Child Welfare Act (ICWA) (Matheson, 1996), which established profound changes in the way Indian children were handled in the child welfare system. The ICWA built in safeguards to protect tribal involvement in the decision making about children in the welfare system in an effort to curtail what had been a serious outplacement of foster and adoptive Indian children to non-Indian families (Matheson; Weaver & White, 1999). The intensity with which American Indian racial duality has been defended by whites can be seen vividly in the social welfare record. Nevada, for decades, delayed instituting an Aid to Families with Dependent Children program, in part because white legislators did not want to pay state tax dollars for benefits going to Indian children (Leighninger, 1987). The state of Arizona, in the early 1950s, eliminated its federal–state Crippled Children's Services program, expelling disabled white children from programs rather than bow to federal pressure to serve Indian children as well (Cates, 2006).

The histories of other racial and ethnic groups are equally distinctive. In the case of Asian Americans, works such as Takaki's (1998) important history of Asian Americans have expanded our knowledge of the experiences of people from a wide range of backgrounds: Japanese, Chinese, Korean, Filipino, and Asian Indian, as well as Vietnamese and other Southeast Asians. The historical record of the intersection of each group with social welfare in general, and social work in particular, is less well developed, although some significant bodies of historical research are available. For example, the specific enactment of racial duality in New Deal Works Progress Administration programs in the territory of Hawaii were analyzed by social worker Heirakuji (1993), who showed the precise interplay of social welfare policy with the prevailing racial hegemony, in which subordination of a variety of Asian Americans was central.

In the realm of Japanese American history, much attention has been given to the World War II tragedy in which approximately 120,000 Japanese American citizens and permanent residents were forced into concentration camps solely on the grounds of their race. A little-known federal Bureau of Public Assistance program was created for residents of the camps, and fuller knowledge of its operations awaits research in the agency's National Archives holdings. Important historical research about the camp experience by or about social workers is available. For example, Takahashi's (1980) research analyzed the administration of the camps as well as the effects of racism on Japanese Americans.

The role of Japanese American community-based services and the general profession of social work in the postwar, coerced dispersal of Japanese Americans from the camps to locations other than their original West Coast homes, although well described in the general historical literature, is generally not incorporated into the social work history literature (Drinnon, 1987; Girdner & Loftis, 1969; Hansen & Mitson, 1974; Thomas & Nishimoto, 1946). The historical research of Brooks (2000) provided a vivid account of Japanese Americans being relocated from the camps to Chicago from 1942 to 1945. In an illustration of the oft-repeated theme of social work assistance embedded in a social control context, Brooks demonstrated how Chicago-based social service workers applied heavy pressure on the newly arriving families to "assimilate" by disavowing their Japanese American culture and not associating with one another in Chicago—the better to blend into the city. As Brooks demonstrated, the newly released Japanese Americans soon learned that they could ignore the pressure not to form within-group bonds, and eventually a resilient, long-lasting network of Japanese American community ties and institutions developed in Chicago despite the pressures of social service providers.

Building on her research into the camp experience, social worker Rita Takahashi became the Congressional lobbyist for the Japanese American Citizens League, an organization that was a key player in passage of the 1988 Civil Liberties Act. This legislation provided to approximately 80,000 surviving internees, more than 40 years after their release, a financial payment and letter of apology from the federal government. Following passage of this legislation, Takahashi then worked with the U.S. Department of Justice to locate people eligible for the payments. For an overview of the long process leading to this national legislation, see the 1992 report of the U.S. Commission on Wartime Relocation and Internment of Civilians, *Personal Justice Denied*. Achievement of this remarkable piece of reparations legislation has influenced subsequent African American reparations efforts (Laremont, 2001).

Incorporating into accounts of the profession's history the varied experiences of Hispanic and Latino Americans in a way that is faithful to the wide range of groups—Chicanos, Puerto Ricans, Cubans, Central Americans, and others—largely remains an unfulfilled scholarly challenge. A significant exception to this statement is the work of Iglehart and Becerra (2000) on the history of social services and American ethnic communities in general and Mexican American self-help efforts in particular. Gordon (1999) also made a valuable contribution with her recent work of "microhistory," (the study of history on a very small scale—as in the study of single communities), which analyzes the intersection of the early 20th-century child-saving movement with powerful currents of Southwestern race hatred and the location-specific nature of racial definitions. She documented the story of 57 "foundlings"—Irish American children from New York who in 1904 were placed, legally and appropriately with regard to the procedures of the day, in new homes with Mexican American families in Clifton, Arizona. The children were accompanied on the trip to Arizona by Sisters of Charity nuns who ran the New York Foundling Hospital from which the children came. Gordon found that when the children boarded the train in the Northeast, they were socially defined as nonwhite because Irish Americans at the turn of the century were not seen as whites in the urban Northeast. When the children exited the train in Arizona, however, Anglos there defined the children as eminently white. Different locales meant different definitions of race, and Anglo determination to preserve racial differences and white hegemony in the Southwest was backed up with force. When white citizens saw what they viewed as white children being placed with Mexican American families, a vigilante group kidnapped them all and distributed them to whichever white family was first to ask for them. The mob threatened the lives of the nuns if they did not turn over the children. Subsequent court challenges by the staff of the New York Foundling Hospital were unsuccessful in their attempts to reclaim the children from the vigilantes. Gordon's work is a compelling analysis of racial hatred, backed up by violence, as it played out in a social welfare arena.

Forrest (1989) offered one of the few historical treatments of the "Hispanic New Deal," a federal social welfare effort to preserve the cultural heritage of northern New Mexico's Hispano villages and to provide economic support. Her study traced the unfulfilled promises of the New Deal effort and of similar efforts in the War on Poverty.

Many other aspects of the Latino and Hispanic encounter with duality in social welfare and social work arenas await attention. For example, the role of social work in Puerto Rico has yet to be carefully interpreted in light of the unique status of the Commonwealth of Puerto Rico and the accompanying special nature of the U.S. social welfare state there (Carr, 1984). Important to such research would be an understanding of the institutional history of schools of social work in Puerto Rico.

Other Diversities in Social Work History

As important as it is, Ringer's (1983) concept of duality based on race does not capture all the diversity and struggles for equality of treatment in American history. Women's encounters with gender discrimination and their role in social work history were discussed earlier in this chapter. Sexual orientation as a basis for oppression and as a source of enrichment to the profession has received increased attention in recent decades. Religious traditions, too, have been an important source of diversity in social work history, a point illustrated here with recent Catholic and Jewish historical research.

An outpouring of new histories of sexual minority communities is now available (Berube, 1991; Bonfitto, 1997; Buring, 1996; D'Emilio, 1983; Duberman, 1986; Duberman, Vicinus, & Chauncey, 1989; Hilliard, 2002; Katz, 1976; Lauritsen & Thorstad, 1974; Marcus, 1992; Sullivan, 1999). Poindexter's (1997) essay on the origins of the modern gay civil rights movement and the relevance of that history to social work may be the precursor to research about the history of the social work profession's relationship with sexual minority communities. As Poindexter observed,

> It would . . . be useful for the profession to review the history of its response to the oppression of gay men and lesbians and to acknowledge its marked absence from the early struggles of this population, as well as its more recent support of some aspects of the battle against oppression. Such knowledge is important for the profession's self-understanding and identity and deserves serious attention. (p. 615)

Regarding the intersection of gay history and social welfare state history, Canaday (2003) made an important contribution with her research into the 1944 G.I. Bill of Rights (Servicemen's Readjustment Act of 1944). The legislation, she pointed out, is a major and previously neglected element of the modern American welfare state. With its support for home purchase and higher education, the act is "credited with moving millions of working-class Americans into the middle class by democratizing higher education and home ownership and with ushering in the postwar economic boom" (p. 935). As Canaday documented, when a 1945 Veterans Administration ruling made the act's benefits out of bounds for anyone discharged for "homosexual act or tendencies," the G.I. bill became the first federal policy to directly exclude gays and lesbians by name (rather than "inadvertently" excluding them through the marriage filter, that is, limiting benefits to people legally married). Thus, for the first time, "Homosexual exclusion was explicit, built into the very foundation of the welfare state" (Canaday, p. 936).

In terms of gay history that is specific to social work, the published record remains thin at this time, particularly regarding social workers whose lives are also part of gay and lesbian history. What our professional history lacks is biographical studies of gay and lesbian social workers comparable to historian John D'Emilio's (2003) biography of African American civil rights leader Bayard Rustin (*Lost Prophet: The Life and Times of Bayard Rustin*). Nominated for a National Book Award, the biography has been acclaimed for bringing to light the previously underappreciated story of a major modern civil rights leader (among other things, he was a key organizer of the 1963 March on Washington) whose accomplishments had been neglected in large part because Rustin was homosexual. Murphy (2001) conducted important work in uncovering submerged gay social work history with his research into Progressive Era "male same-sex eroticism" in the New York settlement movement. His detailed research into the lives and careers of Charles B. Stover (a New York settlement house leader and early advocate of recreational programming for urban youth) and John Lovejoy Elliot (founder of the Hudson Guild settlement house in New York City and president of the National Federation of Settlements from 1919 to 1923) has produced groundbreaking accounts of the intersection of social work and gay history. Murphy (2001) concluded that the lives of these early social workers "embedded a critique of middle-class sexuality and gender roles within their ideal of social brotherhood" (p. 185) and that in defining their settlement house colleagues as "family," they created "an alternative family, one in which sexuality was linked not to reproductive ends. In so doing, they developed a politics of same-sex eroticism that stood in contrast to emerging medical models of homosexual pathology and heterosexual normativity" (p. 185).

Well before Murphy's work on male sexuality, curiosity and speculation abounded about the sexual orientation of many women in the Progressive Era settlement movement. As Murphy (2001) himself put it,

> The settlement house movement. . . occupies a central place in the history of women's sexuality. . . . The prominence of [same-sex] relationships, or "romantic friendships" have raised a number of interesting questions: Were they sexual? Are such "romantic friendships" appropriate subjects for lesbian history? What connections, if any, exist between these romantic attachments between women and the political ideologies and practices of the settlement house movement? (p. 184)

Given the submerged nature of much Progressive Era eroticism, answers to these questions are not easily forthcoming. Inquiries about the sexual orientation of Jane Addams and whether she occupies a place in lesbian history demonstrate how highly charged such questioning can be. What is beyond dispute is that Jane Addams was a woman-centered woman who saw no place for heterosexual marriage in her life and who loved and was loved in turn by Mary Rozet Smith in a relationship that lasted for decades. The two saw themselves as "married," missed each other when they were separated by travel, and saw each other as a principal emotional support in life (Diliberto, 1999; Elshtain, 2002). Nothing is known, however, of specific sexual activity. Is it appropriate to see Addams as part of lesbian history, as many people now do? Diliberto, after considering their exchange of intimate letters, observed,

> As passionate as the letters are, they offer no real clues to whether the relationship was sexual. The emotional bonds between women friends of this era were as strong as, or stronger than, those between husband and wife. The thoroughly heterosexual novelist George Eliot, for example, referred to her closest woman friend as her "spouse." Scholars have long been familiar with the purple language Victorian women employed to describe their feelings for one another. (pp. 185–186)

Elsewhere, however, Diliberto (1999) has speculated about why, in her later years, Jane Addams destroyed almost all of Mary's letters to her: "She [Addams] never explained why. Perhaps she was trying to cover up the sexual nature of their love" (p. 184).

As the modern gay civil rights movement has emerged, an important theme has been the search to uncover hidden gay and lesbian history, and one element of this quest has been to look for people in history who might be called gay or lesbian in today's terms, even if such conceptualizations were not available in the time period studied. This understandable search for a community's repressed history is important and is part of an oppressed group's effort to overcome stigma and exclusion and to claim a collective identity. Such questioning about historical figures is not valued by everyone, however. Elshtain (2002), for example, in her important study of the political thought of Jane Addams, took great exception to curiosity about Addams's sexual orientation. For her, such questions are no more than a reflection of present-day obsession with sex, including sex that is "disconnected from love, devotion and affection" (p. 117). She dismissed curiosity about lesbianism and "speculation about the libidinal lives" (p. 24) of Hull House women as destructive and productive of a "sexualized caricature" of Addams (p. 24). Inappropriate questioning about Addams's sexuality, she repeatedly insisted, is part of contemporary society's "preoccupation with the sexual

[, which] tends to reduce all social and political phenomena to either psychology or sexuality" (p. 24).

In her work, Elshtain (2002) displayed little sympathy with the modern gay rights movement's attempts to excavate its past through biographical inquiry. Her position resonates with the reaction of a graduate social work student who objected to a discussion of such material in her class by exclaiming, "This makes me so mad! Every time a strong woman accomplishes something, someone tries to tear her down by doing something like this!" thereby underscoring the fact that, for some people, it remains the case that raising scholarly inquiries about the sexual orientation of a historical figure such as Addams is tantamount to accusing her of a moral offense.

Turning to religious tradition as a source of diversity, recent research on the intersection of Jewish history and the history of social work and social welfare emphasizes services to Jewish immigrants. Soyer's (1997) work on Jewish immigrant associations and American identity between 1880 and 1939, for example, set the stage for a broad understanding of the Jewish immigration experience. Goldstein (2001) provided a broad and nuanced understanding of the sources of American anti-Semitism in the Progressive Era. Soyer's later work (Soyer, 2000) provided a detailed examination of a specific organization, the Hebrew Educational Society of Brooklyn, and focused on tensions between "Uptown Jews—Americanized, well-to-do . . . of mainly Central European origin . . . and the Yiddish-speaking 'Downtown Jews' they were so eager to assist in becoming proper Americans" (p. 181). Wasserman (2000) provided an account of professional social workers' efforts during the Great Depression to pressure immigrant Jews on New York City's Lower East Side to set aside their immigrant culture and assimilate. Wasserman presents a fascinating story of successful resistance to this assimilationist social service pressure, which at times brought residents in conflict with the Henry Street Settlement.

McCune (1998) demonstrated the role played by social work as Jewish women in the early 20th-century American Zionist Movement sought to carve out a meaningful role for themselves in the movement. The movement was dominated by men who, intent on projecting a robustly "masculine" image for the movement, rejected social work as an insufficiently virile enterprise to include in the movement. McCune showed how "Hadassah ladies" nevertheless persisted and prevailed in significant ways, negotiating gender conflict to create a significant role for social work in the development of Palestine and the American Zionist movement.

Regarding the connection between Catholics and social work and social welfare, Brown and McKeown (1997) provided a sweeping and detailed understanding of the history of Catholic charities in the United States from the Civil

War to World War II. Moloney (2002) provided a broad context for understanding Catholic social work and social welfare as she developed her thesis that "not only did Catholic reforms in the United States appropriate established models of reform from Europe, but concurrent European social and political movements also shaped the activities undertaken by the American Catholic laity" (p. 2). An extensive historical literature is available that examines specific Catholic social work expressions, illustrated by Anderson's (2000) description of how Catholic nuns of the Santa Maria Institute of Cincinnati, Ohio, played a fascinating role in helping to invent social work during the Progressive Era.

CONCLUSION

Social work history, which cannot be understood apart from the history of social welfare and society, can be an energizing part of one's professional identity. Historical understanding provides role models, teaches lessons to inform practice and policy and, at the most fundamental level, fosters critical thinking. History offers vivid examples of once-dominant thinking that are jarring to contemporary sensibilities, such as the COS attitudes toward the poor. For another example, consider Progressive Era social worker John Adams Kingsbury, who, as Commissioner of Public Charities for New York City, reported to Theodore Roosevelt on his accomplishments. Spotlighting reforms for mentally disabled children, but using language and assumptions of his period, he told of his pride in taking the children away from their homes and putting them in large institutions. These "young defectives" were a "burden to their hardworking mothers and a social menace to the community." They needed to be "permanently segregated" behind institutional walls: made comfortable, to be sure, but firmly isolated from the normal world. Children of "normal minds" simply could not be permitted to "mingle with idiots." "Defectives" must not be allowed to reproduce another problematical generation (Kingsbury, n.d.). In describing his policies, Kingsbury was articulating the acknowledged "best" professional thinking of his day. The scientific validity of the eugenic movement's theories was taken for granted by leading intellectuals. The movement's creed assumed "the supreme importance of heredity" and believed that "the unfit must be eliminated or at least limited in number and the fit encouraged to increase their numbers" (Pickens, 1968, p. 55).

Kingsbury's career includes other achievements that are still recognized as remarkably humanitarian in nature. In fact, he was labeled a dangerous radical in his day for the vigor with which he challenged American centers of power in the interests of social justice for the most vulnerable, particularly in the area of national health insurance (Fox, 1986; Kingsbury, 1939; Newsholme & Kingsbury, 1933). That he, like his professional contemporaries, could use eugenics concepts that would be collectively repudiated within two decades is a lesson to us all, because it reminds us of the historically conditioned nature of our assumptions and practice knowledge and underlines the ever-present need to cultivate a critical, reflective, and ethically grounded attitude toward current practice and policy "givens"—an attitude nurtured by the study of the profession's history.

REFERENCES

Addams, J. (1912). The Progressive Party and the Negro. *Crisis, 5,* 30–31.

Allen, R. (1974). *Reluctant reformers: Racism and social reform movements in the United States.* Washington, DC: Howard University Press.

Anderson, M. (2000). Catholic nuns and the invention of social work: The sisters of the Santa Maria Institute of Cincinnati, Ohio, 1897 through the 1920s. *Journal of Women's History, 12,* 60–88.

Austin, D. M. (1983). The Flexner myth and the history of social work. *Social Service Review, 57,* 357–377.

Bell, W. (1965). *Aid to dependent children.* New York: Columbia University Press.

Berube, A. (1991). *Coming out under fire: The history of gay men and women in World War Two.* New York: Plume.

Bonfitto, V. (1997). The formation of gay and lesbian identity and community in the Connecticut River Valley of Western Massachusetts, 1900–1970. *Journal of Homosexuality, 33,* 69–96.

Brooks, C. (2000). In the Twilight Zone between black and white: Japanese American resettlement and community in Chicago, 1942–1945. *Journal of American History, 86,* 1685–1687.

Brown, A. (1991). A social work leader in the struggle for racial equality: Lester Blackwell Granger. *Social Service Review, 65*(2), 266–280.

Brown, D., & McKeown, E. (1997). *The poor belong to us: Catholic charities and American welfare.* Cambridge, MA: Harvard University Press.

Buring, D. (1996). Gay activism behind the magnolia curtain: The Memphis Gay Coalition, 1979–1991. *Journal of Homosexuality, 32,* 113–135.

Calmore, J. O. (1996). Spatial equality and the Kerner Commission Report: A back-to-the-future essay. In J. C. Boger & J. W. Wegner (Eds.), *Race, poverty, and American cities* (pp. 309–342). Chapel Hill: University of North Carolina Press.

Canaday, M. (2003). Building a straight state: Sexuality and social citizenship under the 1944 G. I. Bill. *Journal of American History, 90,* 935–957.

Carlton, I. (1982). *A pioneer social work educator: George Edmund Haynes.* Unpublished doctoral dissertation, University of Maryland at Baltimore.

Carlton-LaNey, I. (2001). *African American leadership: An empowerment tradition in social welfare history.* Washington, DC: NASW Press.

Carr, R. (1984). *Puerto Rico: A colonial experiment.* New York: Vintage Books.

Cates, J. (1983). *Insuring inequality: Administrative leadership in Social Security, 1935–1952.* Ann Arbor: University of Michigan Press.

Cates, J. (1988). Administrative justice, Social Security, and the American Indian. In P. Simbi (Ed.), *Administrative justice in public services: American and African perspectives* (pp. 34–50). Stevens Point, WI: Worzalla.

Cates, J. (2006). *The politics of Native American public welfare*. Manuscript in preparation.

Civil Liberties Act of 1988, Pub. L. 100-383, 102 Stat. 904, 50a U.S.C. § 1989b et seq. (1988). (Title I).

Cornell, S. (1988). *The return of the native: American Indian political resurgence*. New York: Oxford University Press.

Costin, L. (1985). Historical context of child care. In J. Laird & A. Hartman (Eds.), *A handbook of child welfare*. New York: Free Press.

Davis, A. (1967). *Spearheads for reform: The settlements and the Progressive Movement, 1890–1914*. New York: Oxford University Press.

Davis, A. (1973). *American heroine: The life and legend of Jane Addams*. New York: Oxford University Press.

D'Emilio, J. (1983). *Sexual politics, sexual communities: The making of a homosexual minority in the United States, 1940–1970*. Chicago: University of Chicago Press.

D'Emilio, J. (2003). *Lost prophet: The life and times of Bayard Rustin*. New York: Free Press.

Diliberto, G. (1999). *A useful woman: The early life of Jane Addams*. New York: Scribner.

Dreier, P. (1996). America's urban crisis. In J. C. Boger & J. W. Wegner (Eds.), *Race, poverty, and American cities)*. Chapel Hill: University of North Carolina Press.

Drinnon, R. (1987). *Keeper of concentration camps: Dillson S. Myer and American racism*. Berkeley: University of California Press.

Duberman, M. (1986). *About time: The gay past*. New York: Sea Horse.

Duberman, M., Vicinus, M., & Chauncy, G. (Eds.). (1989). *Hidden from history: Reclaiming the gay and lesbian past*. New York: Meridian.

DuBois, W.E.B. (1996). To the nations of the world. In E. Sundquist (Ed.), *The Oxford W.E.B. Du Bois reader*. New York: Oxford University Press.

Elshtain, J. (2002). *Jane Addams and the dream of American democracy*. New York: Basic Books.

Everett, J., Chipungu, S., & Leashore, B. (1991). *Child welfare: An Africentric perspective*. New Brunswick, NJ: Rutgers University Press.

Farley, R. (1996). Black-white residential segregation: The views of Myrdal in the 1940s and trends of the 1980s. In O. Clayton (Ed.), *An American dilemma revisited: Race relations in a changing world* (pp. 45–75). New York: Russell Sage Foundation.

Fellin, P. (2000). Multiculturalism revisited. *Journal of Social Work Education, 36*(2), 261–278.

Field, M. (1980). Social casework practice during the psychiatric deluge. *Social Service Review, 54,* 482–507.

Forrest, S. (1989). *The preservation of the village: New Mexico's Hispanic population and the New Deal*. Albuquerque: University of New Mexico Press.

Fox, D. (1986). Kingsbury, John Adams. In W. Trattner (Ed.), *Biographical dictionary of social welfare in America* (pp. 459–461). New York: Greenwood Press.

Gary, R. (1986). Hope, Lugenia Burns. In W. Trattner (Ed.), *Biographical dictionary of social welfare in America* (pp. 396–398). New York: Greenwood Press.

Girdner, A., & Loftis, A. (1969). *The great betrayal*. London: Macmillan.

Goldstein, E. (2001). The unstable other: Locating the Jew in Progressive-Era American radical discourse. *American Jewish History, 89,* 383–409.

Gordon, L. (1991). Black and white visions of welfare: Women's welfare activism, 1890–1945. *Journal of American History, 78*(2), 559–590.

Gordon, L. (1994). *Pitied but not entitled: Single women and the history of welfare, 1890–1935.* New York: Free Press.

Gordon, L. (1999). *The great Arizona orphan abduction.* Cambridge, MA: Harvard University Press.

Hansen, A., & Mitson, B. (Eds.). (1974). *Voices long silent: An oral inquiry into the Japanese American evacuation.* Fullerton: California State University Press.

Hawkins, B., & Daniels, M. (1985). Inabel Burns Lindsay. *Urban Research Review, 10*(2), 1–3.

Heirakuji, L. (1993). *Hawaii and the New Deal: A case study of the Works Progress Administration.* Unpublished doctoral dissertation, Howard University, Washington, DC.

Hilliard, R. (2002). The San Francisco Gay Men's Chorus: A historical perspective on the role of a chorus as a social service. *Journal of Gay & Lesbian Social Services, 14*(3), 79–94.

Hopps, J., & Collins, P. (1995). Social work profession overview. In R. L. Edwards (Ed.-in-Chief), *Encyclopedia of social work* (19th ed., Vol. 3, pp. 2266–2282). Washington, DC: NASW Press.

Houston, C. (1935, February 6). Houston calls Wagner-Lewis bill a sieve. *Washington Afro-American,* p. 4.

Iglehart, A., & Becerra, R. (2000). *Social services and the ethnic community.* Prospect Heights, IL: Waveland Press.

Jansson, B. (1997). *The reluctant welfare state: American social welfare policies: Past, present and future.* Pacific Grove, CA: Brooks/Cole.

Jones, J. (1981). *Bad blood: The Tuskegee syphilis experiment.* New York: Free Press.

Katz, J. (1976). *Gay American history: Lesbians and gay men in the U.S.A.* New York: Crowell.

Katz, M. (1996). *In the shadow of the poorhouse: A social history of welfare in America.* New York: Basic Books.

Kelly, L. (1983). *The assault on assimilation: John Collier and the origins of Indian policy reform.* Albuquerque: University of New Mexico Press.

Kingsbury, J. (n.d.). Memorandum for Colonel Roosevelt regarding the welfare work of the Mitchell Administration. Washington, DC: John Adams.

Kingsbury, J. (1912). *Notebooks.* Washington, DC: John Adams Kingsbury Papers, Manuscript Division, Library of Congress.

Kingsbury, J. (1939). *Health in handcuffs.* New York: Modern Age Books.

Kirby, J. (1980). *Black Americans in the Roosevelt Era: Liberalism and race.* Knoxville: University of Tennessee Press.

Knight, L. (2005). *Citizen: Jane Addams and the struggle for democracy.* Chicago: University of Chicago Press.

Kusmar, K. (1976). *A ghetto takes shape: Black Cleveland, 1870–1930.* Urbana: University of Illinois Press.

Laremont, R. (2001). Jewish and Japanese American reparations: Political lessons for the Africana community. *Journal of Asian American Studies, 4,* 235–250.

Lauritsen, J., & Thorstad, D. (1974). *The early homosexual rights movement (1864–1990).* New York: Times Change Press.

Leiberman, R. C. (1998). *Shifting the color line: Race and the American welfare state.* Cambridge: Harvard University Press.

Leiby, J. (1984). Charity organization reconsidered. *Social Service Review, 58*(4), 522–538.

Leighninger, L. (1987). *Social work: Search for identity*. New York: Greenwood Press.

Levitan, S., & Taggert, R. (1976). *The promise of greatness*. Cambridge, MA: Harvard University Press.

Lowell, J. (1884). *Public relief and private charity*. New York: G. P. Putnam's Sons.

Lubove, R. (1969). *The professional altruist: The emergence of social work as a career, 1880–1930*. New York: Atheneum.

Marcus, J. E. (1992). *Making history: The struggle for gay and lesbian equal rights, 1945–1990*. New York: HarperCollins.

Matheson, L. (1996). The politics of the Indian Child Welfare Act. *Social Work, 41*, 232–235.

McCune, M. (1998). Social workers in the *Muskeljudentum*: "Hadassah ladies," "Manly men" and the significance of gender in the American Zionist movement, 1912–1928. *American Jewish History, 86*, 135–165.

Moloney, D. (2002). *American Catholic lay groups and transatlantic social reform in the Progressive Era*. Chapel Hill: University of North Carolina Press.

Murphy, K. (2001). *The manly world of urban reform: Political manhood and the new politics of Progressivism*. Unpublished doctoral dissertation, New York University.

Newsholme, A., & Kingsbury, J. (1933). *Red medicine: Socialized health in Soviet Russia*. New York: Milbank Foundation.

Orfield, G. (1988). Race and the liberal agenda: The loss of the integrationist dream, 1965–1974. In M. Weir, A. Orloff, & T. Skocpol (Eds.), *The politics of social policy in the United States* (pp. 313–356). Princeton, NJ: Princeton University Press.

Parman, D. (1976). *The Navajos and the New Deal*. New Haven, CT: Yale University Press.

Parris, G., & Brooks, L. (1971). *Blacks in the city: A history of the National Urban League*. Boston: Little, Brown.

Philp, K. (1999). *Termination revisited: American Indians on the trail to self-determination, 1933–1954*. Lincoln: University of Nebraska Press.

Pickens, K. (1968). *Eugenics and the Progressives*. Nashville, TN: Vanderbilt University Press.

Piven, F. F., & Cloward, R. (1971). *Regulating the poor: The functions of public welfare*. New York: Random House.

Plotnick, R., & Skidmore, F. (1975). *Progress against poverty: A review of the 1964–1974 decade*. New York: Academic Press.

Poindexter, C. (1997). Sociopolitical antecedents to Stonewall: Analysis of the origins of the gay rights movement in the United States. *Social Work, 42*, 607–615.

Quadagno, J. (1994). *The color of welfare: How racism undermined the War on Poverty*. New York: Oxford University Press.

Richmond, M. (1917). *Social diagnosis*. New York: Russell Sage Foundation.

Richmond, M. (1922). *What is social case work?* New York: Russell Sage Foundation.

Ringer, B. (1983). *"We the people" and others: Duality and America's treatment of its racial minorities*. New York: Tavistock Publications.

Ringer, B., & Lawless, E. (1989). *Race-ethnicity and society*. New York: Routledge.

Rogers, W. (1948, February 3). Starvation without representation. *Look Magazine*, pp. 33 ff.

Ross, E. (1978). *Black heritage in social welfare*. Metuchen, NJ: Scarecrow Press.

Rouse, J. (1989). *Lugenia Burns Hope, Black southern reformer*. Athens: University of Georgia Press.

Schiele, J. (2000). *Human services and the Afrocentric paradigm.* New York: Haworth Press.

Schopler, J. H., & Galinsky, M. J. (1995). Group practice overview. In R. L. Edwards (Ed.-in-Chief), *Encyclopedia of social work* (19th ed., Vol. 2, pp. 1129–1142). Washington, DC: NASW Press.

Shoemaker, L. (1998). Early conflicts in social work education. *Social Service Review, 72*(2), 182–191.

Skocpol, T. (1988). The limits of the New Deal system and the roots of contemporary welfare dilemmas. In M. Weir, A. S. Orloff, & T. Skocpol (Eds.), *The politics of social policy in the United States* (pp. 293–312). Princeton, NJ: Princeton University Press.

Skocpol, T. (1992). *Protecting soldiers and mothers: The political origins of social policy in the United States.* Cambridge, MA: Harvard University Press.

Soyer, D. (1997). *Jewish immigrant associations and American identity in New York, 1880–1939.* Cambridge, MA: Harvard University Press.

Soyer, D. (2000). Brownstones and Brownsville: Elite philanthropists and immigrant constituents at the Hebrew Educational Society of Brooklyn, 1889–1929. *American Jewish History, 88,* 181–207.

Spano, R. (1982). *The rank and file movement in social work.* Washington, DC: University Press of America.

Specht, H., & Courtney, M. (1994). *Unfaithful angels: How social work has abandoned its mission.* New York: Free Press.

Sullivan, G. (1999). Political opportunism and the harassment of homosexuals in Florida. *Journal of Homosexuality, 37,* 57–81.

Takahashi, R. (1980). *Comparative administration and management of five war relocation authority camps: America's incarceration of persons of Japanese ancestry during World War II.* Unpublished doctoral dissertation, University of Pittsburgh, Pittsburgh, Pennsylvania.

Takaki, R. (1998). *Strangers from a different shore.* Boston: Little, Brown.

Taylor, G. (1980). *The New Deal and American Indian tribalism.* Lincoln: University of Nebraska Press.

Thomas, D., & Nishimoto, R. (1946). *The spoilage: Japanese-American evacuation and resettlement during World War II.* Berkeley: University of California Press.

Thomas, J. (1967). *My life in white and black.* New York: Exposition Press.

Trattner, W. (Ed.). (1986). *Biographical dictionary of social welfare in America.* New York: Greenwood Press.

U.S. Commission on Wartime Relocation and Internment of Civilians. (1992). *Personal justice denied* (Pub. No. 052-070-06800-1). Washington, DC: U.S. Government Printing Office.

Vann, R. (1966). *The strange career of Jim Crow.* New York: Oxford University Press.

Walkowitz, D. (1990). The making of a feminine professional identity: Social workers in the 1920s. *American Historical Review, 95,* 1051–1076.

Washington, F. (1935, March 9). Washington raps, Jones extols new deal in Atlanta. *Washington Afro-American,* p. 6.

Wasserman, S. (2000). "Our alien neighbors": Coping with the Depression on the Lower East Side. *American Jewish History, 88,* 209–232.

Weaver, H., & White, B. (1999). Protecting the future of indigenous children and nations: An examination of the Indian Child Welfare Act. *Journal of Health and Social Policy, 10*(4), 35–50.

Weiss, N. (1974). *The National Urban League, 1910–1940*. New York: Oxford University Press.

Weiss, N. (1989). *Whitney M. Young, Jr. and the struggle for civil rights*. Princeton, NJ: Princeton University Press.

Willrich, M. (2000). Home slackers: Men, the state, and welfare in modern America. *Journal of American History, 87*, 460–489.

Wilkerson-Freeman, S. (2002). The creation of a subversive feminist dominion: Interracialist social workers and the Georgia New Deal. *Journal of Women's History, 13*(4), 132–154.

Wilson, W. J. (1999). *The bridge over the racial divide: Rising inequality and coalition politics*. Berkeley: University of California Press.

Yabura, L. (1970). The legacy of Forrester B. Washington: Black social work educator and nation builder. In *Proceedings of the fiftieth anniversary of the Atlanta University School of Social Work*. Atlanta: Atlanta University School of Social Work.

Part II

Foundations of
Social Work Practice

8

□□□

Social Work
with Individuals

Mark A. Mattaini

In the Reform Era, when social workers practiced in settlement houses and as friendly visitors through the Charity Organization Societies, they offered their helping services to people as individuals, families, groups, and communities. That was long before the professionalization of social work, and the helpers of the late 19th and early 20th centuries simply did what seemed to be necessary in case situations using common sense. When Richmond (1917) codified a casework approach to helping people, she devised the first methodology in social work, making it possible to replicate and teach casework practice. . . . Thus, casework, or practice with individuals, was the first professionally defined modality in social work. Practices with families (1950s), groups (1940s), and communities (1960s) were similarly developed and, in turn, contributed to the diversified practice repertoire of social workers. . . . The ecosystems perspective has helped to conceptualize the social work practitioner's multiple roles (using the diverse modalities) by laying out the "picture" of a case and enabling the practitioner to determine which modality is most appropriate to use—where and when—in the case. . . . The chief indicator of the progress that has been made from the earliest days of identification solely with a method is that modern social workers first attempt to assess what is needed and is possible to achieve in a case and then choose a modality that is appropriate to the circumstances.

(Meyer & Palleja, 1995, pp. 105–106)

*P*ractice with individuals is still probably the most common modality in social work. We have learned a good deal during the past century about "what works" in helping individual clients shape improved realities; the evidence-based practice movement reflects this progress. Practice with individuals is not always the best choice, however. Family-centered practice, for example, is a powerful and important modality (see chapter 9), and group work (chapter 10) is re-emerging as one of the most important ways to work with people, particularly those who experience vulnerability and oppression.

Given many groups' experiences of collective oppression, advocacy and work on behalf of communities is clearly an ethical imperative; some observers believe such advocacy should preempt work with individuals. Bertha Capen Reynolds, an important social work pioneer (Cotten, 2006; Reynolds, 1934/1982), struggled with this question during the Great Depression. Her resolution, and that of this chapter, is that suffering members of the human web cannot be left alone in their plight because relationship is the core of humanity; all people (and all of life) are connected (Ross, 2006). If one is suffering, we are all affected—and responsible. Building healthy communities is one way to build healthy people (see chapter 11; see also Specht & Courtney, 1994) in which every social worker should participate, but assisting individual people in achieving and maintaining health is also one way to build healthy communities.

The emphasis in this chapter is on work with verbal clients who are of school age or older. Naturally, the process must be adapted, depending on developmental considerations, cognitive capacities, and the nature of the issues to be addressed. In addition, specialized skills are required for certain populations with major developmental problems (for example, autistic adolescents), as well as for work with young children (in which case, some level of family work should usually be primary—see chapter 8 and Mattaini, 1999). Considerable additional reading will always be required for a social worker to be well prepared to work with the populations and issues seen in particular settings.

WHAT IS THE CASE?

One of the core messages of the ecosystems perspective, a view of reality that recognizes the organic unity of life (chapter 2), is that everything is connected. To avoid becoming immobilized by complexity, however, practitioners in partnership with their clients must figuratively "draw a boundary" around the case; that is, they determine which factors to address directly and which will be treated as background or context. This setting of boundaries includes a determination of which people to work with directly or indirectly, what other systems may require attention, and for what period of time to work with the case—the social, physical, and temporal boundaries of the case. To the extent possible, this determination of boundaries should reflect the actual systems present in the case because, as discussed in chapter 2, living systems construct their own boundaries, which effective practice must respect. Ignoring the family system in work with an individual, for example, often limits the potential of the work that can be done. In fact, contact with members of the social network may reduce the need for professional contact while supporting positive outcomes in work with individuals and should therefore always be seriously considered (Gottlieb & Coppard, 1987; Kemp, Whittaker, & Tracy, 1997).

Perhaps the most useful way to conceptualize the process of defining the case is to use a transactional ecomap. Social work students (and, probably, social work professionals) tend to look more evenly at transactional factors in a case if they actually draw the case out for themselves (Mattaini, 1993). Clients also usually respond well to this approach, which communicates a genuine effort to understand their lives and can usefully capture change over time (Hartman, 1978/1995). In some situations, of course, clients would not find this approach useful, but the social worker in such cases should usually at least sketch the situation out for him- or herself. The case of Ms. Todd, a client of mine seen for individual consultation, demonstrates the advantages of ecomapping to understand case dynamics:

Ms. Todd is a 41-year-old African American woman raised in the South who has lived in a large northern city for about a decade. She is being seen in a private, nonprofit agency specializing in individual and family consultation for a range of problems in living. Ms. Todd was referred by her case-worker at a transitional shelter for homeless women with mental illness because of a history of severe depression (which continues to the present) and difficulties between shelter staff and Ms. Todd regarding compliance with shelter policies and procedures.

Ms. Todd had become homeless after leaving a psychiatric inpatient unit. She had moved in with her mother several years earlier but began sinking more and more deeply into depression; she was hospitalized, believing herself to be dying of physical causes, when she could no longer get out of bed. Neither she nor her mother was willing for her to return to her mother's home after leaving the hospital, and she stayed in several temporary arrangements before becoming homeless.

When Ms. Todd was referred for services, she had some minimal involvement with several agencies in what she called "the mental system" and was receiving social security. She was bright, well educated with some college, and had strong social skills when she felt up to engaging. Her vision of her priorities at the time of intake included moving into her own apartment, ameliorating the depression, and moving toward school attendance and an ultimate return to work.

The ecomap shown in Figure 8-1 portrays the shared knowledge about this case between the social worker and the client after a telephone call from the shelter and an initial contact between the client and the practitioner (the case as it evolved over time is presented later in this chapter).

The case boundary here had to be drawn to include the client herself (in all of her behavioral and emotional dimensions), the multiple agencies with which she was involved, her extended family, and her physical world. Also potentially important, although largely missing at that point, were other personal social

FIGURE 8-1

□ □ □ □ □

Transactional Ecomap Clarifying a Client's Situation at Intake

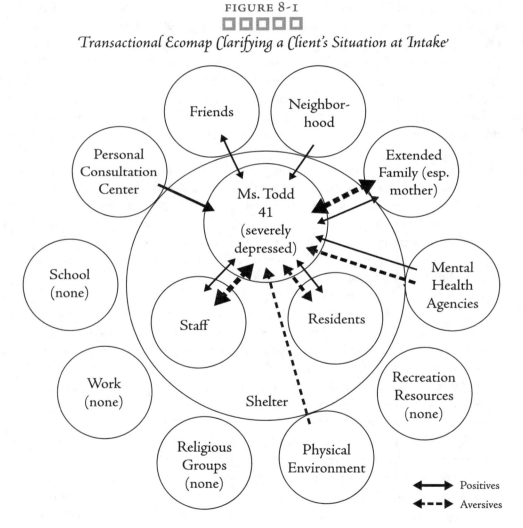

Note: The strength of the transactional exchanges is represented by the thickness of the lines in the figure.

contacts. The foreground in this case certainly included the client's emotional state, housing situation, and the overall scarcity of positive transactions in her life. At the time of intake, it was not yet clear to what extent the client's extended family and some of the other systems in the case configuration might become foci for work or to what extent they would be primarily contextual factors (to be considered in terms of their effects on other areas but not directly addressed). An individual modality made sense initially, although a shift to family work—or at least some contact with her mother—was kept open as a later possibility.

The next decision to be made related to duration of treatment. For many focused issues and goals, short-term, time-limited approaches are demonstrably effective. Open-ended services for people with limited difficulties may be counterproductive, leading to dependence rather than supporting strength (as portrayed in movies, for example, where the "neurotic" patient runs to his or her therapist before acting on any decision). For clients struggling with long-term issues such as severe substance dependence or serious mental illness, however, long-term support is typically required. In some cases, episodic involvement extending over an indefinite period may be needed.

Decisions about length of service should be made according to the needs of the case and the available resources. Painful decisions regarding prioritization and triage may be required when the level of demand is high relative to available professional resources. In Ms. Todd's case, it was possible to offer extended (but not endless) services, which seemed reasonable given the enormous challenges involved in moving from homelessness to stability while coping with a serious affective illness. Goals in a case such as this often need to be reexamined at intervals as the case situation changes, but they certainly focus on helping the client build personal strengths and capacities and connect with natural support networks that can help maintain and extend the gains achieved.

CORE PRACTICE PROCESSES AND SKILLS

A good deal of variation exists among practice approaches (often called "practice models") regarding the central processes, knowledge, and skills required for practice with individuals. Some commonalities exist among approaches—the confluence has been increasing in recent years—but some of the differences among them are substantive and important. The *psychosocial approach* (Goldstein, 1995), for example, focuses on assessment but recognizes the importance of relationship, whereas the *Life Model* (Germain & Gitterman, 1996) acknowledges assessment but places greater emphasis on processes of building relationships with clients and works to understand the case primarily in terms of its ecological surround. The *strengths approach* (Saleebey, 2006), which is increasingly important in the field, places primary emphasis on identification and mobilization of personal and situational strengths, rather than on diagnosis or assessment of pathology or a heavy focus on problems. The strengths approach is one dimension of a shared power perspective. The *ecobehavioral* approach, emphasized in this chapter, is grounded in the four perspectives on practice discussed in chapter 2 (ecosystems, social justice, shared power, and evidence-based practice) while placing strong emphasis on understanding case dynamics in terms of the natural science of behavior (Mattaini, 1997, 1999).

The practice process can be viewed as organic and connected but with four core functions, as shown in Figure 8-2: (1) *engagement* with the client in a relationship of shared power, (2) *envisioning* an improved case configuration to be

FIGURE 8-2
□ □ □ □ □
Schematic of the Recursive Practice Process

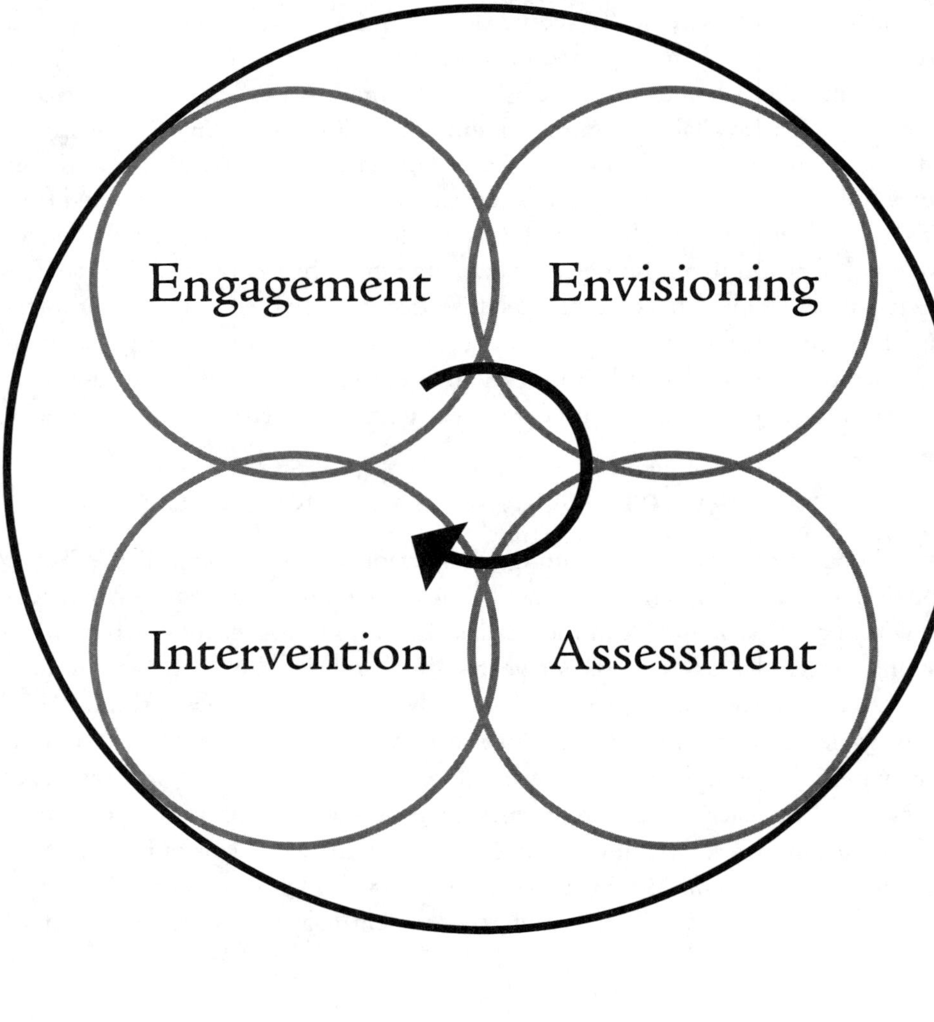

Engagement   Envisioning

Intervention   Assessment

constructed (or a positive configuration to be maintained), (3) collaborative *assessment* of the case, and (4) *intervention* to make or maintain change.

To some extent, all of these functions are present in every practice event, but typically they receive differential emphasis over time. In general, attention is first paid to engagement, which blends (notice the overlap on the figure) into envisioning. That in turn blends into assessment, from which intervention emerges. The arrow in Figure 8-2 shows this general flow. In practice, once engagement is begun, the social worker will continue to work to maintain engagement throughout the rest of the case. The envisioned goal may change, and monitoring progress means that assessment once begun never stops. It is therefore important not to think of these processes as entirely discrete, but rather to recognize that they are interwoven and recursive over time.

The order of these core practice processes is neither rigid nor invariant. In some cases (in crisis situations, in particular) the social worker may act immediately after a time-limited assessment and then shift back to other functions as the crisis abates. A child protective services worker, for example, may quickly determine that a child may be at imminent risk and remove the child from the home, but far more assessment and engagement with the family will be required to develop a long-term plan. Clients who are experiencing natural or manmade disasters or individually traumatic experiences often require rapid cycling between support (active listening) and active concrete problem solving; work with interpersonal and environmental contexts and cognitive and behavioral interventions may be important in later stages of work with trauma survivors (Naugle & Follette, 1998). Determining which steps are appropriate at any moment requires ongoing assessment. Other changes may also dictate shifts among the core functions. For example, a homeless client who finally achieves a reasonably stable housing situation may then be interested in envisioning new directions for the collaboration with the social worker.

Engagement

Some level of relationship is necessary for any useful or effective practice. At a minimum, the client must be willing to interact in some way with the social worker, and for some kinds of cases, an intense relationship may be required (for example, in many cases in which the client is trying to overcome the emotional damage caused by abuse or violence). Many cases seen by social workers are "involuntary," or at least not entirely voluntary, but even in those cases, before a social worker can be useful, some level of relationship is required. For example, if the client is a parent in a child protective services case, the client at least must believe what the worker says; some level of trust must be achieved. To progress very far, the client must also, at some level, contract with the worker to work together (even if only toward an abstract goal, such as "getting my child back").

Constructing a meaningful relationship is essential for obtaining cooperation, convincing clients to return for services, and coming to trust the worker's statements.

When clients have had limited experiences with trusting relationships, achieving authentic engagement in such a relationship can be an important helping experience in itself, but it may require significant time and commitment on the part of the social worker. Engaging and working with involuntary clients is naturally an area of concern for beginning social workers—and sometimes they are self-protectively skeptical about such cases. Effective work with involuntary clients, although challenging, *is* possible, however, given the social worker's genuine commitment, understanding of the dynamics involved, and strong engagement skills, as discussed below. (See, for example, Farabee, Prendergast, & Anglin, 1998, regarding addictions, and Smagner & Sullivan, 2005, regarding involuntary work in child welfare.)

Commitment is critical; engagement may take considerable time, involve a great deal of testing on the part of the client, and challenge the social worker's beliefs that change is possible and that all persons must be respected. Given such commitment, the worker must also understand the dynamics of the case. For example, addiction is "a complex self-organizing system" (Bickel & Potenza, 2006, p. 8) in which "drugs of dependence appear to commandeer evolutionarily old portions of the brain that regulate natural reinforcers of drink, food, sex, and social interaction" (Bickel & Potenza, p. 10). If, however, the social worker believes addiction to be an immoral—and "free"—choice, it will be impossible to work well with an involuntary client struggling with addiction. The worker's judgmental attitude and lack of sophisticated knowledge about the dynamics of the issue will present insuperable obstacles to engagement and subsequent practice processes.

Relationship Skills. Several repertoires (skills) are helpful for constructing and strengthening the professional relationship. Perhaps most important, the social worker can truly listen to the client in a respectful and nonjudgmental way. By doing so, the practitioner functions as a nonpunitive audience, which most people find enormously helpful as they sort out their experiences verbally. Many social work clients have seldom or never had such an audience; many, in fact, have been consistently punished for speaking honestly and from the heart. A nonpunitive audience can help the client to find his or her "voice," and over time, the client will typically share more and more emotionally difficult material.

Responding nonpunitively requires that the social worker somehow come to view the client's actions as natural responses (the best he or she knew how to make) to the client's subjective world, even if the behavior may not be something the practitioner could ever condone. This perspective can be challenging with involuntary clients, but it remains essential. The social worker should be honest with him- or herself and the client, noting when necessary that the actions the client has taken may be disturbing to the worker and perhaps unacceptable to society, but nevertheless expressing a commitment to trying to understand how things happened from the client's perspective.

For some clients, such as those who are struggling with serious loss, the opportunity to simply explore one's experiences and emotions can in itself be a valuable step toward acceptance and, ultimately, moving on. If the social worker can also communicate that he or she can, to some extent, see the client's reality and experience the client's responses (not just experiencing but actively demonstrating empathy), the client's level of trust will increase—sometimes quickly, sometimes slowly and unevenly, depending on the client's previous experience with relationships. If the social worker communicates interest, empathy ("feeling with"), and respect (treating the client as important), a demoralized client is more likely to begin to view him- or herself as valuable through a cognitive process (that is, the construction of an equivalence relation: "I $\approx$ worth listening to $\approx$ valuable"). (Note that the "$\approx$" as used here is a symbol for equivalence *on some dimensions*; it does not mean equal to in all ways.)

A great deal of research indicates that the "core conditions" of respect, empathy, and authenticity are necessary for achieving effective results with a wide range of clients (Hepworth Rooney, Rooney, Strom-Gottfried, & Larsen, 2005). These conditions are actualized in what the social worker does:

+ Respect is communicated through sharing power.
+ Empathy is communicated by expressing a real sensitivity to what the client is experiencing, and why.
+ Authenticity is communicated by being human and real.

There are as many ways to communicate these qualities and experiences of the worker to the client as there are social workers. The nonverbal channel is crucial: Facial expression, tone of voice, body position, physical distance and touch (when appropriate), eye contact, and even arrangement of the space where the exchange occurs are important and will vary a great deal, depending on factors such as age, gender, and cultural expectations. It is particularly useful to role-play and discuss this area with classmates and supervisors, to obtain objective feedback for oneself, and to test those factors cross-culturally. Empathic skills and skills in actively communicating empathy (demonstrating to the client that you are genuinely "feeling with" them) are generally not strong in U.S. society, and active efforts are usually required to achieve the necessary skills for practice. One must learn to listen and to respond as a genuine human being, from the heart.

A wide range of verbal responses can be useful in building the relationship; generally, they involve expressions of empathy (particularly regarding emotions), recognition, and accurate understanding. Statements such as those listed in Figure 8-3 are particularly useful, but they should always be used in ways that are natural to the social worker and familiar to the client.

Sharing Power in the Work. Direct statements recognizing the strengths and value of the client, the importance of the client's voice, the client's potential contributions to resolving whatever issues are present, and statements of shared responsibility for the outcome of the work are critical. The ultimate goal is the co-construction of a relationship of shared power that can be used to achieve the client's goals (Lowery & Mattaini, 2001). In sharing power, each participant has a strong voice in the process, and all recognize and expect that each has his or her own power, own gifts, and own vision to contribute to the work. Every client has strengths, an intimate knowledge of his or her life experiences and reality, and,

FIGURE 8-3

□ □ □ □ □

Worker Statements That May Prompt and Reinforce Client Sharing, Support Client Strengths, and Communicate Empathy in the Engagement Process

- I see . . .
- Can you tell me more about that?
- It looks like this is hard to talk about . . .
- It sounds like you felt really angry, and also maybe a bit hurt, when he didn't come home that night. Is that right?
- I know this may be painful, but can you tell me what happened next?
- And that made you feel better? Did that last?
- Let me see if I have this right: What you are saying is that it was the deception that most disturbed you?
- What strengths do you bring to this situation?
- It's very impressive, given all that, that you are doing so well.
- I'm particularly impressed that . . .
- Hmm . . .
- What was going through your mind at that point?
- Imagine that things changed as you'd like . . . what would be different?
- That must have been pretty frightening.
- Wow!
- Sometimes when something like that happens people feel a certain satisfaction. Was that true for you? Can you tell me a little about that?
- And then you felt . . . ?
- That's pretty normal.
- But . . . ?
- What about now? Do you still feel that way?

often, a wide range of other knowledge and skills; the potential power these factors contribute to the joint work are critical to the outcome. From this perspective, a client is not an aggregation of pathologies, though we all have challenges and damage with which to contend. A better reality can emerge only from power, not from weakness. Similarly, the social worker brings unique knowledge, gifts, and power to the process. Together, the two (and others if involved, which is often important) also carry different but important obligations and responsibilities for the outcome of the work.

A relationship of shared power in direct practice is one of the interfaces between social work and social justice. In a shared power relationship, the social worker gives up a hierarchical stance in which he or she acts as the "expert" and instead takes on a role of one important participant in a practice event in which each party has something essential to contribute and shares responsibility for the outcome. The contrast with early social work, in which caseworkers saw themselves as facilitating moral uplift, or with a practice stance rooted in diagnosis of pathology, could hardly be more stark. A genuine shared power relationship requires that the social worker give up certain forms of ego gratification, not out of sacrifice but out of recognition that they are unjustified. Social workers also need to recognize that people from differing life experiences, social classes, and cultural identities may have perspectives as valid as the worker's own and may know more than the worker in many areas.

The word "empowerment" is widely used in the social work literature. Note, however, that the root of the word is "power" and that real advantages are to be found in talking explicitly about power, both the constructive power that the client, worker, and others bring to their work together and the coercive, oppressive power that clients often experience in their lives. One complication with the verb "empower" is that it is a transitive verb, indicating that someone empowers someone (even if oneself). This concept does not adequately communicate the transactional realities of a shared power relationship. The authors in this book, therefore, tend to write in terms of a dynamic of shared power, which is the basis for empowerment.

A relationship of shared power is constructed gradually, and it can be enriched and deepened during each phase of the work together. No single, "right" way exists to achieve shared power, of course, but the social worker can guide the relationship in that direction at many points. For example, during early engagement, an explanation like the following can be incorporated into the conversation:

I have been working with people to improve their lives for some time now, and I've learned this: We, together, probably have the power to make some real changes in your life. To do this, we need to act as a team; you may not be able to do it alone, given how hard things are right now, and I certainly can't do it by myself. But you know the saying "Two heads are better than one?" Our work is like that. If I do what I can, and you do, too, there's real hope for change. You have a strong voice, I have a strong voice, we do it together . . . how does that sound?

Of course, clients who are experiencing little power in their lives may find this difficult to believe; that feeling is natural and should be accepted. The worker can, in such cases, empathize with the experience of powerlessness and ask the client to give "our team" a chance. In some cases, depending on the client, words like "partnership" or "collaboration" may be a better fit, but explicitly discussing power early on will often prove useful in later stages, can build hope—and, frankly, can be powerful.

Enhancing shared power can occur continuously while engaging in the other core practice functions, and examples are provided throughout the material that follows. During the envisioning process, the client's voice should be primary and taken seriously; the worker, however, brings skills and experience in clearly elaborating a vision, so both participants have critical roles. During assessment, some of the first questions (as outlined in the Interview Guide presented later in this chapter) involve what is going right for the client, what his or her strengths are, the areas of life in which he or she has power. Intervention usually explicitly involves tasks for both client and worker. These tasks should usually be framed in terms of enhancing the client's power to shape a life that works for him or her. In addition, many opportunities to support client power (for example, "I see that as a real strength of yours . . . tell me more about how you achieved that") and to deepen the extent of collaborative power sharing (for example, "Here's a chance for us to really join forces and work this out together") arise in work with individuals.

Many of the same basic strategies are required in work with family members, agency representatives, and other stakeholders (for example, teachers, foster and biological parents) involved in the case because power sharing ought to involve all relevant actors in the case. No standard recipe exists for constructing a relationship of shared power, of course, but constant attention, retrospective evaluation of how well one is using opportunities to share power in work with clients, consultation, and reading the empowerment and shared power literature can all help strengthen skills in building relationships of shared power with clients and others involved in the case.

The process of building a relationship overlaps substantially with the next function—envisioning—and continues throughout the practice process; discussions regarding those other processes often provide the content through which the relationship develops. Relationship construction begins with the first acknowledgments and thoughtful empathic observations the worker makes in the early minutes of contact, and it continues to evolve and shift throughout the work until the time of termination. (By that point, if the use of time has been clarified and honestly discussed throughout the work together, the client should be well prepared to leave without a major emotional or practical disruption. The bigger challenge is sometimes ensuring that the social worker is ready to let go; this should be dealt with through supervision because it can be difficult to acknowledge to oneself.) A good deal is known about how to build and deepen practice relationships, even in particularly challenging situations. Students should pursue this material in depth (see, for example, Germain & Gitterman, 1996; Hepworth et al., 2005).

Envisioning

The second of the major practice functions is working with the client to develop a preliminary vision of what a desirable outcome for the case would look like (including personal, interpersonal, and environmental dimensions). What would change, and what would remain the same? In one way or another, some of the earliest questions to be asked include something like the following:

+ "If we are successful, how will your life be different?"
+ "Who will be doing what differently?"
+ "What would an observer see or hear that would be different than it is now?"
+ "What is your situation like now, and how would you like it to change?"
+ The "miracle question" often asked in solution-focused treatment (Furman & Ahola, 1992): "If you woke up tomorrow and all your problems were solved, what would be happening?"

Envisioning often occurs concurrently with efforts to deepen engagement and can be a useful way of moving the focus toward hope and away—at least to some extent—from problems and pathology. Although empathic engagement requires authentic recognition of the client's pain or struggles, dwelling on the negative without building hope can be demoralizing. In addition, well-established theory related to human behavior demonstrates that it is usually easier to construct new, positive repertoires and transactions (reducing competing problem behaviors indirectly) than to directly attack problems, which often requires aversive strategies (Mattaini, 1997; Sidman, 2001).

At this stage, the social worker's efforts are not directed toward finalizing goals or plans; that usually requires attention to further assessment. Rather, the emphasis is on identifying a general direction for the work with the client and on building hope. In some cases, the client may have a clear vision of how he or she would like life to look. For some clients, the envisioning process may be detailed and relatively specific and may thus facilitate construction of the detailed Goal Ecomap discussed later in this chapter. Other clients may have only the vaguest of notions about direction. That, too, is fine; further specificity can emerge through the assessment process. Some clients, accustomed to thinking about problems and struggles, may find it difficult, especially in the beginning, to focus on goals or the construction of positive alternatives. In such cases, the client and worker may begin at that point ("starting where the client is" is classic practice wisdom in social work) by reaching at least a preliminary agreement about the issues to be resolved. Over time, however, it is important to nudge the process gradually toward a focus on constructing positive change (Goldiamond, 1974/2002).

Assessment

The initial vision developed by the social worker and client is a first step, but in most cases more data are needed to clarify the realities of the client's life and further refine the vision. This refinement happens through the assessment process, which is key to professional practice. Intuitively helpful, positive people may be able to engage others and help them imagine goals, but professional practice also requires the integration of an extensive knowledge base with case specifics—that is, assessment. This knowledge base is one source of power that the social worker can bring to the shared power relationship. The assessment process itself, like the practice process, involves several subprocesses, which naturally tend to occur in a particular order but overlap and interweave and often happen in an interactive way. The reader is encouraged to think about Figure 8-4, which portrays those processes, as a more detailed expansion of the "Assessment" bubble shown in Figure 8-2.

Examples of the kinds of questions that may be useful in completing the assessment functions are provided in the Interview Guide shown in Figure 8-5. It is important that the guide be seen only as a tool to help structure the process; different types of questions will be required in every practice setting and for every case. Questions, observations, and suggestions should occur in the natural flow of an authentic conversation that communicates real concern, support, and interest in understanding the client, not in a rigid, invariant interrogation. Assessment is a collaborative process between social worker and client, not something the social worker does "to" the client; it is emphatically not a process of diagnosing the client's pathology but a process of coming to a joint understanding and plan for the case.

Assessment occurs in every form of practice, including crisis work and very short-term treatment. Even if a social worker in a busy emergency room has only 20 minutes with a person, a professional never acts without having a reason, and what is done is always based on assessment, rapid though it may be. The process

FIGURE 8-4

🔲🔲🔲🔲🔲

Schematic of the Assessment Process

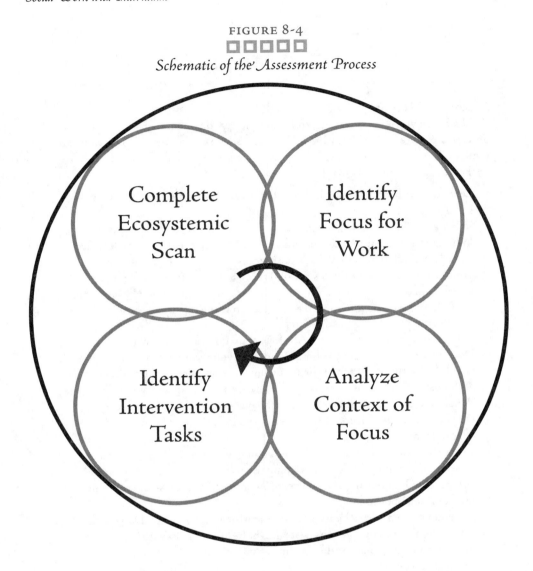

may need to be accelerated dramatically from that occurring in some other practice settings, but it still must occur. It may be helpful to compare this scenario
with those encountered by emergency medical technicians (paramedics), who
must perform a quick evaluation before taking action. Although this evaluation
is much abbreviated from what might be done, say, at the Mayo Clinic, no action
can be taken, even in crisis situations, without some level of assessment. The
assessment conducted by the paramedic on the street is at least as critical as the
detailed evaluations conducted at a medical center. The general framework presented here is therefore applicable regardless of setting or time constraints. Even
if the social worker meets with a client only once, it is still important to know

FIGURE 8-5

□□□□□

Sample Interview Guide

I. Ecosystemic Scan

I'd like to ask you a few questions so I can understand your situation. Let's try to develop a picture of what your life is like. [The social worker may wish to draw an ecomap during this stage or explore systemic transactions that may have relevance to the case, as suggested below.]

- Let's start with what's going right. What areas of your life are currently going best for you?
- What are your strengths? In what areas in your life do you have some power?
- Who are the most important people in your life? [For first person identified: How is that relationship? What's positive about it? How often do those positive things happen? On a scale of 0 (not at all) to 5 (a lot), how much satisfaction do you get from him (or her)? Are there also some struggles? How often do those come up? Same 0 to 5 scale, how much pain do those problems cause you?]
- Who else is important to you? [Ask follow-up questions as above.]
- Does anyone else live in your home? How are your relationships with those people? [For this and each of the following areas, inquire specifically about both positive and negative exchanges, as necessary, and quantify.]
- What kind of contacts do you have with your extended family and kin?
- Do you have many friends? How often do you see friends? How are those relationships?
- What about at work or school? What's going well there? So on our 0 to 5 scale, are there things that are not going too well? About a ___ on our scale?
- Tell me a little about where you live. How satisfied are you with your home and your neighborhood?
- Are you involved with a church or other spiritual community? Do you have any spiritual needs or concerns that I might be able to help with?
- Are you a member of any other groups or organizations?
- Any legal involvement?
- How is your physical health?

---

something about the client's life situation, to identify focal issues and goals, to understand those issues, and to plan what to do.

Ecosystemic Scan. Note that the Interview Guide begins with positives rather than with problems. Client strengths and power, as well as current and potential environmental resources, should be noted, as should challenges and issues. The goal is to capture the entire situation, not only "what is wrong." One impor-

FIGURE 8-5

□□□□□

Sample Interview Guide (continued)

- How much do you drink during an average week? Do you take any medications or use any drugs? What concerns do you have about your use of alcohol or drugs?
- What would you like to do more of? What would you like to do less? [Suggest self-monitoring or observational measures to expand data.]
- What about emotions? What feelings would you like to have more often? Do you sometimes feel sad, tense, or angry? When does that happen? How often does that happen, and how long have you felt that way? [Pursue further depending on responses, including use of self-anchored scales or rapid assessment instruments.]
- Are there any thoughts or memories that disturb you? [Expand discussion as necessary.]

II. Clarifying the Focus for Work

- So out of all of this, where do you think we should begin? What's most important to you?
- You said that you are having some struggles with ___. Is that something we should work on?
- What do you think would be a realistic goal here? What steps might you be willing to consider?
- So specifically, one of your goals might be _____ [state in behavioral terms].
- Is there anything else we should work on at this point, do you think?

[Repeat for additional foci if relevant.]

III. Contextual Analysis of Focus for Work

Now, let's see if we can reach a clear understanding of your first goal, which is ___. [General flow is from current undesirable situation to goal state; this kind of analysis should occur for each identified focus for work, whether it is a behavior of the client (like angry outbursts) or of someone else (for example, a teenage child who is getting into trouble or a landlord who has not made repairs).]

tant distinction between some forms of practice that are based on the strengths perspective and the approach presented here is that identifying strengths is not the end of the assessment process; rather, it is one step toward the process of sharing power to create change. A list of strengths by itself is static, but a list of strengths viewed as capacities and resources for action with a coherent plan can be part of a dynamic process of constructing an improved transactional reality.

FIGURE 8-5
□ □ □ □ □
Sample Interview Guide (continued)

- [If framed as a problem] As near as you can tell, how did this problem start? When was that?
- [If framed as a problem] What seems to trigger the problem? Are there times when it doesn't happen? What are those occasions?
- What are the advantages of the way things are now—for you or for anyone else? Does it "pay off" in some ways?
- Who or what keeps things the way they are?
- What are the costs of the way things are now? What other problems does it cause?
- Are there times when this is not a problem? Tell me about those times. [the exception question]
- What do you think it would take to get from where you are now to where you want to be? [Explore resources, including tangible, personal, and social.]
- Let's talk about what we each can do to help you reach this goal. Some of the power and strengths you bring to our work together are _____. What other resources can you contribute? What I bring to our work is _____. What else might I bring?
- Who else would be willing to help you achieve this goal, or resolve this problem? What could they contribute?
- Who or what might stand in the way?
- How important is this to you? Why? How will reaching this goal enrich your life? How quickly do you think that will happen? [building motivation]

IV. Identification of Intervention Tasks
This part of the interview needs to be highly individualized. It should include exploration of possible intervention options for mobilizing the resources discussed in the previous section and for addressing obstacles identified, emphasizing approaches with the best evidence-based support within the realities of the case situation. Tasks should explicitly involve contributions from everyone involved to achieving desired outcomes. Careful specification of the multiple steps required to work toward the goal is often required. Explore possible reinforcers to be used along the way as well.

To develop a realistic plan, it is essential that the worker and client have a clear picture of the client's life that conveys its contextual complexity. Conducting an ecosystemic scan of the client's life situation begins with and overlaps with the envisioning process but moves deeper, ensuring that the multiple dimensions that may be relevant and important to intervention are considered. The interview guide begins with what is going well, strengths, and personal power. It then moves to examination of relationships with close family and friends, and then more widely into the client's social, physical, and spiritual environment. (In recent years, social work and other helping professions have increasingly recognized the importance of spirituality and religious communities for clients; the Joint Commission on Accreditation of Healthcare Organizations [2004], for instance, now requires spiritual assessment of patients. Hodge [2006] provides an excellent introduction to this area.) Only after all of this has been considered does the process move toward intrapersonal (emotional, cognitive, and behavioral) issues.

A careful review of the relevant dimensions noted on the Interview Guide can help ensure that the full transactional reality is at least noticed. Depending on the issues and goals in the case, it may not be essential to examine all areas in depth, and in modern, fast-paced practice, the time in which to do so is often limited. Using a tool such as the Quick Scan (see Figure 8-6) or other form of transactional ecomap, it is possible to sketch major intrapersonal and transactional dimensions of a client's life in a few minutes, and it may be crucial to do so. It is important to note excesses and deficits of exchanges occurring between the client and other people and systems as well as behavioral, emotional, and cognitive excesses and deficits with which the client is personally struggling. Intrapersonal issues can be noted in the inner circle representing the client, and transactions can be indicated with coded and commented arrows. Although using color is especially effective, if you have only one pen, arrows representing negative exchanges can be distinguished by cross-hatching, and arrows for positives can be plain.

A small preliminary study (reported in Mattaini, 1993, chapter 8) indicated that it is important to actually sketch out such an ecomap (often, but not always, with the client) to ensure that all major areas and dimensions that may be relevant to the case are considered. In addition, most students discover that their clients find developing an ecomap to be an empowering experience, one that communicates the student's empathic interest in understanding the client's life. This process is often recursive with envisioning, because new information that emerges is incorporated into the joint vision of where the case is going.

Although practice can occur only in the present, looking at ways in which the client's circumstances have changed over time is sometimes of value. The roots of current problems can sometimes best be understood in this way; more often, it is important to recognize the temporal trajectory of a case. For example, the current situation may not appear to be too serious, but it may reflect ongoing deterioration that, should it continue, could result in more acute distress over time. In other cases, despite a high level of current stress, a pattern of improvement

FIGURE 8-6
🞏 🞏 🞏 🞏 🞏
Blank Quick Scan Form for Rapid Assessment

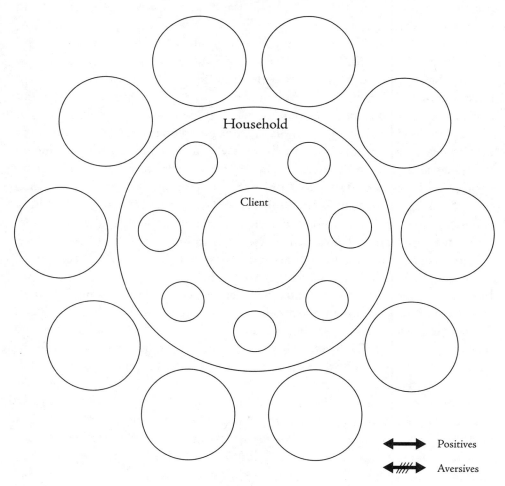

can be identified to build hope and use as a resource. Sequential ecomaps and other instruments, such as timelines or genograms, can be useful for this process (Mattaini, 1993).

In the process of looking broadly at the client's life situation, issues of oppression and violations of human rights and their sequelae may surface. It is essential that those issues be identified and openly voiced when they are discovered; not to do so would be to participate in "blaming the victim" and in the perpetuation of the oppression. For example, in the case of Ms. Todd, while examining her history, the worker and client discussed a problem she had had with a housing provider. This provider appeared to have treated several potential clients differently, depending on race. The open discussion of systematic racism in the network of mental health services that ensued was important for acknowledging the client's experiences and may have contributed to her subsequent involvement in advocacy activities for people involved in that network. Gender dynamics were also involved in the case, because the client had experienced sexual harassment and unwanted advances in the "helping" systems, and those incidents also needed to be acknowledged.

Identification of a Focus for Work. As a result of the ecosystemic scan, the client and worker achieve a preliminary shared understanding of the case as it currently stands and, to the extent relevant, as it has developed over time. Many possible areas for focus—problems, challenges, and opportunities—may emerge from this work, often more than can be directly addressed. (Work focusing on one area may affect others as well, as elaborated by systems theory.) The client and worker should select a small number of foci for work. Usually one to three foci can be managed at any given time. In residential or day treatment programs, where more contact time may be available, it may be possible to devote some attention to a larger number of goals, but even in those cases, most effort usually must be directed toward a very small number of primary foci.

An explicit *contract*—written or verbal—as to the foci should emerge from the discussion between client and worker. If they have different agendas, it is unlikely that the case will move toward an outcome that will be satisfactory. It is essential that there not be hidden, unspoken agendas. Avoiding such unspoken agendas can be more difficult than one may think because social workers naturally have their own opinions and values, which may not be consistent with those of the client. Still, genuine common ground must be found.

Reaching an agreement can be difficult, but it is essential, even in involuntary situations. The client and the worker may not agree on everything, but they must at least have a high-level agreement on goals, which may be as broad as "We both want to keep you out of jail" or as narrow as "We will work to help you find and keep more friends." The more specific the focus for work, the easier other practice processes may be, but the most critical factor is that both participants (and any others involved) leave the encounter with a clear and consensual understanding of where they are going in their work together. When working with an involuntary client, real empathy, frank honesty about what is and is not possible given legal and other limitations, and hopeful persistence in searching for some area of common focus are usually necessary; a sense of humor can also be helpful.

It is sometimes necessary to meet with an involuntary client multiple times before any progress toward agreement occurs. I visited one client admitted to the hospital for a serious suicide attempt multiple times before she ever spoke to me.

She was speaking to no one else, either; in fact she was referred to me by two other professionals I supervised because they could not make any progress. She could not be released until a plan was in place. During each visit, I reminded her who I was, explained how I might be able to help, and offered to do so; I also indicated that it was her choice as to whether she wished to work with me or not. The emotional tone used is important in such cases, avoiding frustration, communicating caring, and giving a straightforward message; it was my job to keep coming back. Finally, on about my fifth visit, after I gave my usual message, she couldn't resist rolling her eyes and laughing, and from that moment we were able to seriously engage. (Such resistance to engaging is also common among adolescents and those in the legal system.)

One useful way to moving toward explicit foci is to think, literally or figuratively, about collaboratively developing a Goal Ecomap—an image of how the overall situation might change as a result of the work with the client. Foci for work can be explicitly noted on the map. Taking this approach reminds the worker–client team to think about focal areas explicitly and in context. For example, the Goal Ecomap shown in Figure 8-7 for Ms. Todd shows a shift in mood but also portrays the kinds of social, environmental, and educational changes that will probably be necessary to stabilize the affective improvement; clarity about such changes is important in the next step (contextual analysis). Attention to the Goal Ecomap will make it more likely that the social worker will assist the client not only with learning new self-talk (a cognitive strategy) but also in planning and problem solving about moving toward stable housing, attending school, and restructuring the relationship with the client's mother.

To achieve the necessary specificity, each focus should involve a change or stabilization of someone's behavior—but "behavior" as used here is a broad concept, including everything from overt motor behavior (for example, battering) to covert verbal behavior (what one says to oneself—self-talk). It includes such things as the physiological processes involved in anxiety or depression and other types of cognitive phenomena, such as memories (Poppen, 1989). The behavior on which to concentrate may be that of the client (for example, to shift from negative self-talk to more hopeful and activating cognitive processes) or that of someone else (for example, the behavior of a child the client is concerned about as a parent). Often, however, the behaviors on which social work practice focuses involve exchanges among actors, transactional patterns that could be tracked on a transactional ecomap (for example, to improve marital dynamics, eliminate child maltreatment, or catalyze the development of mutual aid networks). The focal behavior is also commonly that of systems actors (for example, actions required to have a Social Security eligibility determination reversed).

This level of specificity greatly simplifies the process of monitoring the case. As discussed in chapter 6, practice may be monitored in a variety of ways, many

FIGURE 8-7

□ □ □ □ □

*Goal Ecomap Portraying the Contextual Situation to
Be Constructed through Collaborative Consultation*

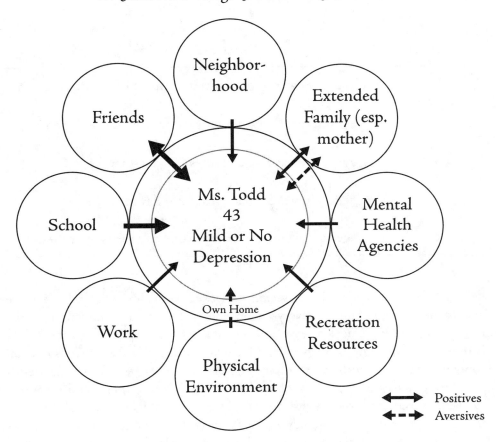

of which apply to work with individuals. Simple counting and graphing of problem- or goal-related events, scores on rapid assessment instruments or behaviorally anchored rating scales, or tracking changes in transactional exchanges using sequential ecomaps are useful approaches that flow directly from envisioning the desired case outcome and targeting specific focal behaviors and transactions for attention. Graphing changes on a behaviorally anchored rating scale developed with Ms. Todd (see Figure 8-8), for example, says a good deal about the trajectory of the case as well as the possible need for adjustments in the work being done.

Contextual Analysis of Focal Transactions and Actions. Identifying the focus for work in a case is an important step but does not immediately indicate what must

FIGURE 8-8

□ □ □ □ □

Behaviorally Anchored Rating Scale for the Extent to Which a Client Engages in Rewarding Activities as One Step for Addressing Depression

Level of Goal Attainment	Rewarding Activity
5	Engages in rewarding activities for most of the day each day
4	Engages in rewarding activities more than once per day
3	Engages in rewarding activities 5-7 days per week
2	Engages in rewarding activities 2-4 days per week
1	Engages in rewarding activities one day per week or less

be done. Not everyone who is seeking a richer social life will find the same approaches helpful, and not every client who is depressed or moving into the early stages of Alzheimer's disease will benefit from the same intervention. What is required is an analysis of those foci for work within the client's transactional context. Consistent with this recognition, Reid (1985) suggested that the identification of causes of problems, obstacles to surmounting them, and resources available or required to deal with those causes and problems are central factors in an adequate contextual analysis; this simple framework still is useful. Of course, in a shared power relationship, the power carried by each person involved in the case is a critical resource.

To complete contextual analysis adequately, the social worker's full professional knowledge base is required. At this point in the assessment, knowledge about human behavior becomes critically important. Genuinely understanding the foci of the work, as well as the factors that may have shaped and now maintain those foci, requires extensive practical and empirical knowledge and a clear theoretical framework for organizing the information collected. One person who is homeless and demoralized may find substance abuse treatment useful, whereas another may require residential stability first, for example. One person with a couples problem may benefit from joint counseling, whereas another may require shelter services.

Cultural-level knowledge can be crucial. For example, a young American Indian man attending a boarding school was experiencing severe emotional distress resulting from dreams of a recently deceased relative. An American Indian social worker called in for a consultation suggested that he set aside a small portion of his meals to "feed" his relative, a traditional way of recognizing, remembering, and expressing respect for an ancestor (and thereby remaining connected with one's collective identity) in certain Native cultures. This intervention was successful. Cultural consultation was required to understand the problem; this intervention would never have been arrived at by chance. In many situations, resources from a client's own culture may need to be intensely involved (for example, using traditional rituals). Only cultural consultation will clarify such options, so social workers should be prepared to work with or refer clients to traditional healers, shamans, religious leaders, and other cultural consultants.

Factual knowledge, theory, and the information gathered in early phases of the assessment must be integrated in a coherent way before the client and social worker can determine what needs to be done. This process is described in this chapter using an ecobehavioral model, although other frameworks are available. Particularly important in an ecobehavioral analysis is an examination of antecedents and consequences of the focal behaviors and transactions. What one says to oneself (for instance, "No one cares about me") can be a critical antecedent to emotional experiences. Environmental events and conditions (severe deprivation, for example) can be important motivating antecedents that make even relatively low-quality payoffs, such as those associated with some substances or abusive relationships, attractive. Problematic interpersonal behavior, such as tantrums or even depressive talk, is often shaped by attention from others (a consequence), a process that can become cyclical.

Attention to constructing more positive antecedents and consequences can be crucial to helping clients take the steps required. If the focus for work is the client's completing school, for example, it is essential to identify the action steps (of the client and others) required to reach that distant goal, determine what kinds of contextual supports (antecedents and consequences) will be necessary to help the client or other target person take those steps, and determine who will provide those antecedents and consequences. All of those steps may then need to be included in the intervention plan. In work with individuals, the two key players always available are the social worker and the client; identifying what each player can do to support the positive actions required to reach the client's goals is a central task in contextual analysis.

Steps in Contextual Analysis. The following four core steps are involved in completing an ecobehavioral contextual analysis:

1. Clarify what action (behavior) needs to be taken by whom to address the focus. If the focus of the work is reducing depression, for example, several actions may be necessary. It may be important that the client become

more active (behavioral activation) and that she change her depression-maintaining self-talk (see Intervention Tasks, below). It may also be necessary, however, to change her exposure to an emotionally abusive spouse, which might involve either limiting contact or taking action to change the interpersonal transactions occurring in the home.

2. Clarify intrapersonal (for example, cognitive) and environmental factors that are obstacles to taking the identified actions. Those factors may include self-talk, but they may also include "pay-offs" for undesirable behavior and transactional interference from others. For example, children often engage in tantrums because they work for them in some way, whether to obtain attention or get what they want. If that is the case, those payoffs may be a serious obstacle to change. Some problematic interpersonal behavior by adults (constant complaining, for example) may also "work" in the short run (often in focusing attention on oneself) but may be quite costly in the long run (as others begin to avoid the person).

3. Clarify antecedent factors that could motivate the people involved to take the desired actions. Keep in mind that it may not be the client's behavior that is the focus for work; the same principles apply regardless of whose behavior is involved. Antecedent factors may include exposure to positive models who can build hope, learning new self-talk, or encouragement to simply "experiment with life" and see how the experiments come out.

4. Clarify consequences that may encourage those involved to take the desired actions. Consequences may include encouragement from the social worker or others, natural consequences that can be expected to occur once behavior changes, or specially planned reinforcers. Making major changes nearly always requires significant shifts in consequences. For example, many people do not enter substance abuse treatment until significant others around them begin to respond differently to their problem behaviors; people who are depressed usually will not immediately find that becoming more active makes them feel better, and they may need strong support from someone else when they take the planned steps.

The kind of chart shown in Figure 8-9 may be helpful in completing this analysis. The tasks that will be selected for intervention will flow directly from this analysis. Tasks are typically directed toward reducing identified obstacles and putting the identified antecedents and consequences in place.

Consistent with principles of evidence-based practice, the social worker will commonly need to take a careful look at the literature, particularly at approaches that have substantial evidence of effectiveness. The social worker–client team will often not know the most promising ways to challenge obstacles and arrange optimal antecedents and consequences without further exploring the knowledge

FIGURE 8-9

*Tool for Ecobehavioral Contextual Analysis of a Desired Behavior
(Behavioral Activation on the Part of the Client)*

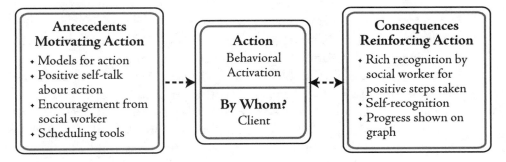

**Antecedents
Motivating Action**

+ Models for action
+ Positive self-talk
  about action
+ Encouragement from
  social worker
+ Scheduling tools

Action
Behavioral
Activation

By Whom?
Client

**Consequences
Reinforcing Action**

+ Rich recognition by
  social worker for
  positive steps taken
+ Self-recognition
+ Progress shown on
  graph

Potential obstacles to be addressed:
+ Messages from spouse and others that "You are
  too depressed to become more active at this point."
+ Limited financial resources
+ Few friends to act as models or offer encouragement

(Long-term, natural
consequences can
maintain activation
without need for
external supports)

Notes: The tool elaborates potentially supporting antecedents and consequences as well as potential obstacles that may need to be addressed. Intervention tasks flow from the diagram, including antecedents, consequences, and challenging obstacles. If the initial efforts to activate behavior prove unsuccessful, a more complete analysis may be required.

base. The evidence-based practice process is designed to help with this task. As stated in chapter 2, the five key steps in evidence-based practice include the following:

1. Develop answerable questions, the answers to which can specifically guide intervention, for example, "What types of social and medical interventions are most likely to slow the progression of Alzheimer's disease for my client?" or "What approaches are most likely to help a young man struggling with being bullied to reach his full developmental potential?"

2. Search for the answers to those questions using the professional literature (including online databases). A major function of graduate education in social work is to prepare the practitioner to independently search for the best information for answering practice questions.

3. Critically appraise the information obtained. In some cases, clear preferences for certain intervention strategies may emerge, whereas in other cases less certain knowledge may be the best that can be located. For example, in the bullying case, the worker would discover that an effort to teach the

youth how to respond to bullying is generally not a powerful intervention, whereas helping him to construct a friendship network and systemic intervention at the school level are more promising.

4. Determine the fit of the strategies and procedures found in the literature, especially given the values and preferences of the client. The data gathered in assessment and organized by the contextual analysis are critical to determining how well those strategies fit the case. In the Alzheimer's example, according to the literature participation in an ongoing socialization and recreation group is likely to help, but the client may refuse these because he or she is "a private person." In that case, other strategies that increase activity and human contact may need to be creatively constructed. To the maximum extent possible, this should be done collaboratively while recognizing that with progressive dementia the client will have less and less ability to participate in such activities over time.

5. Evaluate the effectiveness and efficiency of steps taken, modify the approach accordingly, and clarify outcomes for future reference.

Movement through the evidence-based process often makes selecting specific intervention tasks relatively straightforward, although implementing them may be challenging. In some cases, however, what is found in the literature is limited or only loosely applicable to the case, and the worker and client will need to rely on the contextual analysis, making and testing their best hypotheses as to what may help. Note, as in the bullying example, that individual work is not always the preferred strategy, which is why a professional social worker needs preparation for work at all system levels.

Identification of Intervention Tasks. After the foci for work have been carefully analyzed in their contextual complexity, the worker, client, and others involved in the case are ready to decide what active steps may be useful to work toward construction of the envisioned reality. It is quite useful to think of these steps as tasks (Reid, 1992)—specific actions to be taken—remembering that actions (behaviors) may be overt or private and physical, cognitive, or emotional. Intervention tasks may include actions to be taken by the client, by the worker, or by others involved in the plan. Everyone involved should be expected to make some contribution, although what is done may be quite different for each person, depending on role, talents, knowledge, resources, and others. (Recall also that it is often important to involve others from the social network in the work in some way, which of course expands the base for shared power, so tasks may include making those contacts.)

In many cases, steps to be taken can be framed as processes of *self-monitoring* and *self-management*, which are themselves empowering (Kopp, 1993). Self-monitoring is a straightforward process in which clients track events in their own lives, including their actions and reactions to experiences. In addition to being useful for assessment purposes, self-monitoring can give clients a sense of control over their lives (Kopp, 1993). Methods of self-monitoring range from the simple task of placing a check mark on a chart on the refrigerator each time one compliments a child for good behavior to keeping a detailed structured or unstructured journal to track cognitive self-talk. In some cases, clients' behavior changes as a result of monitoring alone (it is "reactive"); therefore, such monitoring can function independently as an intervention. In other cases, self-monitoring is the first step in a more extended process of self-management in which social or other incentives are added.

The general self-monitoring strategy involves four steps:

1. *Goal:* Clarify the goal to be achieved and the reasons to do so (this involves envisioning, of course).
2. *Pinpoint:* Identify specific actions to take to reach the goal, usually a progressive series of tasks that begin at a level that can almost certainly be achieved (most people tend to set initial goals too high).
3. *Track:* Chart progress on the pinpointed actions (for example, charting the number of healthy meals consumed or the hours spent with one's child).
4. *Provide incentives:* Ensure positive consequences for progress (often, recognition from others, but sometimes small rewards for oneself for achieving a bit of progress). Social or tangible incentives are not always necessary, but when a self-monitoring effort by itself is not working, incentives are usually the best next step to try. In some cases, small penalties (for example, fining oneself $5 for each failure to complete the pinpointed action) may also be helpful; penalties should not be so large that one is tempted to "cheat," however.

Reporting regularly to someone else, like the social worker, is commonly essential to self-management (most people, not just clients, tend not to keep challenging personal resolutions). Lack of progress should be seen as a signal that more assessment is needed to identify obstacles standing in the way, reduce unrealistic levels of expectation, or adjust the positive consequences and/or penalties in order to reach target levels.

Although certain basic types of intervention strategies are commonly used, sometimes the social worker must creatively craft unique interventions that are responsive to case dynamics. Professional social work practice cannot be reduced to a "cookbook" approach, although practice guidelines for particular case configurations can clearly be useful. For example, Reid's (2000) *Task Planner* identified a wide range of intervention tasks that have some empirical support for working with particular client issues. Such resources can provide considerable guidance and point to critical literature that should be examined as part of the evidence-based practice process. Some issues call for specific approaches; for instance, one student was assigned a case of nocturnal enuresis in a six-year-old child. Only a handful of specific interventions, including bladder training, scheduled awakening, and urine alarms, are effective with this problem (Reid, 2000; Sloane, 1979/1988). Generic approaches like empathic listening and examination of family dynamics by themselves will not resolve the problem, but they may be part of the work because contextual supports may need to be addressed to make implementation possible.

Decisions about what steps to take should become part of the collaborative contract between the client and social worker. Such decisions are always tentative, and it is common to revisit the process as needed during intervention. Relative specificity in planning intervention tasks leads to clarity in contracting and can simplify the monitoring process as well. In practice with individuals two levels of monitoring are generally useful: the extent to which intervention tasks are completed and the extent to which goals are achieved. (If tasks are being completed but goals are not being reached, the situation would suggest an inadequate analysis and the need to reassess the case situation.)

The general framework presented here is applicable regardless of setting or time constraints. Even if the social worker meets only once with a client, it is still important to know something about the client's life situation, to identify focal issues and goals, to understand those issues, and to plan what to do, whether the social worker has only 30 minutes or a period of months to work with the client.

Major Strategies for Intervention

The practice process generally moves from assessment to intervention in a relatively seamless way. The worker and client begin to implement the tasks they have identified, some of which may happen in private sessions; others take place in the client's natural environment or as "homework" to be completed by one or more of the participants. In general, three clusters of intervention strategies capture much of what social workers and clients do together: (1) working directly with the web of transactions in which clients live out their lives, (2) working with cognitive and other private events in ways that facilitate new experiences, and (3) learning new skills. In many cases, those interventions are mixed and phased, but it is useful to look at each category separately for analytic purposes. The material here simply touches on each cluster; many books have been written and a great deal of research has been done about each, and social work students must read deeply and widely to be adequately informed about the state of the art (and science) in practice.

Work with Transactional Webs. The purpose of social work is to construct a life reality that is more reinforcing and less aversive for clients, consistent with social justice. Given that social work is ultimately about changing patterns of transactions in the human web, all of social work practice is directed to helping clients achieve a new balance of transactions within their ecological worlds. In some cases, this balance is achieved indirectly (for example, by working with the client to change his or her self-talk, which may then affect his or her experiences). The most immediate way to affect a client's reality, however, is to work with the client to change transactions between the client and environmental actors and systems directly—an active form of practice. For this reason, practice that is directed toward collaborative intervention into the client's ecological world should ordinarily be the first, rather than the last, option considered.

Ways of increasing exposure to positive experiences and transactions include such disparate tactics as assisting the client with accessing benefits to which he or she is entitled, helping the client organize his or her family's living space (as many family preservation programs do), connecting the client to sources of social support (often using the social worker as a temporary bridge to other relationships), or working with family members to construct a more satisfying and less coercive family culture (see chapter 9). In some cases, the social worker may participate in changing other aspects of the client's world (for example, by referring to a group; see chapter 10); by working with neighborhoods, communities, or other larger aggregates (see chapter 11); or by advocating for organizational change (chapter 12).

All of these approaches fall into the "working with transactional webs" cluster of interventions. Many of them also have social justice implications. For example, if one's client is a battered woman, referral to an empowering support group can be helpful in many ways (Tutty, Bidgood, & Rothery, 1993). The client may receive help in protecting her right to security of person and perhaps become an advocate for others to whom this basic human right is denied. Some such approaches are sometimes seen as "merely" tangible services or case management, but if they are grounded in a professional assessment, they are every bit as professional and clinical as family therapy or cognitive restructuring. Many specific types of intervention fall into this general cluster, including network therapies, referrals, and efforts to coordinate the many agencies and systems that may be involved with an individual or family.

One useful framework for thinking about ecological interventions is that of multisystemic therapy (MST), developed by Henggeler and his colleagues (Henggeler, Schoenwald, Borduin, Rowland, & Cunningham, 1998). MST has solid empirical support for work with a range of issues, although like all other potentially effective approaches, how it is implemented is a critical factor. The MST approach is based on nine principles, which are listed in Figure 8-10.

Principle 1, understanding problems (and goals) within their system, refers to assessment, particularly to contextual analysis. Principle 2 offers a way of

FIGURE 8-10
□ □ □ □ □
Multisystemic Treatment Principles

- *Principle 1:* The primary purpose of assessment is to understand the fit between the identified problems and their broader systemic context.

- *Principle 2:* Therapeutic contacts emphasize the positive and use systemic strengths as levers for change.

- *Principle 3:* Interventions are designed to promote responsible behavior and decrease irresponsible behavior among family members.

- *Principle 4:* Interventions are present focused and action oriented; they target specific and well-defined problems.

- *Principle 5:* Interventions target sequences of behavior within and between multiple systems that maintain the identified problems.

- *Principle 6:* Interventions are developmentally appropriate and fit the developmental needs of youth.

- *Principle 7:* Interventions are designed to require daily or weekly effort by family members.

- *Principle 8:* Intervention effectiveness is evaluated continuously from multiple perspectives; providers assume accountability for overcoming barriers to successful outcomes.

- *Principle 9:* Interventions are designed to promote treatment generalizations and long-term maintenance of therapeutic change by empowering caregivers to address family members' needs across multiple systemic contexts.

Source: Henggeler, S. W., Schoenwald, S. K., Borduin, C. M., Rowland, M. D., & Cunningham, P. B. (1998). *Multisystemic treatment of antisocial behavior in children and adolescents* (p. 23). New York: Guilford Press. Reprinted with permission from Guilford Press.

operationalizing the strengths perspective. Not only do the client and worker make lists of strengths, assets, talents, gifts, or power of the client, they determine how to actively *use* that power or those strengths to intervene in the client's ecological world. Principle 3, encouraging responsible behavior and discouraging irresponsible behavior, is valuable but needs to be handled with caution. It is easy to slip into simply blaming the client when things go wrong, when what is necessary is a careful collaborative analysis of why things went wrong and what steps to take to achieve that responsible behavior. Principles 4 and 7 call for the use of specific scheduled tasks; bear in mind that some tasks may be assigned to the social worker. Principle 5 is particularly important because it reminds us that it is the client's transactional web that is the target of our work, not just the client's behavior. Principle 6 reminds us that human action emerges from human development; clients and others in the client's world should not be asked to take action that they are not developmentally prepared to take.

Two important dimensions are included in Principle 8. The first consists of continuous assessment conducted collaboratively with the client and other stakeholders. The second, which is often overlooked, is that it is the social worker's responsibility to determine what action to take if things are not progressing. That does not mean that the client does not have a voice, but it does mean that the social worker's professional knowledge base should prepare him or her to analyze breakdowns in the process and search in an evidence-based way for alternatives. Finally, Principle 9 calls for specific attention to constructing ecological supports for new actions consistent with the client's goals so that progress can be maintained.

In the abstract, work with transactional webs can seem somewhat vague. To make this work real, it is critical to figure out with the client what should and what should not be happening in the ecological situation, what personal and other resources are required to make those things happen, and what obstacles may need to be addressed. In nearly all cases, resources and obstacles involve human behavior, so the social worker's technical knowledge of behavior in context may be required to select the appropriate tasks. If the client is struggling with a serious addiction, to what extent are family members enabling addictive behavior, and what steps might they take to foster sobriety, for example? A great deal is known about these questions (see, for example, Meyers, Villanueva, & Smith, 2005, for a discussion of Community Reinforcement and Family Training [CRAFT]). As the worker, client, and other stakeholders clarify the ecological specifics of the focus for work, the tasks to be taken to intervene in that ecological reality become clear.

Work with Verbal and Private Events. A second cluster of intervention strategies involves (both in the session and as "homework") what clients say to themselves and others, and other private events (those that are not directly observable to someone else, such as memories, dreams, emotional conditions, and self-talk). Generally, private events are the realm of traditional "talk therapy," although the pathological connotations associated with the term "therapy" may not be consistent with much of contemporary social work practice, in which the primary goals are empowerment and building on strengths, as opposed to "curing" dysfunction. (The challenge here, of course, is that "therapy" has a certain contemporary cachet and may be hard to give up for ego-related reasons. The term may insulate and distance the social worker from the client, reinforcing a hierarchical arrangement in which an expert "cures" the disordered person. Healing breaches in the human web is social work's professional function. In many cases other language (for example, "healing," "social work consultation," or "our work together") may be more consistent with a genuine process of shared power than use of the term "therapy.")

Many clients come to the attention of social workers when they are struggling with some sort of dilemma or are faced with a problem for which they have no ready solution. Assistance in sorting out and evaluating the available options is, under those circumstances, a useful task. In fact, one major stream of social work practice theory for several decades was the problem-solving model (Perlman, 1957); that approach was one of the major roots of the contemporary task-centered approach (Reid, 1992). Multiple problem-solving paradigms are found in the literature; a straightforward first approach is "Choices and Consequences" (Mattaini, 1997), in which the heart of the work is identifying the available choices and identifying the usually multiple consequences associated with each. Short- and long-term positive and negative consequences are usually associated with each choice; clients often find decision making much easier if they have carefully thought out and, in some cases, written out all the possible consequences. Note that the concepts of choices and consequences is consistent with a shared power perspective; the worker's role is emphatically not to tell the client what to do but to facilitate the client's own evaluative process.

Work with self-talk (cognitive therapy) is another widely used approach in contemporary practice. The core notion underlying this work is that what one tells oneself is a major determinant of what one does and what one feels. For example, if one tells oneself "I'm a failure in everything I do," it is naturally hard to take action. Many cognitive distortions exist (see, for example, Ellis & MacLaren, 2005; O'Donohue, Fisher, & Hayes, 2003); some common ones are as follows:

- "I am and always will be a failure."
- "I must do everything perfectly."
- "I am powerless in my world."
- "The future looks very bleak."
- "My world (physical and social) is a terrible place."
- "It's awful if things I don't like happen to me."

Note the intensity and rigidity in the statements and the choices of strongly judgmental words. It is easy to see how such statements, repeated over and over by others and oneself until they become automatic, would be associated with stress or demoralization. The current research suggests that changing these verbal patterns by testing them against the real world can lead to behavioral activation (doing something new), which in turn may lead to better experiences and eventual emotional changes. An important cutting-edge variation of this approach is Acceptance and Commitment Therapy (ACT) (Hayes, Luoma, Bond, Masuda, & Lillis, 2006; Hayes, Strosahl, & Wilson, 1999). This emerging approach emphasizes that how one feels is natural, given one's experiences, and that changing experiences will change how one feels. Therefore, one must first commit to acting in new ways despite current feelings. Below are examples of the basic shift through the ACT approach:

+ "I'd like to do something new, *but* I feel too depressed" becomes "I feel depressed, *and* I'd like to do something new."
+ "I'd like to go to college, *but* I am too afraid I will fail" becomes "I'd like to go to college, *and* I am afraid I will fail."

In each case, revised self-talk accepts the emotions present as real and understandable on the basis of one's history and circumstances. Those emotions are not, however, defined as insurmountable obstacles to taking action. As a result, the client can be encouraged to commit to action, which may subsequently produce changes in affect.

Another useful approach for dealing with self-talk under some circumstances is *solution-focused* intervention. Solution-focused work (Franklin, Biever, Moore, Clemons, & Scamardo, 2001; Walter & Peller, 1992) provides another route to building on clients' strengths by helping them do more of what works for them and less of what does not work. This approach is quite accessible and easy to understand. It emphasizes three factors:

1. the *miracle question* (one variation of which is "Imagine that you woke up tomorrow and a miracle had occurred—your problem had disappeared! What would you be doing?, then taking steps to do that)
2. *exceptions* ("Tell me about times when the problem isn't a problem—what's different about those times?" and building more of those exceptions)
3. *compliments* (identifying what the client is doing right). Compliments are directed toward changing the client's narrative about him- or herself; note the connections with the strengths perspective and acknowledgment of the client's power.

Other important techniques are used in solution-focused practice, and students are encouraged to read the emerging literature in this area. It is critical to bear in mind that many client problems may be grounded in systemic oppression and injustice (battering, for example). For such issues, solution-focused or other narrative and cognitive approaches are too limited on their own. Even so, they offer useful techniques, such as the miracle question and discussion of exceptions, that can be used within many practice models.

Many social work clients struggle with significant levels of depression. Both cognitive therapy and interpersonal therapy (which emphasizes resolving relationship problems), as well as certain antidepressant medications, have reasonably strong evidence of effectiveness, depending on the level of depression present. A recent series of studies, however, has indicated that a procedure known as *behavioral activation* is at least as powerful as those listed above, and possibly more so (see, for example, Dimidjian et al., 2006; Lejuez, Hopko, LePage, Hopko, & McNeil, 2001). The core procedures in behavioral activation are identifying activities that the client would be doing if he or she were not depressed, scaling those activities in terms of levels of difficulty, and then working collaboratively to progressively move up that scale, gradually becoming more and more active. The procedures are easier to learn than the alternative procedures and, therefore, are easier to implement with fidelity. (Most cognitive therapy used in everyday settings is done quite differently than the way the supportive research was conducted.) Behavioral activation also requires less "cognitive-mindedness" than the other available approaches. For an accessible description of behavioral activation procedures, see Lejuez et al. (2001).

A variety of other valuable interventions exist for working with this cluster of issues, many of which have strong evidence bases. For example, exposure to the feared situation, event, condition, or object is a critical strategy for working with someone who may be struggling with anxiety-related issues. Even discussion of distressing memories, for example, is one form of such exposure. Relaxation skills can be useful for managing physiological aspects of anxiety, either in conjunction with exposure or separately. Many books and articles by social workers and scholars in other disciplines are valuable reading to prepare for client work involving self-talk and other private events. Two questions for evaluating those approaches are (1) to what extent is the approach authentically congruent with shared power? and (2) to what extent has the approach been demonstrated to be useful with clients similar to one's own? The most interesting and intellectually fascinating approaches may not be those that work best for clients.

Skills Training. Learning new skills for living provides clients with new options for action. Such skills can be empowering by giving clients more voice and influence over their worlds. Although group modalities can be particularly useful for skills training because clients can act as teacher/learners and models for each other within the group (shared power based in strengths), skills training is also helpful in work with individuals.

Some of the interventions discussed earlier are special cases of skills training. Self-management, for example, involves learning a new set of skills, as does cognitive work. One of the most common uses of skills training involves learning new ways to relate socially. Many types of social skills can be learned and refined through skills training, including assertiveness, expressing positive feelings to others, listening empathically, negotiating disagreements, and refusing demands and requests.

Before beginning the social skills training process, it is important to decide with the client which approaches are personally and culturally acceptable; the purpose of this work is to expand the client's options, not to dictate what he or she should do. For some people, particularly those from certain cultural communities (some Latino and Asian groups, for instance), what may be viewed by many white Americans as appropriate assertiveness may be seen as offensive, particularly toward people who are seen as deserving particular respect, such as elders or parents. Great sensitivity may be required in situations involving bicultural or multicultural people who use different repertoires under different circumstances. In all cases, determining what skills to work on must emerge from collaborative discussion, but the collaboration is particularly crucial in cross-cultural situations in which the worker may not know the issues that must be considered.

The general techniques used for social skills training include simple instructions, modeling by the social worker, rehearsal and testing by the client, and feedback, to refine the approaches being used. For example, if a woman is trying to determine how to ask for what she wants more assertively and refuse her husband's unreasonable demands, the worker might briefly clarify what assertive behavior looks like, then role-play a scenario in which the worker takes the client's role while the client takes her husband's role. They would then switch roles and give the client opportunities to experiment with new communication patterns and work collaboratively to tailor even better alternatives for this particular family.

Certain caveats should be noted for social skills training, particularly assertiveness training. If the client faces a risk of violence, assertiveness training may not always be the most appropriate intervention; safety planning and support groups may be indicated instead. Skills training that includes attention to such issues can be powerful, however. There is considerable evidence that unilateral work with the concerned other (usually the spouse) of a person who abuses substances can lead to successful engagement in treatment. The CRAFT model (Meyers et al., 2005) is perhaps the best-developed approach for this work; it includes modeling and rehearsal of skills for

+ reducing the risk of physical abuse to the concerned other.
+ encouraging sobriety.
+ encouraging engagement in treatment.
+ assisting with treatment of the substance-abusing partner.

Social workers interested in this approach should carefully study the detailed research and practice guidelines that are now available (for example, Smith & Meyers, 2004).

Skills training is a common and useful approach for work with children and youth as well. For example, LeCroy and Daley (2001) developed the Go Grrrls curriculum, which includes attention to a wide range of areas including friendship skills, independence skills, planning, body image, sexual health, and actively recruiting help. The material is best presented in a group format, but many of the techniques and materials are also useful in work with individuals. In some cases, skills work with young people is the most realistic intervention in severely troubled families. In one case on which I worked, for example, the parents were enmeshed in long-standing, deep conflicts but refused to address them. The mother also had a dangerously severe problem managing her anger. The 16-year-old daughter, however—perhaps because of her close relationship with a relatively well-functioning grandmother—was quite mature. The most useful work in that case proved to be working with the girl to figure out the best ways to handle her interactions with her parents while helping her with making plans to leave the home as soon as she reached age 18. This work involved extensive role playing and refinement of interaction and situational analysis skills, significant cognitive work, support, and encouragement. Ultimately, the girl learned to have a good deal of control over what happened in her life at home by assessing the situation and using well-practiced skills to respond. Significant experimentation is often needed to determine what actions are most likely to work best.

Clients are not always ready to use new skills in their real world, and their right to set their own pace should be respected. Moreover, some clients have the necessary skills but do not use them under all circumstances. For example, most people can control their anger with their bosses but may not have learned to do so with family members. The issue then involves practicing existing skills on different occasions.

A variation of skills training is *inoculation*, an approach commonly used with anger problems, some kinds of anxiety, stress, and even pain. The process involves breaking typical problem situations into stages (for example, before the provocation, during the provocation, and after the provocation) and learning and practicing particular behavioral, verbal, and cognitive skills that may apply to each stage (Mattaini, 1997).

CONCLUSION

In general, all practice approaches—including those rooted in ego psychology (Goldstein, 1995), those emerging from ecological theory (Germain & Gitterman, 1996), and ecobehavioral and cognitive–behavioral approaches (Mattaini,

1997; Reid, 1992)—rely on variations of the three clusters of intervention strategies outlined in this chapter. Most major approaches deal in some way with working with the client toward exposure to different experiences—in fact, any practice approach that fails to address this directly is too narrow to capture much of what social work practice with individuals must address. All approaches deal with emotions and thoughts, and all deal with changes in the client's behavior. Practice with individuals, like social work practice at other system levels, has as its purpose changing or stabilizing transactions between the client and his or her ecosystemic field in ways that are satisfying to the client and produce better long-term outcomes for the client and the human web within which he or she is indivisibly embedded. Success in this work can only occur, however, within a respectful relationship of shared power.

REFERENCES

Bickel, W. K., & Potenza, M. N. (2006). The forest and the trees: Addiction as a complex self-organizing system. In W. R. Miller & K. M. Carroll (Eds.), *Rethinking substance abuse: What the science shows, and what we should do about it* (pp. 8–21). New York: Guilford Press.

Cotten, C. (2006). *The construction of a social work reputation: Bertha Capen Reynolds.* Unpublished doctoral dissertation, University of Illinois at Chicago.

Dimidjian, S., Hollon, S. D., Dobson, K. S., Schmaling, K. B., Kohlenberg, R. J., Addis, M. E., Gallop, R., McGlinchey, J. B., Markley, D. K., Gollan, J. K., Atkins, D. C., Dunner, D. L., & Jacobson, N. S. (2006). Randomized trial of behavioral activation, cognitive therapy, and antidepressant medication in the acute treatment of adults with major depression. *Journal of Consulting and Clinical Psychology, 74,* 658–670.

Ellis, A., & MacLaren, C. (2005). *Rational emotive behavior therapy: A therapist's guide.* Atascadero, CA: Impact Publishers.

Farabee, D., Prendergast, M., & Anglin, M. D. (1998). The effectiveness of coerced treatment for drug-abusing offenders. *Federal Probation, 62,* 3–10.

Franklin, C., Biever, J., Moore, K., Clemons, D., & Scamardo, M. (2001). The effectiveness of solution-focused therapy with children in a school setting. *Research on Social Work Practice, 11,* 411–434.

Furman, B., & Ahola, T. (1992). *Solution talk: Hosting therapeutic conversations.* New York: W. W. Norton.

Germain, C. B., & Gitterman, A. (1996). *The life model of social work practice* (2nd ed.). New York: Columbia University Press.

Goldiamond, I. (2002). Toward a constructional approach to social problems: Ethical and constitutional issues raised by applied behavior analysis. *Behavior and Social Issues, 11,* 108–197. (Original work published 1974)

Goldstein, E. G. (1995). *Ego psychology and social work practice* (2nd ed.). New York: Free Press.

Gottlieb, B. H., & Coppard, A. E. (1987). Using social network therapy to create support systems for the chronically mentally disabled. *Canadian Journal of Community Mental Health, 6,* 117–131.

Hartman, A. (1995). Diagrammatic assessment of family relationships. *Families in Society, 76,* 111–122. (Original work published 1978)

Hayes, S. C., Luoma, J. B., Bond, F. W., Masuda, A., & Lillis, J. (2006). Acceptance and commitment therapy: Model, processes and outcomes. *Behaviour Research and Therapy, 44,* 1–25.

Hayes, S. C., Strosahl, K. D., & Wilson, K. G. (1999). *Acceptance and commitment therapy.* New York: Guilford Press.

Henggeler, S. W., Schoenwald, S. K., Borduin, C. M., Rowland, M. D., & Cunningham, P. B. (1998). *Multisystemic treatment of antisocial behavior in children and adolescents.* New York: Guilford Press.

Hepworth, D. H., Rooney, R. H., Rooney, G. D., Strom-Gottfried, K., & Larsen, J. A. (2005). *Direct social work practice: Theory and skills* (7th ed.). Belmont, CA: Wadsworth.

Hodge, D. R. (2006). A template for spiritual assessment: A review of the JCAHO requirements and guidelines for implementation. *Social Work, 51,* 317–326.

Joint Commission on Accreditation of Healthcare Organizations. (2004, January 1). *Spiritual assessment.* Retrieved November 24, 2006, from http://www.jointcommission.org/AccreditationPrograms/HomeCare/Standards/FAQs/Provision+of+Care/Assessment/Spiritual_Assessment.htm

Kemp, S. P., Whittaker, J. K., & Tracy, E. M. (1997). *Person-environment practice: The social ecology of interpersonal helping.* New York: Aldine de Gruyter.

Kopp, J. (1993). Self-observation: An empowerment strategy in assessment. In J. B. Rauch (Ed.), *Assessment: A sourcebook for social work assessment* (pp. 255–268). Milwaukee, WI: Families International.

LeCroy, C. W., & Daley, J. (2001). *Empowering adolescent girls: Examining the present and building skills for the future with the Go Grrrls program.* New York: W. W. Norton.

Lejuez, C. W., Hopko, D. R., LePage, J. P., Hopko, S. D., & McNeil, D. W. (2001). A brief behavioral activation treatment for depression. *Cognitive and Behavioral Practice, 8,* 164–175.

Lowery, C. T., & Mattaini, M. A. (2001). Shared power in social work: A Native American perspective of change. In H. Briggs & K. Corcoran (Eds.), *Social work practice: Treating common client problems* (pp. 109–124). Chicago: Lyceum Books.

Mattaini, M. A. (1993). *More than a thousand words: Graphics for clinical practice.* Washington, DC: NASW Press.

Mattaini, M. A. (1997). *Clinical practice with individuals.* Washington, DC: NASW Press.

Mattaini, M. A. (1999). *Clinical intervention with families.* Washington, DC: NASW Press.

Meyer, C. H., & Palleja, J. (1995). Social work practice with individuals. In C. H. Meyer & M. A. Mattaini (Eds.), *The foundations of social work practice: A graduate text* (pp. 105–125). Washington, DC: NASW Press.

Meyers, R. J., Villanueva, M., & Smith, J. E. (2005). The community reinforcement approach: History and new directions. *Journal of Cognitive Psychotherapy, 19,* 247–260.

Naugle, A. E., & Follette, W. C. (1998). A functional analysis of trauma symptoms. In V. M. Follette, J. I. Ruzek, & F. R. Abueg (Eds.), *Cognitive-behavioral therapies for trauma* (pp. 48–73). New York: Guilford Press.

O'Donohue, W., Fisher, J. E., & Hayes, S. C. (Eds.). (2003). *Cognitive behavior therapy: Applying empirically supported techniques in your practice.* Hoboken, NJ: John Wiley & Sons.

Perlman, H. H. (1957). *Social casework: A problem-solving process.* Chicago: University of Chicago Press.

Poppen, R. L. (1989). Some clinical implications of rule-governed behavior. In S. C. Hayes (Ed.), *Rule-governed behavior: Cognition, contingencies, and instructional control* (pp. 325–357). New York: Plenum Press.

Reid, W. J. (1985). *Family problem-solving.* New York: Columbia University Press.

Reid, W. J. (1992). *Task strategies: An empirical approach to clinical social work.* New York: Columbia University Press.

Reid, W. J. (2000). *The task planner.* New York: Columbia University Press.

Reynolds, B. C. (1982). *Between client and community: A study in responsibility in social case work.* Washington, DC: National Association of Social Workers. (Original work published 1934)

Richmond, M. (1917). *Social diagnosis.* New York: Russell Sage Foundation.

Ross, R. (2006). *Returning to the teachings: Exploring aboriginal justice.* (2nd ed.). Toronto: Penguin Canada.

Saleebey, D. (Ed.). (2006). *The strengths perspective in social work practice.* Boston: Allyn & Bacon.

Sidman, M. (2001). *Coercion and its fallout* (Rev. ed.). Boston: Authors Cooperative.

Sloane, H. N. (1988). *The good kid book.* Champaign, IL: Research Press. (Original work published 1979)

Smagner, J. P., & Sullivan, M. H. (2005). Investigating the effectiveness of behavioral parent training with involuntary clients in child welfare settings. *Research on Social Work Practice, 15,* 431–439.

Smith, J. E., & Meyers, R. J. (2004). *Motivating substance abusers to enter treatment: Working with family members.* New York: Guilford Press.

Specht, H., & Courtney, M. (1994). *Unfaithful angels.* New York: Free Press.

Tutty, L. M., Bidgood, B. A., & Rothery, M. A. (1993). Support groups for battered women: Research on their efficacy. *Journal of Family Violence, 8,* 325–343.

Walter, J., & Peller, J. (1992). *Becoming solution-focused in brief therapy.* New York: Brunner/Mazel.

9

□□□

Social Work
with Families

Christine T. Lowery

*J*ulia Loktev's *Moment of Impact* (Loktev & Judd, 1998), a documentary about
her family, was a surprise winner in the director's category at the Sundance
Film Festival in 1998. The Loktevs, Jewish immigrants from Leningrad (now St.
Petersburg), came to the United States in 1979 when Julia was nine years old.
Her parents worked as computer programmer analysts in a suburb in Colorado,
where Julia described herself as "the only brunette in a blond American town"
(cited in Firestone, 1998, p. B2). In 1989, when Julia was 19, her father, Leonid,
was struck by a car while crossing the street to a garage sale—the "moment of
impact." A traumatic brain injury rendered him "neither paralyzed or speechless,
but unable to initiate movement or speech on his own . . . stuck somewhere
between life and death" (Firestone, p. B2).

Loktev's film documented the daily rituals of her mother, Larisa, as she feeds,
washes, and dresses the 50-year-old man who is her husband. Larisa sings, speaks
Russian to him, rages; she talks about the invisibility she feels, which is coun-
tered only by going to aerobics. Intermittently, she and her daughter lie next to
each other, speaking Russian in "intimate and often humorous ways," discussing
their reactions to an unpredictable situation that had endured for more than 10
years at the time of the film (Firestone, 1998, p. B2). The morning comes, and
the rituals begin once more.

The documentary illustrates themes social workers and families may face
together. For the Loktevs, those themes include the aftermath of the accident,
disability and aging, caregiving and caregiver stress, "invisibility," isolation (including cultural isolation), emerging careers and careers interrupted at midlife, daily

rituals, medical interventions, managed care, long-term care, finances, coping and planning over time, family support, and the father–mother–daughter relationship and their tandem development in the life span. Their experiences are sifted through a screen of meanings embedded in ethnicity, cultures, community, the immigration experience and political transition, communication across generations, and the passage of time. Hungry for resolution, social workers sometimes forget the tempo of life pronounced in the repetitive devices (rituals) and themes—credited for the director's prize—depicted in this story.

For a social worker working with this family, what skills and knowledge are required? What assumptions have already been made? What must be learned? What can this family teach about their experience? What interventions can be constructed that combine the needs, strengths, values, and work of Larisa and Julia and Leonid and that take into account their ethnicity, history, U.S. experience, and the overlay of multiple cultures in relationship with the social worker-in-agency, other helping professionals, and community resources in a suburb in Colorado? What religious and cultural resources may be useful? What state, regional, or national resources are available?

Usually, when people have conflict or experience developmental transitions or life-threatening accidents that require additional understanding and help, it is within the context of family life. As family configurations and the multisystem challenges families face become more complex, models of helping families and family groups must prove flexible. Social workers, too, must be flexible and must move away from labels, such as "normal" and "dysfunctional." Social workers must understand how biological family groups or constructed families in neighborhoods and communities work to meet the needs of the group, take care of family members, and deal with internal and external stressors, both positive and negative (Walsh, 1993).

Social workers must rethink boundaries and categories. Not all families are bound by marriage or blood kin, for example. Although they are sometimes rejected by blood relations, gay men and lesbians create chosen families, families of peer relationships, and "fictive kin" bound by love, pushing the edge in new traditions and rights, such as custodial parenting for gay people and domestic partner rights (Weston, 1997). In another example, Boyd-Franklin (1993) indicated that particular values need not be tied to socioeconomic status. Because of their values and expectations for their children, poor and working-class African American families may be seen as middle class in their own communities (Boyd-Franklin, 1993). Family roles do not consistently reflect Western stereotypes. Hamer (1997) reported a qualitative study of 38 black noncustodial fathers who shaped their own roles and functions on the basis of what they wished they had experienced with their own fathers. They responded to their own children by first spending time with them, providing emotional support, providing discipline, being role models, teaching gender roles, and, as a final priority, providing economic support (Hamer).

Larger socioeconomic forces and racial discrimination cannot be ignored. Systemic discrimination in housing, jobs, and education has a telling impact on health and social functioning. Life expectancy is lower for African American men than African American women, and this gender imbalance affects partnering and family life.

> The availability of African American men to participate in relationships is affected by incarceration, mental and physical disabilities, drug and alcohol abuse, and deaths on jobs involving a high degree of danger or health hazards (e.g. military service, blue collar work in hazardous waste, chemical production, or mining), as well as violence of many kinds." (Hines & Boyd-Franklin, 2005, p. 88)

ECOLOGICAL PERSPECTIVE

How do families respond to predictable (births, adolescence, a planned move, a new job, blended families) and unpredictable (natural disasters, accidents, illnesses, sudden job loss) stressors, challenges, and events? What are the coping strategies and consequences used by individuals within the family culture and by family groups within larger cultures and environments? How do these strategies change over time, during the life course? What is the history of adversity and strength in this family group, the person-in-environment fit? What can we build on now?

Germain and Gitterman (1996) outlined the ecological concepts that characterize the life model of social work practice: transactions, person–environment fit, stress and coping, human relatedness, power and vulnerability, human habitats, and the life course. Social workers must see the whole picture when working with vulnerable populations and understand where advocacy is required to make structural changes in society. Transactions between people and their environment act to shape behaviors and consequences. How good is the fit—"needs, capacities, behavioral styles, goals of people and characteristics of the environment" (Germain & Gitterman, p. 9)—between the person and his or her environment? Is there a flourishing relationship (adaptedness)? Adaptation requires continuous change and action geared to benefit human potential and growth and to improve the person–environment fit. What are the life stressors (threats of harm and loss) in the external environment, and what internal stress do they produce? If a client has the personal and environmental resources to address his or her life stressors, these stressors might be perceived more positively as challenges or be considered irrelevant or benign.

Reciprocity is evidence of human connectedness, including connectedness to the natural world; this relatedness enhances competence to support self-esteem, and competence and self-esteem give one self-direction. Coercive power is the "antithesis of growth-promoting, self-healing life forces" (Germain & Gitterman, 1996, p. 19). Disempowerment and pollution destroy life. Human habitats are located in the physical, social, and cultural structures of community and can be neutral, supportive, or disempowering. Within the social structure of the community, rights and protections should shape niches or status for groups and individuals, yet it is tolerance for abuse of power that maintains disempowering

---

◻◻◻◻◻

Sidebar 9-1: Habitat, Neighborhood, and Social Justice: Henry Street Settlement

Helen Hall, a social worker trained at the New York School of Philanthropy (the precursor of Columbia School of Social Work), discussed the importance of settlement work or family-centered neighborhood work in her book *Unfinished Business: In Neighborhood and Nation* (Hall, 1971). Her commitment spanned more than three decades (1933 to 1967) as a resident and director of the Henry Street Settlement in New York City. In 1933, social and health services were centralized to save money, and specialization in social work practice and the influence of psychiatry on social work took hold. City slums were reputed to be fading from American life, and the settlement movement was deemed unnecessary. Hall's experience taught her otherwise: "Neighborhood work had an increasingly important role to play, for the neighborhood is where vulnerability is highest, where observations should be keenest, and services most ready" (Hall, 1971, p. xiii). "Anywhere that poverty degrades a neighborhood and surrounds its children with misery, we are mortgaging our future as a country. It is not only cruel, but stupid" (Hall, p. 107). In Hall's view, to say that settlement houses were no longer necessary was tantamount to a warning by the New York City health commissioner to tightly cover garbage cans to starve the rats while leaving tons of garbage uncollected in the backyards of tenement buildings (Hall).

Hall divided her account *Unfinished Business* into the Depression years (1929–1939), the war years (1940–1944), and the postwar years (1945–1955), when gang warfare was a major concern. Heroin addiction and individual violence were the most disruptive elements in neighborhood life in that period, and it overlapped with the increasingly violent rebellion of youth in the late 1960s, when the fight for civil rights was paramount. The book *Addict in the Street* (Larner & Tefferteller, cited in Hall, 1971) became the most "far-reaching contribution made by Henry Street" (p. 249). *Addict* contributed to social justice awareness when it drew national attention to drug addiction and exposed human suffering to people removed from life in the tenements.

niches for segments of society. Within the intersections of human and cultural diversity and new forms of family groups, life cycles or life stages of development lose consistency. Alternately, life course recognizes shifting norms, global and local environments, and human behavior as "indeterminate" (Germain & Gitterman, p. 21).

PREPARATION, ENGAGEMENT, ASSESSMENT, PLANNING, MONITORING, AND TERMINATION

In quality work with a family, the processes of preparation, engagement, assessment, planning, monitoring, and termination are intimately linked. Each is reiterative; the practitioner should always prepare for the next phase, negotiate relationships as events change them, and gather new data over time in assessment. If workers monitor or feed information back into the system, their planning should be evolving, and the family and the social worker should be able to see what they have or have not accomplished and recognize when their work is done.

Preparing for Engagement and Assessment

As society becomes more complex, quality social work requires that practitioners update their knowledge in the field while they build more specialized knowledge. Preparation includes gathering background information to bridge gaps in knowledge. This preparation should not be limited to a review of the case record or consultation with the social workers in the last agency that worked with the family. Where there are knowledge gaps, practitioners must search the professional literature in health, psychology, social work, and related fields. In the Loktev example, ethnocultural factors intersected with health and social issues of a specific type of disability (brain injury), aging, and caregiving, all of which are critical issues for 21st-century health and social work.

Social workers cannot claim ignorance in this age of information and technology. National resources provide Web sites with links to specific topics. Professional journals abound. For example, *Health & Social Work* alerted social workers to interrelated practice issues on disabilities and aging (Gilson & Netting, 1997). The authors considered lifelong disability and late-life disability and the impact of changing life circumstances on living with disability, including loss of independence and depression. They also highlighted the need for cross-training of aging and disability professionals and discussed stereotypes of client incompetence and worker bias. The article described the crisis of impending nursing home placement and the client's ensuing anger and grief and reviewed alternative services, including home health care services and caregiving by family members. Ethical issues of self-determination and the multiple roles of a social worker, including partnering with the person with disabilities, were discussed. When and how could these issues become part of the intervention process for the Loktevs?

Investing in one's continuing education after graduate school is part of being a well-informed and responsible social worker. For example, subscribing to family services journals keeps recently published material within reach. If one works in a multiservice agency in a multiethnic neighborhood, a resource book (for example, McGoldrick, Giordano, & Garcia-Preto, 2005) on working with families from different ethnic backgrounds, coupled with a resource book (for example, Rauch, 1993) in assessing families in different situations, would prove useful. The *NASW Policy Statements* (National Association of Social Workers [NASW], 2000) and *Encyclopedia of Social Work* (Edwards, 1995) (which includes material on theory and practice) are updated periodically and cover the entire field of social work. These resources could be purchased as part of an agency's commitment to informed social work practice. A working knowledge of community resources and a current community resource directory are invaluable.

As social workers become more practiced, they must not assume that they know the terrain without the guidance of a family's unique experience and perspective. Resources only provide a place to begin. As practice deepens and journal reading reinforces what social work students learn in research classes, social workers can compare information and note changes in the development of a social problem and the response of an agency over time. Documented and researched knowledge provides powerful material for advocacy on behalf of the families with whom social workers work. Such knowledge is imperative for updating agency practices and policies; this, too, is a mandate of social work.

General Preparation for Work with the Loktev Family

As social workers review selected books and journal articles and form questions, they must remember that although this process helps them become familiar with potential issues and ground themselves, it does not permit them to construct the client's reality. The client will define that reality in the assessment, the intervention plan, and the monitoring process.

Disabilities. The U.S. population is living longer than ever before; one in three people will experience some form—or combination—of disability. Disabilities can be physical (arthritis), sensory (loss of hearing, speech), emotional (depression), mental (schizophrenia), cognitive (Alzheimer's disease), intellectual (developmental delays), or health-related (diabetes and dialysis) (NASW, 2000). Rolland (1993) also considered other disabilities, including movement (stroke with paralysis), stamina (heart disease), disfigurement (mastectomy), and conditions associated with social stigma (AIDS). With illness, disability, and death, questions about the type of condition, how serious it is, how long it will last (and, with death, how long the person has to live), rather than "if" one becomes ill, are inevitable (Rolland). As part of end-of-life decision making, social workers may be present in cases of assisted suicide (Callahan, 1997; NASW, 2000), which is permitted in some states, such as Oregon, although it was ruled out as a constitutional right by the U.S. Supreme Court in 1997 (Callahan).

An ecological perspective in assessing families is evident in Rolland's (1993) caution for "goodness of fit between family style and the psychosocial demands of different disorders over time" (p. 447). What is expected to happen in the course of an illness or disability over time? What are the immediate demands on the family? How will demands change as the illness or disability changes through the life course?

Ethnicity and Immigration. After a brief review of two decades of work and study in ethnicity, Levine (1982) declared, "In all of these experiments, one fact stood out. Ethnocultural factors are more powerfully played out in family relations than in any other arena" (p. xi). Chazin (1997) outlined factors that could be relevant in assessment of a family that has immigrated. These include experiences during the immigration process, time of immigration, age at immigration, general condition of families who have immigrated, condition of families who are left behind, policies of country of origin, policies of country of entry, and history of policies since immigration.

What are possible ethnic and cultural contexts for the Loktevs, who immigrated in 1979? Although they have been in the United States for more than 20 years at this time, the immigration experience is not irrelevant because people carry their ethnicity within them. The social worker must be aware of how experiences of the disability, aging, or caregiving are interpreted and what meaning those experiences have for different members of the family, including Mr. Loktev. Although he is without voice, health care and social services providers must not ignore his presence in the family.

In a climate of anti-Semitism after the 1917 Russian Revolution, many young Soviet Jews shed their Jewish ethnic identity and culture and entered the professional ranks in science, government, and industry to help build a new Russian industrial society (Feigin, 1996). The Loktevs were born during Stalin's dictatorship (1934–1953), a period of Jewish persecution by secret police and loss of family members denounced as enemies of the people (Newhouse, 2005). The Holocaust was taking place, and a virulent anti-Semitism limited opportunity; trust and expression of feelings like grief were hidden. The Loktevs would have been young adults during the 1967 Middle East war, when anti-Semitism resurged (Newhouse). How did their families of origin experience oppression during this period? How were the Loktevs affected?

People who come from the urban centers, such as Moscow and St. Petersburg, generally are Russian in culture. Is this consistent for the Loktev family? What other cultural affiliations do they have? In contrast, immigrants from the Ukraine and Belarus are more likely to be craftspeople with a strong Jewish culture and a history of the Holocaust (Feigin, 1996). Feigin noted that Jewish families from Russia "seek support and compassion through verbal expression of their emotional discomfort" (p. 633). Their values suggest collectivity, mutual dependency, and group responsibility versus the U.S. ideals of individualism, self-reliance, and independence (Feigin). How might this orientation be reflected in Larisa's roles of wife, mother, and caregiver and her attention to her individual needs?

Health Care Costs and Caregiving. Leonid and Larisa Loktev are relatively young, but are at an age when health care costs will start to rise. In preparing for the assessment, the social worker must be aware that Larisa Loktev is developmentally at an age where her own health care needs, as well as the health care needs of her husband, will increase.

The cost of health care is initially higher for women because of reproduction but soars for both sexes as they age. The need for hospital care begins to increase by the mid-50s; by the time someone reaches the late 70s, the rate of hospitalization increases by five times one's average lifetime rate; by the late 1980s, this increases to 12 times the average lifetime rate (Foot & Stoffman, 1996). As one ages, recovery time is longer and current home care after hospitalization is limited to a few hours a day. Often convalescent care is required for many with poor health after hospitalization to strengthen the body, allow time to learn how to use the technology (catheters, IV feeds, diabetic self-monitoring, and so forth), and allow time for adjustment to any limitations or therapy schedules. Demographers Foot and Stoffman noted that the baby boomers (those born between 1947 and 1966) will be turning 65 from 2012 through 2031. Health care costs, high in the mid-1990s, will be even higher as boomer aging increases the demand for hospital care in an era in which hospital closures are planned.

Family caregiving first gained attention when community-based resources were required to supplant institutional care for people with mental illnesses in the 1960s and 1970s (Hatfield, 1987). During the past decade, posthospital care, including long-term care, has been transferred from publicly funded hospitals to the home, with serious implications for families and caregivers who must fill the service gaps (Foot & Stoffman, 1996; Tebb, 1995). The issue of caregiving is evident in the literature because of rising health care costs and recent health trends, including attention to people with disabilities and the effects of AIDS (see Lynch & Wilson, 1996). The caregiver's well-being and perception of the burden of caregiving tasks are instrumental in deciding whether an older person (or a person with disabilities) must be institutionalized (Zarit et al., cited in

Tebb). Tebb proposed a caregiver well-being scale that is based on a strengths perspective; factors include resilience and ability to use support to develop and expand strengths that reinforce a positive experience in caregiving.

Tebb's (1995) scale may be useful in the assessment process for Larisa Loktev, because it identifies strengths and areas in which caregivers may need some help. The scale is not available in the article; however, the analysis provides categories of basic human needs and activities of daily living that would be important in the assessment, particularly if one knew little about caregiving. Students are encouraged to contact authors to request information about the availability of instruments or scales.

Not to be forgotten is the daughter, Julia Loktev. What are her developmental needs? Her filmmaking career is beginning, demanding time far from home. What are her concerns? Do her roles as a daughter and a career woman conflict, particularly when seen through an ethnic lens? By scanning the professional literature for relevant research (including information on cultural diversity), community resources, and information the practitioner may receive in a referral, the social worker is initially prepared to meet the Loktevs. The worker should also have identified possible elements of an ecological assessment.

Recognizing that they have much to learn, practitioners must take stock of themselves:

+ What are the worker's apprehensions and strengths?
+ Can the worker talk about disability, illness, loss, grief, and death?
+ Does the worker minimally understand the medical systems within which he or she may have to work?
+ How can the worker get more information about the environment in which his or her clients live and the systems on which they rely?
+ Does the worker understand the ethical issues that need attention now and in the future?

Assessment, Planning, and Monitoring

How does a family function? A family-centered focus treats the family as the unit of intervention; an ecological perspective understands the family as part of the environment within a larger configuration of institutional systems. The interaction of behaviors within the family and with their environment can sometimes be complex and difficult to understand. A good assessment with the family reflects the family's reality—their cultural interpretations of the situation—and adds the perspectives of the professional helpers, outlines potential consequences of different interventions, and helps the family identify priorities for intervention. Ecomaps and envisioning improved life situations (see chapter 8) help give structure and meaning to those interactions while demonstrating what stressors the family is responding to and how those interactions affect individual members and the family as a whole. If a recently divorced, single mother feels fragmented and tired all the time, the complexity of an ecomap may actually provide some relief when she is able to see her situation. In addition, a cultural assessment identifies the meaning of the life event and its causes and points to possible interventions for members of the family within a cultural framework.

Meyer (1993) described assessment as twofold. First, relevant information is gathered to enhance adaptations among individuals, families, and their environments. Practice models (psychosocial, behavioral) guide the process and inform intervention. Second, as a product, the assessment describes "what is the matter" and defines the case situation. The assessment explains the connections relevant in the plan and determines the roles the social worker will take and the levels at which the social worker will operate. Note how the processes are intertwined in the following example:

> When Emily, a young Native American woman from a tribe in Arizona, came to the Indian child welfare agency, she initially requested adoption information. The social worker framed an initial response with information about the Indian Child Welfare Act of 1978, which lists placement preferences for the adoption of American Indian children: family members, tribal members, and other Indian families. In the assessment that followed, it was found that Emily had become pregnant at age 16 and now had an eight-year-old son whom Emily's mother was raising and who was doing well in school. The young woman was now three months pregnant. Abortion had been out of the question with the first pregnancy, as it was in the current situation, because of Emily's religious upbringing. Emily believed she had made the same mistake at age 24, an age when she "should have known better," that she had at 16. Her sisters criticized her for allowing her mother, a widow, to bear the full responsibility of raising her son because of Emily's history of alcohol and marijuana abuse and irresponsible behavior. Currently, she was in a community college program that she would complete about the time the baby was due. Emily was aware of the effects of alcohol, drugs, and tobacco on the fetus; her drinking had lessened since she had started school a year ago. She had not had a drink since she found out she was pregnant a month previously, but she was still smoking.
>
> In the assessment of the family context, it was found that family members were usually supportive when Emily showed responsible behavior. From a cultural perspective, the young woman acknowledged that she could not "give the baby away" without telling her family. The three-month pregnancy introduced a limited time factor, and an intervention was constructed in the first session with Emily.

□-□-□-□-□

Sidebar 9-2: From Deficits to Strengths: The Family Resilience Framework

The research on family resilience has gained strength in the past two decades. It is now recognized that resilience goes beyond adaptation to life's challenges—poverty, mental illness, catastrophic life events, trauma and loss—and involves the recognition of an opportunity to recover and grow from these experiences. Central to this growth is the interplay of multiple risk and protective processes and the mediation of relational influences: intimate partners, kin, mentors, and teachers (Walsh, 2003). Personal growth and the enrichment of relationships are possible. Developmental life stage and timing of events in the life cycle is important.

In addition, events can be viewed and processed as a series of changes over time. For example, divorce involves marital tension, separation, reorganization of the household, changing roles and relationships with children and extended families, and possible remarriage and making new families. Events can be cumulative over a lifetime or coincidental, challenging the family's ability to function under overwhelming stress. A family may deal with a child who is disabled, adolescents in trouble with the law, a job loss for the family breadwinner and financial difficulty, career changes and geographical moves, and the death of parents or grandparents.

Walsh (2003) outlined key processes in family resilience work as an intervention. Belief systems of the family underlie how family members make meaning of adversity, a positive or negative outlook, and transcendence and spirituality. Flexibility, connectedness, and social, economic, and cultural resources are considered family organizational patterns. Communication and problem-solving abilities include open emotional expression and collaborative problem solving.

The essence of family resilience work is that the suffering of the family is recognized. Through sharing stories, members integrate their experience and build support and empathy. In the process, it is affirmed that people intend to do their best under adverse circumstances. In addition, psychoeducational family groups can provide practical information about crisis management, problem-solving skills, social support, and stress reduction.

Work has been done with families in a variety of situations: families changing forms (divorce and stepfamilies; gay and lesbian couples and families); families dealing with job loss and workplace transitions; families with members who have mental and physical illnesses; families with end-of-life challenges and loss; and finally, families with war-related trauma and recovery (Walsh, 2002).

After assessing that Emily had no other reasons for wanting to give the baby up for adoption, the social worker suggested a partnership in which the social worker and client could talk with interested family members in a family meeting. "If you want to do this, I will come with you and talk to them." Although this suggestion made Emily anxious, she was willing. The work of contacting members for a family meeting and disclosing the pregnancy was divided. The social worker visited and informed Emily's mother, who used the news to explain her daughter's recent withdrawal from the family.

At the family meeting the following week, the team of the social worker and the client cofacilitated, taking roles they had previously discussed. The social worker, who was 10 years older than Emily, opened the meeting and voiced the concerns of the client, her doubts, and her fears in bringing this news to the family. Emily acknowledged her own history of multiple partners and irresponsible drinking. She introduced her dilemma of whether to give the child up for adoption. The baby's father had not been a responsible partner in the past, and the family distrusted him because of his history. Emily acknowledged that if she were to keep this child, she would be parenting without his help or support.

Eleven family members, including Emily's mother, Emily's son, a paternal aunt, and three sisters and a brother and their spouses, came to the meeting and took turns speaking. Each acknowledged Emily's chaotic history but also acknowledged her growth in the past two years. Each person talked about how he or she personally supported Emily, about what he or she could do to help, and about making a place for the baby in the family. Even the client's eight-year-old son, comfortable beside his grandmother, spoke his welcome for the baby and was heard by the group. After each person spoke, the final decision always returned to Emily.

Now that Emily could move past some of her guilt and fear, she spent the next week talking more personally with her mother and sisters. Eventually, she decided that she could raise the child within the boundaries of her extended family. Had Emily decided to seek a formal adoption, she and the social worker had agreed to return to the family to discuss the options for keeping the child within the family. If needed, options for keeping the child in the tribe, according to the practices of her tribal group and compatible with the protections of tribal groups under the Indian Child Welfare Act of 1978 would be discussed. A legal advocate from the tribal law program would have been included as part of the planning team, if necessary.

The short-term case required the initial contact and assessment, one home visit and two telephone calls for coordinating the family meeting, two hours for the intervention meeting itself, and a brief follow-up meeting to monitor and terminate care. Emily already had a prenatal care plan in place. Although her family was supportive, Emily realistically recognized that there was much work to be done. It was agreed that nothing else was needed from the child welfare agency, and the relationship ended with the client being encouraged to return if necessary.

Cultural and ethnic priorities will shape how a family responds, to what stressors a family will respond, and how the family may use its support networks. In the example of Emily, values shaped by a specific Native American tribal culture intersect with values from a Catholic religious perspective that, in this meeting, supported family, family interdependence, trust, and honesty. Having the social worker initially "speak" for the young woman; hearing the voices of the entire family group, including Emily's son; and coming to a decision among the women in the family supported tribal practices. In addition, community resources such as child welfare services, health care services, and legal services were all available on this particular reservation.

Elements of Healthy Family Functioning

Emily's example demonstrates elements in a balanced system that Walsh (1993) summarized as important for healthy family functioning. In a family assessment, the following markers of a balanced system must be acknowledged and reinforced as part of the intervention and monitoring processes: connectedness and commitment; respect for individual differences and needs; shared power and responsibilities in family leadership; nurturing and socialization of vulnerable family members; organizational stability and consistency (predictability, clarity); adaptability and flexibility; open communication and allowance for a range of emotional expression; useful problem-solving and conflict resolution processes; a shared belief system; and adequate resources for economic security and psychosocial support (Walsh, pp. 58–59).

At this point in the family's development, Emily's family shared an essence of commitment and connectedness as a supportive family. These elements were balanced by a respect for individual differences and needs, including Emily's decision whether or not to seek adoption. Within this connectedness, intergenerational well-being is fostered (Walsh, 1993, 2002). Although the family was supportive as a group, individual family members were honest and accurate in their communication of their feelings about Emily's past and present behavior (both negative and positive), and the young woman acknowledged their feelings in the family group meeting.

A range of emotions was acceptable in the family communication, and responses were empathetic and provided in an atmosphere of mutual trust (Walsh, 1993, 2002). The sisters acknowledged their own past drinking behavior and how they valued their family life now. Emily cried when she expressed her shame about her own behavior in a "good family"; her mother expressed sorrow about the possibility of "not knowing the baby." Humor balanced the seriousness in the meeting, and the transitions were comfortable, well paced, and affirmative. The family had a shared belief system in its religious background, despite the differing levels of current religious activity. Everyone supported Emily's choice not to seek an abortion and openly spoke of her son's contributions to the family since his birth. Her sisters and mother voiced their concern about Emily's commitment to being a full-time mother for this child. Emily acknowledged their concerns and expressed her own.

Parents who model effective problem-solving and conflict resolution strategies can teach skills that demonstrate ethical values and socialize their children to contribute to the larger community (Walsh, 1993). Problem solving often presents a series of opportunities over time to discuss, act, and re-evaluate. Demonstrating, processing, and evaluating problem solving with the family is the essence of family work.

Predictability, comprehensibility, and flexibility of the family rules within a consistent organizational structure promote trust among members and enhance adaptability (Gravitz & Bowden, 1985; Walsh, 1993, 2002). Children are nurtured and protected, and authority is appropriately delegated (Gravitz & Bowden). For children raised in families in which violence and addiction impinge on their safety and ability to trust, re-establishing predictability and clarity of family rules is vital. Life course transitions, unpredictable stressors, and challenges require that a family group have flexibility and adaptability to respond to internal and external stressors.

Walsh (1993) included sharing of power and responsibilities on her list of elements recommended for couples. Recognizing that each member brings a different kind of power to the family group, shared power and responsibilities could be considered for all members of the family group and between the family and its community. Community-based family support programs recognize that family members are both learners and teachers. Using techniques such as mutual aid, multiple-family celebrations, and family mediation skills, community-based programs demonstrate the sharing of power in learning collectives with families (Lightburn & Kemp, 1994). Delgado-Gaitan (1994) reported a case study of family socialization and cultural change in Mexican immigrant families and first-generation Mexican families in the Carpinteria, CA, school system. Because the families wanted their children to be successful, parents tried to "remake their roles as primary socializing agents and to rethink their goals in the face of historical and current community influences" (Delgado-Gaitan, p. 80). Thus, the home culture became more congruent with the school culture and the community at large. At the same time, the parent and community organization provided structure for immigrant families and a way to participate without rejection of their language and culture. From this participation came a family-based empowerment process—"beyond that of school-mediated interventions" (Delgado-Gaitan, p. 80)—that pushed the schools to improve their programs for Spanish speakers. Contact with other families empowered learning and provided an opportunity for the families to use their own cultural values to create learning environments for their children that met the school's expectations about "expressive language" (p. 80). Many first-generation parents had experienced cultural isolation and loss of their language. In one generation, they turned their own experiences in school into more positive experiences for their children.

Finally, to have a healthy society, the community within larger social systems must provide adequate economic security within which social networks (kin, friendship, coworkers, and social networks) provide psychosocial support for the family group (Walsh, 1993).

WORKING WITH FAMILIES: EMPOWERMENT NEEDED

Belsey, Backett, and Davies (1996) categorized family functioning into three basic levels within an ecological and social justice framework.

1. Families who function within the norms of their culture despite the stress of social development and change
2. Families who are vulnerable but who have not yet experienced serious breakdown
3. Families whose functioning is seriously compromised or who can no longer meet the basic needs of the family members (physical needs, emotional care, individual needs, and development). The family members may have experienced psychological or physical exploitation or abuse or suffered injustice; it may be at risk for breakup because of economic, social, or political forces.

The survival of the family is ultimately threatened by "severe deprivation, inadequate economic resources, unemployment, hunger, isolation, forced displacement or serious disease" (Belsey et al., 1996, p. 412). Under those circumstances, the biological family functions of care and protection are impaired; the economic and social support functions cannot operate; the educational, sociocultural, and socialization functions of the family wither; and the psychological functions (intrafamily relationships and affection) are disrupted. Interventions with families in social work must address the valuable functions of the family and the societal injustices that perpetuate disruptions in family functioning from generation to generation. Social work in the 21st century must incorporate social justice goals with and on behalf of families, emphasize an ecological perspective for intervention plans, and demand empowerment and social action in family work.

Trauma and Immigration

Victims of trauma are rendered powerless by overwhelming force, whether the force is natural (disasters) or conducted by other human beings (atrocities) (Herman, 1997). People may be killed or displaced by natural disasters such as tsunamis, earthquakes, volcanic eruptions, and hurricanes. When posttraumatic stress disorder entered the professional lexicon in 1980, traumatic events were said to be outside the range of usual human experience; however, "rape, battery, and other forms of sexual and domestic violence are so common a part of women's lives that they can hardly be described as outside the range of ordinary experience" (Herman, p. 33). Terrorist attacks and the trauma of war are within the experience of soldiers and civilians, including those in Afghanistan, Iraq, Israel, Palestine, and the Sudan. The worldwide shifts in population caused by war and strife have made refugee camps common, ethnic cleansing a practice, and women and children targets.

McGoldrick et al. (2005) gave attention to the role of war, political unrest, and socioeconomic influences and their impact on immigrating families. Americans may be familiar with stories of African immigrants from war-torn areas such as Liberia, Rwanda, Sierra Leone, and Somalia; however, the largest number of African immigrant families come from Egypt, Ethiopia, Ghana, Nigeria, and South Africa (Kamya, 2005); experiences are varied and should be explored respectfully. The effects of colonization, loss of culture, HIV/AIDS, human rights violations, hunger, poverty, relocation, trauma, and war accompany immigrant families and affect their adjustment in this country.

In another example, Jalali (2005) compared the first wave of Iranian immigrants to third-wave immigrants. Prior experience with Western culture through education, travel, and media aided the cultural adjustment for the first wave. They were affluent and educated, and they brought marketable skills and demonstrated bicultural practices. For the third wave, immigration to the United States was under different circumstances. Some fled their country with hope for return. Political, ideological, and physical separation impinged on family unity and influenced resistance to U.S. culture. "This subgroup's traumatic entry into American culture has often been marked by disappointments, failures, and a sense of hopelessness" (Jalali, p. 460).

Lee and Mock (2005) summarized the diversity of the fifth wave of Asian immigrants, including refugees from China, Hong Kong, Taiwan, and Vietnam. Renewed diplomatic relations between the United States and the People's Republic of China in 1978 spurred student and professional visas, and many people stayed in the United States. Refugees from Cambodia, Laos, and Vietnam faced forced migration, hunger, incarceration, rape, and torture. Sociocultural influences, including the digital revolution, attracted Chinese with specialized technological skills. Changes in the economies of the Pacific Rim and the job market in the United States separated adults who worked in the home country from children who lived in the United States, earning them the moniker of "astronaut" or "frequent flyer families" (Lee & Mock, p. 304).

━━━━▢▢▢▢▢▢▢▢▢▢━━━━

Sidebar 9-3: Genograms and Intergenerational Patterns

(See Appendix C, Exercise 9, for a description of a genogram.)

Family genograms in the context of alcoholism, historical trauma, murder, loss, poverty, and racism can be powerful tools in helping new social workers understand how day-to-day realities are embedded in intergenerational patterns. Genograms can document patterns of immigration, cultural practices, or strengths.

In a pregnancy prevention exercise, preteens might chart the patterns of teenage pregnancies and partnered and unpartnered women and men in their families, including other health and social issues their families have dealt with. In working with blended families, including lesbian and gay families in which children from previous unions are present, a genogram may open discussion of family memberships (kin and fictive kin), role changes, and decision-making processes while examining intergenerational connections. Genograms that emphasize cultural practices can help mixed-race families or families of different cultures explore contrasting or similar practices and beliefs and open doors for sharing cultural practices not recognized before. In parenting classes with Native American families who have experienced intergenerational boarding school placements, charting family members who have been placed and discussing parenting styles may be useful for discussion.

Hartman and Laird (1983) examined the use of genograms in child welfare agencies as part of the adoptive home study; the genograms helped explore how a child would fit into the existing family system and what issues of identity would be considered. A genogram with the natural parents can contribute a family history for the child. In working with foster parents and natural parents, family genograms can guide narratives about child-rearing practices or family rituals and support understanding of dissimilar family backgrounds.

When one or two family members have sexually abused women or children, a genogram exploring intergenerational sexual abuse patterns may be useful in documenting a record of abuses. In such situations, a genogram may encourage those who were sexually abused to share their experiences in an effort to heal and understand. Intergenerational charts for family groups that have experienced alcoholism and drug addiction, divorce and separations, family violence, mental illness (schizophrenia), or physical illness (diabetes, heart ailments) can help family members put disruptive family patterns into perspective. Genograms also may reveal the strengths of family members who have made other choices in dealing with difficult issues.

Multiple-Family Groups

McFarlane (1991) described multiple-family therapy initiated in the 1960s with families of patients with schizophrenia in institutional settings. Deinstitutionalization of mental health patients in the 1970s transferred many functions of state hospitals to families, including "monitoring symptoms, managing medication compliance, instituting rehabilitation efforts, and controlling dangerous and bizarre behavior" (McFarlane, p. 365), all without training or support. Family psychoeducation was an effort to train the family to create an environment that compensated for a complex set of issues: a functional disability or impairment of the brain in a group member, the use of psychotropic drugs, and the difficult and complex burdens on the family group.

The multifamily therapy process was developmental. Initially, the patients and their families met to discuss ward-management problems. Latent benefits included improvement in symptoms and sociability for patients and morale and communication with family members. "Families were sufficiently joined to each other that messages of blame coming from therapists were usually neutralized, while direct emotional support and opportunities for trading successful techniques for managing illness-related behavior often dominated the discussions" (McFarlane, 1991, p. 365). In later stages, families worked on balancing the needs of the patients with their own needs, resisting the clinician's need to categorize the families into "theoretical dysfunctional patterns" (McFarlane).

Boyd-Franklin (1993) recognized the power of multiple-family group therapy (MFGT). Such work strengthens social systems and empowerment in African American communities and counters the isolation that violence and drugs bring to inner-city neighborhoods; it can also bring change to inner-city schools and other nonresponsive systems. These therapy groups are closely related to what McKnight (1997) called "associational communities," from which care or "the consenting commitment of one person for another" (p. 120) is developed. Meezan and O'Keefe (1998) reported that variations of MFGT have been used with battered women and their children (Rhodes & Zelman, 1986); inner-city and multiproblem families (Aponte, Zarski, Bixenstine, & Cibik, 1991; McKay, Gonzalez, Stone, Ryland, & Kohner, 1995); families with difficult parent–child relationships (Cassano, 1989); and adopted adolescents and their families (Lang, 1993).

O'Shea and Phelps (cited in Meezan & O'Keefe, 1998) described a form of MFGT in which trained therapists used psychosocial interventions when working simultaneously with two or more families. Work primarily focused on a specific problem shared by two generations (parents and children) and at least two family members per family (for example, work on decreasing drinking or smoking behaviors of mothers and their pregnant teenage daughters living at home). Patterns of interfamily interaction and alliances among intrafamily members were identified and incorporated across families.

Ideally, MFGT relies on the strengths and experiences of families who have "been there" along with the knowledge and skills of the therapist(s) in an environment of shared power. The power of modeling discussion and problem solving and practicing new behaviors should not be underestimated. The opportunity to learn from one's clients and gain new understanding should not be ignored by the therapists.

Meezan and O'Keefe (1998) evaluated MFGT as part of a package of services (including group therapy and case management services and outreach) to improve family functioning and child behavior with 42 abusive and neglectful caretakers in environmentally stressful living situations in Van Nuys, California. A comparison group of 39 other families, randomly assigned, participated in family therapy with case management services without MFGT. The menu of approaches for MFGT was extensive: "family systems, stress and coping, structural family therapy, group therapy, behavior modification, cognitive–behavioral therapy, reality therapy, parent education, [and] crisis intervention" (Meezan & O'Keefe, p. 33). Goals included increasing social support, fostering parent-to-child nurturing, improving children's behavior, and enhancing children's social competence. Six to eight families at a time worked with four therapists for eight months (34 sessions, 2.5 hours per week) between 1991 and 1995. Developmental issues (such as age-appropriate behavior), discipline, self-respect, feelings, multiple roles and concomitant behaviors, and communication were the underlying themes.

Outcomes measuring family functioning included parent–child interactions, supports to parents, financial management, developmental stimulation, and caregiver interactions. Parent–child interactions produced the only statistically significant difference ($p = .03$) between MFGT and family therapy groups at close of service: Caregivers in the MFGT group reported improvement. Child behavior differences showed that children receiving MFGT were more assertive than children in the traditional family therapy program ($p = .02$). Sixty-two percent of the families in the MFGT group had a planned termination, indicating greater program involvement, compared with 30 percent of the traditional family therapy group. MFGT caregivers were more likely to name a member of their group rather than a therapist when describing interpersonal help. Help in concrete need areas came from informal support systems outside the agency.

Family Support

Family support programs focus primarily on prevention and are family centered and neighborhood based, reminiscent of the settlement house approach. In some programs, an empowerment approach is used, and families work with human service workers to set goals and define activities. Comer and Fraser (1998) listed the goals of family support programs as empowering families as consumers and improving the health, safety, and well-being of children. Services range from informal counseling for stress and life skills training to job searches, child health care, parent education, and organized sports or activities.

Social work, often preoccupied with clinical practice, has not been a leading profession in family support work, and contemporary programs are primarily

multidisciplinary alliances among professionals from the early childhood education, maternal and infant health, and family medicine fields (Lightburn & Kemp,
1994). Recent interest in strengthening communities has been spurred by "a conservative backlash against the War-on-Poverty social programs [and] academic
and practitioner interest in theories of social capital and civil society. Social work,
meanwhile, remains on the sidelines. Some observers even suggest the profession
will have a hard time reclaiming its historic dual mission of changing people and
systems" (Ryan, DeMasi, Heinz, Jacobson, & Ohmer, 2000, p. 8).

Because family support programs use multiple interventions, they are difficult
to evaluate. Comer and Fraser (1998) analyzed outcome data from six family
support projects that had already undergone evaluation using an experimental
or quasi-experimental design. They examined program description, intervention
strategies (home visiting; child development screening; parent training; and
social, emotional, and educational support for parents), target population (multiethnic), evaluation design, outcome measures, and observed outcomes across
the six programs. All program evaluations used multiple measures, including client self-reports. The programs demonstrated positive outcomes with early intervention for young children and parents; however, effectiveness for work with
adolescents and their families was not demonstrated, which suggests that other
approaches should be explored for this group (see Mattaini, 1999). Data for
small samples of families who completed programs and little data on families
who did not complete programs were limitations of the evaluations. Research
has yet to identify the characteristics of the families who complete programs and
those who do not, nor has it explained what environmental elements enhance or
impede growth for the families.

Students should be aware of disclaimers in program evaluations that note that
their services cannot counter the effects of extreme poverty and racism. What
would services to counter economic, social, and political ostracism look like?
McKnight (1997) outlined possible suggestions when he reviewed de Toqueville's
observations and descriptions of Americans acting as citizens in a democracy and
working on local problems through relationships de Toqueville called "associations" (McKnight, p. 119). Decisions were made in "small, self-appointed groups
to solve problems, create new approaches to production, and to celebrate the local
society" (McKnight, p. 119). The plan was simple: Decide what the problem is,
decide how to solve the problem, and organize to implement the solution.
McKnight compared the citizen model to the system model, in which need, clients, and control are relevant. "In summary, systems provide control, mass production, consumption, and clienthood. Associational communities depend on
consent and allow choice, care, and citizen power" (McKnight, p. 120).

Can the citizen model and the system model be integrated to the benefit of
families? Cortès (1997) described the collective work of Communities Organized

for Public Service (COPS), a federation of religious congregations in San Antonio, Texas, and how COPS handles annual block grant negotiation, priority setting, and project selection. For more than 20 years, civics and philosophy have intertwined as community members met in "house meetings concerned with one street or drainage issue, to neighborhood meetings proposing a package of projects, to meetings in each city council district to shape a proposal with the council member" (Cortès, p. 198). With the support of a sister organization, COPS has brought $800 million in "streets, parks, housing, sidewalks, libraries, clinics, street lights, drainage, and other infrastructure to the poor neighborhoods of the inner city" (Cortès, p. 198).

What is the current thinking in family service agencies? Client-centered intervention and community-centered intervention are parallel worlds explored by Sviridoff and Ryan (1997) for the Alliance for Children and Families (formerly Family Service America) and its members. Among agencies surveyed, ideas of community ranged from the place where clients' families live, to a strategic location for delivering services to families, to resource-rich networks to which families can contribute. Counseling remains the standard when working with families

---

Sidebar 9-4: *Families and Substance Abuse*

According to McCrady (2006), unilateral family therapies are supported by research. Families can be taught behaviors to facilitate motivation for change by substance abusers by changing communication patterns, changing consequences of substance use, and attending to their self-care. Assertive communication skills enable families to give specific feedback about the consequences of use and make specific requests for change. Families can be taught to consistently construct negative consequences for use and positive consequences when the family member is not using. Safety and protection from violence in the home is primary for self-care. Although ethnically diverse populations have been studied, unilateral models are not culturally specific. Assertive requests for change, setting limits, and self-care are culturally mediated and may be challenging to implement in different cultures.

Including significant family members early in treatment and in therapy is supported, depending on the level of attachment the individual client has in the family or social networks. Family influence can help develop social networks that do not condone alcohol or drug use. Specific clinical interventions supported by research include contingency contracting for behaviors to support treatment; improving family interactions; increasing reciprocal positive exchanges; teaching constructive communication and problem-solving; and improving family skills to reinforce improvements and to give effective feedback when the substance-abusing family member drinks or uses drugs (McCrady, 2006).

embedded in serious problems; however, housing, school problems, and crime require a community-building approach, a complement to counseling. Family investment in community, such as parents advocating for their children, strengthens the quality of schools and establishes networks for collective work in other areas (Sviridoff & Ryan).

Research-Supported Family Interventions with Youth Who Are Antisocial or Delinquent

Stern (2004) summarized research on the key role of family in working with antisocial and delinquent youth. A host of interrelated issues contribute to risk for antisocial behavior and delinquency: ineffective family management and lack of parental support, conflict and family violence, rejection and hostility, and poor family relationships. Conversely, family closeness, warmth, and positive family interaction are protective factors and decrease deviant behavior. Essentially, an active and close bond with a mentor, adult caregiver, or parent is protective and contributes to resilience. Other factors that may increase the risk of delinquency include isolation, parent criminality, poverty, substance abuse, mental health disorders (especially antisocial personality disorder), and stress.

The family is key in socialization early in a child's life, and the family role is both positive and problematic. Behavior for relationships and interactions is taught, modeled, and learned. Patterson's (1982; Reid, Patterson, & Snyder, 2002) model of coercion demonstrates how antisocial behavior is learned. At home, inconsistent parenting reinforces aggressive behavior because young children learn that their aversive behaviors will curtail discipline. (The process often begins in the first year of life.) Unskilled or overstressed parents attempt to discipline, but they back down when aversive behaviors by the child increase, and they do not enforce consequences for aversive behavior. When the child begins school, the resulting lack of social competence then leads to disruptive experiences, rejection by peers, academic difficulties, and eventual alignment with a deviant peer group, one pathway into delinquency. Antisocial behavior, which has been present all along, then rapidly escalates as the child reaches early adolescence.

Stern (2004) noted a shift toward acknowledging the family not only as part of the problem but as part of the solution in dealing with antisocial and delinquent youth. Functional family therapy (FFT), multidimensional treatment foster care (MTFC), and multisystemic therapy (MST) are three interventions in which the family is central and the environment is considered. Significantly, outcomes for each type of treatment have been favorable as family needs and contexts have changed over years of clinical research and feedback. Although studies like those noted below can be useful for guiding practice, it is also essential to remember that evidence-based approaches for work with families as actually implemented in agency settings involve many variations among professionals, clients, and contexts. As a result, social workers have much to learn from such well-developed approaches, but they need to fit them to the case and consistently monitor the outcomes to determine whether they are in fact helpful for the particular case.

FFT. FFT (Alexander & Parsons, 1973; Alexander, Pugh, Parsons, & Sexton, 2000) focuses on the function of behavior in a family system in which change occurs in phases. Early FFT research found that family processes are predictably different in distressed families than in nondistressed families (Alexander & Parsons). For example, nondistressed families demonstrate a relatively equal distribution of talk time and higher levels of supportive talk among family members. In comparison, in families with delinquent youth, verbal participation was quite unbalanced and significantly more defensive. A major goal of FFT, therefore, is to shift family processes toward those that are characteristic of healthy families.

A second major focus is assessment of family process sequences and determination of the functions (for example, attention or distancing) of those sequences. In treatment, the family-blaming process is disrupted, and a collaborative set of behaviors is introduced. Next, parenting deficits are targeted, and positive communication behaviors are established along with problem-solving behaviors. The family's relational needs and interactions with their environment are recognized in the next phase.

Stern (2004) summarized treatment outcomes showing that FFT decreased recidivism and out-of-home placement for youth early in an antisocial trajectory. FFT can improve family supportive relationships and climate, has favorable sibling effects, and is cost-effective. Results of more than a dozen published studies cited by Stern have suggested that FFT can be particularly helpful with delinquent youth (perhaps more so early in the delinquency trajectory); FFT may be of some benefit with substance-using youth, but the results are not consistently strong (see reviews by Austin, Macgowan, & Wagner, 2005; and Sexton & Alexander, 2002).

MTFC. MTFC is substantiated "for youth at risk of out-of-home placement, for chronic and severe antisocial behavior, emotional disturbances, and delinquency"(Stern, 2004, p. 111). To reintegrate the family, MTFC centers on concurrently developing skills to manage the youth's behavior and develop relationships. Experienced foster families are trained and supervised in the management of the youth's behavior. The youth's family receives parenting skills and family therapy. The youth is removed from the delinquent peer group, is closely supervised, and is taught skills to build relationships with peers. Case management provides coordination among the resource people recruited to assist in the case. MTFC has been shown to reduce incarceration compared with alternative residential care and is a cost-effective alternative to residential treatment, hospitalization, or incarceration (Chamberlain & Reid, 1991, 1998).

Of particular interest is research on MTFC and girls in the juvenile justice and mental health systems (Chamberlain & Reid, 1994). Girls in those systems were found to have a more disrupted childhood, including multiple out-of-home placements. They were more likely to run away from placement and showed more frequent suicide attempts than boys. Relationships with MTFC parents showed a different trajectory for girls than for boys. Unlike boys, the girls initially had low rates of behavior problems, which increased over time; also unlike for boys, relationships with the MTFC parents also deteriorated over time. MTFC was equally effective with girls and boys, however: Program completion rates were equal, and no significant differences were found in arrest rates at one year.

MST. MST (Henggeler, Schoenwald, Borduin, Rowland, & Cunningham, 1998) focuses on the fit between the identified problem and ecological areas in which serious antisocial behavior manifests in the youth's home and community. MST helps parents understand and reinforce change across home, school, peer groups, and community using research-proven behavioral and cognitive behavioral interventions. The assessment is systematic and examines risk and protective factors across systems. Guided by nine core principles (listed in Chapter 8, Figure 8-10), treatment is individualized and is based on family and individual strengths as well as cultural contexts. Treatment integrity is important, and accountability for outcomes is continuously monitored using the multiple perspectives of the participants. "When treatment is not working, the MST therapist, supervisor, and treatment team develop hypotheses about barriers to intervention and generate ideas for overcoming them" (Stern, 2004, p. 113). This last process is well integrated into the MST model.

Strategies for MST include modifying parenting practices and strengthening family functioning at home. Changing peer relationships by developing social competency and problem-solving skills moves youth from deviant peers to relationships with peers who are prosocial. Monitoring peer relationships is key, and MST helps parents develop networks with other parents to help supervise behavior. Parents involved in school life and academic monitoring empower the school–home linkage. The community link is fostered when parents have formal and informal support, know how to use those resources, and have the promise of reciprocal relationships in the informal sphere. Individual problems—for example, substance abuse, mental illness, and victimization—are monitored for intervention.

MST has considerable empirical support. In a number of studies in the United States and Europe, well-implemented MST programs have produced reductions in serious antisocial behavior and rearrest for youth, reductions in maltreatment and neglect, and improvements in academic performance and family functioning (Ogden & Halliday-Boykins, 2004; Sexton & Alexander, 2002). Some evidence suggests that the approach may reduce drug use, although in some studies the impact on substance abuse has been weak. It appears from the research that fidelity to the core principles is important to success with MST and that supervision is important to such fidelity (Henggeler, Schoenwald, & Swenson, 2006). As with most complex psychosocial interventions, not every study has shown strong effects, probably primarily because of differences in implementation. Still, social work clearly can learn much from MST.

Child Welfare and Families: Family Group Conferencing

Family group conferencing (FGC) embodies the cultural values of indigenous peoples from New Zealand, Canada, and the United States; it protects cultural ways and respects family members as human beings (not always characteristic of experiences with child welfare systems). The emphasis is on family responsibility, power, and continuity. FGC is being used in the child welfare system, a paternalistic system in which, in standard approaches, families often find themselves without decision-making authority or the resources to support positive action (Minuchin, Colapinto, & Minuchin, 1998; Pennell & Anderson, 2005). From a strengths perspective, FGC recognizes the collective contributions of the family group, agencies, and community organizations to address threats to the family. Pennell (2005) listed the core values of FGC:

- safeguarding the family members
- ensuring that the family voice is heard by people working with the family
- ensuring social worker accountability
- community involvement, including cultural groups
- consensus building, including shared power, shared planning, and shared action.

FGC is one form of structured *circle processes* (Pranis, 2005), all of which involve bringing multiple actors into a single circle characterized by shared power. In FGC in child welfare, circle participants typically include a varying mix of biological, extended, and foster family members, providers, other family supporters, and often community or cultural representatives. (Note that Emily's case, discussed earlier, is an example of the use of such a circle process.) Effective FGC practice includes careful advance preparation, the conference itself, and follow-up—this is not just a matter of calling an ad hoc meeting. What actually occurs in the conference itself is typically the following: "(1) opening in the family group's traditions, (2) sharing the information necessary for planning, (3) having a private time for the family group to deliberate, (4) finalizing the plan, and (5) closing the meeting" (Pennell & Anderson, 2005, p. xii). Given the sometimes inhospitable environment for processes of shared power in child welfare, structural supports necessary for sustaining the approach have also been clarified (Pennell & Anderson). Social workers interested in conducting family group conferences should carefully review the related literature (for example, Pennell & Anderson) as well as the literature on circle processes in general (for example, Pranis).

Initial findings from well-implemented FGC projects are promising (Anderson & Whalen, 2005). In a study of 70 family group conferences in the state of

---

Sidebar 9-5: *Cultural Gaps in Family Group Conferencing in Child Welfare*

Anderson (2005) reported that assessment of the family culture in family group conferencing (FGC) programs in the United States is generally limited. FGC programs are based on the response of the Maori people of New Zealand to culturally insensitive child welfare practices and decisions harmful to their cultural integrity. Hence, FGC programs stress collaboration in achieving permanency for children. FGC focuses on a team effort that includes the family group, public participants, and community organizations. Shared information, shared education, and shared goals are key. Valuing family strengths and leadership, worker accountability, community involvement (resources available to the family), and consensus building are also important (Pennell, 2005, p. 5).

Often overlooked is the element of *cultural safety* (Pennell, 2005, p. 6). Cultural practices, perspectives, challenges, and solutions must have some way to surface in the formal structures of helping agencies. Time, decision making, planning, traditions and rituals, terminology, and cultural mores regarding child rearing all are influenced by culture, whether professional, agency, or Maori. Family membership is also culturally determined.

On a daily basis, social workers encounter time limits, court petitions and mandates, and the dictates of child welfare workers enforcing agency policies designed to protect the agency as well as children. The role of family members is sometimes considered in case planning and decision making, but it happens inconsistently in the face of differing capacities of families involved with substance abuse or mental health issues in communities debilitated by poverty and with few resources. Cultural competence, cultural sensitivity, training, and supervision of child welfare workers are other considerations. Against those realities, consideration of the culture of the family can be overlooked (Anderson, 2005).

In his analysis of why FGCs in the United States appear to be culturally "neutral," Anderson (2005) posed several hypotheses that social work students might consider:

Washington, family participation and involvement were high (particularly for American Indian families); results showed more children living with family and fewer living with nonrelatives, low rates of repeat referral for abuse and neglect, and stable placements. In a study of 700 family conferences in San Diego, similar outcomes were noted, with children more likely to remain at home, higher consumer satisfaction, and reductions in some types of repeat referral. FGC not only appears useful for achieving child welfare goals but can also lead to higher satisfaction and empowerment for the family.

- "American culture emphasizes commonalities rather than diversity and shapes the implementation of FGC, resulting in ignoring, undervaluing, or misinterpreting the role of culture and diversity" (p. 229).
- For some people, aspects of their culture may be considered a private matter, and some professionals may consider detailed investigation of such elements (for example, spirituality) as an invasion of privacy. Notions of privacy or community knowledge and ways of asking questions, exploring issues, and sharing information are influenced by culture.
- Cultural traditions may play a reduced or underdeveloped role in a family; for example, the isolation that may have contributed to the family's abusive or neglectful behavior may also have ramifications for the family's connectedness to its heritage and traditions (p. 230). Understanding history of oppression and marginalization of the family, whether through immigration or through the consequences of intergenerational poverty, racism, or acculturation would assist the social worker in helping the family make decisions within the cultural context of the child welfare agency.
- "The absence of cultural expressions at family group conferences may be a result of the coordinator's failing to explore this dimension of the family's life and experience; the coordinator's exploring the role of culture with the family, but receiving little, if any, information or guidance from the family; or the coordinator's gaining information from the family, but being uncertain as to how to be responsive to the family's culture" (p. 230). A cultural advocate (not a part of the standard FGC model) has been used to help the FGC coordinator address cultural issues.

Intentional professional commitment, time, and study are required to develop and practice cultural sensitivity, which is a real challenge in the culture of child welfare in the United States.

CONCLUSION: AN ECOBEHAVIORAL MODEL

Lutzker (1997) suggested that it is only logical that treatment for families mirror everyday life. He described Project 12-Ways, a treatment and prevention model for child abuse and neglect, and reviewed several examples of behavioral antecedent procedures, such as using simple prompts (large, bright cards) to help mothers independently start stimulation activities with their babies. Project 12-Ways services included parent–child training, basic child care skills, home safety, home cleanliness, stress reduction, and child abuse prevention strategies.

Lutzker (1997) described a specific example of how a woman who had mental retardation and was unable to read learned nutritious meal planning and shopping skills in order to have her child returned to the family. A match-to-sample procedure was described and evaluated using a pretest–posttest design that assessed one food group at a time (Saber et al., cited in Lutzker). Pictures of food, representing the four basic food groups, were cut from magazines and placed on index cards of four colors: (1) meats on red cards, (2) fruits and vegetables on green cards, (3) dairy products on white cards, and (4) grains and carbohydrates on blue cards. A large planning board was divided horizontally to represent breakfast, lunch, and dinner and vertically to represent the four food groups; each row had a corresponding color-coded envelope. The woman's task was to match the color of the card (with food photograph) at the bottom of the row with the corresponding envelope for each meal she was planning. Seven of the boards were necessary to plan for a week's worth of meals. To shop for food items, the woman matched food photos and placed a second set of photos in a plastic page of a ringed binder, which served as a visual shopping list. When she went grocery shopping, she again matched pictures on her shopping list with items in the store. When a new supermarket was built near her home, she was able to generalize learning from a small grocery store to the large supermarket.

Many social workers working with similar families, however, do not know of Project 12-Ways' procedures, although they have been extensively documented in the literature (see, for example, Lutzker & Bigelow, 2001; Lutzker & Campbell, 1994). What other interventions described in the research literature are waiting to be explored and tested by social workers? What activities for social action have been documented? When looking for effective interventions and monitoring tools for social work with families, one does not have to reinvent the wheel: It usually already exists, complete with technological advances. Social workers should be broad in their reading and specific in their research. One of the most powerful ways to learn is to contribute to the strength of families through teaching or sharing of information and sharing of power in social action. In the process of gaining health, families can then contribute to each other and, in this interconnected way, to society.

SUMMARY QUESTIONS FOR WORKING WITH FAMILIES

+ What level of functioning does the family display?
+ What are the social elements that impinge on their functioning?
+ How long can resources realistically be provided?
+ What types of services must social workers and clients advocate?
+ What societal injustices must be challenged?

REFERENCES

Alexander, J. F., & Parsons, B. V. (1973). Short-term behavioral intervention with delinquent families: Impact on family processes and recidivism. *Journal of Abnormal Psychology, 81,* 219–225.

Alexander, J. F., Pugh, C., Parsons, B., & Sexton, T. (2000). *Functional family therapy: Blueprints for violence prevention* (D. S. Elliot, Series Ed.). Golden, CO: Venture Publishing.

Anderson, G. R. (2005). Family group conferencing and child welfare: Contributions and challenges. In J. Pennell & G. Anderson (Eds.), *Widening the circle: The practice and evaluation of family group conferencing with children, youths, and their families* (pp. 221–236). Washington, DC: NASW Press.

Anderson, G. R., & Whalen, P. (2005). Identifying short-term and long-term FGC outcomes. In J. Pennell & G. Anderson (Eds.), *Widening the circle: The practice and evaluation of family group conferencing with children, youths, and their families* (pp. 123–138). Washington, DC: NASW Press.

Aponte, H. J., Zarski, J., Bixenstine, C., & Cibik, P. (1991). Home/community based services: A two-tier approach. *American Journal of Orthopsychiatry, 61,* 403–408.

Austin, A. M., Macgowan, M. J., & Wagner, E. F. (2005). Effective family-based interventions for adolescents with substance use problems: A systematic review. *Research on Social Work Practice, 15,* 67–83.

Belsey, M., Backett, M., & Davies, A. M. (1996). *The concept of family health. Family challenges for the future.* Geneva: United Nations Publications.

Boyd-Franklin, N. (1993). Race, class, and poverty. In F. Walsh (Ed.), *Normal family processes* (2nd ed., pp. 361–376). New York: Guilford Press.

Callahan, J. (1997). Assisted suicide, community, and the common good [Editorial]. *Health & Social Work, 22,* 243–245.

Cassano, D. R. (1989). The multi-family therapy group: Research on patterns of interaction—Part I. *Social Work with Groups, 12*(1), 3–14.

Chamberlain P., & Reid, J. B. (1991). Using a specialized foster care community treatment model for children and adolescents leaving the state mental hospital. *Journal of Community Psychology, 19,* 266–276.

Chamberlain, P., & Reid, J. B. (1994). Differences in risk factors and adjustment for male and female delinquents in treatment foster care. *Journal of Child and Family Studies, 3,* 23–39.

Chamberlain, P., & Reid, J. B. (1998). Comparison of two community alternatives to incarceration for chronic juvenile offenders. *Journal of Consulting and Clinical Psychology, 66,* 624–633.

Chazin, R. (1997). Working with Soviet Jewish immigrants. In E. P. Congress (Ed.), *Multicultural perspectives in working with families* (pp. 142–166). New York: Springer.

Comer, E. W., & Fraser, M. W. (1998). Evaluation of six family-support programs: Are they effective? *Families in Society, 79,* 134–148.

Cortès, E., Jr. (1997). Reweaving the social fabric. *Families in Society, 78,* 196–200.

Delgado-Gaitan, C. (1994). Socializing young children in Mexican-American families: An intergenerational perspective. In P. M. Greenfield & R. R. Cocking (Eds.), *Cross-cultural roots of minority child development* (pp. 55–86). Hillsdale, NJ: Lawrence Erlbaum.

Edwards, R. L. (Ed.-in-Chief). (1995). *Encyclopedia of social work* (19th ed., Vols. 1 & 2). Washington, DC: NASW Press.

Feigin, I. (1996). Soviet Jewish families. In M. McGoldrick, J. Giordano, & J. K. Pearce (Eds.), *Ethnicity and family therapy* (2nd ed., pp. 631–637). New York: Guilford Press.

Firestone, D. (1998, January 30). From a daughter, scenes of a life in limbo. *New York Times,* p. B2.

Foot, D. K., & Stoffman, D. (1996). *Boom, bust, and echo: How to profit from the coming demographic shift.* Toronto: Macfarlane Walter & Ross.

Germain, C. B., & Gitterman, A. (1996). *The life model of social work practice* (2nd ed.). New York: Columbia University Press.

Gilson, S. F., & Netting, F. E. (1997). When people with pre-existing disabilities age in place: Implications for social work practice. *Health & Social Work, 22,* 290–298.

Gravitz, H. L., & Bowden, J. D. (1985). *Recovery: A guide for adult children of alcoholics.* New York: Simon & Schuster.

Hall, H. (1971). *Unfinished business: In neighborhood and nation.* New York: Macmillan.

Hamer, J. F. (1997). The fathers of "fatherless" black children. *Families in Society, 78,* 564–578.

Hartman, A., & Laird, J. (1983). *Family-centered social work practice.* New York: Free Press.

Hatfield, A. (1987). Families as caregivers: A historical perspective. In A. B. Hatfield & H. P. Lefley (Eds.), *Families of the mentally ill* (pp. 3–29). New York: Guilford Press.

Henggeler, S. W., Schoenwald, S. K., Borduin, C. M., Rowland, M. D., & Cunningham, P. B. (1998). *Multisystemic treatment of antisocial behavior in children and adolescents.* New York: Guilford Press.

Henggeler, S. W., Schoenwald, S. K., & Swenson, C. C. (2006). Methodological critique and meta-analysis as Trojan horse. *Children and Youth Services Review, 28,* 447–457.

Herman, J. (1997). *Trauma and recovery: The aftermath of violence—From domestic abuse to political terror.* New York: Basic Books.

Hines, P. M., & Boyd-Franklin, N. (2005). African American families. In M. McGoldrick, J. Giordano, & N. Garcia-Preto (Eds.), *Ethnicity and family therapy* (3rd ed., pp. 87–100). New York: Guilford Press.

Indian Child Welfare Act of 1978 (ICWA), P.L. 95-608, Nov. 8, 1978, 92 Stat. 3069.

Jalali, B. (2005). Iranian families. In M. McGoldrick, J. K. Pearce, & J. Giordano (Eds.), *Ethnicity and family therapy* (3rd ed., pp. 451–467). New York: Guilford Press.

Kamya, H. (2005). African immigrant families. In M. McGoldrick, J. K. Pearce, & J. Giordano (Eds.), *Ethnicity and family therapy* (3rd ed., pp. 101–116). New York: Guilford Press.

Lang, R. (1993). *A multi-family group intervention to facilitate open communication between adopted adolescents and their adoptive parents.* Unpublished doctoral dissertation, Department of Psychology, Rutgers—The State University of New Jersey, New Brunswick.

Lee, E., & Mock, M. R. (2005). Asian families: An overview. In M. McGoldrick, J. K. Pearce, & J. Giordano (Eds.), *Ethnicity and family therapy* (3rd ed., pp. 269–289). New York: Guilford Press.

Levine, I. M. (1982). Introduction. In M. McGoldrick, J. K. Pearce, & J. Giordano (Eds.), *Ethnicity and family therapy* (pp. xi–xii). New York: Guilford Press.

Lightburn, A., & Kemp, S. P. (1994). Family-support programs: Opportunities for community-based practice. *Families in Society, 75,* 16–26.

Loktev, J. (Director), & Judd, M. (Producer). (1998). *Moment of impact* [Motion picture]. United States: Cinemax.

Lutzker, J. R. (1997). Ecobehavioral approaches in child abuse and developmental disabilities mirroring life. In D. M. Baer & E. M. Pinkston (Eds.), *Environment and behavior* (pp. 243–248). Boulder, CO: Westview Press.

Lutzker, J. R., & Bigelow, K. M. (2001). *Reducing child maltreatment: A guidebook for parent services.* New York: Guilford Press.

Lutzker, J. R., & Campbell, R. (1994). *Ecobehavioral family interventions in developmental disabilities.* Belmont, CA: Wadsworth.

Lynch, V. J., & Wilson, P. A. (1996). *Caring for the HIV/AIDS caregiver.* Westport, CT: Auburn House.

Mattaini, M. (1999). *Clinical intervention with families.* Washington, DC: NASW Press.

McCrady, B. (2006). Family and other close relationships. In W. R. Miller & K. M. Carroll (Eds.), *Rethinking substance abuse: What the science shows, and what we should do about it* (pp. 166–181). New York: Guilford Press.

McFarlane, W. R. (1991). Family psychoeducational treatment. In A. S. Gurman & D. P. Kniskem (Eds.), *Handbook of family therapy* (Vol. 2, pp. 363–395). New York: Brunner/Mazel.

McGoldrick, M., Giordano, J., & Garcia-Preto, N. (2005). *Ethnicity and family therapy* (3rd ed.). New York: Guilford Press.

McKay, M. M., Gonzalez, J. J., Stone, S., Ryland, D., & Kohner, K. (1995). Multiple family therapy groups: A responsive intervention model for inner city families. *Social Work with Groups, 18*(4), 41–56.

McKnight, J. L. (1997). A 21st-century map for healthy communities and families. *Families in Society, 78*(2), 117–127.

Meezan, W., & O'Keefe, M. (1998). Multifamily group therapy: Impact on family functioning and child behavior. *Families in Society, 79,* 32–44.

Meyer, C. H. (1993). Assessment: The idea and the process. In *Assessment in social work practice* (pp. 17–42). New York: Columbia University Press.

Minuchin, P., Colapinto, J., & Minuchin, S. (1998). *Working with families of the poor.* New York: Guilford Press.

National Association of Social Workers. (2000). *Social work speaks: NASW policy statements* (5th ed.). Washington, DC: NASW Press.

Newhouse, L. (2005). Russian Jewish families. In M. McGoldrick, J. Giordano, & N. Garcia-Preto (Eds.), *Ethnicity and family therapy* (3rd ed., pp. 701–707). New York: Guilford Press.

Patterson, G. R. (1982). *Coercive family process.* Eugene, OR: Castalia Publishing.

Pennell, J. (2005). Widening the circle. In J. Pennell & G. Anderson (Eds.), *Widening the circle: The practice and evaluation of family group conferencing with children, youths, and their families* (pp. 1–8). Washington, DC: NASW Press.

Pennell, J., & Anderson, G. (2005). *Widening the circle: The practice and evaluation of family group conferencing with children, youths, and their families.* Washington, DC: NASW Press.

Ogden, T., & Halliday-Boykins, C. A. (2004). Multisystemic treatment of antisocial adolescents in Norway: Replication of clinical outcomes outside of the US. *Child and Adolescent Mental Health, 9,* 77–83.

Pranis, K. (2005). *The little book of circle processes.* Intercourse, PA: Good Books.

Rauch, J. B. (Ed.). (1993). *Assessment: A sourcebook for social work practice.* Milwaukee, WI: Families International.

Reid, J. B., Patterson, G. R., & Snyder, J. J. (2002). *Antisocial behavior in children and adolescents: A developmental analysis and the Oregon model for intervention.* Washington, DC: American Psychological Association.

Rhodes, R. M., & Zelman, A. B. (1986). An ongoing group in a women's shelter. *American Journal of Orthopsychiatry, 56,* 120–130.

Rolland, J. S. (1993). Mastering family challenges in serious illness and disability. In F. Walsh (Ed.), *Normal family processes* (2nd ed., pp. 444–502). New York: Guilford Press.

Ryan, W. P., DeMasi, K., Heinz, P. A., Jacobson, W., & Ohmer, M. (2000). *Aligning education and practice: Challenges and opportunities in social work education for community-centered practice.* Milwaukee, WI: Alliance for Children and Families.

Sexton, T. L., & Alexander, J. F. (2002). Family-based empirically-supported interventions. *The Counseling Psychologist, 30,* 238–261.

Sviridoff, M., & Ryan, W. (1997). Community-centered family service. *Families in Society, 78,* 128–139.

Stern, S. B. (2004). Evidenced-based practice with antisocial and delinquent youth: The key role of family and multisystemic intervention. In H. Briggs & T. Rzepnicki (Eds.), *Using evidence in social work practice: Behavioral perspectives* (pp. 104–127). Chicago: Lyceum Books.

Tebb, S. (1995). An aid to empowerment: A caregiver well-being scale. *Health & Social Work, 20,* 87–92.

Walsh, F. (1993). Conceptualization of normal family processes. In F. Walsh (Ed.), *Normal family processes* (2nd ed., pp. 3–72). New York: Guilford Press.

Walsh, F. (2002). A family resilience framework: Innovative practice application. *Family Relations, 51,* 130–137.

Walsh, F. (2003). Family resilience framework. *Family Process, 42,* 1–19.

Weston, K. (1997). *Families we choose: Lesbians, gays, kinship* (Rev. ed.). New York: Columbia University Press.

10

□ □ □

Social Work
with Groups

Randy H. Magen

The Progressive Era, which spawned the early caseworkers, also produced the first group workers. The ancestors of caseworkers and group workers were mindful of democratic values, critical of the political and economic system, concerned with the needs of individuals, and inspired by religiously based notions of humanity (Schwartz, 1986). Unlike casework, however, the roots of group work can also be found in the recreation movement and the progressive education movement (Germain, 1983).

At the beginning of the 20th century, groups were used for two purposes: (1) to instill democratic values and (2) to socialize individuals. In settlement houses, groups were established for people to learn the skills necessary to participate in their neighborhoods and communities. John Dewey, one of the fathers of the progressive education movement, was influential in settlement houses' development of the democratic purpose of groups. For a short time, he lived and worked at Hull House under the leadership of Jane Addams. Dewey (1922) wrote that groups provided experience in democratic action through participation in activities in which there was shared decision making and a focus on common social problems. This is what Addams (1910/1960) referred to as groups serving as a "building block of democracy" (p. 97). These groups were designed to promote social justice and human rights.

Addams, the founder of Hull House, was also one of the founding officers of what eventually became known as the National Recreation Association (Reid, 1997). From the recreation movement came the use of groups to socialize individuals. In organized associations such as the Young Men's and Young Women's Christian Associations, the Boy Scouts and the Girl Scouts, and, to a lesser extent, in the settlement houses, a variety of small groups were established in which children could play, develop friendships, and participate in recreational activities (Reid, 1997; Schwartz, 1986). Children's participation in groups was believed to promote healthy development through character building—what is now called "the acquisition of social skills."

In comparing early casework to early group work, Toseland and Rivas (2005) listed five differences between the methods:

1. In casework, clients changed as a result of the development of insight and through concrete assistance, whereas in group work, their change was a function of participating in group activities.
2. Whereas casework focused primarily on problem solving, group work focused on both recreation and problem solving.
3. Caseworkers worked with clients, whereas group workers were involved with members. This was more than a difference in terminology; it also resulted in a difference in the quality of the relationship between the social worker and the people being helped.
4. As a result of the differences in their relationship with clients, group workers placed more emphasis than did caseworkers on shared decision making and shared power.
5. The interaction of multiple members in a group required a different set of skills from those developed by caseworkers.

Before World War II, some limited attempts to use group work in settings other than settlement houses and recreational organizations took place, but it was not until World War II that group work moved solidly into rehabilitation settings. Several factors propelled group work into the new settings. The development of group work practice theory in social work (see, for example, Coyle, 1937) as well as research on small groups by social scientists (see Lewin, Lippitt, & White, 1939; Sherif, 1936) helped "clarify the method" (Garvin, 1997, p. 28). At the same time, group work was increasingly taught in the curricula of schools of social work. The influence of Freudian psychoanalysis and the increased collaboration among psychiatrists, psychologists, and social workers as members of treatment teams also led to the use of groups for psychotherapy. Finally, the push for group work came from the thousands of soldiers and veterans who needed assistance for physical and emotional problems. Thus, by the 1950s groups could be found in such settings as psychiatric institutions, veterans' hospitals, correctional facilities, and child guidance clinics. A third purpose developed from the movement of groups into these new settings: the diagnosis and treatment of the individual in the group.

In 1952, the Council of Social Work Education (CSWE) published its first curriculum policy statement. This document, which was the basis for accrediting professional social work education programs, defined social work practice as casework, group work, and community organizing. These three methods became the organizing structure for social work curricula for many years. In 1969, CSWE changed its curriculum policy statement to promote the integration of methods and to encourage training for generalist social work practice. One of the effects of this change in policy has been the precipitous decline in the institutionalization of group work in social work curricula. In 1963, 76 percent of social work graduate programs had concentrations in the group work method. With the growth of generalist and advanced generalist curricula by 1974, only 22 percent of the programs had this concentration, and by 1981 only 10 percent of schools did (Rubin, 1982). After 1982, the *Statistics on Social Work Education* no longer reported the number of schools with group work concentrations (Rubin, 1983). A survey conducted in 1991 of 89 of the 97 graduate schools of social work accredited by CSWE revealed that only six programs (7 percent) offered a concentration in group work (Birnbaum & Auerbach, 1992).

At the same time, a resurgence of interest in group work appears to be taking place. In this era of cost containment and managed care, it is generally recognized that group services are more cost-efficient than individual interventions (Toseland & Siporin, 1986); accordingly, the number of self-help and 12-step–style groups has exploded. If social workers are to continue to stay true to their professional roots and to be responsive to clients' needs, they must have knowledge and skills in social work group work. This chapter provides a basic foundation in social work group work for the beginning social worker, but it is no substitute for the specialized knowledge and training that are necessary to be a competent social work group worker.

APPROACHES TO GROUP WORK PRACTICE

Social work group work has been defined as "goal-directed activity with small groups of people aimed at meeting socioemotional needs and accomplishing tasks. This activity is directed to individual members of a group and to the group as a whole" (Toseland & Rivas, 2005, p. 12). Throughout the life span, people belong to a variety of groups, starting with the family and progressing through, for example, play groups, educational groups, work groups, and task groups or committees (Northen, 1982). Although groups are a natural and constant force in people's lives, social workers need a system for organizing and understanding the various types of "goal-directed activities" that take place in small groups. Presumably, a differential application of professional knowledge and skills is required in distinct types of small groups.

In examining various types of groups, one may logically distinguish between natural and formed groups. A family is natural group, membership in which is gained through birth and adoption. In other natural groups—peer groups and social networks—membership may come about serendipitously. In formed groups, membership is dependent on the fit between the purpose of the group and the needs or skills of the potential members. This distinction may be logical, but the concept of a formed group is so inclusive that it provides little guidance. Moreover, the unique history of natural groups requires a different approach by the social worker, as is evident by the voluminous literature on social work with families.

Papell and Rothman (1966) developed one of the first useful systems for distinguishing types of group work approaches by differentiating group work approaches by function. The differences in function, or group purpose, lead to differences in the focus of the group's activities and the role of the group worker. Papell and Rothman identified three approaches to group work practice: (1) the social goals model, (2) the reciprocal model, and (3) the remedial model. Although Papell and Rothman framed these categories as "models," it is more accurate to adopt the nomenclature of Germain (1983) and hence to conceive of them as "approaches." According to Germain,

> the term *approach* is preferred over the more common *model*, because of the confusion between a theoretical model in science, useful for its predictive value, and a practice model—so called—that merely sets forth the several dimensions of a coherent consistent approach to social work practice but has no predictive value. (p. 31)

The interaction among group function, role of the worker, and focus of the group for the four most common types of groups can be seen in Figure 10-1. The following sections examine the four common approaches to groups in greater detail.

Social Goals Approach

The core function of the social goals approach is the translation of "private troubles into public issues" (Schwartz, 1969, p. 22). The target for this approach to group work is the social order, often defined as a neighborhood or community. The group's work is directed toward action and primary prevention with a focus on the future. The vision of the future, from the perspective of a social goals approach group, is one based on ideals of social justice and human rights. To achieve its purpose, the social goals group requires its members, as one of their first tasks, to increase their "social consciousness" and "social responsibility" (Papell & Rothman, 1966). The group worker in such a group may be a consultant or a convener, whose role is to promote the democratic functioning of the group. Manor (2000) discussed the need for the group worker to prevent the worker–member relationship from paralleling the oppressive relationships

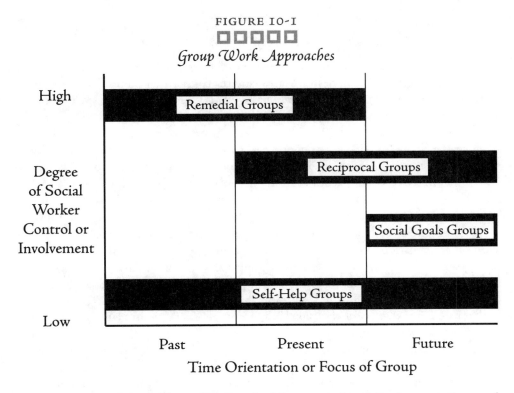

FIGURE IO-I

Group Work Approaches

Source: From Ruth R. Middleman, "The Pursuit of Competence through Involvement in Structured Groups." Reprinted with the permission of The Free Press, a Division of Simon & Schuster, Inc., from PROMOTING COMPETENCE IN CLIENTS: A New/Old Approach to Social Work Practice, Anthony N. Maluccio, Editor. Copyright © 1981 by the Free Press.

members experience outside the group. In a social goals group, the social worker may purposely refrain from exerting power or authority over the group. Clearly, the social goals approach to group work has its roots in the group work of the settlement houses. Today, groups that function within this approach can be found in public housing complexes, where tenants organize themselves to fight crime, or on college campuses where students come together for "take back the night" events.

Reciprocal Approach

What Papell and Rothman (1966) labeled the "reciprocal model" of group work has today become known as the "mutual aid model." The focus of activity in this approach to group work is the reciprocal, or symbiotic, relationship between individual clients and the group. The social worker is an enabler or mediator who seeks to prevent imbalances in the relationship or boundaries between the individual and the group and to help the group release its power to change—to learn

▢▢▢▢▢

Sidebar 10-1: *Teen Inspirators, on the Move*

The "Teen Inspirators," a group associated with the Oak Hill Community Development Corporation in Worchester, Massachusetts, consisted of 20 youths ages 11 to 16, of diverse ethnic, racial, and class backgrounds, and was formed "to improve their lives and neighborhood, and to gain respect from the adults in their community" (Ross & Coleman, 2000, p. 30). The Teen Inspirator project focused both on youth development and on the contributions youth can make to the community and provides a strong example of group work oriented toward social goals.

The project began as part of a community planning effort that involved several working groups, one of which focused on youth and teen issues; it was the only working group that continued to meet after the initial planning meeting. The Youth Working Group originally consisted of parents, service providers, and youth, but adult participation gradually faded, leaving primarily the youth members. Initial projects focused on recreational activities and a food drive; the participants saw the work as positive but of limited impact. The group then moved into a formal action planning process, which included creating a collective vision, identifying problems that stood in the way of their vision, and a series of other exercises culminating in a focused area for action.

The identified focus was to transform a small neighborhood park that served as a drug market and was in a poor state of repair. Improving the park required building bridges with funders, community organizations, local government, and neighborhood residents. The group conducted community mapping exercises (to collectively determine the boundaries of the community as experienced by residents) and focus groups, culminating in a "park planning party." Subsequently, committees and action groups were formed, and the project proceeded with the actual construction of a community park.

The Youth Inspirators also became involved in organizing a neighborhood cleanup and cookout, producing a youth resource directory, and participating in citywide youth planning. The project clearly had substantial effects on the personal and collective development of the youths involved as well as on the larger community. The youth development and resilience research has established that opportunities for participation, leadership, and contribution are critical protective factors associated with resilience, and it is hard to imagine how equivalent opportunities could be offered without work with groups.

Source: Ross, L., & Coleman, M. (2000). Urban community action planning inspires teenagers to transform their community and their identity. *Journal of Community Practice, 7*(2), 29–45.

how to be a mutual aid system. Schwartz (1986) referred to the social worker's role as "the two clients conception, in which the worker's function is to help both the individual and the group, the one to meet his needs within the system, the other to pursue its collective tasks" (pp. 17–18). The reciprocal or mutual aid approach requires the social worker to share power and control over the group with its members. Gitterman and Shulman (2005) gave many examples of mutual aid groups, such as a group consisting of people with AIDS in which they receive support and reassurance and are mobilized to take control over their lives. Groups that are commonly referred to as "support groups" fall within this conceptualization of the reciprocal approach. Schopler and Galinsky (1993) suggested that support groups "lie midway between" remedial groups and self-help groups in terms of their leader's behavior and the control that members have.

Remedial Approach

The focus of the remedial approach is on the treatment of the individual through the use of a group method. In this approach, the group is the means or context for achieving individual goals, and changes in group structure and group process are a means to an end rather than an end in themselves. One of the characteristics of the remedial group is that the social worker exerts a great deal of power and influence over the formation and operation of the group. Group members are selected by the social worker, who is guided in composing the group by the purpose of the group; members are often selected because of similarities in presenting problems or target complaints. In fact, the most critical issue in the effectiveness of remedial approach groups may be group composition. A group that fits the definition of a remedial approach group would be a skills-training and relapse-prevention group for people who are recovering from alcohol abuse.

Mainstream Approach

The broadening of social work practice and knowledge in the 1970s and 1980s resulted in some types of group work falling outside Papell and Rothman's (1966) original typology. Several group work theorists (Lang, 1979; Middleman & Wood, 1990) thus suggested that the practice of group work could be conceptualized with one approach—the mainstream approach. Papell and Rothman (1980) distinguished the mainstream approach from group psychotherapy by the latter's focus on changing the individual through the use of a group context. Group work approaches that fall within the mainstream approach are concerned with developing a mutual aid system within the group, an interest in moving the group through developmental phases, and members' shared goals. The leader role in the mainstream approach gradually shifts from the social worker to the group members as the group develops over time.

◻-◻-◻◻-◻

Sidebar 10-2: Culture Circles for Social Justice

Parker (2003) provided an example of an approach to group work that integrates feminist principles, socioeducation, mutual aid, shared power, and an emphasis on social justice. Services at the Institute for Family Services (IFS) (Somerset, New Jersey) are organized in ways that are distinctly different from most treatment-oriented programs in their work with troubled families. IFS uses a *cultural context* model that breaks through rigid family boundaries that may support sexist practices and that links families to one another and to the community. The primary modality at IFS is group work, using what the program calls "culture circles."

Culture circles are led by staff teams and are generally single gender (especially during the orientation phase), but circles for men, women, children, teens, and couples are offered. All circles have a specific commitment to bridging race, class, sexual orientation, and other structural distinctions. Participation in the circles may extend over a considerable period of time, given the challenging goals of the groups. The content of the culture circles focuses on power, privilege, and oppression within families and in society. Videos, socioeducation (particularly related to power and respect), involvement of sponsors (former clients), contacts with community representatives, and development of critical consciousness within the culture circles all contribute to deepening client awareness of injustice and commitment to lives of nonviolence, equality, and respect within families and communities. The men's circles have a strong emphasis on accountability and personal responsibility, and circles for all participants emphasize power inequities and artificial hierarchies. Staff and other clients within the circle serve in critical witnessing roles as participants commit to taking responsibility and reparation for harms done.

Not all clients remain in the program, in part because what is offered may be distinctly different than what was expected. For example, one man who came to the agency due to escalating arguments with his wife reported that he was "uncomfortable not knowing and unable to control what his wife was saying in the women's group. At the same time, he was put in a situation that required intimate sharing with other men," which was difficult for him, as it would be for many men socialized in certain parts of contemporary U.S. society (Parker, 2003, p. 280). Participants who do remain, however, find that "breaking down barriers," "no secrets," and the collective memory of the culture circle are important to their positive change.

Group work of this kind can be intense and powerful. The use of teams and the sharing of power within the circles reduce the burden that such practice might place on an individual practitioner and bring many more resources into the circle, in the co-construction of a community of empowerment.

Source: Parker, L. (2003). A social justice model for clinical social work practice. *Affilia, 18,* 272–288.

Although the mainstream approach is an eclectic approach that is consistent with the movement within social work to identify a nucleus of practice concepts, I agree with Garvin (1997), who suggested that it is "premature," if not impossible, to encompass all group work approaches within one approach. For example, the mainstream approach does not accurately conceptualize one of the most common types of groups that social workers are likely to encounter—the self-help group. Therefore, the mainstream approach is not included in Figure 10-1.

Self-Help Groups. The best-known and oldest self-help group is Alcoholics Anonymous (AA). AA was founded in 1935, and there are now more than 58,000 groups in the United States and Canada (Kurtz, 1997). Moreover, more than 250 different self-help groups use the name "Anonymous" or a version of the 12 steps (Kurtz). Putnam (2000) estimated that, in the United States at any one time, 2 percent of the adult population is involved with self-help groups and that over the lifetime, participation in such groups is 3 percent. Self-help groups such as AA are typically sponsored by international, national, or regional organizations. These sponsoring organizations often prescribe the format and procedures used in group meetings. Leadership and control of the self-help group lie with the group members. Studies of self-help groups indicate that members of the groups have not only clear goals about the outcome they want, but also clear ideas of how they want to move toward their goals (what the process should be) (Lieberman & Borman, 1979). The primary difference between self-help groups and the reciprocal approach to group work is that in self-help groups the social worker serves as a consultant, resource person, or referral source *outside* the group (Schopler & Galinsky, 1993). Self-help groups can be distinguished from informal helping networks by the existence of a group structure and boundaries.

Other conceptualizations abound in the social work literature as a means for organizing knowledge and skills for group work (see, for example, Garvin, 1997; Toseland & Rivas, 2005). The importance of any typology is in helping the social worker develop a schema for categorizing small groups that allows him or her not only to generalize from group to group but also to begin to understand how to work with specific types of groups.

GROUP PURPOSE AND STRUCTURE

Purpose

Given the definition of group presented earlier, in theory there should be no such thing as a group without a purpose. The failure of many groups, however, can be attributed to the lack of a consensus on the purpose of the group. The purpose of any group should be a clear and specific statement pertaining to how the group

🞐🞐🞐🞐🞐

Sidebar 10-3: Solution-Focused Groups for Junior High School Students

Solution-focused practice (or solution-focused brief therapy) is receiving increasing attention in social work practice as the evidence base supporting it expands. For example, Newsome (2004, 2005) reported on an eight-session solution-focused group for at-risk seventh and eighth-grade students and evaluated the utility of the groups in academic, social, and behavioral spheres. Groups consisted of six to eight students and lasted for 35 minutes per session (total participation time was just under five hours). The content of the groups included the following standard solution-focused techniques:

- Eliciting students' own goals for the semester
- Use of the scaling question (for example, "On a scale of 1 to 10, with 1 being your school goals not achieved, and 10 your school goals fully achieved, where would you rate yourself as a student today?" "Where would you like to be on this scale at the end of the semester?")
- Homework (for example, writing down signs of success)
- Use of the exception question to amplify and reinforce present and future change (for example, "Tell me about a time when you *were* able to complete your homework—how did that happen?")
- Asking the students to imagine themselves as older and wiser: What advice would they give to themselves (or someone in the same situation) today?
- Strategies for dealing with setbacks.

The results of this relatively brief intervention were promising. Modest but significant increases in GPA were found for the intervention group but not for a no-treatment comparison group. Improvements in social skills, classroom behavior as rated by teachers, and homework completion issues as rated by parents were also found. The results found were of a modest but socially meaningful magnitude. The study was small, and it had other limitations, but it nevertheless provided further evidence of the potential power of time-limited groupwork focused on particular issues for this population.

Sources:

Newsome, W. S. (2004). Solution-focused brief therapy groupwork with at-risk junior high school students: Enhancing the bottom line. *Research on Social Work Practice, 14,* 336–343.

Newsome, W. S. (2005). The impact of solution-focused brief therapy with at-risk junior high school students. *Children & Schools, 27,* 83–90.

will address an unmet need of clients. The statement of the group's purpose sets parameters for issues of structure (selection of members, group composition, and orientation), time (duration, frequency and length, and group development), and leadership (characteristics and number). Thus, in group work, structure follows function. From an ecosystems perspective, other systems and forces, such as an agency's policy, affect the composition and structure of a group, but those forces do not diminish the importance of making explicit a group's purpose.

Selection of Members

A great deal has been written in the group work literature about the importance of member selection (Dies & Teleska, 1985; Ormont, 1969; Papell & Rothman, 1966). Members must feel that they fit in and belong to the group (Beck, 1983). The selection of members is the process that affects the goodness of fit between members and the group. Although Shulman (1994) argued that guidelines for the selection of group members are "myths" because leaders take what they can get, this statement does not mean that every applicant is suitable to be a group member.

The guiding principle in the selection of members is that extremes are a problem. When the group has too many members, they lose the ability to interact with each other; when the group has too few members, the advantages of conducting a group are lost. Again, the size of the group depends on the purpose of the group. In general, the group work literature contains examples of groups that have four to 10 members. Social goals groups may be able to tolerate more clients, whereas in remedial groups with clients who are experiencing severe problems, the groups are usually kept small. As the size of the group increases, the ability of each member to participate fully in the group decreases.

Groups with extremely heterogeneous or homogeneous members with regard to individual or group attributes (for example, age, presenting problem) can also be problematic, depending on the goals of the group. For example, in groups of parents who met for support and parent training, mixing parents of teenagers with parents of preschoolers resulted in the failure of the members to identify with each other's problems, whereas a group composed of parents with preschoolers successfully mixed single and married mothers (Magen & Rose, 1994). Similarly, one can imagine how slow and silent a group consisting entirely of people with severe depression would be.

The best rule for avoiding extremes is to never have only one of anything in a group. Yalom (1985) referred to this rule as the "Noah's Ark principle." Some evidence indicates that clients from dominant groups (such as white people and men) prefer groups that mirror the racial and gender composition of society. For black people, however, one study indicated a preference for groups that are composed of equal numbers of white people and black people (Davis, 1979). The literature on women's membership in mixed-gender groups indicates that women prefer large groups, but it also suggests that they are less expressive in those groups (Davis & Proctor, 1989).

The purpose of the group sometimes dictates that the group be homogeneous. For example, a group to enhance racial, ethnic, or gender identity—often referred to as a "consciousness-raising group"—would be most effective with a homogeneous membership. At the other extreme, a group that is designed to decrease racial tensions and to promote social justice and human rights by fighting racism would be most effective with members of different racial groups.

The social worker must assess whether common ground exists between the unmet needs of the client and the purpose of the group. This mutuality of interests is essential for the client to be able to connect with the work of others in the group. Clients must also have the interpersonal skills necessary to participate in a group of five to 10 other members (Rose, 1989) because it is only through interpersonal interaction that the work of the group takes place. Finally, clients must have the cognitive skills to participate in the group at a level similar to that of other group members. For some groups, such skills may be the ability to read and write, whereas for others the skills may be the ability to help problem solve at a developmentally compatible level. Thus, group workers must examine and assess the fit of each client's characteristics, needs, interpersonal skills, and cognitive abilities with those of other group members, as well as with the group's purpose.

Composition

Group composition refers to whether the group can continually accept members (an open group) or whether the membership is fixed at some point (a closed group). Burlingame and Fuhriman (1990) reported that 60 percent of the groups they examined were open, and the remaining 40 percent were closed. An agency's mission affects this aspect of the group as well; for example, acute care psychiatric inpatient units have a fairly high turnover rate; thus, any group that such a unit would operate must be of short duration (such as one session) or must maintain some form of open membership. A support group for survivors of child sexual abuse might maintain a fixed membership to minimize difficulties in relation to trust and self-disclosure.

Fixed membership and flexible membership can be thought of as two poles on a continuum. Some groups have a fixed membership but allow members to drop in and out according to their needs. Other groups may start as flexible-membership groups but become fixed-membership groups at a predetermined point. For example, a large agency in New York City that operates support groups for people with cancer has flexible membership in the first two group sessions. After the second session, though, the group is said to have "formed," and the remaining 10 sessions are held with a fixed membership.

Orientation

Orientation to the group, or what some might call socialization to the client role, is a crucial task of the group worker. Orientation is the shaping of members in their role as group members. It involves both the establishment of ground rules (Tuckman, 1965) and the differentiation of roles (Garvin, 1985). Brower (1988) argued that group members enter the group with their own perceptions—their unique cognitive schema of the group. The task of the group worker, then, is to help members develop a shared cognitive schema of the group—a capacity toward mutual aid and purpose (Glassman & Kates, 1990)—and common perceptions and expectations.

Dies and Teleska (1985) cited evidence that one of the factors involved in negative group experience is unrealistically high expectations. Flowers (1987) reported that members who did not improve were the members who did not agree with others on a rank ordering of curative factors. He suggested that those group members may have come to the group with different expectations than those of other group members; another explanation may be that the group did not initially induce the same expectations in the members who did not improve as it did in the other members. Thus, one of the central tasks for the group worker and the group in the forming phase is to help members develop appropriate expectations for the group. Kaul and Bednar (1986) noted that structure, especially in early sessions, helped induce appropriate expectations and socialize members in their roles.

One method for inducing expectations in a structured manner is through contracting. Shulman (1994) discussed three areas in which contracts can be made in group work: (1) the role of the worker, (2) the mutual needs of the members, and (3) the mutual obligations of the members and leaders. There are many techniques a social worker might use to induce or clarify member expectations. For example, in the pregroup interview the social worker could identify the commonalities between the members' expectations and the purpose of the group. In the first group session, expectations can be made a topic of discussion through the question "What do you want from this group?" Finally, expectations can be grounded in reality by offering a testimonial from a former group member who achieved a successful outcome in the group.

Time

In group work, time can be examined in three ways: (1) the duration of the group, (2) the frequency and length of group sessions, and (3) group development.

Duration. Descriptions of groups that have lasted a single session to several years can be found in the literature. Open-ended groups have no fixed ending point, whereas close-ended (or time-limited) groups have a set termination date. The duration of a group may be constrained by the clients' circumstances, by the agency environment, or by the group's purposes. For example, an inner-city hospital used single-session groups for prevention of HIV transmission in intravenous drug users who were patients in the emergency department.

Although little empirical evidence is available to guide the social worker when planning the duration of a group, one general rule could be stated: More is not necessarily better. A close-ended group means that a termination date has been established a priori; the establishment of an end point facilitates movement toward goals.

Frequency and Length. Across approaches to group work, the most common frequency for group meetings is once a week, and the average length of a group session is one to three hours. Although little to no empirical evidence supports this widespread practice, many practical reasons underlie this type of scheduling, including cost, the availability of meeting space, and the coordination of the members' multiple schedules. Rose (1989) suggested that an optimal approach for close-ended groups would involve fading the frequency and duration of group meetings. Thus, when the group first forms, it would meet frequently, but as the group moves closer to the final session, the time between group meetings would increase or the length of group sessions would decrease. This variability in the time schedule for a close-ended group may be particularly valuable in the remedial approach to groups.

Group Development. A variety of group development sequences have been offered to help the social worker understand changes in groups over time. These typologies have ranged from three stages (Schwartz, 1986) to nine (Beck, 1983). Considerable overlap exists in the labels applied to the stages and, more significantly, in the conceptualization of the stages. Tuckman (1965) suggested four stages of group development that he summarized as *forming, storming, norming,* and *performing.* Tuckman's stages, however, fail to include a termination phase; in keeping with Tuckman's rhyme, I propose a fifth and final stage: adjourning. The crucial issue is not the names of the stages but the group worker's understanding of and skill in helping the group develop.

Although the concept of group development is of heuristic value, the current state of knowledge of group development has multiple problems, including the failure to validate stages of group development empirically, the arbitrary division of the group into phases, the failure to realize that development is not one predetermined sequence, and the attribution of stages as group phenomena when what is actually being described may be the development of an individual member (Beck, 1983; Brower, 1988; Burlingame, Fuhriman, & Drescher, 1984;

Glassman & Kates, 1990; MacKenzie, 1987; Tuckman, 1965). For example, Galinsky and Schopler (1989) pointed out that developmental patterns in open-ended groups are affected by the frequency of turnover among members and the extent to which membership is modified. On the one hand, open-ended groups with frequent and extensive turnover of members would not be expected to move beyond the forming stage of group development. On the other hand, groups with an infrequent and small turnover would develop in a manner similar to close-ended, fixed-membership groups.

Leadership

It is axiomatic that group leaders should have the capacity, skills, values, and attitudes required of any social worker. It is also clear that group work necessitates a set of skills caseworkers do not need. Schwartz (1966) summed up the difference in the requisite social work skills as follows:

> The group leadership role demands that the worker give up much of the interview control to which she has, often unconsciously, become accustomed. Caseworkers have often told me that they had never realized how rigidly they controlled the client-worker interaction until they began to function as group workers, where changes of subject could be effected by anyone in the group, where people often turned to each other rather than to the worker for reinforcement and support, where clients could verify each other's "wrong" ideas, where mutually reinforced feelings could not be turned off when they became "dangerous," and where, in short, one's faith in the client's autonomy and basic strength were put to its severest test. (p. 575)

Recently, the Association for the Advancement of Social Work with Groups (AASWG) published *Standards for Social Work Practice with Groups* (1999). The standards are similar to other standards of practice that have been published by the National Association of Social Workers. The AASWG standards delineate the essential knowledge and values that should guide group workers as well as the primary worker tasks in each phase of the group's development. Although the AASWG standards are rather generic, given the need to be applicable to a wide range of groups, they do provide group workers with a guide for responsible leadership of groups.

Aside from the issue of the group worker's skills, another important issue in leadership is whether to use one or two leaders. No consistent evidence in the empirical literature demonstrates that two heads are better than one. In fact, Kolodny (1980) summarized the literature on co-leadership by writing, "The requirement would seem to be that one's co-leader be someone whom one knows well and is compatible with, who agrees with one theoretically, possesses equal knowledge, and is similar to oneself in competence and professional stature, but is definitely not a friend" (p. 34). Having a co-leader increases the financial cost to the agency or the clients. Another potential problem with co-leadership is that the leaders may dominate the discussion; To put it more strongly, two leaders typically talk too much. In groups with co-leaders, Rose (1989) recommended that the leaders develop a "no back-to-back talking" rule so that they do not dominate discussions within the group.

Co-leadership is desirable in four situations: (1) during training, when it is often helpful for social workers to co-lead their first group; (2) for groups that require specialized knowledge or skills, such as those for children who have been sexually abused or people with AIDS; (3) when issues of physical or emotional safety are involved, such as in groups of men who batter; and (4) in couples groups, when it is useful to have both male and female leaders. The danger in co-leadership, particularly in groups with male and female leaders, is that real or imagined differences in leaders' status may exist. Several studies have found that men are perceived as being of a higher status than are women when co-leading. Similarly, when co-leaders are members of different racial groups, clients have attributed more negative attributes to the group leader who was not from their racial group than to the same-race group leader (Davis & Proctor, 1989).

GROUP PROCESSES

The term "group processes," rather than "group process," is used in this section because many variables have been identified in the literature as belonging to the phenomena of group process. Therefore, it is more accurate, linguistically as well as conceptually, to discuss group process as a composite of phenomena, rather than as a single phenomenon (Fuhriman, Drescher, & Burlingame, 1984).

Novice group workers are often admonished for not paying attention to group processes. However, the problem is usually not that they ignore group processes but that they do not know what is meant by group processes. Even when group workers are given an explanation of group processes, the definitions, such as "process is everything in the group that is not content" (Yalom, 1985, p. 137), are often useless.

Unfortunately, no one clear definition of group processes exists. The following three definitions have been suggested: (1) "the way of working as opposed to the substance of the work" (Gitterman & Shulman, 1986, p. 42); (2) "changes that take place in group conditions" (Garvin, 1997, p. 104); and (3) "an aspect or characteristic of group behavior, the ecological characteristics of the group" (Fuhriman et al., 1984, p. 431). I prefer the third definition because it is specific to group work, includes interpersonal relationship behavior, and also encompasses "characteristics" of the group that are more than individual transactions (Burlingame et al., 1984). The idea that group processes take place across system levels offers a useful connection between group phenomena and the ecosystems perspective. Whichever definition of group processes the reader chooses to adopt, it is clear that a constellation of factors is necessary for the functioning of an effective small group but that those factors are not sufficient for the group to achieve its goals. These "necessary but not sufficient" factors are collectively referred to as "group processes."

Cohesion is an important process variable in group work, but as is the case with group development and group processes, little agreement exists as to how to define it. Kaul and Bednar (1986) remarked that "research on group cohesion ... continues to be based on definitions and methods of measurement so impoverished [they] can only produce a noncohesive body of literature" (p. 640). Despite this criticism, whether one defines cohesion as attraction to the group (Lieberman, Yalom, & Miles, 1973), attraction to other members, or a common schema (Brower, 1988), it is clear that cohesive groups are more likely to achieve their purpose. High cohesiveness has been linked to change, whereas low cohesiveness has been show to correlate highly with members dropping out of groups (Dies & Teleska, 1985; Lieberman et al., 1973). In group work, as in other methods of social work, dissatisfied clients drop out or terminate prematurely. Several suggestions have been made in the literature for maximizing group cohesion, including incorporating a break with a snack, modeling, and reinforcing self-disclosure (Rose, 1977). In fact, intimacy in self-disclosure is associated with members' perceptions of group cohesion (Kaul & Bednar).

The literature generally agrees that clients profit from the group process of self-disclosure (Kaul & Bednar, 1986). Wright and Ingraham (1985) concluded from their analysis of behavior in four interpersonal learning groups that self-disclosure is a function not only of individual differences but of the relationship among group members. This finding suggests that the quality of intermember relationships may affect the quantity of self-disclosure in a group.

Feedback, or what Yalom (1985) referred to as "interpersonal learning," is a group process that has been shown to contribute to therapeutic change (Dies & Teleska, 1985, p. 120). There is widespread agreement that clients benefit from constructive feedback under the right circumstances. The group leader, then, should encourage, if not teach, members to give feedback to each other.

Although the evidence regarding the relative strength of group problem solving over individual problem solving is equivocal (see, for example, Davis & Toseland, 1987), it is clear that the mechanisms involved in group problem solving are central processes in group work. The components of group problem solving have been defined differently by group theorists (see Gitterman & Shulman, 2005; Yalom, 1985), but all agree that problem solving is important in group work.

As Table 10-1 indicates, the nomenclature used to label group processes varies by theorist and by approach to group work. A definitive list of group processes is

TABLE 10-1

□ □ □ □ □

Comparison of Common Group Processes in Remedial and Reciprocal Groups

Remedial Group Processes (Yalom, 1985)	Reciprocal Group Processes (Shulman, 1994)
Instillation of hope Altruism Cohesiveness	Mutual support Strength in numbers
Universality	All-in-the-same-boat phenomenon
Guidance	Sharing data
Identification	Rehearsal
Interpersonal learning Self-understanding	Problem solving Dialectical processes Mutual demand
Catharsis	Discussing a taboo area
Existential factors	Developing a universal perspective
Collective recapitualization of the primary family group	(No exact parallel in reciprocal model groups)

Sources: Shulman, L. (1994). Group work method. In A. Gitterman & L. Shulman (Eds.), *Mutual aid groups, vulnerable populations, and the life cycle* (2nd ed., pp. 29–58). New York: Columbia University Press; Yalom, I. D. (1985). *The theory and practice of group psychotherapy.* New York: Basic Books.

probably not possible, given that group processes are influenced by the group work approach, the stage of the group's development, forces outside the group, and individual differences within the group (Yalom, 1985).

The social worker who is able to identify group processes as they develop over the life of a group is in a position to harness their power in moving the group toward its goal or goals. A social worker who fixes his or her focus solely on the tasks or outcome of the group runs the risk that group processes will serve an inhibiting, rather than a facilitating, function.

PARTICIPATION

A fundamental aspect of the first group meeting is participation by every group member (Rose, 1977). One task of the group leader, unlike that of the case-worker, is to deemphasize his or her role and to stress the value of intermember relations (Dies & Teleska, 1985). Coyle (1947), who wrote the first social work textbook on group work, addressed the issue of participation as follows:

> A full orchestra can have no instruments that are silenced when they should be expected to come in. For that reason the . . . leader needs, first, . . to have all participate and then to be aware of the extent of the existing participating. If his ear becomes trained to this he is then in a position to encourage participation where it is inadequate. (p. 23)

The quality of participation is not the issue; the mere act of participating may be what is crucial. Participation not only develops socializing skills, one of the essential conditions of group membership, but can reduce the probability of members dropping out. For example, in a survey of practitioners, one of the most common reasons given for members dropping out was that they felt socially isolated and were less well integrated into the group than were other members (Dies & Teleska, 1985). In addition, initial participation predicts later, and deeper, self-disclosure. MacKenzie (1987) reported that his analysis of "critical incident reports" revealed that the initial stages of groups were characterized by superficial self-disclosure, whereas the later stages of the group were characterized by deeper self-disclosure.

Although the social worker has the responsibility for maximizing members' participation, certain forms of participation can be a problem. One of the most common types of problems is scapegoating (Shulman, 1994). In scapegoating, one member of the group is singled out for criticism and is blamed as the source of the group's problems. Garvin (1986) suggested that scapegoating in a group is parallel to families seeking change in an identified patient, whereas others, such as Tsui and Schultz (1988), considered it a reflection of larger societal tensions. Whatever the etiology of this form of communication, the group worker has the responsibility to provide help. The question then is what is most helpful when communication is a problem in the group?

Although the group worker may be inclined to "protect" the scapegoat, that strategy generally places him or her in conflict with the group (Gitterman & Shulman, 2005). One tactic is to empathize with the scapegoated individual; another is to confront the group with its here-and-now behavior (Anstey, 1982). Another strategy is to find the common ground between the group and the scapegoat (Gitterman & Shulman); however, that approach has been criticized as taking too long to implement and as being unrealistic (Anstey). Finally, Rose (1989) suggested treating scapegoating as a "group problem" and centering the intervention on defining the problem and engaging the group in a problem-solving process. Whichever strategy the worker uses, it should follow a careful assessment of the problem and be designed to promote the work of the group.

EVIDENCE-BASED GROUP WORK

Although the use of a specific group method should follow and be linked to assessment, group work has several general advantages. First, groups can relieve real or imagined isolation—a characteristic that Shulman (1994) referred to as the "all-in-the-same-boat phenomenon" (p. 44) and that Yalom (1985) labeled "universality." Whatever the exact process, the group offers multiple opportunities for validation and reinforcement. Second, the group is a natural laboratory for learning and discussion. Clients or members are forced to deal with each other's attitudes, behaviors, and feelings; doing so helps them develop social skills either explicitly, as part of the group contract, or implicitly, in the group interaction.

These advantages of group work are theorized or based on practice experience; there is also an increasing body of empirical evidence on group work. For example, Brower, Arndt, and Ketterhagen (2004) examined five years of published research on group work. They concluded that both the quality and quantity of literature on small groups has increased. This empirical evidence has also suggested that group work is effective. In a review of empirically tested social work interventions reported during the 1990s, Reid and Fortune (2003) found that 58 percent of the evidence-based interventions were group-based approaches.

Toseland and Siporin (1986) examined the literature comparing individual and group interventions and asked, "Which is more effective?" In 24 of 32 studies, they found no statistical differences in the outcome of the modalities, but in the remaining eight studies, they found group treatment to be statistically more effective than individual treatment. Toseland and Siporin found no clear pattern regarding the types of problems that are most effectively treated in a group setting. When this study is examined in terms of group versus individual treatment, it seems safe to conclude that the work done in groups is no worse than that conducted on an individual basis. Similarly, in a recent selected review of evaluation studies of group work, Gant (2004), similar to Toseland and Siporin, concluded that, in general, group work interventions are effective, but we must answer the "follow-up question, 'but compared to what?'" (p. 473).

The question to ask is not "Which is more effective?" but "Which is more effective with these particular problems under these conditions?" (Paul, 1967). Toseland and Siporin's (1986) failure to ask this question reflects the failure of group workers to systematically evaluate their practice (Galinsky & Schopler, 1993).

MONITORING AND EVALUATION

Although research supports the efficacy of group interventions, other evidence shows that some clients have negative experiences in groups. Yalom and his colleagues (Lieberman et al., 1973) documented that almost 10 percent of encounter-group participants experienced psychological disturbances attributable to their group experience. Recent research by Smokowski, Rose, Todar, and Reardon (1999) linked negative group experiences to behavior of group leaders. In that study, group members who reported that the leader actively perpetrated inappropriate behavior (for example, pressuring the member to disclose or take action prematurely) or was passive when damaging events occurred were at much higher risk of becoming "casualties" than those who did not report those experiences. Experiencing humiliation or, especially, betrayal in the group was also strongly associated with poor outcomes. Groups can be powerful—that is why they are used—but the leader needs to be manage that power well. Social workers have an ethical responsibility to "do no harm." Given this mandate and the research on negative group experiences, social workers need to learn effective group leadership skills. They must also continuously monitor and evaluate group work practice and attend to both positive and negative processes and outcomes.

All the methods that have been suggested for monitoring and evaluating social work practice (see chapter 6) are applicable to group work. Rose (1984), for example, suggested the use of a postsession questionnaire. This consumer satisfaction instrument allows the social worker to monitor group members' satisfaction on a session-by-session basis. Other forms of monitoring include using observers or co-leaders to record the frequency of participation among group members. The participation data can then be provided to the group to encourage more participation from members who talk infrequently and to diminish the participation of members who talk frequently. Questionnaires have been developed to assess members' perceptions of group processes (see, for example, Yalom, 1985). The questionnaires can be used in their entirety, or subscales (for example, Cohesion) can be chosen to track the development of changes in group processes. Finally, several observational systems can be used to monitor group processes (for a comprehensive review of these systems, see Beck & Lewis, 2000). Regardless of the type of group being implemented, social workers must systematically monitor the group's changing environment

Monitoring the group over time is not enough; social workers must also evaluate progress toward the attainment of the group's goals. This requirement underscores the importance of a clear group purpose; without a clear purpose, it becomes impossible to evaluate whether the group has achieved its goals. In remedial groups, rapid assessment instruments can be used to evaluate changes in individual clients. Goal attainment scaling has also been used in remedial groups to evaluate progress toward individual goals. In groups using the reciprocal approach social goals groups, goal attainment scaling can be used to assess progress toward the collective group goals. Although self-help groups have been subjected to much less outcome research, evidence from a limited number of studies indicates that changes in individual members can be evaluated. For example, Kurtz (1997) suggested that social workers look for evidence of a "conversion experience" or changes in self-perception as a result of self-help group participation. With curiosity, creativity, and tenacity, a social worker will be able to monitor and evaluate group work interventions.

Social workers must move away from a focus on method or approach and start where the client is. If group workers think of themselves as social workers first, they will not prematurely confine themselves to working with one client system or one particular method of helping (Nelsen, 1975).

REFERENCES

Addams, J. (1960). *Twenty years at Hull House*. New York: Signet. (Original work published 1910)

Anstey, M. (1982). Scapegoating in groups: Some theoretical perspectives and a case record of intervention. *Social Work with Groups, 5*(3), 51–63.

Association for the Advancement of Social Work with Groups. (1999). *Standards for social work practice with groups*. Akron, OH: Author.

Beck, A. P. (1983). A process analysis of group development. *Group, 7*(1), 19–28.

Beck, A. P., & Lewis, C. M. (2000). *The process of group psychotherapy: Systems for analyzing change*. Washington, DC: American Psychological Association.

Birnbaum, M. L., & Auerbach, C. (1992, February). *Group work in graduate social work education: The price of neglect*. Paper presented at the Annual Program Meeting, Council on Social Work Education, Kansas City, MO.

Brower, A. M. (1988). Group development as constructed social reality: A social-cognitive understanding of group formation. *Social Work with Groups, 12*(2), 23–41.

Brower, A. M., Arndt, R. G., & Ketterhagen, A. (2004). Very good solutions really do exist for group work research design problems. In C. D. Garvin, L. M. Gutierrez, & M. J. Galinsky (Eds.), *Handbook of social work with groups* (pp. 435–446). New York: Guilford Press.

Burlingame, G., Fuhriman, A., & Drescher, S. (1984). Scientific inquiry into small group process: A multidimensional approach. *Small Group Behavior, 15*(4), 441–470.

Burlingame, G. M., & Fuhriman, A. (1990). Time-limited group therapy. *Counseling Psychologist, 18*, 93–118.

Council on Social Work Education. (1952). *Curriculum policy for the master's degree program in social work education*. New York: Author.

Council on Social Work Education. (1969). *Curriculum policy for the master's degree program in social work education*. New York: Author.

Coyle, G. L. (1937). *Studies in group behavior*. New York: Harper & Row.

Coyle, G. L. (1947). *Group experience and democratic values*. New York: Women's Press.

Davis, L. (1979). Racial composition of groups. *Social Work, 24*, 208–213.

Davis, L. E., & Proctor, E. K. (1989). *Race, gender, & class: Guidelines for practice with individuals, families, and groups*. Englewood Cliffs, NJ: Prentice Hall.

Davis, L., & Toseland, R. (1987). Group versus individual decision making. *Social Work with Groups, 10*(2), 95–105.

Dewey, J. (1922). *Human nature and conduct*. New York: Random House.

Dies, R. R., & Teleska, P. A. (1985). Negative outcome in group psychotherapy. In D. T. Mays & C. M. Franks (Eds.), *Negative outcome in psychotherapy and what to do about it* (pp. 181–141). New York: Springer.

Flowers, J. V. (1987). Client outcome as a function of agreement or disagreement with the modal group perception of curative factors in short-term, structured group psychotherapy. *International Journal of Group Psychotherapy, 37*(1), 113–118.

Fuhriman, A., Drescher, S., & Burlingame, G. (1984). Conceptualizing small group process. *Small Group Behavior, 15*(4), 427–440.

Galinsky, M. J., & Schopler, J. H. (1989). Developmental patterns in open-ended groups. *Social Work with Groups, 12*(2), 99–114.

Galinsky, M. J., & Schopler, J. H. (1993, October). *Social group work competence: Our strengths and challenges*. Plenary address at the 15th Annual Symposium of the Association for the Advancement of Social Work with Groups, New York, NY.

Gant, L. M. (2004). Evaluation of group work. In C. D. Garvin, L. M. Gutierrez, & M. J. Galinsky (Eds.), *Handbook of social work with groups* (pp. 461–475). New York: Guilford Press.

Garvin, C. D. (1985). Group process: Usage and uses in social work practice. In M. Sundel, P. Galasser, R. Sarri, & R. Vinter (Eds.), *Individual change through small groups* (2nd ed., pp. 203–225). New York: Free Press.

Garvin, C. (1986). Family therapy and group work: "Kissing cousins or distant relatives" in social work practice. In M. Parnes (Ed.), *Innovations in social group work: Feedback from practice to theory* (pp. 1–15). New York: Haworth Press.

Garvin, C. D. (1997). *Contemporary group work* (3rd ed.). Boston: Allyn & Bacon.

Germain, C. B. (1983). Technological advances. In A. Rosenblatt & D. Waldfogel (Eds.), *Handbook of clinical social work* (pp. 26–57). San Francisco: Jossey-Bass.

Gitterman, A., & Shulman, L. (Eds.). (1986). *Mutual aid groups and the life cycle*. Itasca, IL: F. E. Peacock.

Gitterman, A., & Shulman, L. (Eds.). (2005). *Mutual aid groups, vulnerable and resilient populations, and the life cycle* (3rd ed.). New York: Columbia University Press.

Glassman, U., & Kates, L. (1990). *Group work: A humanistic approach*. Newbury Park, CA: Sage Publications.

Kaul, T. J., & Bednar, R. L. (1986). Experiential group research: Results, questions, and suggestions. In S. L. Garfield & A. E. Bergin (Eds.), *Handbook of psychotherapy and behavior change* (3rd ed., pp. 671–714). New York: John Wiley & Sons.

Kolodny, R. (1980). The dilemma of co-leadership. *Social Work with Groups, 3*(4), 31-34.

Kurtz, L. F. (1997). *Self-help and support groups: A handbook for practitioners*. Thousand Oaks, CA: Sage Publications.

Lang, N. (1979). A comparative examination of therapeutic uses of groups in social work and in adjacent human service professions: Part II—The literature from 1969–1978. *Social Work with Groups, 2*(3), 197–220.

Lewin, K., Lippitt, R., & White, R. (1939). Patterns of aggressive behavior in experimentally created "social climates." *Journal of Social Psychology, 10*, 271–299.

Lieberman, M., & Borman, L. (Eds.). (1979). *Self-help groups for coping with crisis*. San Francisco: Jossey-Bass.

Lieberman, M. A., Yalom, I. D., & Miles, M. B. (1973). *Encounter groups: First facts*. New York: Basic Books.

MacKenzie, K. R. (1987). Therapeutic factors in group psychotherapy: A contemporary view. *Group, 11*(1), 26–31.

Magen, R. H., & Rose, S. D. (1994). Parents in groups: Problem solving versus behavioral skill training. *Research on Social Work Practice, 4*, 172–191.

Manor, O. (2000). *Choosing a groupwork approach: An inclusive stance.* London: Jessica Kingsley Publishers.

Middleman, R. R. (1981). The pursuit of competence through involvement in structured groups. In A. N. Maluccio (Ed.), *Promoting competence in clients: A new/old approach to social work practice* (pp. 185–210). New York: Free Press.

Middleman, R., & Wood, G. (1990). Reviewing the past present of group work and the challenge of the future. *Social Work with Groups, 13*(3), 3–20.

Nelsen, J. C. (1975). Social work's fields of practice, methods, and models: The choice to act. *Social Service Review, 49*(2), 264–270.

Newsome, W. S. (2004). Solution-focused brief therapy groupwork with at-risk junior high school students: Enhancing the bottom line. *Research on Social Work Practice, 14*, 336–343.

Newsome, W. S. (2005). The impact of solution-focused brief therapy with at-risk junior high school students. *Children & Schools, 27*, 83–90.

Northen, H. (1982). *Clinical social work.* New York: Columbia University Press.

Ormont, L. R. (1969). Acting in and the therapeutic contract in group psychoanalysis. *International Journal of Group Psychotherapy, 11*, 420–432.

Papell, C. P., & Rothman, B. (1966). Social group work models: Possession and heritage. *Journal of Education for Social Work, 2*(2), 66–77.

Papell, C., & Rothman, B. (1980). Relating the mainstream model of social work with groups to group psychotherapy and the structured group approach. *Social Work with Groups, 3*(2), 5–23.

Parker, L. (2003). A social justice model for clinical social work practice. *Affilia, 18*, 272–288.

Paul, G. L. (1967). Outcome research in psychotherapy. *Journal of Consulting Psychology, 31*, 109–118.

Putnam, R. D. (2000). *Bowling alone: The collapse and revival of American community.* New York: Simon & Schuster.

Reid, K. E. (1997). *Social work practice with groups: A clinical perspective* (2nd ed.). Pacific Grove, CA: Brooks/Cole.

Reid, W. J., & Fortune, A. E. (2003). Empirical foundation for practice guidelines in current social work knowledge. In A. Rosen & E. K. Proctor (Eds.), *Developing practice guidelines for social work intervention: Issues, methods, and research agenda* (pp. 59–79). New York: Columbia University Press.

Rose, S. D. (1977). *Group therapy: A behavioral approach.* Englewood Cliffs, NJ: Prentice Hall.

Rose, S. D. (1984). Use of data in identifying and resolving group problems in goal oriented treatment groups. *Social Work with Groups, 7*(2), 23-36.

Rose, S. D. (1989). *Working with adults in groups: Integrating cognitive-behavioral and small group strategies.* San Francisco: Jossey-Bass.

Ross, L., & Coleman, M. (2000). Urban community action planning inspires teenagers to transform their community and their identity. *Journal of Community Practice, 7*(2), 29–45.

Rubin, A. (1982). *Statistics on social work education in the United States: 1981.* New York: Council on Social Work Education.

Rubin, A. (1983). *Statistics on social work education in the United States: 1982*. New York: Council on Social Work Education.

Schopler, J. H., & Galinsky, M. J. (1993). Support groups as open systems: A model for practice and research. *Health & Social Work, 18*, 195–207.

Schwartz, W. (1966). Discussion of three papers on the group method with clients, foster families, and adoptive families. *Child Welfare, 45*(10), 571–575.

Schwartz, W. (1969). Private troubles and public issues: One social work job or two? In National Conference on Social Welfare, *The social welfare forum:1969* (pp. 22–43). New York: Columbia University Press.

Schwartz, W. (1986). The group work tradition and social work practice. *Social Work with Groups, 8*(4), 7–27.

Sherif, M. (1936). *The psychology of social norms*. New York: Harper.

Shulman, L. (1994). Group work method. In A. Gitterman & L. Shulman (Eds.), *Mutual aid groups, vulnerable populations, and the life cycle* (2nd ed., pp. 29–58). New York: Columbia University Press.

Smokowski, P. R., Rose, S., Todar, K., & Reardon, K. (1999). Postgroup-casualty status, group events, and leader behavior: An early look into the dynamics of damaging group experiences. *Research on Social Work Practice, 9*, 555–574.

Toseland, R. W., & Rivas, R. F. (2005). *An introduction to group work practice* (5th ed.). Boston: Allyn & Bacon.

Toseland, R. W., & Siporin, M. (1986). When to recommend group treatment: A review of the clinical and research literature. *International Journal of Group Psychotherapy, 36*(2), 171–201.

Tsui, P., & Schultz, G. L. (1988). Ethnic factors in group process: Cultural dynamics in multi-ethnic therapy groups. *American Journal of Orthopsychiatry, 58*, 136–142.

Tuckman, B. W. (1965). Developmental sequence in small groups. *Psychological Bulletin, 63*, 384–399.

Wright, T. L., & Ingraham, L. J. (1985). Simultaneous study of individual differences and relationship effects in social behavior in groups. *Journal of Personality and Social Psychology, 48*, 1041–1047.

Yalom, I. D. (1985). *The theory and practice of group psychotherapy*. New York: Basic Books.

11

Social Work with Communities

Susan P. Kemp and Edward Scanlon

Social workers have long recognized the salience of community in individual and social well-being. Indeed, community is a natural site for practice, one that reflects the profession's historic commitment to contextual and inclusive practice (Fisher, 2005; Kemp, Whittaker, & Tracy, 1997). Embodied in this chapter is the belief, inherent in social work practice since its earliest beginnings, that geographic and social communities provide singular opportunities for participation, democratic citizenship, and collective action for social justice. At the same time, communities can be just as exclusionary, oppressive, and conservative as any other social structure. Empowering community practice is located in the space between these two realities supporting socially just connections between people and communities and between communities and larger social structures. We are particularly committed to social work practice in and with communities facing multiple economic and social challenges: communities that do not fully share society's benefits and may actively be excluded from full participation and inclusion. Those communities include communities of color, low-income communities, and communities formed around stigmatized identities, such as sexual orientation or disability.

The integrative approach presented in this chapter is consistent with calls for more contextual, integrative, and critically informed approaches to social work practice (Finn & Jacobson, 2003; Fisher & Karger, 1997) and with efforts to create models for community practice that integrate direct practice and community development (Austin, Coombs, & Barr, 2005; Johnson, 1998; Smale, 1995). It neither privileges macro practice nor denies the value of direct practice, viewing knowledge and skills from both domains as essential to effective practice in the community.

This inclusive view of community practice supports the current resurgence of interest in community across practice modalities (Austin et al., 2005; Weil, 2005). In their recent book on community-centered clinical practice, Lightburn and Sessions (2006) called for "practice grounded in a recognition of the profound interdependence of individual and community wellbeing, an understanding that the health of one is highly influenced by the health of the other" (p. 4). Child and family social workers are likewise demonstrating interest in community-centered practice (Ryan, De Masi, Heinz, Jacobson, & Ohmer, 2000); this increased interest builds on more than a decade of calls for a renewed emphasis on the importance of community as a source of resources for individuals and families (Sviridoff & Ryan, 1997; Webster-Stratton, 1997). Coulton (1995a), a leading social work community researcher, noted the need for "a modernized vision of community social work practice" designed to "use the community to strengthen families, create economic opportunity, and protect vulnerable individuals" (p. 439). In health care social work, Poole (1997) described an "urgent need for community capacity building" (p. 165). In prevention practice, renewed interest in community-level change can be seen in efforts ranging from McKnight's emphasis on community assets and strengths (Kretzmann & McKnight, 1993; McKnight, 1997) to programs such as Communities that Care, which focus on engaging communities in supporting healthy child and youth development (Harachi et al., 2003). Recent social work practice models focused on social justice and multiculturalism also emphasize the centrality of the community in contemporary practice (Finn & Jacobson, 2003; Gutierrez, Lewis, Nagda, Wernick, & Shore, 2005).

In addition, several influential foundations have stepped forward to support community-centered approaches to programs and services (for example, the Annie E. Casey Foundation's Family to Family Program, a community-centered child welfare initiative). At the same time, a rich array of grassroots social movements and coalitions has emerged, which has provided new opportunities for community-based social work practice and partnerships. Although community practice still lags in developing a strong quantitative research base, an increasingly robust body of empirical knowledge on neighborhoods and communities is available (see, for example, Brooks-Gunn, Duncan, & Aber, 1997; Chaskin, 1997; Coulton, Korbin, & Su, 1996; Korbin & Coulton, 1997). There is also a rich qualitative literature on community-based programs and practice, much of it based on participatory research models (Chow & Crowe, 2005; Pennell, Noponen, & Weil, 2005).

This chapter has three components: (1) It provides an overview of the meaning of community, a concept that has multiple dimensions; (2) it introduces the reader to the range of models in contemporary community practice; and (3) it describes the core components of a generalist approach to empowering community practice, which is designed to bridge the gap between practice with individuals, families, and groups and practice with communities. Our working premise is that comprehensive strategies are necessary to address the complex issues facing contemporary communities; these in turn create the ethical requirement that social workers understand and have competencies in practice across multiple systems levels. The chapter focuses primarily on theory and skills of immediate relevance to entry-level social workers in a variety of settings and fields of practice. Although both social administration and social policy are highly relevant to community practice, these fields have their own bodies of knowledge and skills and are not explored here. Nor do we examine the more technical aspects of community practice, such as program development and social planning.

MEANING OF COMMUNITY

"Place," as architect and public historian Dolores Hayden (1995) pointed out, "is one of the trickiest words in the English language, a suitcase so overfilled one can never shut the lid" (p. 15). "Community" is likewise a tricky idea, meaning different things to different people and groups, varying across time and place, always in flux. Understanding community is particularly complicated in today's global economy. Flows of capital, people, information, jobs, and culture create the sense that the world is a global village. In many communities, people are linked globally as well as locally by personal connections, the Internet, and global communication systems. Workers and work span the globe: The person at the end of a help line may be anywhere in the world, and many workers labor far from home, sending money back to families in another country or shuttling back and forth themselves. As world economic systems have shifted toward increasing domination by transnational corporations, economic and social inequities have increased, creating huge wealth and advantages for some people and profound disadvantage and dislocation for others. The impact of those shifts is powerfully felt in low-income communities and communities of color, in which historic inequities are further deepened by factors such as the outflow of local jobs, the loss of low-income housing to gentrification, urban development and displacement, and cutbacks in social and human services (Reisch, 2005).

U.S. communities are increasingly diverse, as newly arrived immigrants and refugees, many forcibly displaced by war, political violence, and social upheaval, join established racial and ethnic groups. Like historically marginalized communities, these newer multiracial communities face challenges related to poverty, racism, residential displacement, environmental toxins, and social and spatial segregation. Yet, in an era of rising religious, sectarian, and ethnic conflict, community residents may have difficulties finding common ground for shared struggle. Communities of privilege, meanwhile, increasingly retreat to gated suburbs or create affluent urban enclaves, often in neighborhoods that previously were racially and economically diverse (Fisher & Karger, 1997).

Despite these social and economic divisions, the desire for community is embedded deeply in U.S. social ideology. In a society defined by individualism, the belief nonetheless persists that life is better when people are connected to one another in meaningful ways (Chavis & Wandersman, 1990). For many people, the idea of community evokes nostalgic visions of small-town values and habits, of places where people know one another, look out for each other, and act together for the common good. In their landmark study of U.S. culture, *Habits of the Heart*, Bellah, Madsen, Sullivan, Swidler, and Tipton (1985) found a yearning for "meaning and coherence" in the midst of the pursuit of individualism. They concluded, as has communitarian Amitai Etzioni (1993), that this meaning could be found through renewed commitment to community and civic responsibility. In a similar vein, research on social capital suggests that connections within communities produce tangible social and personal benefits. Warren, Thompson, and Saegert (2001) described social capital as "a collective asset, a feature of communities, rather than the property of an individual" (p. 1). In short, it is a "common good." Yet, the desire for community competes with the equally compelling quest for individual acquisition and fulfillment. Little evidence suggests that dominant groups in the United States readily put the common good ahead of personal advancement, particularly if doing so means relinquishing privilege. Therefore, efforts to develop community as a vehicle for social integration, shared meaning, and collective well-being must confront the reality that the rhetoric of community cloaks deep ambivalence that is fundamentally tied to issues of class, race, and power.

DEFINING COMMUNITY

Social scientists tend to define community as either geographic (connections between residents of a particular place) or social (relationships based in shared concerns and interests). To those definitions, Heller (1989) added a third: community as collective political power. All three definitions assume that in a community, people have something in common that brings them together—"some combination of shared beliefs, circumstances, priorities, relationships, concerns . . . that provides for the possibility of group identity and collective action" (Chaskin, 1995, p. 1). People typically belong to multiple communities, defined as much by shared interests and sense of identity as by geographic proximity. Communities differ according to whether people are linked primarily by affect (the ties of kinship, land, faith, culture, ethnicity, or nationality) or by collective interest. Each type of community presents different issues and challenges for the community social work practitioner.

Community as Place

Many definitions of community link community and place (see, for example, Barker, 1995; Warren, 1978)—that is, community is defined as a group of people who live in a particular geographic area or neighborhood. In neighborhoods, defined by Chaskin (1995) as "a specific *context* of relationships, opportunities, and constraints that, to a large degree are spatially defined or delimited" [italics added] (p. vi), common local concerns are often reinforced by social connections based on proximity, shared social circumstances, and the ties of ethnicity or culture.

Place is a powerful and important site for community and community practice, particularly for low-income communities and communities of color, many of which have been shaped by historical or recent experiences of forced displacement from their original homelands. bell hooks (1990) poignantly described the importance of "homeplace" in the lives of African Americans, who for generations have experienced forced displacement and dispossession. Fullilove (2004) also wrote eloquently about the "root shock"—defined as a "traumatic stress reaction to the destruction of all or part of one's emotional ecosystem" (p. 11)—experienced by the estimated 1,600 urban African American communities destroyed by the urban renewal programs that followed the 1949 Federal Housing Act. Fullilove's detailed ethnography clearly showed the continuing impact of the loss of all that those communities encompassed, not only homes but churches, community newspapers, music halls, and other sites of community identity and connection. "The present state of Black America," she asserted, "is in no small measure the result of 'Negro removal'" (Fullilove, p. 224). In the African American and other diaspora communities, place and placemaking (the processes by which people create a sense of home in the world) are particularly salient in community identity and well-being.

At the same time, one must be careful not to romanticize the role of place (particularly in relation to communities of color) or to assume that geographic proximity automatically defines a community. People who live near one another do not necessarily feel connected, and several communities often coexist in one geographic space. Also, many people develop a sense of investment in their local community as much around specific issues as through profound and ongoing ties to particular people and places (Chaskin, 1995). Some people are interested more in being free of community demands than in developing ties with their neighbors. Others, particularly those who live in neighborhoods that are perceived as dangerous or hostile, may carefully screen their ties with the local community. In a study of "resilient" mothers in a low-income housing project, for example, Brodsky (1997) found that these mothers tended to keep their children close to home; to relate to the community only in limited and strategic ways; and, often, to look to schools, churches, and personal networks outside the community for support and enrichment. Finally, as noted above, understandings of people and place are complicated by the relationships that people and groups have with other places. Thinking about community thus requires the ability to remember that what is local is also, and always, global, just as global processes are eventually expressed and experienced at the local level (Massey, 1994).

Community as Shared Social Ties

For many people, relational communities—communities that are based on shared interests, concerns, and needs—are as important as the communities in which they live. In solidarity communities, an important type of relational community, people share a common heritage (such as faith, religion, ethnicity, culture, or nationality) that provides members with a strong sense of identity and a common system of values and beliefs (Rubin & Rubin, 1992). Ties to such communities tend to be deep and long lasting and are maintained in a variety of ways, including through common language, food, customs, traditions, and religious observances. In emergent ethnic communities, as Rivera and Erlich (1992) noted, relationship-based social networks, informal exchange, and natural support systems are particularly important.

In some instances, social solidarity is imposed on a group by the tendency in the larger society to assume that people who share common demographic characteristics constitute a community (Rubin & Rubin, 1992). People speak of the gay community, the Asian community, the African American community, or the urban poor as though each is a homogeneous group. Although members of such groups may share a sense of commonality, global classifications can be problematic. Not only do they encourage stereotypes, but they obscure the diversity within such groups and the extent to which people vary in their identification with particular communities.

In the preindustrial United States, communities of interest and place were deeply interwoven. As society has become more urban, mobile, and technological, however, communities of interest (also called "functional communities") have increasingly become uncoupled from locality. These "communities without propinquity" (Webber, 1963) may be organized around shared interests (such as environmental issues, professional concerns, or gay rights), common needs and problems (such as parents of children with rare diseases), or both. Nongeographic communities are even more prevalent now that the Internet has become the modern equivalent of the village square. On the Internet, "virtual communities" provide opportunities for sociability, information exchange, social support, and mutual aid (Wellman & Gulia, 1999). At the same time, the mediated and essentially anonymous nature of computer-based networks may dilute what is commonly understood to be community and fragment conventional social solidarities (Wellman et al., 1996). New interactive technologies thus open up possibilities for social intervention yet call for a rethinking and careful analysis of what social workers mean by and expect from community-oriented interventions.

Community as Shared Power Relationships

The United States is not a classless society: U.S. communities are deeply defined by class and race divisions. Social class, which is based on income, wealth, education, and ownership of property (and with the cultural capital that comes with economic assets), determines the degree to which individuals, families, and communities have access to opportunities and resources. Upper-class communities generally have ready access to and control over opportunities and services and a good deal of power over community boundaries and norms. In contrast, the members of low-income communities, such as urban housing projects, often have little access to employment, education, housing, health services, and public amenities; when they do have access to those resources, they often have few options. In addition, members of disadvantaged communities may feel powerless in the face of their vulnerability to external surveillance and containment by public agencies and services (public child welfare services, for example). For these communities, the price of external services and supports is often increased supervision and control, a mixture that fuels feelings of frustration, dependency, and impotence (Murray, 1995).

Although community practice has always been centrally concerned with power, the focus has traditionally been on locating, engaging, and influencing those in the community who already have political or economic power (Cox, 1987). An empowerment perspective highlights the need for a more critical and comprehensive analysis that addresses relationships of power and privilege not only in political terms but also with regard to the reflexive relationships between structural arrangements, personal and collective life chances, and the potential within communities and collectives for agency, resistance, and action (Dodd & Gutierrez, 1990).

MODELS OF COMMUNITY PRACTICE

The past 40 years have seen continuing development, refinement, and specification in community social work practice. As knowledge has evolved and new issues have emerged, community practice has been shaped to fit the needs and concerns of the times. Five major practice domains are typically included in community social work practice (Rothman, 1970; Taylor & Roberts, 1985):

1. community development, in which the focus is on enhancing community participation and competence through, for example, community service programs, self-help efforts such as the prevention of violence, and efforts to enhance social networks
2. program development and service coordination
3. social planning, which is a technical process of problem solving with regard to substantive social problems, such as delinquency, inadequate housing, and mental illness
4. political and social action, in which the focus is on organizing disadvantaged groups to change the policies and services of formal organizations
5. community liaison, which brings into community practice the many community-related activities undertaken by social workers in direct practice, including case management, which has a central concern with accessing, coordinating, and monitoring community resources and relationships.

For many years the tendency was to group these approaches under the general rubric of *macropractice*, defined as practice that "deals with aspects of human activity that are non-clinical in nature, but rather focus on broader social approaches to human betterment, emphasizing such things as developing enlightened social policy, organizing the effective delivery of services, strengthening community life, and preventing social ills" (Rothman & Tropman, 1987, p. 3). From this perspective, community practice and clinical practice are distinct entities.

The 1990s, however, saw a distinct trend toward hybrid models of community practice (Bradshaw, Soifer, & Gutierrez, 1994) characterized by flexible integration of macropractice strategies with strategies focused on the individual and small-group processes that are the building blocks of community empowerment. Emergent perspectives on community practice with women and communities of color endorse the feminist credo that "the personal is political" and highlight the importance of links between individual and collective empowerment. These approaches challenge the construction of community practice in rational–technocratic, expert, and masculine terms and emphasize interventions that encourage process and participation, diminish power and status differentials, and empower vulnerable people and populations (Bradshaw et al., 1994; Hyde, 1996; Weil, 1986, 1994).

Responding to these emerging commitments and to a perceived need for greater clarity about the match between models of community practice and community needs, Weil and Gamble (1995; 2005) developed an eight-model framework for community practice (Table 11-1). The framework includes neighborhood and community organizing (in place-based communities and in functional communities); social and economic development; social planning;

TABLE 11-1

Models of Community Practice in 21st-Century Contexts: Globalization, Human Rights, and Multicultural Societies

	Models							
Comparative Characteristics	Neighborhood & Community Organizing	Organizing Functional Communities	Community Social & Economic Development	Social Planning	Program Development & Community Liaison	Political & Social Action	Coalitions	Social Movements
Desired outcome	Develop capacity of members to organize; change the impact of negative planning and external development	Action for social justice focused on advocacy and on changing behaviors and attitudes; may also provide service	Initiate development plans from a grassroots perspective; prepare citizens to make use of social and economic investments	Citywide or regional proposals for action by elected body or human services planning councils	Expansion or redirection of agency program to improve community service effectiveness; organize new service	Action for social justice focused on changing policy or policymakers	Build a multi-organizational power base large enough to influence program direction or draw down resources	Action for social justice that provides a new paradigm for a particular population, group, or issue
System targeted for change	Municipal government; external developers	General public; government institutions	Banks; foundations; external developers	Perspectives of community leaders; perspectives of human services leaders	Funders of agency programs; beneficiaries of agency services	Voting public; elected officials; inactive/potential participants	Elected officials; foundations; government institutions	General public; political systems

(continued)

TABLE 11-1
□□□□□

Models of Community Practice in 21st-Century Contexts: Globalization, Human Rights, and Multicultural Societies (continued)

Comparative Characteristics	Neighborhood & Community Organizing	Organizing Functional Communities	Community Social & Economic Development	Social Planning	Program Development & Community Liaison	Political & Social Action	Coalitions	Social Movements
				Models				
Primary constituency	Residents of neighborhood, parish, or rural county	Like-minded people in a community, region, nation, or across the globe	Low-income, marginalized, or oppressed population groups in a city or region	Elected officials; social agencies and interagency organizations	Agency board or administrators; community representatives	Citizens in a particular political jurisdiction	Organizations and citizens that have a stake in the particular issue	Leaders, citizens, and organizations able to create new visions and images
Scope of concern	Quality of life in the geographic area	Advocacy for particular issue or population	Income, resource, and social support development; improved basic education and leadership skills	Integration of social needs into geographic planning in public arena; human services network coordination	Service development for a specific population	Building political power; institutional change	Specified issue related to social need or concern	Social justice within society

Social work roles	Organizer, facilitator, educator, coach	Negotiator, promoter, planner, educator, manager	Researcher, proposal writer, communicator, planner, manager	Spokesperson, planner, manager, proposal writer	Advocate, organizer, researcher, candidate	Mediator, negotiator, spokesperson, organizer	Advocate, facilitator

Source: Adapted from Weil, M., & Gamble, D. N. (1995). "Community Practice Models." In R. L. Edwards (Ed.-in-Chief), *Encyclopedia of Social Work* (19th ed., Vol. 1, p. 581). Washington, DC: NASW Press.

program development and community liaison; political and social action; coalitions; and social movements.

In the 21st century, community practice continues to evolve toward a well-defined engagement with a multicultural and globalized world. The following sections draw on recent work that highlights practice principles that support a multicultural empowerment approach to community practice (Gutierrez, Alvarez, Nemon, & Lewis, 1996; Gutierrez et al., 2005). The models are defined by a central concern with social justice (Gutierrez et al., 1996), including explicit attention to the dynamics of oppression and marginality. They emphasize building on the long-standing traditions of self-help and mutual aid present in marginalized communities that have had to create their own structures of support (Gutierrez et al., 1996). They also stress the importance of practice that is based in indigenous institutions and fully incorporates cultural traditions, beliefs, and values (see O'Donnell & Karanja, 2000, on a transformative approach to community practice from an Afrocentric perspective).

Empowering and Multicultural Community Practice: A Generalist Approach

Although knowledge and skills in community practice are used to different degrees in different contexts, they are an important component of the practice repertoire of all social workers. A generalist practitioner may intervene at any system level, applying a wide range of knowledge and skills as the situation demands.

This generalist approach fits well with the practical realities of everyday work with communities. In many communities, a prerequisite for change is to develop shared identity, connections, and the ability to work together among community members (that is, a "sense of community"). Community members must also determine priorities among competing needs. In their ongoing work with individuals and small groups, social workers have many opportunities to support the development of community consciousness and to encourage community participation. These community-building efforts provide a foundation for taking action to address issues of shared concern. As the community moves toward action, the support, advocacy, mediation, and negotiation skills of social workers become increasingly salient. Research, planning, and communication skills also come into play. In ways large and small, on a continuum ranging from radical social action to a concern with enhancing the everyday community contexts of individual clients, social workers are an important source of support for community change. As Germain (1985) pointed out,

> The community is an integral part of the life space of individuals and collectivities that we serve. . . . Reciprocally, when the client is the community,

then the individuals and collectivities within the community must be in the foreground of attention throughout the processes of assessment, intervention, and prevention. (p. 32)

Theoretical Foundations: Ecological Systems, Empowerment, and Multiculturalism. Theoretical support for a generalist approach to community practice comes from ecological systems theory (Germain, 1985; Meyer, 1983), which focuses on the interdependence of people and their environments at multiple and interlocking systems levels. Given the complex challenges facing communities and their residents, effective community intervention typically has multiple dimensions; develops connections among individuals, groups, and social structures; and, as in the following example, may involve several social workers with different roles and perspectives:

> In a multi-ethnic neighborhood struggling with high levels of violence, a community worker working with a group of parents who want to develop a block patrol uses sophisticated interpersonal and group process skills to engage parents and facilitate their planning process. At the local child and family agency, a clinical social worker with many of the parents on her caseload lobbies her agency for the resources to develop an empowerment group in which parents can explore issues of parenting specific to the community. At a meeting convened to coordinate planning for an interagency grant application, the two workers discuss ways in which they might better collaborate with each other and with community members. Both are committed to working in partnership with local residents and want to build links between direct services, community-level interventions, and policy initiatives.

In community practice, as in other fields of practice, the emergence of new ethnic communities, changes in established communities of color, ongoing concerns about women's rights, and the increasing visibility of the gay and lesbian communities have contributed significantly to a growing emphasis on multiculturalism, pluralism, and empowerment (Weil, 2005). Although the wide-angle lens of the ecosystemic perspective ensures a multidimensional approach to the issues and challenges confronting communities, the perspective is largely silent on issues of power and social justice. Social workers must therefore also look to empowerment and multicultural practice models.

A Multicultural Empowerment Perspective.

A concern with community is an essential element of empowerment practice: [Empowerment] suggests both individual determination over one's life and democratic participation in the life of one's community, often through mediating structures such as schools, neighborhoods, churches, and other voluntary organizations. . . . It is a multilevel construct applicable to individual citizens as well as to organizations and neighborhoods. (Rappaport, 1987, pp. 121–130)

A fundamental goal of empowerment practice is for individuals and communities to develop the capacity to resist and to change environmental conditions that negatively affect life chances and access to resources and services. As an outcome, community empowerment is defined by competence, connectedness, a concern for the common good, and a sense of commitment to and participation in the community (Zimmerman & Rappaport, 1988). The process of empowerment involves the development of the personal and collective beliefs, attitudes, and skills that will enable effective action (Parsons, 1991). To become empowered is to perceive oneself and one's community as effective and potent and to develop the ability to act to change the conditions of daily life (Pecukonis & Wenocur, 1994; Simon, 1990). The relationship between capacity and action is reciprocal—each reinforces the other (Zimmerman & Rappaport). Empowering community practice thus has two primary and interlocking objectives: the empowerment of community members and the redistribution of existing power and resources (Mondros & Berman-Rossi, 1991). Both strands are essential to the goal of an empowered community:

> An empowered community is a community in which individuals and organizations apply their skills and resources in collective efforts that lead to community competence. Through such participation and control, the community is able to meet the needs of its individuals and organizations. (Gerchick, cited in Schulz, Israel, Zimmerman, & Checkoway, 1995, p. 312)

A multicultural empowerment approach to community practice is grounded in social work's core commitment to social justice and antioppressive practice (Bankhead & Erlich, 2005; Gutierrez et al., 2005). Recognizing that the dynamics of oppression have many shared features across communities but that each community experiences oppression in it its own way, this approach places a strong emphasis on ensuring that interventions "recognize the unique challenges, triumphs, cultural values, and real and powerful experiences with oppression that create cohesion within and shape boundaries around a community" (Bankhead & Erlich, p. 63). It places the perspectives, interests, and experiences of community members at the center of community change processes, emphasizes collaborative practices, and requires social workers to have the knowledge and skills to engage diverse communities within their own frames of reference.

Connections and Consciousness:
Interpersonal Strategies in Empowering Community Practice

Effective community practice builds on and incorporates the knowledge and skills for interpersonal practice outlined in previous chapters. In working with people around community issues, social workers constantly use their relationship skills. Like empowering practice in general, however, empowering practice in multicultural communities differs from clinical practice as it is traditionally constructed. At the interpersonal level, empowering community practice emphasizes mutuality and collaboration, a commitment to client participation, and a focus on the development of critical consciousness through dialogue as a fundamental building block for change.

Engagement. Members of low-income communities and communities of color have many reasons to mistrust outsiders, particularly those who represent powerful—and frequently oppressive—institutions. Social work's long history of involvement in diverse communities has often involved well-intentioned but normative interventions and services that community members have experienced as culturally inappropriate, punitive, controlling, and disempowering. When contemporary social workers engage with those communities, the historical experiences may continue to reverberate, resulting in reticence toward outsiders and greater trust in community members and informal networks than in external expertise. Writing about community-based research, Reisch and Rivera (1999) highlighted the political complexities in work with communities that perceive outsiders as agents of hostile institutions; they noted that in those contexts, "progressive agendas and cultural sensitivity are not sufficient" (p. 58).

The process of building relationships within marginalized communities takes patience, self-awareness, and the ability to identify trust and power issues (Delgado, 1996; Reisch & Rivera, 1999). These requirements are true for any outsider, even those who share a common identity. The ability to build connections and alliances with community members will vary with the social worker's degree of "insiderness" and identification with the community. Bankhead and Erlich (2005, p. 73) described three levels of identification:

1. primary, involving racial, cultural, and linguistic identity with the community (full ethnic solidarity)
2. secondary, involving similarity of culture and experience but not language fluency
3. tertiary, involving outsiders who are invested in the welfare of the community and committed to advocacy, assistance, and supportive influence despite their lack of linguistic, cultural, or racial similarity.

Collaboration. In empowering practice, social workers aim to replace paternalistic and elitist forms of intervention (those that assume that the worker knows best) with approaches that maximize people's rights, strengths, and capabilities through careful attention to issues of power, social distance, and control. As much as possible, practitioners use their expertise in ways that do not perpetuate oppressive social conditions. The professional skills and institutional resources available to social workers are real and valuable, but they must be offered within a relationship characterized by mutuality rather than professional distance—what Altman (1995) described as a "doing with" orientation (p. 528). Collaboration and consultation are thus key aspects of community practice. Indeed, Altman (citing Mittelman, 1990) encouraged community practitioners to regard community members as the "senior partners" in community-based processes. Appropriate social work roles are those of enabler, facilitator, teacher, resource provider, consultant, compatriot, organizer, advocate, broker, negotiator, and activist (Gutierrez, 1990; Parsons, Jorgensen, & Hernandez, 1994).

Participation. Empowering community practice emphasizes the relationship between people and their sociopolitical environment and the community's right to opportunities, resources, and services. Central to this shift in perspective is the assumption that people must actively participate in defining their needs and concerns and any actions to address those concerns (Maluccio, 1981; O'Donnell & Karanja, 2000). Intentional efforts to enhance community participation and leadership are therefore important (Mattaini, 1993a). Indeed, we agree with O'Donnell and Karanja that "every community practice intervention should deepen the participation of residents and increase their capacity to be self-determining" (p. 77). Incentives for participation may be intrinsic (deriving from the activity itself) or extrinsic (consisting of external rewards, such as food, child care, or other benefits, in return for participation).

Studies of community participation have demonstrated that active involvement and perceptions of influence and control contribute significantly to the personal empowerment of community members (Rich, Edelstein, Hallman, & Wandersman, 1995; Zimmerman & Rappaport, 1988) and result in more positive and durable project outcomes (Itzhaky & York, 1991; Mattaini, 1993a). Participation can take many forms, such as involvement in committees and coalitions, the contribution of a consumer voice in service development and delivery, participation in program planning and management, and involvement in participatory action research.

Participation alone is not sufficient. To be correlated with empowerment, participation must be associated with the belief that one really can influence decisions and actions that affect the community (Schulz et al., 1995). Too often, the involvement of community residents (in community planning, for example) is little more than tokenism. Participation is empty if it is unlikely to result in meaningful change. Halpern (1993) rightly pointed out that in "depleted" communities, real changes in opportunity depend on external social and economic structures. In marginalized communities, projects must be careful not to squander valuable (and scarce) human resources or to further victimize community members by promising more than they can deliver. Thoughtful, patient work with community members and the institutions and services in which they participate is thus required to ensure that participation is meaningful and effective (Briscoe, Hoffman, & Bailey, 1975; Keenan & Pinkerton, 1991).

Critical Consciousness. An essential foundation for empowerment is the development of what Freire (1973) called "critical consciousness"—the ability to reflect experience not just in personal terms but with an awareness that everyday experiences are profoundly shaped by events and conditions in the social and political environment (Parsons, 1991; Weick, 1993). Critical reflection contextualizes personal and community experience (by connecting it to external realities), opens up new perspectives, and enables individuals and communities to visualize alternative ways of "being in the world."

Empowering community practice assumes that workers will engage with community members to understand their experience in political as well as personal terms. Robust models for such engaged practice are readily available in feminist practice (Van Den Bergh & Cooper, 1986) and in the emerging literature on community practice with people of color (Rivera & Erlich, 1992). O'Donnell and Karanja (2000, p. 78) described the practitioner's role as that of "teacher–learner"—someone who learns from and with the community but whose outside skills and perspectives also are valuable.

Consciousness raising involves praxis—a mixture of reflection and action—to ensure that social action is grounded in a critical analysis of the relationship between everyday experiences and wider social and structural issues (Longres & McLeod, 1980). Freire (1973) suggested that it is the development of critical consciousness—the ability to "think against" the status quo—that enables people to act together to change oppressive social conditions.

Discussions of consciousness raising typically focus on creating a vision for change within marginalized groups and communities. Yet, as O'Donnell and Karanja (2000) rightly pointed out, the biases, blind spots, stereotypes, and misinformation of policymakers and service providers also present roadblocks to transformative community change. These (frequently institutional) rigidities can result, for example, in programs and services that overlook structural and collective experiences and mechanisms and focus instead on individual-level analyses and interventions. O'Donnell and Karanja suggested that bridging the gap between internal and external perspectives on community issues requires diligent efforts to build meaningful connections and conversations between external actors and community members—efforts that community-oriented social workers are particularly well positioned to support.

Dialogue as a Basis for Community Action. Consciousness raising is most readily achieved through dialogue, whether between individuals, in small groups, or in larger collectives. The use of dialogue and narrative to facilitate empowerment and social justice has sturdy roots in the women's and other grassroots movements. More recently, dialogic techniques have emerged as an important tool in facilitating conversations among and within groups who have a shared interest in community change but little common ground in other areas (Gutierrez et al., 2005; Roberts, Houle, Kay, Nagda, & Elliot, 2000).

Empowering dialogue differs from conventional therapeutic conversations. First, the social worker joins the conversation with the goal of helping people express, understand, and redefine their daily experiences in social as well as personal terms. Second, empowering dialogue necessarily includes critical examination of the sociopolitical environment and issues of power and domination. Third, dialogue is reciprocal: Transformation will occur in the worker's perspectives as well as in those of community participants. Strategies for facilitating dialogue build on core social work skills: empathy, mutual respect, and active, nonjudgmental listening. The worker is an ethnographer, or "ecological explorer" (Auerswald, 1968): a respectful outsider who, through a process of joint exploration, seeks to be educated about how individuals and communities understand their social reality (Leigh, 1997).

Freire (1973) termed his dialogical strategy the *pedagogy of the question* (p. 35), a technique that encourages people both to find their own answers and to shape further questions (Simon, 1990). In study groups and small-group meetings (O'Donnell & Karanja, 2000), social workers can join with community members to question why things are as they are, what patterns they can see in their shared experiences, and what social and environmental factors contribute to their circumstances. This process of questioning creates a space in which alternative views can emerge. Dominant cultural and social interpretations are challenged, and groups are encouraged to develop explanations that reflect their particular identity and history. In this way, multiple realities and perspectives have the opportunity to emerge and be validated—and to form the basis for new understandings and connections among people with different life experiences and perspectives.

Thinking Contextually. Social workers in all settings know a great deal about their clients' environmental and community experiences, but they often fail to "look beyond the client" (Wood & Middleman, 1991, p. 57) to collective experience. For example, a social worker in a mental health setting who sees a series of low-income women with symptoms of depression will probably feel more pressure to "tool up" on treating depression than to consider the need for a community-level analysis of the structural and social challenges in these women's lives. And even when this analysis occurs, it is relatively unlikely, given the orientation of most mental health agencies, to result in a community-level intervention.

The ability to think flexibly from "case" to "cause" and back again is at the core of generalist community practice. Such practice attempts to ensure that the needs of individuals are connected to efforts to link people who share common experiences and to construct effective and equitable social structures. Attention to community issues is often constrained, however, by assumptions that are deeply embedded in the ecology of practice. Rosen and Livne (1992) demonstrated, for example, that social workers in direct practice tend to attribute presenting problems to psychological factors rather than to environmental factors, even when the client defines his or her problems in environmental terms. Similarly, a study of practice reasoning (Nurius, Kemp, & Gibson, 1999) found that workers tended not to include environmental variables unless they were explicitly prompted, suggesting that a lack of attention to context is not simply an artifact of the worker–client interaction.

To respond effectively to people in their community settings, social workers must develop "habits of mind" that direct attention to context as well as client. Because deliberate effort is needed to overcome bias (Nurius et al., 1999), such habits of mind should be reinforced by the routine use of methods that expand the range of available assessment information. (Many assessment tools, such as clinical diagnostic systems, are designed to reduce complexity; see, for example, Mattaini & Kirk, 1991.) Examples of reinforcers, or prompts, that encourage contextual mindfulness include the use of ecosystemic measures in assessment (such as ecomaps or social network maps; Mattaini, 1993b); regular involvement in the daily life of the community; openness to consumer and community input; and diligent efforts to ensure that consumers actively participate in the planning, delivery, and monitoring of services.

Community Assessment

Effective practice at the community level begins with a thorough understanding of a particular community and its needs. As Poole (1997) noted, "There is little room for formula or 'cookie-cutter' thinking in community capacity-building. What works well in one community may not work in another" (p. 168). A comprehensive community assessment builds on the following general principles:

+ an understanding of different kinds of communities and of the ways in which a particular community is similar to and different from general models

+ the use of multiple methods to generate data, including quantitative and participatory or ethnographic approaches
+ the willingness to approach the community as a "respectful outsider" who is willing to learn about it from its members and who does not impose externally constructed definitions. Meaning should be understood as local and historically situated.
+ a focus on identifying community strengths, competencies, and resources as well as needs and challenges. (See Kretzmann & McKnight, 1993; Parsons, 1991; Saleebey, 1992; and Sullivan, 1992, for material on a strengths approach to assessment.)
+ a thorough commitment to involving members of the community in the generation, analysis, and application of community knowledge.

A collaborative approach that involves community members in defining and assessing community needs and issues is an essential check against misplaced assumptions and external bias. Involvement in the assessment process brings local knowledge and wisdom to the foreground of attention, educates community members (who may not understand the multiple parameters of particular issues), enhances levels of participation and motivation, demystifies the planning process, and facilitates the development of collaborative relationships (Fagan, 1987). Collaboration increases the probability that both problem posing and problem solving will be meaningful and appropriate. As people become active participants—rather than just objects of assessment and intervention—and develop capacities that can be used in other contexts, the likelihood of sustained change increases.

Mapping the Neighborhood Community

An accurate reading of what constitutes a particular neighborhood is critical to the success of a community-level intervention. Johnson and Yanca (2003) and Sheafor, Horejsi, and Horejsi (2005) offered comprehensive outlines for developing a profile of a geographic community. Major domains include

+ physical setting
+ history
+ demographics
+ cultural factors
+ economic system
+ political system
+ sociocultural system
+ human services system
+ major problems and concerns of the community

◆ general aspects of community functioning (such as sense of identity and belonging, decision-making structures, and autonomy).

Mapping Communities Using Quantitative Data. Community-based social workers regularly use quantitative data sources to identify key measures of neighborhood social, environmental, and health functioning (Chow & Crowe, 2005; Coulton, 1995b). Often, these "neighborhood indicators" are chosen by interested stakeholders who identify outcome areas that are of concern to a particular community (Kingsley, 1998). Examples include such indicators as infant mortality rates, homicide rates, child poverty rates, child maltreatment rates, and neighborhood employment levels. Data are gathered that help policymakers and organizers evaluate areas in which neighborhood functioning is improving or worsening. The data provide directions for policy decisions and guide the use of limited funds for neighborhood improvement. Much of the objective data for a community assessment is available from census data and other materials (for example, public health statistics, the Federal Bureau of Investigation's Uniform Crime Reports, city planning data, and labor market statistics) compiled by state and local agencies that are involved in community planning (such as the United Way, local governments, and economic development, labor, and human services agencies). The U.S. Department of Housing and Urban Development has endorsed the use of neighborhood indicators and is currently making better neighborhood data available through the U.S. Census Bureau's (n.d.) American Community Survey (ACS). Compared with the decennial census, the ACS provides data that focus on smaller units of analyses and is released more often.

Specific methodologies and software applications are being developed to make quantitative community data analysis more accessible to people without technical training. Geographic information systems are computer programs that allow the storage, manipulation, and analyses of geographic data (Hoefer, Hoefer, & Tobias, 1994; Tompkins & Southward, 1998). Although many geographic information system programs require a high level of technological skill, recent user-friendly versions developed by the U.S. Department of Housing and Urban Development (n.d.) allow community practitioners to produce high-quality maps of city and neighborhood indicators with relatively little training (Kingsley, 1998). Other software programs, such as those that can analyze mortgage lending patterns in geographically focused areas, have been developed for use by community practitioners without statistical training. Coulton (2005) suggested the importance of using statistical methods that allow for multilevel data and spatial statistics in community-level research. She also called for the use of experimental research designs where possible.

Mapping Communities Using Qualitative Data. Quantitative data provide essential information for supporting community change efforts but do not provide a view of the community through the eyes of its members. For that, community workers and researchers turn to qualitative data, which provide information on the community from the inside out. Such data bring the community to life, allow for more nuanced and valid interpretations of quantitative data (for example, when data gathered from within the community are set against data derived from external sources), and provide important opportunities for community members to be active participants in generating community information.

Strategies for gathering qualitative and experiential data include ethnographic approaches, such as participant observation, field observations, and informal interviews with key community figures and local residents. Participatory action-research models, which integrate research and practice by involving community members in the creation and use of knowledge about the community, are particularly useful (Curtis, 1989; Sarri & Sarri, 1992). Creative strategies for involving residents in community assessments include the use of documentary methods, such as photography, video, and interviews with other residents, that enable residents to construct a living and multidimensional picture of their community (Wang, Burris, & Ping, 1996). PhotoVoice, for example, is a participatory action-research method that involves residents using cameras to document key aspects of everyday life as the basis for initiating change (Wang, Morrel-Samuels, Hutchinson, Bell, & Pestronk, 2004). Other strategies include the use of focus groups, key informant interviews, and resident surveys. The Concerns Report Method (Fawcett, Seekins, Whang, Muiu, & Suarez de Balcazar, 1984) also offers a structured approach to generating consumer input by surveying community members about their perceptions of relevant strengths and problems of interest. It is considered to be an especially useful method for integrating the concerns of marginalized community members.

The value of the social worker's local knowledge must be emphasized. Regardless of the work setting, social workers should be physically acquainted with the community in which their clients live. They should walk and drive around the community, take the time to talk informally with local people, and explore. There is no substitute for knowledge that comes from direct personal experience.

Mapping Community Capacity. Too often, community inventories become a compilation of community deficits and problems. Communities that are the focus of social work attention are frequently defined in the language of risk and pathology—as "high risk," "disorganized," "socially isolated," or "underclass." Such perspectives stigmatize, isolate, and immobilize; they also imply, as Delgado

(1996) pointed out, that resources and skills for change are not available within the community and must be imported from outside.

The 1990s saw renewed research interest in the strengths, capacities, resources, and potentials of individuals, families, groups, and communities. Recognizing that marginalized communities tend to be negatively labeled, scholars of color have emphasized the importance of attention to cultural and community strengths (Bankhead & Erlich, 2005). McKnight (1997) stressed that all communities have untapped resources, skills, and capacities that can provide the building blocks of positive and empowering change. The process of "mapping" those assets is thus an important foundation for community-building efforts. Kretzmann and McKnight (1993) differentiated three major categories of assets: (1) individual level (including households and families), (2) citizens' associations ("a group of local citizens joined together with a vision of a common goal"; p. 109), and (3) formal institutions. Assets include those that are located in the community and under community control and those that originate outside the community and are controlled largely by outsiders. Asset-based community development begins with the premise that "outside resources will be much more effectively used if the local community is itself fully mobilized and invested, and if it can define the agendas for which additional resources must be obtained" (Kretzmann & McKnight, p. 8). It is a bottom-up, relational, and deeply participatory approach to community development.

Mapping Power and Social Justice. At the core of empowering community practice is a concern with understanding power relations, both power as influence (the view from the top) and power as it is experienced in everyday life (the view from below).

+ *Power as influence.* From this perspective, power analysis focuses on identifying those in the community who exert power and influence and who can "get things done" (for a comprehensive discussion of assessing community power structures, see Hardcastle, Wenocur, & Powers, 1997). Strategies include surveys; interviews with key informants; and studies of newspapers, lists of board members, and other documentary sources. Knowing who the key players are in a community (and how to access them) can be essential to the success of community projects, particularly in the early stages of a new initiative.
+ *Power in everyday life.* The analysis of power from the bottom up, in contrast, focuses on understanding power relations from the perspective of community members (Gutierrez, 1990; Hagan & Smail, 1997). Such an analysis, which Hagan and Smail have termed "power-mapping," involves

three key steps, which can be incorporated into consciousness-raising dialogues with community members: (1) It is necessary to map the distribution of power and resources in the community across key domains; (2) it is important to analyze how conditions of powerlessness are affecting residents; and (3) it is essential to identify sources of actual or potential power at the community level.

Such an analysis enhances critical consciousness of the distribution of power in the community and its consequences, provides important information on resources and strengths available to the community effort, and opens up perspectives on what needs to be done for community residents to obtain power in key life domains.

A VALUES FRAMEWORK FOR EMPOWERING COMMUNITY PRACTICE

Although the choice of strategies for community action varies from situation to situation, community-oriented social work practice is always framed by the values and ethics of the profession (Weil, 2005). In addition, Fawcett (1991) suggested that community practice should reflect the following principles:

- Workers should avoid "colonial" relationships with community members—relationships in which power, authority, and ownership of knowledge are vested in the worker. In collaborative and empowering relationships, the contributions of all parties have value for the community effort.
- Project goals should reflect consumer concerns, needs, and perspectives. Criteria for success (outcomes) should be constructed in terms that are meaningful to community members (Rapp, Shera, & Kisthart, 1993).
- Selection of participants and choice of interventions should reflect the "multilevel and systemic nature of community problems" (Fawcett, 1991, p. 625). Change targets should include not only individuals (and their proximate environments) who experience a problem directly but also the institutional and social structures that create and sustain problems.
- Workers should plan for "small wins" at multiple system levels while maintaining a vision of large-scale change. In community practice, where issues often seem overwhelming and intractable, it is particularly important to "think globally and act locally" and to accept that systemic change is likely to be incremental. Fawcett (1991) defined small wins as "those concrete outcomes of modest significance that attract allies and deter opponents" (p. 627).
- Interventions should be replicable and sustainable; that is, they should build on and enhance existing capacity within the community. Fawcett et al. (1984) recommended that strategies selected for community intervention

should, when possible, be inexpensive; demonstrably effective; decentralized (that is, local and small scale); flexible; sustainable with local resources; simple; and compatible with existing customs, beliefs, and values. Although Fawcett and colleagues' view of community change goals may be limited, it is important to ensure that interventions do not come and go at the whim of outside funding or interest (as has too often been the case with university-based, grant-funded research demonstrations, for example).

STRATEGIES FOR COMMUNITY EMPOWERMENT

Empowering community practice focuses on enhancing the capacity of the community to resolve its own problems and needs. Two concepts frequently used to conceptualize this process are community capacity (Poole, 1997) and community competence (Cottrell, 1977). "Community capacity" refers to characteristics of communities that affect their ability to identify, mobilize, and act to resolve community issues and concerns. Key dimensions include participation and leadership, access to and wise use of resources, social and interorganizational networks, sense of community, community history of collective action, community power, shared core values, and the capacity to engage in critical reflection (Poole).

"Community competence," a similar concept, has been defined as the ability of any kind of community to solve problems effectively and, thus, to master social and environmental challenges (Eng, Salmon, & Mullan, 1992). Cottrell (1977) suggested that the process of enhancing community competence typically involves the following:

+ activities that strengthen investment and commitment
+ clarification of issues and interests in the community
+ development of the ability of community members to articulate views, attitudes, needs, and intentions
+ enhancement of communication skills
+ the ability to negotiate differences and manage conflict
+ membership participation.

Community groups can achieve their goals only if their members have the knowledge and skills to negotiate effectively with those who control access to needed resources and services. When these core skills are not available by virtue of social class, education, or experience, they must be developed. Community members also need assistance to identify and strengthen existing skills and resources. Social workers make an important contribution in small groups and community forums when they model, teach, and support skill identification and development. The role of educator, although often overlooked by social workers, is central to effective community practice (Lightburn & Black, in press).

Key areas for skills development include problem solving; assertive communication (public speaking, issue presentation, chairing meetings); conflict management (collaboration, negotiation, and bargaining); political skills (influence and advocacy); and the technical skills associated with identifying, obtaining, and using resources (Cottrell, 1977; Mattaini, 1993a). Strategies for skill development draw heavily on social learning theory and include didactic teaching, experiential approaches such as coaching and role playing, and modeling of effective behaviors.

Leadership development is a critical need in many communities. Natural community leaders may not be effective in negotiations with larger social systems. Supporting the development of informed and effective indigenous leadership, particularly through participation in decision making, is thus an important aspect of community development efforts (Bradshaw et al., 1994; O'Donnell & Karanja, 2000).

Community competence is predicated on the ability of community members to work together on areas of common concern. Here the social worker is challenged to help community members find common ground while recognizing the value and strength in diversity (Bradshaw et al., 1994). Similarly, social workers play an important role in the development of coalitions among different interest groups and organizations in the community. At both the interpersonal and organizational levels, social workers can facilitate dialogue actively, "translate" different perspectives and expectations (a particularly important skill in cross-cultural practice), mediate power relationships to ensure equitable participation, and encourage an open approach to problem solving.

COMMUNITY PRACTICE AND MEDIATING STRUCTURES: GROUPS, SOCIAL NETWORKS, AND COMMUNITY-BASED PROGRAMS

Berger and Neuhaus (1977) envisioned the community as a mediating structure between people and the institutional and social structures of society. In this sense, the community provides a buffer between people and social conditions that are often alienating and oppressive. Four aspects of community practice are particularly relevant to the mediating function of community: (1) the use of small groups, (2) the development of social networks, (3) the construction of communities in social programs, and (4) asset-based social welfare programs.

Small Groups

Groups are the fundamental building blocks of neighborhood and community development (Mondros & Berman-Rossi, 1991; Ramey, 1992). Community workers interact with and facilitate many different kinds of groups, including issues groups, community meetings, planning groups, task groups, self-help groups, coalitions, neighborhood associations, and social action groups. Groups are critical to the process of empowerment (Brown & Ziefert, 1988; Gutierrez, 1990). Cox (1991) described, for example, the progressive empowerment of a group of welfare mothers as they worked together for change in the welfare system.

Mondros and Berman-Rossi (1991) suggested that group work skills are particularly important in the initial stages of a community project, when the social worker brings community members together to explore and validate different perspectives, develop shared understandings, enhance commitment and motivation (and negotiate conflict), and determine a plan of action. Noting that community organizers tend to focus more on the tasks to be accomplished than on the process of implementation, Mondros and Berman-Rossi argued that "organizers invite trouble for themselves if they don't attend to how and why people join groups, the meaning of group experience for individuals, and matters of group process during these beginning efforts" (p. 204). Knowledge of the stages of group development and skills in facilitating group process at different points in the life cycle of community projects are therefore important aspects of community social work practice.

Social Networks

Strong social networks are an essential building block of community capacity. Social workers have long had a interest in identifying, supporting, and creating social networks, both to enhance support for clients and to buttress other interventions (Tracy & Whittaker, 1990; Whittaker & Garbarino, 1983). Rubin and Rubin (1992) defined a social network as "a pattern of linked relationships across which help and information flow on a particular issue" (p. 86). Networks may consist of family and kin, friends, workmates, church members, or people who come together around a shared concern. Social workers are increasingly recognizing the centrality of social networks to efforts to build community, particularly within emergent ethnic communities (Daley & Wong, 1994; Lewis & Ford, 1990). Robust social networks provide members with material assistance and services (caretaking), emotional nurturance and counseling, problem-solving advice and referral, and a forum for collective action and advocacy (Eng et al., 1992). As we noted above, communities of color have always relied on social networks for support, mutual aid, and action, developing parallel service systems in the context of active exclusion from mainstream services.

The Social Network Map (Tracy & Whittaker, 1990) enables workers and clients to assess the nature and availability of social network supports. Developed primarily for use with individuals, it also has the potential to be used with groups to determine patterns of support and isolation in communities. Although natural networks constitute an important resource in community practice, particularly in communities of color, social workers must be careful not to overburden or disempower natural helpers. Nor can it be assumed that all networks are supportive; some, such as those in drug-ridden communities, are toxic to their members, and others may not be perceived in positive terms (Brodsky, 1997). Nonetheless, interventions designed to strengthen the supportive functions of naturally occurring social networks and to encourage new connections between community members are an important element of community building (Gutierrez et al., 2005).

Community Organizations

It is not always possible or reasonable to rely on informal social networks as primary sources of community change. Some communities and their natural support systems, such as those in inner-city neighborhoods, are so overextended that little more can be asked of them (Garbarino, Kostelny, & Dubrow, 1991; Halpern, 1993). In such environments, it is important for community organizations to offer opportunities for connection, safety, support, recovery, and action that in different circumstances would have been provided by networks of kin and friends. Provided they are culturally relevant, the social networks formed in grassroots, indigenous, and community-based programs are an important link in the chain from individual empowerment to community transformation (O'Donnell & Karanja, 2000). Empowering community programs provide a safe haven in violent and isolated environments, enable the development of individual and collective skills and resources, and provide a springboard for action in the wider environment (Lightburn & Kemp, 1994). A commitment to developing, supporting, and working in such programs is thus an important, although neglected, dimension of community practice.

Asset-Based Social Welfare Programs and Community Development

Asset-based social welfare is an approach to community development that focuses on increasing the assets of low-income community members. Sherraden (1990, 1991) argued that government social and tax policies increase the wealth of middle- and upper-income citizens but cause low-income populations to forgo opportunities to accumulate assets. He proposed a shift to social welfare and tax policies that allow low-income citizens to have access to savings accounts, investments, owner occupation of homes, and business opportunities. His asset-based welfare model is influencing neighborhood agencies, housing developers, and youth agencies to construct structured savings programs (Individual Development Accounts), small business development for the poor (microenterprise programs), and targeted low-income homeownership programs (Scanlon, 1998).

All of these programs attempt to build the assets of low-income citizens, often in targeted geographic contexts. Evaluations of recent asset-accumulation efforts demonstrate that the poor do have the capacity to save, invest, and become homeowners, particularly when structured program supports are in place (Sherraden et al., 2000).

Sherraden's (1991) theory of asset-based social welfare is partially rooted in the tradition of community economic development (CED). This work has been described as "corrective capitalism" because it endeavors to extend market opportunities and economic resources to communities bypassed by capitalist development (Peirce & Steinbach, 1987). CED developed in the early 1970s as a response to spatially concentrated poverty, deindustrialization, and economic stagnation (Perry, 1987). CED activities often take place in community development corporations, which have grown in strength and number since the early 1980s (Peirce & Steinbach). Other organizations, such as credit unions, nonprofit housing agencies, community action agencies, and youth job training programs also engage in CED practices. More specifically, those programs are designed to provide housing, jobs, human capital, job training, and access to banking services and business capital. In a similar vein, Midgley (1999) argued that social service programs should be tied to economic investment and positive economic outcomes. He contended that this sort of "productivist" framework offers an alternative paradigm for social work, which he sees as overly focused on service provision rather than on development of the capacities and resources of communities.

CHALLENGING SOCIAL SYSTEMS

Although many community practice approaches emphasize the importance and value of consensus and collaboration, individual and community needs cannot always be met by such an approach, particularly in communities with long histories of exclusion and disenfranchisement. In such situations, social workers often become involved in advocacy and social action in collaboration with community members. It is at this point, however, that many social workers become uncomfortable with community interventions. Middleman and Goldberg (1974) provided a helpful guideline for the use of confrontational tactics, suggesting that social workers should apply the principle of "least contest" in their choice of intervention strategies. That is, less confrontational tactics should be used before those that escalate conflict. Middleman and Goldberg suggested a hierarchy of intervention roles, ranging from mediation to advocacy.

Advocacy at the community level is concerned with improving services and resources for people as a group (class advocacy) rather than for a specific client at a particular time (case advocacy). McGowan (1978), who has promoted a strategic approach to the use of advocacy, listed the following methods:

- intercession (request, plead, persist)
- persuasion (inform, instruct, clarify, explain, argue)
- negotiation (dialogue, sympathize, bargain, placate)
- pressure (threaten, challenge, disregard)
- coercion (deceive, disrupt, administrative redress, legal action)
- indirect (client education, community organizing, system dodging, constructing alternatives).

When the decision has been made to challenge social and institutional structures, social workers have recourse to a range of strategies and can select those that are most appropriate given the issues at hand, community members' level of comfort with conflict, and the nature of the system that is the target of change.

MONITORING AND EVALUATING COMMUNITY PRACTICE

An extensive body of literature is available on the formal evaluation of community-based programs and services. Although a review of this literature is beyond the scope of this chapter, social workers involved in program development and implementation at the community level should certainly become familiar with it (for examples of particular relevance to empowering community practice, see Fetterman, Kaftarian, & Wandersman, 1996).

Quantitative outcome studies of community practice interventions are relatively sparse. A recent review of neighborhood-focused community practice intervention research (Ohmer & Korr, 2006) found only a small number of studies that used experimental designs; that finding is perhaps not surprising, given the applied and activist history of community practice and related concerns about the ethical fit of empirical research designs to the philosophy of practice in the field. Recent work has begun to transcend this concern, bringing quantitative and participatory research methods together within a strong commitment to community partnerships (see, for example, Chow & Crowe, 2005; Two Feathers et al., 2005).

Empowering community practice necessarily incorporates systematic practice monitoring as workers and community residents in partnership learn about community needs, determine actions to be taken, and continuously monitor the efficacy and fit of community-building activities. This collaborative and ongoing process of monitoring and feedback is essential to the integrity of an empowerment approach, which relies at its core on the reflexive interplay between action and reflection (see, for example, Parsons, 1998; Ristock & Pennell, 1996; Sohng, 1998). In empowering community practice, social workers and community residents should together determine how progress and outcomes will be assessed and by what means data will be used as a base for reflection and further action. Preferably, data collection will include both qualitative and quantitative approaches, thereby encompassing the stories that people tell about the process of community change as well as progress on desired outcomes at the personal, interpersonal, and community levels. In the process of generating knowledge, community members become the owners as well as the providers of information about their community, participating as equals and full citizens in defining and redefining the relationships between knowledge and power in their community context (Pennell et al., 2005).

REFERENCES

Altman, D. G. (1995). Sustaining interventions in community systems: On the relationship between researchers and communities. *Health Psychology, 14,* 526–536.

Auerswald, E. H. (1968). Interdisciplinary versus ecological approach. *Family Process, 7,* 202–215.

Austin, M., Coombs, M., & Barr, B. (2005). Community-centered clinical practice: Is the integration of micro and macro clinical practice possible? *Journal of Community Practice, 13*(4), 9–30.

Bankhead, T., & Erlich, J. (2005). Diverse populations and community practice. In M. Weil (Ed.), *The handbook of community practice* (pp. 59–83). Thousand Oaks, CA: Sage Publications.

Barker, R. L. (1995). *The social work dictionary* (3rd ed.). Washington, DC: NASW Press.

Bellah, R. N., Madsen, R., Sullivan, W. M., Swidler, A., & Tipton, S. M. (1985). *Habits of the heart: Individualism and commitment in American life.* New York: Harper & Row.

Berger, P. L., & Neuhaus, R. J. (1977). *To empower people: The role of mediating structures in public policy.* Washington, DC: American Enterprise Institute for Public Policy Research.

Bradshaw, C., Soifer, S., & Gutierrez, L. (1994). Toward a hybrid model for effective organizing in communities of color. *Journal of Community Practice, 1*(1), 25–41.

Briscoe, R. V., Hoffman, D. B., & Bailey, J. S. (1975). Behavioral community psychology: Training a community board to problem solve. *Journal of Applied Behavior Analysis, 8,* 157–168.

Brodsky, A. E. (1997). Resilient single mothers in risky neighborhoods: Negative psychological sense of community. *Journal of Community Psychology, 24,* 347–363.

Brooks-Gunn, J., Duncan, G. J., & Aber, J. L. (Eds.). (1997). *Neighborhood poverty. Volume II: Policy implications in studying neighborhoods.* New York: Russell Sage Foundation.

Brown, K. S., & Ziefert, M. (1988). Crisis resolution, competence and empowerment: A service model for women. *Journal of Primary Prevention, 9,* 92–103.

Chaskin, R. J. (1995). *Defining neighborhood: History, theory, and practice.* Chicago: Chapin Hall Center for Children.

Chaskin, R. J. (1997). Perspectives on neighborhood and community: A review of the literature. *Social Service Review, 71,* 521–547.

Chavis, D. M., & Wandersman, A. (1990). Sense of community in the urban environment: A catalyst for participation and community development. *American Journal of Community Psychology, 18,* 55–81.

Chow, J. C.-C., & Crowe, K. (2005). Community-based research and methods in community practice. In M. Weil (Ed.), *The handbook of community practice* (pp. 604–619). Thousand Oaks, CA: Sage Publications.

Cottrell, L. S., Jr. (1977). The competent community. In R. L. Warren (Ed.), *New perspectives on the American community: A book of readings* (3rd ed., pp. 546–560). Chicago: Rand McNally.

Coulton, C. J. (1995a). Riding the pendulum of the 1990s: Building a community context for social work research. *Social Work, 40,* 437–439.

Coulton, C. J. (1995b). Using community-level indicators of children's well-being in comprehensive community initiatives. In J. P. Connell, A. C. Kubisch, L. B. Schorr, & C. H. Weiss (Eds.), *New approaches to evaluating community initiatives: Concepts, methods and contexts* (pp. 173–200). Washington, DC: Aspen Institute. (ERIC Document Reproduction Services No. ED383817)

Coulton, C. (2005). The place of community in social work practice research: Conceptual and methodological developments. *Social Work Research, 29,* 73–86.

Coulton, C. J., Korbin, J. E., & Su, M. (1996). Measuring neighborhood context for young children in an urban area. *American Journal of Community Psychology, 24,* 5–32.

Cox, E. O. (1991). The critical role of social action in empowerment oriented groups. *Social Work with Groups, 14*(2), 77–90.

Cox, F. M. (1987). Communities: Alternative conceptions of community: Implications for community organization practice. In F. M. Cox, J. L. Erlich, J. Rothman, & J. E. Tropman (Eds.), *Strategies of community organization: Macro practice* (4th ed., pp. 232–243). Itasca, IL: F. E. Peacock.

Curtis, K. A. (1989). Help from within: Participatory research in a low-income neighborhood. *Urban Anthropology, 18,* 203–217.

Daley, J. M., & Wong, P. (1994). Community development with emerging ethnic communities. *Journal of Community Practice, 1*(1), 9–24.

Delgado, M. (1996). Community assessment by Latino youths. *Social Work in Education, 18,* 169–178.

Dodd, P., & Gutierrez, L. (1990). Preparing students for the future: A power perspective on community practice. *Administration in Social Work, 14*(2), 63–78.

Eng, E., Salmon, M. E., & Mullan, F. (1992). Community empowerment: The critical base for primary health care. *Family and Community Health, 15,* 1–12.

Etzioni, A. (1993). *The spirit of community: The reinvention of American society.* New York: Touchstone.

Fagan, T. (1987). Neighborhood education, mobilization, and organization for juvenile crime prevention. *Annals of the American Academy of Political and Social Science, 494,* 54–70.

Fawcett, S. B. (1991). Some values guiding community research and action. *Journal of Applied Behavior Analysis, 24,* 621–636.

Fawcett, S. B., Seekins, T., Whang, P. L., Muiu, C., & Suarez de Balcazar, Y. (1984). Creating and using technologies for community empowerment. *Prevention in Human Services, 3,* 145–171.

Federal Housing Act, P.L. 171, 63 Stat. 413 (1949).

Fetterman, D. M., Kaftarian, S. J., & Wandersman, A. (Eds.). (1996). *Empowerment evaluation: Knowledge and tools for self-assessment and accountability.* Thousand Oaks, CA: Sage Publications.

Finn, J. L., & Jacobson, M. (2003). *Just practice: A social justice approach to social work.* Peosta, IA: Eddie Bowers Publishing.

Fisher, R. (2005). History, context, and emerging issues for community practice. In M. Weil (Ed.), *The handbook of community practice* (pp. 34–58). Thousand Oaks, CA: Sage Publications.

Fisher, R., & Karger, H. J. (1997). *Social work and community in a private world: Getting out in public.* New York: Longman.

Freire, P. (1973). *Education for critical consciousness.* New York: Seabury Press.

Fullilove, M. T. (2004). *Root shock: How tearing up city neighborhoods hurts America, and what we can do about it.* New York: Ballantine Books.

Garbarino, T., Kostelny, K., & Dubrow, N. (1991). *No place to be a child: Growing up in a war zone.* Lexington, MA: Lexington Books.

Germain, C. B. (1985). The place of community work within an ecological approach to social work practice. In S. H. Taylor & R. W. Roberts (Eds.), *Theory and practice of community social work* (pp. 30–55). New York: Columbia University Press.

Gutierrez, L. M. (1990). Working with women of color: An empowerment perspective. *Social Work, 35,* 149–153.

Gutierrez, L., Alvarez, A. R., Nemon, H., & Lewis, E. A. (1996). Multicultural community organizing: A strategy for change. *Social Work, 41,* 501–508.

Gutierrez, L., Lewis, E. A., Nagda, B. A., Wernick, L., & Shore, N. (2005). Multicultural community practice strategies and intergroup empowerment. In M. Weil (Ed.), *The handbook of community practice* (pp. 341–359). Thousand Oaks, CA: Sage Publications.

Hagan, T., & Smail, D. (1997). Power-mapping—I. Background and basic methodology. *Journal of Community and Applied Social Psychology, 7,* 257–267.

Halpern, R. (1993). Neighborhood-based initiative to address poverty: Lessons from experience. *Journal of Sociology and Social Welfare, 20,* 111–135.

Harachi, T. W., Hawkins, J. D., Catalano, R. F., Lafazia, A. M., Smith, B. H., & Arthur, M. W. (2003). Evidence-based community decision making for prevention: Two case studies of Communities That Care. *Japanese Journal of Sociological Criminology, 28,* 26–37.

Hardcastle, D. A., Wenocur, S., & Powers, P. R. (1997). *Community practice: Theories and skills for social workers.* New York: Oxford University Press.

Hayden, D. (1995). *The power of place: Urban landscapes as public history.* Cambridge, MA: MIT Press.

Heller, K. (1989). The return to community. *American Journal of Community Psychology, 17,* 1–15.

Hoefer, R. A., Hoefer, R., & Tobias, R. A. (1994). Geographic information systems and human services. *Journal of Community Practice, 1*(3), 113–128.

hooks, b. (1990). *Yearning: Race, gender, and cultural politics.* Boston: South End Press.

Hyde, C. (1996). A feminist response to Rothman's "The interweaving of community intervention approaches." *Journal of Community Practice, 3*(3/4), 127–145.

Itzhaky, H., & York, A. S. (1991). Client participation and the effectiveness of community social work intervention. *Research on Social Work Practice, 1,* 387–398.

Johnson, A. K. (1998). The revitalization of community practice: Characteristics, competencies, and curricula for community-centered services. *Journal of Community Practice, 5*(3), 37–63.

Johnson, L. C., & Yanca, S. J. (2003). *Social work practice: A generalist approach* (8th ed.). Boston: Allyn & Bacon.

Keenan, E., & Pinkerton, J. (1991). Some aspects of empowerment: A case study of work with disadvantaged youth. *Social Work with Groups, 14*(2), 109–124.

Kemp, S. P., Whittaker, J. K., & Tracy, E. M. (1997). *Person–environment practice: The social ecology of interpersonal helping.* New York: Aldine de Gruyter.

Kingsley, T. J. (1998). *Neighborhood indicators: Taking advantage of the new potential* (Working Paper). Chicago: American Planning Association.

Korbin, J. E., & Coulton, C. J. (1997). Understanding the neighborhood context for children and families: Combining epidemiological and ethnographic approaches. In J. Brooks-Gunn, G. J. Duncan, & J. L. Aber (Eds.), *Neighborhood poverty. Volume II: Policy implications in studying neighborhoods* (pp. 65–79). New York: Russell Sage Foundation.

Kretzmann, J. P., & McKnight, J. L. (1993). *Building communities from the inside out: A path toward finding and mobilizing a community's assets.* Chicago: ACTA Publications.

Leigh, J. W. (1997). *Communicating for cultural competence.* Boston: Allyn & Bacon.

Lewis, E. A., & Ford, B. (1990). The Network Utilization Project: Incorporating traditional strengths of African-American families in group work practice. *Social Work with Groups, 13*(4), 7–22.

Lightburn, A., & Black, R. (in press). *Social workers as educators.* New York: Columbia University Press.

Lightburn, A., & Kemp, S. P. (1994). Family-support programs: Opportunities for community-based practice. *Families in Society, 75*(1), 16–26.

Lightburn, A., & Sessions, P. (Eds.). (2006). *Handbook of community-based clinical practice.* New York: Oxford University Press.

Longres, J. F., & McLeod, E. (1980). Consciousness raising and social work practice. *Social Casework, 61,* 267–275.

Maluccio, A. (Ed.). (1981). *Promoting competence in clients.* London: Free Press.

Massey, D. (1994). *Space, place, and gender.* Minneapolis: University of Minnesota Press.

Mattaini, M. A. (1993a). Behavior analysis and community practice: A review. *Research on Social Work Practice, 3,* 420–447.

Mattaini, M. A. (1993b). *More than a thousand words: Graphics for clinical practice.* Washington, DC: NASW Press.

Mattaini, M. A., & Kirk, S. A. (1991). Assessing assessment in social work. *Social Work, 36,* 260–266.

McGowan, B. G. (1978). The case advocacy function in child welfare practice. *Child Welfare, 57,* 275–284.

McKnight, J. L. (1997). A 21st-century map for healthy communities and families. *Families in Society, 78,* 117–127.

Meyer, C. H. (Ed.). (1983). *Clinical social work in the eco-systems perspective.* New York: Columbia University Press.

Middleman, R. R., & Goldberg, G. (1974). *Social service delivery: A structural approach to social work practice.* New York: Columbia University Press.

Midgley, J. (1999). Growth, redistribution, and welfare: Toward social investment. *Social Service Review, 73,* 3–21.

Mondros, J. B., & Berman-Rossi, T. (1991). The relevance of stages of group development theory to community organization practice. *Social Work with Groups, 14*(3–4), 203–221.

Murray, M. (1995). Correction at Cabrini-Green. *Environment and Planning: Society and Space*, 13, 311–327.

Nurius, P. S., Kemp, S. P., & Gibson, J. W. (1999). Practitioners' perspectives on sound reasoning: Adding a worker-in-context component. *Administration in Social Work*, 23(1), 1–27.

O'Donnell, S. M., & Karanja, S. T. (2000). Transformative community practice: Building a model for developing extremely low income African American communities. *Journal of Community Practice*, 7(3), 67–84.

Ohmer, M. L., & Korr, W. S. (2006). The effectiveness of community practice interventions. *Research on Social Work Practice*, 16(2), 132–145.

Parsons, R. J. (1991). Empowerment: Purpose and practice principle in social work. *Social Work with Groups*, 14(2), 7–21.

Parsons, R. J. (1998). Evaluation of empowerment practice. In L. Gutierrez, R. J. Parsons, & E. O. Cox (Eds.), *Empowerment in social work practice: A sourcebook* (pp. 204–219). Pacific Grove, CA: Brooks/Cole.

Parsons, R J., Jorgensen, J. D., & Hernandez, S. H. (1994). *The integration of social work practice*. Pacific Grove, CA: Brooks/Cole.

Pecukonis, E. V., & Wenocur, S. (1994). Perceptions of self and collective efficacy in community organization theory and practice. *Journal of Community Practice*, 1(2), 5–21.

Peirce, N., & Steinbach, C. (1987). *Corrective capitalism: The rise of America's community development corporations*. New York: Ford Foundation.

Pennell, J., Noponen, H., & Weil, M. (2005). Empowerment research. In M. Weil (Ed.), *The handbook of community practice* (pp. 620–635). Thousand Oaks, CA: Sage Publications.

Perry, S. (1987). *Communities on the way: Rebuilding local communities in the United States and Canada*. Albany: State University of New York Press.

Poole, D. L. (1997). Building community capacity to promote social and public health: Challenges for universities [Editorial]. *Health & Social Work*, 22, 165–170.

Ramey, J. H. (1992). Group work practice in neighborhood centers today. *Social Work with Groups*, 15(2–3), 193–206.

Rapp, C. A., Shera, W., & Kisthart, W. (1993). Research strategies for empowerment of people with severe mental illness. *Social Work*, 38, 727–735.

Rappaport, J. (1987). Terms of empowerment/exemplars of prevention: Toward a theory for community psychology. *American Journal of Community Psychology*, 15, 121–145.

Reisch, M. (2005). Community practice challenges in the global economy. In M. Weil (Ed.), *The handbook of community practice* (pp. 529–547). Thousand Oaks, CA: Sage Publications.

Reisch, M., & Rivera, F. (1999). Ethical and racial conflicts in urban-based action research. *Journal of Community Practice*, 6(2), 49–62.

Rich, R. C., Edelstein, M., Hallman, W. K., & Wandersman, A. H. (1995). Citizen participation and empowerment: The case of local environmental hazards. *American Journal of Community Psychology*, 23, 657–676.

Ristock, J. L., & Pennell, J. (1996). *Community research as empowerment: Feminist links, postmodern interruptions*. New York: Oxford University Press.

Rivera, F. G., & Erlich, J. L. (Eds.). (1992). *Community organizing in a diverse society*. Boston: Allyn & Bacon.

Roberts, R., Houle, K., Kay, S., Nagda, B. A., & Elliot, V. (2000). *Toward competent communities: Best practices for producing community-wide study circles.* Lexington, KY: Roberts & Kay.

Rosen, A., & Livne, S. (1992). Personal versus environmental emphases in formulation of client problems. *Social Work Research & Abstracts, 29,* 12–17.

Rothman, J. (1970). Three models of community organization practice. In F. M. Cox, J. L. Erlich, J. Rothman, & J. E. Tropman (Eds.), *Strategies of community organization: A book of readings* (pp. 20–36). Itasca, IL: F. E. Peacock.

Rothman, J., & Tropman, J. E. (1987). Models of community organization and macro practice perspectives: Their mixing and phasing. In F. M. Cox, J. L. Erlich, J. Rothman, & J. E. Tropman (Eds.), *Strategies of community organization: Macro practice* (4th ed., pp. 3–26). Itasca, IL: F. E. Peacock.

Rubin, H. J., & Rubin, I. S. (1992). *Community organizing and development* (2nd ed.). New York: Maxwell.

Ryan, W. P., De Masi, K., Heinz, P.A., Jacobson, W., & Ohmer, M. (2000). *Aligning education and practice: Challenges and opportunities in social work education for community-centered practice.* Milwaukee, WI: Alliance for Children and Families.

Saleebey, D. (Ed.). (1992). *The strengths perspective in social work practice.* New York: Longman.

Sarri, R. C., & Sarri, C. M. (1992). Organizational and community change through participatory action research. *Administration in Social Work, 16,* 99–122.

Scanlon, E. (1998). Low-income homeownership policy as a community development strategy. *Journal of Community Practice, 5*(2), 137–154.

Schulz, A. J., Israel, B. A., Zimmerman, M. A., & Checkoway, B. N. (1995). Empowerment as a multi-level construct: Perceived control at the individual, organizational and community levels. *Health Education Research: Theory and Practice, 10,* 309–327.

Sheafor, B. W., Horejsi, C. R., & Horejsi, G. A. (2005). *Techniques and guidelines for social work practice* (7th ed.). Boston: Allyn & Bacon.

Sherraden, M. (1990). Stakeholding: Notes on a theory of welfare based on assets. *Social Service Review, 64,* 580–601.

Sherraden, M. (1991). *Assets and the poor: A new American welfare policy.* Armonk, NY: Sharpe.

Sherraden, M., Johnson, L., Clancy, M., Beverly, S., Schreiner, M., Zahn, M., & Curley, J. (2000). *Savings patterns in IDA programs.* St. Louis: Washington University.

Simon, B. L. (1990). Rethinking empowerment. *Journal of Progressive Human Services, 1*(1), 27–39.

Sohng, S.S.L. (1998). Research as an empowerment strategy. In L. M. Gutierrez, R. J. Parsons, & E. O. Cox (Eds.), *Empowerment in social work practice: A sourcebook* (pp. 187–203). Pacific Grove, CA: Brooks/Cole.

Smale, G. C. (1995). Integrating community and individual practice: A new paradigm for practice. In P. Adams & K. Nelson (Eds.), *Reinventing human services* (pp. 59–80). Hawthorne, NY: Aldine de Gruyter.

Sullivan, W. P. (1992). Reconsidering the environment as a helping resource. In D. Saleebey (Ed.), *The strengths perspective in social work practice* (pp. 148–157). New York: Longman.

Sviridoff, M., & Ryan, W. (1997). Community-centered family service. *Families in Society, 78,* 128–139.

Taylor, S. H., & Roberts, R. W. (1985). *The fluidity of practice theory: An overview*. In S. H. Taylor & R. W. Roberts (Eds.), *Theory and practice of community social work* (pp. 3–29). New York: Columbia University Press.

Tompkins, P. L. & Southward, L. H. (1998). Geographic information systems: Implications for promoting economic and social justice. *Computers in Human Services, 15*(2/3), 209–226.

Tracy, E. M., & Whittaker, J. K. (1990). The social network map: Assessing social support in clinical social work practice. *Families in Society, 71,* 461–470.

Two Feathers, J., Kieffer, E. C., Palmisano, G., Anderson, M., Sinco, B., Janz, N., Heisler, M., Spencer, M., Guzman, R., Thompson, J., Wisdom, K., & James, S. A. (2005). Racial and ethnic approaches to community health (REACH) Detroit Partnership: Improving diabetes-related outcomes among African American and Latino adults. *American Journal of Public Health, 95,* 1552–1560.

U.S. Census Bureau. (n.d.). *American community survey*. Retrieved November 25, 2006, from http://www.census.gov/acs/www/

U.S. Department of Housing and Urban Development. (n.d.). *Geographic information systems*. Retrieved November 25, 2006, from http://www.huduser.org/datasets/gis.html

Van Den Bergh, N., & Cooper, L. B. (Eds.). (1986). *Feminist visions for social work*. Silver Spring, MD: National Association of Social Workers.

Wang, C., Burris, M. A., & Ping, X. Y. (1996). Chinese village women as visual anthropologists: A participatory approach to reaching policy-makers. *Social Science and Medicine, 42,* 1391–1400.

Wang, C. C., Morrel-Samuels, S., Hutchinson, P. M., Bell, L., & Pestronk, R. M. (2004). Flint Photovoice: Community building among youths, adults and policymakers. *American Journal of Public Health, 94,* 911–913.

Warren, M. R., Thompson, J. P., & Saegert, S. (2001). The role of social capital in combating poverty. In S. Saegert, J. P. Thompson, & M. R. Warren (Eds.), *Social capital and poor communities* (pp. 1–28). New York: Russell Sage Foundation.

Warren, R. L. (1978). *The community in America* (3rd ed.). Chicago: Rand McNally.

Webber, M. (1963). Order in diversity: Community without propinquity. In L. Wingo, Jr. (Ed.), *Cities and space: The future use of urban land* (pp. 23–54). Baltimore: Johns Hopkins University Press.

Webster-Stratton, C. (1997). From parent training to community building. *Families in Society, 78*(2), 156–171.

Weick, A. (1993). Reconstructing social work education. *Journal of Teaching in Social Work, 8*(1–2), 11–30.

Weil, M. (1986). Women, community, and organizing. In N. Van Den Bergh & L. B. Cooper (Eds.), *Feminist visions for social work* (pp. 187–210). Silver Spring, MD: National Association of Social Workers.

Weil, M. (1994). Editor's introduction to the journal. *Journal of Community Practice, 1*(1), xxi–xxii.

Weil, M. (2005). Introduction: Contexts and challenges for the 21st century. In M. O. Weil (Ed.), *The handbook of community practice* (pp. 3–33). Thousand Oaks, CA: Sage Publications.

Weil, M., & Gamble, D. N. (1995). Community practice models. In R. L. Edwards (Ed.-in-Chief), *Encyclopedia of social work* (19th ed., Vol. 1, pp. 577–594). Washington, DC: NASW Press.

Weil, M., & Gamble, D. N. (2005). Evolution, models, and changing context of community practice. In M. Weil (Ed.), *The handbook of community practice* (pp. 117–150). Thousand Oaks, CA: Sage Publications.

Wellman, B., & Gulia, M. (1999). Net-surfers don't ride alone: Virtual communities as communities. In B. Wellman (Ed.), *Networks in the global village: Life in contemporary communities* (pp. 331–366). Boulder, CO: Westview Press. Retrieved December 1, 2006, from http://www.chass.utoronto.ca/~wellman/publications/netsurfers/netsurfers.pdf

Wellman, B., Salaff, J., Dimitrova, D., Garton, L., Gulia, M., & Haythornethwaite, C. (1996). Computer networks as social networks: Collaborative work, telework, and virtual community. *Annual Review of Sociology, 22,* 213–238.

Whittaker, J. K., & Garbarino, J. (Eds.). (1983). *Social support networks: Informal helping in the human services.* New York: Aldine.

Wood, G. G., & Middleman, R. R. (1991). Advocacy and social action: Key elements in the structural approach to direct practice in social work. *Social Work with Groups, 14*(3–4), 53–63.

Zimmerman, M. A., & Rappaport, J. (1988). Citizen participation, perceived control and psychological empowerment. *American Journal of Community Psychology, 16,* 725–750.

12

□ □ □

Social Work with and in Organizations

Meredith Hanson

We always have been and always will be "group people" (Johnson & Johnson, 2006), and in modern society many of the groups in which we live take the form of complex, formal organizations (Etzioni, 1964). In our organizational society, in which public institutions have taken over many private functions, social workers are the organizational professionals who aid our most vulnerable citizens as they travel through institutional and organizational mazes during times of personal crises. Most social workers are employees and affiliates of social and human services organizations.

The social agency is "the hidden reality of social work" (Weissman, Epstein, & Savage, 1983, p. 3). It is "the locus of practice and professional services" (Vinter, 1959, p. 242). From the earliest days of the Charity Organization Societies and settlement houses, social work's existence has been tied firmly to social agencies. "Unlike other professions, social work was almost exclusively a corporate activity, with little opportunity for independent practice. To carve out a niche, the social worker had to attain hegemony within the agency" (Lubove, 1965, p. 159).

Although most social work practice occurs in social and human service agencies (Hasenfeld, 1983) and host settings such as hospitals and business corporations (Dane & Simon, 1991; Kurzman & Akabas, 1993), many professional social workers do not grasp the extent to which organizational context affects practice, nor do they understand how they can influence their agencies (Gibelman, 2003). Consequently, they miss opportunities to intervene in agency policies and procedures so as to keep the organizations responsive to clients' needs and congruent with social work values and ethics.

Social work practice settings both constrain and facilitate social workers' transactions with clients, professionals, and other key constituents (Hartman, 1993; Zald, 2001). Social agencies legitimize and sanction social services (Hasenfeld, 1983), and they control many of the resources social workers need to assist clients (Hasenfeld, 1987; Toseland & Rivas, 2005). Agency function delimits the forms and goals of practice (Vinter, 1959). Ultimately, by vesting social workers with authority, the practice setting becomes a major source of power for social workers, who embody "the mission, function, structures, and policies of the organization" (Gitterman, 1989, p. 166). Conflicts between agencies and professionals may lead to a loss of benefits and services for clients, low morale among workers, and organizational dysfunction and decline (Lipsky, 1984; Marriott, Sexton, & Staley, 1994).

This chapter is about social work practice in and with organizations. It introduces readers to the work setting as a context, target, and means of professional influence. It defines social and human service agencies; discusses several organizational components that are central to understanding agency dynamics; and illustrates ways to assess, influence, and use organizational structures and processes to promote client autonomy and community well-being.

DEFINITIONS

Social and Human Service Agencies

Social and human service agencies are formal organizations with the stated purpose of enhancing "the social, emotional, physical, and/or intellectual well-being of some component of the population" (Brager & Holloway, 1978, p. 2). They include such diverse practice settings as hospitals, schools, child welfare agencies, nursing homes, settlement houses, employee assistance programs, domestic violence shelters, and prisons. They differ from other organizations with similar aims in at least two key ways: (1) Their "raw materials" are people, who become clients and are transformed, processed, or assisted in some specified manner, and (2) society mandates that the agencies serve both client and societal interests (Hasenfeld, 1983, 1992a).

Human service agencies are created to address personal and social problems and to promote equity and social justice. As such, they are products of ambivalent and contradictory societal ideologies and values (Sarri & Hasenfeld, 1978). Services contain implicit and explicit meanings about the worth of clients as well as societal expectations for how people ought to behave and be treated. Thus, human service agencies engage in "moral work" (Hasenfeld, 1992a).

Because their raw materials are people, and because they owe their existence to societal mandates and political policies (for example, financing and sanction), human service agencies are highly dependent on their external environments.

Consequently, environmental factors, such as a changing political climate and economic conditions, profoundly influence agency operations. Under such circumstances, management can become preoccupied with organizational survival, and individual workers can become absorbed with their personal survival in the agency. In the process, the interests of the clients can be lost. For example, diagnostic practices in mental health settings are affected by insurance coverage; thus, service itself can be shaped by payment policies for particular conditions. Although social workers strive to provide the most responsive and effective care for their clients, they cannot ignore the limits insurance coverage may place on the type of care provided.

Health care agencies, like other social agencies, are accountable to multiple and shifting constituent groups with conflicting interests and agendas (Martin, 1987; Perrow, 1978; Taber, 1987). Attempts to be responsive to one group may interfere with an agency's ability to be accountable to another. For example, the current health care environment is economically driven. Reform efforts designed to contain rising health care costs have affected access to care (through insurance and reimbursement policies) and quality of care (for example, by specifying which services are reimbursable and by favoring outpatient and short-term treatments). Competing mandates to control costs and to provide access to quality care create ethical and role conflicts for social workers, who try to balance the cost-containment interests of insurance groups and other funders with the treatment needs of clients. The resolution of the conflicts affects not only a social worker's decision about what services to recommend but also clients' decisions about undergoing the treatment.

Although social agencies are established to serve particular client groups, agency goals are not defined unilaterally. Goals evolve out of negotiations between human service organizations and their constituents, including funders, political groups, and community members. Although professional codes of ethics may prescribe service ideals that give primacy to client interests, human services agencies are not bound to place individual client interests above those of the agency (Gouldner, 1963; McGowan, 1978; Rhodes, 1991; Vinter, 1959). It is in the context of these organizational arrangements and competing interests that ethical questions emerge and can be understood (Walsh-Bowers, Rossiter, & Prilleltensky, 1996). For example, funding constraints may lead agencies to try to simplify technologies and routinize procedures. As complexity decreases, supervision and staff management costs decrease, thus saving the agency money (Savage, 1987). Those changes, however, may limit and devalue the complexity of clinical practice, and they may actually impede the agency's capacity to meet particular client-related service goals effectively. Thus, social workers must resolve value dilemmas as they decide whether (or how) to adhere to agency procedures while questioning and challenging them.

Formal Organizations

To fully grasp the forces that affect their practice settings, social workers must understand the concept of "formal organization." Writers have proposed literally hundreds of definitions for formal organizations. Some definitions overlap, and others are contradictory, but all reflect particular theoretical perspectives (Bolman & Deal, 2003; Hasenfeld, 1992b; Hatch & Cunliffe, 2006; Katz & Kahn, 1978; Morgan, 1997; Perrow, 1986; Shafritz, Ott, & Jang, 2005). At the most basic level, an organization is any social unit with identifiable boundaries that has evolved or been created to attain some purpose or purposes. Formal organizations, such as social and human services agencies, are social units that have been "consciously designed *a priori*" (Blau & Scott, 1962, p. 5). They are characterized by formal (for example, written) policies, rules, and procedures that guide routine interactions. Formal organizations are usually complex. That is, they employ personnel from several professional disciplines who perform intricate tasks that require specialized education or training (Hage & Aiken, 1970).

Classically, formal organizations have been depicted as goal-oriented, rationally designed, thinking machines. The word "organization" is derived from the Greek word "organon," which means tool or instrument (Morgan, 1997). Thus, it is not surprising that the first definitions of formal organizations emphasized their bureaucratic administrative structures and underscored such rational features as goals (purposes), hierarchical authority structures, divisions of labor, and specialized task arrangements (Gerth & Mills, 1958; Weber, 1924/1947). Classical theorists saw organizations as the means through which goals were achieved. Learning in organizations was linked strongly to professionalization. Divisions of labor and organizational stratification separated the educated "decision makers" from the less educated "doers" (Gould, 2000). Classical theorists distinguished formal organizations from other social systems by their rational–legal nature and the priority they placed on goal attainment. Classical analyses focused on mechanisms of technical proficiency and organizational arrangements that affected efficiency and effectiveness.

As knowledge about formal organizations developed, many scholars became disenchanted with the mechanistic, dehumanizing classical definitions, and they crafted new conceptualizations, which highlighted other organizational features. For example, natural systems paradigms, like the human relations school, emphasized the relevance of noneconomic, social rewards and informal communication and leadership structures for understanding organizational dynamics (Etzioni, 1964; Mayo, 1945; Roethlisberger & Dickson, 1939/1975). The new conceptualizations drew attention to behavioral and normative patterns that emerged as organizational members attempted to minimize stress and organizations tried to survive and maintain themselves (Scott, 2003). Organizational culture—the

□-□-□-□-□

Sidebar 12-1: *Diversity in Organizations*

Organizational diversity has many sources, including the agency membership's professional disciplines, their demographic and personal characteristics, professional interests and job functions, and individual skills and capacities. Effective organizations and work groups accept, value, and promote diversity. A considerable amount of empirical evidence and research demonstrates the positive impact of diversity on organizational climate and productivity. Job satisfaction and turnover, for example, are related to employees' perceptions that they fit into an agency and the agency values their contributions (Chernesky, 1998). Diversity among organizational members deters groupthink and helps ensure that multiple points of view are applied to work assignments. Work groups with members who have heterogeneous technical skills tend to perform better in production tasks (Jackson, 1992). Groups whose members have complementary and heterogeneous abilities outperform homogeneous groups in decision-making tasks (Johnson & Johnson, 1989). Homogeneous groups tend to avoid risks; they lack controversy and may become dull. The "clash of perspectives" and contention that are so important to high-quality performance and creative decision making are often missing in less diverse organizations (Johnson & Johnson, 2006).

Although many benefits accrue from organizational diversity, diversity can lead to undesirable and harmful consequences. For example, the increased conflict associated with heterogeneity raises tensions in organizations. Turnover rates seem to be higher, and cohesion may be lower in diverse work groups (for example, Johnson & Johnson, 2006; O'Reilly, Caldwell, & Barnett, 1989; Terborg, Castore, & DeNinno, 1976). As a result, social agencies that do not attend to the potential negative consequences of diversity may experience divisiveness, excessive bias, stereotyping, and poorer performance.

Organizations that promote and value diversity act in proactive ways to recognize and appreciate the expertise diverse members offer. They strive to transform organizational culture and become multicultural (Chernesky, 2005; Gutierrez & Lewis, 1999; Loden & Rosener, 1991). They become learning organizations (Gould & Baldwin, 2004).

To maximize the benefits and reduce harmful consequences associated with diversity, it must be recognized that diversity is a fact of life that cannot and should not be avoided. Agencies must establish constructive mechanisms and forums for managing conflict when it arises. Policies that bar discrimination and encourage difference must be established (Chernesky, 1998). In-service training activities that enhance cultural competence and appreciation for diversity must be implemented. Rituals that bring agency employees, clients, and others together in ways that celebrate diversity can be instituted. Social agencies should manage diversity not to homogenize themselves but to encourage members to collaborate to attain organizational goals while recognizing and respecting diversity among their membership (Johnson & Johnson, 2006).

shared norms, beliefs, values, symbols, and rituals that give meaning, direction, and guidelines for individual and collective behavior—became a focus of study (Bolman & Deal, 2003; Edwards & Gummer, 1988). Practices that promoted human development and organizational learning were examined more closely.

Open-systems frameworks expanded on classical definitions by underscoring organizations' links with their environments. They depicted organizations as loosely coupled sets of interrelated, interacting subsystems (Buckley, 1967; Morgan, 1997). Proponents of open-systems frameworks argued that an organization's form is determined, to a large extent, through environmental exchanges (Lawrence & Lorsch, 1967; Scott, 2003).

Postmodern theories of organizations drew attention to power differentials, ambiguities, and contradictions that mark organizational life. They challenged efforts to develop universal explanations of organizations and organizational change, and they questioned taken-for-granted assumptions about organizational structures and processes (Hatch & Cunliffe, 2006). Postmodern perspectives on formal organizations expanded the study of organizational learning and the conditions that promote collective learning in social agencies.

Many other definitions of formal organizations, which attempt to integrate earlier perspectives and account for new knowledge, have emerged (see Bolman & Deal, 2003; Hasenfeld, 1992b; Morgan, 1997; Scott, 2003; Shafritz et al., 2005). Each definition is a metaphor, which provides an important, albeit incomplete, image of reality. Taken together, they suggest that formal organizations are rationally based, social entities, characterized by predictable and unpredictable habitual interaction patterns (organizational structures) that are explicitly arranged for the accomplishment of stated purposes. They are organic, dynamic, and open systems in which alliances form and re-form among organizational members and interest groups as they try to meet organizational goals and individual interests. Typically, organizations develop unique cultures and multiple formal and informal power centers that affect their operations. As open systems, they respond not only to internal institutional pressures but also to external political, economic, and social forces in the environment, which can lead to organizational transformation and goal substitution over time.

KEY COMPONENTS OF FORMAL ORGANIZATIONS

Organizational theorists and social work scholars suggest that to comprehend how their practice settings operate, social workers should understand five key components of organizations, depicted in Table 12-1: (1) goals (stated mission or purpose) and other external and internal demands faced by an agency; (2) internal structures and culture; (3) service technologies and programs; (4) membership interests and characteristics; and (5) environmental context, including physical setting, prevailing mood, and resources.

TABLE I2-I
□ □ □ □ □
Key Components of Organizations

Term	Definition
Goals	An agency's officially stated mission and the operating policies that are established to maintain smooth functioning and survival in shifting environments. Typically, agencies have multiple stated and unstated goals, which compete with and complement each other.
Internal structures and culture	Formal and informal habitual interaction patterns. Internal structures provide the framework through which an agency implements its service mission and agency members gain support, validation, and guidance. Informal structural processes in the form of an organization's culture affect an agency's operations by creating a climate that gives primacy to particular values, practices, and goals.
Service technologies and programs	The activities, tools, and practices human service agencies use to assist clients. Human service technologies are intensive, indeterminate, and sensitive to environmental pressures.
Membership interests and characteristics	Organization members are social actors who carry out an agency's work. An organization's members are stakeholders who have an interest in the agency's programs, as well as their own place in the agency. To understand their actions, one must examine the positions they hold, the power and resources they control, their reference groups and linkages with other organizational members, and the impact of specific agency processes and changes on their work lives.
Environmental context	A multidimensional set of interacting external forces that affect an agency's operations and structures. An agency's external environment can be understood as a set of concentric circles that consist of the distal environment, proximal geographic and sociocultural surroundings, and the immediate task environment.

Goals

An agency's goals represent its efforts to respond to multiple demands: to serve clients, to maintain smooth internal operations, and to adapt to shifting environmental conditions. One would expect an agency's goals to complement each other. Several factors, however, can lead to displacement and conflict among goals. Consider, for example, the goals of service. An agency's service goals include official goals, as articulated in mission statements and other public pronouncements, and operative goals that outline actual operating policies (Perrow, 1961). Official goals usually are formulated in vague, overly broad terms to maintain maximum support among key constituent groups. Operative goals, in contrast, are more precise and reveal how an agency makes daily program decisions and allocates scarce resources, such as money and staff. Operative goals reflect not only an agency's efforts to fulfill its mission but also its attempts to maintain itself and remain adaptive.

When responding to competing pressures, official service goals may be subverted and other, sometimes covert, goals may emerge. For example, many mental health clinics establish waiting lists to ensure that clients receive adequate clinical services and to prevent social workers' caseloads from getting too large. Although those procedures may facilitate efficient clinic operations and be consistent with professional standards, they can become organizational barriers to service delivery. Long waiting lists make service unavailable and inaccessible to many people. Moreover, long waiting lists and lengthy intake procedures can serve latent purposes by enabling agencies to "cream" pools of preferred (that is, "motivated") clients who are most likely to accept an agency's "brand" of service (Brager & Holloway, 1978; Gitterman & Miller, 1989). In this instance, agency decisions justified by self-maintenance needs may lead to practices that clash with service goals and interfere with the delivery of care to potential clients.

Internal Structures and Culture

Formal Structures. Organizations' internal structures consist of role sets (networks of related role positions) and predictable patterns of interaction that exist among agency members. They are the means through which services are delivered to clients (Rothman, 2001). Specific organizational structures and administrative practices shape the provision of service and, ultimately, affect an agency's ability to attain its goals (Gutierrez, GlenMaye, & DeLois, 1995). Formal organizational structures are most apparent in an agency's rules and regulations, task specializations, and hierarchical authority structures, as depicted in organization charts and administrative manuals.

No single formal structure is best suited for all agencies. The structure that suits a particular facility depends on such factors as its mission, the nature of its services, environmental conditions, and the training of its staff (Netting, Kettner, & McMurtry, 2004). Decentralized, collegial structures may work well in smaller agencies, such as family services centers, where highly professionalized staff may work independently of each other. More formalized, professional bureaucratic structures seem better suited to large organizations, such as child protection agencies and multiservice centers, which need expert knowledge yet require close coordination and communication among workers (Litwak, 1961). Matrix and project structures (Miles, 1975; Morgan, 1997), in which professionals work as members of interdisciplinary teams assigned to particular functions or projects (for example, intake, discharge planning, aftercare), are better fits for agencies such as hospitals and addictions treatment centers, in which many functional specialties require input from employees who are drawn from several professional disciplines.

Informal Structures and Culture. In addition to formal structures, all agencies have informal structures and networks, which are more fluid than formal structures and more closely linked with members' personal attributes (Etzioni, 1964). These emergent networks include the unofficial interaction and communication patterns that develop as people adapt to their work settings and do their jobs (Monge & Contractor, 2001). They can be thought of as work-based, mutual aid networks. One discovers them by observing who people talk to, where they go for advice, and how they actually complete their work assignments (Weissman et al., 1983).

An agency's organizational culture is an important aspect of its informal structure (Ashkanasy, Wilderom, & Peterson, 2000). Concisely defined, an agency's culture is "the way we do things around here" (Deal & Kennedy, 1982, p. 4). An agency's culture consists of patterns of shared beliefs, behavioral norms, and collective assumptions that have evolved over time as an organization's members struggle with the demands of adaptation and integration (Gibelman, 2003). An agency's culture tends to be ingrained. Thus, although one may be able to identify an organization's primary culture easily, cultural practices do not change quickly in response to internal or external pressure (Meenaghan, Gibbons, & McNutt, 2005).

Cultural practices indirectly affect organizational behavior by creating a climate (that is, perceptions by an organization's members) that gives primacy to particular values and behaviors. Those values and behaviors work sufficiently well that they are taught to new members as the "correct" way to act, think, and feel about their role, their work, and the agency itself (Bolman & Deal, 2003; Schein, 1992). For example, social justice was highly valued in an agency serving an urban homeless population. Veteran case managers told new employees, state auditors, and others that "our job is to make the system work for our clients." Although the agency's mission statement stressed social and vocational rehabilitation and addictions treatment as part of its mandate, new employees learned quickly that case advocacy was a priority. Although efforts were made to help clients change dysfunctional behaviors that contributed to their homelessness, workers' passion and intensity were most apparent in advocacy efforts, when they argued for more resources and persuaded other agencies to "take a chance" with their clients.

An agency's culture reflects the values of the formal system and their reinterpretation in the informal system. Consequently, the organizational culture, as expressed in daily activities of staff, may differ markedly from the agency's purported values as articulated in formal documents. An agency's culture is molded by many factors, including its history, its institutional and physical setting, its staff, its communication networks, and its authority structures (Bolman & Deal, 2003; Katz & Kahn, 1978). Culture evolves over time as workers respond to job pressures, establish social supports, and create comfortable working environments.

Informal, emergent structures and organizational culture can "grease the wheels" of an agency by providing incentives and explanations in areas in which the formal structure is deficient (Barnard, 1968; Perrow, 1986). They can also undermine the formal structure by furnishing competing arguments and legitimizing people who are disillusioned with agency goals, programs, and procedures. The evolution of informal structures is affected by the exchanges that take place among formally designated authority figures, line workers, and unofficial peer leaders. Thus, depending on staff members' experiences with members of administration and their interpretation of administrative motives, they may view a particular program initiative either as a potentially useful innovation or as more "busy work."

Consider, for example, the following situation. In response to a mandate from state auditors, the director of an addictions treatment facility ordered all workers to write "interdisciplinary biopsychosocial summaries" for clients. The purpose of the summaries, which were to be included in the clients' clinical records, was to document that staff members from each professional discipline were involved in developing comprehensive intervention plans with clients. The workers in one clinic embraced the new procedure, whereas those in another clinic opposed it, citing increased paperwork and time constraints.

An examination of the two clinics revealed that the staffs' reactions were directly related to each clinic's culture. In the first clinic, a history of collaboration existed between line workers and supervisors about procedural changes. Power was shared among managers and line workers, and a problem-focused learning culture formed. Thus, when the new procedure was proposed, workers' opinions were sought, and the procedure was modified on the basis of their input. The line workers believed that they were treated fairly, and they incorporated the procedure into their routines. The second clinic had a history of unilaterally imposed procedural changes. Thus, when the new procedure was introduced, staff members rallied around each other to oppose the change. Even when the clinic manager offered to meet with staff about their concerns, staff remained skeptical. No past experience led them to believe that meaningful collaboration would occur. Thus, in the first clinic the informal structure reinforced collaboration and cooperation, but in the second clinic, an emergent, adversarial interaction pattern clashed with the formal structure. In both clinics, staff members' access to organizational decision making affected the organizational culture and contributed to the evolution of informal structures that had a marked effect on agency operations, staff morale, and the care that clients received.

Service Technologies and Programs

Social service technologies are the activities and tools (for example, assessment forms, diagnostic tests, and professional knowledge and skills) agencies use to assist clients. Four of their characteristics have particular relevance for organizationally based practice. First, human services technologies are intensive: They draw on a variety of techniques that are selected, in part, on the basis of feedback from clients (Thompson, 1967). Second, most technologies are indeterminate. Their effects are variable and uncertain, and consensus about desirable outcomes may not exist (Sarri & Hasenfeld, 1978). Third, for many technologies, minimal evidence of effectiveness exists. Fourth, although the technologies are applied within an agency context, they are extremely sensitive to environmental pressures (Brager & Holloway, 1978).

These characteristics can cause dilemmas for social services agencies, which strive for technological predictability and certainty (Savage, 1987). To increase their control over their work, agencies try to seal off their core technologies from environmental and other influences by developing routines and ideological systems that support the use of particular practice theories and service strategies (Hasenfeld, 1992a; Mintzberg, 1979; Thompson, 1967). Although the ideologies and routines fulfill an organizational self-maintenance function by reducing stress and uncertainty, they can become ingrained and resistant to change. Consequently, they may have unintended consequences: Clients seeking assistance may find that they receive what an agency has to offer rather than what they need, and workers who question prevailing practice models may face deep-rooted, ideologically based, structurally supported opposition.

To understand how an agency frames its practice, social workers should identify the core technologies that are central to agency operations. Then they should locate the ideologies and routines that support those technologies. To increase their professional autonomy within an agency, social workers must develop their knowledge of its core technologies. In addition, they must identify and understand the organizational processes and culture that support the core technologies. They should appeal to the agency's own quality control mechanisms to evaluate existing practice approaches, and they should emphasize responsiveness to client need as a criterion for validating the helping process (see Lauffer, 1984). To alter existing "rules" governing the way services are delivered, social workers must appeal to an agency's commitment to fair and responsive service delivery.

They must show how new technologies and service programs can meet client needs for assistance as well as the agency's survival and maintenance needs.

Historically, social workers have relied on authority and expert opinion to guide their professional practices. This tendency has contributed to the proliferation of outdated and ineffective services. Thus, once a professional social worker understands the nature of and rationale behind an agency's core practices, it is crucial for him or her to identify the evidence base for those practices. Drawing on ethical standards that call for the use of evidence-based practices, as well as on information gleaned from a review of the practice research literature, social workers can position themselves to challenge outdated, ineffective practices and gain organizational support for the ethical use of evidence-based technologies (see Gambrill, 2005).

Membership Interests and Characteristics

"Social actors," who perform agency tasks for monetary and other reinforcers, carry out the work of human service agencies. Without them, there is no organization. It is through social actors that organizations gain continuity and change (Scott, 2003). Although members may believe in an agency's mission, their views about agency policies and their actions will vary depending on such factors as their personal attributes, job titles and functions, and involvement in other organizations and groups.

Agency members are stakeholders who are interested in both the success of an agency's programs and their place in the agency. Thus, to understand stakeholders' motives and actions, one should examine an agency's programs and goals and how any changes will affect different personnel. Agency members generally act in their own self-interest as well as the interests of the agency and its clients. If a particular programmatic change adds to a worker's power, prestige, and security, he or she is apt to support it; if the same change threatens his or her position, the worker is more likely to resist it. A hospital social worker, for example, may assume responsibility for coordinating discharge planning because she believes she will be able to help clients. Her enthusiasm for the task will increase if she perceives that her new role will add to her status and influence. Another worker, who also believes that the change will aid clients, may be less supportive of it if he suspects that it will harm his organizational position by drawing resources away from other projects with which he is involved.

Clearly, one must examine many variables to understand agency members' actions and motives. Although people usually act to protect their self-interest, it is often difficult to define their interests. Thus, to predict how agency members may act in particular situations, one must examine their organizational positions (for example, job title and function), the power and resources they control (for example, access to information, materials, and support [Kanter, 1979]), and the impact of specific organizational changes and processes on their work lives. If those factors are understood, one should be able to predict a worker's actions under different circumstances. If those factors remain unknown, it is difficult to anticipate how agency members will react to different organizational practices (Brager & Holloway, 1978; Gummer, 1990; Mechanic, 1962).

Environmental Context

The environmental context consists of a multidimensional set of interacting political, legal, economic, technological, ecological, physical, and sociocultural forces that affect an agency's programs and structures. The effects of those forces can be demonstrated by several examples:

+ Hospitals have become more formalized because of directives from regulatory bodies and concerns about lawsuits. For example, they have developed detailed and prescriptive written policies and procedures for virtually all organizational practices.
+ The public's changed sentiment, welfare reform legislation, and the availability of fingerprinting technologies have supported the rise of an "administrative culture" (Bane & Ellwood, 1994) in some public assistance offices, which puts a higher priority on preventing fraud than on assisting vulnerable people.
+ Whether social workers discuss condom use as a way to reduce the risk of HIV infection with high school students is contingent on authorization from community residents, such as parents, religious leaders, and politicians.

An agency and its environment can be thought of as a set of concentric circles with the agency in the middle. The outer circle is the distal environment—the broad political, economic, and social conditions that affect all agencies. The distal environment changes slowly and cannot be altered by individual agencies. It sets the parameters for the types of services and programs that emerge in society (Hasenfeld, 1983). For example, the political mood that led to welfare and health care reform fundamentally changed the way health and social services agencies operate and the care they provide for clients.

Moving inward, the next circle covers the proximal geographic and sociocultural context. The neighborhoods and communities in which agencies are located have a direct effect on service arrangements. Such agency programs as health fairs and bicultural counseling services are often based on community needs assessments. The way they are delivered may be shaped by input from community members and their representatives (Gutierrez, 1992).

The third circle, and the circle closest to the agency itself, is the agency's task environment, which has the most immediate effect on an agency's daily operations. The task environment includes an agency's beneficiaries (clients and family members), its funders, providers of nonfiscal resources, competitors, providers of complementary services, members of its service network, and "legitimators" (for example, advocacy groups and governmental bodies) (Lauffer, 1984). The task environment directly affects whom an agency serves and how it serves them. For example, agencies that exist in unfriendly task environments, such as those characterized by competitiveness and unpredictable funding, must devote more of their resources to organizational survival, leaving fewer resources for client services. In contrast, agencies with friendlier task environments can direct more attention and effort toward service innovation.

Several dimensions of an agency's environment help explain the variability in the programs that are delivered in different agencies (Brager & Holloway, 1978; Hasenfeld, 1983; Perrow, 1986). First, the practice ideologies and rules regulating different fields of practice limit the types of programs that are permitted. Second, political trends, economic conditions, and personal values affect the public's support for social services programs. Third, demographic changes, as well as competition for scarce resources (for example, funding and clients), spur agencies to become innovative.

Answers to questions such as the following will help social workers discover how the environment affects an agency and its capacity to adapt to environmental pressures:

+ What are the agency's funding sources, and what government bodies regulate its policies and programs?
+ What client populations does the agency serve, and how does it attract new clients?
+ What mechanisms exist to ensure that the agency is responsive and accountable to clients, funders, and other constituents?
+ How does the agency obtain information about the environment?
+ What is the quality of the agency's communication (open or closed, friendly or hostile) with different environmental groups (local politicians, other agencies, and the mass media, for example)?

ORGANIZATIONAL PRACTICE

Competent organizational practitioners see beyond the boundaries of individual cases. They maintain a flexible focus that allows them to understand how the troubles of individual clients represent larger practice issues in their agencies. They often share a worldview distinguished by "a strong sense of what is just in and for the world" (Mondros & Wilson, 1994, p. 15). Like community organizers, good organizational practitioners are "conscious contrarians" (Mondros & Wilson). They are concerned about fairness as well as personal freedom (Figueira-

McDonough, 1993). They are committed to the empowerment of vulnerable and disenfranchised groups, and they have chosen careers that embrace social justice and empowerment and permit them to be the "consciences" of their agencies. They challenge people's thinking and seek different ways of doing things. Whereas other professionals may look for pathology and mental disorders to understand a client's behavior, social workers, who are "conscious contrarians," try to identify client strengths (without minimizing pathology) and locate community supports that can be drawn on to promote adaptive functioning.

When someone is referred to a social services agency, several events can ensue. In an ideal situation, the client's needs fit neatly within the agency's service structure, and he or she receives help. Even in an agency that is carefully designed to be responsive to clients, however, there may be a poor match between a client's needs and the agency's capacity to meet them. When adequate services exist elsewhere and a social worker assesses that a client can be helped by another facility, the worker may refer the client to that agency. In other instances (for example, when the poor fit is an "isolated" case), the social worker may opt to advocate on the client's behalf, creatively interpret policies, and "stretch" existing programs so that they help the client. When the poor fit represents more serious organizational dysfunction that affects a class of clients, social workers have an ethical and professional responsibility to promote organizational change. How they do that is a function of such factors as the nature and severity of the organizational problem, workers' assessment of the conditions in their agencies, support from management and other staff, and their own resources.

An extensive body of social work literature addresses strategies for promoting innovation and change from the ground up in social agencies (see, for example, Bargal & Schmid, 1992; Brager & Holloway, 1978; Erlich, Rothman, & Teresa, 1999; Frey, 1990; McGowan, 1978; Netting et al., 2004; Resnick & Patti, 1980). Although this literature cannot be reviewed in depth in this chapter, seven core practice tasks can be gleaned from it. To produce changes in social services agencies, social workers must

1. define the organizational problems that block service delivery.
2. "read" the agency.
3. pinpoint feasible solutions.
4. develop and select a strategy for organizational change.
5. prepare the agency and themselves for change.
6. initiate the change strategy.
7. monitor, evaluate, and revise the strategy so the change will be institutionalized.

The following case example illustrates aspects of these practice tasks.

Case Illustration

Two social workers employed at the Princeshire Clinic (not its real name), an alcoholism treatment facility affiliated with a large medical school, identified a problem that troubled them:

> Over a three-month period, we noticed that 15 applicants were turned away because they were diagnosed with schizophrenia or bipolar disorder, which the intake workers said made them "inappropriate" for treatment in an alcohol clinic. All had serious drinking problems and would have been admitted if they did not have coexisting mental disorders.

Defining the Problem. Organizational change begins when social workers determine that an organizational element is adversely affecting an agency's responsiveness to clients (Brager & Holloway, 1978; Resnick & Patti, 1980). Problem definitions focus the change effort and suggest its consequences for the agency, clients, and society. Useful problem definitions have several features:

+ They are concrete and operational (that is, they make abstract concepts observable).
+ They are client-centered; they stress the significance of the problem for the care of clients.
+ They locate a problem in the agency by specifying whether it is structural (related to an agency's policies and procedures), technological (arising from an agency's practice modalities), or personnel related (caused by the characteristics or competence of the agency's staff) (Brager & Holloway, 1978).
+ They do not confuse a problem with its solution.
+ They put a problem in context by suggesting why it exists—its history, sources, and adaptive functions.
+ They can be *partialized* (broken down into component parts).
+ They suggest possible solutions.

The two social workers at the Princeshire Clinic developed the following problem definition:

> We discovered that a group home for patients discharged from the state psychiatric hospital had recently opened up near the clinic. Although residents received medication and therapy, some had begun to drink heavily. The case managers referred those people to our clinic. Because we had no policy on applicants with mental disorders, the alcoholism counselors who conducted most of the intake interviews declined to admit them. We clearly had a structural problem in the clinic. We also had a technological problem because we had no services for clients with dual diagnoses.

We believed that the problem was an important one because people in need of help were being excluded from the clinic. Thus, we believed that the services were not being provided equitably.

Because clinic resources were limited and there was resistance to admitting these applicants, we decided to partialize our plans. Specifically, we planned to request that one of us be assigned to intake and that we assess 15 clients with dual diagnoses for admission. We hoped to develop and evaluate one treatment group designed specifically for them.

Reading the Agency. Once an initial problem definition is formulated, social workers must "read" their agency (that is, identify and assess the salient forces affecting its stability). They must ascertain how different constituent groups and individuals perceive the problem and how those groups might react to any proposal for change. They must also identify key people who must be involved in a change effort: critical decision makers, who can authorize change; facilitators, who will support a change and who can influence other key actors; and resisters, who will actively or passively oppose change (Brager & Holloway, 1978). Several useful tools, such as organizational ecomapping (Mattaini, 1993) and force-field analysis (Brager & Holloway, 1992), can be used to analyze exchanges among subsystems and to locate organizational supports and resistances for different change options.

The social workers at the Princeshire Clinic used those tools when they analyzed their agency:

> We completed an organizational ecomap, in which we identified the relevant agencies and personnel that would affect our plans. They included the clinic director (critical decision maker), our supervisor (facilitator), the alcoholism counselors (resisters), other social workers (most of whom were neutral), the clients, the group home, the medical school, and the state departments of substance abuse and mental health.
>
> We used a force-field analysis to assess the prospects for change by identifying organizational and environmental forces that could be drawn upon to support our ideas. Essentially, by constructing a balance sheet that depicted the countervailing forces that support or oppose systemic changes, we were able to clarify some of the factors that would work for us or against us as we tried to initiate organizational change.

A simple force-field analysis is depicted in Figure 12-1. It lists only the major driving and restraining forces that would affect the clinic's plans (see Brager & Holloway, 1992, for an in-depth discussion of force-field analysis in planning organizational change.)

FIGURE 12-1

Force Field Analysis

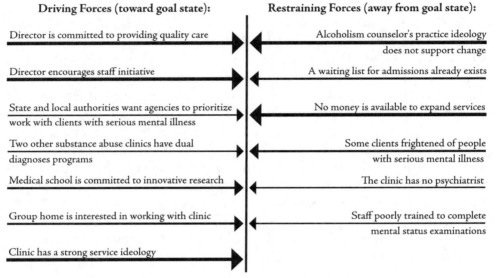

Worst State Likely:	Status Quo:	Goal State:
Clinic policy becomes more restrictive concerning treating clients with dual diagnoses	Current practices continue	Clinic develops a policy that admits and treats clients with dual diagnoses

Driving Forces (toward goal state): | **Restraining Forces (away from goal state):**

Director is committed to providing quality care →← Alcoholism counselor's practice ideology does not support change

Director encourages staff initiative →← A waiting list for admissions already exists

State and local authorities want agencies to prioritize work with clients with serious mental illness →← No money is available to expand services

Two other substance abuse clinics have dual diagnoses programs →← Some clients frightened of people with serious mental illness

Medical school is committed to innovative research →← The clinic has no psychiatrist

Group home is interested in working with clinic →← Staff poorly trained to complete mental status examinations

Clinic has a strong service ideology →

(thickness of arrows represents strength of forces)

The clinic director was committed to providing good client care, and he encouraged staff to be innovative and take initiative. State and local pressure to assist deinstitutionalized patients with serious mental illnesses was growing, and at least two other substance abuse clinics in the city had established small programs for clients with dual diagnoses. The medical school was research oriented and urged the clinic to be innovative. The group home was interested in developing a joint initiative. The clinic had a strong service ideology.

Counteracting these driving forces were restraining forces: The alcoholism counselors' practice ideology did not support a change. They believed strongly that the clinic's purpose was to treat primary alcoholic clients; they were worried about extending existing scarce resources to people who were not primary alcoholics. The clinic already had a waiting list for other applicants, and no money was available to expand services. Seeing people with obvious mental disorders in the waiting room frightened some clients. The clinic had no psychiatrist to consult about the care of such clients, and staff were poorly trained to complete mental status examinations.

Pinpointing Feasible Solutions. Following preliminary analysis of the problem, social workers must develop potential solutions that are acceptable to their constituents and will maximize an agency's responsiveness to the broadest range of clients. Because agency members have interests tied to existing practices and because any change requires effort, social services agencies, like other social systems, will resist change (Frey, 1990). Practitioners can reduce their agencies' resistances and increase the feasibility of proposed solutions in several ways. For example, partializing and introducing a change incrementally will make it more acceptable (Erlich et al., 1999). Feasibility also increases when potential solutions are directly relevant to the identified problem, are simple, do not depart radically from an agency's ideology, are reversible (can be undone), are operational, and are economic (that is, their potential benefits justify the costs involved).

The two social workers described the next steps they took:

> After we completed our assessment, we obtained our supervisor's permission to visit the two facilities providing services for clients with dual diagnoses; we also searched the professional literature. We decided that by modifying our ideas, we might be able to persuade the staff to consider them. We opted to propose that the clinic admit 15 group home residents on a trial basis and that those clients be assigned to our team (an alcoholism counselor who backed the idea was on our team). To gain support, we suggested that our supervisor assess the applicants' needs to be certain we could handle their needs. We also proposed that a nonconfrontational, skills-focused treatment group be formed for the clients. (The empirical literature on best practices and the other facilities recommended this type of group for adults with dual diagnoses.)

Selecting a Change Strategy. Social workers must make two decisions when selecting a change strategy. First, they must decide whether to intervene alone or with a task group. Because of the risks involved, the feelings evoked, line workers' relative lack of power, and the need to delegate tasks and responsibilities, organizational change from below usually involves group-based strategies. Individual strategies are more viable when social workers are more certain about views of key actors or have direct access to them.

Second, they must decide whether to use collaborative, mediatory, or conflict strategies (Brager & Holloway, 1978; McGowan, 1978). A collaborative strategy is characterized by open communication and joint action and works best when little disagreement exists about a problem and its solution, the participants' relative power is equal, and relationships are close. A mediatory strategy, which is distinguished by negotiation, persuasion, and political maneuvering, is used when a social worker hopes to reach a compromise despite some disagreement about the situation (see Fisher, Ury, & Patton, 1991; Simons, 1987). A conflict strategy, which is adversarial and coercive, is used only when the parties fundamentally disagree and a social worker decides that the agency will not respond to other strategies. Because this strategy is volatile, it is rarely used for internal change. In most situations, social workers use collaboration and mediation to influence their agencies, as did the two social workers at the Princeshire Clinic:

> We decided to recruit our supervisor and the alcoholism counselor on our team and form an ad hoc dual diagnosis study group to gain credibility and influence. They agreed, and our supervisor informed the director that we

□-□-□-□-□

Sidebar 12-2: Social Justice and Collaborative Empowerment

Social work is the only profession that identifies the pursuit of social and economic justice as a central organizing value (Marsh, 2005). From the days of the Charity Organization Societies and settlement houses, social workers have been committed to working with marginalized and disenfranchised groups to help them achieve equality and full participation in society. As professional agents employed in social and human service organizations, it is incumbent upon social workers to promote socially responsive, socially just organizational practices.

To ensure that organizational practices and policies remain socially just, it is useful for social workers to incorporate decision-making, monitoring, and evaluation strategies that involve clients and community residents in all phases of program design, implementation and evaluation (for example, Mattaini, 2001). Two practice and research perspectives, in particular, show good promise for authentic client and community partnership: evidence-based practice (EBP) decision-making paradigms (Gambrill, 2005) and participatory action research (PAR) methodologies (Healy, 2001; Weis & Fine, 2004).

EBP, which was developed initially in the field of medicine, is an approach to professional decision making in which social workers use their clinical expertise and experience to integrate the best external research evidence, a client's clinical state and circumstances, and client values and preferences to assist the client in resolving life problems and challenges (Hanson & Sealy, 2005; Haynes, Devereaux, & Guyatt, 2002). It is a transparent approach to professional practice, in which clients are equal partners who can guide social workers toward the assistance that is most acceptable to the clients. Because EBP has so much potential for promoting ethical and socially just practice, social workers should work within their agencies to help them become were meeting to discuss clinical issues that arose in assisting clients with mental disorders. To avoid arousing undue concern from other staff members, we decided not to invite staff from the group home to join the study group. We planned to meet with them periodically to share our ideas with them and to get their input.

We worked collaboratively to develop our ideas. Our limited experience with a few clients with co-existing substance use and mental disorders, who had "slipped through the cracks" in the intake process, suggested that we could help them. We were concerned about medication, but a case manager from the group home told us that the group home's psychiatrist would provide medication and case consultation.

We decided to use a mediatory strategy with the director, alcoholism counselors, and clients. We planned to appeal to the director's commitment to client care (a commitment that was a central element in our agency's culture) and point out how a creative program would impress funders and the

more receptive to this innovative approach to practice. A PAR approach to monitoring, evaluation, and organizational change can be useful in helping agencies adopt EBP decision-making paradigms.

PAR builds on Kurt Lewin's (1951) theory of action research. Two traditions in PAR focus on organizational reform and grassroots social transformation (Healy, 2001). A central premise of PAR is that the subjects of social research are the true experts in their experiences. Therefore, members of the organizations or communities under study are involved with the professional researcher in all phases of the research enterprise, from the initial study design to the presentation of findings and their implications (Roy & Cain, 2001; Weis & Fine, 2004). PAR strategies have been used effectively with a range of social work clientele, including people living with HIV/AIDS and Native Americans who have alcohol abuse problems. In one interesting project, a PAR methodology was used to identify organizational features that would increase a health care agency's capacity for innovation (Thomas et al., 2005). Those features include a clear structure and purpose, the creation of "learning spaces" (both physical and metaphorical) that provide opportunities to reflect and learn from work experiences, and participatory supervisory and management structures.

Although a comprehensive discussion of EBP and PAR is beyond the scope of this chapter, both paradigms complement the approach to organizational practice described in this chapter. Readers will benefit from exploring the references cited in this sidebar and incorporating the principles of PAR and EBP into their practice. As social workers and social work organizations become more collaborative and participatory, organizational processes will become increasingly empowering and socially just for individual clients, groups, and communities.

medical school. To reach the counselors, we considered discussing our limited experiences working with clients who were dually diagnosed at two of the weekly all-staff case conferences. We decided to address client concerns by asking the agency to purchase informational pamphlets on alcoholism and mental illness. We also planned to have the alcoholism counselor on our team speak about psychiatric symptoms in his alcohol education groups.

Preparing the Agency and Staff Members for Change. For change to occur, agency staff must become aware of the organizational problem, be dissatisfied with the status quo, and have hope that realistic options exist for correcting the problem. In short, a system that has organized itself around a problem must be destabilized. One can increase awareness and induce stress in several ways. Social workers can raise their concerns at staff meetings and in discussions with individual staff members. A relatively safe and effective tactic is to ask "informational questions" (Brager & Holloway, 1978). Workers simply ask questions (without suggesting answers) at staff meetings. Social workers can also induce stress if they pick up on any "general" dissatisfaction that exists and use this mood to challenge the myth that everything is okay.

Besides inducing stress, social workers must position themselves personally and structurally to maximize their capacity to promote change (Brager & Holloway, 1978; Mechanic, 1962). They can increase their personal influence by appealing to values and interests they share with other workers and by doing favors for them. They can gain credibility by developing knowledge and expertise on the problem situation and sharing their knowledge with others. Structurally, they can increase their power by aligning themselves with authority figures in an agency, by forming coalitions with informal peer leaders, and by joining committees that allow them to work directly on the problem, as the two social workers at the Princeshire Clinic did:

> Once we decided that our plan was feasible, we tried to increase our coworkers' awareness of the problem. At staff meetings we asked whether anyone was familiar with state initiatives for treating clients with dual diagnoses. We "wondered" what happened to "all the clients" that we sent away from the clinic. We also began to speak individually with some alcoholism counselors and offered to help those who were having trouble with some clients. Our supervisor met regularly with the clinic director and gave him written reports summarizing our agency visits and literature search. She also described anecdotal impressions from our clinical work with clients who were dually diagnosed.

As a result of our actions we began to notice a change in staff attitudes. They no longer reacted negatively when we asked about clients who had mental disorders. They also seemed interested in hearing about our experiences.

Initiating the Change Strategy. When agency members have been prepared, social workers can make their proposal public. At this time, they must decide to whom to make the proposal and how to make the presentation. They must also divide tasks and prepare a negotiating strategy. They should anticipate that they may be asked to modify their plans, and they should think about how to do so. They must shape their arguments, develop alternatives and trade-offs, and identify any leverage they have (Fisher et al., 1991). In this regard, the two Princeshire Clinic social workers took the following steps:

We decided that our supervisor should bring the proposal to the director. He respected her and had accepted her opinions on other matters. The alcoholism counselor and we would float the idea without its specifics among our coworkers. Although we knew that this approach was risky because someone might argue against the plan before it was fully outlined for the director, we hoped to prepare them for change and uncover any opposition.

Our supervisor proposed to the director that the clinic admit 15 group home residents and assign them to our team. A social worker and the alcoholism counselor would form and lead a skills-focused group for them with a goal of helping them establish sobriety. The group would meet twice a week for an hour. The group home's psychiatrist would continue to medicate the clients.

Our supervisor suggested that we monitor the group and make any required changes over the next 12 months. At that time we would write an evaluation report, so that the director could decide whether to continue the program.

The director agreed with our plans, but he decided to proceed more cautiously and incrementally. He agreed to admit only 10 applicants, and he reduced the evaluation period to six months. He also directed the supervisor to give him biweekly reports on the clients' progress. He said that he would expand the program if our initial results were promising. He reserved the right to abort the program at any time.

Monitoring, Evaluating, and Revising the Strategy. Once a proposal has been accepted, workers implement their plans. Among the challenges they face during this stage are maintaining the commitment of superiors, nurturing members of the task group, and maintaining links with other organizational operations. They must also handle any new opposition that arises, alter agency and program structures if needed, and standardize procedures to facilitate generalization and dissemination of the findings (Brager & Holloway, 1978; Gummer, 1990; Resnick & Patti, 1980).

The two social workers at the Princeshire Clinic described their experiences during this stage as follows:

> During the trial period, 15 clients with dual diagnoses were admitted to the clinic. Five were rehospitalized, so more than 10 people never attended the clinic at any given time. We discovered that we could not manage 10 clients in one group, so we formed two groups of five people.
>
> Some of the clients who were less compliant with medication schedules decompensated (experienced dramatic psychotic symptoms) in the waiting room. Much of the decompensation manifested itself as delusional and hallucinatory behaviors that were upsetting to other clients. The incidents also worried some staff who, at times, felt ill equipped to manage the clients. Thus, we had to respond to the fear and concerns that were generated. One activity that was particularly helpful involved having three clients with dual diagnoses and the group home's psychiatrist come to a staff meeting to talk about the problems they faced in recovery.
>
> Our study group continued to meet weekly, and our supervisor gave regular reports to the director. We closely monitored the clients' attendance at group and individual sessions, their drinking status, and their general level of functioning. At three months, we wrote a draft procedure for working with clients with dual diagnoses. At the end of six months, we delivered a final report, which the director presented at a staff meeting. Essentially, the outcomes of our project supported our initial ideas about treating clients with dual diagnoses in the clinic. We confirmed that the presence of clients with coexisting substance abuse and mental disorders did not disrupt clinic operations. Other clients continued to be treated in a timely manner, and clinic resources were not diverted from other areas. Moreover, clients with dual diagnoses seemed to benefit from our help. They attended regularly; six clients established between four and five months of continuous sobriety, and their adaptation to community living improved.
>
> The director accepted and revised our draft procedures and authorized us to continue to admit clients with dual diagnoses. He also began working with members of the agency's task environment to prepare a proposal cosponsored by the medical school to get state funding to expand services for the clients.

Postscript. As a result of the experiences described above, the Princeshire Clinic was able to secure state funding for an expanded day treatment program for clients with dual diagnosis. Over several years, monitoring efforts showed that the clinic continued to provide responsive and effective care for the clients. It was observed, however, that another population of clients with dual diagnoses was not being reached: adults living in homeless shelters. A review of the literature revealed that shelter residents were most effectively reached with shelter-based services. Because the clinic did not have the resources to provide those services, another hospital-based program in the clinic's task environment developed a collaborative demonstration project with a local shelter and the city's department of homeless services. The program secured federal funds to evaluate the utility of motivational interviewing (Miller & Rollnick, 2002), an intervention with a strong empirical evidence base in the addictions field, for treating homeless shelter residents with dual diagnoses. This latest iteration in service delivery illustrates how effective organizational practice can expand beyond an agency to influence service development within an agency's task environment and the community at large.

CONCLUSION

Social workers are organizational professionals who must decide every day how to help clients humanely and effectively. Inevitably, they will encounter agency arrangements that thwart their efforts and obstruct the fair delivery of care. Thus, it is crucial that they be willing and able to look beyond case work and explore all options for assisting people in need. We have learned a great deal about human service agencies in recent years. "No longer are [they] a backdrop, but rather—for good or ill—they are a significant reality" (Meyer, 1979, p. 12) in professional practice. To challenge dysfunctional organizational processes, social workers must develop a reflective skepticism about their agencies. They must be masterful clinicians who are knowledgeable about and skilled at organizational assessment and intervention. They must become conscious contrarians (Mondros & Wilson, 1994) who will question existing service arrangements and prod their agencies and other professionals to think critically about what they do. By starting with an attitude of helping people and a commitment to social justice, they will find the opportunity and courage to use their knowledge and skills to enhance their agency's capacity to serve clients and the common good.

REFERENCES

Ashkanasy, N. M., Wilderom, C.P.M., & Peterson, M. F. (Eds.). (2000). *Handbook of organizational culture and climate.* Thousand Oaks, CA: Sage Publications.

Bane, M. J., & Ellwood, D. T. (1994). *Welfare realities: From rhetoric to reform.* Cambridge, MA: Harvard University Press.

Bargal, D., & Schmid, H. (Eds.). (1992). Organizational change and development in human service organizations [Special issue]. *Administration in Social Work, 16*(3/4).

Barnard, C. (1968). *The functions of the executive.* Cambridge, MA: Harvard University Press.

Blau, P. M., & Scott, W. R. (1962). *Formal organizations: A comparative approach.* San Francisco: Chandler.

Bolman, L. G., & Deal, T. E. (2003). *Reframing organizations* (3rd ed.). San Francisco: Jossey-Bass.

Brager, G., & Holloway, S. (1978). *Changing human service organizations.* New York: Free Press.

Brager, G., & Holloway, S. (1992). Assessing prospects for organizational change: The uses of force-field analysis. *Administration in Social Work, 16*(3/4), 15–28.

Buckley, W. (1967). *Sociology and modern systems theory.* Englewood Cliffs, NJ: Prentice Hall.

Chernesky, R. H. (1998). Advancing women in the managerial ranks. In R. L. Edwards, J. A. Yankey, & M. A. Altpeter (Eds.), *Skills for effective management of nonprofit organizations* (pp. 200–218). Washington, DC: NASW Press.

Chernesky, R. H. (2005). Managing agencies for multicultural services. In E. P. Congress & M. J. Gonzalez (Eds.), *Multicultural perspectives in working with families* (2nd ed., pp. 38–67). New York: Springer.

Dane, B. O., & Simon, B. L. (1991). Resident guests: Social workers in host settings. *Social Work, 36,* 208–213.

Deal, T. E., & Kennedy, A. A. (1982). *Corporate cultures.* Reading, MA: Addison-Wesley.

Edwards, R. L., & Gummer, B. (1988). Management of social services: Current perspectives and future trends. In P. R. Keys & L. H. Ginsberg (Eds.), *New management in human services* (pp. 1–29). Silver Spring, MD: National Association of Social Workers.

Erlich, J. L., Rothman, J., & Teresa, J. G. (1999). *Taking action in organizations and communities* (2nd ed.). Dubuque, IA: Eddie Bowers Publishing.

Etzioni, A. (1964). *Modern organizations.* Englewood Cliffs, NJ: Prentice Hall.

Figueira-McDonough, J. (1993). Policy practice: The neglected side of social work intervention. *Social Work, 38,* 179–188.

Fisher, R., Ury, W., & Patton, B. (1991). *Getting to yes* (2nd ed.). New York: Penguin Books.

Frey, G. A. (1990). A framework for promoting organizational change. *Families in Society, 71,* 142–147.

Gambrill, E. (2005). Critical thinking, evidence-based practice, and mental health. In S. A. Kirk (Ed.), *Mental disorders in the social environment* (pp. 247–269). New York: Columbia University Press.

Gerth, H., & Mills, C. W. (Eds.). (1958). *From Max Weber: Essays in sociology.* New York: Oxford University Press.

Gibelman, M. (2003). *Navigating human service organizations: Essential information for thriving and surviving in agencies.* Chicago: Lyceum Books.

Gitterman, A. (1989). Testing professional authority and boundaries. *Social Casework, 70,* 165–171.

Gitterman, A., & Miller, I. (1989). The influence of the organization on clinical practice. *Clinical Social Work Journal, 17,* 151–163.

Gould, N. (2000). Becoming a learning organization: A social work example. *Social Work Education, 19,* 585–596.

Gould, N., & Baldwin, M. (Eds.). (2004). *Social work, critical reflection and the learning organization.* Burlington, VT: Ashgate Publishing.

Gouldner, A. (1963). The secrets of organizations. In *Social welfare forum 1963: Official proceedings, 90th annual forum* (pp. 161–177). New York: Columbia University Press.

Gummer, B. (1990). *The politics of social administration.* Englewood Cliffs, NJ: Prentice Hall.

Gutierrez, L. M. (1992). Empowering ethnic minorities in the twenty-first century: The role of human service organizations. In Y. Hasenfeld (Ed.), *Human services as complex organizations* (pp. 320–338). Newbury Park, CA: Sage Publications.

Gutierrez, L., GlenMaye, L., & DeLois, K. (1995). The organizational context of empowerment practice: Implications for social work administration. *Social Work, 40,* 249–258.

Gutierrez, L. M., & Lewis, E. A. (1999). *Empowering women of color.* New York: Columbia University Press.

Hage, J., & Aiken, M. (1970). *Social change in complex organizations.* New York: Random House.

Hanson, M., & Sealy, Y. (2005). Evidence-based marriage and family treatment with problem drinkers: A multicultural perspective. In E. P. Congress & M. J. Gonzalez (Eds.), *Multicultural perspectives in working with families* (2nd ed., pp. 339–355). New York: Springer.

Hartman, A. (1993). The professional is political [Editorial]. *Social Work, 38,* 365–366, 504.

Hasenfeld, Y. (1983). *Human service organizations.* Englewood Cliffs, NJ: Prentice Hall.

Hasenfeld, Y. (1987). Power in social work practice. *Social Service Review, 61,* 469–483.

Hasenfeld, Y. (1992a). The nature of human service organizations. In Y. Hasenfeld (Ed.), *Human services as complex organizations* (pp. 3–23). Newbury Park, CA: Sage Publications.

Hasenfeld, Y. (1992b). Theoretical approaches to human service organizations. In Y. Hasenfeld (Ed.), *Human services as complex organizations* (pp. 24–44). Newbury Park, CA: Sage Publications.

Hatch, M. J., & Cunliffe, A. L. (2006). *Organization theory: Modern symbolic and postmodern perspectives* (2nd ed.). New York: Oxford University Press.

Haynes, R. B., Devereaux, P. J., & Guyatt, G. H. (2002). Physicians' and patients' choices in evidence based practice [Editorial]. *British Medical Journal, 324,* 1350.

Healy, K. (2001). Participatory action research and social work: A critical appraisal. *International Social Work, 44,* 93–105.

Jackson, S. (1992). Team composition in organizational settings: Issues in managing an increasingly diverse workforce. In S. Worchel, W. Woods, & J. Simpson (Eds.), *Group process and productivity* (pp. 138–173). Newbury Park, CA: Sage Publications.

Johnson, D. W., & Johnson, R. (1989). *Cooperation and competition: Theory and research.* Edina, MN: Interaction Book Company.

Johnson, D. W., & Johnson, F. P. (2006). *Joining together: Group theory and group skills* (9th ed.). Boston: Allyn & Bacon.

Kanter, R. M. (1979, July–August). Power failures in management circuits. *Harvard Business Review,* 65–75.

Katz, D., & Kahn, R. L. (1978). *The social psychology of organizations* (Rev. ed.). New York: John Wiley & Sons.

Kurzman, P. A., & Akabas, S. H. (Eds.). (1993). *Work and well-being: The occupational social work advantage.* Washington, DC: NASW Press.

Lauffer, A. (1984). *Understanding your social agency.* Newbury Park, CA: Sage Publications.

Lawrence, P. R., & Lorsch, J. W. (1967). *Organization and environment: Managing differentiation and integration.* Boston: Harvard University Graduate School of Business Administration.

Lewin, K. (1951). *Field theory in social science.* New York: Harper.

Lipsky, M. (1984). Bureaucratic disentitlement in social welfare programs. *Social Service Review, 58,* 3–27.

Litwak, E. (1961). Models of bureaucracy which permit conflict. *American Journal of Sociology, 67,* 177–184.

Loden, M., & Rosener, J. B. (1991). *Workforce America! Managing employee diversity as a vital resource.* Homewood, IL: Irwin.

Lubove, R. (1965). *The professional altruist: The emergence of social work as a career, 1880–1930.* New York: Atheneum.

Marriott, A., Sexton, L., & Staley, D. (1994). Components of job satisfaction in psychiatric social workers. *Health & Social Work, 19,* 199–205.

Marsh, J. C. (2005). Social justice: Social work's organizing value. [Editorial]. *Social Work, 50,* 293–294.

Martin, P. Y. (1987). Multiple constituencies and performance in social welfare organizations: Action strategies for directors. *Administration in Social Work, 11*(3/4), 223–239.

Mattaini, M. A. (1993). *More than a thousand words: Graphics for clinical practice.* Washington, DC: NASW Press.

Mattaini, M. A. (with the PEACE POWER Working Group). (2001). *Peace power for adolescents: Strategies for a culture of nonviolence.* Washington, DC: NASW Press.

Mayo, E. (1945). *The social problems of industrial civilization.* Boston: Harvard University, Graduate School of Business Administration.

McGowan, B. G. (1978). Strategies in bureaucracies. In J. S. Mearig (Ed.), *Working for children: Ethical issues beyond professional guidelines* (pp. 155–180). San Francisco: Jossey-Bass.

Mechanic, D. (1962). Sources of power of lower participants in complex organizations. *Administrative Science Quarterly, 7,* 349–364.

Meenaghan, T. M., Gibbons, W. E., & McNutt, J. G. (2005). *Generalist practice in larger settings: Knowledge and skill concepts* (2nd ed.). Chicago: Lyceum Books.

Meyer, C. H. (1979). Introduction. In C. H. Meyer (Ed.), *Making organizations work for people.* Washington, DC: National Association of Social Workers.

Miles, R. E. (1975). *Theories of management.* New York: McGraw-Hill.

Miller, W. R., & Rollnick, S. (2002). *Motivational interviewing: Preparing people for change* (2nd ed.). New York: Guilford Press.

Mintzberg, H. (1979). *The structure of organizations.* Englewood Cliffs, NJ: Prentice Hall.

Mondros, J. B., & Wilson, S. M. (1994). *Organizing for power and empowerment.* New York: Columbia University Press.

Monge, P. R., & Contractor, N. S. (2001). Emergence of communication networks. In F. M. Jablin & L. L. Putnam (Eds.), *The new handbook of organizational communication: Advances in theory, research, and methods* (pp. 440–502). Thousand Oaks, CA: Sage Publications.

Morgan, G. (1997). *Images of organization* (2nd ed.). Thousand Oaks, CA: Sage Publications.

Netting, F. E., Kettner, P. M., & McMurtry, S. L. (2004). *Social work macro practice* (3rd ed.). New York: Longman.

O'Reilly, C., Caldwell, D., & Barnett, W. (1989). Work group demography, social integration, and turnover. *Administrative Science Quarterly, 34,* 21–37.

Perrow, C. (1961). The analysis of goals in complex organizations. *American Sociological Review, 26,* 856–866.

Perrow, C. (1978). Demystifying organizations. In R. C. Sarri & Y. Hasenfeld (Eds.), *The management of human services* (pp. 105–120). New York: Columbia University Press.

Perrow, C. (1986). *Complex organizations: A critical essay* (3rd ed.). New York: McGraw-Hill.

Resnick, H., & Patti, R. J. (Eds.). (1980). *Change from within: Humanizing social welfare organizations.* Philadelphia: Temple University Press.

Rhodes, M. L. (1991). *Ethical dilemmas in social work practice.* Milwaukee, WI: Family Service America.

Roethlisberger, F. J., & Dickson, W. J. (1975). *Management and the worker: An account of a research programme conducted by Western Electric Company, Hawthorne Works Chicago.* Cambridge, MA: Harvard University Press. (Original work published in 1939)

Rothman, J. (2001). Approaches to community intervention. In J. Rothman, J. L. Erlich, & J. E. Tropman (Eds.), *Strategies of community intervention* (6th ed., pp. 27–64). Itasca, IL: F. E. Peacock.

Roy, C. M., & Cain, R. (2001). The involvement of people living with HIV/AIDS in community-based organizations: Contributions and constraints. *AIDS Care, 13,* 421–432.

Sarri, R. C., & Hasenfeld, Y. (Eds.). (1978). *The management of human services.* New York: Columbia University Press.

Savage, A. (1987). Maximizing effectiveness through technological complexity. *Administration in Social Work, 11*(3/4), 127–143.

Schein, E. H. (1992). *Organizational culture and leadership.* San Francisco: Jossey-Bass.

Scott, W. R. (2003). *Organizations: Rational, natural, and open systems* (5th ed.). Englewood Cliffs, NJ: Prentice Hall.

Shafritz, J. M., Ott, J. S., & Jang, Y. S. (Eds.). (2005). *Classics of organization theory* (6th ed.). Belmont, CA: Thomson Wadsworth.

Simons, R. L. (1987). Generic social work skills in administration: The example of persuasion. *Administration in Social Work, 11*(3/4), 241–254.

Taber, M. A. (1987). A theory of accountability for the human services and implications for social program design. *Administration in Social Work, 11*(3/4), 115–126.

Terborg, J., Castore, C., & DeNinno, J. (1976). A longitudinal field investigation of the impact of group composition on group performance and cohesion. *Journal of Personality and Social Psychology, 34,* 782–790.

Thomas, P., McDonnell, J., McCulloch, J., While, A., Bosanquet, N., & Ferlie, E. (2005). Increasing capacity for innovation in bureaucratic primary care organizations: A whole system participatory action research project. *Annals of Family Medicine, 3,* 312–317.

Thompson, J. D. (1967). *Organizations in action.* New York: McGraw-Hill.

Toseland, R. W., & Rivas, R. F. (2005). *An introduction to group work practice* (5th ed.). Boston: Allyn & Bacon.

Vinter, R. D. (1959). The social structure of service. In A. J. Kahn (Ed.), *Issues in American social work* (pp. 242–269). New York: Columbia University Press.

Walsh-Bowers, R., Rossiter, A., & Prilleltensky, I. (1996). The personal is the organizational in the ethics of hospital social workers. *Ethics and Behavior, 6*, 321–335.

Weber, M. (1947). *The theory of social and economic organization* (A. H. Henderson & T. Parsons, Trans.). Glencoe, IL: Free Press. (Original work published 1924)

Weis, L., & Fine, M. (2004). *Working method: Research and social justice.* New York: Routledge.

Weissman, H., Epstein, I., & Savage, A. (1983). *Agency-based social work.* Philadelphia: Temple University Press.

Zald, M. N. (2001). Organizations: Organizations as politics; an analysis of community organization agencies. In J. Rothman, J. L. Erlich, & J. E. Tropman (Eds.), *Strategies of community intervention* (6th ed., pp. 133–144). Itasca, IL: F. E. Peacock.

13
□□□
Generalist Practice: People and Programs

Mark A. Mattaini

A s is clear from the chapters in this book, social work practice includes work with and for individuals, families, formed and natural groups, neighborhoods and communities, organizations, and even nations. The profession developed, in significant part, from separate professional groups that were working at each level; those groups came together as the National Association of Social Workers only in the 1950s. Until the 1970s, most graduate schools of social work were organized by "method"—casework, group work, community organization, and administration—and most students were trained for practice in only one method. With the work of Bartlett (1970) and others in the late 1960s and early 1970s, the "common base" of social work knowledge and values at all system levels was clarified. The result was generalist practice—an effort to expand the worker's knowledge base so that he or she could choose the most promising intervention strategy at the most appropriate level.

There are four requirements for selecting the most effective and efficient approach to dealing with client problems: (1) an understanding of the needs of the case arrived at collaboratively with the client, (2) the skills of practice at multiple system levels (as reflected in the preceding chapters), (3) knowledge of how to mix and phase those skills effectively within an evidence-based practice framework, and (4) a clear commitment to shared power. Much of social work practice happens through organizations and "programs" that—at least ideally—emerge and evolve in response to the particulars of the social aspirations and barriers to those aspirations. Basic program development skills are therefore an important facet of generalist practice. This chapter provides an overview of those skills.

Generalist practice is an organic whole, not simply an aggregation of roles. Although it may be necessary to learn practice in artificially discrete pieces, graduate-level practitioners ideally see themselves not as "group workers," "administrators," and "advocates" at different moments in time but as social workers engaged in activities that have coherence and flow.

Different functions require somewhat different skills (although many skills are useful at multiple levels). Skills for working with smaller systems are often also components of work with large systems. For example, empathic listening skills learned in work with individuals certainly are important in work with families and community members. Group work skills are important not only for small-group practice but also in organizational and community practice. Ultimately, the goal is to achieve a professional identity as a generalist social worker who does what is necessary to work in collaboration with the client to achieve the client's vision, at whatever system level(s) are most accessible and promising. Figure 13-1, for example, is an ecomap portraying the situation of a 32-year-old former client of mine, Robert, who was struggling with several issues, including depression, what he defined as a "sexual addiction" for which he participated in a 12-step group (which had not worked well for him), limited and conflicted interpersonal relationships, and vocational and economic failure.

Even practitioners who define themselves as clinical social workers might intervene with a client such as Robert individually, see him and his girlfriend together, have some contact with his parents, encourage him to try different Sex Addicts Anonymous groups, and refer him to other services. Generalist workers might identify additional potential points of intervention as well; they might design a new form of group service to address the needs of lonely and socially isolated clients (Gambrill, 1996) that includes ties to singles programs in synagogues, churches, and cultural organizations, or they might lead or participate in efforts to build new systems to improve vocational and educational access in the neighborhood. Any point on the ecomap, therefore, is fair game for a generalist practitioner as long as he or she has reason to believe that intervening at that point may help the client address his problems or achieve his goals.

CHANGING BEHAVIOR

All practice is about change, and change always involves action—behavior—of some kind, by someone. In some cases—for example, with people living with severe mental illness—the treatment goal may be to stabilize or sustain a current level of functioning and avoid deterioration. Even under those circumstances, if a need for social work exists, it is because someone must act to provide sufficient support for client action or to change or support actions by others in the environment. The required action may be overt, such as acting more assertively, or

FIGURE 13-1

◻◻◻◻◻

Ecomap Depicting Central Features of Robert's Case

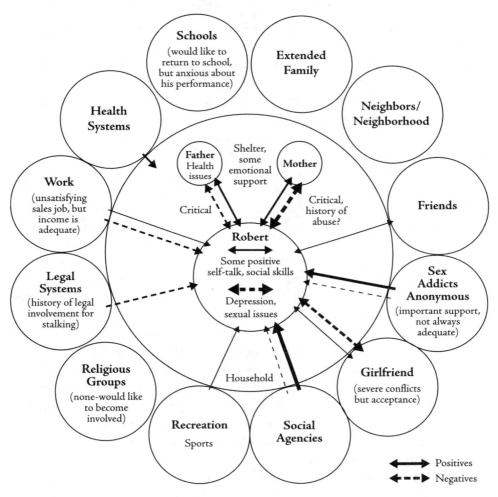

Note: All the arrows that represent interpersonal exchanges in the figure are thin, reflecting a high level of isolation.

covert, such as changing self-talk or learning to manage visceral activity, such as that involved in anger (see chapter 8). The same basic principles apply to the behavior involved, whether the goals in a particular case are to affect the actions of an individual client, modify patterns of behavior in a family, or advocate that representatives of a social institution relate differently to clients. Specific practice tasks, however, as well as ways of understanding the multivariate matrix within which behavior occurs, vary considerably in each situation, partly because of the increasing complexity of the phenomena of interest, which reductionistic thought cannot capture.

If the service contract developed collaboratively with a client calls for helping him or her to feel better emotionally, the social worker may model, prompt, and reinforce behavioral activation (Dimidjian et al., 2006) as well as encourage more accurate self-talk (that is, provide cognitive therapy). If the client's life situation is highly aversive (particularly if the situation involves serious oppression), a further level of complexity needs to be addressed. Under such circumstances, the social worker can work with the client to develop "experiments" in his or her own life space and to begin to take control of the factors that lead to his or her emotional struggles (an empowerment approach). In some cases, strong advocacy may also be required. Simply helping the client adjust to oppression or other very severe life conditions would not be a responsible goal of practice.

In many cases, the client's overt and covert behavior is shaped, prompted, and maintained by the actions of others. Depression, for example, can be deeply rooted in family and other social processes (Biglan, 1991; Brown & Harris, 1978; Jacobson et al., 2001) as well as in biological factors. Family therapists and those who work with people with severe behavioral problems have long recognized that if the behavior of one member of an interactive system changes, homeostatic forces will tend to return that person and the system to their previous state; the problems associated with returning delinquent youths to their previous living situation are a common example (Wolf, Braukmann, & Ramp, 1987). Systems theory and considerable research suggest, however, that if dramatic enough change occurs, the effects may reverberate and be amplified through other parts of the system, resulting in a new configuration. Family intervention often seeks this sort of meaningful and, it is hoped, irreversible "restructuring" (Minuchin, Colapinto, & Minuchin, 1998). Even more complicated patterns are present at higher system levels.

How do these abstract notions work in an operationalized sense? That is, how does one analytically determine the level at which to intervene? Interventions in transactional webs are best selected by identifying access points that are both most powerful and most accessible. For example, family systems tend to maintain repetitive patterns of interaction (that is, "structure," as described by Minuchin, 1974), which may or may not have positive outcomes for the family as a whole. Such patterns constitute the culture of the family. Transactional behaviors maintained by a group, which in the aggregate constitute group culture, are technically labeled "cultural practices" (Mattaini, 1999). A *culture* in this sense is a matrix of interlocking behaviors that occur within the group; ethnic groups have cultures, as do many other organized or self-organizing groups, including therapy and work groups, neighborhoods, organizations, and informal associations. Cultural groups encourage some actions and discourage others; for example,

+ Among some Asian groups, respect for elders is strongly reinforced within the group.
+ Dominant U.S. culture commonly discourages and often punishes actions that may be highly valued in queer culture.
+ In some treatment groups, the level of mutual confrontation is high; in others, confrontation is more tightly managed and contained.

Much social work practice involves working in a process of shared power with clients or participants to change patterns of cultural practices within self-organizing groups.

MULTIPLE OPTIONS IN GENERALIST PRACTICE

Examining the factors that maintain a problem behavior or missing factors that may support a goal behavior can suggest possible intervention strategies at multiple system levels. The contingency diagram in Figure 13-2 traces some of the factors related to instances of overly harsh, aggressive actions by a single parent toward a child (Lutzker, 1998; Mattaini, McGowan, & Williams, 1996). Figure 13-3, by contrast, depicts variables that may be associated with positive, alternative behavior that might be constructed. Both figures can be useful; Figure 13-2 helps provide a fine-grained understanding of why the problem occurs (partially answering the common question "How can someone hurt a child?"). Figure 13-3 suggests options that could support and increase positive parenting behaviors that are required for the family to move ahead. Increasing positive behaviors is usually the most important consideration, as parents typically will not give up problem behaviors unless they have better alternatives available. Careful analysis of the figures suggests that one could have an effect on those patterns in a variety of ways, including individual intervention (teaching the mother to respond to the child's provocation more effectively), family treatment (perhaps focused on reducing coercive exchanges and increasing the rate of positive exchanges), group work (for example, for parenting skills or mutual aid), community organizing (to strengthen social networks and reduce specific environmental stresses that affect the class of isolated single parents), establishing programmatic responses on an organizational basis (broad-based family support programs), or advocating for increased levels of basic resources (policy advocacy for family allowances, for example).

The generalist practitioner regards all of these options as possibilities in planning services and considers combinations that may produce synergistic effects. Within a shared power framework, clients and social workers together can consider the multiple options; each person involved can contribute to planning and

FIGURE 13-2

Factors Contributing to a High Rate of Aggressive,
Coercive Acts toward a Child by a Single Mother

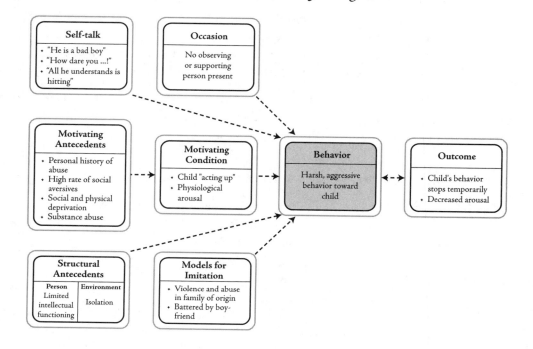

action from his or her own skills and strengths. Because every combination of clients and social workers is different and the context of every case is unique, the particular approach to intervention that is constructed may vary. Both the evidence-based practice process and the shared power perspective emphasize the importance of client voice and choice in decisions related to intervention. The following sections use the case of child maltreatment depicted in Figures 13-2 and 13-3 to illustrate intervention approaches at each level.

Individual Work with Parents

When a parent is overwhelmed, it may well make sense to begin individual work with him or her. For example, in one case, a mother was distressed because she believed her three-year-old son was disobedient; the mother often became enmeshed in verbal arguments with the child. Observations of the mother and son at home, however, indicated that the boy nearly always obeyed his mother and that the primary problem appeared to be that the mother displaced frustrations from other sources onto her child. If the pattern had continued, it is likely that the problems would have escalated because the child had begun to imitate

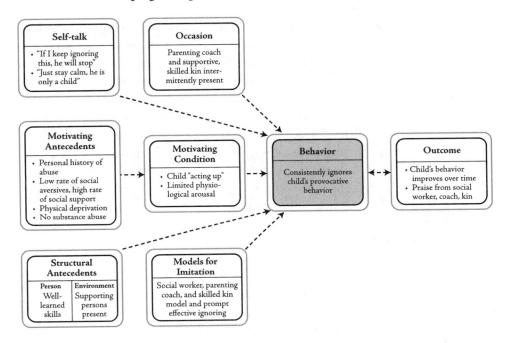

FIGURE 13-3

Factors Contributing to a More Effective Parenting Practice,
Consistently Ignoring the Child's Minor Provocative Behavior

Note: Although certain motivating antecedents (for example, history of abuse and current deprivation) are the same as in Figure 13-2, other stressors have been attenuated as the result of intervention. The level of parental arousal in the face of the child's behavior is therefore lower. Newly learned skills and added social supports in the mother's contextual situation also contribute to improvement in the child's behavior, as well as additional social reinforcement for the parent.

his mother's verbally aggressive modeling, which could lead to an abusive spiral (Patterson, 1976; Reid, Patterson, & Snyder, 2002). Interventions in this case focused on resolving the environmental issues that could be effectively addressed, developing new ways to cope with those that could not be changed, and building positive parent–child interactions characterized by positive reinforcement. Although individual intervention (with attention to environmental factors) was an efficient approach in this case, a primary focus on family interaction patterns may be indicated in other situations.

Family Consultation

Family intervention, which includes work on restructuring interactional patterns within the family, building bridges to external supports, and ameliorating stresses from multiple systems, is a demonstrably effective approach in families in which children are maltreated (Henggeler, Schoenwald, Borduin, Rowland, & Cunningham, 1998; Lutzker, 1998; Mattaini, McGowan, et al., 1996). This intervention strategy can be responsive to many of the multiple transactional factors associated with abuse (see Figure 13-2).

In family treatment, parents can learn new strategies for building relationships with the child and managing behavior less coercively; moreover, older children can be coached to deal with parents differently (Serna, Schumaker, Sherman, & Sheldon, 1991), and problems with other systems can be directly addressed. If the family members are seen at home, they can work with the practitioner to construct and practice new skills in the setting in which they need to be used, which reduces the problem of generalizing what is learned in a training situation to the home. Family consultation is a powerful and flexible strategy, but it can be expensive to deliver and does not offer the same potential for expanding social networks as do some group and community approaches. This network expansion may be crucial for "insular" parents (those who have few supportive social contacts), who have proved a particularly challenging subgroup of maltreating parents to help (Wahler, 1980).

Group Work

Parenting groups are a particularly common approach to reducing child maltreatment, partly because of their cost efficiency and partly because they sometimes offer unique advantages that other modalities may not. Parents who receive group training, for example, often find that the supportive network of the group can help them construct new family repertoires and help them find ways to address problems with other social systems (Brunk, Henggeler, & Whelan, 1987).

Parenting groups can be an effective approach for teaching both coping skills and specific parenting techniques. Nevertheless, evidence suggests that skills learned in a group may not generalize well to the home unless in-home coaching is a component of the program (Howing Wodarski, Gaudin, & Kurtz, 1989). Goldstein, Keller, and Erné (1985) found that the addition of the following four "transfer-enhancing" techniques enhanced generalization:

1. overlearning (the parent is given numerous opportunities to learn the skills to a high, almost automatic level of mastery)
2. stimulus variability (the parent learns to use the skills under an intentionally wide range of conditions, not simply in one way with one co-actor in a parenting group)
3. identical elements (skills learned in the group are practiced in exactly the same way with parent aides in the home at a later time)

4. programmed reinforcement (parent aides are specifically trained to note and reinforce use of new skills in the home).

Without such additional elements, many parents do not consistently transfer what they learn in groups to the home. Research suggests that transfer of skills from one setting to another does not usually occur unless it is explicitly designed into the program; see Stokes & Baer, 1977).

Recent work has shown the dramatic advantages of working with parents or families in multifamily groups. Webster-Stratton, for example, found that parenting education in groups became progressively more effective when it moved from a focus on parenting skills alone to include mutual support, and it became even more effective when an emphasis on building bridges to community systems was incorporated (Webster-Stratton, 1997; Webster-Stratton et al., 2001). The recent movement toward community-centered practice with families (Schorr, 1997; Sviridoff & Ryan, 1997) is consistent with those findings; not surprisingly, for generalist social workers the boundaries between work with families, group work, and community practice must be highly permeable, as seen in the next section.

Community and Organizational Practice

Strong evidence, both on a broad statistical level and from intensive observation of cases, has indicated that parental stress level is a significant contributor to child maltreatment. For example, Wahler (1980) found that a mother's increased number of positive contacts with friends on a particular day was associated with reductions in the number of mother–child problems occurring that day and that to achieve long-term success, it is crucial to address this factor. One effective response to such findings is to work with individual parents to enrich their social experiences. Many communities, however, have a large number of at-risk parents in similar circumstances, and service organizations or community groups can develop practical responses that can serve many individuals at the same time. For example, Wolfe (1991) and associates incorporated informal activity groups in a community setting as a component of an abuse prevention program that also included individual behavioral training, guidance in parenting, and the availability of respite care.

Lightburn and Kemp (1994) described a family support program with which they were associated for some time that not only is deeply rooted in the community but also emphasizes obtaining feedback from the community, developing community among the participants, and using an educational and mutual aid approach that deliberately builds on historic roots in the settlement house movement. As Lightburn and Kemp reported, clients can make excellent use of "learning collectives," which take advantage of resources in the group to develop and test alternative life strategies. This program is an outstanding example of the use of a shared power perspective on practice, and the research indicates that such programs can have multiple positive effects (Comer & Fraser, 1998). Conversely, not all such programs do; in one analysis (Goodson, Layzer, St. Pierre, Bernstein, & Lopez, 2000), no positive effects were identified. The need for an evidence-based approach is clear. In one large example, the Health Realization Institute (2000; see also Saleebey, 2006) reported a wide range of positive changes in family relationships, delinquency and drug trafficking, school performance, and other indicators using emerging techniques of community-building "from the inside out" that rely heavily on shared power, identification of assets within the community, and a focus on the community's own vision of where it would like to be.

Even high-level community interventions, such as those targeting economic development or the reduction of drug-related problems, are likely to have an effect on the incidence of child maltreatment. As suggested by Saleebey (2006), neighborhood empowerment and the resilience of individuals and families within the neighborhood are organically and inseparably intertwined, and the most effective programs, particularly in distressed communities, are those that are not just located in but are deeply embedded in the neighborhood (Schorr, 1997). In fact, the design of effective programming involves all four of the perspectives discussed in chapter 2 in this volume: a view of the ecological field within which family struggles and efforts occur, explicit recognition of issues of oppression and social justice that have an impact on the family, a clear emphasis on shared power within the family and the community that avoids colonial relationships, and a commitment to evidence-based practice. The last two elements need to be considered together; a dynamic of shared power among community participants is essential (Fawcett, 1991) but is not by itself enough. Several studies reviewed in Embry (2004) have suggested that community empowerment approaches that do not include careful attention to effectiveness research may result in no change, or even deterioration; other research clarifies evidence-based kernels (simple, low-cost practices) that can be incorporated into a wide range of programming (Embry).

Policy Advocacy

As powerful as intervention with individuals and collectives can be, sometimes the obstacles to achieving client vision—or the resources needed to do so—lie outside the family and community. They may lie within the social worker's own organization or often in what Bronfenbrenner (1979) described as the "exosystem"—formal social institutions that have an impact on the family despite being at some remove. Addressing those obstacles or accessing those resources may require changes in organizational, institutional (for example, school districts), or local, state, or national government policy. Policy advocacy, too, is part of generalist practice, although the formal skills of policy analysis and policy practice are often taught primarily in social policy courses within schools of social work.

Hoefer (2006) indicated that policy advocacy requires a range of skills, beginning with understanding the issue: Who is affected, and how? What are the main causes of the problem, what options for intervention exist, and what are the social justice implications of each option? In fact, analyzing the causes of the problem and possible steps to resolve it may require an analysis like that shown in Figure 13-3, but the focus is on the behavior of the systems actors who control the resources rather than on the client. What would it take to change those actors' behavior? Who has, or could have, influence on them?

Once the issue is clearly understood, the next steps are strategic and tactical: determining the approach to be used (for example, collaboration, negotiation, persuasion, or coercion) and the specific steps to be taken (Hoefer, 2006; Rothman, Erlich, & Tropman, 2001; Tropman, Erlich, & Rothman, 2001). In addition, the necessary skills for this kind of work involve all levels of practice, including empathic listening, public speaking, working with media, and building advocacy coalitions. In many cases, social workers' advocacy efforts are closely related to their everyday practice, but it is also common for social workers to become involved in social justice issues about which they have deep concerns, even if these issues are largely unrelated to their jobs.

Interweaving Levels

Of course, if a family is referred because a child is in imminent danger, the social worker would ordinarily not devote most of his or her professional energies to economic development or to advocacy for income support. Still, work at every level has the potential to powerfully contribute to envisioned client goals. Multi-level strategies commonly need to be interwoven over time (see, for example, Rothman, 2001, p. 58, who discussed this process as the "mixing" and "phasing" of strategies). One may see a parent in a skills-training group, provide family-based consultation in the home, refer the parent to an ongoing support group, and advocate for support for additional community-level resources. Of course, the social worker can only do so effectively if he or she understands the problem in depth and has the skills to intervene at those multiple levels. For this reason, training in generalist practice is crucial, even though it is not possible to be equally versed in everything. At the very least, the social worker should know when to refer a client to a person with other skills or a program with other resources; ideally, he or she should know how to provide a rich array of services as well.

One way to begin thinking this way is to identify interventions at multiple levels that could benefit one's clients. Although the reader may find it valuable to complete this exercise individually, groups of students (who are likely to have different strengths and perspectives) may be able to develop a richer array of service options. (See Exercise 13 in Appendix C for details of this procedure.) Ideally, a social worker should be able to identify more than one possible intervention strategy at each system level; further analysis and collaboration with clients should then help him or her select the most potentially effective and efficient strategies.

An implicit case-to-class (or case-to-cause) phenomenon is present in generalist practice. If the social worker sees or learns from others in the agency that all the staff members are seeing a number of similar cases, it may make sense to step back and think about programmatic approaches that can efficiently respond to the issues that the class of clients are collectively facing. A "planner" may also propose a programmatic response, but practitioners who are intimately and analytically familiar with the issues, in concert with clients (who are even more deeply embedded in the issues and have a different form of knowledge), may be more likely to develop programs that genuinely address the clients' needs. Practitioners have an organic tie to the realities of the issues, as opposed to an exclusively abstract understanding of them.

PROGRAM PLANNING, DESIGN, AND DEVELOPMENT

Program planning, design, and development are not the exclusive province of administrators or planners, who often have only limited knowledge of the realities and complexities of clients' lives. Organizations and the programs they offer often do not work well for people (Meyer, 1979). Given the stubbornness of many social problems (and the current state of knowledge), even the best-designed and best-implemented programs may produce marginal results in many cases. Effective programs that genuinely meet client needs and respond to social problems are more likely to be designed by or with extensive input from practitioners who have been immersed in the issues for some time in shared power collaborations with clients and other agency staff. Moreover, in an organization that has a genuine commitment to shared power, clients and community members will have strong voices in program planning and evaluation. Every social worker, therefore, needs an understanding of the program development cycle and how to incorporate stakeholders into that cycle.

The following material outlines the typical program development process, which has many variations in practice. Not all programs develop in this way, and the process is usually recursive, circling back on itself. A social worker may be involved only in parts of this process (for example, joining a project after the assets and needs assessment has been completed or being responsible only for reworking program design in response to an uneven evaluation). A general framework for program development, adapted from Kettner, Moroney, and Martin (1999), is portrayed in Figure 13-4. Note that although a general direction (clockwise) is portrayed in the figure, it is common for program developers to circle back to earlier stages, particularly if the program appears not to be working as well as it might.

Envisioning and Problem Analysis

Programs emerge to assist groups of clients to achieve an improved state or to address social problems and common difficulties experienced by a class of people (as opposed to "private troubles" affecting only one individual). Program design should flow directly from analysis of the current (problem) state and the envisioned goal state. One essential point is that issues should not be defined simply as a lack of services (Kettner et al., 1999). For example, a lack of foster care or of inpatient drug rehabilitation facilities is not a social problem, and more foster care homes is usually not the vision that clients or staff really wish to achieve. Those services are responses to social problems or steps toward achieving a desired vision. Defining the problem in terms of lack of a particular service profoundly limits the consideration of alternative options (for example, one would not even consider intensive home-based services to prevent and respond to family breakdown if the problem is defined as lack of foster care). Family breakdown should, in that case, be the problem to be analyzed and family health the vision to be achieved.

FIGURE 13-4

□ □ □ □ □

Program Development Cycle

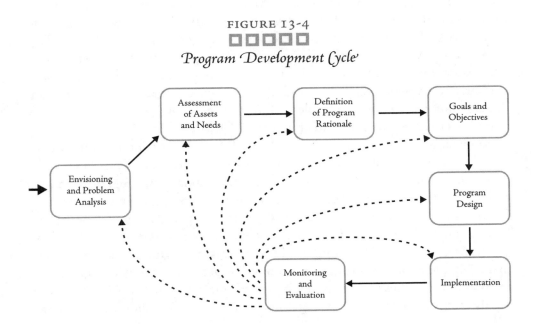

Although they are often excluded, clients, participants, or community members should be key partners at all stages of program planning; the level of involvement may vary at different stages. Client and community perspectives are critical, however, at the level of envisioning. Key stakeholders can always be brought to the table in some way, and no one is more critical to setting program direction than those who are most directly affected by the program. Their vision should be honored to the maximum possible extent. This vision emerges from community values and preferences, which are key to effective and noncolonial programming (Fawcett, 1991).

Traditional approaches to program development have customarily emphasized problems to be solved, but in recent years, a "constructional" approach (Goldiamond, 2002) has increasingly been emphasized. In a constructional approach, the emphasis is on what is to be built rather than on what is wrong. It is the difference, for example, between emphasizing psychiatric diagnosis and treatment for youth versus emphasizing positive youth development by increasing protective factors.

Analysis generally begins by examining what is known about the current (problem) state both locally (by contact with people who are affected) and more globally (by searching the literature to explore the problem's etiology and epidemiology and available responses). Both obvious and subtle social justice dimensions are involved in the social construction of social issues and the development of responses to them. Those dimensions must be explicitly identified and considered in exploring programmatic options. Questions to be explored include the following: Are oppression, injustice, or violations of human rights part of the issue? Who, if anyone, benefits from the current situation, and who is particularly at risk? Do commonly suggested responses genuinely provide adequate help, or do they merely buttress the status quo? Investigation of factors that may affect program design (such as cultural factors that influence which responses are likely to be most acceptable) and of alternative conceptual frameworks for understanding the issue is valuable at this stage and may provide a wider range of options that are more consistent with social justice.

Knowledge of current problems can be useful (and is commonly more widely available than information about the state to be achieved). Problems often serve as a "ticket into services." Quickly, however, the emphasis in program planning should move toward understanding the envisioned goal state and the kinds of resources that could help construct it. What factors protect young people from joining gangs? What resources are helpful to young people as they negotiate dangerous neighborhoods? What kinds of resources assist highly stressed parents in managing their children's behavior in ways that promote healthy child development? Contrast these with problem-focused questions such as "What causes highly stressed parents to beat their children?" Knowledge about the latter can be useful but by itself does not move the program planners toward what needs to be in place. In addition, as in many other areas of practice, an emphasis on what is to be built can be hopeful and energizing, whereas an emphasis on problems and pathology can be demoralizing and have a negative impact on relationships with clients. Problems are not ignored, but they are not the primary focus in planning.

The first step in the program development cycle, therefore, is a clear statement of the problem to be solved or, better, the goal state to be achieved. Some understanding of the answers to questions such as "How are we defining our goals and problems?" "Who is defining the goal or problem as important?" and "What social values are supported by the vision or threatened by the problem?" can help refine the initial statement of goals. The goals statement is likely to be progressively refined throughout the program development process.

Assets and Needs Assessment

The assessment process should begin with a clear definition of the population or geographic area to be served by the program. Although traditional program development has begun and ended by assessing needs, program developers are increasingly recognizing that focusing on needs to the exclusion of assets provides a negatively biased view of the community. All communities include many assets, and those assets can typically be built upon to reach goals (Saleebey, 2006). In some cases, only an inventory of available assets is needed to achieve goals, and a needs assessment can be an unnecessary distraction. In other cases (for example, determining the incidence of certain medical or psychiatric conditions in a community), a needs assessment is required, but without an accompanying assets assessment, it may result in an excessively negative view of what can be a hopeful situation.

Kretzmann and McKnight (1993) provided perhaps the most comprehensive descriptions of completing community assets assessments. They do not begin by inventorying agencies and institutions in a community; rather, they begin by looking at the talents and resources of individuals and voluntary associations within the community—resources that are often completely overlooked by program planners. McKnight's (1997) perspective is that continued expansion of formal agency services over the years has been accompanied by escalating problems—problems always outnumber available services. In fact, McKnight expressed concern that agencies sometimes have a vested interest in increasing the number of clients and therefore have little incentive to work to address root causes of problems.

McKnight (1997) therefore suggested that far more emphasis be placed on community-building and human development efforts that harness other resources: individuals, businesses, churches, police, cultural institutions, libraries, parks, hospitals, physical assets of the community, and citizens' associations. Service agencies are not ignored but are only one necessarily limited sector within this vision. For McKnight, a needs assessment may produce an image of a "needy, problematic and deficient" client community; far better to begin by mapping a community of citizens with capacities and assets.

When traditional needs assessment is required as an adjunct to the assessment of assets, the social worker and the agency must usually learn how many clients or potential clients the problem affects, in what ways, and to what extent. If the agency is responsible for child protective services or preventive services in a large geographic area, with thousands of potential clients who are at high risk for abuse or neglect, its program must obviously be different from one designed to meet the moderate needs of a few families. Needs assessment provides the data required to answer questions about the extent of clients' needs.

Although it is possible—and sometimes necessary—to implement complex and expensive assessments of assets and needs, even a relatively modest strategy may be able to produce adequate data from which to proceed. Neuber and associates (1980) suggested the three-pronged strategy depicted in Figure 13-5. Note that Neuber designed this model for assessing needs, but it is applicable to the assessment of both needs and assets. As shown in the diagram, assessment can begin by examining existing data sources; both quantitative, statistical data and qualitative data may be of value. Another major source of data is key informants, including professionals, community leaders, and others who are immersed in the local situation. Through interviews (or occasionally questionnaires), those persons can provide information that captures the unique dimensions of the problem in the service area.

Potential or actual program participants, clients, and consumers can provide rich, grounded data that are essential to understanding the problem and developing responsive programs. Consumers' perceptions may differ dramatically from those of staff or other key informants, sometimes as a result of cultural or class differences and sometimes simply because their experiences of life, community, and services have been different. A social worker walking into a school experiences an almost entirely different institution than does a second grader who is being bullied, for example.

Although maximizing consumer involvement in needs assessment involves work, the data consumers provide are different from what can be obtained in any other way and are required in organizations that authentically value the sharing of power. Approaches to asset and needs assessment vary along the dimensions of community involvement and empowerment, breadth, and rigor (Kretzmann & McKnight, 1993; Marti-Costa & Serrano-Garcia, 2001). In some cases, questionnaires or interviews conducted at places where current or potential participants or community members are likely to be found may be the most efficient

FIGURE 13-5

□ □ □ □ □

Comprehensive Needs Assessment Framework

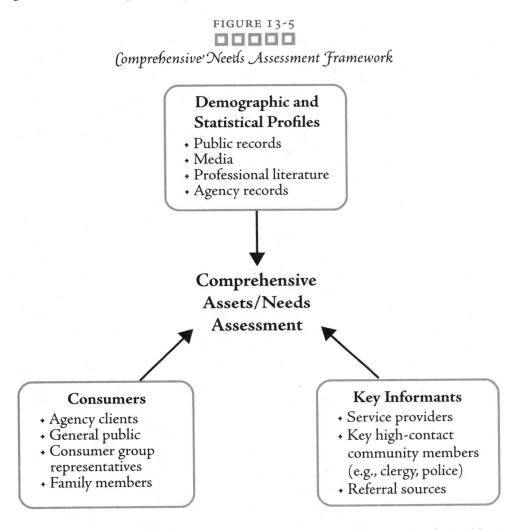

**Demographic and
Statistical Profiles**

+ Public records
+ Media
+ Professional literature
+ Agency records

**Comprehensive
Assets/Needs
Assessment**

Consumers

+ Agency clients
+ General public
+ Consumer group
  representatives
+ Family members

Key Informants

+ Service providers
+ Key high-contact
  community members
  (e.g., clergy, police)
+ Referral sources

Source: Neuber, K.A., & Associates. (1980). *Needs assessment: A model for community planning.* New-bury Park, CA: Sage Publications.

approach. Focus groups are a powerful option when they can be arranged. The use of multiple methods (for example, Weis & Fine, 2004) may provide the richest data for planning. It is valuable to think through multiple options with key stakeholders, including community members and consumers, before deciding how to proceed. Relying only on staff or professional perceptions runs the risk of programming driven by "philanthropic paternalism" (Kissane, 2003), which may satisfy the needs of everyone except the participants, thus perpetuating injustice.

The social worker may not always have the resources or institutional sanction to complete a full assets and needs assessment. An administrator may define the broad parameters of the program on the basis of long experience, essentially using him- or herself as the only key informant, and instruct the practitioner how to proceed. Even under those circumstances, examining the relevant literature to enrich the work is a low-cost strategy (and an ethical imperative), and informal contact with other informants and service participants often can be incorporated seamlessly into planning.

Establishing the Program Rationale

An effective program intervenes in the multicausal chain that could construct the envisioned goal state (or that produces and maintains the problem). Program developers who have not thought this chain through explicitly usually produce programs that fail to work well because they are likely to neglect many of the most important factors involved in complex issues. If an organization is charged with preventing child abuse, a worker may decide, on the basis of his or her own interest, that the program should consist of a six-session educational group to teach at-risk parents about child development and what they can realistically expect from their children. The implicit causal chain suggests that the lack of knowledge and unrealistic expectations contribute to abuse and that increased knowledge will improve parenting. As it happens, the available data do not generally support this model (Wolfe, 1991). Other approaches are better supported by theory and research. For example, it is known from the literature that isolation and poverty increase the risk of child maltreatment. Programs that target those factors and provide explicit guidance for dealing effectively with parenting challenges are much more likely to be effective than the developmental educational model mentioned above (Lutzker, Bigelow, Doctor, Gershater, & Greene, 1998).

In a more detailed example, work conducted by the PEACE POWER Working Group (Mattaini, 2001, 2006) on youth violence prevention suggested that youth participate in a number of subclusters of violent incidents, most of which may need to be addressed in a comprehensive prevention program (Mattaini, Twyman, Chin, & Lee, 1996). One of those clusters involves threatening or violent action to save face (for example, when confronted by someone in authority, such as a teacher) (see Figure 13-6). A number of factors, as shown in the figure, contribute to such behavior:

- a history in which threats of violence lead people to back down from the confrontation and in which threats and violence are associated with gaining or maintaining status
- a life filled with many other aversives that increase the negative valence of confrontation and the positive valence of escaping confrontation

FIGURE 13-6
🞏🞏🞏🞏🞏

Factors Shaping and Maintaining Threatening or
Violent Responses to Confrontation by a Person in Authority

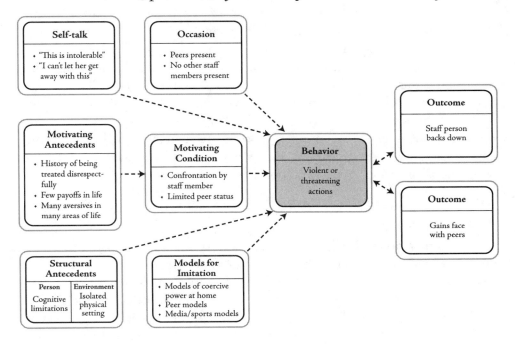

- models of violent response to confrontation
- self-talk suggesting that confrontation is equivalent to intolerable disrespect.

An effective prevention program may address those and other factors. The program rationale, in other words, grows from an understanding of the reasons why the problem occurs and what is known about effective prevention. Participant or community involvement is useful here, as it is in all other stages. The professional, of course, has a special role in that he or she should have a deep grounding in the related knowledge base and strong skills in locating the most current information. Participants or community members, however, are often in the best position to determine how that knowledge maps onto the unique setting and context.

The program rationale can be framed as one or more "if–then–because" statements (for example, "If young people are exposed to models who deal with confrontation in assertive but respectful ways, then the rate of threats and violence will decrease, because through social learning the young people will learn alternative, less socially costly and more effective behavioral repertoires from those models"). The program rationale for a prevention program aimed at youth violence will necessarily involve a number of such statements because we know that causes of and supports for youth violence—and for development of positive alternative repertoires—are multiple. In fact, consistent with the constructional emphasis of this chapter, the most useful programs appear to be those that involve the construction of cultures of nonviolent power in families, organizations, and communities (Erickson, Mattaini, & McGuire, 2004). Also, thinking in generalist terms, multiple options for having an impact on any particular link in the causal network are usually available. For example, models of alternative ways of coping with confrontation could come through individual work, youth–adult collaboration on developing videotapes to model positive action, contact with positive mentors, group skills training, and many other approaches.

Goals and Objectives

Once the program rationale is clear, the goals and objectives flow directly from the conceptual model. The range of real options is constrained by contextual and organizational factors and limited resources. Sometimes, the program may be able to address only a subset of the relevant factors, and in some cases the program may need for political reasons to include components that the social workers designing it do not believe are central but that other crucial stakeholders do.

Goals are usually defined as general statements about what the program is meant to achieve ("to reduce the incidence of child maltreatment in Columbia County"), whereas objectives are specific, measurable parts of the goals. To the extent possible, goals should be stated in constructional terms related to what is to be built, but funding requirements may dictate that goals be stated in problem terms.

Major categories of objectives include the following:

+ Impact objectives, which target changes in the overall incidence or prevalence of a specific goal state or a problem among a specific population. For example,
    – to increase the number of schools adopting the PEACE POWER strategy for constructing cultures of nonviolent empowerment by 20 percent by July 1, 2011
    – to reduce the rate of repeated reports of child abuse and neglect in the county by 20 percent by July 1, 2011.
+ Outcome objectives, which target change (usually short term) among program participants. For example,

- to increase the number of written recognition notes completed by staff by 10 percent per month over a six-month period, as measured by a weekly count of posted recognition notes
- to decrease the use of power-assertive discipline techniques among parents identified by the county child protective services agency by 70 percent after eight sessions, as measured by videotaped observations of parent–child interactions.

♦ Process objectives, which describe program activities or inputs. For example,

- to provide 270 home visits during 2011, as reported by the agency's management information system
- to maintain a monthly average of 200 downloads of positive youth development tools from the project Web site during 2011, as measured by web statistics.

These types of objectives are hierarchical; impact objectives (which may be difficult to evaluate, given limited resources) usually have one or more outcome objectives associated with them. Outcome objectives, in turn, often have one or more process objectives associated with them. Note that each objective, of whatever type, should be clear, specific, and have clear timelines for completion. Statements of objectives should also include strategies for measurement. After goals and objectives have been determined, the social worker and others involved in program development must determine exactly who will do what to achieve the goals—the process of program design.

Program Design

Goals and objectives can be used in at least two ways. First, they should be used as the basis for program evaluation (discussed below). Second, they are important for planning the activities to be included in the program, although by themselves they provide only partial guidance. Setting an objective related to reducing the rate of depression among a group of young single mothers, for example, is a useful starting point. Such an objective, however, does not tell one much about how it will be achieved. That decision is made on the basis of the conceptual program rationale that emerged from the envisioning process and the assets and needs assessment. If social isolation is hypothesized to be a major causal factor in maintaining the young mothers' depression, for example, program activities that flow from this analysis may include support groups and case management to enhance positive connections with natural networks.

Program activities defined at this abstract level, however, are just strategies for addressing the issue; tremendous variation exists among "support groups," for example. Adequate program design includes clear specification of who will do what and when—who will lead the group, who will attend, what the schedule and structure of the group will be, and what activities will occur in the group meetings. Although some relatively clear plans should be in place before the program begins, in most cases activities will evolve over time, on the basis of ongoing evaluation of how well the program is meeting its objectives.

Program Implementation

Program implementation generally requires the cooperative, coordinated effort of groups of people (line staff, supervisors, administrators, support staff, and clients). These individuals often function as members of task groups (staff groups, committees, and interdisciplinary teams) that must work effectively if the program is to be well implemented. Social workers and others have studied effective task groups and have learned that it is possible for social workers, whether as group leaders or as members of groups, to work toward more effective team functioning (Toseland & Rivas, 2005; Tropman, 1996). Specific techniques for encouraging effective teamwork and empowerment are now available, and every social worker involved in programming should be familiar with them (Daniels, 2000).

Beyond the specifics of task group work, agency context and culture also have major effects on program implementation. It is possible—but apparently uncommon—to construct an explicit "empowerment culture" in an organization (Lowery & Mattaini, 1999; Minuchin et al., 1998). Certain practices, including those listed below, are characteristic of such an organization across all levels:

+ authentic dialogue in which all participants have strong voices, as opposed to hierarchical arrangements rooted in adversarial power. Foster parents, for example, feel respected and heard in planning.
+ information freely shared among stakeholders, rather than used to consolidate competitive positions. Line workers are aware, for example, of the fiscal resources available to the program.
+ evaluation activities that are inclusive; all actors are heard in the process. For instance, biological parents review and contribute to evaluation materials that are submitted to courts.
+ case activities that are carried out on the basis of shared contribution and responsibility, so that actors such as foster or biological parents participate from their strengths and their roles can expand as their expertise grows.

Such organizational practices do not emerge automatically; practices in other parts of the organization, particularly groups with administrative and supervisory responsibilities, must be carefully designed to support shared power.

Staff members who are involved in implementing programs must be trained and supervised. It is usually a mistake to assume that staff members already have the knowledge and skills required to implement a program and will apply them effectively. Every program is different, and some level of training is almost always required, in part to give staff members opportunities to think through how to apply their knowledge and talents in a new setting. Even highly competent staff members may not apply their knowledge effectively under new conditions without explicit attention to staff development (Windsor, Clark, Boyd, & Goodman, 2003).

Effective supervision does not involve speaking "longer, louder and meaner" (Daniels, 2000, p. 17) to obtain improved performance. Rather, it primarily involves the following steps, which are usually best done collaboratively with the staff involved:

+ Pinpoint what needs to be done.
+ Find ways to track (measure) whether it is happening.
+ Provide feedback on performance.
+ Reinforce performance, particularly discretionary "extra effort."
+ Evaluate whether staff activity is leading to achievement of objectives.

This model, drawn from Daniels (2000), has broad applicability. By itself, it does not capture every situation, but the framework can help social workers achieve excellence and resolve problems in most situations. The literature on social work supervision provides additional guidance. One important way to pinpoint what should be done clinically, for example, is to ask questions in staff supervision, such as "What does the client want help with?" and "What are you doing to help the client?" (Harkness & Hensley, 1991). Reinforcing what the person is doing right is much more effective than simply giving orders and criticizing inadequate performance. According to research conducted by Komaki (1998) and others (e.g., Daniels, 2000; Malott, 2003), key features of effective leadership include high levels of monitoring (especially in the beginning) that are followed relatively quickly with consequences, particularly recognition of positive contributions, encouragement, and opportunities to describe how one achieved positive outcomes. The concept of the "emotional bank account" is useful; supervisees respond better to corrective feedback if they receive at least three times as many "deposits" (recognition and appreciation for contributions) as "withdrawals" (instances of corrective feedback) (Latting, 1992).

Most graduate social workers develop programs that require staff development, effective team functioning, and supervision of other staff. Generalist social workers should be prepared to take on those functions when the practice situation requires.

Program Evaluation

As seen in previous chapters, monitoring practice is an organic part of all social work practice at all levels. Program evaluation can be thought of as practice monitoring at a programmatic level; in fact, data collected in routine practice monitoring can often be aggregated for program evaluation purposes. Determining what the program is doing and how well it is doing it can be a natural part of the process. Social workers may find it surprising to realize how little effort it takes to evaluate programs if they are designed from the beginning with a curiosity about and a commitment to finding out how well they are working.

Program evaluation is a professional discipline in itself, and some organizations and individuals specialize exclusively in performing evaluations, which can become complex and expensive (Rossi, Freeman, & Lipsey, 2003). Most programs, however, do not need to expend so much effort to make a credible beginning at evaluation. Although program evaluation can be categorized in many ways, it generally is either formative or summative. A formative (Windsor et al., 2003) or developmental (Berk & Rossi, 1998) evaluation takes place as the program is initiated and implemented and is intended primarily to address questions such as the following:

+ Is the program reaching enough of the at-risk population?
+ How much service is being provided?
+ How many resources, and of what kinds, are being expended?

Summative evaluations are designed to determine how a program has fared during a specified period of time, and they examine performance on the basis of process objectives (program activities and inputs), outcomes for clients, and sometimes impact on the target community. These factors can be combined with data about expenditures to perform cost-effectiveness and cost-benefit analyses.

Program evaluation is not about producing reports, of course. It is ultimately meaningless unless what is learned from the evaluation is fed back into the program development process to help sharpen goals and objectives and to improve services to clients. It is a common but serious mistake to think that one undertakes a program evaluation primarily to satisfy funders, although such pressures are real and increasing. Rather, evaluations, if thoughtfully done, are primarily important to the program itself. As is true for all steps of the process, evaluation should be planned and conducted in partnership with the community, clients, and consumers. Different groups of stakeholders may value different outcomes, and they may have different opinions on the kind of evidence that is needed to demonstrate usefulness. As challenging as such collaboration is, evaluations that honor multiple perspectives are more likely to be useful and incorporated into program operations than those that do not.

One emerging framework for program evaluation with particular utility in social work is what has come to be called "empowerment evaluation" (Wandersman et al., 2004). In empowerment evaluation, power and responsibility for evaluation lay primarily with the community of stakeholders, which may include clients, staff, and community. Evaluators partner with stakeholders, and the goal is to build evaluation capacity among them so that, ultimately, evaluation decisions lie with the stakeholder community. Results, as in all good evaluations, are then integrated into a continuous process of quality improvement.

PROPOSAL WRITING

Much funding for social work practice comes from contracts with government entities; grants from private and public sources; and, for many public agencies, directly from budget allocations. Funds are often allocated on the basis of written proposals that are submitted in response to requests for proposals or that are submitted as a regular part of the funding cycle. Proposal writing (and locating potential recipients of proposals) is, to some extent, an art and can be a full-time job, but most graduate social workers will be routinely involved in the preparation of such requests for funding at some point in their work. Excellent books on preparing proposals are available (see, for example, Coley & Scheinberg, 2000), but a few essential points can be summarized here.

Getting funding is not easy. Most proposals (except for regular continuation funding requests) are not funded, so it is essential not to become discouraged if a proposal is not funded. When proposals are not funded, it is important to consider any corrective feedback as nondefensively as possible and to realize that the funding process is often highly political. Frequently, professionals submit proposals in part to become known to funders, to become part of the network, and to test the waters for future submissions; they do not expect to receive immediate funding. Funders tend to support the programs they know, and this tendency is not as unfair as it may seem because funders prefer giving money to entities with a track record, whom funders are confident will use the funds well. A major objective of a proposal is to build confidence in an organization and a program.

Although program familiarity to funders and the luck of the draw (especially which reviewers read a submission) are important factors in funding decisions, a good deal can be done to enhance the chances that a proposal will be accepted. First, the proposal must be on time—extensions are almost never possible. Therefore, back-up staff, back-up computers, back-up copying machines, and so forth are necessary to ensure that a deadline will be met. Second, the proposal must appear professional (with graphs and figures if appropriate) and be neat, grammatically perfect, and pitched to the audience that will read it. Proposals geared to professional peers require a different approach than those to lay advisory boards, for example. Third, enthusiasm and genuine confidence in the suggested approach must be evident. Fourth, most funders have developed guidelines and specific formats for proposals, and it is essential to follow those guidelines scrupulously. For example, some funders prefer to talk with applicants in advance, whereas others prefer that the first contact be a brief letter introducing a possible proposal.

The format requested or required for a proposal is likely to include most of the elements of program design that have been discussed here; if an organization has an effective ongoing program development process in place, much of the necessary material will already be on hand. It is common in strong programs for the staff to know what they would like to do and to have relatively well-developed program plans in place so that when a source of funding is identified, they can immediately move ahead with a proposal. Funding should not drive program development; rather, program development should proceed according to vision and needs, and funding should then be sought to realize the vision.

ALL THINGS TO ALL PEOPLE?

Generalist practice can be overwhelming. Social workers must know so much—and master so many clinical, monitoring, programmatic, supervisory, and other skills—that many workers may be tempted simply to narrow their focus and learn one aspect well. Although specialization has its place, method (work at a single system level) is not that place. Graduate social workers must be familiar enough to select intervention strategies that are based on clients' needs rather than on limitations of their knowledge and to apply their skills effectively as part of organizational structures. In short, they need to be "masters of social work."

By this point, it should be clear that although some practice processes and skills are common across system levels, one needs special skills and relies on somewhat different strategies at different system levels. At all levels, the social worker must find some way to engage or "join" the client system, thus potentiating his or her value as a support (reinforcer) and guide to potentially improved outcomes. With all client systems, one must gather information (explore), organize that information analytically in a way that leads to collaborative intervention strategies (assess), and selectively intervene at points and in ways identified by the assessment. All of this activity should occur within a shared power dynamic, in which social worker and clients share contributions, responsibility, and obligations. In work with an individual, data collected may include emotions, levels of support and coercion within the household, and selected personal history, because such data reflect the salient behaviors and environmental factors (contingencies) that shape them. In work with a neighborhood, one may be most interested in determining who the most powerful figures and organizations are—along with the employment, economic, and educational levels of community residents—because those data tell one a great deal about current and potential asset networks. In either case, one must first obtain the information, organize it, and understand its implications before one moves to intervention planning.

At the same time, social workers cannot be specialists in everything. Most specialization in social work occurs by field of practice; generalist social workers rely on multiple modalities (individual, group, family, community), focused by institutions, social problems, and population groups. They must know about the issues facing their organization's clients; about service structures, resources, and policies relevant to those issues; and about the variety of ways in which to intervene to address those issues. Social workers may be particularly skilled in certain intervention modalities, or they may refer clients to specialists for particular services (for example, to groups for those who batter or programs for children with autism). Still, a sense that one never knows enough may remain—and that is true.

As long as clients come with problems that social workers are unable to help them resolve and goals that social workers are unable to help them achieve, individual practitioners and the field as a whole must remain committed to progressively expanding their knowledge and deepening their skills. Social workers individually and collectively make a special commitment to contribute to the construction of human alternatives, not out of charity but because they recognize that we are all organically connected. Ultimately, as long as some among us are denied our basic human rights, whether by societal oppression or in ways as personal as family violence, more remains to learn and to do.

REFERENCES

Bartlett, H. M. (1970). *The common base of social work practice.* Silver Spring, MD: National Association of Social Workers.

Berk, R. A., & Rossi, P. H. (1998). *Thinking about program evaluation* (2nd ed.). Thousand Oaks, CA: Sage Publications.

Biglan, A. (1991). Distressed behavior and its context. *Behavior Analyst, 14,* 157–169.

Bronfenbrenner, U. (1979). *The ecology of human development: Experiments by nature and design.* Cambridge, MA: Harvard University Press.

Brown, G. W., & Harris, T. (1978). *Social origins of depression: A study of psychiatric disorder in women.* New York: Free Press.

Brunk, M., Henggeler, S. W., & Whelan, J. P. (1987). Comparison of multisystemic therapy and parent training in the brief treatment of child abuse and neglect. *Journal of Consulting and Clinical Psychology, 55,* 171–178.

Coley, S. M., & Scheinberg, C. A. (2000). *Proposal writing* (2nd ed.). Newbury Park, CA: Sage Publications.

Comer, E. W., & Fraser, M. W. (1998). Evaluation of six family-support projects: Are they effective? *Families in Society, 79,* 134–148.

Daniels, A. C. (2000). *Bringing out the best in people* (2nd ed.). New York: McGraw-Hill.

Dimidjian, S., Hollon, S. D., Dobson, K. S., Schmaling, K. B., Kohlenberg, R. J., Addis, M. E., Gallop, R., McGlinchey, J. B., Markley, D. K., Gollan, J. K., Atkins, D. C., Dunner, D. L., &

Jacobson, N. S. (2006). Randomized trial of behavioral activation, cognitive therapy, and anti-depressant medication in the acute treatment of adults with major depression. *Journal of Consulting and Clinical Psychology, 74,* 658–670.

Embry, D. D. (2004). Community–based prevention using simple, low-cost, evidence-based kernels and behavior vaccines. *Journal of Community Psychology, 32,* 575–591.

Erickson, C. L., Mattaini, M. A., & McGuire, M. S. (2004). Constructing nonviolent cultures in schools: The state of the science. *Children & Schools, 26,* 102–116.

Fawcett, S. B. (1991). Some values guiding community research and action. *Journal of Applied Behavior Analysis, 24,* 621–636.

Gambrill, E. (1996). Loneliness, social isolation, and social anxiety. In M. A. Mattaini & B. A. Thyer (Eds.), *Finding solutions to social problems: Behavioral strategies for change* (pp. 345–371). Washington, DC: American Psychological Association.

Goldiamond, I. (2002). Toward a constructional approach to social problems: Ethical and constitutional issues raised by applied behavior analysis. *Behavior and Social Issues, 11,* 108–197. (Reprinted from *Behaviorism, 2,* 1-84)

Goldstein, A. P., Keller, H., & Erné, D. (1985). *Changing the abusive parent.* Champaign, IL: Research.

Goodson, B. D., Layzer, J. I., St. Pierre, R. G., Bernstein, L. S., & Lopez, M. (2000). The effectiveness of a comprehensive, five-year family support program for low-income children and their families: Findings from the comprehensive child development program. *Early Childhood Research Quarterly, 15,* 5–39.

Harkness, D., & Hensley, H. (1991). Changing the focus of social work supervision: Effects on client satisfaction and generalized contentment. *Social Work, 36,* 506–512.

Health Realization Institute. (2000). *The understanding behind health realization: A principle-based psychology.* Long Beach, CA: Author.

Henggeler, S. W., Schoenwald, S. K., Borduin, C. M., Rowland, M. D., & Cunningham, P. B. (1998). *Multisystemic treatment of antisocial behavior in children and adolescents.* New York: Guilford Press.

Hoefer, R. (2006). *Advocacy practice for social justice.* Chicago: Lyceum Books.

Howing, P. T., Wodarski, J. S., Gaudin, J. M., Jr., & Kurtz, P. D. (1989). Effective interventions to ameliorate the incidence of child maltreatment: The empirical base. *Social Work, 34,* 330–338.

Jacobson, N. S., Martell, C. R., & Dimidjian, S. (2001). Behavioral activation treatment for depression: Returning to contextual roots. *Clinical Psychology: Science and Practice, 8,* 255–270.

Kettner, P. M., Moroney, R. M., & Martin, L. L. (1999). *Designing and managing programs: An effectiveness-based approach.* Newbury Park, CA: Sage Publications.

Kissane, R. J. (2003). What's need got to do with it? Barriers to use of nonprofit social services. *Journal of Sociology and Social Welfare, 30,* 127–148.

Komaki, J. L. (1998). *Leadership from an operant perspective.* London: Routledge.

Kretzmann, J. P., & McKnight, J. L. (1993). *Building communities from the inside out.* Chicago: ACTA Publications.

Latting, J. K. (1992). Giving corrective feedback: A decisional analysis. *Social Work, 37,* 424–430.

Lightburn, A., & Kemp, S. P. (1994). Family-support programs: Opportunities for community-based practice. *Families in Society, 75,* 16–26.

Lowery, C. T., & Mattaini, M. A. (1999). The science of sharing power: Native American thought and behavior analysis. *Behavior and Social Issues, 9,* 3–23.

Lutzker, J. R. (Ed.). (1998). *Handbook of child abuse research and treatment.* New York: Plenum Press.

Lutzker, J. R., Bigelow, K. M., Doctor, R. M., Gershater, R. M., & Greene, B. F. (1998). An ecobehavioral model for the prevention and treatment of child abuse and neglect: History and applications. In J. R. Lutzker (Ed.), *Handbook of child abuse research and treatment* (pp. 239–266). New York: Plenum Press.

Malott, M. E. (2003). *The paradox of organizational change: Engineering organizations with behavioral systems analysis.* Reno, NV: Context Press.

Marti-Costa, S., & Serrano-Garcia, I. (2001). Needs assessment and community development: An ideological perspective. In J. Rothman, J. L. Erlich, & J. E. Tropman (Eds.), *Strategies of community intervention* (6th ed., pp. 267–277). Itasca, IL: F. E. Peacock.

Mattaini, M. A. (1999). *Clinical intervention with families.* Washington, DC: NASW Press.

Mattaini, M. A. (with the PEACE POWER Working Group). (2001). *Peace Power with adolescents: Strategies for a culture of nonviolence.* Washington, DC: NASW Press.

Mattaini, M. A. (2006). *Youth violence in context: A Kohonen neural network analysis.* Unpublished manuscript.

Mattaini, M. A., McGowan, B. G., & Williams, G. (1996). Child maltreatment. In M. A. Mattaini & B. A. Thyer (Eds.), *Finding solutions to social problems: Behavioral strategies for change* (pp. 223–266). Washington, DC: American Psychological Association.

Mattaini, M. A., Twyman, J. S., Chin, W., & Lee, K. N. (1996). Youth violence. In M. A. Mattaini & B. A. Thyer (Eds.), *Finding solutions to social problems: Behavioral strategies for change* (pp. 75–111). Washington, DC: American Psychological Association.

McKnight, J. L. (1997). A 21st century map for health communities and families. *Families in Society, 78,* 117–127.

Meyer, C. H. (1979). Introduction: Making organizations work for people. In C. H. Meyer (Ed.), *Making organizations work for people* (pp. 1–12). Silver Spring, MD: National Association of Social Workers.

Minuchin, P., Colapinto, J., & Minuchin, S. (1998). *Working with families of the poor.* New York: Guilford Press.

Minuchin, S. (1974). *Families and family therapy.* Cambridge, MA: Harvard University Press.

Neuber, K. A., & Associates. (1980). *Needs assessment: A model for community planning.* Newbury Park, CA: Sage Publications.

Patterson, G. R. (1976). The aggressive child: Victim and architect of a coercive system. In E. J. Mash, L. A. Hamerlynck, & L. C. Handy (Eds.), *Behavior modification and families* (pp. 267–316). New York: Brunner/Mazel.

Reid, J. B., Patterson, G. R., & Snyder, J. J. (2002). *Antisocial behavior in children and adolescents: A developmental analysis and the Oregon Model for intervention.* Washington, DC: American Psychological Association.

Rossi, P. H., Freeman, H. E., & Lipsey, M. W. (2003). *Evaluation: A systematic approach* (7th ed.). Thousand Oaks, CA: Sage Publications.

Rothman, J. (2001). Approaches to community intervention. In J. Rothman, J. L. Erlich, & J. E. Tropman (Eds.), *Strategies of community intervention* (6th ed., pp. 27–64). Itasca, IL: F. E. Peacock.

Rothman, J., Erlich, J. L., & Tropman, J. E. (2001). *Strategies of community intervention* (6th ed.). Itasca, IL: F. E. Peacock.

Saleebey, D. (2006). *The strengths perspective in social work practice* (4th ed.). Boston: Allyn & Bacon.

Serna, L. A., Schumaker, J. B., Sherman, J. A., & Sheldon, J. B. (1991). In-home generalization of social interactions in families of adolescents with behavior problems. *Journal of Applied Behavior Analysis, 24,* 733–746.

Schorr, L. B. (1997). *Common purpose: Strengthening families and neighborhoods to rebuild America.* New York: Anchor/Doubleday.

Stokes, T. F., & Baer, D. M. (1977). An implicit technology of generalization. *Journal of Applied Behavior Analysis, 10,* 349–367.

Sviridoff, M., & Ryan, W. (1997). Community-centered family service. *Families in Society, 78,* 128–139.

Toseland, R. W., & Rivas, R. F. (2005). *An introduction to group work practice* (5th ed.). Boston: Allyn & Bacon.

Tropman, J. E. (1996). *Effective meetings: Improving group decision making* (2nd ed.). Thousand Oaks, CA: Sage Publications.

Tropman, J. E., Erlich, J. L., & Rothman, J. (2001). *Tactics and techniques of community intervention* (4th ed.). Itasca, IL: Peacock.

Wahler, R. G. (1980). The insular mother: Her problems in parent–child treatment. *Journal of Applied Behavior Analysis, 8,* 27–42.

Wandersman, A., Keener, D. C., Snell-Johns, J., Miller, R. L., Flaspohler, P., Livet-Dye, M., Mendez, J., Behrens, R., Bolson, B., & Robinson, L. (2004). Empowerment evaluations: Principles and action. In L. A. Jason, C. B. Keys, Y. Suarez-Balcazar, R. R. Taylor, & M. I. Davis (Eds.), *Participatory community research: Theories and methods in action* (pp. 139–156). Washington, DC: American Psychological Association.

Webster-Stratton, C. (1997). From parent training to community building. *Families in Society, 78,* 156–171.

Webster-Stratton, C., Reid, M. J., & Hammond, M. (2001). Preventing conduct problems, promoting social competence: A parent and teacher training partnership in Head Start. *Journal of Clinical Child Psychology, 30,* 283–302.

Weis, L., & Fine, M. (2004). *Working method: Research and social justice.* New York: Routledge.

Windsor, R. A., Clark, N., Boyd, N. R., & Goodman, R. M. (2003). *Evaluation of health promotion, health education, and disease prevention programs* (3rd ed.). New York: McGraw-Hill.

Wolf, M. M., Braukmann, C. J., & Ramp, K. A. (1987). Serious delinquent behavior as part of a significantly handicapping condition: Cures and supportive environments. *Journal of Applied Behavior Analysis, 20,* 347–359.

Wolfe, D. A. (1991). *Preventing physical and emotional abuse of children.* New York: Guilford Press.

■■■
Appendixes

NASW Code of Ethics

PREAMBLE

The primary mission of the social work profession is to enhance human well-being and help meet the basic human needs of all people, with particular attention to the needs and empowerment of people who are vulnerable, oppressed, and living in poverty. A historic and defining feature of social work is the profession's focus on individual well-being in a social context and the well-being of society. Fundamental to social work is attention to the environmental forces that create, contribute to, and address problems in living.

Social workers promote social justice and social change with and on behalf of clients. "Clients" is used inclusively to refer to individuals, families, groups, organizations, and communities. Social workers are sensitive to cultural and ethnic diversity and strive to end discrimination, oppression, poverty, and other forms of social injustice. These activities may be in the form of direct practice, community organizing, supervision, consultation, administration, advocacy, social and political action, policy development and implementation, education, and research and evaluation. Social workers seek to enhance the capacity of people to address their own needs. Social workers also seek to promote the responsiveness of organizations, communities, and other social institutions to individuals' needs and social problems.

The mission of the social work profession is rooted in a set of core values. These core values, embraced by social workers throughout the profession's history, are the foundation of social work's unique purpose and perspective:

+ service
+ social justice
+ dignity and worth of the person
+ importance of human relationships
+ integrity
+ competence.

This constellation of core values reflects what is unique to the social work profession. Core values, and the principles that flow from them, must be balanced within the context and complexity of the human experience.

PURPOSE OF THE *NASW CODE OF ETHICS*

Professional ethics are at the core of social work. The profession has an obligation to articulate its basic values, ethical principles, and ethical standards. The *NASW Code of Ethics* sets forth these values, principles, and standards to guide social workers' conduct. The *Code* is relevant to all social workers and social work students, regardless of their professional functions, the settings in which they work, or the populations they serve.

The *NASW Code of Ethics* serves six purposes:

1. The *Code* identifies core values on which social work's mission is based.
2. The *Code* summarizes broad ethical principles that reflect the profession's core values and establishes a set of specific ethical standards that should be used to guide social work practice.
3. The *Code* is designed to help social workers identify relevant considerations when professional obligations conflict or ethical uncertainties arise.
4. The *Code* provides ethical standards to which the general public can hold the social work profession accountable.
5. The *Code* socializes practitioners new to the field to social work's mission, values, ethical principles, and ethical standards.
6. The *Code* articulates standards that the social work profession itself can use to assess whether social workers have engaged in unethical conduct. NASW has formal procedures to adjudicate ethics complaints filed against its members.* In subscribing to this *Code*, social workers are required to cooperate in its implementation, participate in NASW adjudication proceedings, and abide by any NASW disciplinary rulings or sanctions based on it.

---

*For information on NASW adjudication procedures, see NASW *Procedures for the Adjudication of Grievances*.

The *Code* offers a set of values, principles, and standards to guide decision making and conduct when ethical issues arise. It does not provide a set of rules that prescribe how social workers should act in all situations. Specific applications of the *Code* must take into account the context in which it is being considered and the possibility of conflicts among the *Code's* values, principles, and standards. Ethical responsibilities flow from all human relationships, from the personal and familial to the social and professional.

Further, the *NASW Code of Ethics* does not specify which values, principles, and standards are most important and ought to outweigh others in instances when they conflict. Reasonable differences of opinion can and do exist among social workers with respect to the ways in which values, ethical principles, and ethical standards should be rank ordered when they conflict. Ethical decision making in a given situation must apply the informed judgment of the individual social worker and should also consider how the issues would be judged in a peer review process where the ethical standards of the profession would be applied.

Ethical decision making is a process. There are many instances in social work where simple answers are not available to resolve complex ethical issues. Social workers should take into consideration all the values, principles, and standards in this *Code* that are relevant to any situation in which ethical judgment is warranted. Social workers' decisions and actions should be consistent with the spirit as well as the letter of this *Code*.

In addition to this *Code*, there are many other sources of information about ethical thinking that may be useful. Social workers should consider ethical theory and principles generally, social work theory and research, laws, regulations, agency policies, and other relevant codes of ethics, recognizing that among codes of ethics social workers should consider the *NASW Code of Ethics* as their primary source. Social workers also should be aware of the impact on ethical decision making of their clients' and their own personal values and cultural and religious beliefs and practices. They should be aware of any conflicts between personal and professional values and deal with them responsibly. For additional guidance social workers should consult the relevant literature on professional ethics and ethical decision making and seek appropriate consultation when faced with ethical dilemmas. This may involve consultation with an agency-based or social work organization's ethics committee, a regulatory body, knowledgeable colleagues, supervisors, or legal counsel.

Instances may arise when social workers' ethical obligations conflict with agency policies or relevant laws or regulations. When such conflicts occur, social workers must make a responsible effort to resolve the conflict in a manner that is consistent with the values, principles, and standards expressed in this *Code*. If a reasonable resolution of the conflict does not appear possible, social workers should seek proper consultation before making a decision.

The *NASW Code of Ethics* is to be used by NASW and by individuals, agencies, organizations, and bodies (such as licensing and regulatory boards, professional liability insurance providers, courts of law, agency boards of directors, government agencies, and other professional groups) that choose to adopt it or use it as a frame of reference. Violation of standards in this *Code* does not automatically imply legal liability or violation of the law. Such determination can only be made in the context of legal and judicial proceedings. Alleged violations of the *Code* would be subject to a peer review process. Such processes are generally separate from legal or administrative procedures and insulated from legal review or proceedings to allow the profession to counsel and discipline its own members.

A code of ethics cannot guarantee ethical behavior. Moreover, a code of ethics cannot resolve all ethical issues or disputes or capture the richness and complexity involved in striving to make responsible choices within a moral community. Rather, a code of ethics sets forth values, ethical principles, and ethical standards to which professionals aspire and by which their actions can be judged. Social workers' ethical behavior should result from their personal commitment to engage in ethical practice. The *NASW Code of Ethics* reflects the commitment of all social workers to uphold the profession's values and to act ethically. Principles and standards must be applied by individuals of good character who discern moral questions and, in good faith, seek to make reliable ethical judgments.

ETHICAL PRINCIPLES

The following broad ethical principles are based on social work's core values of service, social justice, dignity and worth of the person, importance of human relationships, integrity, and competence. These principles set forth ideals to which all social workers should aspire.

Value: *Service*

Ethical Principle: Social workers' primary goal is to help people in need and to address social problems.

Social workers elevate service to others above self-interest. Social workers draw on their knowledge, values, and skills to help people in need and to address social problems. Social workers are encouraged to volunteer some portion of their professional skills with no expectation of significant financial return (pro bono service).

Value: *Social Justice*

Ethical Principle: Social workers challenge social injustice.

Social workers pursue social change, particularly with and on behalf of vulnerable and oppressed individuals and groups of people. Social workers' social change efforts are focused primarily on issues of poverty, unemployment, discrimination, and other forms of social injustice. These activities seek to promote sensitivity to and knowledge about oppression and cultural and ethnic diversity. Social workers strive to ensure access to needed information, services, and resources; equality of opportunity; and meaningful participation in decision making for all people.

Value: *Dignity and Worth of the Person*

Ethical Principle: Social workers respect the inherent dignity and worth of the person.

Social workers treat each person in a caring and respectful fashion, mindful of individual differences and cultural and ethnic diversity. Social workers promote clients' socially responsible self-determination. Social workers seek to enhance clients' capacity and opportunity to change and to address their own needs. Social workers are cognizant of their dual responsibility to clients and to the broader society. They seek to resolve conflicts between clients' interests and the broader society's interests in a socially responsible manner consistent with the values, ethical principles, and ethical standards of the profession.

Value: *Importance of Human Relationships*

Ethical Principle: Social workers recognize the central importance of human relationships.

Social workers understand that relationships between and among people are an important vehicle for change. Social workers engage people as partners in the helping process. Social workers seek to strengthen relationships among people in a purposeful effort to promote, restore, maintain, and enhance the well-being of individuals, families, social groups, organizations, and communities.

Value: *Integrity*

Ethical Principle: Social workers behave in a trustworthy manner.

Social workers are continually aware of the profession's mission, values, ethical principles, and ethical standards and practice in a manner consistent with them. Social workers act honestly and responsibly and promote ethical practices on the part of the organizations with which they are affiliated.

Value: *Competence*

Ethical Principle: Social workers practice within their areas of competence and develop and enhance their professional expertise.

Social workers continually strive to increase their professional knowledge and skills and to apply them in practice. Social workers should aspire to contribute to the knowledge base of the profession.

ETHICAL STANDARDS

The following ethical standards are relevant to the professional activities of all social workers. These standards concern (1) social workers' ethical responsibilities to clients, (2) social workers' ethical responsibilities to colleagues, (3) social workers' ethical responsibilities in practice settings, (4) social workers' ethical responsibilities as professionals, (5) social workers' ethical responsibilities to the social work profession, and (6) social workers' ethical responsibilities to the broader society.

Some of the standards that follow are enforceable guidelines for professional conduct, and some are aspirational. The extent to which each standard is enforceable is a matter of professional judgment to be exercised by those responsible for reviewing alleged violations of ethical standards.

1. SOCIAL WORKERS' ETHICAL RESPONSIBILITIES TO CLIENTS
1.01 *Commitment to Clients*
Social workers' primary responsibility is to promote the well-being of clients. In general, clients' interests are primary. However, social workers' responsibility to the larger society or specific legal obligations may on limited occasions supersede the loyalty owed clients, and clients should be so advised. (Examples include when a social worker is required by law to report that a client has abused a child or has threatened to harm self or others.)

1.02 *Self-Determination*
Social workers respect and promote the right of clients to self-determination and assist clients in their efforts to identify and clarify their goals. Social workers may limit clients' right to self-determination when, in the social workers' professional judgment, clients' actions or potential actions pose a serious, foreseeable, and imminent risk to themselves or others.

1.03 *Informed Consent*
(a) Social workers should provide services to clients only in the context of a professional relationship based, when appropriate, on valid informed

consent. Social workers should use clear and understandable language to inform clients of the purpose of the services, risks related to the services, limits to services because of the requirements of a third-party payer, relevant costs, reasonable alternatives, clients' right to refuse or withdraw consent, and the time frame covered by the consent. Social workers should provide clients with an opportunity to ask questions.

(b) In instances when clients are not literate or have difficulty understanding the primary language used in the practice setting, social workers should take steps to ensure clients' comprehension. This may include providing clients with a detailed verbal explanation or arranging for a qualified interpreter or translator whenever possible.

(c) In instances when clients lack the capacity to provide informed consent, social workers should protect clients' interests by seeking permission from an appropriate third party, informing clients consistent with the clients' level of understanding. In such instances social workers should seek to ensure that the third party acts in a manner consistent with clients' wishes and interests. Social workers should take reasonable steps to enhance such clients' ability to give informed consent.

(d) In instances when clients are receiving services involuntarily, social workers should provide information about the nature and extent of services and about the extent of clients' right to refuse service.

(e) Social workers who provide services via electronic media (such as computer, telephone, radio, and television) should inform recipients of the limitations and risks associated with such services.

(f) Social workers should obtain clients' informed consent before audiotaping or videotaping clients or permitting observation of services to clients by a third party.

1.04 *Competence*

(a) Social workers should provide services and represent themselves as competent only within the boundaries of their education, training, license, certification, consultation received, supervised experience, or other relevant professional experience.

(b) Social workers should provide services in substantive areas or use intervention techniques or approaches that are new to them only after engaging in appropriate study, training, consultation, and supervision from people who are competent in those interventions or techniques.

(c) When generally recognized standards do not exist with respect to an emerging area of practice, social workers should exercise careful judgment and take responsible steps (including appropriate education, research, training, consultation, and supervision) to ensure the competence of their work and to protect clients from harm.

1.05 *Cultural Competence and Social Diversity*

(a) Social workers should understand culture and its function in human behavior and society, recognizing the strengths that exist in all cultures.

(b) Social workers should have a knowledge base of their clients' cultures and be able to demonstrate competence in the provision of services that are sensitive to clients' cultures and to differences among people and cultural groups.

(c) Social workers should obtain education about and seek to understand the nature of social diversity and oppression with respect to race, ethnicity, national origin, color, sex, sexual orientation, age, marital status, political belief, religion, and mental or physical disability.

1.06 *Conflicts of Interest*

(a) Social workers should be alert to and avoid conflicts of interest that interfere with the exercise of professional discretion and impartial judgment. Social workers should inform clients when a real or potential conflict of interest arises and take reasonable steps to resolve the issue in a manner that makes the clients' interests primary and protects clients' interests to the greatest extent possible. In some cases, protecting clients' interests may require termination of the professional relationship with proper referral of the client.

(b) Social workers should not take unfair advantage of any professional relationship or exploit others to further their personal, religious, political, or business interests.

(c) Social workers should not engage in dual or multiple relationships with clients or former clients in which there is a risk of exploitation or potential harm to the client. In instances when dual or multiple relationships are unavoidable, social workers should take steps to protect clients and are responsible for setting clear, appropriate, and culturally sensitive boundaries. (Dual or multiple relationships occur when social workers relate to clients in more than one relationship, whether professional, social, or business. Dual or multiple relationships can occur simultaneously or consecutively.)

(d) When social workers provide services to two or more people who have a relationship with each other (for example, couples, family members), social workers should clarify with all parties which individuals will be considered clients and the nature of social workers' professional obligations to the various individuals who are receiving services. Social workers who anticipate a conflict of interest among the individuals receiving services or who anticipate having to perform in potentially conflicting roles (for example, when a social worker is asked to testify in a child custody dispute or divorce proceedings involving clients) should clarify their role with the parties involved and take appropriate action to minimize any conflict of interest.

1.07 *Privacy and Confidentiality*

(a) Social workers should respect clients' right to privacy. Social workers should not solicit private information from clients unless it is essential to providing services or conducting social work evaluation or research. Once private information is shared, standards of confidentiality apply.

(b) Social workers may disclose confidential information when appropriate with valid consent from a client or a person legally authorized to consent on behalf of a client.

(c) Social workers should protect the confidentiality of all information obtained in the course of professional service, except for compelling professional reasons. The general expectation that social workers will keep information confidential does not apply when disclosure is necessary to prevent serious, foreseeable, and imminent harm to a client or other identifiable person. In all instances, social workers should disclose the least amount of confidential information necessary to achieve the desired purpose; only information that is directly relevant to the purpose for which the disclosure is made should be revealed.

(d) Social workers should inform clients, to the extent possible, about the disclosure of confidential information and the potential consequences, when feasible before the disclosure is made. This applies whether social workers disclose confidential information on the basis of a legal requirement or client consent.

(e) Social workers should discuss with clients and other interested parties the nature of confidentiality and limitations of clients' right to confidentiality. Social workers should review with clients circumstances where confidential information may be requested and where disclosure of confidential information may be legally required. This discussion should occur as soon as possible in the social worker–client relationship and as needed throughout the course of the relationship.

(f) When social workers provide counseling services to families, couples, or groups, social workers should seek agreement among the parties involved concerning each individual's right to confidentiality and obligation to preserve the confidentiality of information shared by others. Social workers should inform participants in family, couples, or group counseling that social workers cannot guarantee that all participants will honor such agreements.

(g) Social workers should inform clients involved in family, couples, marital, or group counseling of the social worker's, employer's, and agency's policy concerning the social worker's disclosure of confidential information among the parties involved in the counseling.

(h) Social workers should not disclose confidential information to third-party payers unless clients have authorized such disclosure.

(i) Social workers should not discuss confidential information in any setting unless privacy can be ensured. Social workers should not discuss confidential information in public or semipublic areas such as hallways, waiting rooms, elevators, and restaurants.

(j) Social workers should protect the confidentiality of clients during legal proceedings to the extent permitted by law. When a court of law or other legally authorized body orders social workers to disclose confidential or privileged information without a client's consent and such disclosure could cause harm to the client, social workers should request that the court withdraw the order or limit the order as narrowly as possible or maintain the records under seal, unavailable for public inspection.

(k) Social workers should protect the confidentiality of clients when responding to requests from members of the media.

(1) Social workers should protect the confidentiality of clients' written and electronic records and other sensitive information. Social workers should take reasonable steps to ensure that clients' records are stored in a secure location and that clients' records are not available to others who are not authorized to have access.

(m) Social workers should take precautions to ensure and maintain the confidentiality of information transmitted to other parties through the use of computers, electronic mail, facsimile machines, telephones and telephone answering machines, and other electronic or computer technology. Disclosure of identifying information should be avoided whenever possible.

(n) Social workers should transfer or dispose of clients' records in a manner that protects clients' confidentiality and is consistent with state statutes governing records and social work licensure.

(o) Social workers should take reasonable precautions to protect client confidentiality in the event of the social worker's termination of practice, incapacitation, or death.

(p) Social workers should not disclose identifying information when discussing clients for teaching or training purposes unless the client has consented to disclosure of confidential information.

(q) Social workers should not disclose identifying information when discussing clients with consultants unless the client has consented to disclosure of confidential information or there is a compelling need for such disclosure.

(r) Social workers should protect the confidentiality of deceased clients consistent with the preceding standards.

1.08 *Access to Records*

(a) Social workers should provide clients with reasonable access to records concerning the clients. Social workers who are concerned that clients' access to their records could cause serious misunderstanding or harm to the client should provide assistance in interpreting the records and consultation with the client regarding the records. Social workers should limit clients' access to their records, or portions of their records, only in exceptional circumstances when there is compelling evidence that such access would cause serious harm to the client. Both clients' requests and the rationale for withholding some or all of the record should be documented in clients' files.

(b) When providing clients with access to their records, social workers should take steps to protect the confidentiality of other individuals identified or discussed in such records.

1.09 *Sexual Relationships*

(a) Social workers should under no circumstances engage in sexual activities or sexual contact with current clients, whether such contact is consensual or forced.

(b) Social workers should not engage in sexual activities or sexual contact with clients' relatives or other individuals with whom clients maintain a close personal relationship when there is a risk of exploitation or potential harm to the client. Sexual activity or sexual contact with clients' relatives or other individuals with whom clients maintain a personal relationship has the potential to be harmful to the client and may make it difficult for the social worker and client to maintain appropriate professional boundaries. Social workers—not their clients, their clients' relatives, or other individuals with whom the client maintains a personal relationship—assume the full burden for setting clear, appropriate, and culturally sensitive boundaries.

(c) Social workers should not engage in sexual activities or sexual contact with former clients because of the potential for harm to the client. If social workers engage in conduct contrary to this prohibition or claim that an exception to this prohibition is warranted because of extraordinary circumstances, it is social workers—not their clients—who assume the full burden of demonstrating that the former client has not been exploited, coerced, or manipulated, intentionally or unintentionally.

(d) Social workers should not provide clinical services to individuals with whom they have had a prior sexual relationship. Providing clinical services to a former sexual partner has the potential to be harmful to the individual and is likely to make it difficult for the social worker and individual to maintain appropriate professional boundaries.

1.10 *Physical Contact*

Social workers should not engage in physical contact with clients when there is a possibility of psychological harm to the client as a result of the contact (such as cradling or caressing clients). Social workers who engage in appropriate physical contact with clients are responsible for setting clear, appropriate, and culturally sensitive boundaries that govern such physical contact.

1.11 *Sexual Harassment*

Social workers should not sexually harass clients. Sexual harassment includes sexual advances, sexual solicitation, requests for sexual favors, and other verbal or physical conduct of a sexual nature.

1.12 *Derogatory Language*

Social workers should not use derogatory language in their written or verbal communications to or about clients. Social workers should use accurate and respectful language in all communications to and about clients.

1.13 *Payment for Services*

(a) When setting fees, social workers should ensure that the fees are fair, reasonable, and commensurate with the services performed. Consideration should be given to clients' ability to pay.

(b) Social workers should avoid accepting goods or services from clients as payment for professional services. Bartering arrangements, particularly involving services, create the potential for conflicts of interest, exploitation, and inappropriate boundaries in social workers' relationships with clients. Social workers should explore and may participate in bartering only in very limited circumstances when it can be demonstrated that such arrangements are an accepted practice among professionals in the local community, considered to be essential for the provision of services, negotiated without coercion, and entered into at the client's initiative and with the client's informed consent. Social workers who accept goods or services from clients as payment for professional services assume the full burden of demonstrating that this arrangement will not be detrimental to the client or the professional relationship.

(c) Social workers should not solicit a private fee or other remuneration for providing services to clients who are entitled to such available services through the social workers' employer or agency.

1.14 *Clients Who Lack Decision-Making Capacity*

When social workers act on behalf of clients who lack the capacity to make informed decisions, social workers should take reasonable steps to safeguard the interests and rights of those clients.

1.15 *Interruption of Services*

Social workers should make reasonable efforts to ensure continuity of services in the event that services are interrupted by factors such as unavailability, relocation, illness, disability, or death.

1.16 *Termination of Services*

(a) Social workers should terminate services to clients and professional relationships with them when such services and relationships are no longer required or no longer serve the clients' needs or interests.

(b) Social workers should take reasonable steps to avoid abandoning clients who are still in need of services. Social workers should withdraw services precipitously only under unusual circumstances, giving careful consideration to all factors in the situation and taking care to minimize possible adverse effects. Social workers should assist in making appropriate arrangements for continuation of services when necessary.

(c) Social workers in fee-for-service settings may terminate services to clients who are not paying an overdue balance if the financial contractual arrangements have been made clear to the client, if the client does not pose an imminent danger to self or others, and if the clinical and other consequences of the current nonpayment have been addressed and discussed with the client.

(d) Social workers should not terminate services to pursue a social, financial, or sexual relationship with a client.

(e) Social workers who anticipate the termination or interruption of services to clients should notify clients promptly and seek the transfer, referral, or continuation of services in relation to the clients' needs and preferences.

(f) Social workers who are leaving an employment setting should inform clients of appropriate options for the continuation of services and of the benefits and risks of the options.

2. SOCIAL WORKERS' ETHICAL RESPONSIBILITIES TO COLLEAGUES
2.01 *Respect*
   (a) Social workers should treat colleagues with respect and should represent accurately and fairly the qualifications, views, and obligations of colleagues.
   (b) Social workers should avoid unwarranted negative criticism of colleagues in communications with clients or with other professionals. Unwarranted negative criticism may include demeaning comments that refer to colleagues' level of competence or to individuals' attributes such as race, ethnicity, national origin, color, sex, sexual orientation, age, marital status, political belief, religion, and mental or physical disability.
   (c) Social workers should cooperate with social work colleagues and with colleagues of other professions when such cooperation serves the well-being of clients.

2.02 *Confidentiality*
Social workers should respect confidential information shared by colleagues in the course of their professional relationships and transactions. Social workers should ensure that such colleagues understand social workers' obligation to respect confidentiality and any exceptions related to it.

2.03 *Interdisciplinary Collaboration*
   (a) Social workers who are members of an interdisciplinary team should participate in and contribute to decisions that affect the well-being of clients by drawing on the perspectives, values, and experiences of the social work profession. Professional and ethical obligations of the interdisciplinary team as a whole and of its individual members should be clearly established.
   (b) Social workers for whom a team decision raises ethical concerns should attempt to resolve the disagreement through appropriate channels. If the disagreement cannot be resolved, social workers should pursue other avenues to address their concerns consistent with client well-being.

2.04 *Disputes Involving Colleagues*
   (a) Social workers should not take advantage of a dispute between a colleague and an employer to obtain a position or otherwise advance the social workers' own interests.

(b) Social workers should not exploit clients in disputes with colleagues or engage clients in any inappropriate discussion of conflicts between social workers and their colleagues.

2.05 *Consultation*

(a) Social workers should seek the advice and counsel of colleagues whenever such consultation is in the best interests of clients.

(b) Social workers should keep themselves informed about colleagues' areas of expertise and competencies. Social workers should seek consultation only from colleagues who have demonstrated knowledge, expertise, and competence related to the subject of the consultation.

(c) When consulting with colleagues about clients, social workers should disclose the least amount of information necessary to achieve the purposes of the consultation.

2.06 *Referral for Services*

(a) Social workers should refer clients to other professionals when the other professionals' specialized knowledge or expertise is needed to serve clients fully or when social workers believe that they are not being effective or making reasonable progress with clients and that additional service is required.

(b) Social workers who refer clients to other professionals should take appropriate steps to facilitate an orderly transfer of responsibility. Social workers who refer clients to other professionals should disclose, with clients' consent, all pertinent information to the new service providers.

(c) Social workers are prohibited from giving or receiving payment for a referral when no professional service is provided by the referring social worker.

2.07 *Sexual Relationships*

(a) Social workers who function as supervisors or educators should not engage in sexual activities or contact with supervisees, students, trainees, or other colleagues over whom they exercise professional authority.

(b) Social workers should avoid engaging in sexual relationships with colleagues when there is potential for a conflict of interest. Social workers who become involved in, or anticipate becoming involved in, a sexual relationship with a colleague have a duty to transfer professional responsibilities, when necessary, to avoid a conflict of interest.

2.08 Sexual Harassment
Social workers should not sexually harass supervisees, students, trainees, or colleagues. Sexual harassment includes sexual advances, sexual solicitation, requests for sexual favors, and other verbal or physical conduct of a sexual nature.

2.09 Impairment of Colleagues
    (a) Social workers who have direct knowledge of a social work colleague's impairment that is due to personal problems, psychosocial distress, substance abuse, or mental health difficulties and that interferes with practice effectiveness should consult with that colleague when feasible and assist the colleague in taking remedial action.
    (b) Social workers who believe that a social work colleague's impairment interferes with practice effectiveness and that the colleague has not taken adequate steps to address the impairment should take action through appropriate channels established by employers, agencies, NASW, licensing and regulatory bodies, and other professional organizations.

2.10 Incompetence of Colleagues
    (a) Social workers who have direct knowledge of a social work colleague's incompetence should consult with that colleague when feasible and assist the colleague in taking remedial action.
    (b) Social workers who believe that a social work colleague is incompetent and has not taken adequate steps to address the incompetence should take action through appropriate channels established by employers, agencies, NASW, licensing and regulatory bodies, and other professional organizations.

2.11 Unethical Conduct of Colleagues
    (a) Social workers should take adequate measures to discourage, prevent, expose, and correct the unethical conduct of colleagues.
    (b) Social workers should be knowledgeable about established policies and procedures for handling concerns about colleagues' unethical behavior. Social workers should be familiar with national, state, and local procedures for handling ethics complaints. These include policies and procedures created by NASW, licensing and regulatory bodies, employers, agencies, and other professional organizations.
    (c) Social workers who believe that a colleague has acted unethically should seek resolution by discussing their concerns with the colleague when feasible and when such discussion is likely to be productive.

(d) When necessary, social workers who believe that a colleague has acted unethically should take action through appropriate formal channels (such as contacting a state licensing board or regulatory body, an NASW committee on inquiry, or other professional ethics committees).

(e) Social workers should defend and assist colleagues who are unjustly charged with unethical conduct.

3. SOCIAL WORKERS' ETHICAL RESPONSIBILITIES IN PRACTICE SETTINGS

3.01 *Supervision and Consultation*

(a) Social workers who provide supervision or consultation should have the necessary knowledge and skill to supervise or consult appropriately and should do so only within their areas of knowledge and competence.

(b) Social workers who provide supervision or consultation are responsible for setting clear, appropriate, and culturally sensitive boundaries.

(c) Social workers should not engage in any dual or multiple relationships with supervisees in which there is a risk of exploitation of or potential harm to the supervisee.

(d) Social workers who provide supervision should evaluate supervisees' performance in a manner that is fair and respectful.

3.02 *Education and Training*

(a) Social workers who function as educators, field instructors for students, or trainers should provide instruction only within their areas of knowledge and competence and should provide instruction based on the most current information and knowledge available in the profession.

(b) Social workers who function as educators or field instructors for students should evaluate students' performance in a manner that is fair and respectful.

(c) Social workers who function as educators or field instructors for students should take reasonable steps to ensure that clients are routinely informed when services are being provided by students.

(d) Social workers who function as educators or field instructors for students should not engage in any dual or multiple relationships with students in which there is a risk of exploitation or potential harm to the student. Social work educators and field instructors are responsible for setting clear, appropriate, and culturally sensitive boundaries.

3.03 *Performance Evaluation*
Social workers who have responsibility for evaluating the performance of others should fulfill such responsibility in a fair and considerate manner and on the basis of clearly stated criteria.

3.04 *Client Records*
   (a) Social workers should take reasonable steps to ensure that documentation in records is accurate and reflects the services provided.
   (b) Social workers should include sufficient and timely documentation in records to facilitate the delivery of services and to ensure continuity of services provided to clients in the future.
   (c) Social workers' documentation should protect clients' privacy to the extent that is possible and appropriate and should include only information that is directly relevant to the delivery of services.
   (d) Social workers should store records following the termination of services to ensure reasonable future access. Records should be maintained for the number of years required by state statutes or relevant contracts.

3.05 *Billing*
Social workers should establish and maintain billing practices that accurately reflect the nature and extent of services provided and that identify who provided the service in the practice setting.

3.06 *Client Transfer*
   (a) When an individual who is receiving services from another agency or colleague contacts a social worker for services, the social worker should carefully consider the client's needs before agreeing to provide services. To minimize possible confusion and conflict, social workers should discuss with potential clients the nature of the clients' current relationship with other service providers and the implications, including possible benefits or risks, of entering into a relationship with a new service provider.
   (b) If a new client has been served by another agency or colleague, social workers should discuss with the client whether consultation with the previous service provider is in the client's best interest.

3.07 *Administration*
   (a) Social work administrators should advocate within and outside their agencies for adequate resources to meet clients' needs.

(b) Social workers should advocate for resource allocation procedures that are open and fair. When not all clients' needs can be met, an allocation procedure should be developed that is nondiscriminatory and based on appropriate and consistently applied principles.

(c) Social workers who are administrators should take reasonable steps to ensure that adequate agency or organizational resources are available to provide appropriate staff supervision.

(d) Social work administrators should take reasonable steps to ensure that the working environment for which they are responsible is consistent with and encourages compliance with the *NASW Code of Ethics*. Social work administrators should take reasonable steps to eliminate any conditions in their organizations that violate, interfere with, or discourage compliance with the *Code*.

3.08 *Continuing Education and Staff Development*

Social work administrators and supervisors should take reasonable steps to provide or arrange for continuing education and staff development for all staff for whom they are responsible. Continuing education and staff development should address current knowledge and emerging developments related to social work practice and ethics.

3.09 *Commitments to Employers*

(a) Social workers generally should adhere to commitments made to employers and employing organizations.

(b) Social workers should work to improve employing agencies' policies and procedures and the efficiency and effectiveness of their services.

(c) Social workers should take reasonable steps to ensure that employers are aware of social workers' ethical obligations as set forth in the *NASW Code of Ethics* and of the implications of those obligations for social work practice.

(d) Social workers should not allow an employing organization's policies, procedures, regulations, or administrative orders to interfere with their ethical practice of social work. Social workers should take reasonable steps to ensure that their employing organizations' practices are consistent with the *NASW Code of Ethics*.

(e) Social workers should act to prevent and eliminate discrimination in the employing organization's work assignments and in its employment policies and practices.

(f) Social workers should accept employment or arrange student field placements only in organizations that exercise fair personnel practices.

(g) Social workers should be diligent stewards of the resources of their employing organizations, wisely conserving funds where appropriate and never misappropriating funds or using them for unintended purposes.

3.10 *Labor–Management Disputes*

(a) Social workers may engage in organized action, including the formation of and participation in labor unions, to improve services to clients and working conditions.

(b) The actions of social workers who are involved in labor–management disputes, job actions, or labor strikes should be guided by the profession's values, ethical principles, and ethical standards. Reasonable differences of opinion exist among social workers concerning their primary obligation as professionals during an actual or threatened labor strike or job action. Social workers should carefully examine relevant issues and their possible impact on clients before deciding on a course of action.

4. SOCIAL WORKERS' ETHICAL RESPONSIBILITIES AS PROFESSIONALS

4.01 *Competence*

(a) Social workers should accept responsibility or employment only on the basis of existing competence or the intention to acquire the necessary competence.

(b) Social workers should strive to become and remain proficient in professional practice and the performance of professional functions. Social workers should critically examine and keep current with emerging knowledge relevant to social work. Social workers should routinely review the professional literature and participate in continuing education relevant to social work practice and social work ethics.

(c) Social workers should base practice on recognized knowledge, including empirically based knowledge, relevant to social work and social work ethics.

4.02 *Discrimination*

Social workers should not practice, condone, facilitate, or collaborate with any form of discrimination on the basis of race, ethnicity, national origin, color, sex, sexual orientation, age, marital status, political belief, religion, or mental or physical disability.

4.03 *Private Conduct*

Social workers should not permit their private conduct to interfere with their ability to fulfill their professional responsibilities.

4.04 *Dishonesty, Fraud, and Deception*

Social workers should not participate in, condone, or be associated with dishonesty, fraud, or deception.

4.05 *Impairment*

(a) Social workers should not allow their own personal problems, psychosocial distress, legal problems, substance abuse, or mental health difficulties to interfere with their professional judgment and performance or to jeopardize the best interests of people for whom they have a professional responsibility.

(b) Social workers whose personal problems, psychosocial distress, legal problems, substance abuse, or mental health difficulties interfere with their professional judgment and performance should immediately seek consultation and take appropriate remedial action by seeking professional help, making adjustments in workload, terminating practice, or taking any other steps necessary to protect clients and others.

4.06 *Misrepresentation*

(a) Social workers should make clear distinctions between statements made and actions engaged in as a private individual and as a representative of the social work profession, a professional social work organization, or the social worker's employing agency.

(b) Social workers who speak on behalf of professional social work organizations should accurately represent the official and authorized positions of the organizations.

(c) Social workers should ensure that their representations to clients, agencies, and the public of professional qualifications, credentials, education, competence, affiliations, services provided, or results to be achieved are accurate. Social workers should claim only those relevant professional credentials they actually possess and take steps to correct any inaccuracies or misrepresentations of their credentials by others.

4.07 *Solicitations*

(a) Social workers should not engage in uninvited solicitation of potential clients who, because of their circumstances, are vulnerable to undue influence, manipulation, or coercion.

(b) Social workers should not engage in solicitation of testimonial endorsements (including solicitation of consent to use a client's prior statement as a testimonial endorsement) from current clients or from other people who, because of their particular circumstances, are vulnerable to undue influence.

4.08 *Acknowledging Credit*
(a) Social workers should take responsibility and credit, including authorship credit, only for work they have actually performed and to which they have contributed.
(b) Social workers should honestly acknowledge the work of and the contributions made by others.

5.   SOCIAL WORKERS' ETHICAL RESPONSIBILITIES TO THE SOCIAL WORK PROFESSION
5.01 *Integrity of the Profession*
(a) Social workers should work toward the maintenance and promotion of high standards of practice.
(b) Social workers should uphold and advance the values, ethics, knowledge, and mission of the profession. Social workers should protect, enhance, and improve the integrity of the profession through appropriate study and research, active discussion, and responsible criticism of the profession.
(c) Social workers should contribute time and professional expertise to activities that promote respect for the value, integrity, and competence of the social work profession. These activities may include teaching, research, consultation, service, legislative testimony, presentations in the community, and participation in their professional organizations.
(d) Social workers should contribute to the knowledge base of social work and share with colleagues their knowledge related to practice, research, and ethics. Social workers should seek to contribute to the profession's literature and to share their knowledge at professional meetings and conferences.
(e) Social workers should act to prevent the unauthorized and unqualified practice of social work.

5.02 *Evaluation and Research*
(a) Social workers should monitor and evaluate policies, the implementation of programs, and practice interventions.
(b) Social workers should promote and facilitate evaluation and research to contribute to the development of knowledge.

(c) Social workers should critically examine and keep current with emerging knowledge relevant to social work and fully use evaluation and research evidence in their professional practice.

(d) Social workers engaged in evaluation or research should carefully consider possible consequences and should follow guidelines developed for the protection of evaluation and research participants. Appropriate institutional review boards should be consulted.

(e) Social workers engaged in evaluation or research should obtain voluntary and written informed consent from participants, when appropriate, without any implied or actual deprivation or penalty for refusal to participate; without undue inducement to participate; and with due regard for participants' well-being, privacy, and dignity. Informed consent should include information about the nature, extent, and duration of the participation requested and disclosure of the risks and benefits of participation in the research.

(f) When evaluation or research participants are incapable of giving informed consent, social workers should provide an appropriate explanation to the participants, obtain the participants' assent to the extent they are able, and obtain written consent from an appropriate proxy.

(g) Social workers should never design or conduct evaluation or research that does not use consent procedures, such as certain forms of naturalistic observation and archival research, unless rigorous and responsible review of the research has found it to be justified because of its prospective scientific, educational, or applied value and unless equally effective alternative procedures that do not involve waiver of consent are not feasible.

(h) Social workers should inform participants of their right to withdraw from evaluation and research at any time without penalty.

(i) Social workers should take appropriate steps to ensure that participants in evaluation and research have access to appropriate supportive services.

(j) Social workers engaged in evaluation or research should protect participants from unwarranted physical or mental distress, harm, danger, or deprivation.

(k) Social workers engaged in the evaluation of services should discuss collected information only for professional purposes and only with people professionally concerned with this information.

(1) Social workers engaged in evaluation or research should ensure the anonymity or confidentiality of participants and of the data obtained from them. Social workers should inform participants of any limits of confidentiality, the measures that will be taken to ensure confidentiality, and when any records containing research data will be destroyed.

(m) Social workers who report evaluation and research results should protect participants' confidentiality by omitting identifying information unless proper consent has been obtained authorizing disclosure.

(n) Social workers should report evaluation and research findings accurately. They should not fabricate or falsify results and should take steps to correct any errors later found in published data using standard publication methods.

(o) Social workers engaged in evaluation or research should be alert to and avoid conflicts of interest and dual relationships with participants, should inform participants when a real or potential conflict of interest arises, and should take steps to resolve the issue in a manner that makes participants' interests primary.

(p) Social workers should educate themselves, their students, and their colleagues about responsible research practices.

6. SOCIAL WORKERS' ETHICAL RESPONSIBILITIES TO THE BROADER SOCIETY

6.01 *Social Welfare*

Social workers should promote the general welfare of society, from local to global levels, and the development of people, their communities, and their environments. Social workers should advocate for living conditions conducive to the fulfillment of basic human needs and should promote social, economic, political, and cultural values and institutions that are compatible with the realization of social justice.

6.02 *Public Participation*

Social workers should facilitate informed participation by the public in shaping social policies and institutions.

6.03 *Public Emergencies*

Social workers should provide appropriate professional services in public emergencies to the greatest extent possible.

6.04 *Social and Political Action*

(a) Social workers should engage in social and political action that seeks to ensure that all people have equal access to the resources, employment, services, and opportunities they require to meet their basic human needs and to develop fully. Social workers should be aware of the impact of the political arena on practice and should advocate for changes in policy and legislation to improve social conditions in order to meet basic human needs and promote social justice.

(b) Social workers should act to expand choice and opportunity for all people, with special regard for vulnerable, disadvantaged, oppressed, and exploited people and groups.

(c) Social workers should promote conditions that encourage respect for cultural and social diversity within the United States and globally. Social workers should promote policies and practices that demonstrate respect for difference, support the expansion of cultural knowledge and resources, advocate for programs and institutions that demonstrate cultural competence, and promote policies that safeguard the rights of and confirm equity and social justice for all people.

(d) Social workers should act to prevent and eliminate domination of, exploitation of, and discrimination against any person, group, or class on the basis of race, ethnicity, national origin, color, sex, sexual orientation, age, marital status, political belief, religion, or mental or physical disability.

B

□□□

Universal Declaration of Human Rights

*O*n December 10, 1948 the General Assembly of the United Nations adopted and proclaimed the Universal Declaration of Human Rights the full text of which appears in the following pages. Following this historic act the Assembly called upon all Member countries to publicize the text of the Declaration and "to cause it to be disseminated, displayed, read and expounded principally in schools and other educational institutions, without distinction based on the political status of countries or territories."

PREAMBLE

Whereas recognition of the inherent dignity and of the equal and inalienable rights of all members of the human family is the foundation of freedom, justice and peace in the world,

Whereas disregard and contempt for human rights have resulted in barbarous acts which have outraged the conscience of mankind, and the advent of a world in which human beings shall enjoy freedom of speech and belief and freedom from fear and want has been proclaimed as the highest aspiration of the common people,

Whereas it is essential, if man is not to be compelled to have recourse, as a last resort, to rebellion against tyranny and oppression, that human rights should be protected by the rule of law,

Whereas it is essential to promote the development of friendly relations between nations,

Whereas the peoples of the United Nations have in the Charter reaffirmed their faith in fundamental human rights, in the dignity and worth of the human person and in the equal rights of men and women and have determined to promote social progress and better standards of life in larger freedom,

Whereas Member States have pledged themselves to achieve, in co-operation with the United Nations, the promotion of universal respect for and observance of human rights and fundamental freedoms,

Whereas a common understanding of these rights and freedoms is of the greatest importance for the full realization of this pledge,

Now, Therefore THE GENERAL ASSEMBLY proclaims THIS UNIVERSAL DECLARATION OF HUMAN RIGHTS as a common standard of achievement for all peoples and all nations, to the end that every individual and every organ of society, keeping this Declaration constantly in mind, shall strive by teaching and education to promote respect for these rights and freedoms and by progressive measures, national and international, to secure their universal and effective recognition and observance, both among the peoples of Member States themselves and among the peoples of territories under their jurisdiction.

Article 1.
All human beings are born free and equal in dignity and rights. They are endowed with reason and conscience and should act towards one another in a spirit of brotherhood.

Article 2.
Everyone is entitled to all the rights and freedoms set forth in this Declaration, without distinction of any kind, such as race, colour, sex, language, religion, political or other opinion, national or social origin, property, birth or other status. Furthermore, no distinction shall be made on the basis of the political, jurisdictional or international status of the country or territory to which a person belongs, whether it be independent, trust, non-self-governing or under any other limitation of sovereignty.

Article 3.
Everyone has the right to life, liberty and security of person.

Article 4.
No one shall be held in slavery or servitude; slavery and the slave trade shall be prohibited in all their forms.

Article 5.

No one shall be subjected to torture or to cruel, inhuman or degrading treatment or punishment.

Article 6.

Everyone has the right to recognition everywhere as a person before the law.

Article 7.

All are equal before the law and are entitled without any discrimination to equal protection of the law. All are entitled to equal protection against any discrimination in violation of this Declaration and against any incitement to such discrimination.

Article 8.

Everyone has the right to an effective remedy by the competent national tribunals for acts violating the fundamental rights granted him by the constitution or by law.

Article 9.

No one shall be subjected to arbitrary arrest, detention or exile.

Article 10.

Everyone is entitled in full equality to a fair and public hearing by an independent and impartial tribunal, in the determination of his rights and obligations and of any criminal charge against him.

Article 11.

(1) Everyone charged with a penal offence has the right to be presumed innocent until proved guilty according to law in a public trial at which he has had all the guarantees necessary for his defence.

(2) No one shall be held guilty of any penal offence on account of any act or omission which did not constitute a penal offence, under national or international law, at the time when it was committed. Nor shall a heavier penalty be imposed than the one that was applicable at the time the penal offence was committed.

Article 12.

No one shall be subjected to arbitrary interference with his privacy, family, home or correspondence, nor to attacks upon his honour and reputation. Everyone has the right to the protection of the law against such interference or attacks.

Article 13.

(1) Everyone has the right to freedom of movement and residence within the borders of each state.

(2) Everyone has the right to leave any country, including his own, and to return to his country.

Article 14.

(1) Everyone has the right to seek and to enjoy in other countries asylum from persecution.

(2) This right may not be invoked in the case of prosecutions genuinely arising from non-political crimes or from acts contrary to the purposes and principles of the United Nations.

Article 15.

(1) Everyone has the right to a nationality.

(2) No one shall be arbitrarily deprived of his nationality nor denied the right to change his nationality.

Article 16.

(1) Men and women of full age, without any limitation due to race, nationality or religion, have the right to marry and to found a family. They are entitled to equal rights as to marriage, during marriage and at its dissolution.

(2) Marriage shall be entered into only with the free and full consent of the intending spouses.

(3) The family is the natural and fundamental group unit of society and is entitled to protection by society and the State.

Article 17.

(1) Everyone has the right to own property alone as well as in association with others.

(2) No one shall be arbitrarily deprived of his property.

Article 18.

Everyone has the right to freedom of thought, conscience and religion; this right includes freedom to change his religion or belief, and freedom, either alone or in community with others and in public or private, to manifest his religion or belief in teaching, practice, worship and observance.

Article 19.

Everyone has the right to freedom of opinion and expression; this right includes freedom to hold opinions without interference and to seek, receive and impart information and ideas through any media and regardless of frontiers.

Article 20.
(1) Everyone has the right to freedom of peaceful assembly and association.
(2) No one may be compelled to belong to an association.

Article 21.
(1) Everyone has the right to take part in the government of his country, directly or through freely chosen representatives.
(2) Everyone has the right of equal access to public service in his country.
(3) The will of the people shall be the basis of the authority of government; this will shall be expressed in periodic and genuine elections which shall be by universal and equal suffrage and shall be held by secret vote or by equivalent free voting procedures.

Article 22.
Everyone, as a member of society, has the right to social security and is entitled to realization, through national effort and international co-operation and in accordance with the organization and resources of each State, of the economic, social and cultural rights indispensable for his dignity and the free development of his personality.

Article 23.
(1) Everyone has the right to work, to free choice of employment, to just and favourable conditions of work and to protection against unemployment.
(2) Everyone, without any discrimination, has the right to equal pay for equal work.
(3) Everyone who works has the right to just and favourable remuneration ensuring for himself and his family an existence worthy of human dignity, and supplemented, if necessary, by other means of social protection.
(4) Everyone has the right to form and to join trade unions for the protection of his interests.

Article 24.
Everyone has the right to rest and leisure, including reasonable limitation of working hours and periodic holidays with pay.

Article 25.
(1) Everyone has the right to a standard of living adequate for the health and well-being of himself and of his family, including food, clothing, housing and medical care and necessary social services, and the right to security in the event of unemployment, sickness, disability, widowhood, old age or other lack of livelihood in circumstances beyond his control.

(2) Motherhood and childhood are entitled to special care and assistance. All children, whether born in or out of wedlock, shall enjoy the same social protection.

Article 26.

(1) Everyone has the right to education. Education shall be free, at least in the elementary and fundamental stages. Elementary education shall be compulsory. Technical and professional education shall be made generally available and higher education shall be equally accessible to all on the basis of merit.

(2) Education shall be directed to the full development of the human personality and to the strengthening of respect for human rights and fundamental freedoms. It shall promote understanding, tolerance and friendship among all nations, racial or religious groups, and shall further the activities of the United Nations for the maintenance of peace.

(3) Parents have a prior right to choose the kind of education that shall be given to their children.

Article 27.

(1) Everyone has the right freely to participate in the cultural life of the community, to enjoy the arts and to share in scientific advancement and its benefits.

(2) Everyone has the right to the protection of the moral and material interests resulting from any scientific, literary or artistic production of which he is the author.

Article 28.

Everyone is entitled to a social and international order in which the rights and freedoms set forth in this Declaration can be fully realized.

Article 29.

(1) Everyone has duties to the community in which alone the free and full development of his personality is possible.

(2) In the exercise of his rights and freedoms, everyone shall be subject only to such limitations as are determined by law solely for the purpose of securing due recognition and respect for the rights and freedoms of others and of meeting the just requirements of morality, public order and the general welfare in a democratic society.

(3) These rights and freedoms may in no case be exercised contrary to the purposes and principles of the United Nations.

Article 30.

Nothing in this Declaration may be interpreted as implying for any State, group or person any right to engage in any activity or to perform any act aimed at the destruction of any of the rights and freedoms set forth herein.

(Adopted and proclaimed by General Assembly resolution 217 A (III) of 10 December 1948)

Source: United Nations. (1948). *Universal Declaration of Human Rights.* New York: Author. Retrieved December 2, 2006, from http://www.un.org/Overview/rights.html

C

□□□

Sample Classroom Exercises

𝒇ollowing are examples of exercises that can be used with this text, in class sessions, in associated skills laboratories, or in other ways. Because the foundation course covers so much content, it is important that students have an opportunity to process what they are learning, to organize the material for themselves, to put their learning into words, and to practice skills. Many approaches exist for this kind of experiential learning, and the exercises here are merely suggestions. Teachers and students likely will find a style that works for a particular class; it may include some mixture of role-playing, small-group discussion, and other participatory presentations. What is important is that students act on and express their grasp of course content so that they experience some of the dilemmas, ambiguities, and challenges that are inevitable in practice. Exercises such as these do not lead to "right answers"; they thus help students become more comfortable in taking risks and living with uncertainty, using their own judgment, and co-constructing new and creative responses to real-world situations.

The material that follows includes an introductory exercise on empathic listening, followed by one exercise for each chapter of the book. (Students and faculty are encouraged to send feedback regarding these exercises to ctlowery@ earthlink.net as a means of shaping the text for the next edition.)

PRELIMINARY EXERCISE:
SELF-KNOWLEDGE FOR PRACTICE

Personal life experience is one source of knowledge on which every social worker depends. Your own life experiences mold and influence not only your personal life but also your professional practice as well. If you had a strong family background, for example, you will draw a great deal of emotional strength from those experiences, but it may be more difficult for you to deeply understand experiences of clients with very different histories. If you come from a family in which substance abuse was a factor, this will have multiple effects on your practice. It is crucial that you deepen your self-awareness, including knowledge of areas about which you need to be particularly sensitive as well as strengths you draw from your personal history. This exercise is designed to help you begin such exploration, which you will want to continue throughout your career because you will need to periodically discover new facets of yourself in your work.

Divide the class into small groups of four to six people and have everyone take a moment to individually write down their own answers to these questions:

+ In what two areas of my practice do I need to be especially sensitive to possible interference from my personal history?
+ What are two particular strengths I bring to practice from my personal history?

Do not bring to the surface issues that you do not feel comfortable sharing (although you should process such issues at some point, preferably with someone you trust).

When everyone has completed this step, the members of each group should take turns going around the circle, first discussing your responses to the first question. Use a Native American Talking Circle method: Each person takes his or her turn and speaks without interruption; when that person is done, the next person takes his or her turn. Save general discussion until everyone has taken a turn. Be sure to listen to and support each other in this exercise and to keep your own comments brief; avoid self-absorption! After you have processed the first question, use the same procedure to examine the second question. Conclude with a brief classwide discussion of the importance of self-awareness in practice.

EXERCISE 1: EMPATHIC LISTENING

A basic skill for all forms of social work practice is empathic listening, which is a way of expressing respect for others (clients, colleagues, and so forth) and building relationships, as well as for collecting the information needed to develop intervention plans. Crucial aspects of empathic listening are as follows:

+ actually hearing what the other person is saying (listening for both content and associated emotions)
+ communicating verbally and nonverbally that the listener is hearing what the other person is saying

+ listening nonjudgmentally, being careful to avoid even subtle punishment for honest expression (for example, the question "So you didn't mean to treat your child so abusively?" includes a subtle punitive message).

In this exercise, the class should be divided into groups of three (one or two groups of two can be used if necessary). Each group's members should decide among themselves who is to take each role (roles are rotated after about 10 minutes). One person should take the role of a "person with a problem"—which can be a real (but not overwhelming) issue or one borrowed from someone else the student knows. Another person should be designated as the "listener," and the third should be designated as the "observer," who will identify what the listener did well and what the listener might do to listen and communicate empathy even more effectively. (Note that the role is not to criticize what was done incorrectly!)

For the first two minutes (the instructor may want to announce the times), the listener is to simply listen without saying anything at all but should try to communicate interest and empathy nonverbally. For the next two minutes, the listener can only use one- or two-word "furthering" responses, like "um-hmm" or "I see." Then, for the remaining time, the listener can ask brief questions meant to elicit information and use empathic paraphrasing (for example, "It sounds like you were feeling very frustrated when she said that"). The listener should completely avoid making suggestions or asking leading questions that have suggestions built in. When the role play is complete, the three partners should discuss the experience briefly. (These instructions should be either posted on the board or given in handouts.)

After brief discussion, the roles in the triad should be rotated, with another student taking the role of the listener and using the same progression; after another 10 minutes, the roles should again be rotated so everyone has taken every role. The class may then want to pursue a general discussion about the experience, why the skills are so important, and why they are so challenging.

EXERCISE 2: TAKING AN ECOSYSTEMIC PERSPECTIVE

Divide the class into groups of six to eight, each of which is to draw an ecomap that captures the dynamics of the following case (or another provided by the instructor) on a large sheet of paper:

An 18-year-old single mother of a two-year-old daughter was referred to child protective services (CPS) by an emergency department physician of a local hospital. The two-year-old had been brought to the hospital by her mother, Ms. Chin, a second-generation Chinese American woman, because the child was crying in pain from severe burns on her buttocks. The mother's explanation was that the child had backed into the open oven door when the mother was removing cookies she had just baked. The mother was extremely agitated and fearful.

The social worker at CPS learned from the mother that she had somewhat limited social supports—the father of the child visited occasionally and her parents, who were in poor health, lived on another floor in the same building, but she did not work or socialize outside her apartment house. Beyond the family, she had only one real friend, an elderly woman living alone in the apartment next door. Ms. Chin had not finished high school because she had become pregnant; she had no job skills, and although she seemed intelligent and aware of the seriousness of her situation, her affect was flat and she seemed to be quite depressed. The child appeared to be developmentally normal, affectionate with her mother, and outgoing in the social worker's presence.

Ms. Chin was worried that her description of the accident would not be believed and that CPS would remove her daughter from her care. The social worker had the impression that the mother was concerned about her daughter's welfare and that this might have been a true accident, not an instance of child abuse. When the social worker later talked with the neighbor who knew the mother, she learned that the mother often became impatient with the child, but the neighbor had not observed hitting or anything else that she regarded as abusive.

The social worker had to make a decision about the immediate health and welfare of the child: Did this case require immediate placement to protect the child? Was this a woman who would respond to help, and what would the interventions be? The assignment for the small groups, however, is not to make a decision, but rather to organize case data in ways that could be helpful for planning—to "see" the case ecosystemically, including social and cultural factors, and to identify possible points for intervention on the ecomap.

Creating the Ecomap

In drawing the ecomaps, consider the interrelatedness of the case variables, what is known and not known about the case, and what limitations and potentials for help are present in the case. Ecomaps drawn by different groups might emphasize different points for intervention, depending on the way they are drawn. A typical ecomap will include

+ circles depicting the case variables in sectors
+ arrows to depict exchanges among systems and variables

+ shading or colors to identify the point or points of intervention indicated by the perspective taken on the case.

Groups should share their ecomaps with the class, followed by a discussion focused on understanding the case in its transactional complexity.

EXERCISE 3: MORALITY AND SOCIAL JUSTICE

Working in dyads or triads, the class should discuss the following questions:

+ What groups or institutions provide guidelines or taboos for your moral behavior? For example, what was considered taboo in your family of origin (disloyalty, sexual behavior, drinking)? Who established those rules?
+ What moral expectations do you have of yourself as a social worker? How consistent are those with the moral expectations you grew up with?
+ What moral expectations do you have of your colleagues?
+ Recognizing the essential interconnections among all people, institutions, and the natural world, as well as the impact of larger sociocultural and corporate forces, what personal responsibility do you have for constructing a just world?

After the small groups compare their answers to the questions, the class as a whole should discuss and record how actualizing one's moral perspectives could contribute to a "just" world. Do not attempt to define a just world at the outset; build a just world from the moral standards that are operating in the class.

EXERCISE 4: ETHICAL PRACTICE

Part 1

One of the most difficult—but crucial—demands of the *NASW Code of Ethics* is that the social worker intervene with impaired colleagues when issues such as substance abuse or personal problems interfere with their work with clients.

Break the class into dyads (groups of two). In each dyad, have one student take the role of the impaired worker and the other the role of a colleague. (The instructor may wish to model a minute or two of an interaction between the two in front of the class first.) Each dyad should now role-play a serious conversation in which the colleague expresses his or her concern, listens to the impaired colleague, and clarifies the next steps that he or she will take if the impaired colleague does not take appropriate action.

After about five minutes, the class should discuss the experience, its emotional effect, and the importance of taking such steps. Then the members of each dyad should switch roles, this time discussing another issue with serious ethical or values implications, such as a worker who appears to be becoming romantically involved with a student he or she is supervising, a worker who is treating colleagues in the organization disrespectfully, or a worker who is making ethnically offensive comments. Again after about five minutes of interaction, the entire class should process their experiences.

Part 2

Using the decision-making strategy presented in chapter 4, each person in the class should complete a systematic analysis of the ethical dilemma described in the case below. Each person should determine what action he or she would take in the case and justify the choice of action.

> Margaret, a social worker at the local counseling center, has been counseling the Patterson family for about seven months. Recently, while Mr. Patterson was temporarily unemployed, Margaret became aware of an incident of harsh parental discipline that she had questions about. Margaret discussed the incident with the family and decided not to file a report with the CPS agency at that time. As a result of recent experiences with CPS, it was Margaret's conclusion that CPS intervention "may do more harm than good." Margaret was convinced that she could reach the family through their established relationship, which was reported to be quite strong. It was Margaret's judgment that the incident was an isolated one and that if she reported the family to CPS, they would resent the reporting and would not return for counseling. "Having worked with CPS before in this community," said Margaret, "I am convinced the family would get no help at all there."

EXERCISE 5: DIVERSITY AND CULTURE

Before beginning this exercise, it is important that everyone in the group recognize the need for mutual respect and curiosity when discussing core personal and cultural values. Start by giving each member of the class the opportunity to answer the question "How do you self-identify culturally?" For purposes of this exercise, cultural groups can be loosely defined as including any group that mutually supports particular practices, beliefs, and values over time within the group. This broad definition includes, for example, ethnic, religious, and national cultures as well as many smaller social networks. The instructor or group leader should usually go first to act as a model. It is important that each person be allowed to define him- or herself in his or her own way—for many students, race and religion may be the most salient factors, but for others sexual orientation or cohort factors may be most important. (It may be necessary to remind the class of this fact because, on occasion, members of the class may interrupt to question whether a person is using the "right" categories.)

As each person provides his or her self-identification, list it on large sheets of paper or on the chalkboard. Then break the group into small groups having one or more central features in common. Those who do not fit into any simple system of grouping can form their own "diversity caucus."

Each small group is then given 20 minutes to discuss the following questions and to prepare a report to give to the larger group. To encourage honesty, it is important to remind participants that many cultures teach and encourage biases toward those who are not members of the group and that, as a result, we all carry biases that we need to recognize.

- What messages (positive and negative) did you receive in childhood about your own group?
- What messages (positive and negative—honesty is critical here) did you receive in childhood about those of particular other groups?
- What do you not understand about one particular culture that is not your own?
- How may your cultural background and values affect your practice—now and in the future?

After 30 minutes, each group sends a reporter to participate in a panel discussion in front of the larger group. After the reporters summarize the group discussion, the instructor and other members of the class are given the opportunity to ask members of the panel questions to clarify and deepen mutual understanding.

Source: Nakanishi, M., & Rittner, B. (1992). The inclusionary cultural model. *Journal of Social Work Education, 28,* 27–35.

EXERCISE 6: MONITORING

Part 1

Examine the graphs shown in Figure 6-3. In small groups, students should describe what they see and answer the following questions:

- How is the couple doing at various points in the case?
- What variables seem to be interrelated in some way?
- If you were the social worker, how might you use the graphs in practice with the clients?

Part 2

It is important to experience what clients experience, to the extent possible, in order to build sensitivity and empathy. For example, social workers who use tools such as rapid assessment instruments may want to try them out themselves first. This is an exercise in which students prepare sequential ecomaps that reflect changes in their own lives.

To begin, students should individually draw an ecomap of their own life six months ago (or one year ago, if the changes over that period are more noticeable) and one for the present. Each student should then share his or her ecomap with another student. Students should discuss the experience of seeing their own lives visually and of sharing them with someone whom they probably do not know intimately.

EXERCISE 7: THE PROFESSION

Break the class into groups of five to seven people. Ask each group to spend 20 minutes answering the following questions, noting their answers with markers on large sheets of paper that can be hung on the wall:

+ Why did you enter a graduate social work program?
+ What is your biggest concern about social work as a profession?
+ How important to you is social work's historic commitment to social justice? Why?

After the small-group discussions, each group should report back to the full class. After the reports, general themes should be extracted in a large-group discussion.

EXERCISE 8: PRACTICE WITH INDIVIDUALS

Distribute the following case example to the class (other sample cases can be substituted using the process outlined here):

José is a 28-year-old graphic artist who is seeking help at the community mental health center because he has been experiencing anxiety and depression. Since he recently learned that he tested positive for HIV, he has been unable to concentrate on or to complete his work assignments, to sleep at night, or to eat regularly. Although he is married and has two children, José, a first-generation Mexican American, has also had occasional sexual liaisons with men, and his physician assumes that is how he contracted the virus. Although he is largely asymptomatic, José is concerned about his health, his job status, and his ability to care for his family. However, his most immediate concern is that he does not feel that he can disclose his health status to either his wife or his parents. José's parents now live with his younger brother in a small town in another state. José feels that his diagnosis would be particularly hard for his parents to accept for cultural reasons.

In spite of his good health, José has missed days at work and has received several warnings from his supervisors, who are baffled by the recent deterioration in his work performance. His wife is also concerned about his lack of motivation at work and his "hypochondria." At home, he makes excuses for not being near his children and is avoiding sexual contact with his wife.

Engaging and Envisioning

Divide the class into two circles, with two empty chairs in the center of each. Have one student take the role of José and the other that of a social worker in each circle. The students should role-play the first 10 minutes of an initial interview, with a focus on engagement and envisioning an improved situation toward which the worker and client might aim. The student playing the social worker can interrupt the role play at any point and ask the observing students to make suggestions about how to move ahead at difficult points; the other students in the circle should remain quiet except when their help is requested by the social worker. The instructor can move back and forth between the two circles, leading brief discussions of the process thus far and periodically asking other students to take one of the roles.

After completion of one or two 10-minute segments of role play, the entire class can discuss the following questions:

+ What value dilemmas or ethical issues did this scenario raise?
+ What did the social workers do that contributed to engaging the client?
+ What else might they have done to further engagement?
+ To what extent were the worker and client able to move beyond describing the problem situation to envisioning a better reality they might work toward?
+ To what extent did the role plays exemplify shared power? How?

EXERCISE 9:
SOCIAL WORK WITH FAMILIES—
THE GENOGRAM

The genogram is a visual intergenerational family tree. Charting and recording intergenerational patterns, including causes of death, can be useful in health histories (Hartman & Laird, 1983); for understanding family immigration patterns

and connections in different geographical places; for adoptions; for understanding intergenerational patterns related to substance use; and in other circumstances
in which relationships relevant to the work being done need to be clarified.

To understand the patterns in one's own family history, each student begins
by drawing a three- or four-generation (grandparents, parents, self and siblings,
children) genogram. Each can select one or two patterns they want to explore at
this time (for example, types of losses, twin births, alcoholism) and chart these
with the usual gender, age, marriage and divorce, and birth and death categories
in the genealogical chart. For example, the model (Figure C-1) includes occupations and alcohol histories for a family in treatment. Note how the primary client
system is boxed off and located within a larger household system.

Students should share what they have learned from this exercise, including
their reflections on when constructing genograms may or may not be helpful in
work with clients.

Reference

Hartman, A., & Laird, J. (1983). *Family-centered social work practice*. New York: Free Press.

EXERCISE 10: PRACTICE WITH GROUPS

Background

Distribute the following case example to the class (other sample cases can be
substituted using the process outlined here):

> You are the leader of a group of ninth and 10th graders (15- and 16-year-
> olds) in a school-sponsored group for underachievers (students who do not
> do homework, talk a lot in class, or do not concentrate on schoolwork). The
> students do not have many friends in school and have been identified by
> classroom teachers as those who make trouble for other students. They
> hang out together after school and outside the group.
>
> The purpose of this group is to help the students develop skills and atti-
> tudes that will lead them to succeed in school. The group was formed about
> three or four months ago and is now in the work, or ongoing, phase (Tuck-
> man's [1965] "performing" stage of group development). For example, in
> recent sessions, the group members have talked about their families and
> discussed how to respond when they are angry with other students and
> teachers.
>
> Several of the group members went dancing at a club on Saturday night,
> and this is the first group meeting since the dance. While she was dancing
> with Ellen, Jane said to her, "You look gorgeous. I could really go for you."
> Ellen left abruptly and did not return to the dance.

FIGURE C-I

□ □ □ □ □

Sample Genogram

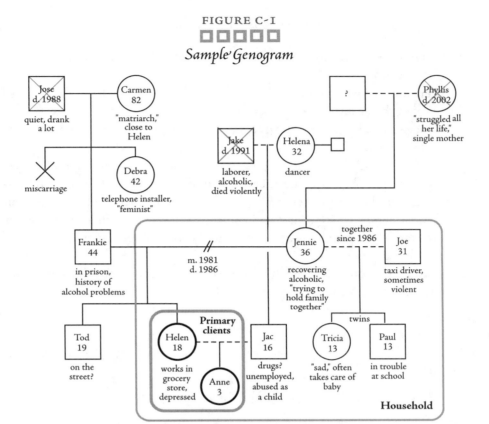

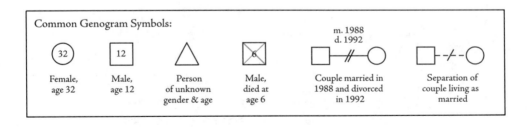

At the next meeting Ellen came in a little late. When she arrived, several group members immediately asked her, "Where did you disappear Saturday?" Ellen responded, pointing to Jane, "Ask her!" Jane says, "What are you talking about?" There is some arguing back and forth, but finally Ellen is persuaded to tell her story. Then the group members criticized and "dumped on" Jane.

Instructions for Role Plays

1. Assign the roles of the leader, Ellen, Jane, and two to three other members of the group.
2. There are two ways to begin this role play:
   + Begin the group where the scenario left off.
   + Have Ellen leave the room and start the role play with her coming to the group late.
3. The leader and the members (especially the leader) must respond to this interpersonal obstacle. The members should stay in their roles. The role play should last five to seven minutes. After that time, one leader and one member should switch roles and continue the role play. Before the switch, however, members should give feedback to the leader about what helped and what did not help.
4. Finally, one group member should serve as a recorder who will report back to the class the feedback given to each leader.

Reference

Tuckman, B. W. (1965). Developmental sequence in small groups. *Psychological Bulletin, 63,* 384–399.

Suggested Reading

Shulman, L. (1967). Scapegoats, group workers, and preemptive intervention. *Social Work, 12,* 37–43.

Note: This exercise was developed by Renée Solomon, formerly of Columbia University School of Social Work, New York.

EXERCISE 11: ELICITING MULTIPLE PERSPECTIVES IN COMMUNITIES

Any community group will have a wide range of perspectives on issues facing the community, even when there seems to be a high level of shared concern. For the social worker, this situation raises the problem of how to ensure that multiple perspectives, particularly those that are typically silenced, get heard and validated. In the following exercise, students use their everyday experiences to learn a strategy for providing all members with a voice in the process. The exercise uses Freire's "pedagogy of the question" to elicit various perspectives and to encourage critical reflection on their meaning.

- Select a topic that is part of the everyday experience of all students in the class (such as some aspect of their experience in the class or as students in the school). Choose something likely to be substantive that has dimensions of social justice.
- Pose the topic to the class in the form of a series of questions, such as "How do you experience issues of race (or gender, respect, sexual orientation, or another thematic issue) in this school (or in your field placements)?" "How could this issue be better addressed?" "What obstacles do you see to addressing this issue honestly and helpfully?" Write these questions on an index card.
- Use a talking circle format, with everyone seated in a single circle. Encourage students to speak genuinely and from the heart. One student or the instructor, holding the card, reads the first question aloud and answers it in his or her own way. Answers should be relatively brief and as thoughtful as possible. The card is then passed to the next person, who answers to same question. Only the person holding the card may speak, and no one else may interrupt. Participants may pass, but they must wait until the card comes around again to speak. The card should go around the circle three times, using a new but related question each time (a single question can also be used for multiple rounds if it is proving very rich).
- After the circle has been completed three times, the class can discuss together what they heard in the responses. Use newsprint and markers (so a record exists) to record the various points of view. Ensure that both minority and majority perspectives are captured. Also focus on what people are learning about what other people think. Encourage critical reflection on both content and process. Note any general (or generative) themes that connect the students' experience to wider institutional, social, and political issues. Encourage discussion of these issues from multiple perspectives.
- Close by exploring with the class ways in which the material might be used as a basis for further discussion and action. How can the multiple voices that emerge from this process be nurtured and encompassed in the long term? How might this process be useful in other groups? To what extent is it consistent with various cultural norms, and is that an advantage or a disadvantage?

This exercise is useful at three levels:

1. It generates thematic material from the students' experiences that will be similar to content that they will encounter in the community.
2. It models a strategy that students can use in their own practice.

3. It provides a vehicle for enhancing students' empowerment (if material relevant to the class gets a response). Each of these three levels should be identified by the instructor in the discussion that follows the exercise.

EXERCISE 12: PRACTICE WITH ORGANIZATIONS

Divide the class into groups of six to eight people. Each group should prepare a five-minute role-play scenario about a problem in service delivery (a situation in which agency procedures or service arrangements do not "work for people") drawn from one of their fieldwork placements. The scenarios selected should be real and reflect a general organizational issue.

Each small group should present its scenario to the class, followed by a discussion of the following questions:

+ How is the client not being well served in this scenario?
+ What alternative service arrangements could realistically be constructed that might work better?
+ What resources would be required, and what obstacles overcome, to make these changes?
+ What could be one small, realistic first step toward the identified goal?
+ How is a process of shared power relevant to the arrangements being discussed here?

The same process should be used with each scenario prepared by each of the other small groups.

EXERCISE 13: GENERALIST PRACTICE

Part 1: Practice Possibilities at Multiple System Levels

A social worker can, and sometimes must, respond to a client's needs in many ways and at multiple system levels. The material in chapter 13 discusses such responses to the problem of child abuse and neglect, but a similar approach is important in working with many other social problems. This exercise is designed to encourage creativity and analytic thought in deciding on effective intervention strategies.

In small groups of four to six people, choose one type of case that at least one student in that group is currently working with (if possible, choose something other than child maltreatment). In each small group, do the following:

+ On large pieces of paper, draw a hypothesized causal chain involved in maintaining the problem in at least some cases. Do not aim for perfection; spend no more than 10 minutes developing this conceptual model.
+ On another large sheet of paper, develop a three-column table. In the first column, list system levels (individual, family, group, neighborhood, community, organization). In the second column, list at least one possible and useful intervention strategy for each system level in the first column. In the third column, note the reasons for identifying each strategy, based on the conceptual model of the problem that has been sketched. Spend no more than 15 minutes on this table.
+ Next, a reporter from each group briefly explains to the full group, without interruption, the conceptual model and table of interventions outlined. When all groups have reported, open the floor for general discussion, with particular emphasis on areas of contrast among the small groups.

Part 2: Fields of Practice

Divide the class into three or four groups by field of practice (for example, family and children's services, health services, school social work). Each group should role-play an interview with the following client (or one selected by the class and instructor) for about 10 minutes and then answer the questions listed after the case example below. The groups should then report their conclusions, and the class can contrast the differences in responses across fields. Note that a client like this may surface in practically any field of practice; the question is how the case would be dealt with in each.

At your fieldwork agency, your supervisor has asked you to help Gina, a 38-year-old single, European American homeless woman who has two children in foster care. She was recently picked up by the police following a mugging in which she was beaten severely. She had told the police, "I just want to be left alone—by everyone." Until five years ago, when she was hospitalized for six months for what she called a nervous breakdown, Gina worked as a laboratory technician in a local hospital. For the past four years, she has been in and out of the shelter system, which she entered after her boyfriend battered her. Her two children (ages six and eight) were removed from the home for neglect about six months ago, and she has lived on the streets since shortly thereafter, in the process losing all benefits. Outreach workers have recently observed Gina raving and ranting at pedestrians. She also has a history of drinking heavily (although she is sober at the moment). She reports no extended period of sobriety for the past four years. When asked about her drinking, Gina says, "I drink because I have problems."

Questions

+ What kind of services could Gina receive from your agency? What barriers are present?
+ Thinking across all system levels, what other services and systems might be relevant to providing assistance in this case?
+ What policy dilemmas does this case raise within your field of practice?
+ Does this case raise any values dilemmas for you?

Index

⬜⬜⬜
About the Editors

Christine T. Lowery, PhD, is associate professor, Helen Bader School of Social Welfare, University of Wisconsin–Milwaukee. She is from the Laguna (New Mexico) and Hopi (Arizona) tribes and has 12 years of social work experience with American Indians in both urban and reservation settings. Her research has focused on substance abuse addiction and recovery processes with American Indian women and sociocultural change among Indian elders on the Pueblo of Laguna.

Mark A. Mattaini, DSW, ACSW, is associate professor, Jane Addams College of Social Work, University of Illinois at Chicago. His writing, research, and current practice focus on youth violence prevention, the dynamics of nonviolent social action, practice theory, and the analysis of cultural systems. He is editor of the journal *Behavior and Social Issues* and author or co-editor of nine books on social work practice and social issues. He has experience in family services, residential care, developmental disabilities, substance abuse, mental health, and prevention settings.

About the Contributors

Jerry R. Cates, PhD, is associate dean of the Jane Addams College of Social Work, University of Illinois at Chicago. He is writing a book on the politics of American Indian participation in public assistance and has published on the historical development of social security and public assistance.

Meredith Hanson, DSW, is professor and director of the PhD in Social Work Program at the Graduate School of Social Service, Fordham University, New York. He teaches courses on the evidence base for social work practice in the doctoral program and courses on direct practice and social work with alcohol- and drug-involved individuals, families, and groups in the MSW program. His teaching, practice, and scholarly interests include agency-based practice, program design and development, addictions treatment, international social work, and social work practice with adults with coexisting substance use and mental disorders.

Susan P. Kemp, PhD, is associate professor, School of Social Work, University of Washington, Seattle. She was formerly a member of the practice faculty, School of Social Work, Columbia University, New York. Dr. Kemp's research interests include community-based and environmental social work practice and social work history.

Randy H. Magen, PhD, is professor, School of Social Work, University of Alaska, Anchorage, and is coordinator of the MSW program. His research interests include group work and domestic violence. He has recently published on domestic violence in rural Alaska and measurement in groups. In addition to publishing and teaching, Dr. Magen also facilitates a weekly group for men who batter.

Marian Mattison, DSW, ACSW, is chair, Social Work Department, Providence College, Providence, Rhode Island. Dr. Mattison has published articles and book chapters on the subject of ethical decision making and routinely presents workshops and training seminars on ethical decision making for both local and regional venues.

Edward Scanlon, PhD, is associate professor, School of Social Welfare, University of Kansas. His current areas of scholarship include asset-based social welfare and the social work profession's involvement in the political process.